A MORAL TEMPER

The Letters of Dwight Macdonald

A MORAL TEMPER

The Letters of
Dwight Macdonald

EDITED WITH AN INTRODUCTION BY
MICHAEL WRESZIN

Ivan R. Dee

CHICAGO   2001

Frontispiece photograph courtesy of Mariette Pathy Allen.

Library of Congress Cataloging-in-Publication Data:
Macdonald, Dwight.
     A moral temper : the letters of Dwight Macdonald / edited with an introduction by Michael Wreszin.
          p.   cm.
     Includes index.
     ISBN 1-56663-393-1 (alk. paper)
     1. Macdonald, Dwight—Correspondence.   2. Intellectuals—United States—Correspondence.   3. Macdonald, Dwight—Political and social views.   4. United States—Politics and government—1945–1989.   5. United States—Social conditions—1945–   I. Wreszin, Michael.   II. Title.

E748.M147 A4 2001
973.91'092—dc21   2001028380

For Michael Macdonald

and Nicholas and Elspeth Macdonald

CONTENTS

ACKNOWLEDGMENTS

John Lukacs, the historian and good friend of Dwight Macdonald's from the 1950s until his death, was the chief inspiration behind this book. Besides offering me his own files of correspondence with Macdonald, he played an important part in finding a publisher and getting the project under way. Albert Fried, the historian and my close friend, read every version of this collection and offered invaluable editorial advice. Judith Schiff, chief archivist at the Sterling Library of Yale University; Dean M. Rodgers of the Vassar College Library; and Ed Desrochers of the Phillips Exeter Library all helped me acquire photographs. Dwight Macdonald's sons took an interest in the book, and Nicholas dug up some of the family pictures. My former student Vitoria Lin helped with a good deal of the clerical work involved in retyping the letters for publication. Finally, I am indebted to Ivan Dee and his associate editor, Hilary Schaefer, for their considerable editorial assistance and consistently sound advice. While I am grateful for the interest, encouragement, and help of all of the above, I bear sole responsibility for the judgments made in selection and editing, and for any errors that unfortunately occur in the reproduction of these letters.

M. W.

New York City
May 2001

INTRODUCTION

Dwight Macdonald's life story as revealed in his vast correspondence is the story of an American awakening. It is an account of an upper-middle-class white male, schooled in the elite institutions of the establishment, who started out with all the prejudices and provincialisms of his class—anti-Semitism, racial bigotry, sexist patronizing—and through the force of his inquiring mind managed to jettison a footlocker full of dandyish pretensions and become one of the most penetrating critics of politics, society, and culture in twentieth-century America.

This intellectually colorful life can be traced through a vast correspondence, more than seventy-three linear feet, housed in the Sterling Library at Yale University. It ranges from childhood through his school, college, and professional life—a full sixty years of consistently vivid and exciting material. The correspondence is rich, diverse, and well catalogued, with letters to[1] and from a variety of significant figures in twentieth-century American intellectual and political life. To name just a few: Daniel Aaron, James Agee, Hannah Arendt, W. H. Auden, Daniel Bell, Isaiah Berlin, John Berryman, William Buckley, Nicola Chiarmonte, John Dos Passos, T. S. Eliot, Abbie Hoffman, Sidney Hook, Irving Kristol, John Lukacs, C. Wright Mills, Mary McCarthy, Norman Mailer, George Orwell, Ezra Pound, David Reisman, Arthur Schlesinger, Jr., Stephen Spender, Diana and Lionel Trilling, Edmund Wilson. There is a wealth of family correspondence and an entire section devoted to his Trotskyist period, as well as correspondence regarding his involvement with various organizations both professional and political.

When the editor of a British periodical praised Dwight Macdonald as a "good American" despite his scathing dismissal of American culture in the fifties, Dwight wrote in reply:

---

1. Macdonald Papers, Manuscripts, and Archives, Yale University Library; Macdonald made copies of most of his correspondence, often even handwritten letters.

Sir:

In your editorial preceding my "America! America!" you write: "We would not publish Mr. Dwight Macdonald's spirited and witty comment on American life were not Mr. Macdonald himself a good American." I must object to this on both factual and logical grounds.

Factual: How do you know I *am* a "good American"? I do have a purely personal affection for some aspects of my native land (and a purely personal dislike for others), but patriotism has never been my strong point, and I don't know as I'd call myself A Good American. I'm certainly a critical American, and I prefer your country, morally and culturally, to my own.

Logical: You confuse the source of criticism with its validity. A Bad American, cynical and traitorous, might still make perfectly sound criticisms of his country. And if they were sound it would be your editorial duty to print them. It's in that other place to the East that civic virtue is the indispensable passport to print.

Dwight Macdonald was indeed a critical American, but it was a criticism that transcended pejorative denunciations—though, as he once wrote, he was "a specialist in abuse," "a technician of vilification," "an expert mudslinger" whose responses fit "the barbarism of our social institutions and its rationalized lunacies." His approach was carefully analytical, and he had, as Hannah Arendt observed, "an extraordinary flair for the significant fact and significant thought." For more than fifty years, from the 1930s to the 1980s, he was a prolific and influential critic of politics, society, and culture in the United States and abroad. He could invariably be found at the center of the major controversies and confrontations of his time. His own extraordinary journal, *Politics* (1944–1949), was described by Daniel Bell as "the only magazine that was aware of and kept calling attention to changes that were taking place in moral temper, the depths of which we still incompletely realize."

Macdonald is perhaps best remembered by his peers as a pivotal figure on the anti-Stalinist left and a ferocious critic of what he called "totalitarian liberalism," which, he charged, often apologized for Soviet tyranny. Cultural critics from Adorno to Eliot have judged his theoretical analysis of mass culture as a seminal contribution to the literature. In today's postmodern accommodation—not to say exaltation—of popular culture, Macdonald's analytical dissection of that "spreading ooze" remains a powerful statement with which contemporary critics are obliged to deal.

His correspondence does not simply trace the personal journey of an exciting and provocative publicist, or illustrate an indigenous American dissenting tradition; it also illuminates the character of elite education in the 1920s, the radicalization of an important group of writers and intellectuals in the thirties and forties, the loss of radical and liberal confidence during the postwar years, the debate over the relationship between mass culture and totalitarianism in the fifties, and the crisis of culture and values during the era of the Vietnam War. Although he died in 1982, he remains to this day an essential reference in the historical confrontation between the canon and multiculturalism.

Macdonald was born to upper-middle-class parents in New York City in 1906 and was educated at the Barnard School for Boys, Phillips Exeter Academy, and Yale University (B.A., 1928). He was an astonishingly precocious youth. Determined to be a writer and scholar, at the age of fifteen he informed his father that he could read no more modern literature (meaning nineteenth-century classics) until he had mastered Greek and Latin. While at school and college, he had no apparent political interests, but his intellectual self-assurance and inability to suffer pretense foreshadowed his later slashing political polemics and his sometimes acerbic literary criticism. As a freshman he wrote to the president of Yale, James R. Angell, to denounce compulsory chapel because a sermon by one of the college dignitaries was "full of puerile and stupid twaddle" and an insult to his intelligence. As an editor of several Yale publications, he threatened to publish a protest against William Lyon Phelps's teaching of Shakespeare on the grounds that the venerable professor was incompetent. When the dean gave him the alternative of quashing the piece or being expelled, he chose the former. In an interview shortly before his death he recalled this decision as a deplorable compromise of principle.

During his senior year Macdonald wrote enthusiastically about the can-do businessmen he had encountered on his searches for a job after graduation. He had a brief and often hilarious tenure in Macy's executive training program. It was his plan to learn the retail trade and then go into advertising, but he quickly lost his taste for the "romance of rayon" and sought escape in journalism. Through Wilder Hobson, a Yale classmate, he found his way to Henry Luce's new venture, *Fortune* magazine. For his first few years with the Luce publication he spent much of his time researching and writing profiles of successful businessmen. He was well paid but did not find the work terribly satisfying. He took every opportunity to pursue his literary interests by writing reviews and pieces for literary magazines. He also founded and edited a journal, *The Miscellany*, with two former classmates, G. L. K. Morris and Fred Dupee. He was surprised and disappointed when Henry Luce expressed displeasure that he was dividing his time. *Fortune*, Luce insisted, was a full-time job!

Macdonald met Nancy Rodman, the sister of Seldon Rodman, at editorial meetings for the quasi-socialist journal *Common Sense*, which Rodman edited with Alfred Bingham. Initially Macdonald was interested in contributing reviews and literary articles. The evidence suggests that it was Nancy who did much to radicalize him. Not only did she introduce him to Marxist literature (*The Communist Manifesto* and Trotsky's autobiography, among other writings), she complained that his work for *Fortune* was often frivolous and served no useful purpose at a time when sharp social criticism was essential. She took him to radical meetings and encouraged him to insist that he report on more politically relevant topics than giant crabs in Japan, the best prep schools, and nervous breakdowns.

As he became more aware of and interested in political issues, Macdonald found the wealthy business executives he interviewed to be narrow-minded, "stupid and scared" people whom Roosevelt had saved from their own folly, yet they continued to grumble. Although Marxism never really absorbed Macdonald, and he felt that Communists were often pretentious and humorless, he nevertheless appreciated their critique of laissez-faire capitalism. In an article about the Communist Party U.S.A., he stated explicitly that they served a useful purpose in pointing up the contradictions and failures of the capitalist system.

When Dwight and Nancy took a delayed honeymoon in 1934, Dwight spent much of his time in Majorca studying the rise of dictators and the danger of a too powerful state, and taking a cursory look at *Das Kapital*. Both he and Nancy felt compelled to pursue an intellectual calling and returned to pursue serious work. They devoted time to Communist front organizations, the Newspaper Guild, the Share Croppers Union, and a strike of the elevator operators, supporting with enthusiasm the striking operators in their own apartment building. It was Macdonald's extended articles on the United States Steel Corporation, with his closing tribute to Lenin, that led to a bitter dispute with his editors and his resignation from *Fortune*.

By the fall of 1936 both Dwight and Nancy were staunch fellow-travelers. The evidence suggests that Dwight voted for the Communist Earl Browder in that year's presidential election. As the fear of another war approached, Macdonald became obsessed with the power of the state to lead people into war. His growing pacifism was far more compatible with the anti-imperialist war position of the Socialist Workers Party than the program of the Communist Party. He joined the SWP in 1939 and quickly became a leading intellectual contributor to its publications, carrying on spirited debates with Leon Trotsky, James P. Cannon, Max Shachtman, and James Burnham. Trotsky was, according to legend, irked by Macdonald's constant criticism and remarked that "every man has a right to be stupid on occasion but comrade Macdonald abuses it."[2] He left

2. Although Trotsky did refer to Macdonald as stupid, I have discovered no source for the quip except in secondhand mentions by such figures as James Burnham and Harry Roskolenko. Macdonald seemed proud of the attack and quoted it often. I think he made it up.

the party in 1941 because of the leadership's undemocratic insistence on strict adherence to the party line. Macdonald could never tolerate editors interfering with his prose.

After an intense political argument with Phillip Rahv and William Phillips, Macdonald was persuaded to serve as an editor of the revived *Partisan Review* during these years (1937–1943), but his belligerent anti-war stance led to an acrimonious break with his co-editors. In 1944 he invested his considerable talents, his savings from his *Fortune* job, and his wife's inheritance in the creation of *Politics*. It served as a personal vehicle to express his growing anarchistic fear of statism and his pacifistic as well as ethical approach to politics. The journal developed an international reputation in intellectual circles for its lively, unorthodox position and its literary quality. Dwight and Nancy's apartment and the office of *Politics* became the center of an "international fraternity" of like-minded young people who shared a vision of the postwar world as a "complicated and terrifying place." It is astonishing to consider the youthful unknowns whom Macdonald introduced to American readers: Simone Weil, Albert Camus, Bruno Bettelheim, Nicola Chiaromonte, Lewis Coser, Victor Serge; and the young American social scientists, historians, and essayists Daniel Bell, C. Wright Mills, Irving Howe, Paul Goodman, Kenneth Stampp, Richard Hofstadter, Frank Freidel, Mary McCarthy, and so many more who later became leaders of the postwar literary and intellectual scene — and with whom he corresponded.

By 1948, Macdonald was losing his taste for politics and for editing *Politics*. His anti-Stalinism had become an overriding feature of his political perspective, and as a consequence he found himself supporting the main features of Truman's cold war policies. This blunted the critical edge of his writing, and he became increasingly depressed with the political scene, which he described as a "desert without hope." At the same time, as he approached middle age his marriage to Nancy was crumbling. The cement of political activism that had been their main bond was no longer strong enough to keep them together. Macdonald began the first of two affairs that ultimately led to his divorce and 1954 marriage to Gloria Lanier.

With the election of Eisenhower, Macdonald — having lost much of his verve and optimism for reform — turned his attention away from organized politics to a broader assault on the quality of American life and the commercialization of its culture. He fashioned the concepts of "masscult" and "midcult," which shaped the dimensions of the lively debate over mass culture and its intricate relationship to what Macdonald saw as a creeping totalitarianism that threatened all modern nation states. Like Orwell, Macdonald feared the corruption of culture by capitalist commercialism as much as he feared the corruption of politics by Stalinist totalitarianism. While he remained a democrat in politics, he called himself a cultural conservative. He defended classical principles and standards and evaluated the arts and literature on the basis of his classical education and tastes. He denounced the Revised Standard Version of the Bible and was appalled by the "permissiveness" and "debasement of language" found in *Webster's Third New International Dictionary*. Again, like Orwell, he thought that the degradation of politics in the forties and fifties was directly connected to the decay of language. When it came to culture, Macdonald made it his business to defend the achievements, standards, and traditions of the past. Despite the obvious conservatism of his cultural perspective, his attack on mass society and mass culture had important political implications. It was seen by conservatives as an assault on American values. In effect Macdonald was using cultural criticism as a substitute for traditional political criticism.

Throughout the fifties and early sixties, Macdonald was a staff writer for the *New Yorker* magazine, where he published some of the most incisive critical and cultural commentary of the period. His famous review of Michael Harrington's *The Other America*, the longest review in the history of the magazine to that time, is considered by many to have been a main catalyst for the subsequent war on poverty. It was unquestionably one of Macdonald's most effective political acts.

The 1960s brought him back to the barricades. He was now lecturing on campuses throughout the country, teaching literature, film, and cultural criticism. He also lectured on anarchism and was quick to take up the fight against Kennedy and then Johnson's interventionist foreign policy in Cuba and more vociferously in Vietnam. He also wrote film criticism for *Esquire* (he considered film a genuine art form) and a column entitled "Politics," which amounted to a monthly assault on the administration's Vietnam War policy. No longer did his anti-Stalinism blunt his political critique. While he was never one to support the North Vietnamese, he felt that cold war anti-communism was a dead end and in large part responsible for the tragedy.

Macdonald's last decade was largely confined to a series of visiting professorships. He often suffered from severe "writer's block" and found that teaching helped solve his need to make his opinions known and became a welcome escape from facing a blank page in the morning. He had always been a heavy drinker, but age made it all the more difficult for him to handle his drinking. It also obviously interfered with his writing. His last piece was a long essay review of a biography of Buster Keaton, published in the *New York Review of Books*, a publication he had helped found. He died of congestive heart failure in New York Hospital on December 19, 1982.

One thing missing in this volume is the visual aspect of Dwight Macdonald's letters. He was a master of the typeover, the marginal insertion, the explanatory footnote wedged into the bottom margin, as well as interminable postscripts. When he was angry, serious, or reflective, he had as much trouble ending a letter, even a note, as Henry James. He had to get it right. As his good friend John Lukacs has observed, Macdonald "knew that the choice of every word was not only an aesthetic but a moral choice." He labored over his published work, producing endless drafts. In those pre-computer days he would begin typing from the beginning again and again. His letters appear casual, but one often finds several drafts with a plethora of cross-outs, insertions, and marginal notes. Unfortunately facsimiles were impossible to include here. Typos, puzzling punctuation, and occasional spelling errors have been corrected in the letters, but Macdonald's word creations and other syntactical eccentricities have been retained.

One of the most dedicated Macdonalites—and there are a healthy number to this day—has remarked on how open and fresh his letters were. Perhaps it was because, as Paul Goodman crankily charged in an attack on Macdonald, "he thought with his typewriter." Macdonald responded that one had to start somewhere. What you hear in these letters is a person thinking and working out the ideas as he writes. Goodman offered the left-handed compliment that Dwight was "our best journalist" but that he was not a serious "writer." Dwight was defensive about this charge, because, as he said, he had never "written a book in cold blood." Even his books about Henry Wallace and the Ford Foundation were really collections of articles published initially in *Politics* and the *New Yorker*. When he was not being defensive he called himself an intellectual journalist. Like Hannah Arendt, he had a remarkable knack for getting to the core of a contemporary issue. That is what makes these letters so rewarding. Through them one can enter that world of intellectual ferment that followed World War II. Perhaps most compelling is Macdonald's continuing recognition that, as Daniel Bell noted, "changes were taking place in the moral temper." Czeslaw Milosz, another writer whom Macdonald helped, saw him as a "totally American phenomenon . . . the completely free man, capable of making decisions at all times about all things strictly according to his personal moral judgment." As he insists in these pages time and time again, "the Root is Man."

CHRONOLOGY

1906   Born March 24 in New York City to Dwight Macdonald, Sr., and Alice Hedges Macdonald.

1916–1920   Attends the Barnard School.

1920–1924   Attends Phillips Exeter Academy.

1924–1928   Attends Yale College.

1926   Death of Dwight Macdonald's father.

1927–1928   Serves as chairman of the board of the Yale *Record*, the university's humor magazine.

1928   Spends six months with Macy's executive training program in New York City.

1929   Becomes an editor for Luce publications—works on *Time* and as an associate editor of Henry Luce's new magazine, *Fortune*.

1930   Publishes six numbers of a literary magazine, *The Miscellany*, with Yale classmates George L. K. Morris, Geoffrey Hellman, and Frederick W. Dupee. Begins writing serious film criticism as well as literary criticism.

1934   Marries Nancy Rodman in November.

1936   Resigns from *Fortune* in dispute over editing of his articles criticizing the United States Steel Corporation.

1937   Becomes an editor of the revived *Partisan Review*; his first article for *PR* is a critique of the *New Yorker*. Publishes a three-part article on Luce magazines in *The Nation*.

1938   Birth of a son, Michael Dwight. Begins writing for *The New International*, a Trotskyist publication. Writes *Fascism and the American Scene*.

1939   Joins the Trotskyist Socialist Workers Party. Becomes acting secretary of the League for Cultural Freedom and Socialism and signs its cable to French President Daladier protesting the imprisonment of French pacifists.

1940   Writes *Jobs, Not Battleships* for the Socialist Workers Party. Sides with Max Shachtman's Workers Party in its split with James P. Canon's SWP.

1941   Resigns from the Workers Party over issues of intellectual freedom and party organization.

1943   Resigns from the editorial board of *Partisan Review*, protesting what he sees as a shift away from political commentary to a narrow focus on literary criticism.

1944   Begins publishing *Politics*, and in the first issue writes "A Theory of Popular Culture."

1945   Birth of a second son, Nicholas Gardiner.

1946   Writes "The Root Is Man" for *Politics*.

1948   Publication of *Henry Wallace: The Man and the Myth*.

1949   Discontinues publication of *Politics*, confessing to a "stale, tired, disheartened and . . . demoralized" feeling.

1951   Joins the staff of the *New Yorker*.

1953   Publication of *The Root Is Man: A Radical Critique of Marxism*; publication of "The Bible in Modern Undress" in the *New Yorker*.

1954   Divorced from Nancy Rodman Macdonald; marries Gloria Lanier.

1955   Publication of *The Ford Foundation: The Men and the Millions*.

1956   Lives for a year in London as a staff writer for *Encounter*; publication of *Memoirs of a Revolutionist*.

1957   Death of Macdonald's mother, Alice Hedges Macdonald.

1958   "The *Encounter* Row," in which Macdonald complains of the editorial control wielded by the Congress of Cultural Freedom. His article "America! America!" is rejected by *Encounter* editors and published in *Dissent*.

1960   Publication of "Masscult and Midcult" in *Partisan Review*. Becomes film critic for *Esquire*. Publication of *Parodies: An Anthology from Chaucer to Beerbohm*.

1962   Publication of *Against the American Grain*.

1963   Review of Michael Harrington's *The Other America*, "Our Invisible Poor," in the *New Yorker*.

1964   Publication of "Fellini's Masterpiece," a review of "8-1/2," in the *New Yorker*.

1965   Publication of *Selected Poems of Edgar Allan Poe*. Leaves the staff of the *New Yorker*.

1966   Drops the *Esquire* film column.

1967   Writes a political column, "Politics," for *Esquire*, in which he consistently denounces the war in Vietnam and the Johnson administration.

1968   Publication of *My Past and Thoughts: The Memoirs of Alexander Herzen* with a lengthy introduction by Macdonald.

1969   Publication of *Dwight Macdonald on Movies*.

1970   Reissue of *Memoirs of a Revolutionist*, retitled *Politics Past*. Selected for membership in the National Institute of Arts and Letters.

1974   Publication of *Discriminations*.

1974–1980   Visiting professorships and speaking engagements throughout the country.

1980   Last publication, essay review of a study of Buster Keaton in the *New York Review of Books*.

1982   Dies December 19 in New York City.

A MORAL TEMPER
The Letters of Dwight Macdonald

Dwight Macdonald (left), Justin O'Brien, and Dinsmore Wheeler—the
Hedonist Club at Exeter, 1924. (Photograph by Donald B. Straube, courtesy of
the Class of 1945 Library, Phillips Exeter Academy)

CHAPTER ONE

THE EDUCATION OF A GENTLEMAN, 1920–1929

"I have trained my mind." — Exeter Journal, 1923

These prep school and college letters include Macdonald's accounts of his brief and often hilarious experience in the executive training program at Macy's department store. From his first day away, he was an inveterate letter writer and determined to keep his parents and later his very close friend Dinsmore Wheeler up to date not only with his intellectual activities and interests but with his inner life as well. This is particularly evident in the letters to Wheeler.

To Theodore Dwight Macdonald [father]

October 19, 1920

I hope my other letter did not scare you. I am doing as well as most of my class. On the 18th we had the exam for Oct. I did very well in relation with my class. There are 14 fellows in my class and 9 of them got E– (that is a failure) or E. One got C and the rest got either D, D+, or D–. I got D–. So as the exam determines your standing to a very large extent, I am among the first 5 of my class! Write me when you get my package of *Exonians* and exams.

Greek is pretty hard but I am glad I took it. Dr. Jacobi is a peach. There is to be no more golf as the links are so bad. I will write you what I go out for. I should like to take walking there are a lot of good walks around Exeter. I must close now as I have a lot of work to do.

P.S. I like Exeter more every day I think it is a great school I am so busy that I have not had time to be homesick.

To Parents

April 30, 1923

. . . I sent you a copy of the new *Monthly* yesterday, in which my Dunsany essay appears. Write and tell me what you think of it. Well I didn't get the Lantern Club prize after all; Lamb's story was first and poor little me second. What atrocious taste most fellows have, don't they? (Answer: *YES!!*)

I am busy on two great *opus*, or perhaps *opa* would be better. The first is my Merrill Prize Essay. I have decided to write a comparison of Erasmus and Luther. You can see that since they were the two greatest figures in the Renaissance, and since they were widely different in personal character, they will make a vivid contrast. At present I am reading up on Luther. I have a 400-page tome on his life and letters which I am reading now. It really is absorbing, contrary to my expectations. When I finish that, I will read parts of four or five other books on Luther and then Frat's Erasmus again, and I will be "all set," as the expression is. The other opus is my next story for the *Monthly*. I have not definitely decided on the details of the plot, but I can tell you that it will be a story of school life—either here, or in some school very similar to it—and will be a sort of study in the struggle of a fellow against the opinions and prejudices of the students and profs at large. This is not at all what I want to say, but I can't seem to express it, you know.

To Father

February 12, 1923

My very dear Pater: I have just received the correspondence between you and Henry Seidel Canby, the *Sat. Rev.* editor, and while I very much appreciate the compliment you pay me when you calmly ask Canby for a book for me to review, don't you think that is putting it on a little thickly?

I do! You must think I am an infant Dr. Johnson or Macaulay, or something. Ye Gauds! (As a very dear friend of yours says) I could no more review a book than I could—well, make first base on the Varsity (in spite of my build). All the same don't think that I don't appreciate your ambitions for me and O Boy wait till you see my next story.

To Parents

November 28, 1923

I am talking up Browning now and really like him immensely. When I get home for Xmas . . . I'll show you what to read, how to read and why to read in him. For the present it will be enough if you read the following and report on same in your next letter. Here are the poems:

(1) Johannes Agrigola
(2) Fra Lippo Lippi*
(3) The Bishop Orders His Tomb at St. Praxid
(4) Caliban upon Setebos
(5) Confessions
(6) Soliloquy in the Spanish Cloister
(7) My Last Duchess

They will probably be hard to understand at first, but just think a little about them and I am sure they will become clear. The ones with a star are more difficult.

To Parents

CYNICISM

ESTHETICISM

CRITICISM

PESSIMISM

THE HEDONISTS[1]
Exeter
December 6, 1923
Pour epater les bourgeois

———

monocle & dagger

. . . Is this paper attractive in your opinion? We three Hedonists printed it ourselves at the Academy press. We have also single white sheets for less formal correspondence.

The following books have just arrived from Glazier, my English bookseller. *The War of the Worlds* by H. G. Wells—that was for you father. I read it myself yesterday afternoon and find it readable; *To Let, A Man of Property,* and *In Chancery,* by John Galsworthy—these three compose in part the *Forsythe*

———

1. Dwight and a select few of his classmates formed their own elite society, The Hedonists, designed to separate themselves from the surrounding mediocrities.

Saga as it is called; *Regiment of Women*, and *First the Blade*, by Clemence Dave. I have also just received two copies of *Reginald*, that book I told you of this summer. It is only 35 [cents] a copy—new with a lemon yellow jacket! So now I am sending this morning for 10 copies which I will use as Christmas presents. . . . In spite of all my spare time, I find myself kept pretty busy. Writing for the *Monthly*, attending meetings of the Exonian and Lantern Club, and *above all* talking, talking, talking—at the Hedonists with Bob Lamb, Eddie Mills, Johnny Seawall, Johnny Haven, Johnny Burr, Anyone! Ye Gods! I should be a most brilliant conversationalist by this time if practice means anything. . . .

To Parents

n.d., 1923–1924

. . . Well I am glad you liked the story. I am quite a "lion" now with the fellows. They are awfully complimentary about the story, but I suspect that their praise is mostly tact! I have decided I should get a good foundation in the Greek and Latin Classics before tackling modern literature, so I have given up Swift and am now engaged in laboriously translating Livy and Thucydides. I asked Pinks for a good author to read in conjunction with Caesar and he recommended Livy. He was very decent about it—he even lent me a small Latin dictionary to look up the unfamiliar words. Dr. Peacock said Thucydides was a good one to start on, so I bought a Greek dictionary which I will need later on anyway and started. Whew! You never realize how little you know about grammar till you tackle something like Thucydides! . . . I sounded out Mc Cann [a classmate he has just met] on the question of books and found that he is not a great reader. He said he would like to read, but always thought books were "dry." I am going to take him over to the library tonight and pick out some good books for him. We have had long talks on religion in which I maintained that there was no *God* and he said there was. It was quite interesting. I wish I could talk to you about that, I bet you would be on your knees after a few minutes of my irresistible logic. (I hear church bells ringing so I will continue after church.) Went to church where an Andover prof preached! What is the academy coming to!!

I just read a wonderful book about English school life called *The Hill*. It is by Howard A. Vachell. It isn't the regular "Tom, Dick and Harry at Fairweathers" sort, but a real work of art! The scene is laid at Harrow. One of the leading characters is a fellow named Edgerton who is always *well-dressed and immaculate* (mother please note) and a regular old aristocrat. He is the type that uses "one" instead of I. He is in my mind the most interesting character in the book. I won't ask you or Hedges [Dwight's younger brother] to read it bec. I realize that you wouldn't (ha! ha!). Seriously, though, I wish you would at least start it and *make* Hedges read it.

To Alice Hedges Macdonald [mother]

March 6, [1924]

. . . According to your oft-repeated advice, I am "cultivating" with more or less success two very fine chaps. (I think I have told you about them in my last letter, but in case I didn't their names are (1) McCann and (2) McVitty. The first has only one serious fault: he comes from Rochester, New York, and he believes he is a descendant of Pepin, the founder of the Carolinian dynasty in France (look him up in the Britannica under "Pay to Pol," (I think). I think he is mistaken after argue, — er discuss[ing] the matter with him. I am trying to get him interested in reading. He has promised to come up to my room between the hours of 8:30 to 9 on Saturday for reading. He is coming up tonight and I am going to start him on Kipling's *Drums of the Fore and Aft*. Last Tuesday night I went to a lecture by a Frenchman (in English) on "Moliere" with McVitty. After the lecture the Hampton Quartet played with great energy but unfortunately, without a like degree of success. Nevertheless they got quite a hand.

"Business before pleasure," say I, so I'll start off with my marks. In Greek I got B, as I expected. The best scholar in our class only got a B+, so I guess I am not so bad after all! In Latin I got C (comments both unnecessary and undesirable), as usual. In Math I sunk to a lowly B– since I only got C– on the big test. Doc is not good at all, I think he wastes hours talking and gassing about everything under the sun and then bawls us out for not knowing enough. Well, enough of *that*! Let's pass on to the great surprise I have up my sleeve. IN ENG. I GOT C!!! I almost fell over when I heard it! I don't know why or how I did it, and I don't care! The fact remains — I got a C in English. Now you can't ask me why I only get Ds in my favorite subject — ha! ha! In French I got C+. This is the only mark I am not proud of. I know I should be able to get a B and I am straining every muscle (or perhaps brain-cell would be more appropriate) to get it.

To Parents

[Spring] 1924

I have just returned from the Prize giving, and find myself — much to my amazement — owner of (1) $45 in gold, (2) the Stedman Woodberry edition of Edgar Allan Poe, (3) four selected volumes of Rudyard Kipling's works — *Stally and Co.*, *The Jungle Book*, *The Light That Failed*, and *Captains Courageous*.

The evening began very pleasantly, and the Greek and Bible prizes (Hedges got one of the latter!!) were run off. Then Tuffie read "The Pits-Duffield Prize, awarded to that member of the Senior English Class who shall do the best in a written examination, awarded to (*long pause*) Dwight Macdonald." As I wrote you, I did not have very much hope of getting it, so I was more or less unprepared. I dashed up, however, and received a warm, moist hand-shake by Doc Perry, (2) a "dummy" set of Poe (the real set had not yet arrived), and (3) a parting smile. A few more prizes were read off and then—"The [Seighton] prize to be awarded to that student who does the most towards fur-thering interest in creative writing in the Academy. Awarded to (*pause*) Dwight Macdonald." I did not even suspect that I would get that, and so I was totally unprepared. I went up amid much clapping, and, feeling very much stunned and surprised, received four leather-covered volumes of Kipling. The very next prize was the Chesterfield prize, so you can imagine how foolish I felt going up again. There was a great demonstration and much laughter as I pocketed the money. I certainly was "quite the boy" raking in (3) prizes!. . . .

AT YALE: *"To be fair, the administration did not prevent us from using the library."*

To Parents

October 2, 1924

. . . I have been in New Haven a week now. The Exeter men here are pretty ter-rible; the Robbinshowardcornishthomas type; the rest are Lamonclendennin-michaels, if you get what I mean. Just now I rather envy you and Pinny[2]—at least you can whisper the name of Anderson without someone saying, "Oh, yeah! That Dry League feller that's in the jug." Most of the past week has been consumed in standing in line waiting to see Deans, Advisors, Inspectors, and Officers of one sort or another who, when one finally does come face to face with them, growl something and push a pink card at you to fill out. Then you go to another room and give the card to someone else, etcetera ad inf. I'm be-ginning to hate the whole damned business of officialdom and authority as much as you do—a large order. Classes here are imperceptibly less boring and childish than at E, the teachers are more intelligent, I believe. The one ray of sunshine in the whole Plutonian outlook is the great prestige of the *Lit* and the *News* among even the gin-soaked. . . .

I have just received 10 copies of France's *Penguin Island* and 5 of his *The Red Lily* from England. I'm going to spread them about where I think they will do the most good—so to speak. Have you them? If not, say so and I'll send you a

2. Nickname for Justin O'Brien, later to be the biographer of Camus and professor of French literature at Columbia University.

pair. *Penguin Island,* especially, is superb. No one of sound intellect could read this—not even Pinny, by the way—and fail to see the ridiculous side of the Roman Catholic Church. I don't wonder they put him on the index.

To Dinsmore Wheeler[3]

October 19, 1924

. . . Your letter was really very absorbing. I ran into two peanut-stands and almost got run over myself twice in the attempt to read it while on my way to History class. Seriously though, AS SOMEONE WE BOTH KNOW IS FOND OF OBSERVING, I enjoyed the perusal of it almost as much as if I had written it myself—than which there is no higher praise! . . . *Penguin Island* is something to thank the gods for—not The God, that chill bungling, "silent Cal" person, but the jolly pagan gods, who at least took some sort of interest in the men who danced and groaned at their feet. I suppose you know France's dictum: "the highest form of writing is that which combines irony and pity," or something like that. How utterly true that is! And also how hard to attain For irony *vide* Aldous Huxley, Bodenheim, Dean Swift, Voltaire, Shaw, etc.; for pity *vide* "Elizabeth," Frederick Niven, Mrs. Humphrey Ward, Dickens, Harold Bell Wright. For both *vide* Anatole France; and . . . W. M. Thackeray.

Speaking of irony, remember that story about Exeter I told you . . . that I have written called "Mr. Townley"? I think I have a little irony in it, but no pity—as is usually the case with young barbarians like you and me. It's a study of a *very* hateful prof. (he is a half-breed, part F. N. Robinson, part E. A. Barret [two of Macdonald's teachers]—mostly F.N.R.) and I'm sure you will agree with the thesis of the story—which is simply that some prep. school profs are, to use my own words, "mere Tyrants of Boys, whose heart and spirit are alike dust." Anyway, I handed it into the Lit., and—Allah be praised—it was accepted! So you see I seem in a fair way to "arrive" up here as far as writing is concerned. Probably from now on I will meet with a series of rebuffs, and become so discouraged that I'll never touch a pen again! I will send you a copy of the December Lit when it comes out. . . . It's 8:45 P.M. and I have had three experiences, so to speak, since I laid down my pen at 5 to go to the President's reception. (1) was, of course, the reception, which was crowded and boring—al-

3. Dinsmore Wheeler was a classmate at Exeter who became a very close friend. He and Dwight maintained an intense and confiding correspondence until well into their adulthood. Dwight spent several summers at the Wheeler family farm in Ohio. He also had a romantic relationship with Wheeler's sister, Dorothy. Dwight used his correspondence with Dinsmore as a kind of personal diary, writing to him often, even on his trip to Europe, which was a delayed honeymoon with his wife Nancy. Later he used the correspondence as source material for his psychiatrist and also for his brief memoirs.

together a silly affair: people trying to be pleasant to me with about as much comprehension as a bachelor uncle trying to amuse an infant nephew. I met President Angell himself, and was reminded of Lou Perry, not in size, for Angell is small, but in a certain flushed joviality, which must be very effective in securing funds. I also talked for a long—too long—time with a Mary Cabot, who lives here and who is a cousin to Blake Cabot, and one of the Boston Cabots. . . . [I went to the talk] by Professor Jack Crawford, director of the Playcraftsmen, author of *I Walked in Arden*. . . . He spoke on "A Philosophy of Life." He said much that was original and much that was sound, but unfortunately what was original was not sound and what was sound was not original (a bon mot of Richard Brinsley Sheridan). Fortitude, tolerance, curiosity, humor, and something else constituted his right little, tight little philosophy. Very admirable, a bit whimsical, and quite respectable—but not for me.

Your verses to the little waitress are *very* good. I mean this. You have expressed in what seems to me an effective, lucid, and original way a feeling that I myself have often experienced: a sort of delight in knowing something or someone who is perfect in dainty frailty. Poe's *To Helen* has the same emotion as your II verse:

> "Thou wast that all to me, love.
>   For which my soul did pine;
> A green isle in the sea, love,
>   Where every tree was mine."

This is from memory, and may be wrong in places. But you see the sense: the aching for something absolute, beautiful, and unbreakable to which you can turn and be refreshed and renewed—and which shall be yours only. Call it Helen of Troy, Utopia, Penelope, or a fat bank balance, the idea is the same. Still commenting on the little waitress, I observe that she is dainty, petite, fragile, etc. And precisely the opposite of you yourself. You are attracted by your opposite, but I am drawn to tall, slender, long-legged girls—now isn't that strange. . . . I really can't break off without a word about the main theme of your letter. So you are *toujours miserable*, eh? Much as I disliked his talk, I can't help referring you to Prof. Jack Crawford. Fortitude, humor, tolerance, *and* curiosity. The first two you possess in some measure, the third not at all, the fourth—I once *did* think—in abundance. Now the first three aren't 1/2 so necessary for wellbeing in a place like Yale or Harvard as the last. And it seems that the last must be greatly restricted. Curiosity about how Paris looks in the winter or what the Australians really are like (VIDE Kangaroo, of course) cannot obviously be satisfied. But curiosity—or I think *interest* would be better—interest, then, in books, people (not necessarily all male), and ideas can be very well satisfied. As you saw from my last letter I am not exactly a Smiling Sam all the time, but I owe the fact that I am not a Dismal Jenny all the time to my interest in such things as Browning, *The Lit.*, China, Morris, Mrs. Noyes (wife of my English Prof. and possessed of the simplest, freshest, most human soul in the world; she is also young and handsome), several fellows I've met this fall, my Victrola and collection of records, and my bloomin' self. This sounds whimsical and professorial. Ah well! You know, I desire to be just what you write: broad-minded, free from prejudice, and clean in body and—oh, hell—soul. I also refuse to become a lifeless lump of clay, dull, uninterested, stupid, sketchily read, and impervious to 1001 of the finer sensations and experiences. To be open to all thoughts, experiences, loves, etc. Is my one aim. To become thus, one must read much and eagerly thrust himself into contact with all things, and preserve his own integrity. D. H. Lawrence said a very profound thing I think when he said that sin is something which violates one's personal, spiritual integrity. If the mirror is flawed and cracked, one can get no truth from it.

But how I rave on. This letter is written, as you may have perceived, in one of my exalted moods while the last one was written in one of my black despair moods. I would give a lot to help you out of your Doubting Castle, but I feel I haven't done much in the pages above. I'm really just as badly off as you, except that I am only *quelquebois miserable*. But when I am, all the savor of life is gone. I wish to hell I could see you soon, but it is too close to the Christmas Holidays to make a trip down East, so I will have to wait till next term. . . . Next time I will write you some letters that will arouse your interest in *something* at least. Damn, I talk like a Y.M.C.A. director.

Of course you haven't any *talent*. If you possess anything, it is (loud crescendo of music offstage) GENIUS. This is a rather abrupt way of putting it, but I think I am right. Twenty years from now—etc.

To Parents

n.d., October 1924

Mr. Townley was accepted! Isn't that great? My first two things were potboilers, but now I feel I have really arrived! A regular story is always a much better test of one's writing abilities than any quantity of verse—that is, if one has a prose mind, as I believe I have. I've just reread the thing in the light of its acceptance and I find it much better than I ever did before. Isn't it absurd what a difference such things make?

This weekend I have been busy with two productions of the pen: (1) An article on Kipling for the Course, and (2) the first two numbers of At the Window, my proposed column in the *Exonia*. . . . My identity will be shrouded under the name Argus. I also have been writing *Record* "drool." So far I have the fol-

lowing things either complete or roughly written: a dialogue called "Ya Know?";
a description—humorous, of course—of the Dean's Tea Dance, to which I
went last week (I enclose the invitation); some very light verse; and some odds
and ends from Exeter. I hope to work this all up in its finished form before the
next "criticism" on Wednesday, which will mark my entrance into the lists as a
[heeler—a staff contributor to the *Yale News*]—until I go out for the *News* this
winter, at which time I'll have to drop out for a bit. . . . Stayed up till 12:30 last
night reading *The Light That Failed* and missed breakfast and chapel this morning. It was worth it. I carried freely over *The Light*. Got A+ in a Greek test (i.e.,
95). . . .

To Dinsmore Wheeler

n.d., February 1925

. . . Your reproachful remarks on my reception of the Young Idealists' Cult were
very vexing. Of course I am earnestly seeking a Philosophy of Life just as you
are, and God knows I didn't think for a minute that I was stifling a delicate
flower with my ribaldry. But I don't see how two heads can be better than one
in this case, because a P. of L. must be *all* your own or else it is a mere pose.
That is, such things are not interchangeable between two minds—even between 2 such gifted ones as ours, my dear.

What in hell do you mean by saying: "your genius consists of your ability
and capacity to work." I *hope* you mean "your ability and your capacity to
write." Otherwise I'll never, never forgive you. First you stick me up on a
pedestal on which I have no especial desire to stand and where I look foolish,
and then you proceed to pull me off the pedestal and cast me into the mud by
saying that I'm a hard worker, a go-getter, a steady, reliable, industrious little B.
Franklin, a—but you get the idea? That is just as flattering as to tell me that "I
mean well"—and I suppose you would have told me that too if you had thought
of it. I admit I *do* work, but so did Dickens, so did Carlyle, so did quite a lot of
other old boyos that make your tea-for-a-penny Chicago *literati* look like so
many orangutans. But this outburst of spleen is not conducive to the elevated
frame of mind. I will conclude with a general god damning of you all.

To Dinsmore Wheeler

n.d., early 1925

. . . Lately I have begun to get rather sick of writing, and even reading has lost a
lot of its savor: you know how it is, one can't even concentrate on a page of
print, and at times every book becomes utterly loathsome. However, I think it
was partly the rainy, foggy, cold weather, because now that the air is warm and

the sun is out, I feel what Pink Gillespie would call my "pristine vigor" coming back to me. In fact this morning I read Ring Lardner's *How to Write Short Stories* with great gusto; it is really a perfect gem of vulgarity and bourgeoisie, and I wonder if Ring fully realizes how close he comes to life. It is, of course, also very funny. If you do get a hold of it, I would recommend "The Facts" and "The Golden Honeymoon," the latter of which Mr. Gilbert Seldes, former editor of *The Dial,* says is perfect of its kind. I've been more or less specializing in Dickens of late because I decided to take him up next in a course in English Letters which I am giving to Messrs. Vernon Munroe and Hedges Macdonald. I write a paper on someone twice a month and send it to them at Exeter; they read the paper, and the books by and about him that I recommend. So far I have taken up Jane Austen, Robert Browning, Rudyard Kipling, and Charles Dickens. If you want to raise your naturally low estimate of Dickens, take *Martin Chuzzlewit* and read all the parts in which Mrs. Sarah Gamp figures. She comes in toward the end of Vol I;. . . . Everything she says is funny, I do believe even if she only asks the time. . . .

P.S. I saw the great Henry Seidel Canby in the library today. He was next to me at the delivery desk, and he looked like a rather seedy normal schoolteacher. Very small and insignificant, half bald and half scraggly hair, pince nez, utterly commonplace, businesslike face, faded greenish brown suit, funny shirt, and a rather agreeable but quite undistinguished voice. He looks like the sort of man who would take a pedantic pleasure in collecting pre-revolutionary political pamphlets and in talking about them at great length. Another idol shattered! If I'd only listened to Papa Mencken, I would have known him for a dummy all along.

To Dinsmore Wheeler

n.d., February 1925
. . . Your dislike of rules, formalities, outlines, etc., strikes a very responsive echo in this old gizzard. But I suspect that my motives for dislike are just the opposite of yours. That is, I despise and avoid them because they fail to accomplish what they attempt—but I do not at all despise their goal. You, on the other hand, hate them because you don't believe in their goal—which is order. Don't you see—I see the futility, sterility, the pedagogy of most existing attempts at order, but I still cherish a sneaking feeling that my own system may be all right. To parody *Alice*—"And this is very odd because I haven't any system." As yet, that is. But ever since I can distinctly remember I have always been a great one for making outlines, summaries, etc., the one object of all of which was to compress and classify such subjects as Ancient History, "David Copperfield," Gaius

Pompey, and Erasmus. In fact my present COURSE IN ENGLISH LITERATURE is easily traceable to this passion for order, for clarity, and completeness. This is a typically French quality, I believe, while your murky, uneven, and disorganized view of this is typically English. And yet I recognize with joy a considerable streak of your hatred in my own self. I say "with joy" because the spontaneous, irregular genius of a Dickens has always appealed to me more than the rule-observing, clear-eyed genius of a Flaubert. "Spontaneity is the soul of art," however, as an unqualified credo leaves much to be explained away, this same Flaubert among other things.

You say, "Life itself seems to be without outline, without definitiveness, and so I seldom care for them in drama, in books, in art, or in poetry." Well, if you mean that you think the disorganized meanderings of a *Dreiser* are better than, say, the highly [centralized] and thematic stories of Poe—why, I must disagree. For it seems to me that one cannot hope to even *approximate reality* in art, and that therefore any attempt to imitate the diffusiveness and lack of outline of life in a work of art is utterly futile. The object of a story—and, in a lesser degree, a novel—is to "put across" something to the reader. What this something is depends on the time, place, and inclination of the writer and is of minor importance; how valuable it is depends wholly on the amount of genius or talent possessed by the writer and is of major importance. The means of "putting across" this something is, it seems to me, what is termed "art," and more restrictedly, "technique." Now the best means of telling a story—i.e., the best "art"—is by adhering to certain principles, call them "conventions" if you will, such as good construction, such as harmony between the units of the story, etc. etc. You will say: "Look at Shakespeare's "Romeo," look at Thackeray and Dickens and The Illiad," the plots of which or whom, are all feeble, utterly senseless. Well, I can only reply that if those plots has been better, the works would have been. But anyway, all this stuff about "art" and "life" comes down to this: art can never create a complete or even successful illusion of reality, and therefore any attempt at so doing is futile and a diversion of its energy. WHAT UTTER RANT AND CANT AND PLAIN B L A A H H H!!!!

I also have found that any of my own or other people's pet dogmas, theories, philosophies, religions, creeds, moralities, or standards fade into utter [nullity] whenever I really *think* about them instead of *feeling* them. Which proves, I maintain, that my mind is [inferior/superior] to my—shall I say "soul"? In fact, I was seriously considering writing a paragraph or two about it for my own satisfaction when I received your letter.

To Dinsmore Wheeler[4]

n.d., May 1925

Your last letter very gratefully received and read. It seemed to me, however, that it lacked the sparkling . . . play of wit and cleverness which your previous epistle have displayed. Indeed, much of it seemed to me "one long melodious whine"—though possibly the "melodious" doesn't belong. At any rate, I gather that you are even more depressed, dispirited, damnatory, and misanthropic—ah, fooled you that time!—than usual. I'm very much the same way, only more so. My spleen and bile, however, are much more horrible than yours because I pour it down my own throat, while you let fly at the world with your little squirt. That is, I am introspective and morbid, also oversensitive, also overanalytic, also weary to death of this goddamn thinking, *thinking*, THINKING! Somewhere I once read a plea of Mark Twain's for a moment's respite from the ceaseless churnings of his mind. Don't you ever feel that you would go mad some night when your mind won't leave you alone? My case is all the worse because I am in love—and not with a girl either. But "in love" is such a vague and meaningless word—perhaps I mean something a great deal more than that, and perhaps a great deal less. You remember up at E[xeter] I was "in love" for all the Spring term with Vernon Munroe? Well, the same thing has happened here with George Morris—the fellow you met in the Grand Central Terminal with me. It is largely a matter of looks that is, just as with Munroe. Of course you couldn't get a very good idea of George's looks in two minutes . . . but I think he is the most enchanting-looking boy I ever knew, except Vernon, of *course*. But besides his looks he has the "added attractions" of intelligence, culture, and breeding—oh, how stiff and silly this all sounds. Anyway, I have made myself quite miserable over him for only too much of the last few months. "I don't know why I tell you all this" is what I might write, but it wouldn't be true. Because I do. It's partly from a quite selfish desire to relieve myself a bit by blowing off steam, and chiefly because we know each other so well that I don't need to keep back things. I wouldn't of course write to any one else. For why write each other at all if we keep up the same subterfuge and pretensions that one must keep up with everyone else. Of course I don't need to ask you not to let Bob Lamb, Pinny, or anyone else read this. Also, if you think I am a homosexualist, please disburden yourself of that idea; my amatory feelings have little that is physical about them. Also I hate to have little boys like you at 47 Oxford St. [Cambridge] thinking about such things. It's just not manly, that's all.

4. Dwight had anxiety about his sexuality for a good part of his life. While in prep school and college at non-coed institutions, he was frequently attracted to a classmate and revealed these interests to Dinsmore, who advised him that they were perfectly normal.

To Marian Isaacs

August 13, 1925

. . . As you so keenly perceived, my attitude toward you at the [Wheeler family farm in Ohio] was on the whole one of hostility. I think that whatever else I may criticize in you, you possess a mind remarkably flexible and free from prejudice and pride — pride in the stiff-necked sense, of course. Therefore I am going to do a very unusual and what would be with most girls a very foolish thing. I'm going to tell you more or less plainly just what I really think of you. I do this partly because I think you are worth it, partly in compliance with a request of Dinsmore's that I do so.

I suppose the thing which I most abhorred in you was what seemed to me your lack of sincerity, of naturalness. Almost everything you said grated on my nerves, seemed out of place and affected. You seemed perpetually to labor under the strain of making yourself agreeable, or — when alone with Dins and I — of appearing ultraintelligent. I felt that you replied to everything not so much what you really felt to be true or sincere but rather what you thought would please or impress your hearers. In short, you were playing a game and, while I am very fond of games as a diversion, I dislike making of one's social relations a careful and studied game. I can forgive much, but I must have a feeling that the person is also sincere and open in what he says. This lack of naturalness on your part, however, was, I am sure, caused by the strain you felt yourself under all the time you were at R.D.3. But it rendered all intimate relationships — intellectual or otherwise — out of the question for me.

Another thing I noticed in you was a lack of — what shall I say — character, individuality. You seemed to flow too easily into the molds Dins or I indicated. Dins is, I admit, something of an overwhelming personality, is difficult to stand up against him. But you seemed to be only too willing to follow the lead of even so unimpressive a person as myself, and this leads me into another channel. You appeared to be soft-soaping me at a great rate. You were, in fact, only too obviously attempting to raise my estimate of you, and ironically enough, the more you tried, the lower it fell. For I missed in you a certain dignity, an aloofness and sense of personal pride that I fancy is a sign of the lady — or gentleman. When Mrs. W[heeler] made her ungracious and nasty attack on your morals, race, etc., you did not become angry or even disgusted. You cried — for which I do not blame you — and became penitent and tearful. What you said and did after Dins and I had left, I do not know, but I fear you went even further and quite convinced Mrs. W. that she was in the right after all. Humility is one of the Christian virtues, but as G. K. Chesterton paradoxically points out, humility is merely pride carried to a splendid extreme.

And then too there was the fact that you are a Jewess, and are rather obviously one, to make me react unfavorably. For I dislike rather violently the Jews as a race, and although you are in my opinion superior to your race, there are certain Jewish characteristics that are present in your makeup. The two that I have tried to expound above are the most offensive to me. I say you are superior to your race because I think you possess a—what shall I say?—"heart," that your emotions and feelings are not relegated to a back seat but control and determine your actions *almost* as much as your intelligence. Your feeling for Dins is, I am quite convinced, not only genuine but disinterested—insofar as any human emotion can be disinterested. And also you seem well disposed, "decent," not at all malicious or evil. . . .

. . .I feel all this is rather fruitless, for I express myself so poorly that I fear you may get a wrong impression from it all. However, the very fact that I do write you 6 pages of criticism is some proof that I have respect and feeling for you. I am afraid this all sounds cocky, patronizing, and most offensive, and I apologize beforehand for it all.

To Dinsmore Wheeler

Fall 1925

. . . As Marian Isaacs has probably told you, I went and called on her one afternoon in N.Y.C. She was, on the whole, better than at R.D.3. I didn't like her over-self-conscious attitude toward my letter, though. She had obviously erected defenses of her own dignity rather than tried to understand and, possibly, apply my criticism. She passed it off as "ridiculous," which it was not, and tried to impress me with how little effect it had on her. "*Of course*, I didn't take it very seriously—you're only eighteen after all, and how can you set yourself up as a critic?" But such a reaction, is, after all, very human and even more very feminine. And M.I. is, in spite of this episode, in my opinion of greater intelligence than most of her sex. . . .

. . .This is one hell of a college, I have at last concluded. If I don't meet someone soon with brains, individuality, distinction, *something*, I shall go mad. Mr. G. L. K. Morris is the only subtle and sinewy intellect I have yet encountered in the g.d. class of 1928, that awful "Sahara of the Bozarts." If I ever am blessed, or cursed, with a son, I shall tell him to go wherever he damn pleases— except Princeton. All the intellectuals up here are either "nice boys" with a gentlemanly inclination towards the better-known works of Keats and Arnold, or embryo pedants and fakes. To be intellectual, nay, intelligent, reserved, individual, and sensitive is to be solitary. About four-fifths of the undergraduates are, or aspire to be YALE men. The remaining fifth are either the Peoria High School mental incompetent type, or "cranks." I am of necessity driven back on myself—from which I escape by reading and writing. Perhaps it is just as well for me after all. For I do get a lot more reading done than I might otherwise.

To James Rowland Angell, president of Yale University

December 1, 1925

The sermon which D. Stearns preached in Battelle last Sunday was without exception the worst I have ever heard. And this includes four years of sermons at Phillips Exeter. Before I heard that sermon I was strongly against compulsory chapel: now I am rabidly, unreasonably, fantastically against it. To be forced to listen to such puerile, stupid twaddle is an insult to any intelligent person. Perhaps I should now give a few reasons for my condemnation of last Sunday's sermon. As Sheridan once remarked of a youngster's maiden speech, Dr. Stearns said much that was original and much that was sound, but unfortunately the original parts were not sound and the sound parts were not original. He seems to have a remarkable power of hypnotizing himself with the magniloquent platitudes such as "The family is that institution which is the foundation of all our civil and social structure"—or about twice as many words to that effect. His sermon was absolutely lacking in any plan or coherence; he drifted from tradition to convention to "the younger generation" to women's rights to somewhere else, etc. And not one intelligent remark did he make. It was a mass of platitudes, generalities, offensive admonitions against cynicism and that terrible Devil, Radicalism, and words, words, words. If I was a liberal before I heard that sermon, I am a red red Radical now. In short, Dr. Stearns preached a very bad sixth-form-Sunday-evening talk. When I left the chapel I was literally quivering with rage.

Please don't think I am condemning Stearns because he presented, or rather failed to present the conservative point of view. Not at all. I don't object to a person's disagreeing with me; I enjoy Stuart P. Sherman as well as H. L. Mencken. But I do most strenuously object to a human animal getting up on his hind legs and making a fool of himself—and me—and that is what Dr. Stearns did last Sunday.

I would have written to the *News* about this, but they would probably not print it—and they are right I suppose. And so since you were there and heard the sermon for yourself, I make this protest to you. I'd be very glad to talk this over with you if you want to. All I have said here I am quite sincere in. Be assured.

To Dinsmore Wheeler

March 23, 1926

. . . Did you see Mencken's uproarious criticism of *An American Tragedy*? I say "uproarious" because the poor fellow is so obviously writing on the horns of a dilemma: he can either massacre the book as it deserves and thus puncture the balloon he has been blowing up for several decades, or he can preserve his balloon intact at the sacrifice of that critical integrity which he flaunts in his colleagues' faces so often. He chose the best way out, I must admit: tempered truth. . . .

To Mother[5]

n.d., Spring 1926

Your letter struck terror and dismay into me, mother, and although I realized the truth of your remarks about my being too anti-social and proud and shy, still I must violently object to your advising me to be politic and diplomatic. You say, "One must be politic all of the time in life whether you like it or not." Now I say it all depends on what you mean by "politic." If you mean that one should not injure other's feelings wantonly or through sheer egotism, that one can use tact in dealing with people in matters that are not important, I agree with you. But if you mean that one should keep silent in the face of cant and lies and evil and silliness and stupidity and injustice merely in order to save one's own hide, I do not. I believe that no one of any intelligence or justice is going to think any the worse of one for speaking out his mind. And as for the others, I don't much care what they think. You say, "but at least one must be agreeable to one's fellow creatures or go jump in the lake." If one's fellow creatures are asses and swine, one might as well jump in the lake. . . . In print I am always going to take the hide off such silly charlatans as Mr. B. B. T. Coffin, author of the book I reviewed so violently. Just because it was Yale University Press was no reason for not exposing it. If the Press is good, criticism will not hurt it. If bad, it should be criticized. Anyway, that book made me sick at my stomach, and I think it would make anyone so who has any taste or intelligence.

5. His mother chastised him for a harsh review in the Yale paper of a Yale professor's book. She was concerned that Dwight think about the impressions he made and the friends he cultivated. He frequently apologized to her if an acquaintance was Jewish.

To Dinsmore Wheeler

Fall 1926

... J. A. BRIDGETTS [an Exeter classmate] I had in for lunch at the invaluable Yale Club the other day. He is not at all changed. He wore an abominable hat and almost was ejected by the doorman. He is now working (sic) in a Greenwich Village antique shop. He told me wild tales of the Village and its parties. Everyone gets soused there every night, he said. He has met Maxwell Bodenheim, E. E. Cummings, Edna St. V. Millay, and all that sort of crowd. He says that all they think of seriously for any length of time is Sex—homo or otherwise. Joseph A. is as amusing as ever; he is an original if ever there was one. His favorite expression is, "He (or she) is a riot." Rather good.

I HAVE SEEN TWO very good movies: SIEGFRIED and THE BIRTH OF A NATION. ... You probably have seen *The Birth of a Nation* when you were very young. So had I. But I had completely forgotten it. I now have rediscovered it, and in my opinion it is a great picture. It is oozing with sentimentality, but, as I remembered before, I don't dislike that at times. The marvelous thing about it is that it can absolutely sweep *you* off your feet even today. It's emotional kick is tremendous. You want to tear in pieces the cocky insolent niggers and carpetbaggers of "after-the-war" days, and when the good old Ku Klux Klan comes sweeping down on horseback and rescues the besieged whites, you want to cheer. In spite of my prejudice against the modern K.K.K., that was the way I felt. The most convincing proof of the vitality of the picture is that several times the audience burst out into applause as some daring rescue was made or some heroic deed done. I don't think I ever before heard a New York audience applaud a picture—except, of course, the Pathe news. ... Of course there is a lot of what R. K. [Morris] calls HOOEY or WHOOEY in it, but the thing is *alive*. I saw it twice the other night, and was not at all bored the second time.

To Dinsmore Wheeler

Winter 1926

... Why aren't you around here? You are the only person I have ever known whom I felt was my equal, possibly my superior. You are the only one of my intimate friends of whom I am really proud. This is not a slur on the rest; rather a compliment to you.

All this being true, I am sure that sooner or later I will join you on the farm, that we will live together a life such as few can live in this rotten age. Whether we do anything or not will make no difference. If it is in us to write, we will do so. If it is not, we won't. Certainly we will read and talk, eat and sleep, work in the sun, sweat, and absorb the peace of open hills and fields. It may take five, it may take ten years for me to get out of the city, but I know I will—sooner or later.

To Parents

[Spring] 1927

. . . Tomorrow I start on a rather interesting experiment. I figured out my total waking hours and found they were 108 a week. Of these 16 are consumed in classes, 12 in preparation of lessons, 14 in eating and dressing, 7 in exercise, and 7 in miscellaneous jobs and errands. This leaves 52 free hours a week—or about 1/2 my waking time. Not bad! I am going to try to spend 25 of these 52 hours each week in study and reading. (By the way, I shall have about 55 free hours next term, as my Bible course doesn't extend beyond this term—thank God.)

These 25 hours I shall spend as follows: 10 in reading Brandes's *Main Currents of 19th Century Literature* (6 vols). And the principal works of the writers he takes up. (This will take me several years, I guess!) 5 in reading works of English Literature. 5 in playing records and reading about operas, etc. And 5 in studying Greek, outside of the regular assignment. So that I won't leave all of this to the last two days of each week, I will do a minimum of 20 minutes a day in each of the 5-hour "courses" and 45 minutes in the 10-hour course.

This all sounds very complicated and hard, but it is worth trying. I ought to get a lot more done than I do now. I may extend the idea and force myself to write so long each day.

To Dinsmore Wheeler

May 19, 1927

. . . Dins, I'm in love. Head over heels, hip and thigh, horse, foot, AND dragoon! I can't sleep nights and I spend my days looking forward to my next meeting with her. I've never before felt anything half as strong as this. I am in Elysium and in Inferno at the same time. Despair gnaws at my vitals while Hope fans my fevered brow with perfumed wings. (WOW!) No kidding, Dins, I'm nutty about her. I met her two weeks ago and I've seen her about 12 times since then—every day since last Saturday too! This afternoon we are going on a picnic, tête-à-tête, after I finish with this damn exam. We're going to drive down to the shore in her car—and listen to what the wild waves are saying. This is pretty incoherent, but I will try to explain the situation in my letter. Expect one soon.

P.S. Oh yes! The lucky girl's name is HARRIET ADAMS AND SHE IS THE DAUGHTER OF J. C. ADAMS, of the English Dept. She graduated from Vassar two years ago and she works in the Public Library. Sounds awful doesn't it? Also she is a college widow from way back, and she was one of the most popular girls in her class at Vassar. Sounds horrible, n'est-ce pas? On the other hand she is full of pep, very good-looking (she was on the Daisy Chain!), and oh how unconventional! DETAILS IN OUR NEXT.

To Dinsmore Wheeler[6]

June 17, 1927

. . . In the past month Fate has amused itself by making me its punching bag. I've received so many major injuries that I don't even *know* how much of me is left intact. A little more and I'll look like Lon Chaney. This refers to nothing physical, of course. I still possess the usual quota of arms and legs.

So much has happened that I could never begin to tell it all to you. During the past few months, as you probably know, I've come into conflict with the dean, my fellow students, and the chief of police for various crimes against the commonweal—such as criticizing Doctor Phelps and printing a *Record* which contained several nudes by Titian, Corregio, etc. For these tales sown in the wheatfields of New Haven I reaped my reward on Tap Day when I got nothing. Wilder got Keys. That made me pretty sore and sour. Then my beloved uncle wrote me that since I had made a fizzle of this year at College I had better give it up and go into business at once. With all that hanging over my head, I was imprudent enough to fall violently in love—as you know. When I wrote you I was on top of the wave. At present I am several fathoms undersea among crabs and seaweed. She doesn't love me; she never has; and she doesn't think she ever will. She *likes* me immensely, oh she's just crazy about me—just like a sister! Christ!

She'll give me everything except what I want. She'll do anything for me except what I want her to do. I don't give a damn for all the friendship in the world *from her*. So that's my situation and that is really the only thing that keeps me awake at night. I'm still as much in love with her as ever, and when I think of her that horrible, hopeless feeling comes over me. Right now everything is indifferent to me. What makes it all the worse is that she had one affair three years ago with a fellow who was a Big Man, chairman of the *News*, in Bones, on the baseball team, a Rhodes Scholar, etc. Things went wrong and she couldn't marry him when he wanted her to—and now he is married to someone else. She hasn't got over it yet—and she talks about Frank all the time and how he was the only person she has ever loved and how she can never love anyone else

6. Dwight had ridiculed William Lyon Phelps of the English department and inserted his criticism in the *Yale Record*. The printer was shocked and sent it to the dean. An edition of the *Record* was delayed because he had printed classic nude pictures in a parody of a film magazine.

like him, etc. Could anything be more exquisite torture? I won't see her for 6 months, thank God. . . .

To Dinsmore Wheeler

n.d., October 1927

Since I returned to Yale this fall, about a week and a half ago, I seem to have changed a good deal. For the first time in my life I can make myself do things I don't want to do—not once or twice but day after day. I've been intending all my life to get up earlier in the morning. This past week I have been up by 7—or 6:30—every morning. I also force myself to do my hardest lessons first and not to read when I should be studying. For the first time I have some control over myself. I take a savage, sadistic delight in making my poor mind and body do as they oughter.

Another thing I have noticed is that people don't seem to mean much to me—at least the people around here don't. I've not called on a single person since I got back, have not sought out anybody on my own initiative. I find that I would just as soon be alone, even at mealtime, as in company. In short, I don't give a damn for anybody. When people talk to me, I answer, but I never take any thought of what I say. When they leave me I am relieved, and all the time they are with me I am more or less impatient for them to go. In CRIME AND PUN-ISHMENT, which I am now reading, the central character, Raskolnikov, a young student, feels precisely that way toward people, even the most friendly and well-disposed.

Two other things that perhaps have in part caused the foregoing. First, I am for the first time without much economic support. Mother can spare a couple of hundred dollars a year, but the rest I really should get myself. I keep a strict expense account and so far I am astonished at how little one can spend—and yet live. If nothing throws a monkey wrench into the works, as probably will happen, I should get $13.20 regular income a week: $7.00 from my afternoon class for kids that I've started again, $3.00 from the INQUISITOR column which I run once a week in the *News* and which I managed to get the *News* to pay for, and $3.20 for checking coats at the University Library. Then I am going to contribute to LIFE, HARPERS, THE MERCURY, ETC. and see what luck I have.

The other thing is the excellence of the courses I am taking. Later I will describe them to you.

These two interests have made me more self-contained and self-controlled, maybe. Or what do you think?

. . . Lately, I've been wondering why it is that, in spite of long absences, radically different temperaments, and innumerable petty—and thus all the more irritating—misunderstandings, I consider you without question my best friend. Dupee is more sympathetic, Hobson better balanced, etc. I never get as angry with them as I do with you, nor do they get on my nerves so often. And yet beside you, O Wheeler of Ohio, they dwindle to mere geometrical points, which, as you know, have no length, depth, or width and are abstractions only. The only reason I can discover for this phenomenon is the simple fact that you are *bigger* than they are. You'll probably go to hell and make a mess out of most of your life, and Dupee and Hobson are as likely to succeed as anyone I've ever met, and yet you will always be more admirable, interesting, and important to me than they will. I like 'em and I respect 'em, but there's a difference, dearie, there's a difference.

Well, I've got to do some work on the *Seven Against Thebes* of Aeschylus, so no more. Write me when you feel like it.

To Dinsmore Wheeler

December 8, 1927

. . . It's a funny thing, but the older I get the less things seem to matter to me. I still get as excited as ever about things, and I still work as hard as ever at writing, reading and studying—BUT I feel more and more that nothing makes any real difference to me. I feel that I can get along without anything, that I don't need books, friends, money, entertainment, glory, respect, or anything. If some prophet were to convince me that I am to completely fail in life and end up knowing myself a mediocrity and sans money and friends—well, I don't think I would lose much sleep over it. (Perhaps largely because I could not imagine it.) Somehow I feel self-sufficient and careless. I read good books because I want to be well-read and because I enjoy it. I write for the *Record* because I have to, for the *News* because I want the money, for the *Lit* because I feel I ought to. I write essays for my various courses because if I don't I won't pass. But I write practically nothing because of any creative urge. That is, I don't need to write at all, and if tomorrow the *Lit., News,* and *Record* were to suspend publication, I probably wouldn't write a line for a long, long time, nothing at all. Maybe never again. Maybe I haven't what is called the "creative spirit." I don't care whether I have it or not.

It has just occurred to me that the reason for this indifference is that I know damn well that I have the creative power and that I *am* good. Therefore I look on the future with indifference—since I know that I *can't* fail. Therefore I am indifferent to what Fate may do to me—since I know she can't do anything very serious. I know I am good, and so what if I never do anything at all? That wouldn't alter the fact that I know my power. It is just in the last few months that this conviction has come over me. (It was probably the summer at R.D.3 which sowed the seeds.) Before that I used to doubt myself and to be depressed or elated at what other people thought of me. I used to sweat and worry about whether I was a "genius" or not. Now I don't much care what people think of me, nor am I uneasy about my "genius." Has this bored you? I had no idea that it would take so long when I started out. I never talk to people around here about myself, so that's probably why such a flood of introspection came forth.

Dupee was down here over a week ago, and we had rather a good time. Some good talk. . . . Freddie is a good friend but too damn earnest and sweet. Sometimes I take a perverse pleasure in being nasty to him. When he gets sore, he bristles up like an enraged little rooster. I fear he bears an ineradicable stamp of priggishness. He would be a world-beater, though, if he were more caustic, careless, callous. To him literature is always a serious matter; he approaches the great writers on his knees. My own theory is that if one is not bored at times by *Hamlet* or *The Divine Comedy*, one is perhaps intelligent but certainly not human. And I don't get down on my knees for nobody! The final word on Dupee: he has a first-rate mind, but he is too lacking in fire, originality, power to ever do first-rate stuff himself. I need not tell you that all of this is between you and me.

To Dinsmore Wheeler

April 12, 1928

Well, I have a job—got it this vacation. It is at *Macy's* in their "training squad," which means that for 6 months I will be put in every department of the store and perform every conceivable function. At the end of that time, if I have made a success, I will get a fairly good regular job with good prospects of advancement. The main reason I am going with it is for the training, which will be rigorous but, I think, very valuable. The salary is very good: $30 a week. Strangely, I am anticipating *Macy's* with more pleasure than dread. (That's a strange sentence itself.) I mean that I am looking forward to my work there. I probably will eventually go into advertising work. This past week I saw four of the biggest agencies in the city: J. Walter Thompson, which is about the biggest in the country, Barton (i.e., Bruce), Durstine and Osborne, Charles W. Hoyt Co., and George Baltler, Inc. I think I have a rather good chance with this last as soon as I graduate, but I will probably take the Macy job for a year or so for the business training. Then I can go into agency work and land a pretty good job on the strength of my Macy experience.

The four or five interviews I had with men pretty high up in the different agencies have had an enormous effect on me. Whether this is merely temporary or not I do not know. All I know is that right now I feel as if last week was a century. All my life here at college is or seems to be right now changed. Up to this time, as you know, literature was my be-all and end-all and my greatest ambition was to someday create it. Well, right now I honestly don't care very much whether I ever set pen to paper again. And this is the queerest thing of all: I really am interested in business and I really am ambitious to succeed in the business world. This may be just a reaction or a rationalization or something that in time will disappear. . . . The slight glimpse I had of the business machine in my contact with the men I talked to at first terrified me, depressed me, and yet fascinated me. These men were so cold, so keen, so absolutely sure of themselves and so utterly wrapped up in business that I felt like a child before them. They were so sure of their values that I began to doubt mine. Then my courage began to return, and it occurred to me that the sort of power these men had was the dominant power in America today and that it was what I wanted for myself. Last week I perceived how feeble, shallow, infinitely weak American art and letters are besides American business. I thought of profs here and back at Exeter who represented culture: they made a poor showing besides these men. I tell you Dinsmore, that American art, letters, music, culture is done. There are hundreds of businessmen, thousands of them, that are better in their line than the best poet or painter we have today. The power is all in business: these men I saw were all of them keener, more efficient, more sure of their power than any college prof I ever knew. THIS IS ALL TOO EXAGGERATED—I HAVE NOT FORGOTTEN OUR CHICKEN FARM, NOR HAVE I ENTIRELY GIVEN UP LITERATURE—I'M JUST RIGHT NOW VERY EAGER TO START IN BUSINESS AND SEE WHAT IT'S ALL ABOUT.

To Dinsmore Wheeler

May 24, 1928
. . . This afternoon Wilder [Hobson] and I went over to a tea dance at one of the Staff Clubs and heard two hours of Fletcher Henderson's band. Sassy, boy, that's some band. I admit that I never have known what jazz meant until this afternoon. Those niggers played like men possessed. Something outside them and bigger than anyone of them seemed to have them in its power. The remarkable thing about them is this: although one gets a sense of utter, wild abandon—as in most colored orchestras—at the same time the form is never broken. The disciplined passion they exhibit is the very essence of the greatest art. This direction of their energy is, I think, rather unusual in negro jazz. Its what gives Henderson's outfit its preeminence: there is an intensity, a power in their playing that one misses in the equally passionate outbursts of the others. It is the personality of Henderson himself that is at the root of all this. He is a rather pale, quiet-looking fellow, who remains calm through the most lyrical trombone shrieks. When every other nigger in the orchestra is cutting loose for all he's worth, Fletcher remains cool and unmoved at the piano. His playing is cold, clear, and very brilliant technically; he never pounds the keys though he always makes the piano heard—rather by the almost classical clarity of his play-

ing, in which the notes comes out vigorously but never bombastically, than by any force. As he plays he looks around at his band, gentle and serene, sometimes smiling indulgently at some particularly wild piece of savagery, and one feels that he controls every player, even the outlandish gentleman who goes berserk with the saxophone every so often.

To Dinsmore Wheeler

May 29, 1928

. . . I would come up on Friday if it were not for a class . . . which is given by the way, by no less a man than the great Henrico Seidelias Canbinious, the distinguished editor of that God-awful sheet, *The Saturday Review.* In certain parts of Ohio this gentleman is also known as "Pants" Canby. This course I'm taking is jokingly called "Advanced Literary Composition"; Henry and I often have a good laugh over that one together. As a matter of fact, though, the course isn't as bad as it might be, and it would be valuable if for no other reason than for the opportunity it gives me to observe Henry Seidel at close quarters. He is one of the leading critics, in the opinion of many people *the* leading critic, of the day. At first, I could not understand it. He seemed utterly commonplace, dull, mediocre. Now I begin to comprehend it better: he is a queer combination of common sense (a not at all despicable commodity of which he has a great deal) and uncritical enthusiasm. Whether this last is assumed for his dear public's sake or not I don't know—don't think so, however. The effect of such a combination of elements is rather pathetic: his pumped-up, English-prof-with-a-pipe sort of literary enthusiasm is all the time leading him into extravagant eulogy of such dodoes as Galsworthy, Christopher Morley, and A. A. Milne, while, on the other hand, his common sense generally prevents him from recognizing a deep and original writer, in fact, makes him rather distrust such fellows. Once they have arrived, helped in their ascent by such critics as Nathan and Mencken, he is always ready to give them the glad hand—but he is not going to put himself out before that. Or perhaps he does not dare. A very curious thing about his classes—and one that is typical of many of the played-out English profs around here—is his inability or unwillingness to praise or blame. He finds good points in every paper read, no matter how poor, and he finds bad points in the best of them. From his reaction everything read in the class might be about on the same level. This shrinking from making critical judgments naturally has a deadening effect on the creative activity of the class. And, on a larger scale, it is thus that Canby affects modern letters. There is no fertility in the man, no promise or encouragement for creation, merely a stagnant level of acceptance of good and bad for their own sake. If the future of our letters rests in such hands there is no hope.

MACY'S: THE ROMANCE OF RAYON
"Dins. . . . I really am interested in business and I really
want to succeed in the business world."

To Dinsmore Wheeler

October 28, 1928
. . . All the past week . . . [my position] has remained the same—a standing position behind a counter piled with rayon damask yard goods for drapes. . . . Tomorrow it changes once more, this time to a sort of guide in a "Rayon Exhibition" which is being put on for Monday, Tuesday, and Wednesday by the Rayon Institute of America, yes sir!, in order to educate the public about rayon, that is, in order to delude people into believing that rayon is about twice as cheap a material as silk which is true, and also twice as good, which . . . is also true of course. My duties are to stand around the various booths and explain to people that rayon is—wait a minute—a fabric made from vegetable fiber by means of chemicals, or words to that effect. I must also inform anyone who is sap enough to question me that at eleven and three each and every day there will be shown at no charge a motion picture with the title, *The Romance of Rayon*, followed by an exhibition of rayon dresses on Lovely Mannequins. This letter might be pretty hot stuff, eh, Ed? But as to hot stuff, why there's a bit in *The Romance of Rayon* that shows a girl dressed in rayon pajamas get out of bed and put on a rayon negligee that's not so slow either! Of course she doesn't really get out of bed—I mean it's a sort of couch effect—but the idea is there because if not why would she be wearing pajamas?

To Dinsmore Wheeler

n.d., October 1928
There is a sign in each of the elevators reading: The operator of this elevator, NAME, has pledged himself to courtesy and service. One of these reads:

THE OPERATOR OF THIS ELEVATOR
J. CUMBERBATCH
HAS PLEDGED HIMSELF TO COURTESY
AND SERVICE

J. Cumberbatch is a sawed-off nigger with bow legs. Every time I ride in his elevator I have an internal snicker at Mr. Cumberbatch. He has his revenge on me, however, for his name runs through my head day and night like Mark Twain's "A blue slip for a five-cent trip, a buff slip for a ten-cent trip, Punch, brothers, punch with care; Punch in the ticket of the passenjaire!" Or like Poe's bells, bells, bells, hear the clanging and the danging of the bells, bells, bells. Or like the water that came down at Lodore, in so maddening a fashion.

To Dinsmore Wheeler

December 10, 1928

. . . I am deeply depressed about Macy's and my work in life. One month of executive work—in a small way, to be sure—has almost convinced me that I am not made to be an executive, because (1) I am not practical, (2) I cannot command, (3) the 1001 details that one meets every day baffle and irritate me and do not stimulate me to cope with them, (4) I have no deep pleasure or interest in performing practical works. Spengler says there is the man of Truths and there is the man of Facts, the philosopher-idealist and the man of action. I realize now that I am entirely the first, and it seems to me insanity to have attempted to function in the world of Action. Until I can throw myself heartily into some work, "get on fire," as your father says, I will never amount to anything, and the only thing I could ever grow enthusiastic over would be some work with ideal or moral rewards rather than worldly ones. I could work hard for an abstraction, a theory, or an art, but never for a business concern, which does not seem to me at all of first-rate importance. And even if I wanted to give myself to my work at Macy's, my talents are scarcely those most required for success there. The man of action who can master facts and make them serve him instead of submitting to them, the adroit opportunist whose easy grace of action in meeting each situation is not inhibited by a thousand doubts, self-consciousness, hesitations, theories, principles, such as are constantly retarding me—it is he who can get ahead in business, where there are no "truths"—moral or even intellectual— that is, no general principles, that is, no abstractions, but only Facts. So my situation is dark enough: I have never known so many weeks on end of uninterrupted depression. In the morning I get out of bed with loathing for the day ahead of me, and at night I return home tired out and thankful for the end of the day. . . . At college I would have laughed if someone had told me that in less than a year I would look back to the academic barnyard as a delightful mode of existence. I will probably end up by going back to the universities as the dog returns to his vomit, and having despised the race of college professors above all others, end up by becoming a second-rate one myself.

To Dinsmore Wheeler

January 8, 1929

. . . You got some good ones in the literature way this Xmas, and you got some lemons. I would nominate in this latter category Dr. James's opus . . . [*Varieties of*] *Religious Experience*, which I have never read. But I have been looking into that gentleman's collected correspondence, and if his letters are any test of the man, I cry beware! As a philosopher he is dangerously like Browning (Robert), full of vim, gusto, and vigor, but, alas, not blessed with any taste, that is, sense of proportion. For instance, he praises highly the notorious Josiah Royce, than whom there exists no more drearily bourgeois a thinker. And James too, like Browning, is bourgeois (I hope you have mastered this word; the last time I used it on you brought forth a denial of any knowledge of what it meant). To return to James: without any acquaintance with his philosophical work, I deeply distrust him for the vulgar show he makes of being open-minded, liberal, etc. Oh my, yes, we are just too sensible and free from prejudice! Bring us all your little problems, children, and we will put on our nice clean thinking cap and Think them through for you. Bertrand Russell, H. G. Wells, and in some of his stuff Havelock Ellis, these belong to the same priggish school. The reason they are so dangerous is that they make such pretense at thinking things out when really they are quite without imagination and insight. They remind me of the Jeremy Bentham school of philosophy—weren't they the famous "utilitarians"?—and of that prize hygienic-scientific-level-headed-and-open-minded prig Herbert Spencer. Such men are essentially vulgar, materialistic (i.e., James and his pragmatism, and Wells and his hygienic-sunlit-incubator utopias). They are so damn sensible about things that they see no good in anything unless it makes for the Betterment of the Race. No thinker satisfies me who does not meet the tragedy of life with something better than an expression of regret and dismay. Those fellows are constantly trying to "prove" something; they attempt (madmen) to harness the Truth and make it pull them towards a millennium. But the only truth that will let itself be thus used is a sorry nag. The stallion of the higher Truth would kick James and the rest into oblivion if they ever ventured near him. It is only the Nietzsches and Spenglers who can throw a leg over that steed (CYMBALS, DRUMS, ETC.). . . .

Things are going from bad to worse at Macy's. . . . Now I realize what a fool I was to go to Macy's and from now on I freely accept that I am an intellectual-artist-man of ideas—what you will and *not* a businessman, chemist, banker, engineer, bourgeois, or Cherokee. . . . The men of business can direct and administer with marvelous efficiency the various business institutions on which the whole social and political structure of the country rests, but they have even less ideas of the ultimate end than the statesmen and warriors who directed things in the past. The only end is a further development of the means of extending our conquest and organization of the material world so that we may possess more of it. But Hoover and the rest are silent as to any abstract, ideal end of liberty, truth, love or justice to be attained. . . . My days at Macy's are numbered.

To Dinsmore Wheeler

February 15, 1929

. . . Perhaps I can permit myself a few words on *Point Counter Point.* My main objection to it was that it degraded humanity in a small, mean, cold-blooded way. I don't mind attacks on the human race, but they must be warm and vigorous. I relish and admire the works of Swift, Nietzsche, Stendhal, to name at random those of the great traducers of man. There is a power in their very hatred that vitalizes the reader. But Huxley's intellectual toying with people, like a highly intelligent cat amusing itself with some mice, only depresses me. It is impossible to feel any noble emotion, such as respect, awe, love, hatred, pity, terror, towards any of his characters. They seem like so many insects crawling about, liable at any moment to be killed or mangled—and for no good reason except their creator's caprice. There is not the slightest inevitable rhythm that determines the outcome of any series of actions. I take this back on second thought. The passages from the notebook of Philip Quarles were very good—by far the best thing in the book—but their excellence was not part of the novel. Let Huxley stick to essays and light verse and stories, but he is neither broad, tall, nor deep enough to sustain a serious novel.

Well, I am sorry I had to be so rough on your Aldous; he'll survive it, however. I am presently reviewing for *The New Republic* a group of six books on frontier life, the only notable one being Agnes Repplier's life of Pere Marquette, the discoverer of the Mississippi—or rather the explorer of that river. De Soto, I think, was discoverer. One of the books was on a priest who tried to aid the Central and Latin American Indians against the early Spanish conquerors, who butchered them by the thousands for no good reason except that they were weak, decadent, and defenseless. Another was about the extermination of the buffalo. There is a curious parallel between the two cases: both the Indians and the buffaloes were practically defenseless, at the mercy of the first comers. And both were slaughtered, many exterminated in very short order. There is apparently small room in this world for the weak and the naked, at least not in the frontier world. . . .

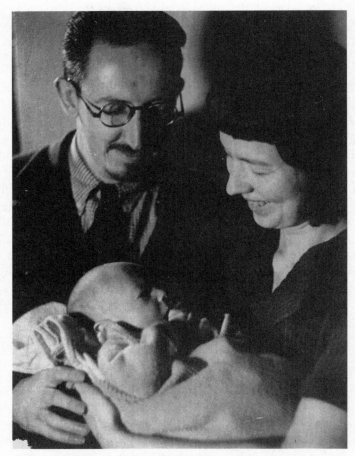

Dwight and Nancy Macdonald with new son Michael,
1938.

CHAPTER TWO

FROM LUCE TO LENIN, 1929–1936

"I wish you could know Nancy. She's a sweet girl, even if she does let me in for drearily long-winded left-wing political meetings."

These letters trace Macdonald's radicalization during his tenure as a writer for the Luce publications *Time* and *Fortune*. Nancy Rodman played an important role in this transformation, for it was she who first introduced him to some of the classics of leftist literature, and her own deep social consciousness was infective. Without Nancy, Dwight might have remained simply an articulate Luce journalist.

To Dinsmore Wheeler

March 13, 1929

. . . We work on Sunday and get these two days off in the middle of the week. I am in an entirely different division of the magazine from Hobson. This is the situation: for some time they have been experimenting with a new magazine, to be called FORTUNE. It will be a *de luxe* mag, in format like *Vanity Fair* or *The Spur,* and will be devoted to glorifying the American businessman. You get the idea? A business magazine written and got up as attractively, cleverly as possible. The personal and the dramatic will be played up—much as *Time* itself does. My position is an anomalous one: I write some of the business section for *Time* and I do articles for the as yet unborn *Fortune.* That is, I will do both of these—unless I am fired. Last week I devoted most of my time to new mergers and financing deals (for *Time*) and to a map of automobile exports all full of quaint and useless information. . . . To make a quick, flashy impression—in a way, to write an advertisement—that seems to be the thing they're after. Well, maybe they can find some place for my talent nonetheless. Here's a bit of irony: at college I dashed off stuff that got me all sorts of publicity, was wonderful journalism—and it did me nothing but harm. That is, I got publicity but only bad, never good. And no money at all. Now here I am trying to make some money, and I see that what journalists are looking for is just the clever, hasty, crackling sort of stuff I used to write at Yale—and I find it impossible to do it. The book reviews I have written have all been positively *heavy* in comparison to those I did at college. And so, since I don't shoot off a lot of smart, pretty-colored fireworks as I used to, the editors don't want my reviews. I haven't been able to get any more at the *New Republic* or the *Herald-Tribune*, and the *Forum* just sent me back one I did for them.

In this connection, this is interesting: I had a talk with a woman who writes for the *Delineator,* gives radio talks, and so on, is an enthusiastic, agreeable, plump matron of forty. She had read an article I wrote called "Genius Slips into the Movies." "This is good stuff," she said. "You have some *fascinating* ideas, but you want to break it up more. (I had sweated to get the thing into form, make it whole; but of course the reader would find it easier to digest if it were broken up. That's almost a law of modern journalism: break the form! It gives novelty, rests the eye. To take in a *whole* might cause some slight disarrangement of the cerebral molecules, God forbid!) Make it gayer! Yes, that's it. That's what it needs—a gayer, lighter touch. Write it as if you were talking to someone, telling them all about it." (Another Rule: be personal! I wonder if that is an adjustment, a shortsighted one, to the growing impersonality of our journalism. All these cigarette testimonials written by dukes and sea captains, trying to kid the straphanger, the homo boobiensis, that he is entering into some sort of *personal* relationship with the dukes and captains, that *they* are telling *him* how smooth *Old Golds* are. By the way, even your hero, Count von Luckner, has succumbed to this virus and written a Lucky Strike ad. It's a knockout, though! Have you seen it? "By Joe!" every 2 words.)

To Dinsmore Wheeler

April 3, 1929

Having finished my story on Fashion Expert Parrish, I find myself unemployed, for a time at least. . . . It is a warmish, hazy afternoon. No fresh air flows in at the wide-open office window. I am leaning over my desk, in shirtsleeves and vest, a combination that I vaguely recall as being considered improper, but one of which I am very fond, of course. I turn my head to the right and look out the window at my side. My eye travels over four large buildings, each of them famed in the city. Farthest to the left, on crowded, important, 42nd Street, arise the 40 or 50 stories of the new Chanin Building, which dominates the central Manhattan skyline. Straight ahead, separated from my window only by the block from Third to Lexington Avenue, is the Commodore Hotel, a square block of windows. Within six months this will be shut off from my view by the steel framework of the new Chrysler Building; the foundations for this tallest building in the world are now being blasted and scraped out of the Manhattan rock. I look down on tall orange cranes in a pit walled by reinforced concrete. Next to the Commodore looms the enormous Graybar Building, whose total floor space must rival the 15 square miles of the American Telephone and Telegraph Building. Through a narrow slot between Commodore and Graybar, a slot that once was 43rd St. and now is a blind alley, I glimpse a single great arched window of the comparatively low Grand Central Station. The fourth building, neighbor to the Graybar and in line with the other three, is the newly completed New York Central Building, whose thick square central mass, capped by a gilt cupola, reminiscent to me of a Ringling Bros. circus and the Academy Building at P.E.A. [Phillip Exeter Academy], sit solidly on a base of building a block by a block and a half square and twelve stories high. This base alone is larger than most office buildings. Thus drawn up for my review, these four monsters toe the line from 42nd to 46th street.

Turning my head, on the other hand, to the left, my eyes rest on Parc Lorenty, the movie critic of *Judge*. And even that is denied me at present, for the suave Mr. Lorenty has clapped his felt Homburg on his head and gone away from here.

My meeting with [Sherwood] Anderson was to me both enjoyable and important. Since it was raining, we did not walk but sat in the hotel lobby for a couple of hours. I found that my idea of him was quite false. Instead of a hollow-eyed, monologuenous mystic, peering sadly out of dark "wise old eyes" and groping for understanding of the . . . beauty and mystery of Life—instead of any such dreary creature, I found a middle-aged advertising man, who diffused a faint aroma of whiskey. Only Anderson was much more intelligent and richly, warmly human than most advertising men. His face was not drawn with pain but was rather flabby and ruddy. And most of the time he talked in a light, semi-humorous way, always ready to laugh at any joke or wisecrack I made. He was extremely easy to talk to—without pride and also without that subtler and more deadly form of pride, an affectation of humility. Mainly he talked about the need for a conscious artist class in this country, a class that would not be ashamed or proud of being artists, that would accept it as a fact. Until that comes about, he said, there can be no firm basis for letters over here. He told me that he felt no understanding with the older writers of his generation. "I used to go down to the Authors' Club. I don't any more. All they talk to each other of is how many volumes their latest book is selling and what high-priced editions they are bringing out." He said he got more out of talking to painters than writers, that painters today in America seem more interested in their work as art, in its technique, than do writers. He's absolutely right about the artist's life being recognized as a normal mode of existence. Until we writers stop apologizing for being writers there's no hope for us. His idea is the creation of an "artistic" class, the members of which can communicate to each other, can *understand* each other. Now we're all fallen apart, separated from each other. Anderson told me the remarkable thing (to him) about my essay was that it considered his work as art, judged it by aesthetic standards. Can you imagine it? He says hardly any of the "critics" care anything about aesthetic value of the books they criticize, don't know what he is trying to do at all. And that's true. Most criticism of novels is sociological, philosophical, historical, descriptive, comparative—almost any angle except the only important one, namely, its value as a piece of literature. Anderson said that he would like to see me do for the other big writers today what I had done for him, criticize them as literature, relate them together and to the times. Wouldn't I like to do it! You remember last summer we plotted buying the *Milan [Ohio] Ledger* and going into the publishing business? I told Anderson of our idea, and he said that he made a comfortable living out of his two newspapers in Marian, Va.—5 or 6 thousand dollars a year. What he likes best about them is that people in the vicinity are slowly forgetting that he is the great Sherwood Anderson the writer and are thinking of him as Mr. Anderson, editor and publisher of their newspaper.

To Dinsmore Wheeler

October 17, 1929

. . . These days it is almost physically impossible for me to write after office hours, because I write so much during the day. You see, almost two weeks ago I started to work on an ambitious project of my own (approved by my Boss), namely, to recount the story in some detail of the three railroad merger campaigns of Leonore Fresnel Loree, president of the Delaware & Hudson. The story is about 3/4 done now; I expected, when I began it, to have it finished a week ago. It is just like writing history: you have to assemble reams of notes, choose the important facts out of them, organize them in some sequence, and, hardest of all, narrate them in a graceful and interesting way. It's a monstrous task! I never worked half so hard on anything at FORTUNE before. I have written steadily, or tried to, all day, so that at night my flesh crawls at the idea of taking up a pen or pencil.

. . . I'm sorry to hear you are one of these cover-to-cover readers of TIME. I thought they were all automobile salesmen or professors of sociology. You must be hard up for something to do. Please forgive me if I take this golden opportunity for a little homily, BUT why do you read so many magazines? THE ARTS is worth reading every month, but you are lucky if you find one article per month in the MERCURY or the FORUM really worth reading. Worth reading, that is, in comparison with what you might read: i.e., the accumulated volumes of a couple of millenniums. Good God, man, why not use the abundant leisure that is now being thrust upon you in exploring Plato, Dante, Cervantes, and so on? Even Tolstoy and Dostoevsky would be infinitely more valuable than all this magazine froth. Do you ever read any solid stuff? If so your letters never indicate it, no references, I mean, to it. But now I'm becoming irritated (though it looks a lot more angry on paper than I really feel). Or not irritated but indignant. My greatest vice is my easily aroused indignation—also, I suppose, one of my greatest strengths. I can work up a moral indignation quicker than a fat tennis player can work up a sweat.

As to the Pullman movie: of course, you have no sources at the farm. My idea was to spend a couple of afternoons in the Public Library and get together a mass of notes on the subject. Then type them, send you one copy and keep one myself. Then we could either work up separate scenarios and compare them; or we could—well, I don't know just what else we *could* do. It's a pretty impractical idea, I'm afraid. Yet if you are interested it might be good sport.

I accept the Hemingway rebuke with a chastened spirit—though I think your opening blow, viz., "Your reaction to Hemingway was what I expected," was rather below the belt. If you "expected" me to take such a boneheaded attitude as you proceed to outline, you could hardly have enough interest in my mentality to write me a 12-page letter. And there were a couple of cracks in that part of your letter that were just plain nasty. . . . But, as far as my criticizing *A Farewell to Arms* without having read it, you are, alas, only too justified in your censure. That is one of my worst habits, getting off a lot of prejudice about things which I have explored only in the most casual way. I shall read *AF to A* before I jump on it any more, or make a gallant attempt to read it, at least. Dupee has a long review of it in the first number of *Black and White*. He develops several very interesting critical ideas, as, The Sentimentality of the Understatement of Emotion vs. The Ditto of the Overstatement of the Ditto. Example of the first: TRISTRAM by E. A., Robinson; example of the second, MAUD by Tennyson.

To Dinsmore Wheeler

December 12, 1929

. . . Our literary disagreements may not be so profound, after all. I can certainly go with you to almost any extent in your damning of Whitman. Wait till you read my destructive analysis of the Good Grey Poet in my essay on Jeffers! As for *All Quiet*, you say that you find its chief virtue in the sense it gives you of the author's being overwhelmed by the war. Whereas that to me is its defect. I think the explanation is that I am considering the book aesthetically, and you are looking at it more from a personal emotional point of view. The same with *Farewell to Arms*: you probably get quite an emotional kick out of it, eh? Did I tell you that, goaded by your reproaches, I spent another half-hour trying to read the book, only to find it much worse than had been my first impression? It just bores me: the conversation seems thin, trivial, and pointless; and the writing seems wire-drawn, drearily mannered, and dull, dull, dull. Your suggestion that I may be influenced against the book merely because it is so popular does not move me: certainly the writer of our day whom I have admired most and longest—Sherwood Anderson—has as great a vogue and standing as Hemingway.

But this letter is getting slightly acid with justification and argument. Hell, I'm sweating here at the club—I've just taken off my coat. In an hour I leave for Washington, D.C., on the B&O. Tomorrow at 9 A.M. I am to interview Claude Porter, author of the forthcoming Interstate Commerce Commission's R.R. Consolidation Plan. I am writing a big story for *Fortune* about railroad consolidation, I've been working on it a week or two, and will be at it for another equal period. Does the idea of it bore you as much as did the Loree story?

By the way, if you still read TIME you'll be interested to know that in recent "Business and Finance" sections I've written the stories entitled BULLISH BUSH, BATTLE IN THE WEST, and CHRIS THE WHITTLER. Not bad of their paltry kind, either.

No kidding, Dins, don't get the idea that I look on myself as doing a man's work in the world and being on the broad highway to success, etc. My job is not unpleasant, but it doesn't satisfy! Always at the back of my head is the idea of getting out of this insane city and away from this ridiculous job of mine (which, no doubt, is much less ridiculous than most jobs around here) and beginning to Live (instead of to nervously exist) and to do what God intended me to do— read, talk, think, write. I do all these things now, but in a hasty, worried way. My life is barbarous: 8 hours of mental tension (not always high, I admit) at the office and then I must tear off raw hunks of leisure, conversation, reading and bolt them hastily, always with the idea of the "Job" at the back of my head. I want to live solidly, sanely, with some dignity and reality, to use my body and to see, smell, hear, taste, and touch real, natural things instead of the stone and glass of the city. Back to the Farm, boys. There are consolations in the city of course: wine, women, art. As for wine, I am all for it. For instance, I went to dinner with the James Hamills, drank 3 cocktails, and just managed to stay above the table. It was a very pleasant evening, the wine easing up the tension-strain of the city which may be why New Yorkers drink more than folks down on the rutabaga patch. As for women, la belle et pale Laura Biddle Stewart seems to have given me the go-by. And I've found she is not at all the unworldly, solitary, ethereal, spiritual being I once thought her. Alas and alas! She has been going on one round of social activities ever since she came to the city a month ago. So busy has she been, in fact, that she hasn't been able even to see Honest old Dwight, her Hayseed Admirer. Also G. L. K. Morris tells me that she had a Swiss admirer in Lenox after I left with whom she would retire to the bushes and shrubbery at county-club dances. Frailty, thy name is woman!

To Dinsmore Wheeler

December 20, 1929

My one-day visit turned out to be a momentous one, did it not? For me it meant a great deal, probably more than any 24 hours I have ever passed. It revealed to me something that I have long dimly felt, but never quite accepted: that you and your family (Dot, Dick, and your mother) are an inseparable part of my life. Up to my visit, when for some reason I was angry with you, I would mentally wash my hands of you, resolve to go my way and let you go yours. Of course, in a day or two I would forget my resolution (which was never at all fixed or definite: it was rather a *threat*, a feeling that I could cut loose from you, than an actual resolve to do so). Well, my visit revealed to me how deeply you and I are linked together. Our bond is one of friendship, respect, intellectual sympathy, and more than all these, one of nature. That we should be together—not *be* together, but rather exist in close relationship with each other, regardless of where we happen to be—seems to me now the natural order of things. And more than that, I feel that I naturally belong with The Farm and Dot and your mother and Dick and you, and all of you together as a group. For you all I feel something more than affection: we are all bound together by natural and necessary ties.

You yourself, of course, are the center of The Farm for me. Around you are your mother (whom I began by hating, and for whom I now feel a deep affection), Dot (whom I love), and Dick (whom I respect and like for his purity, sweetness, and gentleness of nature). You see what my visit has done to me? God knows I am surprised at myself. Such emotions I have not felt in years. And just think—if I had not come out to The Farm, I would have discovered none of these things about myself and all of you. Sooner or later, however, it would have become clear. Only I'm glad that it came so soon. I feel that the great edifice of our relationship has been completed—or better, I have had a glimpse of the solid foundations on which the building rests, and so I can turn back to the work of carrying it higher and farther in *Time* with a quiet heart.

Since my return I have been hopping around the office as hectically as if I had never had a deep breath of the country. Already I am pretty sick of writing, especially since I had to work most of this (Saturday) afternoon, and will have to do some work tomorrow. As the magazine draws near publication, the strain gets worse and worse. If I believed in FORTUNE and gave a good goddamn about it, I might endure with a grin to work most of my holiday on it. But since I have no interest in it, no deep or living interest at least, I resent having to work so incessantly for it. My evenings and Sundays are my own, I feel, and I don't like to give up the reading and writing I might do in them.

To Dinsmore Wheeler

February 2, 1930

. . . By now you should have received the *Sketches of a Sportsman.* Sherwood Anderson first told me of them—when I met him last spring—and it was not until a month or so ago that I remembered his praise of the book, and read a couple of sketches in the Yale Club library. I was at once delighted, and as I read more from time to time my pleasure became deeper. As Anderson had told me, one gets a fine sense of life from the book, of the rustic, outdoor, provincial life that was lived in the villages and on the estates of the old Russia. The people in the book are real, as is the setting. Turgenev is the reporter at his best: almost all the sketches I've read so far have been pure description—quite different from the *creative* work of Dostoevsky. But the comments of an intelligent man on life, and descriptions of real persons and situations by a sensitive and talented observer—these have their place in letters as well as more ambitious creative work. What I object to is when, as in Proust, this chronicle and description are puffed up into something as lengthy and pretentious as a great creative work. In these sketches Turgenev, as Anderson in his HELLO TOWNS, does not load his medium with more than it will bear—and so his impressions of the countryside and his delineations of the people he comes across remain true, understated, balanced, sane. His literary talent and his intelligence make the book a delight to read—how in a few words he gets the "feel" of the countryside, how in a few words he strikes out some little scene (boys in swimming, two old men fishing) that comes to the reader almost as directly and freshly as it did to Turgenev! The sketches remind me somewhat of Hawthorne's little sketches of the New England countryside and people.

. . . About Dos Passos and Edison, in fact, about Edison only: Edison inferior to Steinmetz because he "cashed in" on the machine or because he was chiefly interested in the "industrial side of invention." That's silly, of course, and Dos Passos is silly to say it—though I didn't get that impression from his review. But, from what I've read about Edison, he seems to be pretty small potatoes *as a man*. I don't think the friendship between Ford and Edison is merely fortuitous. The two men—who are undoubtedly the two greatest geniuses of our industrial age—are deeply similar. They believe in Facts, and they have little understanding of intangible, philosophical concepts. They believe in direct action, childishly, pathetically so: as Ford and his Peace ship, or Edison and his Scholarship Contest, or Ford and his reconstruction of old villages. Ford is confronted with a great war, whose roots go down for centuries, whose issues and implications are so vast that an Aristotle, a Thucydides would not dare even *pronounce an opinion* on it. Yet Ford hops in his little steamboat and actually sails to Europe to stop it. Such lack of understanding of the nature of abstract, as opposed to practical, forces can almost be termed insanity. And Edison thinks he can perpetuate what is doomed to perish—his genius—by so childish a piece of direct action as gathering together 48 bright boys and picking the best mind from them by an examination. The exam, by the way, was rather eccentric. Edison and Ford are "practical men," the highest, most intensified form of the practical man. They are so damn practical that they are insane. And they are both so fabulously one-sided. Their blind spots are so big. They have conquered the forces of the industrial age as no other men have—and they have made the conquest in spite of, or rather because of their terrific limitations, mental and spiritual. They have demonstrated what a poor, puny, lopsided thing this industrial age *is* when it can be conquered by two such men. They are petty in spirit, barbarous in intelligence, either dull or fantastic when they act. Their philosophy is one of shrewdness, hard work, ingenuity, and always a blind and childish faith in "Facts"—they change the face of America—and are so limited in their vision that they don't know what they've done! Take Ford out of his factory and he is indistinguishable in spirit, in taste, in intellectual scope from millions of Americans. Take Edison out of his laboratory and he begins to chirp prosperity and efficiency with the rest of the salesmen and copy-writers. My God! If these men are the Lincolns and Napoleons of today, the human race has gone to hell.

. . . The fact that FORTUNE is at last appearing makes it more interesting to write for it, but gives no more meaning to my work there. It's fun to throw the purple spotlight on industry—but the fun is wearing thin with me. I'm wondering how much longer I can go through the motions—you see, the basic and simple fact is that I don't give a damn whether FORTUNE is "good" or not, that I can't think of it in terms of "good" or "not good." The essential purpose, the general direction of FORTUNE is one which has no meaning for me. And the time is sure to come when this simple fact will become so prominent in my consciousness that I will stop working for FORTUNE. There will be no decision to make, no effort of the will: the balance will simply swing in the other direction. . . . I've recently read Mann's DEATH IN VENICE, a story so carefully and skillfully contrived that one is afraid to breath while reading it. If you ask me, it is a little too conscious, a little too perfect in structure—rather precious, in short. Still, a first-rate tale. It's odd the way Mann is obsessed by the idea of decay, dissolution, disease—whether physical, spiritual, moral, social, or mental. Often they are all combined. His BUDDENBROOKS, which I hear is his masterpiece, shows the decay in three or four generations of a bourgeois family. And DEATH IN V. and THE MAGIC M. are obviously concerned with the same theme. So incessant preoccupation with one theme shows a rather serious deficiency in artistic scope, what?

. . . In the letter before the last you asked whether I had any plans for myself or for us, and whether I thought the future worth speculating on. Well, I don't know how to answer, Dins. I am so hurried from day to day that I get no chance to plan or speculate. Constantly I have a belief underneath everything that New York is no place to live a reasonably satisfying life. But, goddamn it all, I am so rushed that I get no chance to think or feel my way towards something better. The Farm, you and I raising enough to live on and reading, writing, talking, engaging the good air and earth—that's a nice picture. But what about your Mother and what about your family? How could we all adjust ourselves to one another—not for a summer, but for good?——But hell, this is no answer to your question, all this piddling stuff. But can't do any better tonight.

> God, I'm weary—not physically
> But mentally. I'd like to lie on a
> Sun-hot beach a million years! I
> Want to bathe in peace and plenty
> Quiet and reality, none of which
> Are found in this city.

To Dinsmore Wheeler

June 13, 1930

I would have written you long ago except for the pressure of work I've been laboring under. Henry R. Luce, the Great White Father of the mad journalistic tribe who work on TIME and FORTUNE, has taken over FORTUNE of late. And, as a bondbroking friend of mine remarks about J. P. Morgan: "They all step when Luce (Morgan) cracks the whip." You've got to work if you don't want Massa

Luce to sell you down the river! The man is a driver of the first order—not offensively so, however. He is human underneath it all, and if he drives his writers, he certainly drives himself even more fanatically. His trouble (and genius) lies in the fact that he is a parson's son. In the last month I have written stories of some length on Baldwin Locomotive, American Can and Foundry Co., and the New Turkestan-Siberian R.R. in Russia. Also a brief survey of the match industry and several short pieces for TIME. . . . The article on the Diesel is good, though I say it myself. In re Mott of General Motors, the complete picture of the man could not be presented. We had a lot of information on him, and he seems a pathological case. He has been married three times. Each time he took his bride on a honeymoon to his ranch out West. The first lady died there in a few weeks, the second went crazy, and the third hurried back home and began suit for divorce. There's a plot for Sax Rohmer, eh? . . . I've started Stendhal's LE ROUGE ET LE NOIR, the first half of which I read several years ago in college. Even way back then I recognized its greatness and preferred it to all the other novels we read in the course, including MADAME BOVARY. It is so uncompromisingly truthful, accurate, almost scientific in its analysis of human behavior that it takes on a certain grandeur from that fact alone. In addition, of course, Stendhal was an extraordinary acute observer of the human comedy. And an artist always fully in control of his work. Rarely does one find such complete detachment on the part of an author from the passions and feelings of his characters. In this respect the contrast could not be greater, in my opinion, between Stendhal and Ernest Hemingway. Stendhal in the first few chapters of the book has described and satirized the small town better than Lewis did in BABBITT and MAIN STREET COMBINED. Where Lewis feebly and unimaginatively piles detail on detail to get his effect, Stendhal strikes to the root of the matter in 1/100th the space. He doesn't describe; he analyzes, reduces the plethora of raw material that life offers, to some sort of order. At the end of the first chapter are some prophetic, amazing words: "The Tyranny of public opinion, and what opinion!, is as stupid in the small towns of France as in the United States of America." Here's another excellent crack: "There's the great word that decides everything at Verrieres: TO MAKE MONEY; by itself, it represents the daily thoughts of more than three-quarters of the inhabitants." In another place Stendhal remarks of M. Renal, the Major of the town and most substantial man of wealth, "He was very polite, except when money was the subject of conversation." Stendhal has no style to speak of, but he does smite the nail mightily upon the head, an accomplishment even rarer than a fine literary style. . . .

AT THE OFFICE, Next Morning

Last night, after I stopped writing the letter, I happened to pick up Nietzsche. By God, I didn't put him down for an hour! Why do people read the tripe they do when such superb stuff can be had? It was a revelation to me, though I had always admired Nietzsche immensely. What think you of such apothegms as these:

It is not the strength but the duration of great sentiments that makes great men.

A man of genius is unbearable unless he possesses at least two things besides: gratitude and purity.

The degree and nature of man's sensuality extends to the highest altitudes of his spirit.

He who fights with monsters should be careful lest he thereby becomes a monster. And if thou gaze long into an abyss, the abyss will also gaze into thee.

Our vanity is most difficult to wound just when our pride has been wounded.

To him who feels himself preordained to contemplation and not to belief, all believers are too noisy and obtrusive; he guards against them.

When there is neither love nor hatred in the game, women's play is mediocre.

It is a curious thing that God learned Greek when he wished to turn author—and that he did not learn it better.

A nation is a detour of nature to arrive at six or seven great men—yes, and then to get around them.

What a person *is* begins to betray itself when his talent decreases, when he ceases to show what he *can do*. Talent is also an adornment; an adornment is also a concealment.

The one seeks an accoucheur for his thoughts, the other seeks someone whom he can assist: a good conversation thus originates.

In revenge and in love, woman is more barbarous than man.

The belly is the reason man does not so readily take himself for a God.

It is not enough to possess talent: one must also have your permission to possess it; eh, my friends?

Objection, evasion, joyous distrust, and love of irony are signs of health; everything absolute belongs to pathology.

Jesus said to his Jews: "The law was for servants; love God as I love him, as his Son! What have we sons of God to do with morals!"

To vigorous men, intimacy is a matter of shame—and something precious.

Christianity gave Eros poison to drink; he did not die of it, certainly, but degenerated to Vice.

One begins to distrust very clever persons when they become embarrassed.

In affability there is no hatred of men, but precisely on that account a great deal of too much contempt of men.

Discovering reciprocal love should really disenchant the lover with regard to the beloved. "What! *She* is modest enough to love even you? Or stupid enough? Or—or—

A sign of strong character, when once the resolution has been taken, to shut the ear even to the best of counterarguments.

One loves ultimately one's desires, not the thing desired.

What say you to these? There's enough meat in most of them to keep talking for a day—would that we could talk together once more. . . .

To Dinsmore Wheeler

December 10, 1930

You want MORE about my latest, if not greatest, feminine (sic) delusion. Well, she is tall and wonderfully filled-out, with a Victorian figure. She dresses almost wholly in black . . . usually rather tightish about the bosom and belly (rightly so . . .). She's rather hard-looking, with a small, rather hard mouth—prettily shaped and insolent, and a pair of large-pupilled eyes. . . . Any mother would throw a fit if she found her boy within 100 feet of her. Her voice is rather strident, and her laugh is the least humorous thing about her. . . . Her face is unlined—never looks tired, always smooth and fresh. At the most, a faint shadow appears under her eyes, making them even lovelier.

Her mental, moral, and spiritual qualities are about as bad as possible. I'm sure the reason her face is unlined is that she has never experienced a real emotion or fairly met a human situation. She's an actress (at present in a dramatic school) and has every theatrical vice . . . absurdly affected . . . plays the part of the "girl about town" . . . phony . . . utterly selfish and indescribably callous to the feelings of others. Even I can see she has no tact whatsoever. In any social group, she never seems to fit in . . . gaucheries and "breaks" . . . a child, a barbarian, unable to understand other people's feelings and to conceal her own. Therein, of course, I have much in common with her. My only advantage is a fairly keen mind and a pretty good disposition. Her disposition would be hellish were it not that she is such a child, after all, and so can be diverted with simple expedients. Her one serious defect is that she seems almost incapable of any feeling for anyone outside herself. Whether she is "shallow" or just "unawakened" my researches have not yet established. (1951: nor ever did)[1] For one so selfish, assured and insolent, she is curiously ineffectual. Her lack of social sense, perception, sensitivity is so enormous that, with the advantages of great beauty and heartlessness, she still cannot cope with life—that is, with man.

1. Much later, in the 1950s, Macdonald studied these earlier letters to prepare for his visits to a psychiatrist. He made marginal comments and inserted some notes.

Even a simple fellow like me can see through her artifices. The funny thing is that although I can hardly find a good word to say for her except physically—I am as fascinated now as when I first saw her. Were she a little more complex, the affair would be morbid. But even her evil qualities are so rudimentary, so childish in their forthrightness, that she cannot be called a Vampire. All I've spent on her is some money (too much) and some idle thoughts. Any deep emotion is practically impossible—thank God! Were I to love her seriously! . . . Last night she remarked out of a (fairly) clear sky, "I'm tired of you," a remark all the more uncalled-for since she's so far allowed me nothing but a few kisses. (1951: THAT WAS ALL I EVER GOT) . . . I wish I was harder, and subtler.

So now you know all about her but her name, which is Edith Atwater. . . .

To Dinsmore Wheeler

February 2, 1932

If I don't write you, it's not from lack of thought about you but because I am passing through a mental and spiritual hell. Work on FORTUNE is more unsatisfying every month, and yet I can find nothing to cling to in its place. The only times I'm alive now are when I'm either drunk or Godawfully miserable. And I'm in love with a gal who doesn't reciprocate. For the first time in my life I am beginning to feel continuously inadequate to living and to wish I had never been born. The fact is I'm grotesquely unfit for contact with my fellow men and (Oh God!) Women, and will only be happy when I retire to my tropical desert island. Which I hope will be soon—and for good. I continually feel that I am the ugliest, dullest, weakest, most cowardly and altogether ineffectual human being on God's earth. And all because Fay [Williams] doesn't love me—that plus several dozen minor reasons.

To Dinsmore Wheeler

January 8, 1934

Nancy Rodman and I are reading Shakespeare together and finding it very absorbing. We've done *Othello* and are beginning *Coriolanus*, which T. S. Eliot and G. L. K. Morris agree is Shakespeare's greatest production. I wish you could know Nancy. She's a sweet girl, even if she does let me in for drearily long-winded left-wing political meetings. (I went to one last week which lasted for four hours. Best speaker was Miles Reno, who had a rustic Iowan charm and little else.) We're going this afternoon to see the Brancusi show, which seems to be just about the finest thing in the art way to be seen this winter. . . . Had dinner with my Rich Uncle . . . whom I damn near converted to communism. . . .

To Dinsmore Wheeler

June 16, 1934

. . . As for my coming out to the farm, my vacation will begin when I've finished the piece I'm now working on (subject: The Communist Party in the U.S.A.) which will be around August 1, and will last a month. I'm going to spend the first two weeks with Nancy Rodman, probably, possibly only a week, depending on where she is staying then (she's with her mother in New Hampshire now) and certain other factors. . . . I am pleased Dot had such a good time when she was here and that she liked Natasha [von Hoershelman, research assistant]. (The feeling was reciprocated. Natasha felt an emotional sympathy, instantly, with Dot, she told me, which she could never feel, for example, with Nancy.) . . . Last weekend Hellman [Geoffrey—Yale classmate and colleague at Luce publications] and I, plus Walker Evans who is doing the photographs for the Communist piece, went up to Camp Nitgedaiget (Yiddish for Sans Souci) and saw some Communists at close range. It was An Experience. Ask me about it when I next see you. People in crowds are obscene, aren't they, or am I psychopathic?. . . . Today I talked with Earl Browder, secretary and big shot of the U.S. Communist Party. He's a little man with a shrewd smile, cigar clamped in yellowish teeth, and the ready, somewhat evasive answers of the small-town lawyer or politician. Neither a worker nor an intellectual, certainly not a revolutionary. He sits at a desk in a bare room in the shadow of a gigantic (five feet high) bust of Lenin. An amusing contrast between his prosaic shrewdness and the melodramatic, scowling, insanely enormous bust of Lenin. . . .

To Nancy Rodman[2]

July 1, 1934

The city's not the same without you. Here I am working away at the office at 10:15 (P.M.) simply because there is nothing else I especially want to do. My desk

---

2. Macdonald met Nancy Rodman, a Vassar graduate (1932) and sister of Seldon Rodman, the poet, in Seldon Rodman's apartment. At the time Rodman was editing the left democratic journal *Common Sense*. Macdonald was writing literary criticism for the journal and frequently encountered Nancy at editorial conferences. At the time of his courtship of Nancy he was also involved with two other women, including Dinsmore Wheeler's sister Dorothy. Despite the fact that Nancy was a debutante and came from a well-to-do New York family—her grandfather had been the president of the New York Stock Exchange, and her grandmother ran a settlement house in the city—she inherited a deep social consciousness and strong political commitments. Although diffident, she had an intellectual as well as a moral and political influence on Macdonald.

is submerged in Communist literature, and I wish you could help me plow through it. All day I have been talking to Communists, and tomorrow I am going to run through the following strenuous program under the auspices of your brother.

10:00 Trotskyites

11:15 Gitlowites

12:30 Lovestoneites

5:00 Weisbordites (which I'm told consist of Weisbord and his wife). These Communists are a maddening race for an outsider because of the great air of mystery and conspiracy they adopt. They never answer a question but always find a pretext for preaching a Communist sermon instead. They won't answer such simple questions as what their dues are and who is on their central committee. And they are shocked if one is blasphemous enough to question any of the innumerable dogmas they rigidly hold. As someone said today, "The trouble with the Communists is they are always in church. They'd all make good Jesuits."

This weekend I'm going with Walker Evans up to Camp Nitgedaiget (Yiddish for "Don't worry") to see the Communists at play. He's going to take some pictures to illustrate the article. I hope the article turns out well, because it may be my valedictory at FORTUNE.

To Nancy Rodman

July 7, 1934

... I've done practically nothing in the last few days but read a little on the Communist Party in the U.S.A. That [Elizabeth] Dilling women's who's who in radicalism is especially entertaining. Its high point so far is the slogan of the American Anti-Bible Bookstore: "If it's Against the Bible, we have it." That book, *Rebel America* [by Lilian Symes and Travers Clement] is fairly good but written in a wordy, academic, lifeless style. I wonder why people think that a stuffy style must always go with an impartial point of view.

To Nancy Rodman

July 16, 1934

It now appears I'm not to write about those big nasty Japanese crabs[3] [a *Fortune* assignment] and that after I've finished my piece on communism I'll be free to

---

3. This potential assignment sparked Nancy's criticism that Dwight was wasting his time on trivial matters during the nation's economic crisis and that he should insist on more substantial pieces.

do as I please. . . . The weekend at Nitgedaiget came near making a fascist out of me. I discovered a lot of aristocratic reactions (as, to bathing in a slightly dirty pool with the other comrades and eating on slightly soiled plates with the other comrades and applauding mass-level violin solos with the other comrades) which quite surprised me. Also a fundamental, individualistic dislike of living as one of a herd. The comrades were 99 and 44/100% pure Yiddish and they had that peculiar Yiddish love of living in each other's laps that you can observe any day at Coney Island. But I feel disgusted by humanity, whether Yiddish or Racquet Clubbish, when it presents itself as a squirming mass. Hellman's reactions were amusing, however, and in general I'm glad I went. By Sunday noon we could stand it no more and we stole away to the Westchester Embassy Club, to which Geoffrey belongs, where we bathed in a clean if capitalistic pool and drank a couple of Tom Collinses in capitalistic solitude.

To Nancy Rodman

July 20, 1934

It's terribly hot and I'm sitting by an open window dressed simply in a pair of pajama bottoms, a costume I hope won't shock any passersby on the Queensboro Bridge. . . .

Yes, I agree entirely about communism. Last weekend didn't change my belief that, all else aside, communism is the only way out of the mess our society is in. Whether it's a blind alley is another question, but it's the only alley that has any chance of *not* turning out to be blind. The way Johnson, Wagner, and even Perkins, whom I'd thought a liberal and intelligent dame, have applauded the brutal and illegal persecution of the "reds" now going on in California as a result of the San Francisco strike has made me boiling mad. I'm going to flay them in my article—which is turning out fairly well so far. I'll bring you a copy.

The other day I had a two-hour argument with Luce about *Fortune* not having enough social consciousness. I think I upset him a bit, though I don't think I made my prospects of "getting ahead" any better. Not that I care. I'm going to quit soon anyway, unless I'm fired first as a "red." Remind me to give you a full account of my argument with Luce—you'll be interested. (Or I'll know the reason why!)

To Nancy Rodman

n.d., July 1934

. . . You can't imagine how I'm looking forward to seeing you again and being at Nantucket (my favorite summer resort anyway) with you. *Please* take good care of yourself, darling, at least until I arrive. Life begins on Wednesday.

How do you like *What Maisie Knew?* I'm curious to know, for I'm just taking up *The Wings of the Dove* again—having just finished *P. of a L*. Have you that Hound and Horn Hank James tome with you, by the way? I hope so, as I'd like to read it. The James problem must be faced!

You've discovered that men don't like their judgment questioned by women, you say? I hope you consider me an exception to that, because I think I am. (Don't unkindly say that I don't like my judgment questioned by either man or woman!) Curious, I have a great deal of literary vanity but very little personal or even intellectual vanity. I care less and less what people—even those I like and respect—think about me and my actions.

To Dinsmore Wheeler

January 31, 1935

. . . You mentioned a little essay you were thinking of sending me. If it wasn't cut short by your fall, I'd of course very much like to see it. If you still feel self-conscious about my legendary "snorts of disgust," I've worked in vain. Really, Dins, you should know what a gentle mild fellow I am at heart. . . . No, I don't think either Love or Sex or individuals are old-fashioned. Nor have I yet seen a proletarian or class-conscious novel which was good for any other reason than its effectiveness in those fields. You speak of learning to write about male & female as if that were a funny little province of letters like writing the goldfish column in the SUN every Saturday. I say, "It was good enough for Stendhal, it was good enough for Proust, it was good enough for Henry James, and it's good enough for me." (Add "That Old Time Libido" to the front of this and you have something pretty damned amusin'.) . . . I don't smoke much when I'm writing—though when I read your query as to whether I did, I at once got out a cigarette and lit up. (A Count Condossis, by the way, in a lovely orange and gold package with a gilt coronet, and are they lousy.) . . . I'll send you a complete list of books I take with me. As yet I am still deciding. My plan is to get a small, light, sturdy trunk and pack therein some 30 tomes and possibly a typewriter. I can leave that at some convenient place if we do much traveling around, which we probably won't. . . . If your father really wants to give us a w.p., we would very much like William Henry Chamberlin's *Russia's Iron Age*. . . . Tell him it will be packed in my trunk as I want to read it along with some other books. . . . That quotation from E. M. Forster was very interesting. Like most of his stuff it was slickly phrased and intelligent, with even a certain amount of originality. But the contrasts are a little too neat to be convincing. I see no reason why one can't be utterly absorbed by and faithful to one woman and also highly civilized. Forster reminds me very much of Aldous Huxley: he's persuasive, facile, highly intelligent, rather witty, deficient in depth, emotional warmth, intellectual integrity.

. . . We are sailing on February 21 (I think it is) on the *Saturnia* of the Italian Lines—used to be a Cosulich boat, I think, until Il Duce said "Let there be one Line," and there was. The trip takes about 12 days, includes stops at the Azores, Gibralter, Lisbon, Algiers, Naples, and Palermo, where we get off. We will stay in Palermo or somewhere in Sicily until it gets too hot or we get too something, when we will go somewhere else. No plans yet. The idea is to do a minimum of traveling because I want to try and get some work done. Sicily ought to be a perfect place at this time of year, and Il Duce, surely one of the great comic characters of all time, has decreed that all hotels chop fifteen percent off their rates and all railroad tickets be reduced to half—just for the benefit of such touristy mice as Nancy and me.[4]

. . . The Soviets have finally produced an excellent sound film—*Chapayev* or *The Red Commander*. It's nothing compared to the early Eisenstein or Pudovkin films because it has no great aesthetic merit (by which I mean that its form is purely narrative and that the moving isn't constructed out of pictures in the dynamic fashion of POTEMKIN) but it is as good a nonaesthetic film as I have seen. It has an "epic" (much misused word) quality: it is full of action, humor, and even a little human pathos, and it tells a story which is already deep in the national consciousness. I'm sending you a copy of the NEW THEATER, after I've read it, which has an article by Eisenstein on the Soviet movies, which hails *Chapayev*. The article is pretty poor, unfortunately, and doesn't seem to be written with Eisenstein's full force. There's a piece on Meyerhold's theater which looks interesting.

Have you read either HEAVEN'S MY DESTINATION or FORTY DAYS OF MUSA DEGH? And would you like to read either? And if not, what books would you like to read? I'm determined to send you a couple, and if you don't pick any out, I'll have to do it blindfolded.

For the last two weeks I have been living in a new and exciting world, the realm of the neurotic and insane. . . . I am doing a piece on the nervous breakdown. So I've been reading Freud, talking to psychiatrists, visiting sanitariums and hospitals. I am now composing for your special benefit some notes on a

---

4. Macdonald had arranged a six months' sabbatical from *Fortune*. He and Nancy planned to tour Italy and then spend the rest of the time in Majorca to pursue his writing interests. It was to be a kind of second honeymoon since the first had been short and hectic due to the pressure of writing deadlines. But his career ambitions were very strong, and both he and Nancy often seemed worried that they did not produce enough scholarly work to justify their trip.

visit to Butler Hospital in Providence I made last week. The subject, which takes in practically all abnormal psychology—though I try to keep clear of the psychoses, i.e., things like paranoia, manic depression, dementia praecox, i.e., definite insanity—is the most interesting I've ever worked on. I think I will compile a bibliography of literaria neurotica—Strindberg, Hamlet, Lear, William Ellery Leonard, Julian Sorel in THE RED & BLACK ("first neurotic in European literature," at least first one to be described with clinical insight by his author), etc. I suppose you've read Freud. He writes extraordinarily well, don't you think? . . . I'm sorry this letter is so chaotic. The typewriter always makes my style even jerkier than it usually is. I'm about to buy myself a fountain pen, however, and I'll write you again this week with that.

To Dinsmore Wheeler

March 8, 1935

Tomorrow morning the *Roma* sails for Sicily and the happy isles of the Mediterranean, and we on it. . . . I'm glad you agree about Roosevelt going to the right. I'll be interested to see how far he has gone by the time I get back. And whether Huey Long is dictator or in jail by then. . . . Curious coincidence, my deciding that Roosevelt was going right and picking out the very same week's facts to prove it as TIME did in *its* calling of the turn the same week. I'm told that it was Luce's idea in TIME, so maybe I've a smart journalistic sense at that. . . .[5]

[James] Agee, by the way, is in poor shape psychologically. No interest in his work here, and small ability at faking. He spends three times as long on his pieces as he should, and has a devil of a time with them. I've advised him, and I think he's going to do it, to ask for a six- or ten-month leave in which to collect himself and get back into decent condition again. Also he might be able to reach some happier solution of the il-faut-vivre problem in that time. . . . One more remark anent your objections to communism. I agree perfectly with your dislike and skeptical amusement, but I think there is one point to be firmly made. And that is that the Communist point of view is more often right than any other when it comes to realistically interpreting current political and economic trends. It took liberals like you and me two years to be disabused of our illusions about Roosevelt, but the Communists saw him for what he is from the very first. We were taken in by (1) his fine words and (2) his really sincere intention to do right. But the Communists saw that he wasn't strong enough to re-

5. *Time*, February 18, 1935, had carried a cheerful account of FDR's move to the right: Richberg's anti-labor policy in the NRA; the conservative Social Security program; the opposition to prevailing wages on public works projects. See Arthur Schlesinger, Jr., *The Politics of Upheaval* (Boston, 1960), p. 213.

dress the balance between capital and labor, and that his putting the federal government into the capital-labor fight would merely result in capital being strengthened, i.e., the federal power is a weapon that will be used by whichever side is stronger, and Roosevelt merely got it into good fighting trim to be taken over by the capitalists.

To Dinsmore Wheeler

March 20, 1935

In about three hours we will come to anchor off Palermo, tenders will come alongside, and Nancy and I will disembark to set foot for the fourth and first time respectively on Italian soil. . . . There's been so much to do, it seems. Shore excursions to the Azores, to Lisbon, to Algiers ate up much of these days. . . . We have been exercising violently in the sala gymnastica, and doing a lot of reading. Nancy has plunged deep into Indian folklore as the first step in her ambitious project of writing a history of oriental art—a nontechnical, "Intelligent Man's Guide" to the subject. . . . For my part, I've been reading Chamberlain's *Russia's Iron Age* (given us by your father), which is very good. Read it if you can possibly get hold of it. Also Malraux's *La Condition Humain* ("Man's Fate" to you) and the *Iliad* (in Greek), both of which are very fine. I've also started a notebook of ideas, on the order of the ones we kept years ago, only less personal.

We have no definite plans as yet, except that we have a rendezvous with the Italian Line at Trieste at the end of May. There we take an Italian liner to Greece, whence we sail for Spain, getting there around July 1. (All this sea voyaging can be done on one round-trip ticket, you see.) We will probably stay in Spain the rest of the time, reading and writing in some retired country town. (Nancy knows Spain well, having spent many months there.)

In Sicily we are leaving Palermo in a day or two—it's not especially attractive or interesting—and making for Taormina (didn't Lawrence write *Sea & Sicily* about it?) and, maybe, Syracusa.

Seeing foreign places is an exciting and exhausting business. One reacts so strongly to the utterly new and foreign (you can . . . feel the foreign-ness of places on your skin) that one is soon tired.

Once you asked me for a list of the books in our library trunk. Since that's now in the baggage room, consigned to Trieste, where we will pick it up in two months, I can't give you a complete list. But we are taking with us to Sicily a small suitcase of tomes, selected for immediate use:

(1) Iliad, books I to XII
(2) Autenneth's Homeric Dictionary
(3) Nivedita & Coomaraswamy: Myths of the Hindus and Buddhists

(4) Coomaraswamy, Indian and Indonesian Art

(5) Moore: History of Religions

(6) Grosset: Civilizations of the Orient, Vol II India

(7) Burkhardt: The Renaissance in Italy

(8) Machiavelli: The Prince

(9) Auden: Poems

(10) Spender: Poems

(11) Oxford Book of English Verse

(12) Hopkins poems (Grazia signore!)

(13) The Random House Selection from Donne

(14) Proust's Swain's Way

(15) Marlow: Edward II

(16) Sterne: Tristram Shandy

(17) Joyce: Ulysses (in an excellent little white-bound Albatross edition, no bigger than a Modern Library book)

(18) Selected Papers of Bertrand Russell

(19) Baedecker's Italy

(20) Freud: A General Introduction to Psychoanalysis

(21) James: The Art of the Novel

(22) Richardson: Maurice Guest

(23) Richardson: The Fortunes of Richard Mahoney

Written out, that seems quite a lot of the world's wisdom to pack into one fairly small valise.

P.S. Add to list of books: (24) Jane Austen: Emma

To Dinsmore Wheeler

June 6, 1935

. . . This journey so far has been in many ways the most fruitful and contented part of my life. Now after two and a half months of inquiry into Italian art and antiquity, after absorbing such elements—however superficially—as the nobly high gold-crested mosaic interior of Monreale, those sponge-pitted, chalky quarries of Syracuse where the Athenian prisoners died in thousands, after entertaining for a month the full shock of ROME, and after two weeks' hasty inventory of the Florentine treasure house of painting and sculpture, after all this we now are settled here [Palma di Mallorca] for the remaining three and a half months. And it is an ideal place to be, to read and create and live. Altogether I should say I am extremely lucky.

But to answer your letter, which is the most moving reminder I've yet had of the U.S.A., which both of us have felt a nostalgia for ever since we left on the *Roma*. Palma is all that one could want any place to be, and yet it is to the

United States—to R.D.3 [Wheeler family farm in Ohio] and Brookfield, Conn. [Dwight and Nancy's summer cottage], rather than New York City—that I feel myself attached. The rough grey granite fences of Connecticut, the Ohio spring you so eloquently describe have for me, I find, that unique, peculiar, irrational, poignant charm which the lover savors in the eyelids or the breasts of *one* woman, and only one. To them I belong and they are my destiny. But I'm rising to heights I won't be able to sustain—better undo the gas valve and come down a bit. . . .

Your description of the spring at The Farm made my mouth water. O to be in Milan now that April's here! Spring is lovely in Italy, too, but with none of the charm of the American season. The earth is too old, too mellow with experience to venture the mad, fresh profusion of an Ohio spring. . . . I too feel the insecurity of natural, peaceful human happiness in this world of Hitlers and Stalins. The problem of why men insist on destroying whatever is lovely and good in their lives is becoming an obsession with me. Much of my reading and writing is directed toward a solution, or rather an explanation. The best I can do in the way of a latter is to blame wars, depressions, dictators all on Western man's lust for power as an end in itself, as indeed the highest, and regardless of whether in achieving or preserving it he destroys everything else including life itself. And my best solution, achieved after a hint from Bertrand Russell, is the Chinese worldview, which submits to force and would rather be weak and happy than powerful. I'm soon going to look into Latorettes' history of Chinese culture. . . . The [Westbrook] Pegler columns are especially appreciated. Send us a lot more, please! The whole batch passed around the dinner table tonight. Pegler seems to have found himself in the wider field of politics at last. These columns seem much better than any I've seen for a long time. I relished especially his remarks on the Italians defending the Gates of Rome in Abyssinia and on Mr. Hoover's late noble experiment. . . .

June 8: Day after tomorrow we move into a house of our own—white stucco, three bedrooms, garden full of pink and purple flowers, wide prospect down the slope of a hill with a blue bay of the Mediterranean in one corner— all for $28 a month. . . . I expected to find Mallorca a sort of debauched Provincetown, with drunk American minor poets, suspicious and hostile natives, touristy shops, jazz and cocktails. Nancy has been here for long stays twice before. . . . Her enthusiasm caused us to decide to stay here for the last half of our time. So far the place seems almost ideal. The natives are nice-looking, polite, pleasant, a great relief after the aggressive and usually unpleasant way Italians assert themselves. It is a relief not to have to continually defend one's pocketbook and one's individuality from the rapacious brigandage of the Italians. (Travel sometimes causes bad feelings to arise toward other people, I'm afraid.) . . .

But cheapness is a negative virtue at best. The satisfaction of Majorca for me is partly that here I can read and write outdoors all day in the sun and partly that the people are so good-natured and their life so philosophically free from the tension of dynamic American and European 1935 civilization that I feel free to think and read as much as I like. Relieved of any inhibitory counterstress of dynamic materialism, my normal mental energies are asserting themselves in a remarkable way. I've never read so much at a stretch (reading outdoors doesn't give me that unreal, blood-pounding-in-temples, withdrawn-from-life feeling that a couple of hours indoors does) and never felt so perceptive, so teeming with ideas, so able to look down on the world from a lofty point of view—the altitude one of intellect rather than morality, you understand. Nancy says she feels the same way, and she reads and makes notes a good deal. One is ashamed to accept a banal paradise like Mallorca—how much more satisfying if one could think, "We were the first that ever burst into that silent sea"—but I can't escape my fate. Don't despise me too greatly. . . . I think I am getting even more development out of this vacation than I expected. The crucial issues of the modern world are defining themselves to my fascinated eyes. I'm beginning to realize that almost all man's sufferings are brought on by his own stupidity, and to understand why he refuses to pay attention to the good and the wise. Recently I've been reading about the World War for instance. All 800 pages of Winston Churchill's brilliant history of the war, *The World Crisis* have been explored, annotated. I've just read J. M. Keynes's admirable *The Economic Consequences of the Peace*, a cool, humane chain of logic which demonstrates that reason and humanity *with* basic prejudices are more to be desired than a basically correct viewpoint *without* reason and humanity. Although he believes (the book came out in 1920) that Germany was "guilty" of causing the war and that Bolshevist Russia was a land of the devil, he nevertheless recommended that the Versailles Treaty be scrapped as unfair to Germany and that the Allies recall their internationalist armies from Russia. He also predicted the speedy collapse of German reparation payments and the default on the allies debt to the U.S. His appreciations of the personal qualities of the Big Four at Versailles are very sensitive. Altogether, a book you should read (it's only some 200 pages long) if you haven't. Have you ever seen Colonel Repington's *The First World War: 1914–1918* . . . that war diary is amazingly frivolous, stupid, brutal, malicious, snobbish, and frank? It's the most damaging testimony on the sort of people who ran the war and their behavior that I have ever seen. Repington, who was an important, or at least widely known and powerfully connected, British staff officer and strategist, is a sort of modern Pepys, with the humanity of Pepys but with all his delight in bean-spilling. His diary is full of excellent ammunition for the Bolshevik and pacifist, some of which I'm storing in my notebook—I've all sorts of theories about the war and how it was bungled, and why. The heroes of one's schooldays, Joffre and Kitchener, seem to have been as dunderheaded a pair of obstinate old men as you could find on the Supreme Court bench. But you can learn all about this when I see you next.

To my amazement I've succeeded in reading from 50 to 100 lines of the *Iliad*, in Greek, more or less steadily every day for the two weeks we've been here. I'm getting really interested in it. The poetry, of course, is very beautiful. But the heroes are very interesting as studies of personality. Most fascinating character is Homer himself. To what extent he was serious, to what ironical (his heroes often act in obviously absurd or outrageous ways), whether he was at heart a civilian making fun of soldiers and a Bolshevist satirizing the "bosses" — these are intriguing questions. Read the first half of Book Two, the Thersites incident, and see what you think. If the rest of the *Iliad* (I'm only in Book Three) equally bristles with such questions, latent though not recognized by the scholars, who take Homer with deadly seriousness, I may attempt a Marxian Commentary on Homer.

The other day Esther [Hamil—a friend from New Haven whom Macdonald met at Yale] wrote me that she is going to Reno for a divorce, by this time is probably there. "Good," said Nancy, and I agreed. I like Jim, but he has acted in the stupidest, most reactionary and male-possessive way toward Esther as a wife. He made it necessary for her to choose between him and her mental-literary interests, and of course he lost. She apparently is taking the children. It's a mess only because of them, but kids have to take their chance. I'd always be for the adults putting their happiness ahead of their children. Esther sounds very upset about it all, poor gal. I wish I could be with her. Writing, she says, is her one rock of safety, and she is taking a typewriter and a lot of poetry books to Reno. She's writing a play about a psychoanalyst. . . .

If I had any production of my own I'd send it to you. But several score pages of notes, about 20 pages of pencil notes on H. H. Richardson's *Maurice Guest* and *Fortunes of Richard Mahoney*,[6] and some rough beginnings of so-far abortive projects are all I have to show for my three months of idleness. But I am absorbing, arranging, reflecting, or conjecturing more than I ever have before. And I have decided to ripen my mind with reading and thinking before trying anything ambitious. I could write an essay on Richardson now, I could by an effort of the will aided by a talent for words complete several projects, perhaps even a shortish book, while I'm here. But I am learning at last the virtues of humility. There's so much to be known about the world, so much that, for me at least, *must* be known before I'll be ripe for anything good.

6. H. H. Richardson was the pen name of Henrietta Richardson, an Australian novelist thought well of in the 1930s. *The Fortunes of Richard Mahoney*, the first of a trilogy, was regarded by many critics as an outstanding achievement.

My main reading for the past week has been in *Middletown*, which you should look through if you haven't already. Next I'm going to take up [A. A.] Berle's *The Modern Corporation and Private Property*.[7]

... Last week we went to a bullfight—a very good one, with fierce bulls who charged on a dead run into the arena and skidded in the sawdust as they hurled their brute bodies at the deceptively waved cloaks (which are a dark pink rather than the scarlet I had imagined). It's all as tense and primitive and beautifully stylized as Ernest says it is, but I'll never go to another. Banal as it is to cavil about the horses, I do. To see a half-ton of heavily muscled bull charge at full speed, sharp horns lowered, into the side of a rickety, blindfolded, pathetically shambling old horse, mercifully so doped he doesn't seem to show much fear—that's cruel, unjust, and unsporting, in my opinion. The horses are heavily padded on the sides toward the bull, but when the horse goes down completely as happened once in this fight, he's often de-gutted in a revolting way. The one I saw was, anyway, and I didn't like it. No symbolic values are enough to reconcile me to such tortures. Six bulls were killed that afternoon. ...

To Esther Hamil

n.d., July 1935

... Your appreciation of *Letters to a Young Poet* is all the more welcome because a young married couple here (man, Yale, rich, a Hartford boy and, at 25, a fully trenched snob and reactionary; girl, Vassar, whimsical, talented, poetically once, though lately unproductive, the most brutally illogical woman I've ever met) to whom we lent the *Journal* were shocked, even disgusted by the monstrous conceit of the author—a curious reaction to Rilke, who always seems so humble an artist. They went so far as to find egotism in what to me is the supreme repression of disinterested sympathy in literature, the episode in which he follows the neurotic with the convulsive tic. To them Rilke's minute description was coldly analytical, and his following the man was an act of heartless curiosity. That he was trying to impart some of his own strength, this was incomprehensible to these sensible bourgeois souls, who would have politely averted their eyes and phoned for an ambulance. I resent the implication when you write, "What obscure intuition moved your factual and realistic mind to give me that book just when you did?" It's not fair to damn me as "factual and realistic and then give the credit for everything good to some "obscure intuition." I think I'm much more intuitive than most people realize, more than I want to be even, though in this case no intuition was involved. The book ex-

---

7. Berle was one of the more famous of FDR's brains trust.

presses so admirably and movingly what we both feel about writing that I wanted you to have it.

. . . Three days ago we moved from Hotel Victoria, a swank terraced affair at the bay's edge, to this place, Villa Soleil, a furnished house we sublet for $25 a month. We like it very much. There is a terrace with a wide view of the sea, hills, a lighthouse, and a colony of huge silver oil tanks. . . . Most of the time we spend reading, taking notes, and writing. . . . I have made a lot of notes on H. H. Richardson; but for various reasons, or rationalizations, I've done nothing with them. There is so much to be read and assimilated, I want to know about so much, *must* know, in fact, in order to do the, well, the sort of philosophical-historical criticism that interests me—that any puny effort I might make seems absurd. I've been reading *Middletown*, that anthropological study of life in a small U.S. city which the Lynds did, lately. I've finished Winston Churchill's history of the World War (*The Crisis*), a brilliantly written book, and J. M. Keynes's *The Economic Consequences of the Peace*. I read 50 or 100 lines of Homer every day, and I've noted down several, to me, exciting speculations about the *Iliad* and its author. Yesterday I began Stendhal's *Charterhouse of Parma* and liked it much more than I did several years ago when I read some 100 pages of it. I've also read Henry James's *The Art of the Novel* every now and then. . . .

I'm concluding this letter in the afternoon shade on our terrace, which faces East. We both heartily wish you were here. It's a life as close to ideal as I've yet come. Both of us feel more mentally alive—which is our particular way of being alive—than ever before in our lives. I've never read so continuously and with such continual awareness of what I'm reading, so that my life here, which to most people would seem complete idleness, is really more strenuous than my former construction from 9:30 to 5 of elaborate and often quite clever factual fairy tales for tired tycoons. . . . Not until this prolonged absence from the U.S. did I realize how great a charm my own country has for me. Wordsworth put it more lyrically when he wrote

> I travell'd among unknown men
>   In lands beyond the sea
> Old, England! Did I know till then
>   What love I bore to thee.

Nostalgia for the United States, where conditions for working and thinking are as hostile as they are favorable here, this irrational and even immoral (to a pacifist and internationalist like myself) sentiment is always with me. When I first came abroad, I tried constantly to awaken myself to the miraculous fact that *this* tree, *this* pebbled path that my feet scraped along, this green hillside seen from the train was ITALY or PORTUGAL or whatever. But now I try to forget that, and sometimes I can almost imagine that a line of telegraph poles marches over a Connecticut (and not a Mallorcan) meadow and that the lulling [sic?] of frogs at dusk rises into heavy New England marshland air and not into the soft tropical atmosphere of this island.

To Esther Hamil

July 20, 1935

. . . We are coming back a few weeks early, partly because we want to consult books we haven't here, for purposes I'll later mention, but chiefly because we want to see the U.S. and our friends—you not least—again. Six months is longer than it seems when one is in an alien land, friendless and hence, except for what can be contrived tête-à-tête, conversation-less. I am a great deal more of a social animal than I realized. So we are coming back on the *Roma* around the middle of August—leaving here on the tenth. . . . Nancy has done a lot of work on Oriental Art—you know her project to write a one-volume history of it. . . . And I have read a great deal—Stendhal's *La Chartreuse de Parme*, which I finally finished with relief, I confess; Trotsky's readable and interesting *My Life*; James's *The Golden Bowl*, whose tenuous subtleties I'm still struggling with; that thorough and intelligent study of provincial American manners, *Middletown*, and a great tome of Nancy's on Chinese history and culture. After several months of indecisive hovering, in which I rejected the idea of a long essay on H. H. Richardson, after taking pages of notes, because after closer inspection her value didn't seen to warrant such an expenditure of effort (and also because I didn't seem to think very clearly or fruitfully on the plane of literary criticism, a state of mind I hope won't be permanent)—and after a long period up in the air, anyway, I finally lighted, at Nancy's suggestion, on a subject which has turned out to be extraordinarily well suited to my talents—judging by the vast number of ideas I seem to produce under its stimulus. It is, not to keep you in suspense through anymore subordinate clauses, the modern dictatorship—Hitler, Stalin, Mussolini, Kemal [Atatürk] etc. I've spent the last two days ordering my voluminous thoughts on the subject, and I now have four major subdivisions: WHAT life is like under a 20th-century dictatorship, WHY these dictators have arisen, HOW they keep in power, and finally what the future may be expected to bring forth. . . . The outline alone now comes to 8 pages, so it's clearly pretty complex. I've read a lot here for it—Nietzsche, books on Russia and Germany, Marx, etc. There are a score more I'll look into when I get back to New York. It all should result in a book which, if I can bring it off properly, should, or at least could, be rather good. You will have to do some critical reading for *me*, now, and I'm well aware that my style, verbose, heavy, banal, will read poorly to so sensitive an ear as yours. I hope you'll be lenient.

Do you know James—the late James of *The Wings of the Dove* and *The*

Golden Bowl? You might absorb something of value from him, although his complexities and proclivities may be hopelessly at loggerheads with your own simplicity of statement. He seems to be markedly conscious of just what effect he wants and how to produce it, and he has an extraordinary command of technique. No writer I can think of at the moment is so blandly, easily, triumphantly sure of his mastery of language. Whether his style isn't perhaps a bit too precious, hair-splitting, and persnickety—this is a question, but there's no doubt about one technical achievement of his: the use of metaphor. An interesting survey of metaphor through the ages could be made, probably has been. I think you'd have to go back to the seventeenth century to find such originality of metaphor, such a precise use of so powerful an instrument as James delights in—for his pleasure in bringing off a literary conceit is as obvious as that of any Elizabethan poet. I'll stick in some pages from my notebook to give you an idea—I want 'em back.

Were off to bathe in the sea—translucent, green, crystalline, quivering with bright light, quite different from the somber Atlantic—so I must stop.

To Dinsmore Wheeler

August 25, 1935
We're home, after a hectic time getting here. The *Roma*, packed with 500 Chinese people in tourist class alone, docked the day before yesterday. We made two new friends on the trip—a Rabbi Goldfarb, the most progressive man of God I've ever met, and a Mrs. Wooschin, an attractive Russian woman, whose husband (not on boat) is a Jewish doctor and whose brother directs Soviet movies. The last three days of the voyage was one long conversation—mostly on Soviet Russia, where several of the tourists had spent time.

Your letter was waiting for me. I'll answer it presently. I've got to call off the visit to R.D.3, I'm afraid, because *Fortune* wants me back a week earlier (Sept. 9) and I've an enormous load of reading and writing to do on my dictatorship thesis, too much for two months, let alone weeks. If my conscience would let me, there's nothing I'd rather like more than to see The Farm and Ohio again after months of exile—also to tell you about what we did and saw abroad. But 4 days driving and a week at R.D.3 would eat up my two weeks in one gulp—and I want to get my project under way enough to be able to carry it along all winter in my leisure.

To Esther Hamil

August 28, 1935
Already, you see, I'm deep in the midst of American life. We are going up to spend the Labor Day weekend (again, how American) with Selden, Nancy's

brother, and his wife. They have a house on Martha's Vineyard in the midst of a literary coterie of more-or-less radical gentry. We've been told we must profess deep pink political opinions or must not object to nude bathing. The former will be easy—we've grown more and more socially conscious in the last six months—but I've not made up my mind about the latter. It's a subtle question. Rationally I've no objection to emerging clothesless in public. YET there is a certain sense of privacy, almost of property which protests. Where do you stand on this great question?

I promised you some impressions of the U.S. . . . They are scantier than I expected, so scanty that I'll not try to inflate them beyond remarking, very generally, that this country is astoundingly *richer* than either Spain or Italy. The American landscape, to one fresh from the brown, sun-blasted, waterless Spanish countryside, is as prodigal, as recklessly profuse as an American grocery store is compared to the dingy, poverty-pinched little food shops of the continent. As for bathtubs, electric iceboxes, and such—there's no comparison possible. Materially, only the very rich abroad can live as we do over here. New York was moderately depressing to me, though to Nancy, who likes the place, quite otherwise. But even she was appalled by the sordid inhumanity of the subway. But I'm afraid this very sketchy (there's a lovely lady with violet eyes sitting next to me!) account is all that comes to mind right now.

We came home two weeks early to get some reading done (the trunkload of books being exhausted and the local libraries specializing in fiction). We've been here a week and I've read just one book, done no writing. The rush of social life, "seeing" people, was something we didn't count on. It's the great peril of writing or even reading in New York City, a temptation that so far I've been unable to conquer. Last night we mutually (she with the violet eyes just asked me for the time!) agreed to lead a better life this winter. Are you going to be in N.Y.C.? . . . I wish we could all get inextricably snowed in deep in . . . the Vermont winter. (She is leaving, with a vague, extremely vague, smile in my direction.)

I hope you won't find us too socially conscious, leftish in orientation, for comfort. The injustices and absurdities of the capitalist system for some reason are increasingly preoccupying my thought. Last night we had a much too spirited argument with Geoffrey Hellman and Natasha.[8] In fact, my relations with Natasha seem to be threatened by this ever growing gulf. A pitiful thing, if it really happens. Perhaps you can help me here.

---

8. Natasha von Hoerschelman was Macdonald's research assistant at *Fortune*. He had been keen on her just before his marriage to Nancy.

To Esther Hamil

November 2, 1935

. . . Sorry not to have answered your note sooner. For the last three weeks I have been busier than ever before in my life, writing and revising a long and extremely financial article on Republic Steel Corp. It was also complicated by a spirited and endless row with the company and with the editor about some left-wing sociological cracks I took at Republic. Finally [Archibald] MacLeish was delegated to rewrite my remarks, which he did so skillfully that both the editor and I were satisfied (or at least willing to let it go at that). The company remains intransigent, however. Today the final proof goes back to the printer, so I am at last free. Nancy and I may celebrate my freedom by making a brief tour of New England at the end of next week. I'm next going to write a long two-part article on U.S. Steel Corp., and there are plants and people in Worcester, Mass., and New Hampshire I have to see. Nancy wants to see art museums. So we may drive around. If we do we will probably go right to Boston a week from today, and we do hope we will see you. . . .

Republic Steel has so filled my life of late that I've done nothing else of interest. I reviewed Freud's AUTOBIOGRAPHY (which is interesting but not exciting—a reissue of a sketch he wrote ten years ago) and [Robinson] Jeffers's SOLSTICE (which is pretty poor—the vein has run thin) for my brother-in-law's magazine [*Common Sense*]. I'd like to do more reviewing and maybe I will, if I can get books. Fred Dupee is back in town after four years' exile in Mexico. He looks precisely as he did when he went away, which is somehow gruesome. We are now living at 425 East 51 Street and like it very much. . . . Too bad about Dashiel Hammet not taking the extra room. I saw an unfavorable review in THE NEW MASSES recently of his book on how to write short stories, so maybe he just doesn't recognize merit when he sees it.

. . . I saw Dinsmore in Akron, O., three weeks ago. I was out that way seeing Republic Steel's plants, and so I spent the weekend with him at Tom Polsky's. . . . Physically he is in splendid health, but psychically he seems to have given up the struggle (not that he ever fought very hard). As a person he has developed a great deal, but I think he will never be really fulfilled until he writes.

To His Excellency, The Governor of Georgia

November 4, 1935

We wish to register a protest against the eighteen-year sentence of Angelo Herndon [well-known black Communist]. Apparently Herndon was guilty of no crime or misdemeanor—unless to express Communist opinion be such in your state. His conviction on a technicality found in an antiquated "insurrection law" seems to us so outrageous a violation of his civil rights as a citizen that it is difficult to see how you, as a sworn upholder of law and order, can countenance such a blatant injustice.

We are neither Communists nor members of any radical organization, but we have an interest in seeing fair play done. If the newspapers of New York City have misreported this case, we should very much like to hear the other side of the story. [Signed by Dwight Macdonald and Wilder Hobson, a colleague at Luce publications]

To Dinsmore Wheeler

November 6, 1935

. . . The Republic article is considerable of a success—less superficial than most FORTUNE articles. I spent three weekends, many nights on the thing, and I finally worked out a thought-structure which was strong enough to remain unchanged through a lot of stress & strain caused by violent objections from the company. They didn't like it because the tenor of the article was mildly critical, whereas they are a big advertiser in both TIME and FORTUNE, and also have always received marvelous publicity in these sheets hitherto. But there were things that had to be said the more I got under the surface, and so I said them. At the end I had a long sociological disquisition on the duties of management to stockholders, implying that possibly the Girdler management was none too scrupulous that way. [Tom] Girdler [CEO, Republic Steel] read it, banged his fist on the desk, and said, "Why, this is socialism." God knows what he would do if he ever came across a real socialist. The editor (Hodgins) wanted to leave most of the guts out, but I appealed to Luce, who had MacLeish work out a compromise which satisfied me if not Hodgins. For all his lousy poetry, MacLeish has his uses around here as a left-wing social force. I feel that FORTUNE can be made somewhat more critical and socially conscious, and in my next piece, which will be on no other corporation than U.S. Steel itself, arch-capitalist company. It will be in two parts and will be the most important corporation story we have ever had. After some doubts as to the kosher quality of my economic attitude, they let me have it. I'll do a lot of traveling—to Birmingham, Ala., to Gary, Ind., to Pittsburgh and West Virginia, even perhaps to the Lake Superior mines.

. . . They gave me a raise here the other day, and I now get the absurd sum of $10,000 a year. In return I'm staying over until July 1 before beginning my next six-month period. They don't want me to take six months a year off, and I suspect they will refuse to let me go away when and if they feel sure enough of their staff here to get along without me. If I could only find someone who could take away my job from me! . . .

Our apartment is beginning to be quite attractive. We have a baby grand piano, lent us by Nancy's Aunt Lee (at whose house was our wedding), and we will in a few weeks have an elegant desk in modern style, 32 by 56 inches. We spent yesterday looking at modern furniture and wishing we could afford to chuck out everything we have and replace it by modern stuff. I don't understand why anyone buys Grand Rapids Chippendale (or real Chippendale for that matter) when they can get modern. . . . We have quite a decent library with Nancy's tomes added to mine: three large bookcases full. . . .

[G. L. K. Morris and his wife] took us to see JUBILEE the other night, you know, the musical show Moss Hart and Cole Porter wrote on their trip around the world. They should have stayed home, I'm afraid. The East inspired them to nothing more profound than a song called "Let's Begin the Beguine" and to some cheap chromatic effects in the music which sound like Chinese Sandman. Its not bad, but it's far from being good. Mary Boland was the only one in the cast with much to offer, and she had no situations that called into play her peculiar talents. The lyrics were the usual painful doggerel (except for one song, JUST ONE OF THOSE THINGS, do you know?)—forced rhymes and mechanical meter. When the Elizabethans could get such subtle and moving effects in song verses, why can't we?

To Nancy Macdonald

November 26, 1935

It's six P.M. and the city [Pittsburgh] is swathed in what they call "smog" (get it?). And I'm exhausted after a day of trying to extract information from reluctant steel barons. Natasha [his research assistant] and I seem to be famous already here—the local paper had a report of my Republic article, and someone asked her this morning to give an interview over the radio! God knows why or on what. I lunched at the Duquesne Club, the city's hangout for tycoons. Imagine me sitting at the head of a long table, looking down two lines of beefy, predatory steel magnates. Enclosed is an official document of the affair.

To Nancy Macdonald

November 28, 1935

This afternoon I discovered that the Steel Corporation, with its usual brilliance, had just sent back to New York two letters that had come to me care of Mr. Fairless. They had assumed I was going back, although I am staying here till Friday night. One of them, they told me, was from you. All I could do was swear, which I did freely. This is about the stupidest outfit I have yet come across—though Natasha met a vice-president today whom she swears is interesting and even sensitive. He's sixty-six and he took her out and bought her FOUR cocktails. She was pie-eyed when we met for dinner, and extremely put out that I did not become so too. But I felt in no drinking mood, and also I thought (just a little) of you. In a few minutes Harvey O'Connor [well-known left-wing radical in the thirties] is coming over to talk about USS and labor, and tomorrow we are going to Youngstown to see the big Macdonald plant there (recently renamed after me as a delicate gesture) and also to talk to Clarence Irwin, leader of the steelworkers' left-wing union group. On Friday we get up at 7 A.M. and spend the day seeing the Homestead, Braddock, Duquesne, and Clairton works, which means just about the biggest collection in the world. Then we go to Birmingham, where we'll be by Saturday evening (it's a 24-hour trip). Write me at the Tutwiler Hotel, dear—the Tennessee Coal and Iron C. would probably send the letter on to Ramsey Macdonald in London. (Tutwiler—nice name, what? So damned quaint.) . . . Last night the smog was so thick everything looked like a Whistler nocturne, especially the Monongahela River. Natasha and I went to see the Marx Brothers in their new opera film, which was fairly good, and then walked for miles through the poor districts across the river. We found a Communist newsstand where I bought a magazine on the U.S.S.R., and we peeked in at a solemn Socialist meeting in a small restaurant. When you come with me on our tour, dearest, we must come to Pittsburgh. The president of the Bessemer & Lake Erie has promised me (and you too if you act like a lady) a ride all the way to Lake Erie on his railroad, and President Moses of the H . C. Frick Coke Co. is wild to take us through one of his mines. So you see we'd have fun. . . . Here comes O'Connor so I must stop.

To Nancy Macdonald

December 2, 1935

My trip so far has been extremely full and exciting, though how much grist it will yield to my mill is to be seen. Thanksgiving dinner we ate at the table of Clarence Irwin of Youngstown, leader of the left-wing in the national steel-worker's union. After inspecting a big new plant of the Steel Corporation, we had ourselves driven in a big shiny corporate limousine—a nice touch of irony, what? Irwin is a handsome, honest, and intelligent fellow—rugged and deep-voiced, also curly-haired. . . . He and his wife pressed us so to stay that we did, and liked it and the Irwin family very much. Friday we got up at 7:00 A.M. and set out with a benevolent old blockhead named Captain O'Neill to look over the Homestead, Braddock, Duquesne, and Clairton works of the Steel Corporation, which are strung along the Monongahela River beginning some 10 miles outside Pittsburgh. Since each is from one to three miles long, we came back that evening in a state of wild insanity. It was in many ways the most stimulating day I ever spent, however. Those are the classic plants of the Steel Corporation.

Worcester was small potatoes in comparison. We left Pittsburgh Friday night, spent two hours Saturday walking about Cincinnati, then entrained again for Louisville, where we spent Saturday afternoon entraining for Birmingham and getting there early this morning. . . . This morning I spent with Bill Mosey, the Communist organizer . . . and a group of local radicals, arranging a lot of visits for Natasha who oddly enough must talk to the workers while I talk to the bosses. . . . This afternoon we drove around looking at the "company towns" where the workers live. They were mostly sordid and rotting with no plumbing even.

To Henry Luce

n.d., 1936

For some time I have felt that *Time* was not as journalistically impartial as it might be, that it has a bias toward the right. This distresses because (1) after six years of working for Time Inc., I have a considerable affection for the enterprise; (2) any bias impairs TIME's greatest journalistic asset, its reputation for fairly reporting both sides of a question; (3) my personal sympathies happen to be liberal. This doesn't mean that I advocate TIME going "left"—any more than I want FORTUNE to do so. In times like these, a truly objective and impartial magazine would perform a unique and extremely valuable service. This is what FORTUNE, it seems to me, is beginning to do.

Perhaps [Eric] Hodgins and [Wilder] Hobson and myself are wrong about TIME's bias. You can make up your own mind on the basis of the attached exhibits, worked up in a few hours' review of recent TIME issues. I should like to make one thing clear: the two cases in which I think TIME's bias shows itself most clearly, the Gauley Bridge and the Shoemaker lynching tales, happen to be stories which I know a good deal about personally. There probably would be other such cases unknown to me now, which would become apparent if I knew much more about the raw material from which TIME's stories were written.

I hope you won't think all this presumptuous. It has been on my mind for some time, and for my own good and that of the organization I am hereby getting it off.

COMMENTS ON EXHIBITS

EXHIBIT A: TIME has a way of being pretty brutal and cold-blooded about things that appall most people (myself included). This callousness (to be noted also in TIME's gusto in recording full blood-curdling details about gruesome murders and accidents) is probably one reason for the often-heard charge of "fascism" leveled at TIME. The sentence underlined is reeking with implications that liberals and radicals who "howl" about lynchings are naive and even a bit sissified. (The term "affray," by the way, is misleading: Shoemaker and the others were beaten by a gang; there was no fight involved.) Let TIME report lynchings without emotion or bias, but let it refrain from sneers at protesters against lynchings. The tone of this piece is all the more unjustified in that the Shoemaker lynching was far from being just one more incident in the class war. Shoemaker was not a Communist, and in any part of the country except the South he would hardly be called a radical. He was actually working inside the Democratic party precisely as Upton Sinclair worked inside it in California, and he was trying to promulgate a "Plan of Transition" which is backed by people like John Dewey and Congressman Amlie. So shocking was his murder to the people of Tampa that the following Sunday most of the town's ministers devoted their sermon to a demand for punishment for his abductors. And another fact TIME should have recorded, the local American Legion post actually adapted a resolution calling for an investigation. (To say nothing of a lot of newspaper editorials also calling for action.) In other words, it was not politics-playing Bill Green and howling liberal Norman Thomas who kept the case from cooling down, but the pressure of public opinion in Tampa itself.

EXHIBIT B: This is too long a story to be told here. It seems to me to illustrate pretty well the positive and negative results of TIME's bias. The background facts are briefly these. Between 1929 and 1932 some 2,000 men were employed building a tunnel at Gauley Bridge, West Va. Although it was through solid quartz, no precautions were taken against silicosis, with the result that to date some 500 men have died, and the rest are probably going to die in a few years. Last summer the *New Masses* uncovered the story, almost by chance. Last fall the *People's Press*, a radical tabloid, sent a reporter down and really dug into the case in a big way for the first time. Hobson saw an early *People's Press* account, sent it down to TIME. Nothing happened. Two weeks later I got a lot of unpublished, original material on the business and sent it down to TIME, with the result that the attached piece appeared. I object to this article on two grounds. (1) Negatives. Journalistically, it seems to me TIME missed the beat badly in not digging into the facts and coming out with a complete, detailed story. It would have been the very first treatment of the case outside radical publications. There was a lot of excellent human interest material. And when 500 men die on one job and nothing is heard about it until three years later by the rest of the country— it seems to us that the magazine which first cracked open the story would have scored something of a scoop. Since the attached article came out, Gauley Bridge has been featured in the *World Telegram*, has made headlines in a special congressional investigation . . . and is heard from more and more. TIME could have done some pioneering here. Instead, it lamely had to print an amplification of its totally inadequate story. My positive (2) objection is to the two sentences underlined which imply that the radical press was trying to revive an old scandal, long since recorded and forgotten by other papers. This is precisely the reverse of the fact, as I told Billings at the time. There was no treatment of the story in any big newspapers, so far as anyone has been able to find out, until the *People's Press* took it up. TIME's justification for implying there had been a lot printed already about Gauley Bridge rests on a single support: a wire from United Press saying merely, "This case has been treated in the newspapers already." TIME didn't ask in what newspapers or when or anything (obviously local papers must have had something about it). On this slender evidence, TIME makes not one but two insinuations which are neither true nor [sparing.] Incidentally, another positive objection to the pieces is that it plays up the sensational, purely external, and melodramatic side of the case (the cemetery planted to corn, etc.). In just as cheap fashion as the *People's Press* did. You get no sense of the important social and humanitarian issues involved in the case. Also the silicon dust is kicked up by the drilling, not by the blasting.

EXHIBIT C: The pictures are swell, but the captions are almost ludicrously biased. They give the impression that Mr. Morgan and his partners are being put to the torture. Actually, as the article itself points out (marked passage, page 18), and as all journals, right or left wing alike agree, the investigation was conducted in the friendliest way. Morgan and Nye parted on the best of terms, Raushenbush was no Untermeyer nor even a Pecora, the late President Wilson was the only person to be seriously attacked. In view of all this, why these melodramatic captions, throbbing with sympathy for the poor bedeviled Mr. Morgan? Especially uncalled-for cracks: A, the "cold stare" of committee clerk Lois Corey—Mygod, can the girl help it if she looks that way? B, and "downy-lipped investigator" Brown, who "pipes more questions." The implications here are that clerk Corey bears some animus against nice old Mr. Lamont, and that investigator Brown is a shrill-voiced adolescent not to be taken too seriously by these whose lips aren't downy and whose voices don't pipe. TIME, by the way, has developed a technique of implying things by shrewdly chosen adjectives and neatly turned phrases. This trick enables the writer to put a prejudiced twist on his story without having to back it up with documentation: the meaning comes out quite clearly, but the words are literally quite true and checkable. (I know, for I've done it myself in my brief experience writing for TIME.) This is legitimate enough if the facts are really such as to justify such a slant, but it becomes very dangerous when writers are prejudiced and are not adequately controlled by the editor. Both these criticisms, to some extent, seem to me true of TIME at the present moment.

EXHIBIT D: It seems to me that the NATION (attached) did a better job of reporting on the Gustloff affair than did TIME. The NATION paragraph marked in red, especially, brings out the essential facts about the Nazi movement in Switzerland—and very curious and interesting they are. TIME can't be expected to be omniscient, and if this were an isolated case it would mean nothing. But I've been reading the *Nation*, the *New Republic*, and the *New Masses* in the last few months, and I have frequently found their reporting of events far more revealing and complete than TIME's account. For years TIME has had a contemptuous attitude toward these magazines as mere journals of opinion and as prejudiced and nonfactual. Comparing TIME with the NATION, I can see no ground for this point of view. I urge that TIME's editors read these prejudiced magazines for a few months with open minds. There is a great deal that TIME can learn from them, and I see no reason why TIME can't in its own way do as thorough and complete a job of reporting on labor & social issues as the liberal journals do. At present, the chief difference between TIME and the NATION seems to be that the NATION is consciously left-wing (and can therefore allow for its own bias and make an honest effort to dig down to the facts) whereas TIME is ostensibly impartial but naturally (perhaps unconsciously) right-wing (and therefore, its bias being unadmitted and perhaps even unrecognized by its own editors, unable to allow for its prejudices). I should like to see TIME become really impartial.

EXHIBIT E: This little piece is frankly slanted in an anti-Communist direction. It may be quite justified, but, in view of the general tone of FOREIGN NEWS, I should like to see some supporting evidence. What do current wages in Russia, figured on the same basis as those quoted food prices, amount to in dollars? And can these commodities be termed necessities in Russia today—however necessary they are in the U.S. today? Is the bread white or black, for example? Throughout large sections of Europe butter is a luxury, not eaten by the masses, and costs damn near $2 a pound. Do Russians drink coffee as Americans do?

EXHIBIT F: This is another example of the liberal journals doing a much better job of reporting than TIME. I realize that their special field is involved here, and that they had their correspondents in Pekin. But TIME should have been able to discover (1) the strike was won when Governor [Herter], for political reasons, refused to send in militia; (2) that Police Chief Donahue, whose picture is shown, is an ex prize-fighter; (3) that it was not a union vs. union strike (since a company union cannot be called a real union—see NARA labor reports *ad infinitum*) and that the cause of the strike was not the pretext offered by an engineer being fired but rather a long and complex series of wrangles over collective bargaining, of which this was just one episode; (4) that this was the first big strike in the Chicago area since NRA; (5) that the strikers had been waiting vainly for two years for NRA to do something about their complaints. TIME has never shown an intelligent interest in labor news. More and more people are coming to take more interest in masses of workers and strikers than in picturesque individual tycoons. When TIME was founded this wasn't the case. But times have changed. Let TIME continue to chronicle the spectacular and romantic individual, but let it also pay some attention to the masses—less spectacular, less romantic, but, I submit, currently of more significance. Specifically, why not a full-blown Labor section, written by someone interested in labor? This will probably necessitate going outside for a writer.

EXHIBIT G: Pieces like this one are one reason for the charge of "fascism" so frequently made against TIME. One gets a distinct impression that whoever wrote the piece was not shocked by this vicious and brutal attack on Blum, that he was rather stimulated by the violence and bloodshed. The whole business, which seems clearly an unprovoked and murderous assault on an unarmed man who had given no provocation, is made to appear almost as much Blum's fault as that of his attacker's. Blum is pictured as a peculiarly irritating and hateful person ("the peculiar detestation Leon Blum is capable of arousing"), who could only expect such treatment as he got. But I fail to see anything peculiar in a politician's capacity for arousing hatred in his enemies. The account of the attack could have been written by one of the cane-swinging "stalwarts" of the Action Française. The splintering of glass, the spurting of blood, the mauling of Blum, "bleeding and gasping"—these are described in heroic fashion. One gets an impression that a traitor is receiving a well-deserved punishment and that it's all very exciting and romantic. (Also note his attempt to make Blum appear the aggressor in the description of how his car "edged too close" to the funeral procession. This is patently absurd. What is "too close"? And would a Blum-ist agree with a Royalist on the definition? For completely unfair implication, however, consider "The snout of Socialist Monnet's car incensed the mourning Royalists." That single word "snout" is a fine example of what can be done with one word. Why does the front of a car become a snout? Answer: "snout" is an opprobrious, disgust-awakening epithet. The sentence beginning "Almost before Blum's blood clotted on his bandages, Leftist leaders were screaming over every wire . . . demands . . ." is also worth noting. The morbidly specific reiteration of the bloodshed theme—not the slightest reason for dragging in surgical details here, except TIME's fascination with bloodshed—and the "screaming" Leftist leaders—these are typical. Why must radicals always be presented as screaming or howling? Do their protests appear so silly to TIME? If so, small wonder TIME appears silly to them.

To Dinsmore Wheeler

March 16, 1936
. . . Have you seen the first Steel piece? If not, I'll send you a copy—it's my chef d'oeuvre. Everyone from G. L. K. Morris to Louis Dembitz Brandeis has

praised it. (Brandeis, I'm told by John Chamberlain, new *Fortune* recruit, who heard it from Felix Frankfurter, read the piece and thought well of it. Few men's praise could be sweeter to me.) It really is a damn good piece of work. Part Two, on Prices, comes out next month, Part Three, on Labor (by Bob Cantwell) the month after, and Part Four, a grand finale full of high philosophical speculation, the month after that.

Besides U.S. Steel I've also been doing a lot socially. On Thursday last we gave a cocktail party for forty-five people, collected $27 for the sharecroppers down South—the Communist effort to unionize them is my chief left-wing interest at present. Esther Hamil was down last week and stayed a few days with us. She has developed into quite a person—well-poised, extremely intelligent, tolerant, mature, conscious of her motives and emotions. I wish you could know her—and she, you. The elevator strike has also taken our time and attention. The landlords are acting with almost unbelievable arrogance and stubbornness. We got a document up in support of our operators and got 22 out of 60 apartments here to sign it. Then we sent it in to the landlord, with a note saying "Enclosed do *not* find this month's rent." A few days later—no connection, though—the mortgage company that owns this and 150 other apt. buildings broke the landlord's united front and signed up with the strikers. Nancy and I are, of course, now on the friendliest possible terms with the elevator people. It's swell to feel such a warm sympathy flowing back and forth between us and them. The class struggle makes you love your fellow man, if you're on the right, that is the left, side.

If you know any wealthy liberals, you might get them to contribute to The League for Southern Labor—the sharecropper's outfit. I've an extra copy of a book, *The Collapse of Cotton Tenancy*, which is a remarkably good little account of the whole situation. Shall I send it on to you or aren't you interested?

On two successive nights last week I shouted violently at Geoffrey Hellman and George Morris (each on a separate occasion), and I became so outrageous that there's now a wide chasm between me and them both. The subject under discussion was the elevator strike. Geoffrey enraged me by taking an anti-union position and stubbornly clinging to it despite all that reason could do. George was merely "liberal" and disposed to think the whole business can be ignored by the detached artist. I regret the break with George, who is at least intelligent and open-minded, but Geoffrey can go to hell—after all these years. He's both stupid and ignorant, and he's grown soft and lazy and smug with the years. I'm growing more and more intolerant of those who stand—or rather squat—in the way of radical progress, the more I learn about the conservative businesses who run this country and the more I see of the injustices done people under this horrible capitalist system. I hope you are keeping me company on the pilgrimage to the left. Geoffrey I lost with slight regrets, George I would miss more, but it would be too much if *you* appeared among the enemy. But unless you've changed a lot since I saw you last, there's no danger of that.

Do you see the *Nation* and *New Republic* and *New Masses?* We subscribe to all of them and would be delighted to pass on our copies if you want them. Let me know. . . . I've been reading Spender's *The Distinctive Element*, fascinating criticism for we Jamesians. Also Alfred Bingham's *Insurgent America*, a badly written but clearly thought-out book. He's done some independent thinking on a foundation of Marx and Veblen.

. . . I'm bound to *Fortune* till next August 1, when I get another 6 months leave—which I hope will be financially able to be turned into a permanent absence. Some time after that we project a trip of a month or so through the American countryside, and I hope we'll be welcome for a few days at R.D.3.

Did you see my review of Dennis's book *The Coming American Fascism* in *Common Sense.* I may do some books for the *Nation*—negotiations (begun by me) now afoot. Why don't you review?

To Geoffrey Hellman

March 24, 1936

Your letter stimulates me to reply briefly to several points. (1) Union monopoly might lead to abuse of power, but so long as the employer has the strategic position he does under capitalism, the union can't get a monopoly. Today the landlord has all the power. No one proposes the union be given all the power, merely that it be given enough power to counterbalance that of the landlord. It's absurd to put up a bogeyman of "union monopoly" in any capitalist state. (2) I'm not exclusively interested in things which interest you only slightly. I'm as keenly interested as ever in writing and books—in fact I'm now reviewing a biography of Raleigh for the *Nation*—and I'm not looking for any class angle either. Isn't the real truth that you aren't interested much in anything, that you've let yourself get shockingly slack and smugly comfortable since you left college? Also, by the way, I'm still interested in movies—enough to go to special showings whenever I can. Also in people, and not necessarily left-wing people either. Among my conservative or neutral friends I can think of Esther Hamil, George Shepherd, Lola and Del, Tom Prideaux. I'd like to know more such people, only whenever I meet people nowadays they always turn out to be radical or liberal—too bad. (3) I really sympathize with your hatred of fanaticism and dictatorship. Temperamentally, I'm at least as individualistic and nonconformist as you are. I hate submitting to authority, and I personally cherish individual liberty—my own and that of other people. But in this country today we live under the dictatorship of a small class of capitalist—mostly those who control the great corporations—and the only way we can get free is to submit to discipline.

You can't fight dictatorship with anything except dictatorship. Yes I'm fanatic and egotistical and hard-boiled, and precisely because such things as the Liberty League exist is it necessary that I be so. You personally aren't much affected by the economic autocracy which weighs so heavily on most people in this country, nor am I. But I can feel for the others (to you apparently they are merely the least fit), and I can see that only by meeting the conservatism of the ruling class with an equally fanatic and intense radicalism will the masses ever get control in their own hands. Your position as a detached lover of fair play has no meaning today, and whichever side wins—the capitalist (i.e., fascist) or the democratic (i.e., Communist)—you will get it in the neck. After this letter, you probably won't want to see me again. I hope, though, that All is not Over permanently.

To Dinsmore Wheeler

April 23, 1936

It looks as though my long association with FORTUNE were drawing to a close. The final installment of the Steel articles seems to be destined for a thorough sabotaging by the editors, and I've served notice that if it is wrecked, I'm leaving. Trouble is that, while the article is really damned good (as they themselves admit), it is both theoretical and critical. It attacks directly the present management of the Corporation, and *Fortune* just doesn't do that sort of thing. It's a disgusting business and I'm depressed as the devil—as well as being bored to death with the Steel Corporation and with all business enterprise. I think I'll take a few years off to study seventeenth-century poetry or Chinese fan painting. For your amusement, I'm enclosing a copy of the final installment, as it *won't* appear.

I feel too low to write much of an answer to your long and very much enjoyed letter of March 19. . . . Yes, FORTUNE is getting to be a nest of liberals. Chamberlain is a very nice fellow, though not at all inspired and far from being radical. He's a typical open-minded liberal, with leanings to the left but also a healthy respect for the powers that be. MacLeish is more complicated psychologically. I'm glad he has taken a leftish position, but I don't place any great reliance on his feelings for the masses or his revolutionary ardor. He's too anxious to score personal triumphs, to impress the right people. (But I'm in a bitter mood, and these judgments are perhaps too harsh. . . . I bought Dutt's book [*World Politics*] and have read about half of it with great admiration. It's the best thing of its kind that I've seen. It should be read by every citizen of every capitalist state. . . . The break with Hellmen and Morris has, of course, been at least superficially patched up. But I'm no longer on intimate terms with either, and I'm increasingly aware of profound and rapidly increasing differences in our points of view. I feel more sympathy with Morris than with Hellman, probably because Morris is more intelligent and alive. Smugness and stupidity are unforgivable sins—in people who have had a chance, through education and money, to be better. Yet, in another way, Hellman is much warmer humanly than Morris. It's confusing, but I feel I won't bother much longer about it. There seems no dearth of new people with more radical views in our lives. . . . I am very glad you are also journeying leftward, though I had no real doubts on that score anyway. . . . Interesting of you to talk to Dewey. I read a little book of his last fall, *Liberalism and Social Action*, which was a sound piece of thinking—though unsatisfactory in the end, as all liberal thinking is to me, because it funks the brutal, head-on issue of the class struggle. I don't mean class struggle necessarily in a Marxist sense, but simply the clash of interests in modern society and the natural disinclination of those at the top to give up any of their power without a fight. The liberals want to get somewhere by sweet reason, by education and reform, but I don't think such things amount to a damn in this modern world. . . . I agree with you partially about Medley Butler [former military officer and sharp critic of American imperialism in Latin America], but I've got tremendous reservations about him. How much he is a clown is the question. Also the crackup of Al Smith, to mention only one example, makes me suspicious of untutored public figures who lack the backbone of some kind of theoretical knowledge. Butler is anti-fascist now, but it is not hard to imagine him being taken in by sugarcoated fascism just as Smith was deceived by sugarcoated plutocracy. . . . You might like to collaborate in a small book I'm projecting: a book which would put forward each of the banal misconceptions about capitalism, communism, fascism, etc. which so many people in these states hold. The idea would be to gather in a little notebook, on the scene of the crime, verbatim if possible, the most characteristic of these misconceptions— right out of the mouths of their perpetrators. Example: Communism wants to reduce everybody to the same level. Or: You can't change human nature; people are naturally selfish, fond of property, etc. Or: Look at our American standard of living. Isn't that a pretty good recommendation for capitalism? And so on. The book to answer these banalities in simple, good-humored, if possible witty terms. Clarity and readability being the two main qualities aimed at. . . . I'm about to go around with a notebook, jotting down the thought-patterns of my conservative friends on social and economic topics. Would you be interested in joining me? . . . Good idea to start a local chapter of the League Against W[ar] and F[acism]. From what I know of that body, it's all right. . . . I'm sending the *Collapse of Cotton Tenancy* under separate cover. Hope you like it as much as I do. . . . [Robert] Cantwell, I've talked to a lot recently. He's a great discovery, no opportunity to write more about him now.

To Dinsmore Wheeler

June 10, 1936

. . . The big news is that I've left *Fortune*, for a six-month leave of absence anyway, and maybe for good. I had not intended to go until August, but the bitter taste of the Steel sellout was reducing me to a stage of psychic impotence. Toward the end of May I realized that *Fortune* was dead for me, and that I was just dragging out a lifeless, dried-up existence there. So on the principle that life is short and two dead, lost, wasted months not to be thought of, I up and left. A weight has been lifted off my shoulders. I feel free, free to see what life is all about, to really read scores of books that I've long wanted to. Especially I hope to orient myself politically. I know that I don't believe in capitalism, but I'm still hazy as to what course to take from there. On the other hand, a new kind of weight has descended on me—a kind which you have probably felt for years. I mean the responsibility of doing things on one's own. I feel like a man newly discharged from the Army—how difficult to decide, to act instead of doing what one is told! I've been away a week and three days now, and I've accomplished very little even of reading. Ordering one's life so as to get something accomplished isn't easy. A job is demoralizing that way. . . . Nancy and I are embarking on a scheme for self-education. American history, we find, is a blank to us. And, of course, essential to people with our interests. . . .

This is a very poor day to write a letter, or anything. I drank too many cocktails yesterday, and I have a hangover. My brain is vague, slightly out of focus as if some important nerve connections had been cut. . . .

The editorial board of *Partisan Review*, 1940: Standing (from left), G. L. K. Morris, Philip Rahv, Dwight Macdonald. Seated, F. W. Dupee, William Phillips.

CHAPTER THREE

AMONG THE PARTISANSKIS AND TROTSKYISTS, 1936–1943

"Dear Trotsky: We are all opponents of Stalinism and committed to a Leninist program of action."

These years record Macdonald's further radicalization, his work as an editor for the revived, independently radical *Partisan Review*, and his writing for Trotskyist publications and brief tenure in the Socialist Workers party. His developing anarcho-pacifism and opposition to the United States role in World War II led to his resignation from *Partisan Review* and the subsequent founding of his own journal, *Politics.*

To Dinsmore Wheeler

October 24, 1936

To think I should ever actually be living in Cambridge—and you not here. . . . We finally landed here, right next door to Esther Hamil, in a furnished room for which we pay a genial New England spinster $7 a week. I often think of you wandering about Cambridge—in fact all my place associations here center about you. For some reason the place that is most redolent of my past visits here is the walk between Widener and the president's house, the one leading out through an archway in a row of brick dormitories to the main street. . . . We read a bit [while staying in Esther Dette's summer house in Walpole, New Hampshire, for a few weeks] the *Spoils of Poynton* by James, a very good story in his most gossipy and delicate manner; part of the *Portrait of the Artist*; and the first 200 pages of *Capital*, Vol. I. They are tedious, repetitious, hard to follow, and yet somehow they produce a feeling of awe. Marx goes so directly to the heart of the problem. And his argument, as much as I can follow it, seems irrefutable. Can't see any possible way of accounting for the phenomenon of profit except through surplus value. The learning of the man is something appalling: the list of books to which he refers in this volume takes pages and pages. We're almost up to the comparatively easy and lively part: the long chapter on The Working Day, in which he shows by specific detail how surplus value is obtained by British capitalists.

Our days we spend at Widener digging into steel data.[1] Today, for example, I read the report of the Senatorial Investigation into the 1919 steel strike—chiefly testimony by [Samuel] Gompers, Mike Tighe [Elbert] Gary, and [William Z.] Foster—while Nancy plowed through a long doctorate thesis on cartels in the German steel industry. The strike investigation is a rich mine. Gary for pages rants in an unbelievable manner. Do you know his classic pronouncement on hard work: "It is largely machinery (work in steel mills), almost altogether machinery. That is not saying there is no work in that, because of course there is; I would not belittle it, of course. It's hard work to work hard whatever one does, and to the extent one does work hard, he, of course, is doing hard work. That is evident." Believe it or not. Tighe and Gompers are almost as stupid and nauseating. They talk like cheap politicians, with lots of flag-waving and red-baiting. Foster shows up remarkably well. He was savagely cross-examined on his alleged radical views by the senators, and he was at once well tempered and dignified. His remarks about the strike were a breath of reality—one saw at last what the men were fighting for, what the issue really was. And his level of intelligence was much higher than that of his inquisitors. I must find out more about him. Next week we attack the Baker Library in the Business School. There seems to be lots of data there. Alan Sweezy took us over the other day and got us properly introduced. He's been very helpful—you know he teaches economics here, don't you? And that he's active in the teachers' union?

Speaking of unions, the last couple of weeks in NYC I spent largely in organizing a unit of the Newspaper Guild at Time Inc. We had our first meeting the night before I left, elected Wilder Hobson chairman. We've got 50 out of a

1. Macdonald planned to expand his *Fortune* articles into a book on the steel industry in the United States. It was one of many book projects that never came to fruition.

possible 200 members in the organization. Not bad, what? The *Fortune* writers are in it almost to a man. *Time* is the great problem, of course.

Yesterday I was taken to lunch by Felix Frankfurter. (I sent him a copy of the last U.S. Steel piece, and he was much interested.) I liked him very much — he's warm, "stimulating," dynamic, full of questions, and, of course, intelligent. He's no radical, Mr. Hearst to the contrary notwithstanding. Just an old horse-and-buggy liberal of the Brandeis-Borah anti-monopoly school. He was mildly disturbed when I told him I was reading *Capital* and that I intend to write my book from a Marxist angle. Warned me against two much "theory," and he's to some extent right. He asked me to meet some of his students and discuss things with them — also to disclose my intellectual history: from Luce to Lenin, so to speak. And he's promised a note to Brandeis when I go down to Washington! He quoted a revision of an old aphorism. Originally it ran: "He who is not a socialist at 20 has no heart. He who is a socialist at 40 has no head." New version inserts "not" in Part II. Not bad?

To Dinsmore Wheeler

December 6, 1936

We've been in Pittsburgh just a week this evening. And a full week it's been. We've seen, once by day and once by night, the two great outlying steel districts: Ambridge and Aliquippa thirty miles up the Ohio, and the Monongahela River nexus: Homestead, Braddock, Duquesne, Clariton, McKeesport. Tomorrow we drive over to Weirton (32 mi) with Rose Stein to witness, and we hope, take part in a "flying squadron" demonstration on the steps of the Weirton post office. The town was opened up a couple of weeks ago by a flying squadron of 50 organizers who drove over in 18 cars, set up tables at the mill gates, and openly signed up hundreds of Mr. Weir's peasantry. The company cops didn't dare molest them because several employees of the La Follette committee went along in a car bearing a huge sign: LA FOLLETTE CIVIL LIBERTIES COMMITTEE OF THE U.S. SENATE. Yesterday I saw Clinton Golden, the regional director of the Steel Workers' Organizing Committee (it's always SWOC around here, not CIO), and he told me this story. Today Nancy and I drove out to Aliquippa and went to a mass meeting — held in a Romanian Hall, up a steep flight of stairs, decorated with crude frescoes and Slavic fraternal signs. About 400 workers, mostly old-world, Slavic, with leathery faces, spiky mustaches — unskilled labor, I should say. Fine-looking people, lots of juice, character to them. Two Pennsylvania mounted policemen were there, looking very trim and smart in grey whipcord, tall domed helmets, chin straps and all. Golden spoke — he's a big, drawling fellow, a bit on the ministerial side but good at this sort of thing. Mostly jokes and stories designed to put Jones & Loughlin in a ridiculous position. After the meeting the two policemen went up to Golden and the other organizers, who had been on the platform with him, shook hands and talked pleasantly. Quite a change since 1919. One old worker said to Nancy proudly, showing a mouth full of gold teeth: "They used to beat us up, but we call 'em over now. They're on our side this time!" Last week I also talked to various savants at the University of Pittsburgh, which has an active and quite liberal Bureau of Business Research; worked a couple of days in the Carnegie Library here; and spent at least 24 hours all told trying to find my way around this most confusing of all cities. It's built on steep hills and not one but three (confluent) rivers must be coped with in orienting one's self. This hotel is out in the Schenley Park district, a good four miles from the "golden triangle" of downtown Pittsburgh and which has been building since 1929 and is still full of cement-mixers and plank walks at odd places; the bleakly classical Mellon Institute; the big expensive Schenley Park Hotel, where Ben Fairless and Ernie Weir live; the U. of P. Stadium; various other U. of P. structures; and the huge Carnegie Institute (library + dinosaurs + stuffed birds + concert hall + international art exhibition, which Nancy reports is even worse than she expected)—all these buildings are grouped around big grass areas in a sort of civic center, halfway between the office buildings of the Triangle and the Monongahela steel mills.

We are still talking about the swell time we had with you at R.D.3. I feel that our friendship, approached, each time we see each other, in a gingerly, tentative way, almost with some apprehension as to whether it will bear our weight (and time's weight)—I feel it still stands firm. For the future, of course, who can say? (I do wish you would do some Marxist reading. I'm going to send you that Engels book.) But for the present I feel one week of talk leaves the structure more solidly based than ever.

Rose Stein (she writes for leftist papers and is a swell person, a small Jewess with great quantities of vitality and a refreshing belief in the workers—refreshing because she sees them all the time) just called up to say a special little preliminary rumpus is to be staged tomorrow at 10 A.M. in Weirton, some kind of demonstration—and so we are going over for *that* as well. Look for our names in the teargassed list—hope it's no worse.

After the atmosphere out your way—the deadness, speaking socially and politically—it was inspiring to talk to Stein the other night and learn that *all* Americans aren't Babbitts. Of course, unhappily, industrial workers aren't typical of Mr. U.S. Citizen, but there are a lot of them. And from the accounts Stein gives (and the limited contacts we've had here so far), they are alive, eager for more life and knowledge, shrewd, humorous, full-blooded sort of people. We'll know more after next week, when we expect to attend various night-school classes which Stein is getting started. She gets a group of speakers—current events, sociology, anything—who give short, informal talks to groups of workers. Most of the sessions given up to discussion. Stein says there has been a huge response to the project. We're going down with her this Friday while she starts a group going in Donora and Monessen, tinplate towns. Unlike the Pyramiders, these people can't be induced to *quit* talking, says Stein. People pop up all over the room—everyone wants to have his or her say. Doesn't your mouth water?

This is a chaotic letter—there's so much to write about. I haven't even mentioned what has impressed us the most here—the unbelievable beauty of the landscape: the mills, enormous and smoke-washed, the river bottoms and the frame houses of the workers perched on the steep hills above them—Sylvia Saunders says it is the most photographable place she's ever been in.

To Dinsmore Wheeler

December 27, 1936
. . . [My throat infection is] in fact an honorable wound, acquired that cold Monday we drove over to Weirton and stood around giving out papers at the mill gates. That day was the high point of our stay in Pittsburgh. Then we got a glimpse under the surface. We drove over early in the morning with Rose Stein. We went to the home of Kenneth Koch, the local C.I.O. organizer, where we talked to Koch and other leaders and had lunch. (I enclose a piece by Stein which gives Koch's secret—but pre–our visit history. Will you send it back please?) These workers are very hospitable, you know. While we were eating, two young college boys from the La Follette Committee came in to see if Koch knew where some of his "hatchet gang" attackers were. They are trying to serve subpoenas on them, but Weir has shipped them up to his Detroit plant, apparently. After lunch, we all went out and met a "flying squadron" from C.I.O. headquarters composed of about fifty members of the glass workers' union, now on strike. Protected by them, the local leaders put on a two-truck parade for several hours through the streets. Two of them broadcast from a sound truck, with great fluency and humor. They were followed by a truck with big C.I.O. signs on it, which was followed by a sedan full of strong-arm men to keep order. We followed, too, for a while. Then we gave out "Steel Labor" at one of the gates. (The plant is huge, employs 12,000.) There was no "trouble" at all, though the company police looked rather annoyed. The workers were swell, and we came away with great hopes for social progress in general and the steel drive in particular. (Out of several hundred men we offered the paper to, only one refused it.) What I saw of the CIO technique at headquarters also encouraged me. We spent an evening talking to the CIO research director, a U. of Pittsburgh graduate and former instructor named Harold Ruttenberg. He made a lot of excellent data available to me. They've got a small but well-chosen morgue built up already! . . .

Things look much better abroad, with Italy detached from Franco and

Hitler probably going to follow suit. The great question is: Did Soviet diplomacy foresee all this? If so, a great triumph, I must admit, Trotskyite as I am. By the way, let's all go down and see Trotsky in Mexico. Fred [Dupee], I suppose couldn't, but he might tell us the best routes.

Laski arrived and looks very interesting. Thanks for it. I'm saving it until Newburgh, when I'll have plenty of time. Meanwhile I've been finishing up: [J.H.] Bridges's *Inside Hist. of the Carnegie Steel Co*; [Samuel] Yellen's *American Labor Struggles*; Engels's *Socialism Scientific & Utopian*; Dutt's *World Politics*; great masses of magazines. Did you get the handbook? The Workers Bookshop is supposed to have sent it. For Xmas we got the new Bible, which is certainly improved as literature in the new format; the new Boswell's *Journey to the Hebrides*, which promises to be a lot of fun; and quite a large sum of money from Nancy's various relatives. What did you draw?

I'm sending you a subscription to the *Marxist Quarterly*. The first number is very good. Hope you'll enjoy it. (This is the semi-Trotskyite new Communist sheet. The Stalinist one, *Science & Society*, is dull and disappointing. The Trotskyites certainly seem to attract the intelligentsia.)

Have you any books not too old and not too abstruse, which you don't especially want? Rose Stein . . . is starting a circulating library to travel around to the industrial communities around Pittsburgh with the speakers in her Workers Schools. . . .

Let me know what you think of (1) *The Marxist Quarterly*, (2) the distressing tendency to Right Deviation in the Odd Fellows, (3) Life, not the mag., in general.

An Open Letter to John Dewey

January 1937

Your article "Democracy is Radical" in the January *Common Sense* compresses into a brief space so many ideas with which I disagree that I am moved to attempt a reply. The one point in which I find we agree is your title. Democracy *is* radical, no question of that, and it is our mutual objective. But we seem to have totally conflicting conceptions as to how to reach it.

In your opening paragraph you cite as gestures the new Soviet Constitution and a pronunciamento by Goebbels that National Socialism is the democracy of the future. Although the wording gives that impression, I can't believe you intended to imply that both are equally valid or invalid. At any rate, from these phenomena you draw a moral: "Possibly there is some faint cheer for those who believe in democracy in these expressions. It is something that after a period in which democracy was scorned and laughed at, it is now acclaimed."

The implication is that the Soviet Union has changed, in fact completely re-versed its attitude toward democracy. Surely you are better acquainted with Marxist theory than this. Unlike Hitler, whose *My Battle* exhibits a passionate hatred of democracy as such, Marx limited his attack to capitalist democracy—a form of which in your next paragraph you yourself declare to be no democracy at all. The celebrated dictatorship of the proletariat is merely the means which Communists believe to be necessary to their ultimate goal: classless, and therefore real, democracy. And so instead of the Soviet Constitution represent-ing a *volte face*, as you imply, it means precisely the opposite: a big step toward the fulfillment of Communist theory. At no period was democracy "scorned and laughed at" by responsible Marxists. On the contrary, the necessity for a proletarian dictatorship was considered a heavy burden, a burden it is a great relief to set down at last. In times like these not to recognize that the fascist and Communist dictatorships are traveling in opposite directions—this seems to me intellectually irresponsible.

Your answer is, as, you write later on: "The fundamental principle of democracy is that the ends of freedom and individuality for all can be attained only by means that accord with those ends." There is undoubtedly danger lest the continued use of force corrupt the ends, no matter how noble, to which it is directed. Furthermore, no reasonable, humane person—and even in the ranks of the Marxists will you find such—prefers to use force if his ends can be gained by what you define as "voluntary action based upon public collective intelli-gence."

President Azana, of the Spanish Republic, is a man with whom you would, perhaps, find much in common. Up to a few months ago he believed in your formula, so completely that he made the error of applying it in practice. Placed in power last fall by a sweeping majority, Azana, a man of letters as much as lib-eral politician, felt the battle was over. In the spirit of benign reason he pro-ceeded to carry out certain mild reforms to which the electorate has clearly given its approval. The result is well known. It is reported that Señor Azana, dis-mayed, retreated to France and is solacing himself with the Latin classics.

Later in your article you yourself give the explanation for Azana's failure when you state, apparently without realizing the implications of the remark: ". . . reliance upon superior physical force is the reactionary position." If this is true, and I think it is, we should expect the reactionaries to use this force against any effort to threaten their position through "voluntary action." The rul-ing classes are by definition in possession of "superior physical force." And in a period of revolutionary progress like this one, they are also by definition, reac-tionary. They have the force, and they never hesitate to use it. In every country in which a left-wing movement has threatened their position—in Italy, in Germany, in Poland, in Hungary, in Austria, in China—the pattern has been the same. The rulers have not reasoned. They have not debated the issue. They have struck with all the power at their command. The struggle is going on in Spain and may soon be forced in France. The question, as I see it, is not whether reason is to be preferred to force. That seems to answer itself. It is whether in this postwar world the things you and I both value—democracy, civilization, freedom, peace, humanity itself—whether these can be successfully defended by sweet reason alone. After what has happened since the war, your trust in the amenability to reason to our capitalist rulers seems unrealistic to say the least. It seems to me that your point of view tends to disarm the forces of progress at a period when they have never before so desperately needed to be armed.

As a pragmatist, you are not so impervious to past experience as it might appear from the above. And indeed, to cite European examples does not fully meet your argument. For although you grant the Marxist contention that capitalist democracy means democracy for the bourgeoisie but for no one else, you make one exception to this universal law. The exception turns out to be precisely the United States of America! Thus you are able to maintain that Europe's unhappy experience with the liberal path to democracy does not necessarily concern us.

Your entire argument, then, would seem to rest on the unique quality of bourgeois democracy in this country. I wish you had illuminated this crucial point a little more clearly. For you came no closer to a definition than: "It is fundamentally an attempt to realize democratic modes of life in their full meaning and far-reaching scope." This means very little to me. Nor do you support your opinion with any data. If you had, I think you might have found yourself in difficulties. "The United States," you write, "is the outstanding exception to the statement that democracy arose historically in the interest of an industrial and commercial class. . . ." Surely few contemporary historians would support this statement. Is it not generally agreed that the Revolution was caused by the oppressive measures of the English crown which, in accordance with the then dominant mercantilism economics, tried to penalize colonial trade for the benefit of the mother country? Not on the farmers, not on the poor artisans and apprentices, but on the merchants and manufacturers did the British Crown's taxation policy bear most heavily. How could there be a purer case of a democracy arising "in the interests of an industrial and commercial class"? Even the French Revolution presents less of a clear-cut picture, since its motive power was drawn from the misery of the peasants as well as from the desperation of the bourgeois.

It is true, however, that at one period this country was an exception to the

Marxist generalization about capitalist democracies—or rather, that it wasn't a capitalist democracy. The golden age of American democracy—which is possibly more prominent in your mind's eye than you realize—begins with Jefferson's annihilation of the Federalists in 1800 and lasts until the Civil War. In that period, and then only, I think, was the United States a democracy. The Southern planters, aided by their allies, the intensely democratic frontiersmen of the West, were able to hold in check the Northern industrialists for a few decades in which a kind of agrarian, almost pastoral, democracy flourished. It was the age that produced our great democratic heroes—Jefferson, Jackson, Emerson, Lincoln. Even Karl Marx was impressed. When he wrote in the spring of 1852 "The Eighteenth Brumaire of Louis Bonaparte," he specifically excepted from his damnation of bourgeois republics the United States "where, though classes, indeed, already exist, they have not yet become fixed, but continually change and interchange their elements in a constant state of flux, where the modern means of production, instead of coinciding with a stagnant surplus population, rather supply the relative deficiency of heads and hands, and where finally, the feverishly youthful movement of material production, that has a new world to make its own has left neither time nor opportunity for abolishing the old spirit world."

The Civil War brought to a bloody close this idyllic democratic interlude. Once more the oligarchy was established in power, based this time on industry rather than trade and land. Since the Civil War the United States has rapidly overtaken the bourgeois democracies of Europe in industrial production and in its correlative: the political dominance of the capitalist class. So vigorous has been our economic expansion that probably never in history, except perhaps in the France of Louis Philippe, has a capitalist class been able to dominate the state so completely as in post–Civil War America. The old agrarian democracy of the West struggled bravely on, now trying populism, now Henry George and the single tax, now Bryan and free silver, erupting in the Granger movement and the nonpartisan league. It was a gallant attempt to restore the golden age of American democracy, the age which I suspect you have in mind when you speak of the unique quality of our democracy. Of necessity it failed, since the social and economic conditions under which it could be realized existed no longer. The attempt was, indeed, essentially reactionary, since to succeed it would have had to overthrow all our industrial progress in favor of reversion to an agrarian economy.

It is quite true, then, as you say, that in this country we have a tradition of democracy which is not wedded to capitalism, as in Europe. But the tradition seems to me ineffectual today, a nostalgia for an era which has no chance of being resurrected. Messrs. Tate, Agar, and the Southern Agrarians to the contrary. We must abandon such dreams and apply ourselves to the real problem: how to overthrow the most strongly entrenched capitalist class in the world. When we, and I hope you, address ourselves to this task, I think we shall discover that our ruling classes, though they may not share the democratic enthusiasms of their forebears of the frontier, are just as quick on the trigger.

To Dr. James B. Conant, Harvard University

May 4, 1937

I have not replied to your letter of April 14 sooner because I wanted to acquaint myself more fully with the facts in the Walsh-Sweezy case. Now that I have read the available material and talked with informed Harvard people, I find it impossible to believe that Sweezy's dismissal, to quote your letter, "had nothing whatsoever to do with what some people call his liberal or radical opinions." (Don't you consider them liberal, by the way? Or is your awareness of liberalism limited to your commencement addresses?)

With your letter you enclose the statement you made to the Harvard Board of Overseers, remarking: "This statement I realize will be misinterpreted in some quarters, but it has been interpreted just as I intended it to be in this morning's *Herald-Tribune*." Surely you are a bit ingenuous when you mention, as a point in *favor* of your statement, that the bitterly reactionary *Herald-Tribune* gives it editorial blessing.

However pleasant as a profession of liberal faith, your "explanation" doesn't explain anything. The only concrete excuse given therein is that "In our large departments less than half the instructors eventually obtain promotion. . . ." But the question is: on what grounds has Harvard decided that Walsh and Sweezy are not to be in the successful minority? Is *Time* correct in reporting that they were recently voted the most popular instructors in their courses? Is it true that Dr. Walsh recently received a Wertheim fellowship and that this is a notable academic distinction? What formidable talents do the men possess in whose favor Walsh and Sweezy are being passed over? Is it true that when Walsh and Sweezy are eliminated, Harvard's economics department will be overwhelmingly conservative in temper? And so, what steps are being taken to replace them with equally "liberal or radical" instructors?

Questions like these can't be answered by the elementary treatises in liberal theory to which you have confined yourself so far. When you issue a statement in the case which gets down to the real issues (and which the *Tribune* doesn't approve), then one may be able to credit you at least with honorable intentions.

To Dinsmore Wheeler

May 7, 1937

. . . We've started a magazine again, only don't say nothing about it to nobody. "We" means Dupee, Morris, myself, and two critics named William Phillips and Philip Rahv, who used to run an excellent (the best, in fact) leftist literary magazine called *Partisan Review*. Morris, as usual, is putting up the money with his usual tenderheartedness. (Even I may contribute something if TIME stock goes up far enough.) Our idea is to make it a nonpolitical Marxist journal of literary criticism and general cultural interest. Stories and poems too. The old *Partisan Review*, some of whose subscribers we'll inherit (it stopped coming out last fall), was somewhat tied to the C.P., which Rahv and Phillips feel was a mistake. This sheet will have no affiliations and will print no polemics or articles on immediate political and tactical problems. Rahv and Phillips, whom I've spent several long evenings with lately, seem to be extremely well informed and very intelligent—even brilliant, to use a horrible term. We'll put out the first issue next fall. How about becoming a contributor? Put on your thinking cap, eh? And, remember, not a word to a soul.

The steel book, delayed by these *Nation* articles, is about to get under way again. I've moved the publication date back to the first of 1938. And even then I'll have to drive myself to get it done. The material is so abundant and so rich that I'm scared I won't make the most of it.

I must get back to Part III of the *Nation* series.

To Editor, *The Nation* [written with Seldon Rodman]

May 13, 1937

As frequent visitors and part-time residents in one of the most notoriously backward open-shop communities in America, it has been our good fortune to become associated with an intensely dramatic and significant "labor disturbance." Out of the 1,100 employees of the Firth Carpet Company at Firthcliffe (just outside of Newburgh), 1,050 walked out last week under the leadership of the C.I.O. Textile Workers Organizing Committee. Axminster weavers in the United States average over $30 a week, but at Firthcliffe the best paid were making $20. Unskilled labor was paid as little as $11; everybody worked over 40 hours a week, and not a few averaged twelve hours a day, six days a week; twenty minutes out for lunch was the maximum.

So labor-hating are the city and its one newspaper that it has been impossible to rally any citizen support to get a column of even neutral publicity. The owner of the plant, a patent violator of the Wagner Act, is Lord Askroyal and is said to be in England attending the coronation. His huge daily advertisements in the local paper cunningly lay the blame on "outside agitators," "undesirable characters," and "communistic influences." The courage and militancy of the strikers have been magnificent, and the picketing has been uniformly peaceful and disciplined. "Violence" occurred Tuesday when scabs tried to drive through the picket line and ran down a deputy sheriff. The sheriff was so mad he gave the driver a ticket and told him never to come back. Yet the workers continue to be represented as a bloodthirsty, atheistic, and lawless mob.

The company is taking steps to organize a vigilante committee. No decent humane citizen of Newburgh or Cornwall would join if he understood the real situation. We hope that everyone within a radius of twenty miles who reads this letter will communicate with us immediately at Hemlock Glen, Grand Avenue, Newburgh. The strikers must have support. Anonymity will be scrupulously preserved if you desire it. But act *at once.*

To the Editor, *The New Republic*

May 19, 1937

In his lengthy review of "The Case of the Anti-Soviet Center" [*The New Republic*, April 7], Malcolm Cowley somehow overlooked what seems to me, after reading the book, the crucial problem. That a conspiracy of some sort was going on and that most, if not all of the defendants were involved—this Mr. Cowley is at great pains to demonstrate, and this I think, becomes quite plain to anyone who reads the testimony. But the important question, I suggest, is not: Were the defendants guilty? But rather: Of what precisely were they guilty? It is interesting to know that some, at least, of the defendants were wreckers and terrorists—of peculiar interest, of course, to Stalin. But radicals outside the U.S.S.R. are, or should be, more vitally concerned with the political meaning, the ideological background of those acts of terrorism than with the acts themselves. Were the defendants cynical adventurers, as charged by the Soviet, prepared to restore capitalism with fascist aid if such was the price they had to pay for power? Or were they a responsible political opposition, perhaps even the true heirs of the October Revolution, driven to underground plotting because Stalin has made all open opposition impossible. Above all, what was their connection with Trotsky. Is counterrevolution and even fascism the logical outcome of "Trotskyism"? The answers to these questions cannot but influence radicals the world over, not only in their attitude towards the present regime in Soviet Russia but also in their political tactics within their own countries.

It is these questions which the two Moscow trials have made the greatest effort to answer, and it is precisely these questions to which the answers are least satisfactory. Mr. Cowley scarcely seems aware that it is important that they should be answered. After showing in detail that a great deal of the testimony appears to be reasonably truthful, he continues: "But there are other points in the indictment which seem less firmly established." Those "other points" so casually introduced turn out to be all the major points, namely, the charges of counterrevolution and fascist conspiracy and the charge that Trotsky was implicated with the defendants. "On these points," Mr. Cowley writes, "I think we must suspend our judgment until more conclusive evidence is produced by one side or the other." This is all very well, but Mr. Cowley's suspension of judgment seems to be purely nominal. He adopts Prosecutor Vyshinsky's line of reasoning, implying that the logic of Trotsky's political theories leads straight to fascist alliance in order to overthrow the detested Stalin. He even goes Vyshinsky one better and suggests that Trotsky calculated that, once established in power, "he could turn against his allies and by the force of his genius rouse the rebellious spirit that sleeps just under the surface in Germany, Italy, and Japan." This bit of romantic melodrama is the best Mr. Cowley can do as an explanation of Trotsky's "line." To believe him capable of such a harebrained scheme, which thumbs its nose at every tenet of Marxist politics, one must also believe him in the last stages of senile dementia. And to believe this, one would have to take care not to read *The Revolution Betrayed*.

It must be granted that the trial explains the Trotsky line only a little better than Mr. Cowley. It is certainly not for lack of trying. The defendants vie with the Prosecutor in eagerness to hammer home, with endless repetition, the loathsome tenets of "Trotskyism." Radek gives the best summary (p. 114) of what was in store for Mother Russia if Trotsky and his fiends (including, of course Radek) had ever achieved power. The Ukraine was to go to Germany, the Amur region to Japan. Vast concessions were to be granted to foreign capitalists. Private capitalists were also to be sold outright "important economic enterprises, to be specified by them." "The collective farms would have to be disbanded." As the logical climax, Radek quotes (from memory) a letter he received several years ago from Trotsky: "There can be no talk of any kind of democracy. The working class has lived through eighteen years of revolution, and it has vast appetites; and this working class will have to be sent back partly to privately owned factories and partly to state-owned factories, which will have to compete with foreign capital under most difficult conditions. That means that the living standards of the working class will be drastically lowered. . . . In order to hold power we shall need a strong government. . . ."

But on what beside "a strong government" and fascist bayonets was Trotsky, the leader of the 1905 revolution and the partner of Lenin, counting? Vyshinsky and Sokolnikov cooperate to clear this up (p. 55):

Vyshinsky: "Specifically, on what forces within the country did you calculate? On the working class?"

Sokolnikov: "No."

Vyshinsky: "On the collective farm peasantry?"

Sokolnikov: "Of course not."

Vyshinsky: "On whom, then?"

Sokolnikov: "To speak quite frankly, I must say that we reckoned on being able to rely on the elements of the peasant bourgeoisie."

Vyshinsky: "On the kulaks, on the few remnants of the kulaks?"

Sokolnikov: "That is so . . .

Even Trotsky, obviously none too bright all the way through this conspiracy, dimly realized that "the few remnants of the kulaks" was not a very broad base for a counterrevolution. And so he planned nothing less than "the creation of elements of a new bourgeoisie" (Sokolnikov, p. 159). Talk about your social transformations: Lenin's task in 1917 was nothing compared to what Trotsky was willing to undertake in 1937. Trotsky's tactical line, in fact, was conceived on such a grandiose scale of lunacy that even his henchman Radek, whose appetite for the politically fantastic was God knows keen enough, was taken aback at times. Describing his receipt of one of those remarkable letters from Trotsky— "which unfortunately I burned" (p. 543)—Radek says: "For nothing at all, just for the sake of Trotsky's beautiful eyes, the country was to return to capitalism. When I read this, I felt as if it were in a madhouse" (p.124). One agrees with him, but the question is whether the head-keeper is named Trotsky or Stalin.

The trouble with the trial is that it proves too much. No one could be as crackbrained and malevolent as the Trotsky of these confessions. Word for word, the testimony dovetails into Stalin's foreign and domestic policy. Has *Pravda* been plugging the newly won higher standard of living? Trotsky was plotting to lower it. Are Soviet citizens justly proud of their splendid collective farms? Trotsky would break them up and restore the kulaks. The Five-Year Plan? Trotskyites tried to wreck it. The Stakhonivite heroes? Trotskyites murdered them. According to Vyshinsky, whose final speech is as vindictive a bit of chauvinistic ranting as has been heard since the Reichstag fire trial, Trotsky even planned to liquidate the intelligentsia (p. 930), presumably beginning with himself. The docility, or rather the downright fervor,with which the defendants play Stalin's game is most bewildering. They are fairly bursting with eagerness to destroy any last lingering influence their former leader might still have in the Soviet Union. Unanimously they excoriate Trotsky and all his works. Piatakov (p. 589) speaks of "my loathsome past . . . this filth . . . this vileness, festering sore . . ." Drobnis (p. 553) of "the stuffy, stinking, foul, evil-smelling Trotsky underworld . . ." Ivan Muralov, the old soldier who once followed his leader with devotion, calls Trotsky (p. 551) "that agent of the Fascists, enemy of the working class . . . who deserves every contempt."

Finally, it is impossible not to observe that Radek and Sokolnikov, the only defendants to give lengthy and detailed accounts of the Trotskyite political line, and the self-confessed high priests of "Trotskyism," were the only major defendants to escape the death penalty. They were let off with ten years apiece "as members of the anti-Soviet Trotskyite center, responsible for its criminal activities but not directly participating"—although Radek testified (pp. 89–92) that he not only knew in advance about the accusation of Kirov but even suggested a likely man for the job. Radek, in particular, plays an equivocal part in the trial. His testimony is by far the most damaging to Trotsky, and it is also by far the most open to suspicion. He dramatizes shamelessly, he dictates long editorials which neatly prove just what he wants them to prove, and in general he is that trap for the unwary exemplar, the all-too-willing witness.

I bring up these points not because I think they offer a complete explanation of perhaps the most baffling state trial in history, but because I feel that Mr. Cowley should have reckoned with them. I quite agree with him that the evidence is as yet insufficient to enable one to reach any judgment. And in the hope of stimulating the production of more evidence, I have joined the Committee for the Defense of Leon Trotsky. Mr. Cowley began his article by confessing, with disarming candor, a personal prejudice against Trotsky. Perhaps it is not too late to try to match his honesty by confessing, on my part, an equally deep-seated prejudice in Trotsky's favor. It's hardly necessary to give my reasons. They are about the same as Mr. Cowley's. [A much-edited copy of this letter appeared in *The New Republic*, May 19, 1937.]

To Leon Trotsky

August 23, 1937

I am writing you to answer some of the questions you raise in your letter to us regarding the *Partisan Review*. We feel that we have not made ourselves clear in describing the nature of the magazine. The enclosed circular may give you a rough idea of our approach, but I wish to supplement it with a few remarks.

From our point of view, the magazine, being exclusively a cultural organ, with its main emphasis on creative literature and criticism, cannot take any specific position on questions of Marxist strategy in the fashion of a political party or grouping. In this sense, we are ideological in character, rather than political. Furthermore, our conception of the relation of revolutionary literature to revolutionary politics is such that it excludes our taking part in *immediate* political controversies. As individuals, of course, the editors have a political life of their own and hold various beliefs concerning the present situation: all of us are opponents of Stalinism and committed to a Leninist program of action. We believe in the need for a new party to take the place of the corrupted Comintern.

But as editors of a literary periodical we cannot impose such ideas on the literary contents, although our political ideas do shape—in some ways—our work as editors. We shall attack all forms of reformism, including Stalinism primarily because of its devastating influence on revolutionary culture; and it was the Stalinist antics with the intellectuals that first stirred us to examine critically their political line.

Because of its connections and the character of its contributors, most of whom are more or less allied with your program, the *Partisan Review* will doubtless be branded as Trotskyist by the local Stalinist litterateurs. In fact, even prior to the appearance of our first number the *New Masses* gang is already describing us as stooges of the Fourth International. Although we think the description inaccurate, we are by no means ashamed or frightened by the connection they establish between your ideas and our magazine.

We are very eager to have you write for us on cultural and literary questions, knowing, of course, your approach to cultural problems fully involves your entire political position. As you remember we suggested several subjects in our first letter. In case you wish to write on other subjects do not hesitate to disregard our suggestions.[2]

To Freda Kirchwey [editor of *The Nation*]

December 10, 1937

I've long had—and I still have—the idea that the NATION exists to tell the truth about social issues. But I'm beginning to wonder whether this belief may not be mistaken. You won't mind, I hope, if I indicate a few reasons.

For some time liberals and radicals have watched with anxiety and bewilderment what's been happening in Spain and Russia. The question in each case is the same: Are the policies of the Stalin regime building socialism or are they destroying it? This would seem to be an important question to be asked, and yet so far the NATION has scarcely recognized that the issue exists. Its news of both Russia and Spain is conveyed almost wholly through Louis Fisher, an ardent partisan of the Stalinist regime. This is not to criticize his journalistic ability, nor is it to criticize the NATION for making use of his talents. "Objectivity" is a God-like and perhaps not always desirable journalist attitude—cf. Time Inc.! But must Mr. Fisher have a monopoly on Spain and Russia?

In a recent *Modern Monthly*, Anita Bremmer had what seemed to me the most intelligent and most thoroughly documented exposition of the war in Spain that I have yet read. An article, or a series of them, of this sort would have

2. Trotsky did not bite. He felt the magazine was too independent and politically undisciplined.

interested the liberals who read the NATION, I should think. Bremmer is a NA-
TION contributor of long standing. When the Spanish War broke out, she was
allowed to write for you a long article on it. But as soon as the Stalinists began
to crack down on the anarchists and socialists, Bremmer was no longer welcome—except in your letters column. Was it, perhaps, that her views on the
Spanish conflict would be not only interesting to your readers, but also persuasive?

The thing that immediately stimulated this note was a report in the
Evening Post that you had declined to attend the Trotsky Commission meeting
Sunday night because you are "out of sympathy with the Commission." I suppose it's none of my business, but I can't help wondering why the editor of a liberal magazine should feel this hostility towards the work of the Commission.
Are you completely convinced by the Moscow Trials? I've read the court
records together with most of the literature pro and con, and the whole case
against Trotsky seems to me vulnerable at a dozen vital points. (To say nothing
of the suspicious conformity of the "confessions" to every bend of the Stalinist
political line). If you have some doubts about the trials, then perhaps you think
the present Commission is not competent to render a verdict. In that case, what
alternative method of getting the truth would you propose? And—excuse the
impertinence—what have you or the NATION done to further any such alternative? Or perhaps you think it is (a) undesirable; (b) unimportant that the truth
or falsity of the charges against Trotsky be established. If so, how does either
square with a liberal position?

There are many other points at which I find myself in serious conflict with
the NATION. Recently you printed two feature articles, by Stone and by Lore, arguing the case for another world war in defense of democracy. When may we
expect a word on the other side (which I and most people I see happen to favor
quite strongly)? Your editorial attitude towards the New Deal in its current
swing to the right is timid and much to stuffy-genteel. The *New York Evening
Post,* it seems to me, has been speaking out on this theme more boldly and effectively than the NATION. When will Lerner stop licking the boots of every
New Deal big shot—his article on Black was the crudest piece of chicanery I've
seen since I wrote that sort of stuff myself for *Fortune* (with, I insist, a little more
respect for my data). It seems to me the NATION is mistaken if it thinks it can dispose of difficult (and unpleasant) issues by closing its eyes to them. This war
problem, the Stalinism question, and the nature of the New Deal, these can't
be understood by professions of faith. If the NATION wants to keep the confidence of its readers, I think it must adopt a more realistic—and, possibly, a
more honest—editorial policy.

While I was at *Fortune*, the NATION was always to me the great symbol of
honest, truthful, intelligent journalism—everything that I missed at *Fortune*.

But it now appears that the NATION, too, has its commitments, its investments, so to speak, just like *Fortune*. A journalistic investment in Soviet Russia seems to me no more admirable than a like investment in the Greatness and Goodness of Big Business. And telling only one side of the story smells no sweeter journalistically when it is done to protect Stalin or F.D.R. then when it is done to attack them.

I hope you'll forgive me for speaking frankly. I'm genuinely disturbed by what seems to me to be the recent decadence of the liberal tradition in the NATION. There's not much left journalistically if one can't trust the NATION.

To Freda Kirchwey

January 14, 1938

Thanks for your letter. I can't say it makes me feel any better about the NATION. It's not so much that we disagree, it's rather that you don't even admit the basis for disagreement. Anyway, you are evidently either unwilling or unable to make any concessions, so that's that.

I resent, naturally the crack about my "professed friendship" for the NATION. Your note of January 7 was friendly, even conciliatory. What has caused you to suddenly doubt my attitude towards the NATION? And what right have you to assume that I'm being hypocritical (rather an ugly charge, by the way) in criticizing the NATION as a friend? Surely the tone of the war letter—which I helped draft, as I mentioned—should indicate that I don't look at the NATION through barbed wire. But if you insist on regarding me as an enemy, I suppose I'll have to accept the role.

To Dinsmore Wheeler

May 30, 1938

. . . Thanks for your advice, both by word of mouth and in your note, about my future course. I've taken one step which is, characteristically, a compromise. Beginning with the July issue, I'm to write a monthly column (literally, it will be a page) for the NEW INTERNATIONAL, the Trotskyist magazine. I think you already subscribe. If you don't, I'll give you a sub. (But I think I did give you one, no?? It's the best thing of its kind, including the *Nation* and *New Republic*, now going, I think. In writing for it, I'll be reaching a wider audience than in PR (they print 4,000 copies, [James] Burnham [leftist theoretician, Trotskyist] tells me) and, more important, to some extent a working-class audience. And at the same time I won't have to water down what I have to say, as would be necessary in writing for labor papers. (Not that I'm not constantly turning over in my mind the idea of trade-union journalism.) I've got a swell idea for the column: it will be a column on columnists, a survey of the months thinking of [Westbrook] Pegler, [Heywood] Broun, [Dorothy] Thompson, [Walter] Lippmann, [Alvin] Johnson, [Raymond] Clapper, [Mark] Sullivan. Have you any suggestions as to others who should be included, by the way? These seem to be about the most widely read, wouldn't you say? The idea will be to analyze the main currents of bourgeois ideology, to discriminate between the black reaction of a Sullivan, the dark grey of a Thompson, and the Zebra stripes of a Pegler.

The FORUM is running my article on Pittsburgh (5,000 words) in its August issue. I'll send you a copy. My reward $100—and the hope that the piece will be of some possible help to the leftists in P. It's pretty rough stuff—I give the Business Community the works. FORUM seems well pleased, though.

I enclose a bit on the Steel Corporation's annual meeting, which I recently did. It's been turned down by the *Nation*, the *New Republic*, and even, I'm ashamed to say, by my fellow editors on PR—the latter, it should be said, not precisely saying they don't like it, but merely that it doesn't seem that PR is the place for it. Nancy likes it some, so do I—neither of us too much. What do you think?

The enclosed quote from Eisenstein is interesting, especially in the light of my unfortunate half hour with Joyce, when I suggested that ULYSSES was cinematic in form and ought to be made into a movie—to get no discernible response from The Master. But maybe I put an idea in Joyce's head, to germinate and eventually be harvested by Eisenstein!

PR publishes in the June issue, out next week, what I think is the best thing we've yet had—[Rosa] Luxemburg's letters from prison, or some of them at least. The editorial foreword and the "newsreel" at the end are my work.

I've actually discovered a Trotskyist—a member of the Socialist Workers Party, not a mere sympathizer like myself—who was in my class at Yale! Unfortunately he's not very interesting, aside from that.

There's a move on foot to organize a committee to defend victims of capitalist and Stalinist persecution (strikers here, POUMists in Spain, etc.). The PR boys are in it. Would you be interested in taking some part? We had a preliminary organization meeting the other night, which was disappointing, but when and if something more occurs, I'll let you know. (Disappointing not because there was any lack of attendance or enthusiasm—that is, about 35 people, mostly quite intelligent and articulate, turned up—but because the Trotskyists are the prime movers, and their chief, Cannon, acted in a discouragingly sectarian and stupid manner.)

If we can rent our apt., we'll go off to the seashore for the summer. If not, we'll spend a month or so anyway in Newburgh.

Your NATION review looked quite nice in type, I thought. Are you doing any more for them? What do you think of [Margaret] Marshall's series on the columnists. I think she muffed a swell chance.

For the past couple of weeks I've been laboring at my survey of the Soviet cinema, 1930–1938. I've dug up a great deal of extremely interesting stuff, and the article ought to be of some value. It's going to be pretty dismal reading for the Friends of the Soviet Union.

It's late (11 P.M.) now, and I must arise at 6 to "do" the baby, so I'll have to stop. By the way, his name is now Michael Dwight Macd. How do you like? We decided on Michael chiefly so we can call him MIKE. But if you disapprove, and can implement your disapproval with sufficiently telling arguments, we can easily call him something else.

To Harold Rosenberg

June 7, 1938

I'm sending you a copy of the new issues—3 copies, in fact, to be used where you think they'll do the most good. Yes, something should be done to get PR better known, and I'm trying a few things now. We're taking a quarter-page in the *New Republic* and we're having large exchange ads in the APPEAL, the CALL, the NEW INTERNATIONAL, and the INTERNATIONAL REVIEW. Some shoots should come up from so much broadcast seeds. . . . Speaking of the League of American Writers, have you heard about their current suit against Rahv to collect $100 they lent the old PR? We're trying to settle for less, but they seem more interested in persecuting Rahv than in getting cash. Calmer is also involved, as is Phillips, but they haven't done much about those two. . . . Glad you approve the Column-on-Columnists idea.

I was very much impressed by your Mann article. It seems to me by far the best thing I've ever read about Mann, as well as one of the most brilliant pieces of Marxist criticism I've yet seen (the latter being, perhaps, a qualified compliment). I liked especially the way you related Mann's literary ideas about change to the old prewar Bernsteinian "Socialist" doctrines. And in the last part especially (I thought the beginning a bit heavy) you arise to heights of eloquence—as in the comparison of capitalist contradictions to "pistons of progress" in capitalism's apogee which now "clash in a wild disorganization of the machinery of society." I was so impressed by the piece that I took the liberty of showing it to Dupee and Rahv (hope you don't object). They are equally enthusiastic. We all think (1) it is just the sort of piece PR exists to print, (2) it's a great shame (a crime, even) that your work hasn't appeared in our pages so far. I know how you feel about Rahv and Phillips and I know why you feel so—since, to a large extent, my reactions are the same. But I don't think you would deny they are extremely intelligent (admitting serious limitations), and I have lately found that, with a certain amount of tact, patience, and persistence, one can work with them quite satisfactorily. And it seems a great pity, considering how few really good minds "our" group (I say "our" since politically and intellectually you seem to have much the same outlook as we of PR do) can commend—it seems to bad to have you split off from us by personal animosities. Whatever may be said about Rahv—and a great deal can be said—he is intensely interested in the same things that you are, and I have never known him to let his personal feelings interfere with his editorial judgment. His reaction to your article, for instance, was as enthusiastic as though you were on the friendliest of terms. But perhaps I am exaggerating the friction between you and the Rahv-Phillips camp anyway. I hope so. To come down to practical things, if it weren't that Phillips' article covered much the same ground as yours (and incomparable less adequately), we would ask at once to print your piece if *Virginia Quarterly* and *Life & Letters* don't want it. (The length of Troy's piece is also a consideration— though his approach doesn't conflict with yours at all.) But even though I would like to ask you to send the piece back to us if you don't dispose of it elsewhere. We haven't completely made up our minds one way or the other. . . . There's a new book we would very much like you to review for us: Christopher Caudwell's *Illusion and Reality*. Dupee and Rahv have both read it, and they say it is the most important analysis that has yet been done of the relationship of Marxism to literature.

To Dinsmore Wheeler

August 4, 1938

. . . PR is going on next year, as a quarterly, however. Monthly publication is too expensive and too arduous, we've found. Morris will put up the cash again. He doesn't seem at all worried by the Trotskyist drift of the magazine in late months. There's a liberal for you of the old school! How do you like recent issues? We think they are the best we've put out—and comment we get seems to bear out that idea. I'm curious to know, especially, how you like Rahv's notes on Dostoevsky. By the way, we're continuing you on the subscription list free for nothing—we can't afford to drop one of our few contacts with the Soil!

Morris has just returned from Europe full of direct observation of fascism—they were in Italy and Austria most of the time. He says you have no idea how barbaric and revolting the Nazification of Austria is until you see the process yourself—says that when he first saw a shop window plastered with a huge yellow sign, DON'T BUY FROM JEWS, he felt as he had when in China he saw a bandit's head stuck on a pole in the street. He described Hitler's visit to Mussolini as a great flop—the Italians hate the Germans, and failed to respond to Hitler at all. At one big demonstration, when Hitler and Mussolini appeared on a balcony together, they were many cries of DUCE!, not a peep for Hitler, although Mussolini kept pushing Adolf forward and even pointing to him. Finally, Mussolini had to send soldiers among the crowd, to shout HEIL HITLER!

Have you seen Jerome Frank's SAVE AMERICA FIRST? I've just finished it— I'm reviewing it for the NI next month, together with the two other how-to-save capitalism works, from the Brookings Institution and the Harvard Business School respectively. It's interesting how similar Frank and the conservative Brookings people are in their remedies. The Frank book is rambling and, in my opinion, rather superficial, but quite lively and intelligent. It puts the case for the New Deal about as well as it can be put, I imagine. I think you would enjoy it, I'll send it out to you after I finish with it. If you like.

To G. L. K. Morris (college classmate, abstract expressionist, and financial supporter of the *Partisan Review*]

September 2, 1940

I'm coming to think that we just can't let PR die at this point. From talks I have had with "our" public, from letters, and from trying to think myself what sort of platform I could find for my own stuff half as good—from all these, plus Nancy's exhortations, I've come to change my mind. When we talked last, I had a vague idea of killing PR and then, after some months of reflection, perhaps you and I getting some new people and starting up a new magazine. But I don't think we should let the winter months go that way. A new magazine, and new editors, those seem to be clearly necessary, but PR should be changed into its successor if at all possible.

What crystallized the whole thing in my mind was a talk Nancy and I had the other night with Rahv, who's just got back from the Cape. I was surprised, and rather moved and inspired, by the vehemence with which he insisted it would be a great blow to all we believe in to let PR die right now. When I indicated your and my feelings about the present editorial staff, he admitted that he himself didn't think the board at all perfect the way it exists. . . .

We talked a good deal, and although Rahv demurred at the idea of liquidating Dupee and Phillips, he put up a comparatively feeble fight, mostly on grounds of sentiment. I think a board with Rahv and two or three new people, and without Fred and William, would function well and would be fun to work with. Rahv at least is a functioning writer, and his ideas are practical. And his Russian pessimism could be overcome and compensated for by some new people on the board. But the dropping out (or off) of D and P seems to me essential. To try and put through the kind of new ideas that seem to be necessary in the face of Rahv, D, and P united, this is more than I can face, after two years of struggle. And you feel much the same way, I gather. So it seems to me we should start our new magazine right now, without waiting for things to settle down—and minus 2 of the present editors.

Could you get down to NYC in the next week to talk about all this? If you could meet with me and Nancy and Rahv and Clem G., we could explore the possibilities a bit more.

For this next issue, what would you think of asking about ten people—Sidney Hook, John Dewey, Burnham, Edmund Wilson—to write not over 1,000 words each on some aspect of Trotsky and his significance to them? We ought to make some such gesture, I think, to the memory of the man whose thinking colored our whole editorial policy.

I enclose a rough draft of some ideas on the new magazine I made the other day. It will indicate what I think are the possibilities.

To G. L. K. Morris

September 9, 1940

Just a word in reply to your note of Sept. 7. I think you exaggerate to yourself the difficulties of starting a new magazine. It would be no harder to begin publishing the kind of magazine I suggest than it would to continue with the present PR. To change the name, format, and editors takes no special amount of money or time—the new format in fact would be . . . cheaper. I am in favor of this "new" magazine against the present because I think it could strike in just that direction which, in talks with you, I had gathered you, too, felt the magazine should go—less academic, more bold and experimental, more receptive to new ideas and writing and with a board of editors who would actively participate, lead, and create, instead of sitting back and moaning about the sad state of things. Greenberg is far from ideal as an editor, but he seems to me to be as intelligent and well-inbred as either Fred or William, and to have the great virtues over them of being (1) able to write (the new *Horizon* has as its lead article a piece by him) and (2) enthusiastic and positive in his approach to the business of editing. Also, there is Rosenberg, whom even Rahv admits would be an excellent addition as an editor—he's extremely brilliant, with original and often profound ideas of his own. Again, he is given to positive ideas and wants to try things, to do something. And, like Clem, he can write and can work hard.

As to going on with the old PR: I've really come to the conclusion that I'm unwilling to take on another year the job of acting as spark plug in the outfit, of having to plan and propose to three colleagues who seem to me by now to be pretty much out of touch with the literary-political field (except for Rahv, who still writes and therefore has at least a foot in it), and whose temperamental limitations (timidity, exaggerated respect for established expectations, fear of being laughed at), make it discouraging and constantly irritating to try to work things out with them. You haven't been around the magazine as constantly as I have, and you probably don't realize how wearing and nerve-fraying this kind of sterile endless conflict can be. I see no reason why it must continue. Fred and William have ceased to contribute anything (except two votes to Rahv's overcautious negativistic policies) and it is stifling the life of the magazine to drag them along with it. You write, "If there is a burning enthusiasm to continue PR as is, let's try it a while longer." (There really IS a surprising enthusiasm for the magazine, by the way. Two Midwestern contributors—Sylander and Koos— just dropped in today and talked of PR as the one hope of Western culture!) But what's the use of "trying it a while longer"? Don't we know by now what's wrong with the magazine? Do you think things will work out better this winter on the old basis? I know they won't, because already the literary sources for the present PR are drying up, because unless the magazine gives more of a lead, unless its editors write more themselves and give more of a tone to the magazine and take more trouble to cultivate and revise and criticize writers with some talents—unless this is done, PR will stagger on through the winter and go into a steady decline.

Possibly the exact formula I suggest for a new departure may not be right, possibly (whether it is a good one or not) it doesn't please or interest you—on this we can and of course will talk. But I think it would be (for me, at least) much more of an "effort" to go on with the present PR than to try something new with some new people. (Or rather with three old editors and two new ones.) If you want to continue to finance a magazine—and I fervently hope you do—I see some chance of success—in the sense of broadening the circle of readers and of stimulating intellectual life and striking a few paths in the wilderness that surrounds us all more and more—with a revised editorial board and a different type of magazine; but with the present setup, I see no reasonable chance of success.

I think you and I should get into an hour's talk before the meeting on Thursday night. (Can we have this meeting at your place, by the way, because our place is being used that night for another gathering?) If we can agree on a basis, it would be better if we presented a united front at the meeting. Would you drop me as to when and where on Thursday you want to meet? . . .

Best to Susie—see you Thursday,

P.S. My own position on continuing the present PR is this: Such a magazine would certainly be better than none at all; if you decide, finally, that you would rather back such a magazine, I would be glad to continue as editor, but only on condition that PR takes an office and that all five editors take equal shares of editorial work and responsibility on their shoulders. I would plan to devote much less of my time to the magazine, and I would consider it my responsibility to do nothing more than read and write an article now and then. To run the office would take a business manager, and it would probably be necessary, knowing the level of energy and efficiency of our colleagues, to have the business manager function also as a sort of managing editor.

In other words, the magazine could be carried on as a repository for the best that is sent in, an anthology, a place where if someone writes something good, he can get it published. This is by no means a negligible function for a magazine, of course. But it's not the sort of magazine I would want to give any large amount of time to right now. But more of this when we meet. . . .

To Victor Serge

June 1941

A friend of mine who is experienced in refugee work has suggested that the American authorities might be more willing to grant you a visa if you formally offered to testify before the Dies Committee on methods, personnel, etc. of the OGPU abroad; also on what you know of the Stalinist movement in general today. The Dies Committee is, as you perhaps know, a body of the U.S. Congress which for two years has been investigating "subversive activities." It is very reactionary and anti-labor. On the other hand, its hearings receive much attention and it should be possible to formulate your testimony in such a way that its effect would be on the whole progressive, helpful to the real interests of labor. I might add that the Old Man [Trotsky] was willing to testify before this committee. You must make the decision yourself. If you decide favorably, you should write Nancy a letter (typed) stating that you would be willing to testify and outlining the kind of information you would give.

The reason it is so difficult to get you an American visa is that your case comes under a certain section of the Smith Act, a law which forbids the entry into this country of any persons who at any time have ever been members of an organization which advocates the overthrow of the American government. We finally, after much effort and use of influence, were able to obtain from the Board of Immigration Appeals an exception in your case. But the State Department up to now has sabotaged this decision by simply doing nothing. It is now eight weeks since the Board ruled that an exception should be made in your case, and—despite letters, phone calls, telegrams—the State Department still refuses to, and how long this can go on we don't know.

Dear Comrades [officials of the Workers Party]

July 1, 1941

In my letter of March 22 (published in Internal Bulletin #9) I wrote: "But I must state quite explicitly that if the party as a whole supports the kind of organizational procedure the present P.C. has adopted, I will feel obliged to leave the party."

It is now over three months since my letter was submitted to the Plenum of the N.C. (which unanimously sustained the P.C. against my complaints). It is over a month since the letter was published in the Internal Bulletin. This is a reasonable length of time in which to see what response, if any, the party membership would give to my complaints against the P.C. The response, so far as diligent inquiry reveals, has been zero. Whether from conviction or passivity, the rank-and-file of the party appears to be solidly behind the P.C. in this matter.

I am forced to submit, therefore, my resignation from the Workers Party.

I wrote "forced" because I regret having to take this step. So far as political action today goes, I am still in basic agreement with the Party, as I think the "Ten Propositions on the War" in the current *Partisan Review* indicate. But I have long since come to believe that the replacement of capitalism with collectivized property form is only part—and perhaps no longer even the major part—of the task of social revolution today. The insurance of political democracy in the new regime seems to me equally important. The fact that in Germany capitalism has yielded to a planned, collectivized economy which nonetheless is marked by the most extremely reactionary social features seems to me one indication of the inadequacy of the traditional Leninist conception. The terrible degeneration of the Russian Revolution is, of course, an even more dramatic warning. I don't think this can be explained only by Russia's economic backwardness. Certain authoritarian and anti-democratic features of bolshevism, pointed out before 1917 by such critics as Luxemburg and . . . Trotsky, played a major role as well.

From the time I first began to write for the Trotskyist press, in 1937, I have criticized the movement's hierarchical, undemocratic organization, its sterile and narrow-minded Marxist "orthodoxy," and its superstitious veneration of Trotsky and the Leninist tradition he represented. The factional struggle last year—at the beginning of which I joined the party—seemed to show that part at least of the Trotskyist movement was breaking with these methods. The Stalinist practices of the Cannonite Majority, wholeheartedly backed up by Trotsky himself, in the course of the struggle seemed to make crystal-clear the end to which traditional methods led. For various reasons, however, the defection of [James] Burnham being the chief one, the leadership of the Workers Party began what might be termed a Retreat to Moscow almost as soon as the new party was formed. The same old atmosphere which disgusted many of us with the Socialist Workers Party is back with us again: the intolerance of even the most well-meaning criticism, the abusive and intemperate polemical tone, the smug assumption that the Party has a monopoly of all political virtue and wisdom, the religious approach to Marxist doctrine, the interminable rehash of stale platitudes and catchwords with which the Party leadership covers up (or rather, reveals) its political bankruptcy when confronted by a new situation, above all, the "defensive reflex," in Trotsky's memorable phrase, with which the Party leadership meets any suggestions for change.

So far has the Retreat to Moscow proceeded by now that adherence to "bolshevism" as an organizational doctrine seems to have been established in the Workers Party as a requisite for membership. If bolshevism means the organizational and intellectual tradition of the American Trotskyist movement, then I am opposed to it now as I have been in the past. Whether the evils I protest against are inherent in bolshevism, or perhaps even in Marxism, or whether they are mainly the specific fault of the American Trotskyist tradition, this is something I haven't yet made up my mind about. But that they are evils, that they stand in the way of reaching any socialist goal, this I do know. I have delayed taking this final step for months, hoping either that I could be convinced I was wrong or that the Party leadership would change its views. The stalemate has not been broken. The membership apparently backs up the leadership. I must therefore leave the party. I am opposed to this kind of a party because I think the political tradition it represents, for all its admirable (in the past) qualities of courage, devotion, and revolutionary intransigence, is one which today is obsolete and tomorrow will prove more of a hindrance than a help in the achievement of revolutionary socialist aims.

For some time I—and doubtless many others still in the party as well—have based my support of the Trotskyist movement on a sort of "lesser evil" argument: It's true that it has great faults and is far from perfect, but—where is there a better movement? I must confess I have no alternative organization to propose. But the argument no longer seems to me valid, for two reasons. (1) After a year of the W.P., I can't take it seriously as a revolutionary movement; its top leadership seems incapable of reaching any clear, principled theoretical basis, split as it is between Shachtman's opportunism, Johnson's semi-religious "Leninism," and Allen's routinist orthodoxy; its rank-and-file, understandably, is confused and demoralized; in practical actions there is the same incompetence, routinism, and lack of spirit and energy we used to criticize in the old S.W.P. (2) Reading, discussion, and experience have at least taught me what perhaps I should have seen earlier: that the kind of organizational procedures described in my letter of March 22 are stepping-stones to Stalinism. The first condition for effective action in a revolutionary socialist direction in the future must be a sharp break with the organizational tradition of the American Trotskyist movement.

To James Farrell

September 18, 1941

Thanks for the invitation to join the Civil Rights Defense Committee. I see that the Committee has now sprouted a complete set of officers. Who elected or appointed them? So far as I know, there has not to date been held any general meeting of those interested in forming such a committee. Nor, judging from the phrase in your letter of Sept. 17 about "keeping you informed of all important developments," is there any intention of holding such a meeting.

This seems an odd procedure to adopt for a group that is defending democratic rights. I'm not willing to lend my name to such a Committee, especially since I have a very low opinion of the moral standards of the SWP. As I wrote [George] Novack several weeks ago, I'm all for forming a democratically run defense committee, with properly elected officers, and with some controls and checks over Novack and the other SWPers who do the administrative work. But I'm not joining a Cannonite vest-pocket committee in which eminent nonparty people are appointed to honorary posts, from the top.

The way this committee has been handled from the beginning is a scandal—just like the old Stalinist paper "front" outfits. I'm not having any, thanks.

To Edmund Wilson

n.d., November 1941

It's your own business, I suppose, but I think you're making a mistake in keeping silent on this [Van Wyck] Brooks business [denouncing American writers who did not meet their patriotic responsibilities in their work]. If you approve, as you wrote earlier, of my piece, then I take it you agree it's a serious matter, going far beyond Brooks's own personal failings and asininity—a symptom of growing cultural repression and regimentation. And in that case it would seem the responsibility of writers on *our* side of the fence to stick their necks out now, to speak out publicly against this sort of thing. Personal letters don't do the job at all. (You'll recall we had the same disagreement at the time Cowley made his smear attack on PR in the *New Republic*—and I still think the personal letter you wrote him at the time (instead of a public statement) was the wrong tactic.

In this case, also, it seems to me you have an especial responsibility to repudiate Brooks publicly, since he has actually invoked you as a supporter of his ideas. You have a large "following," with whom your word carries much weight. Don't you think you have an obligation to at least inform them (as well as Brooks) that you don't back up Brooks in this issue?

To Delmore Schwartz

December 22, 1942

Your letter so charms and annoys me that I sit down to answer it the very morning I get it.

First, God save me from my friends, if you're atypical! So you defend me, you rat, against your genteel-academic colleagues by saying that neurotic antagonism is the basis of my intellectual existence and my predictions never come true, but that I am a master of exposition and also openhearted. In future, do me a favor and either keep silent or join the Enemy. [Macdonald was involved in a bitter controversy over the position of the PR toward the war; he opposed American involvement.]

My political beliefs, which I take seriously, are not based on mere love of brawling and being "different," but on some experience (mostly my years on *Fortune*), on sympathy for human beings (who are brutalized and oppressed in every way by the social system we have), and on intellectual conviction which I've arrived at by a wide (and still continuing) reading in politics and economics. Goddamit, that nasty crack about being just a congenial sorehead is the way the conservatives have always everywhere brushed aside any kind of criticism from a radical standpoint. It's the easiest way to dispose of embarrassing criticisms, and undoubtedly the genteel-academic circles in which you so gallantly defend me are only too delighted to agree with your "defense."

On rereading your letter, I see you except my political (and cinematic) views from this, so formally all the above must be stricken from the record. But how in the devil can I be responsibly antagonistic in political and films and neurotically so in other matters? In literature? How does the fact I admire Eliot's later poetry, which you for some wacky reason affect to dismiss as worthless, fit in with this alleged anti-everything pattern? Eliot is certainly well established and his later poems are certainly right in fashion, and a fashion which I oppose violently, as you know. As for [Weldon] Kees, all of us, including Rahv, were for printing the review. Later on, it's true, Rahv got cold feet, as he usually does, and changed his mind. But anyway, it wasn't a peculiar aberration of mine. And if, as you say Levin and Rukeyser deserve to be raked over the coals, and if you're so superior as to the abilities of [Lionel] Abel and Kees to do it, then why in the devil don't you yourself do it? Why don't you ever have the guts to speak out in print on anything? [Schwartz did trash Muriel Rukeyser, but anonymously.] As I told you a long time ago (a prediction that has come true), you're ruining your career (not to speak of your moral being as a man) by trimming your sails to prevailing winds, by keeping silent on any hot, controversial issues, by excessive diplomacy and hush-hush attitude toward all the fakery and shoddiness that's for years been growing so in our whole intellectual atmosphere. I can see how the fact that I insist on talking out on a few such themes might seem to you practically mentally unbalanced. But I assure you the shoe is on the other foot.

Second, you have a lot of gall to say you helped PR out in its early struggling days and now I don't even reply when you suggest a reviewer for your poetry. PR helped you, my dear fellow, in your early career—we printed your stuff first and notably "In Dreams [Begins Responsibility]," which others had turned down and which made your reputation, initially at least. And once you were established, then you stopped writing for PR completely. I'm glad you're beginning again, but for a long period you sent us nothing at all. As for my not replying to your suggestion of [R.P.] Blackmur as a reviewer, I didn't object to Blackmur, whom we did ask (but he's committed elsewhere, apparently) and I did pass on your recommendation to the boys.[3] But why should I write you back? I don't approve of your making the suggestions and so preferred to pass it over in silence.

Thirdly, you're more than a little right in objecting to my having once told you that you should write not criticism but poetry only. I've now come to think it was bad advice and that I badly underestimated you as a critic. And I want to say that, if my manner towards you has been condescending (as your crack about my laughing at your jokes, sealing you in Martinis and then telling you're a fool to write anything serious, would indicate that you feel it has been), I assure you you are mistaken. Angry as certain moral traits in you make me (as you can see from the above), I've always had the greatest respect for you as an intelligent and a literary man, and also sympathy for you as a person. The length of this letter testifies to that, I think.

Fourthly, I should say that your essay on Eliot should not be too much over 5,000 words.

Fifthly, please read this letter in the spirit in which I read yours, i.e., with the realization that it is quite serious and should be taken seriously, but also on a typewriter (especially if one is somewhat irritated), and that my attitude towards you is at least as ambivalent as yours is towards me. I'm really very fond of you, believe me.

---

3. Dwight frequently referred to Rahv and Phillips as "the boys." It was used pejoratively, suggesting a conspiratorial collaboration.

Sixthly, I'll never quite get over your failure to commit yourself in print (as [Paul] Goodman did) on the war, after the views that you expressed to me privately.

Seventhly, I probably am a bit too much on the anti-all-that side, but the conjunction of the really fearful decadence and inhumanity all about me and the discreet silence of those (like you) who by virtue of their talents and brains should be the leaders of a protestant movement against it all—this unhappy conjunction probably tends to aggravate a temperamental bent into a kind of professional, official attitude. The results of a deformation in this direction, however, I think are likely to be better, qualitatively, than those of the more prevalent (in intellectual circles) opposite deformation, towards a silent and passive conformity.

Eighth, You brought all this on yourself with your request, "Please answer." Was every wish more fully granted?

Ninth, do write me, either breaking off all relations or, I hope, not, at this address: c/o Dinsmore Wheeler, R.D.3, Huron, Ohio, where I'll be until Jan 2.

P.S. I see that, Freudian-wise, I omitted to ask you about one crack that particularly aroused me—about my predictions never coming true. It seems to me that what's happening now in the world, and in the war, is a pretty good vindication of what I've been saying for years about the nature of the Roosevelt administration, the prospects of liberalism, and the real nature of this war. What had you in mind?

To Selden Rodman

April 18, 1943

I can understand your not liking [Otis] Ferguson's review, but I'm puzzled as to why you think Nancy and I are in some way to blame for Ferguson's low opinion of your book. Perhaps it will clear up things if a few matters of fact are established:

1. You asked me particularly, as you'll recall, to see that PR reviewed "The Revolutionists." So I made a point of having a review done, and think you should give me credit for that.

2. You seem to think that I knew Ferguson was going to pan the book. Why do you assume that? I have never met him and know nothing about him except that he contributed some good pieces to the "Hound and Horn" and is a specialist in poetic drama. He therefore seemed a logical choice to review the book, and I agreed when Rahv suggested him.

3. Ferguson is as much or as little a member of PR's "gang of little hatchet-men" as Auden or Isherwood, if less so in fact if the closeness of his association

with the editors and the number of contributions is the criteria. Before the review, he had contributed just one thing to PR—a poem. As I said, I don't know him and am not sure any of the other editors do. Anyway, he is certainly not particularly identified with PR.

There are a couple of questions of our values which also need clearing up. Just what would you expect Nancy and me to do once Ferguson had written his review? (And don't forget, a. we didn't know what he'd say, and b. he was well qualified for the job.) Try to get the other four editors to reject it on the grounds that you were my brother-in-law and Nancy's brother? That would have been both unsuccessful, and in my opinion, wrong. You can't seriously propose that kind of logrolling. Furthermore, your appeal to "family feeling and other human emotion" would seem better addressed to yourself than to us. On no evidence, you're quite willing to write your sister a venomous letter accusing her of plotting to have your book knifed in PR—and you end up suggesting that it's not at all beyond her (and me) to print this personal letter in PR if we can thereby "defame" your "reputation" among our "circle." It seems to me family feeling should not give way so completely merely because Nancy is unfortunate enough to be connected with a magazine that reviews a book of yours unfavorably. There is finally this business of talking about PR's "sterile academics," "ingrown critics," and "minor obscurantists," when what you really mean is that PR takes literary values seriously and therefore often criticizes books adversely. If PR is so sterile and ingrown, why were you so anxious to have us review your book? That's really cheap stuff, the usual complaint of philistinism against intellectual values. I'm sure it's your feeling of the moment, not a considered opinion.

Again, I can understand your disliking the review, but you really have no right to take this line towards Nancy and myself. Come around and see us next time you're in town.

To the Editors, *The Nation*

June 2, 1943

What kind of doubletalk is my friend James Agee handing us in his review of "Mission to Moscow?" He seems to approve the film's political objectives—except for the Moscow trials, where he shifts into tripletalk—and to detest its moral, aesthetic, and intellectual qualities. It might have occurred to him, in the course of his fancy ruminations, that there is generally a connection between the human and artistic value of a propagandist work of art and the quality of the cause it promotes. If "the deeper effect [of "Mission to Moscow"] is shame, grief, anesthesia, the ruin of faith and conscience and the roots of the intelligence"—he certainly throws the language around—one would expect so painfully scrupulous a reviewer to suspect something rotten in the film's thesis. The simple fact is that "Mission to Moscow" is what it is because it has a very dirty job to do.

The bias with which Agee, for all his protestations of political virginity, approaches "Mission to Moscow" emerges clearly when he admits a "painful impotence" to take any stand on the truth or falsity of the Moscow trials—after having written the following extraordinary lines: "It is good to see the conservatives of this country, Great Britain, France, and Poland named even for a fraction of their responsibility for this war. It is good to see the Soviet Union shown as the one nation, during the past decade, which not only understood fascism but desired to destroy it, and which not only desired peace but had some ideas how it might be preserved. . . ." How can Agee be so agonizingly indecisive about the trials and so blatantly, unqualifiedly cocksure about the even more complex questions of the Soviet Union and war, fascism, and appeasement?

Reluctant as I am to widen the area of Agee's impotence, I must ask him: (1) If Munich's appeasement was shameful, as it was, why not also the super-appeasement of the Nazi-Soviet pact? (2) If the conservatives bear heavy responsibility for the war, as they do, why not also the Kremlin, whose pact was the match that touched off the explosion? (3) If the Soviet Union "understood fascism" so well, how does Agee explain (a) the "Social Fascist" theory of the late twenties, and the refusal of the Communists to make a united front with the German Social Democracy against Hitler; (b) Stalin's failure to send decisive aid to Spain, because of respect for the "nonintervention" farce, and his followers' joining with the conservative democrats within the Loyalist government to strangle the developing social revolution, which might have brought victory over Franco; (c) the Communist slogan in 1933, "After Hitler, our turn"— hardly a good example of "understanding" fascism; (d) Molotov's famous remark in 1939 about fascism being "a matter of taste"; (e) the support given to Hitler's peace drives, after he had conquered Europe, by Communist groups throughout the world—up to June 21, 1941, that is?

My friend Agee has the right to whatever opinions he likes, but he also has the obligation to harmonize these opinions one with the other. To leave unresolved the internal contradictions in his criticism, in the hope of somehow pleasing everyone, is doubletalk at a time when clarity on the kind of issue posed by "Mission to Moscow" is of vital importance.

To the Editors, *Partisan Review*

July 3, 1943

Please accept my resignation from *Partisan Review*, effective next issue. Naturally, I regret severing connections with a magazine to which I have given much time and effort. I feel, however, that the divergence between my conception of the magazine and your own has become too great to be bridged any longer. This divergence is partly cultural: I feel *Partisan Review* has become rather academic, and favor a more informal, disrespectable, and chance-taking magazine, with a broader and less exclusive "literary" approach. But the divergence is mainly political.

When we revived *Partisan Review* in 1937, it was as a Marxian socialist cultural magazine. This was what distinguished it from other literary organs like *Southern Review* and *Kenyon Review*, and this orientation, in my opinion, was responsible for much of the magazine's intellectual success. The war, however, has generated sharp political disagreements. Not only has the Marxist position been reduced to a minority of one—myself—but since Pearl Harbor there has been a tendency on the part of some editors to eliminate political discussion entirely. For my part, I have opposed this retreat and I have insisted that precisely because of the urgency of the crisis, social questions should bulk even larger in the magazine. The conflict has reached the point where there remains little of the *esprit de corps* necessary to put out a "little" magazine. I should have liked to carry my viewpoint. This being impossible, I am withdrawing. From now on *Partisan Review* will devote itself to cultural issues, leaving the thorny field of politics to others.

What interests me, however, is a magazine which shall serve as a forum and a rallying-point for such intellectuals as are still concerned with social and political issues. A magazine which, while not ignoring cultural matters, will integrate them with—and yes, subordinate them to—the analysis of those deeper historical trends of which they are an expression. The degeneration of the liberal magazines seems to render this kind of publication important today. I hope it will be possible to launch such a venture this fall.

Finally, I should add that Nancy Macdonald, who has functioned in the demanding capacity of business manager of *Partisan Review* for the greater part of the past five years, is also severing connections with the magazine. Her reasons are about the same as those indicated above, and she will work with me on the new project. Both of us wish the new *Partisan Review* the best of luck.

To Phil Rahv

July 3, 1943

Congratulations on raising the money! Nancy and I feel a bit sad at getting out after all these years, but such are the fortunes of war. (I think I had a sneaking hope you would not get the money and that I would be the survivor, so to speak.) GLKM writes me you've urged him to continue with the magazine and suggests I consider also keeping on, and leading my political life "elsewhere."

That would be impossible, of course—though I would have no objection to writing a little for the new PR if the occasion presents itself—and if you want my stuff. And anyway Nancy and I are going to see what can be done about launching the kind of magazine we think the times require.

Enclosed is a letter of resignation, to go into the new issue. I've tried to keep it as impersonal and good-tempered as possible. I felt it was necessary, however, to be explicit as to the reasons I am now withdrawing. You'll understand, I'm sure, that one doesn't resign from a magazine with which one has been intimately connected for five years without making clear precisely why one is doing so.

Enclosed is also a copy for a one-page back issue ad, and also for a half-page exchange ad which I had arranged with Ivan Goll's new magazine. You can run or not run them as you see fit (though I'm afraid I did rather promise Goll, who is, as you know, very persistent).

Please keep my name on this next issue, since I helped edit it.

I meant to ask about the identity of the recipient of Luxemburg's prison letters before I left town, but forgot. You can find out by calling Rose Laub, at WA-9-5994 (217 W. 14 St.). Suggest you state in an editorial note, in any case, that these letters have not been published before in any language.

I just received the complete proof of my article. It looks about the right length—I cut and resorted it quite a bit. I'll send in corrections right away, direct to Schoen.

By the way, be sure to include that review by Dan Bell—it will mean a lot to him, and I believe I'm entitled to at least that much space under our one-third-politics division of the review section.

I sent in Schapiro's riposte several days ago. Hook, I think, must be given a chance to reply, though it will be OK with me if he doesn't.

Your arrangement with the Mercury sounds very good, on the pay side at least. And I suppose you will get all the new books, which on the whole should be fun.

Let me see proof on the resignation letter, please.

To Phil Rahv

July 16, 1943

Our letters must have crossed in the mail. Glad to finally hear from you.

I accept the omission of the point about popular culture from my letter. You're right, it was quite unfair in its implications. But the other change won't do. Makes no sense, for one thing, since PR has always been "in the main a cultural magazine." I don't insist on my old wording. Put it: "From now on *Partisan Review* will devote itself to cultural issues, leaving . . . etc." I assume of course it's not too late to make this change, since you could hardly alter the text of a letter signed by me without consulting me. You'd better head the letter "A RESIGNATION" or something—looks peculiar without a head.

You should have let me know long ago you don't want to run [Meyer] Schapiro's piece. He's rather disturbed about it, as am I. It was sent in over two weeks ago, after you wrote you'd "try to fit it in." I think we have an obligation to print it; Mike is an old and valued PR contributor, his letter is certainly on a printable level. [Sidney] Hook did attack him in a nasty way personally (everyone I've heard from or talked to thought Hook's tone very bad, much more personal and venomous than Mike's—and this includes people who didn't especially sympathize with Mike's position), and it's only editorial decency to give him space for a reply. I simply can make no sense of your criterion for printing or not printing it: namely, that we should print it "if he (Hook) wants to answer it." Why should it depend on that? Anyway, I think we should run it next issue (or rather you should, the editorial "we" being about to be fractured!) and should appreciate your letting me know right away what your plans are.[4]

A pleasant surprise for you: George apparently owes not $250 but $366.90 more. At least he wrote me recently to that effect. Nancy has asked him to send in the money, but he hasn't yet.

Nancy thinks it would ball things up too much to try to settle the transfer of the bank balance, etc. (including the business about the Foundation for Cultural Experiment) at long distance. She has the checkbook up here and has been sending out checks as needed. So wait till we get down, in mid-August, and meanwhile she will send out checks as Joan lets her know. You'd better jog up Morris on the $366 because Schoen wants to be paid.

Be sure to send me 5 or 6 issues, won't you?

P.S. Will it be OK with you and Will if I use the PR subscriber list to circularize for my new magazine (if any)? I assume it will, but bring up the matter to forestall possible future misunderstanding.

---

4. In the January/February 1942 issue, Sidney Hook wrote a devastating critique of what he saw as a revival of religious neo-orthodoxy in an article entitled "The New Failure of Nerve." He singled out the "frenzy of Kierkegaard" and Reinhold Niebuhr, who has successfully revived the doctrine of original sin as a political tool. Meyer Schapiro, using the pseudonym David Merian, responded with "The Nerve of Sidney Hook: Socialism and the Failure of Nerve," an exchange in the May/June 1943 issue. He denounced Hook as a sell-out and defended the angst of Niebuhr, Kierkegaard, and other religionists of despair as similar to the sensitivity of many modern artists. Macdonald tended to side with Schapiro in this debate because he distrusted Hook's mechanical faith in rationalism. He was already skeptical of Marxist determinism.

To Delmore Schwartz

July 21, 1943

I should have written you long ago. Sorry. We've been up here a month. It's very quiet. We see the Schapiros, half a mile off, and that's all. The other day we visited Brattleboro—first time we've seen a movie theatre or a drugstore in a month. Nancy is working on the involved, fascinating, and endless Negro Question. I'm slowly getting up steam in my study of the labor movement. And I've "discovered" (via Schapiro) two books: [Alexander] Herzen's memoirs (vol. 2), and Harold Frederick's *The Damnation of Theron Ware.*

Please forgive me for not writing you about the change-of-life at PR. Most of it happened while I was up here, and I figured the boys were probably keeping you informed. I've written a note of resignation, which will appear next issue along with my piece on democratic values (which I hope you will read, despite your ban on periodical reading). When Morris announced he wouldn't continue his subsidy beyond the next issue, I decided, as I imagine the boys did, too, that the magazine had better go all one way or the other. I've been sick of the eternal friction with the boys (and also of their eternal gloom and negativism) for a long time. So I suppose that if Phil could get backing for an all-literary mag, he and Will should take it over. Otherwise, Nancy and I would take over completely. Phil got the dough, as you must know. . . . Nancy and I will probably start something else this fall. I suppose you will become an editor of the "new" PR. I'll be curious to see what comes of it, though of course I myself regard the shift to culture as a cowardly retreat and nothing more dignified.

I would like to talk about the Rahv-Schapiro set-to with you. The report I had from Schapiro was that Rahv was the one that blew up, shouted, and behaved in a most boorish way. I must say from past experience that Rahv does tend to become very overbearing and monopolistic in a political discussion.

On *Genesis:* I bought and read the book. Delmore, you should ask yourself what you want to do. Go through the motions of writing "serious," "important," "experimental" poetry; or write what is real to you, what fills a need for you, as an individual, not as a performer for a certain audience (however sophisticated and learned—not that they are so damned much of either, really!)? The prose parts were good novel writing, often, although, overstylized and oversimplified for the most part. But at least a bite and humor and concreteness which conveyed a real experience. The poetry parts I found unreadable and, in fact, did not read after the first 100 pages (could not read). The versification was flaccid, monotonous; the speakers never clearly identified; the whole effect pompous and verbose. Intellectually, the trouble is that the comments made by the poetic ghosts are rarely necessary; the narrative carries its implications clearly enough, and the poetic commentaries merely raise the points to a congressional-oratory sort of level. (A Congress made up of Freud, Marx, etc., but still a Congress). On the whole, I agree with Goodman's review (though the form in which he communicates his ideas struck me, as I wrote you, as petty and "catty"). I thought Matthiessen in PR was bumbling and unperceptive— also it took the poem much too seriously. Delmore, why in hell don't you stop trying to be the Eliot of the Thirties and exploit your real talent: for satire, humorous, intimate, realistic description and commentary? *Genesis* is dead, believe me, a frog that burst in the effort to blow himself up as big as an ox. You should—if you want my opinion, which you've been gratis for many years now—write (1) lyrics (2) novels.

To Delmore Schwartz

August 13, 1943

Thank you for your letter of July 25. Once more our visit to Cambridge must be put off—sorry to have bothered you about it. A couple of days after I wrote you, I got a letter from G. L. K. Morris telling me the PR boys had composed a most unfriendly reply to my note of resignation and were even inclined to refuse Nancy and me a copy of the subscriber's list for use in starting our new magazine. Up till then I had innocently assumed the break was a friendly one—in fact, Phil had carefully avoided in his letters any adverse comment on my note of resignation and, of course, any hint of a blasting reply—or of trying to keep the PR list from us (as though Nancy hadn't created the damn thing!). Anyway, we had to go therefore direct to NYC, without a visit to Cambridge. Things are now patched up, we have the list, etc. We found the boys had taken the most fantastic legal and other precautions against (I suppose) a possible attempt on my part to "capture" PR! (Of course the first step in such a coup would be to go off to the country for the summer, leaving everything in the hands of one's adversaries.) Ah well. When Phil was reassured, he behaved in a more human fashion.

Phil says you disapproved of my note and approved of their reply. If so, I'm grieved. Their reply was abusive (as against the reasonable tone of my note), personal (I made no personal remarks), and false. Do you really think I wanted to reduce PR to a Trotskyite propaganda sheet, that either I or Trotsky have ever believed in subordinating culture to political interests (what I said was to political analysis, and the boys misquoted me and then smugly moralized for a paragraph), or that PR, under Rahv's direction, won't shy away from political articles more than it has in the past?

So it's "Mr. Delmar Schwartz" who joins the PR staff! That was an unfortunate slip, betraying just the academic touch I claim the boys' editing has. Mr., for Christ's sake! Why not Professor?

The enclosed is a counterreply by Schapiro to Hook's letter in May–June. Would you please read it and send it on to Phil with a note as to whether you think it should be printed as is, or cut, or not printed at all. Morris is for it as is, as am I. Phil hasn't officially made up his mind, but isn't keen about it. I think it should be printed because it's on a decently high level, because Schapiro is an old and valued PR contributor who has a right to the magazine's letter columns, and because in this kind of controversy freedom of expression should be given a wide margin.

Thank you for all you write about *Genesis*. I hope you are right and I am wrong about its genuine quality.

Nancy and I are sorry to hear that you and Gertrude are living apart, and we hope you will be together again soon as we are very fond of you both.

You are always welcome here if you can get a few days off. It's quiet as hell, the only sounds being the fall of pine cones in the immemorial woods and the discourse of M. Schapiro.

How did you like "The Future of Democratic Values"? (Now's your chance. . . .) Did it affect your views at all?

The Italian events are the most heartening to "our" side—if you're still on it—in many years. The people haven't forgotten—after twenty years!

Do you think you could find out by discreet inquiry why Thoreau's "Civil Disobedience" is included in the navy textbook? A very curious choice. Could it be a kind of Liberty League individualism, verging on anarchism, as the doctrine of the old-style Republican industrialists, in Hoover's day, used to? Would this perhaps illustrate the III law of the dialectic?

I'm doing some thinking about the new magazine. You'll doubtless contribute, if occasion offers, won't you? (Just as I'll contribute to PR.)

Dwight Macdonald and friends at the East 57th Street apartment of Mary McCarthy and Bowden Broadwater in the late 1940s. Front, Macdonald and Kevin McCarthy. Rear (from left), Broadwater, Lionel Abel, Elizabeth Hardwick, Miriam Chiaromonte, Nicola Chiaromonte, Mary McCarthy, John Berryman. (McCarthy Papers, Vassar College Library)

CHAPTER FOUR

||||||||||||||||||||||||||||||||||||||||||||||||||||||||||||||||||||||||||||||||||||||||||||||||||||||||||||||||||||||||||||||||||||||||||||||||||||||||

POLITICS AND THE SEARCH FOR RESPONSIBILITY, 1943–1949

"In a terrifying world, the root is man."

These are the *Politics* years. The correspondence records Macdonald's political deradicalization, his abandonment of Marxism, his increasingly vigorous anti-Stalinism to the point of obsession, his growing disillusionment with mass political movements. A growing weariness evident here not only reflects his political despair but the growing failure of his marriage. During this period the first of several affairs begin.

To Delmore Schwartz

September 30, 1943

I didn't reply to your letter of August 30 because it was so malicious and so clearly designed simply to hurt and humiliate me that there seemed little point in answering. There was also such a discrepancy between the provocation which my previous letter (quite unwittingly) offered, namely, the matter of [Paul] Goodman, and the abusive tone of your letter as to make me suspect that you had some deep-lying subjective motive unknown to me, perhaps that you have been storing up a whole series of slights and rebuffs and insults from me (again these being not deliberate or conscious, I assure you) and my remarks on the Goodman business, in the midst of a perfectly friendly letter, must have touched off the whole powder magazine.[1]

Anyway, I simply can't and won't carry on our relations on this plane. I'm less thick-skinned than you probably realize, and it is upsetting in the extreme to be abused in this way by someone I consider a friend. I'll neither defend myself nor make a counterattack. The field of battle is all yours.

As to the new magazine—it is definitely going ahead, and I've raised already most of the funds needed to get it under way. First issue, I hope, will appear December 1, and I also hope, will contain something from you. As to the Review of Reviews you suggest, I'm not sure it would fit into the formula, which is, roughly, to cover the social-political scene and to treat of cultural matters only in one of two ways: either popular culture, or else as symptomatic of social and historical trends. In other words, no purely literary criticism, or consideration of literary criticism in itself. There are many other magazines, including PR, which print literary criticism, so there seems no point in duplicating. But if what you have in mind would fit in, by all means do it. With absolute freedom to say what you like, of course, that being the editorial policy I'll follow with all contributors.

However, I'd much rather you wrote a piece inaugurating the Popular Culture department. Why not take a couple of days to quarry something out of the 60 pages of notes you already have on the subject? I'm placing much reliance on Popular Culture to sell the magazine, and I'd like to begin with something really strong, such as I know you would do.

Deadline for the first issue will be Nov. 10. Let me know what you can do, if anything.

As for our personal relations, please make up your mind whether I'm friend or foe and behave according to one or the other hypothesis. If you think I'm the fatheaded prig your letter of August 30 describes with such gusto, then I really don't see why you want to have any relations with me—or why I should want to have any with you. Friendship requires a minimum of mutual respect.

1. The tension between Schwartz and Macdonald stemmed from Dwight's defense of Paul Goodman's critical review of Delmore's long poem *Genesis*. Macdonald generally agreed with Goodman's critique and also judged the poem "unreadable, flaccid, monotonous, the whole effect pompous and verbose." He was also angry that Schwartz had not made a strong statement against the war, whereas Goodman had. Macdonald and Schwartz often squabbled but remained close friends.

To Dinsmore Wheeler

November 29, 1943

. . . Didn't you get the prospectus I sent? I want, in fact, to combine the best features of Time, PR, New Essays, and a three-ring circus. Also, I don't share your high esteem of [Paul] Mattick as a theoretician; [Karl] Korsch is the only one of the New Essays crowd whose stuff I admire.

Yes, wrote a piece on the convention, it's in the current *Common Sense* (after hot argument with Hertzberg who didn't like critical attitude towards that boy scout labor faker [Walter] Reuther).

The [Lillian] Symes piece, and the [Rosa] Luxemburg letters, were holdovers from the old PR. My colleagues, as you might imagine, weren't enthusiastic about either.

For Christ's sake, Wheeler, get the lead out of your pants and read "The Future of Democratic Values"! Who did you think I wrote it for?[2]

Way to understand the paradox of a socialist fighting for the right of Negroes to die more often in a lousy war like this one is to think of it as a question of status. Making the Negroes do labor battalion stuff and keeping them out of danger is just as humiliating to them as jimcrowing them in buses, and is felt as such by them. Also, there's real social dynamite in training Negroes to fight with planes and guns, not clean out latrines. I'm sure this is the big reason for army's policy. On the other hand, it's true there's something odd about fighting army jimcrow on this basis. It's a complicated age we live in, and if one is to act at all, one must decide what ends one wants and hew to the line letting the chips fall in often peculiar places.

To William B. Hesseltine [University of Wisconsin historian]:

December 8, 1943

I might as well get it over with without any polite shilly-shallying, and confess that the Progressive piece isn't at all what I'd hoped for. As you can see from the copious and frank notations, almost every paragraph seems to have weak spots. The general tone is not at all critical or even serious—it reads like a bit of campaign literature. I don't at all object to your praising the Progressives—only to the fact that your praise is so unconvincing. To be convincing, the piece would have to be much more factual with some discussion of the concrete specific po-

2. Macdonald's essay appeared in the *Partisan Review* (July/August 1943). It was an eloquent denunciation of the meaningless futility of the war and a stout defense of socialist collectivism as the only way to humanize the prevailing bureaucratic collectivism that was developing throughout the Western world. He was very proud of this piece as a part of the "Failure of Nerve" series initiated by Sidney Hook.

litical program of the party (beyond the fact it is for sane, decent Common Man). And it would have to try to meet some of the more basic criticisms that can be made of the party, instead of sliding over them with phrases.

Also, I don't understand you when you say that you are a Socialist but that you can't criticize Progressives for not being Socialists too since "they never claimed they were." You can certainly show that in not being Socialists they get into some very peculiar and undesirable fixes, just as Roosevelt's New Deal did, and that their program is one of superficial reform which won't work in a crisis period like this one. (In fact, that's one reason they are in such a weak state today.) Instead, you seem to take them completely on their own terms and write entirely with a Progressive frame of reference.

If you want to recast the piece so as to answer some of the questions and meet the objections noted, fine. Please believe me—it's not the pro-Progressive slant I object to, it's the superficiality and (in places) cheap campaign slogans.

Enclosed is a revised circular for the mag, just off the press. Thought it might interest you. Awfully sorry about this business, but what can I do? I have to call them as I see them. Do rework the piece if you're still interested in it (and if you agree my criticisms have some validity). In any case, I do hope you will still want to write the full-dress article on the South, at some later date.

To Al Goldman ([labor lawyer and Trotsky's attorney during the Dewey hearings in Mexico; he was indicted and imprisoned for violation of the Smith Act in 1941]

August 7, 1944

. . . There's some compensation in the presence, a mile away, of the Nicola Chiaromontes.[3] Do you know him? He's a wonderful fellow—deeply cultured in the European way, very intelligent, and honest. He's a kind of Proudhonian anarchist. We have many discussions about Marxism (with me in the defense attorney's role—you'd probably disavow me!). Jim Farrell was up staying with him a couple of days; Jim and I had a terrific row the first night he arrived about politics (with and without a capital P), but by the time he left all was forgiven on both sides. (Though differences still exist.) Chiaromonte is now engaged in a long correspondence with Meyer Schapiro, as to the relative merits of Marx

---

3. Nicola Chiaromonte became Macdonald's closest friend. He was an Italian independent radical who had fought in the Spanish Civil War and was the inspiration for Malraux's character Scali in his novel *Man's Hope*. Among many members of the New York intellectual community, Chiaromonte was seen as Dwight's guru. William Phillips once charged that Macdonald had sought out a "disciple who would tell him what to think." Their long correspondence puts the lie to that charge. Nevertheless Chiaromonte did have a profound influence on Macdonald.

and Herzen (and Proudhon), the alleged (by C.) oversystematization of Marxism, the problem of political power, and socialist and other weighty matters. I find myself somewhat in the middle of the discussion, though if I had to choose a side, it would be C's, I think.

The magazine is going very well. One thing that constantly surprises me is the number of objections we get, from readers who seem to be quite sincere liberals or radicals and not fellow travelers, to criticism of the Soviet Union. Apologies for Stalinism which I had thought had been disposed of years ago are still raked up. And a new tendency is observable, new that is since the Trials period: instead of denying the facts about tyranny, class divisions, low living standards, etc., as used to be done in the old days, these facts are now admitted, even taken for granted, and the further argument is made: what do you expect, human nature is "fallible," Rome wasn't built in a day, only sterile "perfectionists" refuse to compromise "realistically," etc. This seems to me very significant, showing the demoralization and the loss of hope of the left. I've got a letter, five single-spaced pages, from a man in Ohio who describes himself as "a middle-aged factory worker" (and obviously, from his style of writing and arguing, is not a trained intellectual) which argues the case for Stalinism in those terms. It will probably appear in the next issue, with a rejoinder by myself. The military success of the Red Army, plus the increasingly dismal aspect of Allied foreign policy, makes people, it would seem, cling all the more desperately to the illusion that socialism can be advanced via the USSR. In England it's much worse: had a letter from George Orwell the other day telling me that the *Manchester Evening News* (published by the *Guardian*, much the most honest bourgeois paper in England, acc. To Orwell) had rejected a review he did for them of Laski's new book, apparently because Orwell criticized Laski's whole-hog acceptance of Stalinism and ventured to point out a few blemishes in the USSR. (He enclosed the review, which I thought much too favorable to Stalinism!) He writes that England is in the grip of a "Russomania" which makes it impossible to publish even the mildest criticism of Russia in any of the big papers.

Well, perhaps this is long enough for now—I note by the printed instruction sheet there is a limit on length. I'll write you next week, and hope to hear from you before too long on how you are, what you are thinking and studying, etc. (I quite understand you can't write often.)

Nancy sends her very best, so do I—and give our regards also to Comrades Cannon, Dunne, Morrow, and Dobbs (all of your band that I know personally).

To Al Goldman

August 18, 1944

Trust you received my first letter, written last week.

It's been incredibly hot here, a real drought, grass seared brown, trees limp and faded. I can only imagine what it must be like in the city. How have you fared out there?

I've been reading the Marx-Engels correspondence for the first time; an exciting experience; it's very rich and lively. I wonder if this edition, the International Publishers selection, is politically edited. Does the complete German Collection give a much different picture? I don't read German, unhappily. One of my favorite remarks is Marx's to the effect that a good polemic must be both brutal and subtle. Trotsky knew this and practiced it; his followers have mostly specialized in the first quality only.

I'm growing more and more worried by the political backwardness and softness of us Americans—only the British surpass us. Two current indications: (1) the recent convention of the newborn Michigan Commonwealth Federation, which, from the accounts in the *Militant* and *Labor Action*, was a rather dismal fizzle; they didn't even dare put up a candidate for governor, apparently so as to avoid conflict with the PAC; and their statement of principles was awful double-talk; and this is the best, the very farthest reach of radicalism and independent action which the American Labor movement has produced in this crisis year! (2) This morning's mail brought in a clipping from the N.Y. *Post* quoting Isaac McNatt, one of those 18 Seabees who got such a dirty deal from the Navy (you may have seen his "I Was a Seabee" in the June *Politics*) to this effect: "I am appealing directly to President Roosevelt in the firm belief that he, great humanitarian that he is, will not fail me." McNatt, whom I know personally, is an intelligent chap and seems to be quite militant about fighting for his rights. Yet such a remark! I've written him a letter asking how come, giving the many reasons why FDR is no friend of the Negroes—hope he answers it; I'd really like to understand how such illusions can exist.

I've been talking of late with Nick Chiaromonte about the very important and interesting question of the responsibility of peoples. To what degree—to take the most currently hot issue—are the German people "responsible" for the absolutely inconceivably horrible mass executions of millions of Jews in the death camps? This involves the whole question of cultural conditioning, the formation of special groups for special tasks (the murders apparently are carried out by elite guards who are systemically brutalized by scientific methods for years before they become inhuman enough to do this kind of work), the powerlessness of the individual, and even of vast groups, before the concentration of state power in a modern "advanced" society, what the masses can and cannot be expected to do in opposition to their rulers (for instance, those who believe the Germans are responsible as a people for the horrors of Nazism say, "Why don't they make a revolution, then, if they are really serious about their objections to Nazism?"), etc. Nick suggests it might be well to try to formulate the problem in detail and then ask a number of people to discuss it.

The widespread feeling over here that the Japanese are, as a people, sub-human—there's of course much more of this kind of hatred than anti-German feeling—may produce terrible consequences in the next few years. In this connection, I think the following paragraph, from G. B. Sansom's *Japan: A Short Cultural History*, a remarkably good book, is to the point:

"Throughout Japanese history until the restoration of 1868 the whole trend of social ethics, both in the native tradition and in the Chinese systems of philosophy as borrowed by the Japanese and adapted to their own requirements, has been to emphasize the duties of the individual and to neglect his rights. The group came first. Loyalty, other obligations. This strong sense of social discipline was not seriously impaired by the emergence of the Japanese people from isolation in the middle of the 19th century. It was preserved, partly by the habit of behavior, and partly by the deliberate choice of the leaders of Japan who, when they were converting their country into a modern state, took care not to destroy those features of the feudal tradition which would serve their purposes. Their object was to unify Japan, to increase its strength and its wealth; and they knew the value of obedience . . . the culminating phase (was that) in which the leaders of the country were able to impose upon the people a full-fledged worship of the state . . . it is interesting to speculate as to how much of the people's active consent to totalitarian rule derives from ancient habits and how much is due to recent and intensive indoctrination. On the answer to this question depends the prospect of changes in the nature of political thinking in Japan after the war."

Similarly, one might say that Stalin has preserved as much as possible of the old half-Asiatic Russian traditions which Ivan and Peter the Great also exploited and preserved—that short history by B. H. Sumner (Louis Clair reviewed it in the last *Politics*) suggests there is more of this tradition in Stalin's system than we Marxists have been aware of. I wish I knew more about anthropology.

The war is moving fast these days, isn't it? The *U.S. News* reports that optimists in Washington think Germany will collapse in one month, while "pessimists" think it will take four. The news that it was General Patton who was responsible for the brilliant stroke that broke the stalemate in Normandy pleases me a lot. He's a straight fascist type, and he's also the best general (it would seem) we have. I can't wait to see the liberal weeklies draw the logical conclusion from these facts. . . .

To Owen Campbell[4]

November 1944

I regret that I am only one person, and hence incapable of serious political comment. Being a single individual has been a weakness of mine since birth, and I doubt if anything can be done about it at this late date. But this, of course, does not excuse *Politics* for being so unlike, say, *"The Militant,* which has indeed most successfully eliminated vacillating refinements of thought and over-scrupulousness. It has also achieved a high degree of crudity, as for that matter, has Comrade Campbell himself.

To Victor Serge

February 27, 1945

. . . Our political views, my dear Victor, seem to be diverging rapidly. I am convinced that you are making a great mistake (as you no doubt are convinced about me). It pains me to have you speak well of Ruth Fischer, whom I know and whom I think is morally impossible and intellectually half-crazy on the subject of Stalinism. (She is an intelligent, in some ways brilliant person—but anti-Stalinism has become an obsession with her.) The *Network* seems to me on the same level as the Stalinist press, except with reverse political content. How can one adopt such methods—slander, amalgams, hysterical and vulgar abuse, wild generalizations on the basis of scanty data—to fight the CP? It simply makes one into the image of what one fights. I'm also very sorry to see you becoming a regular contributor of *The New Leader,* which is an extreme right wing . . . paper, of a low intellectual level and which has become the organ of exhausted and bourgeoisified former leftists like Max Eastman (did you see his polemic against me and *Politics?*) and Sidney Hook. Once again *The New Leader* has no political ideas or principles except anti-Stalinism. . . . Ruth Fisher[5] (about whom I hear some very ugly stories, from several independent sources), the N.L. is willing to make a bloc with anyone—and specifically with our ultra-reactionary State Department in order to fight Stalinism. The only reason I can see for someone like yourself, with your past record and your fine moral and intellectual sensitivity to the real needs and interests of the masses, to

4. Campbell had written complaining that the "running of a magazine called *Politics* and dedicated to politics by one man, all by himself, is, in a sense, highly ludicrous." *Politics,* November 1944, p. 318.

5. Ruth Fisher was the sister of Heinz and Gerhardt Eisler. She had turned away from communism and become a virulent anti-Stalinist. She testified before the House Committee on Un-American Activities that her brother was guilty of spying for the Soviets and murder.

accept such a political milieu is that anti-Stalinism is becoming your own basic political principle.

Now of course Stalinism is a great danger in postwar Europe, perhaps *the* great danger. But just as you didn't adopt a "lesser evil" theory in fighting fascism in the thirties (which was then the greatest menace), just as we didn't accept any ally in the fight, but insisted on conducting the fight in accordance with our general socialist principles and with a view to the progress of the working class and masses and not simply to the military defeat at all costs of the Nazis—so now in Europe I think we must have a more flexible, subtle, and sophisticated ("realistic" if you will) policy than simply damning every popular movement in which the Stalinists play a leading part.

I wish I could talk this over face to face. It is, of course, a great problem and one which cannot be easily solved. . . .

To Victor Serge

March 30, 1945

. . . Sorry you don't want me to send your MS to Orwell in London. I don't agree with you about there being less freedom of expression in England than here. On the contrary, there are two English liberal political weeklies—the *Economist* and *Tribune* (for which Orwell writes)—which are much franker and more critical about the war and about Russia than any of our own liberal journals. Also, the English have (1) a higher cultural level, more of an intelligentsia than we do, and (2) a much more deeply rooted tradition of free speech and thought. These factors would also be in favor of your book being published over there. Finally, Orwell, who is an influential journalist and editor, has actually asked to see your book for Secker & Warburg—no publisher here has shown that much interest. Of one thing, anyway, I'm now sure: no American publisher will touch your book at present; I've tried half a dozen, also the Polish firm of Roy, without the slightest success. Furthermore, the American publishing business is much more mass-commercial than the English is; publishers think in terms of big sales, because they have higher operating and advertising costs; your book is on too serious a cultural level for the American public in general; it might be that even if the political situation changes, this would still prevent it being published over here. (In England in 1940, for example, two books were brought out, somewhat of the nature of yours as to socialism— [Paul] Froelich's *Rosa Luxemburg* and [Anton] Ciliga's *Russia Enigma*—which never appeared over here.)

For all these reasons, I think you are mistaken in not having me send MS to Orwell. But I shall of course abide by your instructions.

Thank you for your frank and friendly response to my criticisms of your present political position. I was sure that you would take my disagreement in a friendly way (as it was of course intended to be taken). I wish we could meet and talk about all this face to face.

I accept your objection to the tone of my polemic against Eastman—in fact, I regret that tone myself; I suppose I was momentarily irritated into adopting it by the tone of his original article. But that's no excuse. Our personal relations, by the way, are still good. I have always considered Eastman honest and personally decent; it is his mental processes which shock me!

I enclose the part of a letter I have just sent to [Jean] Malaquais (who has submitted, by the way, a really excellent article on Louis Aragon, which will appear shortly in the magazine). The letter is self-explanatory; I show it to you so that you may not feel I am discussing things behind your back. The rupture between you and the others—word of which has come to us from several sources—distresses me. From what I know of all of your political ideas and personalities, I cannot believe there is a real basis for such extreme feelings on either side, and must attribute it to the terrible isolation you are all forced to live in. I don't want to presume to moralize, but believe me, my dear Victor, no one gains by such breaks and ruptures. Is there no possibility of reconciliation?

Again, my best wishes to Laurette and yourself.

To Art Wiser [pacifist, conscientious objector, and communitarian]

January 16, 1946

It is hard to write you because our situations are so different. You have too much leisure, I too little; you seem—from what Mary writes me—to be thinking and enriching your internal life, while of late my own existence has become busy and externalized to an almost frightening extent. Both of us are alike in this at least, that we are dominated by external compulsions (though in my case there is an appearance of free will and choice).

Mary just wrote me a long and very informative letter about your life in prison. She says you asked whether I know why the discrepancy between the official count of dead in air raids in Germany and Japan and the newspaper accounts. I don't, and have long intended to look into it, for I was struck by it too.

Am I wrong in detecting a Farberish influence on one of the poems you have been writing—the one beginning "A riffle, a raffle"?

The reason I'm so occupied now is that the magazine is flourishing almost too much, and on top of that I am trying to finish the final draft of *The Root Is Man*, which I actually first projected over two years ago and which will have to at least outline a clear and consistent position on the whole crisis we are living in. Questions like Marxism, the scientific method, the role of the working class in social change, etc. And on top of that, we were imprudent enough to reprint 10,000 copies of my article on European starvation in the last issue. We felt we had to do it because the suffering is so great over there and the US Government has done so disgracefully little to relieve it. But it was rash, for 10,000 pamphlets are quite a lot, and so I've been wrapping parcels frantically.

By the way, an old comrade of yours helped me a bit yesterday—Olcutt Sanders. He's just back from Puerto Rico and is bound for Texas, where he will be field secretary for the Friends. . . .

A number of people have been much impressed by your letter to a Judge in the last issue (the printer dropped out the word "a," giving it a curiously clipped title.) They welcomed—as I did—the assumption behind your whole approach: that the state's demands on the individual may be, and indeed must be, rejected if they conflict with one's own basic morality. This is the line that Jackson's indictment at the Nuremberg trials took; practically, it is limited there to the Nazis and their generals; but Jackson was naive enough, or fuzzy-minded enough, to state as a general principle that the individual must be responsible for a decision to obey the state, and cannot plead "orders" or "legal duty" if his actions are immoral. It remains to be seen (or rather, we know quite well already the answer) what Jackson will do after he finishes with the Nazis. We have a little satirical piece on this in the new (Jan.) issue.

I suppose you've read by now Simone Weil's article on *The Iliad*. The response to it has surprised me; I thought it was a great political article, dealing with the moral questions implicit in the terrible events one reads about in every day's newspaper, which was why I played it up so prominently in the issue. But I had not expected such an overwhelming reaction from readers. Nothing I've printed yet seems to have made so deep an impression. The only people who didn't understand how such an article had a place in a political journal were— and I think this is profoundly significant—all of them Marxists. To a Marxist, an analysis of human behavior from an ethical point of view is just not "serious"— even smacks a little of religion.

Write me when you have time. You'll hear from me soon again.

To Arthur Steig [*Politics* reader who complained that the magazine was too tolerant of Proudhon's anti-Semitism]

January 16, 1946

Have you ever read Marx's "On the Jewish Question" (in Stenning's translation, *Selected Essays* by Karl Marx)? I'm told that anti-Semites have been buying up that volume to get it. Also have you read the Marx-Engels letters with their use of the word "jew" as a slighting epithet?

Marx, like Proudhon, identified to some extent the jew with finance capital, and drew, also like P, unflattering conclusions from this fact. Are we to say therefore that M and P were precursors of fascism—were even anti-Semites in our modern sense of the word? When you imply that P—at least—was such, and that Chiaromonte is Jesuitical in pointing out that the jew-capital amalgam had some real foundation, aren't you overlooking the historical factor? Why was it, after all, that these two great socialist theoreticians entertained such ideas (prejudices if you like)—and one of them a jew himself at that!? Is it not because in the earlier phase of capitalism the Jewish financier played a big role, really was a force for evil (if you're a socialist)? What was then a prejudice (with some justification, as C points out) has now become a monstrous and cold-blooded and pathological lie; what was then a small matter—like someone today saying they detest Scotsmen—now has become a central historical issue. But you should be able to see that the different historical setting makes all the difference in the real meaning of P's (and M's) anti-Semitic attitudes.

See Engels's long letter of April 19, 1890 (pp. 469–472) in the "Selected Correspondence" for a good historical sketch of anti-Semitism; or perhaps you know it already.

And—as before—let me urge you to keep your shirt on—talking about the "murder of Jews" as a result of C's defense of P is just adolescent.

To Clem Greenberg

February 11, 1946

Nick Chiaromonte has told me of your attack on Lionel Abel. He has seen Lionel and says his face is bruised from several blows. As you know, I rang you up this morning to make sure that it was you who began the fight. You told me you had hit first (and most) but said that Abel had insulted you. I gather from Nick, however, that you were plenty insulting yourself. And anyway, it seems to me uncivilized to end a verbal clash with physical violence, as you did here, and as you have done on other occasions.

You told me on the phone that this is your personal affair with Abel, and none of my business. Perhaps. But since Lionel is a friend of mine, I think it is proper for me to tell you that I consider your attack on him a cowardly (you weigh about twice as much as he does) and brutal action. And that I don't see how it will be possible for me in future to have any personal relations with you.

To Clem Greenberg

February 15, 1946

I'd like to withdraw the remark about breaking off personal relations. It was hasty and unwarranted. After talking to Harold, Nancy, and William, I realize that the affair was more complicated than it had seemed to me, the chief complication being that Lionel to some extent degraded himself to your level by accepting your challenge to fight. So I don't want you to think I am passing judgment on you but rather on your specific act. Also, so far as I am conscious, I have come of late years to dislike passing moral judgments on individuals, and indeed hesitated writing you in the first place because it did seem to me a little pompous and priggish of me to set myself up to judge you. I decided to do it, however, and don't regret the decision, because of the extreme abhorrence I have to physical violence in itself, and also because of the repugnance I felt, and feel, to a person giving a beating to another person in every way much his physical inferior. Your action I still feel is inexcusable, but I also feel, as a friend of yours of long standing, that it doesn't so to speak sum you up.

(copy to Lionel)

To Norman Thomas

March 20, 1946

Although I favor asking the Nuremberg Tribunal to look into the Moscow Trial charges, I cannot sign your appeal because it commits the signers to the view that the Tribunal is a court of justice, worthy of respect.

The "respectful" attitude of the signers and the "honorable" nature of the court are emphasized. The signers "look for justice" to the court. "The Tribunal has the opportunity, in line with the task assigned to it, to exercise the spirit of full justice to" Trotsky and Sedov.

Since I have no respect for the court, consider it not honorable but dishonorable, think it either naive or disingenuous to look to it for justice, and think that rendering justice is not at all "in line with the task assigned to it" — for all these reasons, I cannot sign the letter.

I would gladly sign the appeal by Wells, Koestler, and other English intellectuals which you enclose, for this is quite cold and objective and gives no implication of approval of or confidence in the court in general.

I should like to say why this implication was needlessly and gratuitously given to the letter. And to suggest that a revised version be prepared which commits the signers only to the point at issue: the investigation of documents relating to the Moscow Trial charges.

P.S. I am especially puzzled by the letter's endorsement of the Nuremberg court because I know that at least two of the original endorsers listed in your note view the court in pretty much the same way I do.

To Albert Camus

May 17, 1946

. . . I don't need to tell you that your proposals—for an international magazine and the formation of groups of individuals in various countries committed to some statement of principles—attract me very much. They are the first practical suggestions for activity which seem to me to offer some possibility of taking me where we want to go.

The reason that I'd like to read carefully your Columbia [University] speech again, and discuss it with you—and the reason I hope you will have a chance to read soon the first 3 or 4 pages of my own *Root Is Man*—is because I feel that before we can begin as serious an undertaking as you suggest, we must get to know just how each of us sees the problem and what kind of activity we would favor, etc.[6] At present I don't feel clear enough on this. For example, you took part in the Resistance, and I gather you feel (I may be wrong) even now that this violence was permissible. I'm not sure that one can really draw a line anywhere as to violence; that is, I'm coming to think violence is a means that corrupts the end under any circumstances. This is the sort of difference—if it exists—that we must be aware of and if possible resolve.

Another thing that's occurred to me: would a big publisher like Gallimard support a magazine that would—if it is to fulfill the function we have in mind—very probably get them into trouble with the authorities? For example, if our magazine were being published right now, I'd propose a strong article against the denial of free speech to Trotskyists and anarchists by the present French government. We might even offer each of these groups some space in each issue of the French edition of our magazine, to print the political material the police won't allow them to print in their own papers. This might mean suppression of us. Would Gallimard stand for this sort of thing?

We must also talk about first steps practically, before you go back. Perhaps the best way to discover just what each of us thinks will be to begin to work together towards the goal. The very first step would seem to be the pamphlet stating our reasons for rejecting the traditional large-scale mass-historical kind of activity and our ideas on how to make a new approach from the bottom, from the level of personal relations and issues. Shall this be a number of statements each by a different person? Or a single statement, the product of you, Nick [Chiaromonte], myself, and whatever other people any of us want to ask to take

6. On March 28, 1946, Camus spoke to a crowd of twelve hundred in the McMillin Theater on the Columbia University campus. The thrust of his talk was that there was no substantial distinction between the victors and the vanquished in the war. It was a world of efficiency and extraction where everything was permitted. Macdonald, however, was not sure that Camus condemned violence absolutely, which was the position he was currently holding.

a hand? In the latter case, which I favor, some one person must write the thing, editing and adapting the others' ideas, etc. I think you would be the best person. Could you and would you do it?

Another point: cannot we begin right now, you in *Chroniques* (or whatever it is to be called) and I in *Politics* to exchange ideas and articles? You could send me the advance proofs of an article by yourself or someone else which you are about to publish in *Chroniques* and which you think should be known to American readers, and I could do the same. In this way we could learn to work together, could exchange ideas and keep in touch, and could lay the foundations for the international audience and the sense of international communication we'll need to get the magazine started. This has the advantage of beginning in a small, unpretentious, practical way.

To Mr. Ludowyk [*Politics* reader]

June 28, 1946

. . . Re: the 4th International. I was for two years a member of the American Trotskyists, but got out in 1941 because they seemed to me authoritarian in organization and politically sterile. I've never regretted my decisions, and feel farther from them than ever. As *The Root Is Man* will show you (I'm sending you the 2 issues with it in by first-class mail) . . . it is my opinion that serious political activity towards socialism is not now possible on a party or a mass basis and that we must begin again in a much more modest, and directly personal, way. I've heard about the Ceylonese Trotskyists—the movement is strong there, I gather, at least relative to its weakness elsewhere. The split you mention was probably between followers of the official US Trotskyists (led by [James Patrick] Cannon), who control the IV Int., and those of the Workers Party Trotskyists (led by [Max] Shachtman). I belonged to the latter, in fact went through the 1940 split here which produced the two factions; the Workers Party people are very much more decent, democratic, and intelligent than the official group, which here in USA is almost Stalinist in policies and in its organizational practices. I'd strongly advise you not to get connected with them, at least. And not to join either for that matter, for reasons which I try to make clear in part 2 of *The Root Is Man.*

To Daniel Bell

July 1, 1946

. . . To some extent, part 2 of the *Root* will give you an idea of my present thinking on the absolute-value problem and also the question of political action today. You are right about the necessity of redefining Justice and other values in the light of concrete historical conditions, but there must also be an absolute, nonhistorically relative content to be redefined. Also, unless one clings to such an absolute content, one is at the mercy of events, and must accept Stalinism (if one lives in Russia) or USA progressivism (if here). More and more I come up against the fact that we must face and live with contradictions of this kind (Justice is both historically relative, as Marx said it was, and absolute, as Plato did), must live dangerously intellectually in a way which the Marxians and Deweyans, with their scientific monism, shrink from doing; their attitude, too confident in one way and too timid in another, seems to me 19th century and not appropriate today.

To Mr. Hardisca [*Politics* reader]

July 15, 1946

Thanks for your letter. The *Rubiat* is a great poem—or rather, a great tradition—but I don't think one should base a political philosophy on it. if people are as irrational as you think they are, then we're cooked. To edit a *Politics* which would lure 5 million readers by preaching a new religious revival would bore the hell out of me. So I hope you're wrong about people.

To Mary McCarthy

August 24, 1946

. . . No excuse [for not writing] except that for some reason I seem to have less time here than in the city. Writing and editorial chores take a lot of time, more than they should: this summer has not proved at all fertile for me, don't know why—one seems to run into such barren spells, at least I do; but with a monthly one just cannot afford them. . . . The social life this summer has been terrific, too much really. We see people almost every evening somewhere, much more than in the city. It's foolish, for the bloom gets rubbed off social occasions when they become as habitual as this, and it becomes a kind of athletic performance. . . . You probably want some news first of all about Ruel [Wilson, Mary McCarthy's son with Edmund Wilson]. He and Mike get on much better than they did last year, which I think is partly because Ruel seems much happier and more outgoing than he did last year (and partly because Mike too is in a more elevated state of mind). Ruel's an awfully nice kid, and I think it's done him a lot of good to be with you alone last winter. I've had no opportunity of observing him with Edmund (we seem to be on his blacklist along with the Walkers[7]; at least he's never had us, or even Mike, around, and appears hurried and

---

7. Charles and Adelaide Walker. Charles Walker wrote a book on the life of a steelworker; Adelaide was an actress. They often attended the same parties on Cape Cod as Dwight and Nancy.

constrained whenever I run into him on the street), but from what others say, Edmund treats him "correctly" on the whole but with no warmth or understanding. He doesn't seem to feel any attachment to Edmund, certainly nothing as compared to his feelings for you. It's a great pity his year should have to be divided. . . . The car has run beautifully, except for a crankiness on hills (stalling, difficulty in starting again. Only one flat (I've now got a lovely hydraulic jack). Steering wheel still has play, but not too badly. . . . Had dinner at Dos Passos other night, dull; DP has become a simple Republican, scared to death of Russia and communism, fattish and complacent. . . . We spent an evening at the Matsons with George Grosz, the painter; he got drunk, abused socialism and art, praised Hollywood and moneymaking; pathetic because violence of his attack showed how little he can believe in it (or in the US business culture he wants to merge himself into). . . . In D and G you see the wreckage of the leftism of the 20's; they're lost without a movement; memento mori. . . . Must stop now to go to a beach picnic—The C's [Colebrooks], Joan Colebrook, the Berrymans. As usual, cold grey day. . . . We hear from Ruel that you left Paris for Italy several weeks ago, maybe you are now en route home. . . . We missed you a lot—Cape society lacks something without you.

To Daniel Bell

November 26, 1946

You seem genuinely surprised by my lack of cordiality on the phone. But why? You don't answer letters, you don't even reply to an invitation to stay with us in the country, you don't bother to do a small favor and advise me on that Ceylon college opening. And then when you do finally write, you write a letter which—this will probably surprise you, too: you are obtuse on such matters— made me sore as hell and had the same effect on Nancy (before we had exchanged a word on the subject).

The reason your letter irritated and depressed me was that it was nothing but a lengthy and detailed account of your own little academic busy-nesses, and appeared to both of us to be full of complacency and self-satisfaction. Not a word about the Ceylon business (which you've evidently forgotten completely), nothing that might relate us in the context of either friendship or interest in ideas. Just a smug retailing of your doubtless high-powered activities, in few of which I could take much interest.

I drew the conclusion that, no doubt without being quite aware of it yourself, you had made a snug career, or were making one, in the U of C and other reputable environs, and that this catalog, unaccompanied by any show of interest in the kind of world I still live in, was meant to tell me: here's the kind of thing I'm devoting myself to, so you see there's not much in common between us any longer. When I added this impression to your avoidance of *Politics* in favor of lousy (both politically and intellectually) sheets like *New Leader* and *Antioch* [*Review*] as a way of communicating via the printed page; and when I read in your letter that you consider working for the Third Party group a sacrificial labor of idealism—then I decided your letter was a signpost at the crossroads, if you will excuse the metaphor.

It appears I was wrong about the tone of your letter—that it was not meant to express any personal break or disinterest. Good—I don't like feuding either. But let's not kid ourselves—there is much less in common now between us than there was several years ago. I haven't changed much, that is, so far as my attitude towards society goes. But I think you have—or at least that a streak of careerism which always bothered me about you has widened a lot. It's not that you teach at Chicago—heavens, one must eat, and I've never even as a Trotskyist made such silly points. But that (and I refer again to your letter) you seem to accept it, to have become a serious academic type, to have, in a word, found your niche in this rotten system. (Thus you consider it an idealistic, even rather bohemian and revolutionary action on your part to have taken a post at Chicago because you turned down a better job at *Time* to do so. Now really, Dan!)

Well, why should I lecture you. Maybe I'm all wrong, and certainly I'm not such a model of virtue myself. But anyway that's how it looks to me. I just don't see that we have much in common; we've come to live in different worlds, and I think you'll realize it yourself later if you don't now.

I wouldn't have written this much if I weren't still personally fond of you, I suppose.

To Simone de Beauvoir

February 12, 1947

After we talked on the phone several things occurred to me.

(1) The book is one I should have given you with the others. It's generally considered "a minor work" but it's a personal favorite of mine among Hawthorne's writings. I think you will enjoy it. The first half, about Brook Farm, gives a wonderful sense of the atmosphere of the best period of our history—between 1800 and 1860.

(2) Two people who might be worth looking up in California are: Carey McWilliams, who knows more about the class struggle there and especially about the migratory farm workers than anyone else; don't know his address—and don't know him personally—but you could get it through either John Steinbeck or McWilliams's publishers, Little Brown. The other—quite a different type to say the least—is Kenneth Rexroth, an eccentric and genial poet who lives at 692 Wisconsin Street in San Francisco; he is the center of a little group

of anarchist-bohemians; this is the only intellectual group, so far as I know, on the whole West Coast; so they're of interest, if only by default.

I hope you will keep a travel journal, and I need hardly say that I'd be delighted to print it in *Politics* if you want to. No one knows anything about the USA over here—we have to find out from you people! . . .

To Paul Beeck

February 28, 1947

Thanks for helping get people to send packages to Germany, and for circulating the German Catastrophe. . . .

Your reference to that earlier snide crack of yours about me was most handsome, also. I was amused rather than annoyed by that crack, as the main point seemed to be that I'm a snob (which I can assure you I am not) because I am of an upper-middle-class family and went to prep school. That struck me as funny that this charge in itself was snobbish—the kind of proletarian snobbery that the left has been cursed with for too long. We can't all be proletarians, you know, and if some of us public school boys see the light, we should be welcomed as returned prodigals. There is more rejoicing in Heaven over one sinner that repents than over 99 just men, you know!

To Daniel Bell

April 8, 1947

I quite understand about the delay in completing the Reading List. There's no hurry now, as in the next (May–June) issue I'm running a special section on Russia and am including a Reading List on USSR; so there would not be room for two Reading Lists in that issue. . . .

Distressed to hear that you and Nora are getting divorced: had been hoping you would work it out; only bright spot: better now than after 10–15 years of jangle wrangle.

As you probably know by now, the change is to a bi-monthly, not a quarterly. Reasons are mostly editorial: I kept getting so far behind in the monthly that I didn't have time to plan it recently (let alone read or think). I believe the first bi-monthly issue, which you've probably gotten by now, shows the good effects of the slower pace. Maybe next fall the old mad monthly pace can be resumed.

Good for you to break with the *New Leader* (especially as it was such a personal wrench) over their war-drums beating. Harold Rosenberg believes that the Burnham-PR-New Leader set is even more of a threat to decency and sanity on the left today than the Commies were in the 30s. I think this is exaggerated, but certainly the neurotic intensity with which those circles pursue a hate-Russia policy is making it easier for the black rightists to push the country still faster towards something damned unpleasant as in the red purge now projected in govt. offices.

But why didn't you send *me*, instead of *The Call*, your break piece? Don't you want it to be read? (*The Call* is not read, so far as I can determine.) That is just the sort of thing *Politics* wants to tell its readers about—now I suppose I will have to pick it up from *The Call* if I want it.

What will happen when the S[ocialist] P[arty] and the S[ocialist] D[emocratic] P[arty] merge, as I hear they are about to? What in God's name will be the line on Russia of the combined groups? (Same query could be asked of the merged Trotskyists, in fact; there is a neat parallelism in the mergers in other ways too. . . .)

So there is a *Politics* club (I assume you mean the mag and not the subject) at Chicago and you're their adviser! Why don't they let me in on the secret? Your letter was first I'd heard of it. Or maybe you do mean Politics as a subject—can't imagine Shachtmanites crowding under this banner. . . .

To George Woodcock

April 24, 1947

. . . I hate to say it, but I don't much like your May–June letter. It seems routinized, written not because you had much to analyze or report but because you had contracted to write a bi-monthly letter. There was nothing of significance in it which *Time* and the N.Y. *Times* had not already reported. And it was written in a diffuse and dull journalese, quite different from your previous letters. Am I right in suspecting you didn't get much kick out of writing it yourself?

The thing to avoid in writing a regular letter is this routine aspect, and I'm afraid your last was just that. So I'd rather not use it—though of course I'm paying you for it. Would you reread it and see if you think my reaction is at all legitimate?

Your Dutch Letter, on the other hand, is very good (perhaps because a fresh subject, not routine). I hope to get it into the next issue. . . . Re: Godwin—Houghton Mifflin returned it to me, not interested. (Damn fools) But I should think your agent should be able to get some US publisher to do it—although the intellectual level of books published here is definitely lower than London's.

. . . P.P.S. You should have done some blue-penciling on that Rexroth letter in the last NOW. His opening paragraphs are fantastic. For instance, the description of the homosexual orgies in our public squares. I've lived in NYC all my life and I've never seen these allegedly nightly exhibitions. Rexroth, whom I know well by correspondence (or rather by his letters to me), is a brilliant crackpot. And I don't mean just a crackpot: he really has imagination, wit, and a sense of the heart of the matter. But he's also a kind of comic-strip anarchist in his wilder moments, and that kind of thing does no good, in print, either to him or to the ideas all three of us share.

To Philip Young [student writing a thesis on *Politics*]

May 27, 1947

. . . As for your other questions: The editor comes from the upper middle class. Exeter and Yale. Was on *Fortune* staff 1930–1936, $10,000 a year during last 2–3 years. Pitzele (Mel, I suppose) is romantic when he says I saved $75,000 — $20,000 about it. Main source of financing of *Politics* is my wife Nancy's money (she also from upper middle class—grandfather was pres. of NY Stock Exchange, brother is Seldon Rodman, poet, late of *Common Sense*), plus $1500 from anonymous donor. Losses to date: about $7,000. (Including $1500 on packages abroad. I became an editor of PR, incidentally, after I left *Fortune*; financing of PR while I was on it was by George L. K. Morris (college friend), i.e., 1937–1943.

As to the kind of people who came to *Politics* meetings—hard to say— NYC intellectuals, for most part; lower middle class and middle class, mostly former. Plus perhaps 30% Trotskyists, anarchists, Socialists. No meetings this year—I was too busy—other groups have taken up idea, held meetings at which doubtless many of same people were present. Should say there IS a rather vaguely defined *Politics* group—not in terms of political program or party but of feeling that all old answers, whether Marxian, Deweyan, religious, or New Deal, don't satisfy; also that ethical, individual approach needs more emphasis. As to a formula for salvation, I know it doesn't exist in mind of the editor and don't think it does in minds of most readers—or at least, don't think they read the mag to get one.

My natural opinion is that *Politics* has now reached, or is reaching, the stage where some kind of general principles can be arrived at, some sort of weltanschauung that will be peculiar to it. But it isn't there yet—and so far, its readers are a group only in that (1) they approach politics on a fairly high intellectual level, and (2) are dissatisfied with the traditional answers. . . .

To Maurice Merleau-Ponty

July 17, 1947

Thank you so much for your letter and for the MS of your forthcoming article, "Apprendre a Lire." I am very glad you wrote. After consulting with Lionel Abel, who acted as special editor on the [French] issue, I have omitted the

[Jules] Monnerot article[8] and have substituted for it an article of yours which we had hoped to include (but had found no space for): "Marxism and Philosophy," from the *Review Internationale*.

The reason we originally decided to print Monnerot's article without printing the one of yours to which it replies was that Monnerot seemed to both of us to give a fair idea of your main trend of thought and to deal accurately with it. However, when we got your letter, we realized that you think his article unfair; so, although (even after reading the MS you enclosed) we still felt M's interpretation was just, we concede your right to insist on at least a reasonable portion of your original articles being printed along with M's article.

In an early future issue I hope to present the whole controversy with your original articles (in part—they are too long to reproduce in full) plus M's analysis, perhaps some of your "Appendre a Lire." Maybe I will have a few words to say myself.

I hope that this will somewhat reassure you as to the coolness of some American intellectuals on the Stalinist issue. Not at all a coolness so far as Stalinism is concerned: it is, in my opinion, the great danger today, and only in minor ways to be distinguished from Nazism. But a coolness rather in the sense that it must be rationally discussed, and those who, like yourself, are sincerely deluded about its revolutionary nature, have a right to loyal and friendly discussion, not abuse. As you know if you read *Politics*, my approach to Stalinism is quite different from that of *Partisan Review* (see Dec. 1946 issue).

To Mr. Gurian [editor of a Catholic publication]

August 31, 1947

. . . Naturally, I don't think there is the slightest obligation to exchange advertisements with *Politics*. And it is quite possible that no material benefit would come to either of us from such an exchange.

But—and this is The Point, it seems to me—the only reason you give for not exchanging is that you don't like some of the remarks we have made about the Catholic Church. What in the world has this to do with exchanging ads? Good heavens, I heartily dislike many things I read in *Partisan Review*, or *The*

---

8. Macdonald refers to the French issue of *Politics* (July/August 1947). Monnerot's article, *"Liquidation et justification," La Nef* 37 (1947) was a powerful attack on Stalinism and particularly the purge trials. Merleau Ponty was charged with defending the trials in the previous issue of *Politics* by Macdonald's French correspondents, Gelo and Andrea Delacort. Macdonald had little respect for what he regarded as the French Stalinist intellectuals, particularly Jean-Paul Sartre. For a polemical and provocative account of these politics in France, see Tony Judt, *Past Imperfect: French Intellectuals, 1944–1956* (Berkeley, 1992).

New Leader, or you own magazine. Yet I have willingly exchanged ads. Your attitude implies that one makes a total judgment on a magazine—and one, furthermore, related to a very small (in my cosmogony, at least) point, i.e., its attitude toward Catholicism) issue—and then refuses even the minimum degree of friendliness and cooperation suggested by exchanging house ads, if the magazine is not wholly pure.

This reminds me too much of Stalinist mental procedure for comfort.

I'm quite willing to accept your statement that my decision was fully my own, but I don't see how that changes anything.

This trivial episode confirms me in my hunch that a liberal open-minded Catholic is a contradiction in terms, since the Catholic Church (like the Communist Party) is both (a) an institution with vast and important interests in the status quo, and (b) the repository of The Truth. Hence for practical and ideological reasons, the heretic (or simply the critic) must be cut off, put beyond the pale; and that tolerant, free intercourse on certain planes which is possible to antagonists free of these burdens (as, *The New Leader*, which I have attacked more and more violently than the Catholic Church) must be given up as a luxury.

To return to the specific point: I maintain that it would occur only to a Catholic (or a Communist) to give as a reason for not exchanging ads with another magazine in the same field the fact that this magazine had criticized the Catholic (or Communist) position. This is the reason you gave in your letter of June 25. Either you think it sufficient, in which case you should remain a Catholic. Or you think it insufficient, in which case you should become a liberal (here used as meaning a freeman).

Please excuse the sharpness of this note, but the problem of the Catholic liberal has long fascinated me, and I feel I'm beginning to understand it at last.

To Art Wiser [a pacifist radical conscientious objector involved in the founding of the Macedonian Community in Georgia]

October 2, 1947

. . . I'd like to print something on the community but the report isn't it. Something more critical, human (this report is full of academic-bureaucratic jargon, doubtless because it is angled to impress possible angels), informal; more about the human, psychological problems (and rewards) of such a venture, and less about the practical side. What do you people get out of it as individuals? Do you ever get drunk? Do you paint, write poetry, get spiritual illuminations? How does your experience compare with Hawthorne's account of the similar venture at Brook Farm, as described in the first half of the *Blithesdale Romance* (to my mind the classic hostile criticism of intellectual communities on the land)?

What about your relations to the local folks? How about sex? Etc. etc. I've been purposely provocative in these queries, so as to suggest a line quite different from that of the report. What I mean is that there are, for instance, various ways of looking at the life of a family: (a) domestic economy (Who washes the dishes? How will the new living room furniture be financed? Which is more urgent—a new washing machine or repairs on the car?); (b) political (What is the family's role in society? What does it "do" about war, oppression, etc.); (c) psychological (How do the members get on with each other sexually, emotionally?); (d) ethical (What are they living together for anyway? What values do they strive to live by? How does their life as a family help—or hinder—them from drawing closer to what (1) they, (2) the observer, thinks of as a Good Life? . . .

To *Politics* Subscribers

November 17, 1947

As you may have noticed, the last issue of POLITICS was dated July–August. POLITICS has a long and dishonorable tradition of coming out late, but the present lag is something special even in our history. There is only one reason for it: POLITICS has been a one-man magazine, and the man (myself) has of late been feeling stale, tired, disheartened, and—if you like—demoralized.

For a while I thought of indefinitely suspending publication. But the reactions to this proposal were so unfavorable, even indignant, as to suggest that perhaps POLITICS still has, or could have, more of a function than I thought. Further, there is still no magazine for which I would rather write. Thus obligation and inclination both point to an attempt to continue POLITICS on a more satisfactory basis.

The first step towards such a revival is the analysis of the editorial mood noted above. It seems to be due to three factors: (a) the ever blacker and bleaker political outlook; (b) my own growing sense of ignorance, which requires more time to investigate and reflect before sounding off in print; (c) the psychological demands of a one-man magazine which, at first stimulating, have latterly become simply—demands.

Not much can be done about (a). But the other two may admit of solution by (b) changing the frequency to quarterly for a while, and (c) drawing others into the work of planning and editing POLITICS.

The next issue will therefore appear in January. It will be dated "Winter 1948" and will be the first of a new quarterly series. It will have more pages and will cost more (present subscriptions will be honored on a pro rata basis). I think it will be possible to get together an editorial group to put out the magazine beginning with the Spring 1948 issue. What the new POLITICS will be like will depend on what kind of group can be formed and what they decide to do. I hope it will be possible to give more details of future plans in the next issue.

P.S. Nancy asks me to remind you that the need for packages abroad this winter is as great as it has ever been. And to urge those who have not yet taken part in our package project to try if possible to adopt a European family. If you can take a family, send your name to Nancy in the enclosed envelope, telling them how often you will send packages. Even if you can't send regularly, $10 will buy a Care package for Christmas.

To Jack Jessup [*Life* Magazine editor]

November 21, 1947

I couldn't, or at least didn't, think of any subject for a LIFE profile, so didn't call you. If you fellows have someone you think I could do for you, let me know.

Most likely way for me to get some of LIFE's corrupting money . . . now seems to be to sell LIFE what it wants of the Wallace book before publication. The obstacle you mentioned the other night—the Ingersoll-*Fortune* footnote— is now providentially removed from the book. The lawyers insisted on it; in fact they thought my language re Ingersoll was closer to libel than anything else in the book. So I yielded (especially since the publisher had previously insisted it was a false note) thus combining necessity with expediency. Page proofs will be-coming through in a week or two, and I'll send you a set on the chance LIFE wants to do something with the book (which will be out in Feb.).

Re Your objection the other night that I shouldn't "support," by writing for it, a magazine I had criticized so strongly as I did the Luce papers: I don't see the area of my responsibility as going beyond what I write and sign my name to. If that is too seriously affected by the truth-distorting policies of the Luce papers (or any big commercial outfit), then one can withdraw one's name (as I did with NYorker in the Somervell profile) or, if the imposture seems too great, even withdraw the whole business. But I'm sure it's possible to get an honest piece printed in LIFE or FORTUNE, so why not write one? Just as I write for PR even though I have also criticized it rather strongly at times. Another point: aren't you proposing a kind of total condemnation, an excommunication really? And who am I to pronounce any such awful sentence on the Luce papers? And I couldn't, honestly, anyway: I read *Time* every week, and usually find a half-dozen things in it of the greatest value and interest. Even things which I have been delighted to print in *Politics*—such as that cover story on Jackie Robinson, and much of the reporting on Germany.

Tell Eunice [Clark, nee Jessup] she did a swell job in that discussion with Mayer; he's basically a very good fellow but needs to be morally browbeaten a little. . . . *Time* just called, may run a Press story on my letter explaining why no *Politics* for so long! They evidently consider it *Time*worthy.

To Jean and Andrea Delacourt

December 19, 1947

. . . As to restoring some of the cuts in the article—I fear it is too late, since it is all set up in type. . . .

Please believe me: the necessity I felt for cutting your article had nothing to do (so far as I am conscious of my own motives) with the fact that I am more pessimistic than you are. It was purely for technical-journalistic reasons. You political people always think editorial decisions are connected with ideological matters, but believe me, they usually are not—in my case at least. I'm a writer, editor, journalist primarily, and by now I know when an article is "overwritten"—i.e., labors points which an intelligent reader can grasp without elaboration, and uses a kind of academic-pompous style which takes 20 words where ten would do the trick. Now your stuff—and the last article in particular—is too often guilty of this journalistic sin; hence it was necessary to cut drastically. . . . [Lewis] Coser, I think, will back me up on this criticism of your journalistic technique (and he is not a pessimist like me, but seems to pretty much share your—relative—optimism). Do you ever see "Time" magazine? You might get some ideas on how to present material briefly, with maximum effect, from it. ("Time," of course goes much too far the other way—but some of its technique is good.) I'll send you a few issues if you like.

Now as to pessimism: It is true that I am very pessimistic these days—and indeed last fall very nearly decided to give up the magazine itself as a result. I now feel somewhat more cheerful—partly because of the super response of the readers to the enclosed letter, which states frankly my difficulties. Anyway your reasons for feeling relatively optimistic don't satisfy me. You write (1) the masses are still oppressed and exploited and still aspire to a better society, and (2) the political situation is still "open" in the sense that totalitarianism is still limited to Russia. I agree with both statements; but what I don't see is any mass movement, or even any political theory, which shows reasonable promise of taking advantage of (2) to lead us toward a better society. The monotonous series of failures of such movements and theories in the past 30 years, I admit, makes me suspicious now of all such proposals. But is not this suspicion justified? Concepts like "working-class democracy" cannot be expected to rouse one to the virginal enthusiasm they did in the 20s; they have been "devaluated" just as "free enterprise" and "war for democracy" have been. And, unhappily, every failure makes success later on more difficult. . . . That's how things look to me. I'm always open to conviction—and hoping for it!

To Mr. Hirsch

December 26, 1947

. . . No apologies, however, for not bringing out *Politics* for six months. A man cannot work if his heart is not in it; and that was my state for a long time this fall. As to the "contract" to put out a monthly or refund subs, why of course: you can have your money back anytime you want it. But naturally I cannot bind myself to put out a magazine forever for your (or anyone else's) pleasure. Especially since Nancy and I have to meet the annual deficit and it is much too big for our modest income. You really shouldn't write such nonsense—unless you think the magazine makes money, an even more fantastic idea. Our deficit last year was slightly over $5,000. . . .

To Niccolo Tucci[9]

January 21, 1948

. . . Thanks for the *Harper's* story and the Einstein piece. Former seemed to me inflated, didn't much enjoy it. Latter is extremely well done, and you've hit on something new and good in journalistic techniques: putting the reporter in too gives a dialectical interplay much more interesting (and true) than the conventional one-dimensional formula. (Perhaps you overdid it a bit in the beginning—I mean the part up to E's entrance.)

I was disappointed in the piece, however, from an ideological viewpoint. You gave me the impression that you had gone into the question of responsibility with E at length, and that you had argued about it—I mean that you had pressed him, and he had replied. But there's almost nothing on the theme, and, far from either arguing with E or leading him to expose his position (which I think is not a defensible one—is indeed rather hypocritical), you set up a question for him which enables him to score very easily. And when he makes that sophistic point that, if the atomic scientists are to be held responsible, then so must Newton be because the law of gravitation also played its part in the Bomb, you not only don't object but underline his point by saying that such an attitude towards scientific responsibility as E repudiates "would amount to a form of censorship on all our actions and thoughts."

As indeed it would. But the objection to E's part in The Bomb is not that

9. Niccolo Tucci was an Italian aristocrat and former member of the propaganda wing of the Italian embassy in Washington. Disillusioned with politics, he contributed a witty but cynical and satirical account of nearly everything. Macdonald liked the erratic whimsy of his writing. He kept him on the staff throughout the life of the magazine despite critics' demands that he be fired.

he years earlier worked out the equation which made it possible (nor is Newton held responsible by any reasonable person) but that he went to Roosevelt in 1940 and convinced him that an atomic bomb was scientifically possible and thus directly helped bring it about. E's point is thus sophistry, and it's too bad you let him get off the hook so easily.

Also, there are lots of other aspects of the scientist's responsibility which you might have gone into with him—though he's obviously a slippery customer and probably would have evaded and escaped.

I know you won't take these undiplomatically direct criticisms in bad part.

To Arthur Schlesinger

February 28, 1948

(1) Thanks so much for the review; glad you liked the book [on Henry Wallace]. Friends kept calling me up the day the review appeared congratulating me on it, till I began to think I'd written it myself. Sales to date are 2500—not bad but not brilliant. However, your review will probably have an effect.

(2) The ADA membership (and especially the SDA [Students for Democratic Action], since much of Wallace's support seems to be on the campuses) should be the ideal group to sell the book to. Vanguard is willing to sell ADA copies at the usual bookstore discount of 40%, for resale to its members. I'm writing Loeb about this: if you see him, and if you agree of course, you might put in a word.

(3) The success of Henry's demagogy is alarming in view of the Czech business. I've been thinking of ways to deflate or at least embarrass him. What about a Master List of Awkward Questions, which would be formally submitted to him, and which (if he doesn't answer, which he probably won't) could be brought up persistently at all press conferences? Such things as the Stratton Bill, the Brooks-Douglas episode, last year's endorsement of the Stalin regime against internal opposition, etc. I'll work something out and send you a draft; Jimmy Wechsler should have some ideas too. (Maybe we should form a Brains Trust to make the Great Commoner chronically unhappy.)

(4) Why in hell doesn't ADA come out for a liberal candidate to put up against Truman for the Democratic nomination? The convention's stand was dismal: neither yes or no on Truman, and no other candidate in sight. If ADA is just part of the Truman forces, what's the use of it? No wonder Henry steals all your thunder.

(5) Thanks for the invitation to see you in Cambridge. I may be there for a couple of days at the end of March; if so, shall hope foregather.

To Nancy Macdonald [written from Washington, D.C., while Macdonald was on book tour]

April 1, 1948

. . . Drove down to the Library of Congress. . . . No trouble getting a card to use stacks. Dropped in on Robert Lowell (poet in residence this year—cushy job) in his large chintzy-curtained office. He was very cordial and I have taken a great liking to him. (How could I have baited John [Berryman] so maliciously at the Cape on subject of Lowell? I'd never even met him. Must stop this sort of judgment on people, as you have often advised.) He is tall, husky, looks like champion basketball player—squared-jawed, but with a diffident, intense manner that reminds me very much of [James] Agee. He carves the air with his hands the same way. I found him very simpatico. (Writing is bad because B&O roadbed is bad. I am ordering another whiskey to steady my hand!)

Lunch with Laura and Adrienne Koch, who works in MS division too—on Jefferson and Madison papers. Have to admit (again) I found her lively, shrewd, and pleasant. (WHY did I have to sound off on her that evening at Margaret's? People always seem to be much better when you meet them than when you think about them.) Also not unattractive. . . .

By the way, I told Lowell that I was reading his book but found it hard going. He said it is much easier than his earlier things. (AH! Train has stopped.) And that he is making his verse more and more comprehensible. Good news!

The Washington Pacifist meeting was that night. It was a frost as far as attendance went—only about 100 or so, in the Friends Meeting House, which seats about 300. But I was quite good, especially in the discussion period. The audience was good too—I mean they asked really serious and difficult questions. It was the best such discussion I have ever taken part in—perhaps the small audience was an advantage. Lowell was there, and brought Ezra Pound's 23-year-old son (who looked 17). (Lowell sees Pound regularly at St. Elizabeth's. I've promised to send Pound *Politics*.) After the meeting I went out with Bill Gausman, local head of the S.P. and a very smart and likable young journalist (though a 100% Thomas man) and a half-dozen boys and girls including a very pretty one who works for the Woman's International League (D. Detzer's outfit) and who quite charmed me though I don't (as usual) have the faintest idea of her name. Also Lewis Corey's undergraduate assistant was there now doing his "field work" in the AFL; he says the Wallaceites are very strong in Antioch and that Corey jumped at my offer as the drowning man at a straw. . . .

Dinner at the Press Club with Jimmie Wechsler. . . . Like Spender, he looks much redder and coarser than his photos. (Maybe the camera does lie!) An outgoing, harassed, sincere fellow. He had been following Wallace around for months, on his speaking trips, and is now completely fed up with him. Says he is a liar and a bore, and nothing else. (He told me that on plane trips, C. P. Baldwin, W's manager, makes everybody draw lots and the loser has to sit next to Wallace.) . . .

Met Lowell at Cosmos Club, where he lives (and where I met Russell Lord when I interviewed him on Wallace). The Randall Jarrells also were there, plus two unidentified and not-pretty females. Literary Talk + Responsibility of Peoples (atom bomb vs. death camps). . . .

Last night I stayed up till 2:30 finishing *The Steeper Cliff* [novel by David Albert Davidson about West Germany]. Worth reading—something real to say, but, oh dear, he just is not an artist. Literary quality low—characters not developed much—a bit sentimental—not vigorous, inventive, doesn't really get under the surface very far. But does treat a great theme, the great theme of our day (of moral responsibility and courage) in a serious way. We must have him around. . . .

That's all, darling—rather a bare account, I'm afraid. But traveling numbs me. . . . You don't know where you are. That's enjoyable and exciting in a way, but also numbing. I feel distant from NYC and also from myself (who exists at 117 E. 10 but not at Destler, O., which we just passed through). . . . Tell Mike [oldest son] I am collecting souvenirs: have a miniature whiskey bottle, in which my drink came, for him, . . . give him a big kiss and hug for me. And ditto to Nick [youngest son] and double ditto to yourself.

To Mr. Brumm

March 28, 1948

Debunking Wallace affords me satisfaction for two reasons: (a) on the basis of a thorough study of his words and actions since 1932, I am convinced he is a phony, that is, that he pretends to be something he is not; I place value on truth for both aesthetic and ethical reasons. (b) If he pretended to be a good Buddhist and was not, I would deplore it and would do a little to expose him; but he pretends to be something which I regard as much more important: a man of goodwill who values peace, democracy, and human freedom; thus I regard him as dangerous to those ideals, which are mine, and so am willing to spend a lot of time trying to persuade others, through reasons and the citation of evidence, that Wallace is not on "our" side but is on the enemy's side. In the last six weeks, his presidential campaign has become simply an instrument of Russian foreign policy, in my opinion. And since I regard Russia as a totalitarian social system diametrically opposed to my own values, I feel even more obliged to attack Wallace. The fact that you yourself, I might add, seem to regard Wallace as at least a "lesser evil" to Truman, only confirms my conviction that his demagogy is dangerously effective.

I'm shortly leaving on a tour of the Midwest, speaking on Wallace (and debating wherever possible) to as many student audiences as I can get. I'm sure you'll agree that open, public discussion is one way by which we can all arrive at a just view of Wallace. I'll be in Detroit, probably, for a couple of lectures (at Wayne and to a UAW audience) between April 8 and 11. Is there any possibility of a debate or lecture at Ann Arbor? Do let me know, if so. Should be delighted to run out from Detroit.

Thanks for writing, and I hope I've been able to at least explain my motives, whether you agree my judgment of Wallace is well founded or not.

To George Orwell

April 23, 1948

It was good to hear from you again. But distressing to learn of your TB; I hadn't known. Glad you are getting well, and will be up and about by summer. But a year's work lost is indeed, as you so Britishly understate, a bore.

Thanks for writing to [Victor] Gollancz [British publisher] re the Wallace book. He wrote me first a quite enthusiastic letter, and then, a few weeks later, concluded it was no go—he couldn't get it out in time; God knows why he couldn't have figured that out first, but publishers don't seem, as a class, overly intelligent. No other nibbles from London. Over here, the book is going badly—only 3500 copies in 2 months. Don't know why—the reviews have been many and mostly quite favorable; and Henry has helped a lot. Maybe Americans are too positive-optimistic minded to pay $2.50 to find why they should NOT vote for Wallace.

But I'm having a lot of fun speaking around the country at colleges on Wallace, doing what I can to expose the man's lies and demagogy, and the almost 100% Commie entourage which writes his speeches.

By now you should have received the Winter *Politics*; please let me know if you haven't, and I'll ship you another.

Next issue will be mostly on Russia, with special attention to the great cultural purge. Should be a good issue, I think.

I'm mailing you several books you may not have read and which may pass some time away for you pleasantly. [Joseph Wood] Krutch on Johnson and Polner on Tolstoy are two of the best modern biographies I know; the first is especially impressive, considering that Boswell already is in the field—but I think he adds a good deal, and of course, from a scholarly viewpoint, he puts in much new material. I wonder if you share my private enthusiasm for Dr. Johnson? I imagine you do, for some reason.

So Middleton Murry has done an about-face! I never followed his stuff because its solemnity and fluffy prose style repelled me, but I did know vaguely he was some kind of pacifist. The fact that he so absurdly thought of Russia as a peaceful country 10 years ago probably explains the violence of his revulsion now.

The enclosed may interest you. We've held one meeting so far—on the Russian culture purge. Speakers: Nicolas Nabokov, Meyer Shapiro, Lionel Trilling, and myself. It was a success—about 400 people, $300 profit, and solid speeches.

Do write again when you feel like it. And I hope your streptomycin is continuing to work well. Let me know if there is anything I can get for you over here—particularly books or magazines, or some luxury not available in Scotland.

To Harold Orlansky [a young conscientious objector who contributed to *Politics*]

July 21, 1948

. . . On the death camp comparison: I wish you'd meet this objection to it (I'm not at all suggesting you omit the comparison, merely justify it better): the Nazi camps were not rational because the Nazis took millions of people who were not dangerous to them and, at a big expenditure of manpower, rolling stock, materials, etc., killed them because of their race alone; a rational course would have been to let the Jews alone because unless they threatened the regime enough to justify the effort of killing them; the death camps were not even useful as propaganda—to strike terror in others, like the concentration camps—since their existence was carefully concealed. The authorities who run our asylums, on the other hand, don't go out and pull in victims; they have the insane dumped on them, and must do something about them; as you show, the most convenient thing to do is to first reduce them to subhuman objects, and then help them perish as speedily as possible; this is abhorrent, of course, but rational, since it's the easiest way out for normal, callous, lazy men. The Nazis went to great and needless trouble in creating their camps.

That is the point I'd like answered. An interesting way to do it might be to add the above, as written, as a PS to the article (stating that the editor objects as follows); and then to answer it. Or handle it any way you like.

Yes, I should certainly like you to do an English Letter for *Politics*; know it will be good—you've got the real journalistic sense of the concrete. . . .

To Anonymous[10]

July 28, 1948

I'm asking T. S. Elliot to pass on this note to you.

In our Spring issue, of which I've sent a copy to Mr. Eliot for transmission to you, I reprint most of the chapter, "The Background," from *The Dark Side of the Moon*. I did this because it seemed to me such an admirable presentation of the historical and psychological reasons for the kind of society we see in Russia today. The book as a whole is the most reasonable and convincing expose of USSR that I know of, with the exception of Jerzy Gliksman's *Tell the West*. And it is well known, from a literary point of view, which makes it almost unique in its field. . . .

To Ralph Manheim[11]

August 17, 1948

No, I don't think you're insane on the "Perspectors"[12] business. But I do think you give too much weight to Lionel's feelings in the matter. For one thing, he's dished out plenty of venomous gossip about others in his days, and it seems unreasonable of him to claim immunity now. (Of course, no one is so thin-skinned about the aggression of others as the aggressive person.) For another, if the PR boys don't have this peg to hang their malice on, they'll have another. For a third, it seems likely to me that another, and perhaps even more vivid, reason Lionel doesn't want the story to appear is that it satirizes most shrewdly and funnily (and one thing L cannot stand is to be laughed at) the intellectual type he and Harold belong to. And I see no reason why such censorship should be permitted him. For a fourth, against your friend's outraged feelings (and he is easily outraged, and frequently, so what's one more nail in his cross between friends?) have you sufficiently weighed the loss in pleasure and understanding which the readers will suffer if the story is not published, not to mention your own interest as an author, or mine as an editor?

In short, I think the story is altogether excellent and grieve at not being

10. The author of *The Dark Side of the Moon* was a woman, T. S. Eliot wrote the preface to the book, and it was published by Scribner in 1947.

11. Ralph Manheim was a translator with an international reputation who often did translations for *Politics*.

12. A story written by Ralph Manheim in which the main characters are based upon the personalities of May and Harold Rosenberg and Lionel Abel. Manheim refused to let Macdonald publish it for fear of damaging his friendship with Abel, because the character representing Abel is stealing money out of May's pocketbook. The story is in the Macdonald Papers at Yale.

able to print it. And I cannot take L's anxieties very seriously; he's anxious always, because of guilt about his own unrestrained aggressions, which he projects on others by accusing them of aggression toward him. Not that the PR boys are not indeed in actuality apparently on the offensive against Lionel. But what does their gossip amount to, really? So you think it will change anyone's opinion of Lionel? I don't.

Well, it's up to you. I've put down what I think, in the hope of persuading you once more to change your minds.

Best to Mary.

P.S. Cape is hecticer than ever this summer. Katie Carver dropped in on us for the weekend recently, with some news of your neck of the woods. The Hivnors are living in Truro; Saul Bellow is visiting two miles away; etc. etc. et al. et al. . . .

To Joe Reilly

September 24, 1948

. . . I'd rather not sponsor your committee until I know a bit more about it and its work. Must say frankly that pacifists whose judgment I trust are cool; they say (a) you got the Philly Youth Council against Conscription into a bad split by holding a rally in which you (without authorization) linked the names of the YPSL [Young Peoples Socialist League] and the Young Friends with the National Youth Assembly against Conscription; (b) that this stems from your wish to have a "united front" with the Wallaceites, who, in my judgment, are controlled by the Commies; (c) that in picketing a registration place in Philly last month you gave the press a statement naming as supporters of the Peacemakers' nonregistration program some people who are not supporters.

You write that you are neither pro- nor anti-Communist. I am quite definitely anti-Communist. Your position does not seem to me a liberal or tolerant one, so much as a stupid one. Cannot see how a pacifist or socialist can compromise on the Commie issue.

To Albert Camus

October 21, 1948

We were delighted to get your letter. It heartens and encourages us over here to know that you and your friends in Paris show such sacrificial enthusiasm for our joint enterprise (or rather, enterprise-to-be). Mary McCarthy especially sends her greetings.

The thing you could do at once that would most help us over here to raise money and to broaden the interest in Europe-America Groups (EAG)[13] would be to let us know right away—or as soon as you can—in some detail just what you would like to do in the way of independent writers in France. A list of writers and intellectuals whom you propose to help financially, with biographical details and an account of the kind of work they are now doing—this would be one desirable bit of information. Also as concrete as possible a sketch of what other activities might be undertaken, assuming we—and you, too, of course—can raise sufficient funds; with an indication of how much funds would be needed for each project. (It all sounds more and more like the Marshall Plan!) The more information of this kind you can give us, the easier it will be to interest people over here.

Last night we held the first meeting of EAG since last spring: about 20 members came, including Sidney Hook, Elizabeth Hardwick, Barrett and Phillips of *Partisan Review*, Paul de Man, Nicholas Nabokov, Mary, and myself. It was mostly devoted to discussing the Stalinist issue: we all condemn Stalinism, and most of us believe it to be "the main enemy" in Europe today; but some of us—Hook and the PR editors, notably—put more emphasis on fighting Stalinism and less on more general matters (such as the war issue and socialism) than others do (notably Mary and myself). The discussion was very friendly, and I see no reason why the two viewpoints cannot work side by side in such a group as EAG. But it does exist, and last night it showed itself practically in a tendency of the Hook group to be less interested than I am in aiding and working with French and Italian groups and more interested in anti-Stalinist Russians and Germans in Germany. I think EAG should concern itself with, and link itself with, both; also that anti-Stalinism should by no means be the only card-of-admission to our little fraternity, so to speak. I mention all this, although there is actually less disagreement in the group than the above schematic outline suggests, to show you how important it is that you and your friends write us in detail about your plans. Hook and Nabokov last night were able to give some convincing evidence as to both the desperate material needs and the political possibilities of the refugees from Soviet Russia who have arrived in the West, especially Germany, since 1945. I favor helping and working with them, naturally. But I should like to have equally concrete information from you as to the needs and possibilities in France.

13. The Europe-America Groups was a neutralist, third-camp group founded by American and European intellectuals to promote an internationalist community in the interest of peace and culture, and was initially critical of both superpowers. Mary McCarthy and Nicola Chiaromonte were its leading figures.

To Irving Howe

December 19, 1948

Thanks for sending me the Reuther piece—and I do hope you WILL later on take part in the New Politics (which I've put off till next fall, to give plenty of time for planning and fund-raising).

I hope you'll realize that what I'm about to say about the article is said because I like you and think you've got a great talent; hence want to warn you of what seems to me a serious danger for your intellectual future.

Briefly, I thought the article (with the exception of the left-hand column on p. 15) was lousy; indistinguishable from the runofthemillpieces in the *Progressive*. More briefly, it shows that you are in danger of becoming a liblab. The style is full of liblab cottonwool orotundities—cf. The last sentence; and such gems as "democratic mass organization," "major streams of the AM political tradition," "How Reuther will respond to this challenge." Further, the style is full of dreary cliché: "tasted the sweet awareness of his power to persuade men," "clash of ideologies," "threw himself into the campaign," "dim awareness," "threw his weight around." . . . Now, Irving, you write better than that in *PR*, *Politics*, and the *Nation*—even in the *NR* or *Labor Action*.

I think you've unconsciously assimilated the style of Reuther and the UAW liblabs. If your book is written in this dismal patois, it will be a flop.

Also, you follow in Charley Mill's footsteps (in that embarrassingly bad *Commentary* article of his on the UAW) in accepting the flimsy, liblab-bureaucratic ideology of the UAW "left" wing when you write about the UAW. The split you describe in R's personality is real enough, or rather was real at one time; but how sentimental and overoptimistic to slant your analysis so that it becomes essentially another appeal to R's "better nature"—just like the sad editorials the *Nation* used to address to FDR on national policy. Can you seriously think that R is going to take the Debs path, or that he can? I hear that even [Ernie] Mazey has flopped in his top post, that he's disappointed all his liblab-SP followers.

To sum up: your wish and hope for Reuther and the UAW to realize your own socialist values has made you look at R not with the sharp, cold eye with which you regarded, say, Matthiessen, but with very rose-colored spectacles. There is a split between your intelligence and your hopes, and so you develop that horrible vague orotund style which honorifically and humorlessly "takes seriously" things which your brains tell you aren't to be taken seriously. And makes you "go easy" on R and the UAW because you have sentimental hopes for them.

Your article shows that, as I've insisted for some time, there is much less difference between the Trotskyist and the liblab than is generally assumed—

since they both share the same basic "progressive" values which no longer can bring about socialism but only, at best, the kind of thing we see in England today.

But what I object to—and I know you will take this seriously, since you yourself have on occasion shown an appreciation of the importance of this sign-post—is the STYLE. The style is the man—and also the politics. Read your piece over again and see what you think.

Again, apologies; but I speak this way only because I'm concerned about your writing.

Memo to Himself

December 1948

Talked with Will and Edna [Phillips] night of Jan. 20 three hours or so. They said this is what happened:

Phil Rahv said [William] Arrowsmith in *Hudson Review* had violently attacked PR. I said fine. Phil said there were anti-Semitic overtones to the attack. (Not true—or at least only in minor degree—see A's article.) Whereupon I turned on assembled PR editors & wives and said: You Jews are no better than anyone else. Then harangued them (all this being quite drunk) on their obligation as Jews to show concern about the Arab refugees, said I would start a committee to help the Arab refugees, damned the Israeli govt. for its lack of concern, etc. At one point, William said some remark, and I said to him: Oh, you sharpshooters! You shift gears too quick for me—I can't keep up with you. (Will thought this anti-Semitic—though I think it may well have referred to my own past experience with the Boys and their shifty logic, which I don't connect with them being Jews.) Then as we were all leaving, Will said: Well, anyway, Dwight, I do admire you for being so frank and honest, and for not sneaking around corners. To which I replied: Well anyway, Will, I don't admire you for not being frank and for always sneaking around corners. But you can't help it, you were born that way. (Here may indeed have been anti-Semitism—though it's possible I was irritated by Will's usual sanctimonious, solemn-sweet manner; and that I was indicting him as himself (born that way) rather than as a Jew. Consciously, I don't think of Jews as especially sneaky or unfrank. But of course there may be unconscious anti-Semitism. Will and Edna both agreed I had made no overtly anti-Semitic statements; they however felt the overtones were in this line.

To Mrs. [Elizabeth] Ames [director of the Yaddo writers' colony]

March 3, 1949

Thank you for your second note, saying that "because of certain conditions" at Yaddo, all guests are leaving on March 1, and inviting me to come nevertheless, "if you do not object to solitude."

Yesterday I had a long talk with Elizabeth Hardwick, one of the March 1 walkers-out, and what she told me of the present situation at Yaddo forces me to now decline your invitation. This I do reluctantly, for I don't at all object to solitude, and I had looked forward to two weeks' uninterrupted work on my book.

I agree with the position, and the action, taken by the four guests who left March 1, of whom I know three personally. Yaddo is supposed to be a refuge for writers and artists, not a center for pro-Soviet propaganda. That a figure like Agnes Smedly [writer and left-wing supporter of the Chinese Revolution], whose lifelong activity has been as a full-time journalist apologist for communism and the Soviet Union, should make Yaddo her headquarters for years, that she should—because of her friendship with you—occupy a specially privileged and influential status, and that, now that the whole scandal has come out in public, you should actually defend this transaction and should insist that Smedley is just another of those nice old Jeffersonian (or maybe agrarian?) Democrats—all this seems to me to indicate that, as Hardwick and her associates charge, the Communists have had, and still do have, a strategic behind-the-scenes position at Yaddo.

The objection, of course, is not to pro-Communist writers and artists being invited to Yaddo, but to persons like Smedley, who have no connection with cultural life and activity, making Yaddo their base of operations. I know how the Communists work, and I know that once they get the kind of hold they apparently have over your administration, they will use it ruthlessly to reward the faithful and knife the heterodox. The details Hardwick told me confirm this generalization.

Yaddo has been perverted from the intention of its founders, and until this mess is cleared up, I don't want to have anything to do with it. So I must regretfully, believe me, my dear Mrs. Ames, decline your invitation.

P.S. I'm sending Elizabeth Hardwick a copy of this letter, to use as she thinks best.

To Elizabeth Ames[14]

September 8, 1953

You must remember me with small favor, and I should have long ago written you and apologized for my rude and, what's worse, foolish and unfounded letter at the time of the Robert Lowell fracas. I'm usually fairly objective and level-headed, but that time I must admit my political prejudices ran away with me and I accepted a flimsy "case" against you and Yaddo on spectacularly insufficient evidence. Long ago, from talking with others quite familiar with your policies at Yaddo, I concluded I had been sold a bill of goods, and I should have written you. Sorry I did not, but I hope this belated apology won't be TOO belated.[15]

To Joan Colebrook[16]

March 9, [1949]

. . . Joe Gould[17] spent yesterday afternoon here, reading the *Satevepost*, drinking coffee, and making phone calls to get dough (care of the Minetta Tavern); he got three promises of checks, one from a J. Walter Thompson v.p. He remembers you from Truro, and also in NYC; I told him you had planned to visit him in Bellevue, and he was touched. Or seemed so—hard to tell, poor fellow.

I wish you could have been here last night; we had in for dinner two members of he Paraguayan Hutterite community, bearded, gentle, yet alive young men, both English. We talked about everything, the Hutterite communities in North and South Dakota (about 80 of them, completely isolated from US life, which they'd just been visiting), god, and the historicity of Jesus. Latter subject was expounded chiefly by John Berryman, who dropped in (after not seeing

14. This second letter to Elizabeth Ames is deliberately out of order because it is so pertinent to the issue raised by Macdonald in 1949.

15. Elizabeth Ames replied, September 12, 1953: "I am glad to have your apology for having taken part in the infamous witch-hunt of 1949. Your doing this is, for me, evidence of your self-respect. If great numbers of my friends had not rallied to my defense, I should have been more terribly dismayed than I was, for I would have had to wonder what our future in this country would be if a majority of intellectuals could be so easily misled. Your apology with those of others received from time to time has helped to restore my confidence.

16. Joan Colebrook had come to America from Australia in the forties by way of Great Britain. She was unhappily married to John Van Kirk, had three children, and lived in Truro on Cape Cod. She was a novelist, short story writer, and journalist. Macdonald helped her in her career and began an intense affair with her in the summer of 1948 that lasted several years. It was common knowledge among many of the members of that summer colony.

17. Joe Gould was a famous Greenwich Village character, allegedly engaged in writing the history of the world in several volumes.

him for 3 months); he was in pretty good shape, though very worn and tense-looking, and at times inclined toward mild hysteria-euphoria. He's going out to the University of Washington to teach for 10 weeks at $200 a week, and has also got a grant of $1,000 from the Nat. Academy of Arts and Letters; so moneywise, he (they) are not doing badly right now. But I gathered they have great debts and without these windfalls might have foundered. It's a great pity about John—such energy, intelligence, and completely selfless love (of learning, poetry, people), yet so crippled by infantilism and narcissism. Actually, he's not selfless, the reverse rather—other people are to him what you once called a mirror for his own personality. Yet he has the capacity for being so, and he tries to be so, and is genuinely warm and outgoing. But there's something wrong, so that he just can't take any responsibility, can't really love anything outside himself (yet wants to desperately)—and loving anything, whether learning or art or other people, means taking responsibility—no?

Again, I'm running on—forgive me.

On the Hutterites, one revealing and rather depressing fact came out: a year or so ago, they took in 110 DPs from Germany, selected by their own people over there. NOT ONE of these has become a member of their community; most have by now left to try their luck elsewhere in Paraguay or Argentina, a few still live with them but only until they can get away. I asked how come. Anderson (one of the two) explained it as due to (1) rough, primitive living conditions, (2) materialistic temper of the DPs, (3) moral disintegration the DPs had undergone as result of their horrible suffering for so long, (4) fact few people anyway feel strongly about God or live in community. Nancy thought this satisfactory explanation, I didn't. Seems to me this is a very serious criticism of the way of life the community has developed; if it cannot provide enough pleasure and interest and satisfactions (including materialistic ones, what's wrong with them anyway—part of life) to interest at least some of such a large number of people, then it is failing; I can't believe that there are not some basic human needs that a good community would satisfy well enough to make converts of least say 10% of 110 people. What do you think?

. . . You know, we both look Jewish, or at least Semitic—our big, floridly curved noses and also a certain sly, reflective, withdrawn look we have. I'm glad. We also have in common: love of walking and other forms of exertion, tactlessness plus honesty and gregariousness, talkativeness, flirtatiousness, feeling for the underdog, recklessness plus practicality (with lapses in latter), interest in ideas, some degree of vitality and spontaneity, and . . . love. So endeth today's lesson.

To Dr. Counts [George S. Counts, liberal educator and disciple of John Dewey]

March 11, 1949

I enclose three letters which have been sent me recently and which I think of interest to our new enterprise. Would you please submit them for consideration to the new executive committee?

The two from George Fischer reinforce me in a view which I've come to since the meeting last week, as a result of talking with others invited to that meeting. This is that the present statement of the Friends of Russian Freedom—which I think on the whole very good—puts far too much emphasis on propaganda. I have come to feel that the most worthwhile activity such a group can engage in is helping Russian refugees and DPs, and, above all, setting up the proposed Institute. And I have come to believe that the group's propagandistic activities (except for certain occasional and special cases, such as the countermeeting to the Waldorf cultural congress) should be of an informational nature and should consist in making available to the public material produced by the Institute.

(I know, incidentally, that others have also come to this general conclusion, namely, Hans Kohn, Meyer Schapiro, Mary McCarthy, Hannah Arendt, Edmund Wilson, and Arthur M. Schlesinger, Jr. This letter expresses only my own specific views, but I know directly, or from others, that the above share the general viewpoint.)

My reasons for this evaluation are:

(1) The idea of showing, in action, that American citizens really do consider the Russian people their friends and allies against the Stalin regime—this is the novelty, the real appeal of our statement. And to implement it by helping, with funds and moral support, the neglected and potentially invaluable Russian DPs, and also by setting up a Russian Institute over there—this is a really bright idea and one that shows more clearly our bona fides than any amount of spoken and/or written denunciation of Stalinism.

(2) For this reason, I think we'll attract much wider support if we concentrate almost exclusively on this aim than if we divert any considerable amount of our energies into anti-Stalinist propaganda. Abroad, a concrete and generous action of this kind may be expected to win more friends for our anti-Stalinist position than any amount of words. And over here, where there is certainly a need for rational and sober exposes of the real nature of the Soviet regime, I don't see that this task can be more effectively done—except in special instances like the notion on the Waldorf congress—by a committee than by individuals. Which brings me to:

(3) The channels of communication in this country are not, to say the

least, now closed to criticism of the Soviet system. Nothing prevents members of the committee, as individuals, from performing the very necessary task of enlightenment on their own nook, as speakers, writers, or whatnot. This kind of effort—which could draw heavily from the firsthand information we may expect our Institute and our contacts with DPs abroad to provide—will be more effective if done individually because (a) individuals generally write better and think more clearly than committees do, and (b) there is inevitably in a broad group, such as the Friends of Russian Freedom propose to set up, much political disagreement between individual members, which means that either a lower common denominator is arrived at and the group expresses only ineffectual banalities, or else that one particular political tendency gains the ascendancy and those who hold other views are put in an uncomfortable position. . . .

To Nick Chiaromonte

April 7, 1949

Well well well (three holes in the ground—ask Miriam to translate) . . . so you are now a UNESCO official! I always knew that was where you belonged, spiritually; now you and Julian Hurley can really get to know each other. Seriously, I'm very glad for you, moneywise, and do hope it won't be too dull and dispiriting. I've been collecting UNESCO literature, by the way, and hope to have a few satirical words to say about UNESCO (which to me is on a plane with United World Federalists and Garry Davis) in the next issue. Send me some espionage reports—why don't you do, anonymously of course, a reportage piece on some especially excruciating sessions for me?

. . . Enclosed material will interest you. We all had a wonderful time at the conference. I've sent Tousset at "La Gauche" a proof of the *Politics* article, told him he can publish it there or in *Les Temps Modernes,* cut or uncut as he likes. Prod him along if you see him, will you? They're putting on a Paris conference along same lines, as you know, and the French intellectuals should get the facts on the Waldorf affair right now.

. . . No, I didn't say Europe should not get any more US help (as I'm sure you know I wouldn't) at that meeting. I said the US should intervene more in the internal affairs of European governments, should make a condition of aid certain reforms; I pointed to Greece as example and suggested no more economic aid until wages are raised, income taxes made higher, social services improved, trade unions made free, martial law lifted, etc.

Don't agree that Olivier's Hamlet is so bad as all that—in fact, must say I liked it more than I expected to. It IS a bit vulgar, but also has virtues: clear, good diction; fine acting (by everyone except Olivier); dramatic effects (though often at expense of the deeper, more spiritual & intellectual meaning of the play). Anyway, that's how I felt. I liked much more than Henry V.

The real swindle is *The Madwoman of Chaillot*—what a slick, sophisticated, empty, and lazy sleight-of-hand performance. Giradoux is a real "operator," a pickpocket! He gives you everything—even anarchist ideas, so fashionable today everywhere except in politics—but it turns out to be nothing at all. It takes centuries and millennia of a great culture to make such a play possible—such easy manipulation of style and concepts, such a show of profundity and wit and style—without the slightest solidity or seriousness or even intention behind it.

The Last of the Free Individuals over here (me) hasn't yet vanished—that is, I haven't taken a job after all, and now won't, for we're going to spend the summer on the Cape as usual (very economical, too, that is). In fact, I haven't even got around to writing any money-articles, though any day now I shall get down to polishing up a piece for *Fortune*. My whole life and work has so long been oriented in a nonmoney (in fact an anti-money) direction that I can't seem to get it pointed the other way. Everything I get involved in seems to be a way of not making money, or of losing it. But I really must cut it now—our capital (except for Nancy's inherited trust fund of $4,000 a year) will be very close to extinction after we've paid for the Spring issue, the kids' school, and Nancy's analyst. (You know, or do you, that she has been going to a psychoanalyst four times a week for a year now? It's apparently worked out very successfully—at least she feels it has, and the analyst thinks she'll be all finished by this summer.)

I now have four projects on the fire, for the next two months: "The Dream World of the Soviet Bureaucracy," a speculative piece on the essential nature of bureaucratic thinking (for *Fortune*); "Semitism," a quarrel with Jewish nationalism which I shall try to get printed in *Commentary*; "Goodbye to Utopia," presenting my proposals for a limited, inconsistent, and modest kind of political thinking (for the next issue); and a critical analysis of US foreign policy (for the next issue). In case of first three, I have lots of material, notes and even some MS completed. After I get through these, I hope to really attack, this summer, *The Root Is Man* book. (Did you see the French "Spartacus" edition yet? Tell me if you see or hear any interesting reactions.)

Give Lionel Abel my best when you see him and ask him to tell me where he is so I can send him some copies of new issue. I liked his PR Paris Letter very much, and would welcome a Paris Letter for the Spring issue from him if he wants to do one, tell him. I also enjoyed your Rome Letter in PR, by the way.

Have you read *The Oasis* yet? Almost no one likes it around here except me. And I didn't like it the second time I read it anywhere near as much as when I heard Mary read it originally. Do you think it is vicious, malicious, and nasty? (I won't pass on your remarks to Mary, so write freely.) I've seen (via Rahv) Kaplan's remarks on it; they seem to me extreme. . . . More rows, clashes, feuds, and factional conflicts in the NYC literary world this winter than at any time in the past—maybe it's all breaking up—rather frightening, really. . . .

To the editor, *The Socialist Leader*

April 11, 1949

I'm so grateful to Mark Holloway, and yourself, for passing on to your readers so faithful a summary of the discussion, in *Politics*, of the difficulties pacifist thinking faces vis-à-vis Soviet imperialism. It's a question that must be faced up to by all who call themselves pacifists or socialists.

Holloway suggests that the USA may be forced, by the dynamics of capitalism, to take the offensive against USSR (while my own assumption was that this would not, or at least has not, taken place). I do not agree wholly, since I think it unlikely there will again be a really severe economic crisis in this country: capitalism—rather, state capitalism—in America has learned how to use the state power to avoid such recessions, in my opinion. But this is admittedly speculative, and Holloway may be right. What I want to query here is his use of the word "socialism," when he writes that "the only hope of eliminating Stalinism without war" lies in the socialization of both Western Europe and America.

Does he mean by "socialism" the victory of a political party based on the trade unions and with a liberal domestic policy and a program of economic nationalization—the kind of change that took place in England in 1945, in short? If so, I disagree. Such a change, in my opinion, would not make any important difference in the international situation, as far as war with USSR goes, any more than the British Labor Party victory did. I cannot see that Churchill's policy in Palestine, Greece, or the United Nations would have been any worse, from a socialist viewpoint, than Begin's has been. Nor does it seem likely to me that a substitution of Walter Reuther for Dean Acheson in our own State Department would make any differences so far as defeating Stalinism without war goes.

If Holloway, however, means by "socialism" what I do—namely, a much more profound and revolutionary change in both ethical values and social institutions—then I wonder if he agrees with my statement, in the article under discussion, that such a change is so unlikely as to make it unhappily not a factor to be taken into consideration at present? If he does agree, then his "only hope" (as quoted above) is merely a pious wish and not a political calculation or recommendation. And if he does not agree, then either he or some other of your contributors should try to demonstrate, by analysis of the present historical situation, the basis for such a hope. For only thus can the dilemma be resolved.

he china-shop metaphor: Holloway mistakes my mean-
at the encounter would take place in our own territory
r that it would destroy our own cultural and ethical val-
re it takes place. Even if the USA should wipe out the
by atomic bombing without suffering any material dam-
uld still be in the position of the china-shop proprietor,
s we should have to smash our most priceless porcelains
enemy—namely, our concern and respect for other
vould be left of the fragile fabric of "civilization" which
t st re usly preserved and (slightly) extended in the past two
—not the question of how much material damage we
might suffer—is what makes it, for me, impossible to support a third World
War.

To Nick Chiaromonte

April 14, 1949

. . . Mary's story: yes, too literal; also too much on the surface; yet I think the reaction against it is excessive; some very witty and penetrating remarks; most serious criticism I've heard is that the people cannot learn anything about
themselves and their weaknesses from it; as one, I have to agree; YOU of course
are the Holy Ghost, hovering over the scene but exempt, by virtue of your sacred character, from either criticism or (alas) specific description; by the way,
have you seen your patron's (Kaplan's) letter to Rahv on the subject—ask him
to show it to you—true to some extent, but just as bitterly inhuman as Mary's
story, really, and even more exaggerated; maybe I'm a centrist; I know the intensity of the feuds and polemics now running about repels and frightens me
(except, of course, in the case of the attack on the Stalinists, which I think CAN-
NOT be too drastic—though it can be too unscrupulous and immoral, i.e., too
Stalinist).

God, I'd like to come to Paris for a while. To share Garry Davis's happy ob-
scurity, leisure, and lack of Connection.

But I've got to meet Paul Goodman in 1/2 hour, and then to see a would-be
editor of a forthcoming little mag, and then to preside over #1 of our Packages-
Aboard lectures at the Rand School (Bertram Wolfe on Stalin).

The real point is that the alienated, radical, Bohemian left wing is becoming an institution as complexly articulated and interrelated as Luce's organization.

Do write soon.

P.S. I must add this—and do ask Miriam, to whom my love, to give me her reactions and judgment too; am I mad or is there an upsurge of what I call "Semi-

tism" (Jewish nationalism) lately? The other night at a party, Clem Greenberg, slightly but not very tight, came up to me and asked me why I used the adjective "Jewish" in describing the delegates at the Waldorf Conference session I attended (I enclosed a copy of my piece in case you didn't get the earlier letter). I said because the ones who spoke had Jewish names and looked Jewish. He began to talk about anti-Semitism. I said it seemed to me true that they were Jewish, and if so it was a sociological fact. He said only a Jew could properly have made the observation, and then began to shout at me, "faker," "you're a horse's ass, Macdonald," etc. I turned my back and walked away, saying I would not discuss it on that level. Later, as he was leaving, he spied me and (he was on some stairs, above me), began to denounce me as a faker again to suggest that what I needed was a good punch in the nose. I restrained myself, partly out of aversion to violence and partly because it seemed irresistibly funny to me at the time, and finally bewildered him by admitting he had convinced me I am a faker and what does he want me to do then? As he went out the door, my host (also a Jew) told me later, Clem said that he (my host) should ALSO be punched (in the nose) for inviting "such a person" to his house. (Phillips and Barrett of PR were there and, according to my host anyway, seemed to think Clem's reaction a normal one.) Now this is all balled up with Clem's personal hostility to me, but what I want to know is whether you and Miriam have yourselves noted lately, as I have on other occasions, a super-sensitivity and a super-aggressiveness on the part of the Jews about their Jewishness. I mean the same kind of thing which the Marxists used to show in regard to the question of the class struggle. Clem's reaction was much the same way as that of a Stalinist or Trotskyist who has finally "caught" some centrist temporizer in a statement which is "pro-bourgeois." The assumption is that the Workers (or the Jews) are pure, and any one who implies otherwise is a Petty-Bourgeois Agent of Reaction (read: Anti-Semite).

The cream of the jest is that Fadayev, the person I was heckling, now turns out to be the prime mover in the current Soviet purge of Jewish intellectuals in the USSR (See NEWSWEEK April 4—a story based on State Department research—by the way, the State Department has been uncovering a lot of first-hand data, from the Soviet press, on what is actually happening in Russia today in cultural meter—if you have not seen the 36-page digest, released March 24 last, on "U.S. Efforts to Establish and Cultivate Cultural and Scientific Exchange with the USSR" you should; it is USSR which is "resigning" from Western civilization, and not USA; if you cannot get it, and need it for use in the Camus-Sartre counteraction in re the coming Paris culture-conference of the Stalinists, let me know and I'll mail you my own copy; it is the best possible ammunition for Us (not US) since it is pedestrianly and overwhelmingly factual—anyway to get back on the track of the above sentence, if it is grammatically possible—the cream of the jest is that Fadayev, the very person the predominantly Jewish audience at the Writing & Publishing panel was applauding, is also the functionary who had already, before he came to this country, been carrying out the purge of Jewish (read "cosmopolitan," apparently the euphemism used by the Politburo) writers inside USSR.

In short, everything is hopelessly balled up—but do let me have your and Miriam's reactions to the above minor (in big-scale political terms) but major (in terms of our milieu) question.

To George Orwell

April 18, 1949

I finally got around to reading *Burmese Days*, which you so kindly sent me, a week ago; and what was my surprise when out of it fell your letter. Hence my failure to reply sooner.

I'm glad to report that Nancy was able to round up 2 copies of Gissing's *New Grub Street* at the first 2 secondhand bookstores she tried! So I've mailed you one, and shall keep the other for myself. (Just finished it last night, by the way, and agree with you that it's a fascinating and quite strong novel, and should certainly be revived.) You owe me $1.35 for the book; let me know if you want us to hunt up more copies for you, or of other Gissing books. Delighted to help out.

Yes, you have a subscription, which expired with the last (Winter) issue. As stated there, the mag can continue only if I can raise money, which I'm trying to do. If you want to renew and take a chance, it's $3 a year. I've sent the last issue to your new address.

I must tell you how much I liked *Burmese Days*; it's excellent both as a novel and as a picture of colonialism; cannot understand why it's so little known over here (Edmund Wilson, I now recall, "discovered" it and other of your novels several years ago; but I don't know whether he said much publicly about them; I do know he admired them a lot.) What struck me especially about it was the richness of its effect because of the different kinds of sensibility you show in it. The love story (if one can call it that) is as moving and unmerciful a description of unequal love I know; the plot is wonderfully worked out, and the triumph of evil over good has the "existential" quality now so fashionable; the colonial sahibs and their native colleagues and antagonists are presented with a detached justice and humor which reminds me of Forster's *Passage to India*; and you give the "feel" of Burma very powerfully. It's been some time since I read a novel I enjoyed so much; in fact, I found myself reading it in two sittings, more like a detective story, quite absorbed in it and anxious to see how it was "coming out."

George Woodcock, I think, is now in Canada; at least he wrote me recently that they were sailing early this month. I'll probably hear from him soon.

If you meet some rich English brewer who wants to become a patron of the (political) arts, do suggest he send me a check for *Politics*. Our (Nancy's, really) money has run out, and we've got to raise about $10,000 from the readers to carry on *Politics* if it is to go on.

I'm sending you separately a report I did on the recent Waldorf Conference which will interest you.

To A. J. Muste

April 19, 1949

I'm honored to be asked again to serve on Peacemakers' national committee. But I must decline, for two reasons:

1. I feel less and less interested in committee and organization work. People, including myself, seem to behave more stupidly and mechanically on a committee than they do as individuals. Meetings have come to be pure chore and boredom for me, so that, as you know, I scamp my share of the job, which makes me feel guilty. Maybe I'm a psychological 4-F when it comes to committee work.

2. Probably connected with this feeling is a growing doubt about pacifism as a political tactic today, a doubt as to both its possible effectiveness and also its ethical justification. Also a skepticism about any consistent, basic ideology: I'm beginning to suspect that the ethical losses are greater than the gains. These doubts are as yet only doubts; but until they are resolved on way or the other, I think it best to withdraw from pacifist activity.

So, with real regret and even some embarrassment, I must resign from Peacemakers. (I'm also resigning from the WRL [War Resisters League].) I hope it will later be possible for me honestly and enthusiastically to again take part in the pacifist movement. In whatever event, good luck to all of you.

P.S. If I can help Peacemakers with any technical skills I have, do call on me. Consider me, for the moment, the first of a new species: the pacifist fellow-traveler!

To Irving Howe

April 21, 1949

It pains me to write this letter, and, as you can see, I've been putting it off. Another reason for delay was that my reaction on first reading p. 427 of your PR mag chronicle was so violent that I wanted to count to ten, so to speak, before letting go.

Now I've counted ten, and have just reread what you wrote, and I still feel just as strongly. The depressing thing is—and believe me, this is not just cant—

that I'm unable to see any justification for your omission of a reference to *Politics* in that passage. Depressing because it seems to indicate that our codes of behavior are not only different but opposed, so that, unless we can perhaps in a later talk clear this up, I have to regard you with distrust, at the very least.

It's bad enough that you fail even to mention *Politics*, though you comment at length on its closest similars: the liberal weeklies and *Commentary*. But, with the best will in the world, I simply cannot see anything but a description of *Politics* in your last two paragraphs—the very climax of your chronicle:

"We need in America a magazine that will . . . engage in political and cultural criticism from a generally radical point of view, will not be afraid of being labeled highbrow or destructive (GODS!), and will resist both Stalinist demagogy and liblab verbiage. There are more than enough literary magazines in America, but hardly a serious non-academic and non-party political one."

How is that not a description of *Politics*? The very terms, "radical" and "liblab" were given currency by *Politics*. Has P been afraid of being labeled highbrow? Hasn't a constant complaint in P's letter columns been precisely that P is "too destructive"? Isn't P "serious"? And nonacademic? As for "non-party": in your card, you write you consider P a party magazine. Clearly, it's not in a literal sense: on the contrary, one of its main insistences (and justification) has always been its independence of parties. Then is the party—me? If so, this is a special use of the term and should have been explained (which would have made you look foolish, of course). And even if so, you would then have to show that *Politics* has been more partywise exclusive, in its editing, than *Commentary* or the liberal weeklies (which you apparently don't consider "party" magazines); that is, that in editing it I have kept out viewpoints contrary to my own in the way that real party magazines like the N[ew] I[international] or the F[irst] I[nternational] do. This I don't honestly think you can demonstrate; I've tried always to allow, even to encourage the greatest variety and freedom of viewpoints—if only because my own political ideas for years, as your Trotskyist comrades have often pointed out, have been tentative, contradictory, and deplorably vague.

The next paragraph begins with a lengthy protest against the disdain for politics now shown by American intellectuals. Here again the silence on *Politics* is pointed: unless of course you don't consider it an intellectual magazine (in which case, what the devil is it and why the devil do you want to be connected with it in the future?). It concludes with a description of "the one kind of politics" needed to fill the gap and to brush aside academicism, mystification, and reaction: "the politics of intellectual criticism, secular intransigence, devotion to radical and scientific values; and a refusal to raise the flags of power." Now, really, hasn't *Politics* been secular, radical, and hasn't it refused precisely to raise the flags of power? (True, it has been predominantly (at least since 1945) critical of "scientific values.")

So then, as I add it up, your very specific description of your ideal "little magazine" for the time exactly fits *Politics*, with the possible exception of the "party" point (I mean a very strained argument can be made that P is a party mag—a fallacious one, as I tried to show, unless you also include *Commentary* and the liberal weeklies) and the quite legitimate exception of the scientific-values point.

Then, why, in a long chronicle covering the whole little mag field, is *Politics* omitted? Why don't you state, if you like, that P fits the description except, alas, that it is a party organ and that it does not accept (or at least the editor does not accept) scientific values? And why don't you praise it, and give it a puff and helping hand, because it does come so close to what you want?

Further—assuming that you think P fails to meet the specifications in many other ways beside the above two—why not at any rate go into the matter, make whatever evaluation you think correct, but at least not pointedly ignore it?

The mystery becomes all the deeper because of our own personal and professional relations over some years, so that I am sure there is no element of personal dislike or hostility involved. And also because of your remark to me a few weeks ago, after the Waldorf Conference, that after going through the current crop of little mags (precisely for this very chronicle, good heavens!) you had concluded that it was essential to continue *Politics* and that you therefore wanted to once more be included in plans for a new editorial board to run the mag if money can be raised.

You may say that you were talking of a quite new magazine which *Politics*, with a five- or six-man board, might become. In that case, is it your "perspective," as we used to say, that the new *Politics* would break so sharply with the old *Politics* as to become something drastically different, and even contradictory to the old? And in that case, what is supposed to be my role? After all, the old, or existing, *Politics* is the kind of magazine I, and no one else, want to put out (since there is only one editor). And in working out a new *Politics*, the initiative apparently is still to be mine, both in working out a program and also in raising funds (at least up to now, you have shown no desire to carry the ball). So is it your idea that I should, with your editorial cooperation, simply turn my back on the magazine I've created and labored on for years, and write it all off as a loss? I'm driven to this hypothesis—which is fantastic psychologically and repugnant ethically—by the fact that the existing *Politics*, judging from your chronicle, apparently strikes you as either so wrongheaded or inconsequential as not to be worth even mentioning. And also by the fact that you apparently don't recognize that your description of the kind of mag needed in the future applies closely to the kind of mag *Politics* has been and is. In short, your conception of a highbrow, nonacademic, radical, secular, destructive, independent, anti-Stalinist, and anti-liblab political magazine is apparently widely different from mine, since these adjectives describe just the kind of magazine I've tried to put out. I do think you might have given me at least a hint of this, and also of just how you would editorially conduct such a magazine, when I invited you to join the board of a possible new *Politics*. The only hypothesis I can see (and do suggest another, for I would like very much to be wrong on this) is that you had some idea of "capturing" the mag for science, for Marxism, maybe even for, God save us, Trotskyism.

The most deadly, and poisoned, form of polemical attack is simply to ignore the opponent's existence, in the context where the opponent clearly does exist. This is what you've done to *Politics*, a magazine whose editorial board (assuming I raise the dough) you have just lately indicated you would like to join. This, you can be sure, is not exactly unpopular with the PR boys, who for obvious reasons would not object to a little magazine survey which excluded *Politics*. (Your six lines on PR itself I thought cowardly: if you have the objections you hint at, you should have accepted the responsibility of developing them, or even stating them explicitly and not in a mumbled aside; after all, PR is the biggest and most influential of all the little mags you considered.) I call this a real stab in the back.

I hope you'll reply, either in writing or in person. Maybe we'd get farther— if there is any place to get—in a talk; you know my number. One thing please don't do: don't brush it all off with a wisecrack or some flip remark. It's a serious matter for both of us, and not only for our personal relations but also for our own personalities and values.

To Allen Tate

May 3, 1949

Thanks so much for your note. The editorial[18] seems to have pleased most readers, except for Pound himself, who scrawled a note so vituperative and hot-tempered that I took a great personal liking to him. He is of the opinion that if an ape could use a typewriter, he would write the way I do.

---

18. In the spring of 1949 the first Bollingen Prize for poetry was awarded by the Fellows of the Library of Congress to Ezra Pound who was at the time in St. Elizabeth Hospital for the Criminally Insane. He had served as a propagandist for the Italian fascist government and was a notorious bigot and anti-Semite. The judges nevertheless awarded him the prize for the *Pisan Cantos* as the best book of poetry published in the United States during the year 1948. It contained ample evidence of his virulent prejudices. Macdonald wrote an eloquent cover-page editorial, "Homage to Twelve Judges," in *Politics* (Winter 1949) applauding the judges' decision not to allow the poets repulsive politics and bigotry to interfere with their judgment of his skill as a poet. He also turned it into a cold war propaganda statement by pointing out that "There were few other countries and certainly none east of the Elbe where this could happen." This was a cause célèbre, particularly among Jewish intellectuals, who did not appreciate Macdonald's editorial.

Glad to know about Luther Evans; I shall certainly praise him publicly first chance I get. Omission of Leonie Adams name was due to ignorance: my source (*Manchester Guardian Weekly*) failed to list her name. Shall also repair that omission. My source also failed to mention Schapiro's public adverse note, which several friends have told me about since my editorial appeared.

Yes, [William] Barrett's [*Partisan Review*, April 1949] editorial was indeed cant. My printer (who also prints PR) first drew my attention to it while it was going through the press. "Say, read this and tell me whether he's for or against it, or am I just dumb?" I read it and told him he wasn't at all dumb, that it was a chef d'oeuvre of double-talk, but that I believed Barrett was against the award. Later, I ran into Barrett and, after some fencing around, he said that "of course" he meant the editorial as a criticism of the award. Final turn of the screw: the *Daily Worker* recently devoted a column to denouncing PR's editorial under the impression that it favored the award! And the lines which Barrett quotes as (implied) evidence of Pound's anti-Semitism the *Worker* thinks are quoted favorably—and goes to town on the relation between formalism, Trotskyism, and anti-Semitism!

It's bad enough that PR should oppose the award for political reasons, but it's disgusting that it should try to have it both ways, expressing its opposition with an ambiguity calculated to lull those favoring the award while tipping the wink to those against it.

Distressing about [Robert] Lowell; you must have had a sad time; but Elizabeth [Hardwick, Lowell's current wife] says he is much better now; hope so.

To Davis Herron

May 3, 1949

Glad to hear that [Bruno] Bettelheim will be with you in August; should be a real addition to Cape society. (We're hoping to get up early in June, ourselves.)

The head of the Downtown Community School (where Mike and Nick go) is looking for a place in July. We told him to write you. Just he and his wife, both nice, non-Commie, uninspired liberals; should think they'd be good tenants. You might drop him a line, if you like: Mr. Reece, DTS, 235 East 11 St., NYC.

Your crack about [Howard] Fast & me being like two Britishers meeting after a long stretch among the natives and drinking scotches together was uproarious. I laughed out loud and still chuckle. May I extract it, as a letter to the editor? Too good to waste on just me. (But wait till you get into a similar situation with Fast, or a reasonable facsimile thereof; you've been far more isolated among the natives (i.e., the non-Marxians) than I, and I'll bet you down many more scotches than I did, thinking of Polly Boyden, Phyllis Duganne, & Co.! It really IS like the old school tie, this having once been part of the Bolshevist movement, and no matter how much one's reason and ethical values tell you now otherwise, one still has a sense that one "belongs" to the club. Just as I still can't resist reading Trotskyist polemics, as Max's 112-page (mimeographed) denunciation of renegade Erber. . . .[19]

To M. Cordier

May 13, 1949

I regret to have to inform you that last week Europe-America Groups held a final meeting, at which it was voted to dissolve it, at least for the time being. The difficulties were twofold: (1) technical, or immediate, none of us could or would give the time to run EAG, so that all last winter EAG held only one public meeting (which was a failure) and did nothing else either; (2) general: there was a certain vagueness about our aims, and also a justified doubt as to whether a special group was needed to carry out those aims; concretely, since we are all writers, it appeared to us that if we wanted to communicate our ideas abroad, and vice versa, this could be done simply by sending articles or letters to European publications. There was also another difficulty: a basic conflict between what might be called the "radical" wing of EAG (McCarthy, myself, others) and the "realistic" or respectable wing (Rahv and Phillips of *Partisan Review*, Sidney Hook, etc.). This conflict centered around the policy of the U.S. State Department, which the realists accepted to a much greater degree than the radicals did. This conflict, also, was so basic and so intense that it made it impossible for EAG to be the kind of fraternal, communal group it aspired to be. . . .

To Abe Kaufman

May 21, 1949

. . . On your query: I haven't yet put my doubts about pacifism's ethical defects into writing, shall do so this summer. My general point is that, while the pacifist is of course quite ethical about his own personal behavior (more so in my opinion, than the nonpacifist, which is why I'm still a pacifist fellow-traveler); his inability to suggest a reasonably workable pacifist approach to the problem of Stalinist aggression means that he washes his hands of the fate of his fellow men in areas more menaced by Stalinism than the US is. I cannot honestly see nonviolent resistance, beginning with a withdrawal of US troops from Berlin, as

19. Macdonald refers to a meeting with Fast after the notorious fellow-traveling Waldorf Conference. He was surprised that on other issues he had much in common with Fast and that their meeting had been amiable.

doing anything but deliver over to Stalinist terror and dictatorship the peoples of Europe. When I made this point at a meeting of pacifists at the New School a year ago, several professed themselves amazed that I should, as a pacifist, consider the consequences of an action. If the act is good, then it should be performed regardless of the consequences, they argued. Of course, the point is that my definition of "goodness" includes the consequences as well as the act itself.

So that is what I meant by pacifism's ethical deficiency: not enough concern for the fate of others, too much concentration of one's own moral purity.

Regards, and thanks again for writing.

To C. Wright Mills

May 28, 1949

Nancy and I were delighted to be invited to Temagami, and I was about to write and say Fine, when I prudently looked at the map. Ye gods and alas—from the Cape it is a good 1,000 miles, which, in our decrepit car, means at least 2-1/2 days and probably 3, each way. So, unless we win a better car in a raffle, I just don't see how we can do it. (To get to the Cape each year—260 miles—is a hard and adventurous full day's work.) So we'll have to say no, at least for this summer. I'm very disappointed, as I'm not only curious about your private Utopia, but also had looked forward to discussing politics both with and without a capital P.

On that: I'm wondering about having a board at all. I keep running into evidences of such deep (and often unexpected, to me at least) differences of opinion and of values between myself and others of the proposed board that I wonder whether the result of all of us cooperating, on equal terms, might not be a kind of lower-common-denominator compromise which would cancel out each of our sharpest and most lively ideas and reduce everything to a tepid common ground. Or else, the board would be rent by violent ideological clashes, endless wrangling and bitterness—all the more bitter because the arguments would be not on any minor points that could very well be "settled," but on really basic assumptions.

Thus I was amazed and distressed by Howe's PR magazine chronicle, which ended with what seemed to me a close description of *Politics*, but without mentioning *Politics*. I've had quite a correspondence with him (all friendly) and discover he thinks *Politics* has been eccentric, sectarian, and out of the mainstream of radical thought; in short, he basically is out of sympathy with the mag as it is and has been. I'm unwilling to revive *Politics* with an editorial policy which would break sharply with its past tone, yet this seems to be what Howe had in mind all along.

Also, your own proposal of "getting together" with the N[ew] I[nternational] seems to me impossible. I had a long talk with Conley, who impressed me as personally decent and politically open-minded but also not very acute. I've come to regard Bolshevism with about as much affection as I regard Fascism, yet these N.Y. boys are, after all, Bolsheviks, in however diluted and shamefaced a way. (I found that Conley, who seems honestly to oppose the Bolshevik orthodoxy of his party, himself wrote a review of Shub's *Lenin*, which I'd set aside to flay as a specially crude example of smearing!) He just couldn't see any inconsistency, whence I (charitably) conclude he's not too acute.[20]

Briefly, it now seems to me that I, and probably you, underestimated the depth of the differences between us—on such questions as the labor movement, the possibility of socialist action today, the application of scientific thinking to politics, etc. Maybe not, and maybe all the above is a mood rather than a serious conclusion.

Hope so.

To Ray Kinder

June 8, 1949

. . . On Pound: it's true that the various Pounds interact and can't be completely compartmentalized, but it's also true that (at least in the opinion of the Bollingen judges) the fascistic, anti-Semite, and funny-money Pounds did not affect the poetic Pound enough to make the poetry bad. If they think this, then they are right to give him the prize, since the prize is for Pound's poetry and not for Pound the man. You seem to imply that the award will have evil consequences—by which I suppose you mean that it will give aid and comfort to the political ideas for which Pound stands. This may be true, but these are far outweighed, in my opinion, by the good consequences I tried to indicate in my editorial: namely, that we have eminent critics able to evaluate a man's work without bringing in his life and personal ideas in other fields. You imply that Pound's deplorable political views DID corrupt his poetry in the Pisan Cantos; if so, then the judges erred, of course. But their error could be shown without any reference to, or even knowledge of the poet's political views: by considering the poetry itself and showing wherein it is not good poetry. This would be exactly the same operation as the judges presumably performed, though with a contrary result. But the big thing is to consider the poetry, not the poet, if one is awarding a prize for poetry. The more common procedure today—esp. in the USSR—is to confuse a judgment of the poet with a judgment of his poems.

20. Conley may have been a pseudonym. A former member of the Workers' Party remembered that Shachtman had attacked Shub's book.

The fact is that some pretty lamentable types have written good poetry, while some horrible political and even moral ideas have also produced poetry (Ex. Of the latter: the Old Testament *passim*.) I see no reason why we cannot award Mr. P the poet while at the same time denouncing Mr. P the fascist and anti-Semite, just as one can admire Napoleon's military genius while abhorring his ethics.

Does the above at all explain my view?

P.S. The same difficulty is posed, for the democrat and equalitarian, though in a less intense form, by the whole development of English literature since 1900. The indisputably great names: James, Joyce, Eliot, Yeats, Lawrence, Shaw, Pound. Except for Shaw (and he is at the least ambiguous, with his former praise for Mussolini and for dictatorship in general), all held social and political views which are distressing to the socialist, the anarchist, or even the liberal. All were, in short, deplorably reactionary. Yet they wrote great literary works, Ergo, bad politics does not result in bad novels or poems. Ergo, reality is not constructed as neatly as one might wish. Ergo, the only way to find out if a poem is good or not is to consider it by itself and not in connection with the ethical, political, or social views of its creator.

To Robert Bone (young Columbia professor and devout *Politics* subscriber, angry at Macdonald's anti-Soviet position]

June 15, 1949

You're right when you detect a change in me, and in *Politics*. In WWII, I said to hell with both war camps (Axis and Allies), originally as a revolutionary socialist, finally as a pacifist. This doesn't mean I said, as many if not most of my colleagues in both the socialist and pacifist movements said, that there were not important qualitative differences between the Nazi and Allied war camps. On the contrary, in *Partisan Review* (around the summer of 1941) Clem Greenberg and I wrote a little article opposing the war which began by admitting such differences. But other considerations then seemed to be more important than these differences. As a socialist, I opposed the war because I thought it would not solve the problem of totalitarianism (it hasn't) and because I thought a revolutionary "third camp" had a historical possibility of coming into existence, as it did during WWI, and solving this and other problems. And the first condition for such a third camp coming to be was to oppose the war, since the logic of support of one side in the war was that the victory of that side would solve the problem. Then, as a pacifist (after the atomic bombing of Japan) I felt that the very methods of modern warfare are so atrocious that no good can come of a war.

The reason I no longer take the revolutionary socialist view in opposing a war is clear: no third camp materialized, and the chances of it doing so in WWIII seem to me negligible. Pacifism still has a hold on my thinking, though I should tell you, if you don't already know, that I have felt obliged to resign from both the War Resisters League and Peacemakers. I tried to show the dilemma which as (then) a pacifist, I found myself in today in my questions and answers in the fall issue. This dilemma hasn't been resolved, for me, so that I felt it necessary to resign from pacifist groups. (For while I'm not a nonpacifist exactly, neither am I a pacifist; in short, I'm still in a dilemma.)

Politics has, as you write, taken a different line toward the national enemy in WWIII-to-come than it did in WWII. While we didn't print much about the evils of Nazism or the comparative virtues of the USA in WWII, in the past year we have harped on this theme vis-à-vis Russia, rather insistently. The reasons for this change are partly, so to speak, technical: *Politics* is a radical magazine; no appreciable proportion of its readers or their acquaintances had any illusions about Hitler's system, hence there was no point beating a dead horse; in the case of Stalin's system, however, this is not the case. While probably not a large percentage of our readers feel friendly to Stalinism, it seems to be the case that (a) many of them still cherish illusions about it, that is, still see it as much less threatening to socialist-pacifist values than Nazism was (whereas the fact is, because of its greater ideological depth and consistency and because of its greater appeal to the masses, the youth, and the intelligentsia, Stalin's communism is far MORE dangerous), and (b) almost all of them move in left-of-center milieus where illusions about Russia and communism are still widespread. I know for I went on a lecture tour, on Wallace, a year ago, speaking at various big Midwestern universities, and found that there was a great deal of friendly sentiment among the students (the people whom radicals must look to first for action) toward Stalinism and the USSR.

These, however, are as stated above, technical reasons. The more important reason for the shift you discern is this. On the one hand, I no longer think that the American people are going to make that revolution, that drastic break with ancient evil and hoary iniquity, which I once hoped they would make; so I no longer see any political (or, if you want, historical) reality in such utopian, all-or-nothing doctrines as revolutionary socialism or pacifism. (I don't see any other people making the break either, but am less certain about it because I don't know as much.) On the other hand (and doubtless it is in large part the result of these expectations of basic change for the better being disappointed) I have become very conscious of late of how very much better things are ordered in this country (so far as the interests of the great mass of human beings are concerned and also so far as my own interests are concerned) than they are in Russia and in countries which are now within the Russian sphere. I could also see that there was such a difference between Nazism and democracy, but, since I then felt there was a THIRD choice, the differences seemed less important. Now that I see no third choice (that is, no victory for either Trotsky or Gandhi over here), I'm more aware of the importance of the difference. I also tend to ask myself more than I did; what would be the actual effect, here and now, on the people directly involved in a victory of USA or of USSR in this or that area of their global struggle? Formerly, I was willing to sacrifice myself and to demand similar sacrifices from others, under the formula of future benefits demanding present losses—with the idea that the Third Camp policy might mean the temporary extension of Nazism but that the ultimate result would be favorable. Now I have been forced, by what I think is the logic of events, to abandon this ultimatist, utopian perspective, and to think in much more limited empirical, here-and-now terms. I simply cannot see the withdrawal of the US Army from Berlin and the consequent giving over of the Berliners to the terror and repression of the Soviet system, as a good thing. I don't think peace would have come nearer, and I know that a lot of people would have at once suffered a very great change for the worse in their lives.

But let me come now to your concrete points.

(1) By "West" I mean the non-Communist part of Europe plus the USA, that is, those nations which still are part of "Western civilization," which still are somewhat linked to the whole development from the Greeks through the 18th century of Western culture. Russia, as I have made clear in this very issue (p. 10) and elsewhere in *Politics*, breaks today sharply with this tradition. It is closer to the pattern of Asiatic despotism. So (also see p. 10) I do indeed mean "Acheson and I" as against, let's say "Vishinsky and Howard" (p. 10). [Macdonald was responding to a *Daily Worker* columnist in *Politics*; he was "choosing the West."] Whether this distinction is "simpleminded" or "meaningless" or "imprecise" depends on whether you agree with my interpretation of the facts; if you can show me that the Soviet system is not so dramatically opposed to Western culture as I think it is, I'll gladly change my terms (and my mind).

. . . What has changed in the last two years in my political and ethical thinking is that I have lost my faith in any general and radical improvement in modern society whether by Marxian socialism or by pacifist persuasion and ethical example. So I have come to look at any situation, or policy, in immediate terms—that is, to judge it by what I estimate its effects will not be just tomorrow, of course, but at least in a relatively short time, that is, the few months or years that I can with any clarity look forward, estimate the results. Looking at things this way, one realizes that often, perhaps usually, the effects of absolute perfectionist, logically harmonious, and ethically pure doctrines like socialism or pacifism are, here and now, quite bad for people. Take the question of the bid for world power by Soviet communism. Pacifists (and your letter shows this clearly) instinctively tend to underrate the threat of Stalinism and to deny that it is not only far worse than the US or Western European political systems but also a new kind of total human degradation which is to the old tyrannies of our epoch as the atom bomb is to the Gatling gun. So they say, don't contribute to war hysteria—let's try to "understand" Russia (by which they mean really what Wallace, for whom many of them voted, meant: let's moderate our criticisms, let's give her what she wants—I claim that I myself "understand" Russia, or rather the 4 million bureaucrats who run Russia, and that the more I learn about their system and psychology and ethics, the more I am forced to conclude that only force and hostility, not necessarily and not preferably military, will protect pacifist and socialist values against the Soviet threat). Pacifists also cannot possibly favor keeping the US Army in Germany or elsewhere (or even having an army). But the first result of withdrawal and disarmament on our side would be the spread of Russian power throughout most of the rest of the world, and the second its extension to this continent. The pacifist says that maybe, but by then our pacifism and brotherly love will win over the Russians themselves. This I no longer think would be the case. It might work if we had to deal only with the Russian people, directly; but there has arisen in Russia (as there arose in Germany) a new kind of state and of power politics which uses both the utmost of brutal force (killing off the Jews and the kulaks and other oppositionists) and also of psychological pressure (getting inside people, as in the Mindzenty[21] and the Moscow Trials, making them actually different people—the kind of broken zombies George Orwell's 1984 describes); and whose government apparatus is so powerful and so unchecked by any classes or social groups outside the government that it operates with a maximum force on all opposition, whether pacifist or not. There is no "public opinion" to appeal to in a Russian and a Russian-dominated country; I might even say there is no "human nature," at least none that has any perceptible effect on the policies of the ruling class.

. . . The difficulty in arguing with socialists and pacifists, I find today, is that, while our basic values are much the same, our intellectual picture of the world, our estimate of what is actually happening, is so different that to discuss any single point leads one into a discussion of the whole picture.

. . . So to your point: Yes, I'm quite proud of what I and others did at the Waldorf Conference [challenged the Communists]. I don't agree with [Sidney] Hook's policy on CP teachers. On the other hand, I also don't agree that a

21. A Roman Catholic clergyman who resisted the Communist regime in Budapest. He was sentenced to life in prison and was set free during the uprising of 1956. When the Communist government gained control, he sought asylum in the U.S. embassy. He spent fifteen years in voluntary confinement there and was permitted to return to Hungarian society in 1971, at the entreaty of President Nixon.

Commie teacher would not distort the truth more than either a Catholic or a bourgeois; in fact I am quite sure he would distort it a great deal more. Again, I think you don't know enough about the CP press, movement, ideology, actions. As for looking at my bedfellows, that's always the last resort, in a political argument, of I won't say a scoundrel but rather a sophist. Before the war, I constantly attacked the New Deal alongside Westbrook Pegler and Colonel McCormick; during the war, the Nazis were on my side throughout and the Stalinists until mid-1941; today you are in bed with the Stalinists on issues like peacetime conscription (as I am also). Etc. . . .

I prefer Truman, atom bomb and all, to Stalin because while the atom bomb is horrible, Truman (and US society) is NOT summed up in it, there are also virtues, even humanity; while Stalin is 100% (or at least 95%) pure evil, and his system IS summed up in death camps and police terror, with not enough mitigating virtues to be worth talking about.

. . . I agree that Pound, like [Norbert] Wiener,[22] must be judged as a whole man, fascism and all, and not just as a poetic specialist. But I didn't praise Pound (but on contrary explicitly condemned him—he wrote me an abusive letter about it) but the Bollingen judges. And I think if you are judging poetry, you should judge it only as poetry, without regard to the personality or ethics of the poet. . . .

To Will Phillips

July 18, 1949

We're all fine—Cape has never been nicer—our house this year is big, and I have a detached studio in the woods where I should get a lot more done than I do. And you and Edna? Trust you have been able to be at your country place at least part of time in this terrible heat.

So [Mel] Pitzele[23] doesn't recall telling me you said what I told you he told me you said. Indeed, we'll need a Lloyd Paul Stryker to get to the bottom of this! (By the way, weren't you pleased with the result of that trial? I'm fairly sure

22. In the Winter 1949 issue of *Politics*, Macdonald wrote a column dealing with what he called "uncommon people" who had committed individual acts of courage and principle. Norbert Wiener, an MIT mathematician, had refused to give information to a colleague working on guided missiles. He had acted as a man first and a scientist second. Robert Bone felt that in supporting the decision to give the Bollingen Prize to Pound, Macdonald was being inconsistent in not seeing Pound as the fascist first and the poet second.

23. Mel Pitzele was the labor editor of *Business Week*, a former Trotskyist who had moved to the right and become a spirited anti-Communist. With his friend Arnold Beichman, he had played a role in the struggle against the Waldorf Conference. This cryptic reference is probably about behind-the-scenes strategy in those protests.

Hiss is guilty, and the verdict was a real triumph considering the judge's behavior, etc. The day the jury was out, I bet Francis Biddle (yes, the ex-atty-genl) $5 that Hiss would be convicted, so the jury saved me $5 (all the smart money was on Hiss, I gather). Biddle said he, if he had been on the jury, would have had to vote for acquittal, on grounds of reasonable doubt. I have the impression the Old New Dealers, and Truman, really hoped that H would get off, that they're afraid of the case. Or maybe a psychoanalyst. Pitzele is a very curious fellow. I know he told me what I told you he did, because I at once cross-questioned him, since the remark appeared to me out of (your) character. And I have another trivial story, re P., which also involves a statement he made—tell you when I next see you. . . .

. . . And reading a lot—most recently, Hulme's *Speculations*, a very disturbing and brilliant book; I agree with half of his basic points, disagree violently with the other half; I imagine you would disagree almost wholly; have you read it? Also Sorel's *Reflections on Violence*, which so far is disappointing— more of Mencken than of Nietzsche, I'd say.

A neighbor up here—Paul Magriel—wants to review Nat Fleischer's current book on heavyweight boxing for PR, and I said I'd suggest the idea to you. Paul is a very learned and lively fellow—an expert on baseball, boxing, and ballet (was curator of the dance at the Museum of Modern Art for a while, also edited "Dance Index"; has published scholarly books and bibliographies on boxing, and has a big collection of boxingiana. He thinks Fleischer, who is the Meyer Schapiro (or thought to be) of boxing lore, is an ignoramus and a self-advertiser; and he wants to demolish, definitively, Fleischer's claims to scholarly rating (Fleischer is often referred to as "Mr. Boxing.") Might be a lively item for PR; sports scholarship is a neglected branch of Popular Culture. If you're interested enough to tell him to have a try, drop him a note, address Wellfleet, Mass. He has the book already.

To George Orwell

July 19, 1949

How are things going? I admire your energy and courage in building a house, farming the land, etc. . . . I'm writing this mainly to tell you not to worry about the loan. Our finances are not really too bad, and perhaps we alarmed you too much. All we meant to say was that, when repayment is convenient to you, it would be nice for us. But we weren't thinking of getting anything at all back in less than a year, and we perfectly understand that what you can do on it depends on how well things work out as to climate, etc. So please don't make any sacrifice—there's no hurry at all.

Looking forward to M. L. Berneri's book on utopias, a subject peculiarly close to my own current interests. I read *Freedom*'s special supplement on her, and felt that the photographs bore out the enthusiastic praise in the articles. I mean that she seemed to have been much more of an anti-intellectual (and even anti-life, or at least anti-enjoyment and spontaneity) party organizer than I myself like or admire; I got the impression she believed in sacrificing one's more "difficult" and "esoteric" ideas (that is, one's real ideas, as against party slogans and moral tags) in order to "educate" and "be understood by" the common people. I have long believed this to be a bad idea anyway, and especially foolish because I don't believe the masses are thus educated, or even moved (at least not in a socialist direction). On the contrary, I'd say the most effective popularizers of socialism were men like Bakunin and Marx who didn't have this idea at all, who wrote to the top of their bent always, without this vulgar modern mass-market idea of hitting at the lower common denominator. She reminded me of C. Zaccaria, of Naples (her husband's uncle?, anyway some relation), with whom I talked at length several years ago in NYC, and whom I found quite antipathetic for the reasons just noted. I'm sure he regards me as a perverse dilettante, and I know I felt him to be the same kind of pious, simpleminded "organization man" I used to know in the Trotskyist movement. Finally, I must say I thought M.L.'s pamphlet on the Russian workers a bad job—tritely written, a badly organized mass of undigested facts. This confirms my above suspicions. Am I wholly wrong?

Future of *Politics* is uncertain, as enclosed will show. Meanwhile, I'm at last getting down to revising and expanding "The Root Is Man" for book publication. Am also doing a lot of swimming, walking, clamming, and (as always) talking.

Best to Inge.

To Nicola Chiaromonte

September 14, 1949

. . . I cannot agree, however, when in reply to [Arthur] Koestler's choose-the-grey, you write: "There is a grey side to Stalinism, too, if we start going in for nuances." IS there really? Only yesterday, [I] was discussing point re Nazis with a neighbor, who teaches sociology and has pro-Wallace leanings, and she said: "There's nothing that's all black, after all." So I challenged her to give the white, or even grey, side of Nazism, and all she could think of was [Erich] Fromm's point that the Nazis gave the youth a feeling of belonging to a community, and the institution for some kind of common cooperative living. But when I asked what this communal-cooperative relation was used for, she was embarrassed. So just what is this grey side to Stalinism? I really don't see it. I think that since 1930 we have seen the growth of totalitarian political formations which, as the name suggests, really ARE total (as much as anything human and hence finite and fallible can be) and that totality is an evil one. That is, I think it can be shown that Stalinism is all black, and that if the Russian people get anything good out of it, it is because they evade or resist it. Whereas the European or American political-economic systems seem to be mixed, that is, grey. For example, I can publish *Politics* because Nancy has some capital; I can use The System to further a good (in my view, and yours) end; the ideology and the control is not yet total. For the ownership of capital, even if it is used for anti-Capitalist purposes, is sanctioned and protected by the system; hence, a cranny, a loophole. So too the worker in the West can move from one place to another, can change jobs, can have some degree of personal security from punishment by the state if he obeys certain written and well-known laws. Also, he (and the petty bourgeois intellectuals like ourselves) has SOME choice of his political and cultural foods; can read books and periodicals which attach different values to things; etc. You know all this of course. But I really would like you to attempt an answer to the question: just what, concretely, is grey in the Stalinist system. I ask this because the more I compare the present systems in the East and in the West, the more I am driven to the conclusion that the East really IS black as compared to the West's grey. So, as an internationalist and pacifist, I'd like to see as much grey as possible in the East. . . . Do help me out, Nick![24]

To Readers of *Politics*

October 10, 1949

I have reluctantly decided to suspend publication of *Politics*. My reasons are partly financial, partly personal.

Financial: So far, we have raised slightly over $900. This is being returned to the donors. The minimum needed to guarantee a year's monthly publication is $8,000. (My own income, for example, is so depleted that I would have to get a salary of $3,000 out of the magazine if I gave full time to it.) That means at least $7,000 more to be extracted from friends and readers, a job for which at the moment I have neither heart nor stomach.

Personal: Although I had all summer to draw up the promised prospectus for the new *Politics*, I did absolutely nothing on it. So I conclude that I don't really want a magazine right now. For several reasons: the general political situation, which gets less interesting and more depressing every month; reluctance to assume again the many routine chores involved in putting out a magazine

---

24. Chiaromonte replied that with respect to international power politics, the guilt was shared by both the superpowers, and that Macdonald's "pure evil" argument weakened criticism of American foreign policy.

(these are stimulating for a time, but after five years they pall); the fact that my own values and interests are changing even more rapidly than usual, so that I want to spend more time on my own writing and less time tinkering with other people's.

It's painful, naturally, to let the magazine go, especially since many of you have expressed so personal an interest in *Politics*. But, for the above reasons, I feel it must be done. Perhaps later on things will look different. If so, you will hear from me.

Meanwhile, please be sure that Nancy and I won't forget the support, encouragement and friendship so many of you have given us.

P.S. Nancy's "Packages Abroad" will continue to use the office. The need is still great, and contributions will continue to be most welcome.

To Joan Colebrook

October 12, 1949

It's nine A.M. and I'm sitting in the office, alone, with my shirt off (it's very hot). I'll begin work soon (this morning it must be stuffing envelopes, some 1500 of them, announcing the end of *Politics*, a sad task), but first I want to write you, dear.

Your (1), (2), (3) letter came—how do you manage to write so often? It's amazing (and, for me, wonderful) with all the things you have to do. On the job: you know, after we parted, I thought of the same thing myself: that you might do some research, for which I'd pay you out of proceeds. (I'm seeing Phil Horton, of *The Reporter*, on Friday; they pay $.10 a word, and Phil wants me to write for them; I will.) That will work out all right, I'm sure. And it would be a way that we might legitimately see each other more frequently (in addition, of course, to the illegitimate times). I'll think of something shortly, and we'll confer about it. One idea I had was a series, some kind of human-interest expose, for the N.Y. *Post*, which runs a lot of such material, and whose new editor, Jimmy Wechsler, I know. They had a series on teenage gangs this summer; it was not good, but might have been. For that matter, you might do, on your own, a series on that Jefferson Market women's prison you want to get into—get yourself arrested and tell just what happened to you after that. I'd give you an introduction to Wechsler, and with your personality, and your literary standing, you ought to land the job.

On your "Thirdly": God, did I really say "No wonder V [reference to Joan's husband, John Van Kirk] socks you if you etc.?" How could I have? I don't recall it at all. Wasn't I kidding?—even so, what brutal jest. Darling, I am distressed, and you're right, it was "insensitive" to say the least. I'm sorry. "What prompts them?" you ask about such statements. This: in my school and college days I felt rejected, scorned by women—longer than that, in fact: for most of my time on *Fortune*, that is until I met Nancy in 1934. This feeling still was dominant, though not so painful, until three years ago. The result of this long time of fear and frustrating and (in the early years) successive rejections (doubtless in part engineered by myself unconsciously because I was really afraid of women and wanted NOT to have to do with them)—the result is that I have become very suspicious and anxious, really unable to believe that a woman could love me and not let me down or dismiss me or betray me. So I attack you, because I can't believe you really do love me, and because I want, unconsciously, to prepare myself for disillusionment (she really wasn't loving, I could see it all the time. . . .).

. . . But when I wrote you last week, I was very depressed, and still suspicious, fearful; so I projected on you my fears and doubts. If I do it again, darling, remember, it's not so much me as my past speaking. (But, nota bene: the foregoing is in no way intended to apply to all future criticisms or complaints I may have—in general, on the contrary, they will be extremely acute, completely justified, and should be listened to with the utmost respect by JVK!).[25]

To T. S. Eliot

November 14, 1949

Thanks so much for your very kind letter of last summer about *Politics*. As you know by now, I finally decided to suspend publication for a while. I don't by any means regard this as permanent; in fact, I hope to revive the magazine, in some form or other, next fall. One reason, not the least, for my wanting to do this is the response from readers to the notice of suspension: many of them—more than I'd realized—seem to feel that *Politics* was valuable to them in a personal, unique way. So I feel that more of a group, an audience has been created than I'd thought, and it would be a pity not to continue the relationship later on—such relationships being so rare and difficult in our dehumanized commercial culture over here. Meanwhile, I'm doing some writing for money, as the family is broke, and also revising and enlarging my two-part article, "The Root Is Man," to make it into a book.

Again, thanks for your encouragement, which means a good deal to me. I do hope we can meet again next time you are in this country.

25. Joan's current husband, John Van Kirk.

To Joan Colebrook

November 15, 1949

Dear, I'm dashed you cannot come up today, intense disappointment, as it's been so long and I had much to tell you. Then there was all that typing—though since you had that same typist's cramp you did last time you were in town, perhaps it was as well you couldn't come after all. Not really, though. . . .

However, must be "philosophical" about things like this (interesting use of the word, implying that the philosopher is one who gets above human miseries by an act of disinterested, objective looking at them as a whole—as indeed he does). I'm drinking gin and water (don't worry, in moderation) even though it's morning; it helps one to be philosophical, at least it helps me. . . .

Thank you for your two letters. No, you shouldn't conquer your reluctance to go to the Cape next summer. Don't you feel, as I do, that the Cape has become too easy and familiar a routine, and that one wants new, possibly exciting or possibly pleasurable or maybe both, experience? Paris and Rome are the two places I want to go most, and if you too were able to be there, how marvelous! Think in these terms, will you darling? . . .

Thomas Cook says there's a special winter round-trip rate (if you return within 60 days) on Transworld Airlines, NYC to Rome, of $597.60; doesn't sound very special to me, but regular rate is $800; children under two are free, over are half-fare. You could also fly NYC to Paris, thence second-class rail to Rome, for about $10 less; the air round trip there is $493.40. Further information, consult Miss Rogers, Thomas Cook, 587 5th Ave., Vo-5-1800.

Are you REALLY thinking of doing it?

Oh yes, you can get space, she says, but advisable to reserve it right away. You can cancel reservations, without loss, up to 3 days before sailing, or rather flying.

Awfully dangerous, air travel.

Sorry I sound businesslike on the phone, but the instrument inhibits me because I can't see the other person (also, in our case, because one doesn't know who's listening in); you know I don't feel businesslike, don't you?

What is this important new thing that has happened down there? Take pity on my curiosity and give me, in your next letter, at least a general idea. Is it anything bad? Please tell me.

Yes, we should see a wider variety of people than we do, and yes, we should find some way to appeal to people by reason (I liked Schweitzer, in his autobiography, insisting that he still held an 18th-century belief in reason despite its current unfashionableness; I do too.) But what to do, concretely? Don't you feel that we've all been on the wrong track all our lives—by "we" I mean myself and the milieu I've lived in so long here in NYC; your life and milieu have been, until recent years at least, different, but I suspect you too feel this.

I'll see what I can dig up on the two research topics (I seem to reverse letters in typing a lot these days, wonder what it means, maybe suppressed homosexuality—inversion, that is? If so, it sure is suppressed!) Why are you interested? And why were you reading back issues of *Time* at Princeton? I mean, what is the connection with your novel? Just curious (as usual).

Sat up till 3 A.M. the other night finishing *The Age of Innocence*. A very good second-rate novel (I mean on the Trollope–Dos Passos level as against the James-Proust level); interesting to compare it with James, whose pupil she was; two differences struck me at once: there's comparatively little tension, formal interest in her prose style; she describes from the outside where James dramatizes from the inside, thus she gives a much better idea of the mores of the time, is better as a social satirist, while tells me far more about life in general. The epilogue, 30 years later, is very amateurish; out of key and sentimental. Thank you for the book, which meant something to me, and which I enjoyed a lot. . . . Did you, by the way, in giving it to me have any kind of parallel in mind? If you don't know what I mean, you didn't.

The other night we went to a little party for Ruth Fischer (you know, "Stalin and German Communism"—Eisler's sister) at, of all places, Bertha Gruner's apartment, on Greenwich Avenue. I had a long talk with Karl Wittfogel, whom I'd like you to meet some time; he is probably the foremost Sinologist in this country, and that doesn't mean a sinus specialist, and a wonderful type of passionate scholar. Bertha, who works for him, has put his latest work, a huge $15 volume, first of a vast History of Chinese Society which he is directing, on her table, and he began to tell me about it. His voice trembled with intensity and excitement, as if he were in love. Which he is, with knowing about things. There's something very moving, and attractive, about anyone who is really serious and passionate about anything, isn't there? It's odd this intensity about his "subject," because he is a big blonde stolid-looking fellow, very courteous and collected for the most part. What set him off, I think, was some remark of mine which indicated that I thought the book much too specialized for a layman like me to make any sense out of (and thus by implication not of interest to me); so he set about showing that it wasn't just "scholarship" but that it had something to tell me, too. Which shows he is not just a specialist but something much more. . . . We're driving up on Sunday to spend the day with the W's, in Cornwall. They said we should come for the weekend if without the children, for the day only if with them; they seem to regard children with considerable anxiety, like strange hostile animals, and each blames it on the other—very curious.

Darling, it's sad you're not here today, and I cannot tell you face to face that I love you and have missed you every day. But I'll come down next Monday surely. Can I stay the night? . . . I'll call you Friday or Saturday. . . . Enclosed some things, let me have back some time. . . . I wish I could kiss you. . . .

To Bob Hatch [*New Republic* editor]

November 23, 1949

Look. You need a political adviser. Of the six people who are doing major reviews in your forthcoming Books on Russia section (a good idea, by the way), five are Stalinoids, that is, persons who are relatively sympathetic to the present Soviet regime. The sixth, Bergson, is neutral. There is not one anti-Stalin writer, as against 5 of varying degrees of pro-ness. What goes on? Furthermore, I'm something of a Soviet "spetz" myself, in a small way. Why didn't it occur to you to ask me to do something? Or Bert Wolfe, or Dallin, or Solomon Schwartz, or Nikolaevsky, or Shub, or Karl Wittfogel, to name the first people in the definitely "unsympathetic" camp that come to mind? Each of these is as well qualified as any of the ones you did ask, and better than Barnes and Lauterbach.

Or maybe you think your five are either neutral or anti-Stalin? In that case, I repeat, you need a political adviser. Will you liberals never learn the Facts of Life?

More in sorrow, believe me, than in anger.

To Joan Colebrook

December 7, 1949

. . . On [Henri] Bergson: try it this way, maybe: read 3 pages a night, no more; that kind of writing is very hard for one not used to it; I'm not as adept as you seem to think at it, have never had any training in philosophy, and there is something in me which prefers the concrete always; but in our age it is necessary even for nonphilosophical types to learn this kind of thing, because things are corrupted at the root and only by this kind of thought can one get down that far. B's message is essentially that we should think in terms of time rather than of space; things change ceaselessly in time, since each new second changes one's perception by adding itself to the total, so that in looking at an apple one sees a different apple every second (the apple plus one second of apple-view, the apple plus two, etc.). Modern man, scientifically minded, thinks in space terms, since one can lay out a thing in space, can diagram it so to speak, and it will stay put, to be analyzed and catalogued by scientific investigation. But in time nothing stays put, even for an instant, there is no way to hold it down, and intuition is the only recourse, the typical method of the poet, the artist—and, dear, of the woman. B also sees space-thinking as deterministic, and time-thinking as instance of free will. I'd say that YOU (like Molière's bourgeois who discovered he had been talking prose all his life) have been time-thinking all your life without knowing it. So do attack B again, when you feel like it.

Goodbye now, darling, and I couldn't love you more.

Dwight Macdonald with Norman and Adele Mailer in Provincetown, Massachusetts, 1960. (Courtesy of Sabrina Lanier)

CHAPTER FIVE

CRITICISM AS A SUBSTITUTE FOR POLITICS, 1950–1959

*"A tepid ooze of mid-cult is spreading everywhere. . . .
Americans have been made into permanent adolescents by
advertising, mass culture—uncritical, herdminded, pleasure-
loving, concerned about trivia of materialistic living, scared
of sex, death, old age. . . ."*

Increasingly disillusioned with politics as a "desert without hope," Macdonald hoped to revive his interest in life by engaging in cultural criticism. It became a substitute for politics in that it allowed him to maintain a critical stance toward American culture while at the same time accepting the major establishment premises of the cold war. Abandoning his earlier life as a political partisan, he was also abandoning his marriage and embarking on one and then another affair, culminating in his marriage to Gloria Lanier. In some subtle way, his discontinuing *Politics*, leaving Nancy, marrying Gloria, moving out of the Village to the Upper East Side, and becoming a staff writer for the *New Yorker* confirmed that the old camp of the New York intellectuals had indeed broken up. His work for the American Committee for Cultural Freedom and his tenure at *Encounter* brought him much closer to the American establishment. Closer, perhaps, but he remained a loose cannon.

To Nicola Chiaromonte

January 6, 1950

. . . Alas, whoever told you I was "fine, working hard on a lot of things" was misinformed—though I *am* discovering Schweitzer (also Bergson's wonderful little "Introduction to Metaphysics"). I'm sure I'm at least as demoralized, stale, and disoriented as you are. And not even for any good external reason, such as an obnoxious job. I'm still not getting down to serious writing, my work habits are still very bad, and my life is still disorderly, slack, and self-indulgent (only that in the city, as against the Cape, there's little pleasure in it). . . . I *am* doing some money writing—a piece on the *NYTimes* for the *Reporter* ($330). And a profile of Richard Weil, president of Macy's New York, for the *NYorker*, for which I hope to get $700 or $800 when it is done; also other projects, still in early stage. . . . But otherwise God knows what becomes of the days, weeks, months; they slip by. . . . At least I'm aware of the nature of my present life, and at least I am still struggling against it and trying to live better. But the long crisis that set in at the end of 1946 is still with me. . . . Greenberg as Paris editor of PR—well well well. It belongs in the No Comment department. The degeneration of everything is frightening. I don't think I could stand another winter in New York. Nancy likes it better, but we may move abroad this spring, for a year at least. Depends on finances and such personal factors as Mike's new school, which he likes very much. Don't even dream in your worst moments of coming back here: nothing is happening, all ties of sociability and intellectuality have snapped, people just don't see each other, and yet one, or I at least, spends half one's time either dining or cocktailing with people one doesn't know and finds flat and dull, or trying to get out of it. . . . That love affair I wrote you about is still going on, to say the least, wonderful and satisfying but full of frustrations, difficulties, dangers, guilt, complications. . . . I seem to have written myself into much too somber a mood; actually, things are not so bad as this letter sounds, if only because my native optimism is too great. Things are depressing and even desperate, but not hopeless, and enjoyment, even satisfaction, is often in my life. . . . Thanks again for your note, and believe me, Nick, there's no weakening on my part, either, of love and affection. When my life becomes more orderly and productive, which I'm taking the new year—and a fresh half-century, too—as a pretext to resolve that it *shall*, I'll write you a real letter.

To Joan Colebrook

[January 26 or 27] 1950

Darling—this will be a short letter because I want to get some work done on The Book. I took Mike to a hockey game at the Garden tonight. Sweet, how *are you?* I hope there will be a letter tomorrow morning. I am going through scores of volumes looking for usable stuff on labor—found some, but its amazing how *abstract* most books are. We saw "The Devil's Disciple" the other night. Disappointing—very thin as a play, and badly acted—the one good part (and actor) was "Gentleman Johnny" Burgoyne (Dennis King). Dinner at Weils[1] last night was quite an affair: 12 people at table, including Herbert Bayard Swope, who was as impressive and socially charming as he's supposed to be. We all had a violent argument over Acheson's not "turning his back" on Hiss. Nancy and I supported him, the rest all thought he acted improperly. I couldn't make them see that it is one of the good features of our system (as against totalitarian ones) that the individual is *not* wholly merged in his office, that he can act as an individual. Terrible about Matthiessen [who committed suicide]! I saw him in action at the Waldorf Conference—he fronted for Fadayev [chief Russian delegate to the Waldorf Conference] and Howard Fast [American novelist and Communist Party member]—was clearly not happy about it all, yet too weak to break with the comrades. What an age we live in. Saw the American Abstract Artists show yesterday. Ghastly! No pleasure—Abstract Art has reached The End. Like Marxism. There was only *one* canvas I liked, out of about 40. Must go now, darling—I love you, adore you, goodbye for a while *Write!*

To Joan Colebrook

February 16, 1950
Darling—I want to call you up just to hear your voice, but I don't not because of the expense (tell you why in a minute) but because I fear my voice will be too businesslike and yours may not exist at all; also I have the sense of all those potential Listeners, which cramps an already cramped telephone style. . . . So, I write, a bad third to (2) phone, (1) you, in the flesh. . . . I returned feeling depressed, not actively so as on one famous previous occasion, but quietly so (and, sure enough, fate, the very next day—yesterday—Mary McCarthy called up, was in town putting her *Post* series[2] to press—I'll clip them for you when they begin next week—and we had her around for drinks; don't worry, no more beans were spilled) and quite exhausted. Darling, we weren't at our best, were we? So many clashes over little (hair pulling, bus schedules) and big (state of my health, my obtuseness about our feeling about publicity) things. Both of us, I especially, insist on points too much, are too articulate, don't find out just

---

1. Richard Weil, Jr., the forty-two-year-old president of Macy's New York store. Macdonald was working on a profile of him for the *New Yorker*.
2. "Greenwich Village at Night." The first installment appeared February 20, 1950.

what IS the situation before plunging in with judgments. And you were so wretched with your cold and headache and things, and, darling, I was not anywhere near sympathetic enough, or understanding enough. . . . How I loved you when you went walking in that bone-chilling rain both days, you with your cold, and how patient and loving you were with me, when I insisted on TALKING TALKING everything through to the bitter end, and you must really have been feeling so lousy. . . . I want to verbalize things too much, sometimes it is better not to try to analyze everything, from a radish to love, which does best if left alone. Too much will-reason in me; yet that is also one of my good points; does anybody really ever know themselves; sweet, do continue to bear with me. . . . Also you were right, of course, about it's being unnatural to see each other so briefly and at such long intervals, so that we sit around all day exhausting each other with much too much emotional-personal talk. . . . I'm a rich man. Shawn of the *New Yorker* actually called me up yesterday, less than 2 days after he'd gotten the profile, and accepted it with enthusiasm; said it was superb, very strong, that I was writing better than ever, etc. etc. And it will be in two parts, which means at least $3000. . . . Can't you think of something . . . for me to do within a radius of 50 miles? . . . What's in Philadelphia, for instance? I could take a room (double) in the Ritz for a week, on my expense account! . . . One more thing: are you still, normally, as distressed and unhappy and upset by the present situation—fact we can see each other so little—as you sounded when I was down [to Bucks County]? I feel guilty about it, yet I cannot, at the moment, resolve it without doing something I don't think ought to be done, now. I love you, and because I love you I cannot bear to have you suffer so much. I didn't realize you were until I came down—this is what saddened me more than anything; from your letters, I got the impression that things were not so bad; but your mood when I was there was or seemed to be that if we couldn't go off together now, or soon, you almost wished we had never begun anything. Joan, I know that in most ways I am much better off than you, but I can't help that, can I darling? And can't remedy it except by the one thing that, now, is unthinkable; you'd agree if you could see, know, as I do. . . . Dearest, do you want to feel free of me? Do you feel it's now or never, so far as I'm concerned? I didn't dare, coward that I am, to put it so directly when I was there. . . . What I am trying to say is that I love you and want you to do what you feel most deeply is best, right for yourself without considering me. . . .

To Mr. [or Miss] Hawes [student doing a study of *Politics*; Macdonald was not sure of gender]

June 25, 1950

... Flattered you think my political philosophy worth a thesis—and hopeful that you will be able to define it more clearly than I ever have!

... I consider myself an anarchist—that is, the free development of the individual seems to me the only reasonable purpose of political institutions, and this I think must be a "here and now" matter, not some distant goal, as with Marx, to be won by coercion, suppression, and other means which bind the individual, cramp him even more than he was under 19th-century capitalism; also, I see the state as the great political enemy today, both here and in Russia; private capitalism seems to me much less menacing to my values than the growing power of the state.

I WAS a Trotskyist from 1937 (when a careful reading of the full transcript of the second Moscow Trial—issued by the Commies over here in a burst of stupidity—convinced me that the trial was a frame-up and that hence the Soviet regime was a corrupt one) up to 1941. At school and college (Exeter '24 and Yale '28) I was a rebel and dissident but not in a political sense; had no interest in politics. From 1929 to 1936 I was a staff writer on *Fortune*, for first 3 or 4 years again completely unpolitical: about 1931 I put out with three friends (2 of them Morris and Dupee, later editors of *Partisan Review* with me) a little literary, purely literary mag called *The Miscellani*, which the public library has. Wrote a lot in it about the movies, especially the Soviet cinema. My years on *Fortune* slowly convinced me that US capitalists were stupid and corrupt, and that capitalism was ditto—I saw things from the inside. Climax came with a big series of articles I did on the U.S. Steel Corporation early in 1936 (the first is especially indicative of my viewpoint then, which was à la Brandeis anti-monopoly liberalistic) as a result of which I got into increasing hot water with Luce and his satrap, Ralph McAllister Ingersoll, who was then editing *Fortune* and was as reactionary as a couple of years later he was pro-Commie. Left *Fortune* around May 1936, worked for a year getting material on a projected book on the steel industry (which never got done), then became editor of the revived *Partisan Review* (Morris, Dupee, and myself joined with the old editors, Rahv and Phillips, to revive it—they had broken with the Commies, who had put it out before that in late 1937) Began to write for Trotskyist *New International* in 1938. . . .

You misread (as I admit others have done) my statement about "critical, support" of the last war, in *Politics*. I meant to reject such support, from a revolutionary socialist viewpoint. (In a footnote in my reply to Don Calhoun's "The Political Relevance of Conscientious Objection," later on, I tried to make that clear.) After the atom bombing of Japan, I became a pacifist, joined the War Resisters League and Peacemakers. But as I wrote in my "Dilemma" article — *Politics* — the Soviet threat has put me in a dilemma, and I no longer consider myself a pacifist, and a year ago I resigned from the directing committee of both the WRL [War Resisters League] and Peacemakers.

To answer your specific queries:

I can imagine a justifiable war, but cannot imagine such a war today because of the technological and social nature of modern warfare.

Violence sometimes is justified.

Bureaucratic Collectivism I take to be what obtains in Russia today. I regard it as an even greater threat to human values than Nazism was (greater because it exploits the idealism of the Marxian socialist movement, and so deceives many who were able to see the infamy of Nazism; Stalin is able to do the same things as Hitler did but without incurring the same disapproval, hence he is more dangerous). Democratic Collectivism I take to be what obtains in England today. I view it about as I view our own political system, that is, compared to Nazism or Sovietism it is good and well worth defending, but in itself it is far short of what I want or even what I think might be possible. I don't know whether collectivism is possible without bureaucracy, but so far it has not been, and I think there are certain theoretical reasons for this. As an anarchist, I don't like collectivism and prefer individualism. Cooperation and free association are what I believe in, following Proudhon and Kropotkin, that is, we must begin with the free individual and let him voluntarily cooperate with other free individuals to achieve such ends as they can all agree on. But I have no confidence in the mother-knows-best psychology of collectivism, whether the mild British and social democratic kind, or the brutal Stalinist kind. Politics for me is something to be worked from the bottom up, not from the top down. The great political problem of our century is how to stimulate the individual to insist on running his own life, on doing things for himself and willingly disciplining himself to work with others for modest, practical human ends, such as educating children, making his community more attractive, and feeding and clothing his family. I think people usually act more decently and more reasonably when they are thinking of their own "selfish" immediate interests than they do when they "sacrifice" themselves and make themselves parts of some grandiose ideological machine to change the course of history. My attitude toward history is about that of Tolstoy in the latter part of *War and Peace*. I'm not scared of people individually, but I am scared of the mass man, impersonal institutions like the state or an army. Nice decent young American boys, thousands of them, tens of thousands, burned to death or disintegrated into dust tens of thousands of "enemy" women and children in the war; they did it as part of the army, as a "job" that was sanctioned by the state, though probably not a dozen of them would have been capable of pouring jellied gasoline over a child and touching a match to it. But it's too painful to write about. . . .

P.S. My views have not changed essentially since *Politics* stopped. I'm even more pessimistic and less able to see any immediate course of political action than I was then.

To Danny Rosenblatt [young union organizer from Michigan who worked on the *Politics* staff and became a close friend of Dwight and Nancy]

August 8, 1950

(Note my wife addresses you as Dearest Danny—hmmm.) . . . No, my summer is not very productive so far, about all that can be said is that it is more productive than last summer, which resulted in a big round $0. I've done a longish review for PR of Bruno Bettelheim's *Love Is Not Enough* (have you seen? much good stuff in it, though perhaps only a parent or one concerned professionally with kids would find it absorbing), and am about to turn out a 900-word job for the *NYTimes* on Louis Fisher's new life of Gandhi, which so far as I've read is vulgar and wretchedly written. Amazing how incompetent, just as a writer, Fisher is: his sentences are all short, all are direct statements with no subordinate clauses (or few at least), and they cohere in a paragraph the way marbles do in a bag. And he's such a toady to power and fame. . . . Mainly I've been hacking away at the [Roger] Baldwin profile, which is to be in 3 parts (at least they've agreed to consider that length) which means about 25,000 words. Alas it will not be done in a week, as poor Nancy (and poor me) thought when she wrote you. It just goes on and on. And I am not, or have not been up to now at least, very articulate on the typewriter. So it is slow work. . . . On Korea, as Nancy wrote you, I'm for the US-UN action. Because the Communist invasion seems just one more in the long series of "have-nots" (and mostly totalitarian) powers use of force to reshape the status quo in their favor: Manchuria, Ethiopia, Rhineland, Austria, Czechoslovakia (Munich), invasion of Poland by the Nazis, of Finland by the Commies. The first five were not resisted by the "have" (or "democratic") powers; result was that Hitler finally invaded Poland, stronger for not having been stopped earlier, and WW2 began. Can see no alternative except use of force to repel force; appeasement didn't work, and certainly wd work even less with Stalin. BUT it now looks as though (even if we with great bloodshed push the Koreans back to the 38th parallel) we are being maneuvered into fighting the whole damn continent of Asia, partly because our own lousy policies (Formosa defense, refusal to seat Chinese Communists in

UN, lack of any policies that appeal to Asiatic masses as against Chiang), partly because of the bold demagogy of USSR (Malik is turning the UN into a madhouse, is proving what Hitler said, the power of the Big Lie confidently and tirelessly repeated). Fact that Indonesia is at best neutral on Korea and India only a little on our side there, this alarms me. Yet what else could be done? It's beginning to look as though Truman has gotten into a Dilemma. Maybe I should send him my Dilemma issue. . . . Re my discussion on Korea etc. with Howard Griffin, (a) his attitude toward USSR seemed to me very wishful and uninformed, like that of the goddam Quakers; he kept talking about "understanding" Russia, to which I retorted that the more I understood it the more sure I was that force was the only way to stop it—in fact, it was my studies in Soviet kulture that finally made an unpacifist out of me; (b) he later admitted he was shaken by some of my arguments (and facts), which shows, as of course we know, that he is a reasonable man. . . . Have been reading D. H. Lawrence's collected poems—he is both more readable (and understandable) than more recent poetry and also, to me, much more moving: he actually wrote love poems that don't read like class problems. . . . This letter doesn't say much, but it seems impossible to talk about most of the things that really matter and Make a Difference. Everything seems so complicated these days, yet I feel myself so simple. Perhaps that's the trouble—a simple soul in a complex situation—and age. . . .

To Joan Colebrook

August 28, 1950

Joan darling, just called, you were not there. So must write. Don't know how serious to you last night's estrangement was then, is now. Hope not too serious. But it is serious to me, at least very painful. Here's what happened, my truth anyway, as it seemed to me. We all went swimming, for my part because it seemed an "opportunity" to perhaps be alone briefly with you. X [Gloria Lanier, whom Dwight was to marry in 1954] hung back from going in, and I took her hand and put my hand on her back and playfully pushed and pulled her in. Then I swam over to you, made advances, was rebuffed. ("No, not with everyone looking." "But no one is, and why do you object?" "Some people don't object," and you swam angrily away, just like the other time.) So I went back to X for a moment, angry too, and feeling your reaction out of all proportion to the offense which did not seem to me an offense at all but merely the slightest demonstration of playful affection toward X. Then we all went back and I followed you to the house, distressed and hoping to make it right, and you again rebuffed me and I said, "Why do you always refuse to take advantage of opportunities." And you: *"You* don't anyway!" "Darling, why do you undervalue yourself so?" "You're the one that undervalues, I think." Then breaking away, cutting it short, leaving the wound to fester. It did. I woke up at 3 —nervous, depressed, guilty, resentful, hurting, anxious—finally got up and read your poems ("First to a Woman" moved me especially, it's a good poem, more than good, and so is "Child"), and when I came across the notation you had added on one of them about the hurricane, I realized it was written for me, and it was as if you were speaking to me kindly and lovingly, and I put my head down and couldn't cry. This sounds literary, and is in expression, but it all really happened. I'm a literary person, as you are. . . . So that's it. Behind it there is more, as you know. Because there *is* more is why I feel upset and guilty. You were, or seemed to me to be, quite unjust about the specific occasion, but there was more. Not much, almost nothing in one way. Something serious, in another, not about me and X, but about me and you. Or maybe just me. (Joan, I love you, and that means more to me now than ever it has.) This. A few weeks ago some of us had an hour to kill here one evening, waiting for the kids to get back from a movie, so we danced. X and I got on very well as dancing partners, so I enjoyed dancing with her. (I'm not a good dancer, don't know steps, and worse, can't or don't hear music, so don't keep proper time; my dancing is more pantomime, in imitation of dance steps, than dancing; you know all this since you've danced with me; I like to dance, though.) Then, at Libby's dance, we did a lot more dancing, X and I, and I found her again pleasurable and attractive as a partner; also vice versa. Toward the end of the evening I kissed her, a hasty embrace just outside the porch; she had asked me to come out and see the stars, and I knew what she wanted and felt a tenderness, and an attraction, for her. But I did not want more than that, because of you. And because, beyond this sexual attraction (curiously fixated on dancing), she means and I think can mean, nothing. She is now ardent, awkwardly so. I had thought to let things slide, perhaps out of cowardice, perhaps to avoid hurting, perhaps because nothing has been at all explicit and maybe I'm assuming or presuming too much. The party last night I did make efforts at avoidance, I certainly did *not* make or take advantage of any opportunity, but you were as contemptuous and hurt as if I had. If you sensed I felt an attraction and were reacting to that, then haven't you yourself admitted such feelings to others? If it was the incident in the water just described, wasn't your reaction excessive? And didn't you practically drive me back to X by your withdrawal, so abrupt, so decisive, so completely breaking off (the hardest thing for me to stand with you is this kind of cutting me off from you; it's a surgery justified in extreme situations . . . too brutal, too hurtful for last night? No?). This is all too defensive and one-sided and perhaps excessive, but I feel last night was in a way more serious to us . . . simply because of the apparent triviality of the cause of the misery on both sides.

To Joan Colebrook

November 2, 1950

. . . Thanks for your note, darling, and for all the trouble you took to give me the straight dope on Hauserism.[3] I'm going to give it a try, at least partially, as there's certainly something wrong with my personal relations with food. . . . The one big light midst the encircling gloom . . . is that I have been able to talk with N[ancy] about Things (you know, things) and she reacted nobly, generously, wonderfully; as I knew she would; and more than that, she herself seems to be in a really altered and improved state of mind: the analysis helped her a lot, she thinks, to get over the feeling of inadequacy and inferiority she felt with me so long, partly because she felt out of it with me and my friends and associates from an intellectual point of view, partly because she did not get the emotional response from me she needed, I didn't make her feel a woman (nor did she make me feel a man, of course, this being just another way of putting it). Her relations with R [Robin Lanier, Gloria Lanier's husband] have been very good for her, and it is very serious; she finds in him a tenderness and response that was lacking in me; she says he is very like her, temperamentally and in his troubles and problems (perhaps too much so, she adds); and I see what she means. . . . We talked about possibilities of breaking up, and she says she could face it if need be. In general I believe she has developed amazingly towards independence, has become much more outgoing, has made friends of late—not lovers, friends, women as well as men—in a way a couple of years ago wd have been quite impossible for her. So I really feel much less guilt and anxiety about that since I have returned. (Our second, and really explicit and thorough, talk just took place this morning, and I feel in much better spirits than heretofore.) . . . I think we were never really "right" for each other, emotionally and sexually, but that we loved and respected and had so much in common with each other in all, or at any rate, many other ways (but not the basic, vital ways) that our marriage was good for a long time. Then 3 or 4 years ago, for whatever reasons or perhaps just a kind of cumulative process, we each began to find it increasingly difficult, whence lovers, psychoanalysis, and other disintegrative symptoms. . . . I'm deeply glad we didn't just try to rub along (rubbing each other "the wrong way" in the process, because now things seem to be getting resolved. . . . We even talked about the children, and she said she felt a separation wd. not necessarily be too bad for them, since "we're all decent people and will work it out." . . . She does think, before any final decisions, that I should have

3. Gaylord Hauser, author of a popular dietary program for weight loss and health. Macdonald was beginning to have a weight problem and a particularly large belly, which embarrassed him.

some talks with a psychiatrist, and I agree, since, ghastly as it is to break up a marriage that for so long has been at least much happier and more productive than most marriages, I feel the creative paralysis and the depression I've been in for so many months is perhaps excessive even granting so serious a cause. Also I've been unproductive and depressed since 1947. So maybe there's something queer about me—I mean even queerer than most people are. Anyway, it seems reasonable enough to submit myself to at least a look-see by the experts. So I'm talking to her analyst . . . and shall also possibly have nine sessions with a psychiatrist I've reason to believe is good. I don't have terribly much confidence in it, and I will not go into a regular psychoanalysis (because I don't have enough faith, or hope, or maybe charity about the results). (Though I must say *something* has made a real difference in Nancy.) But I would like to know more about myself, especially since I've been feeling so disoriented and so to speak floating of late. ("I'm not myself today"—odd how penetrating such conversational clichés are sometimes!) And I think I owe it to N, and to you too for that matter, to at least submit some of my problems to some kind of expert diagnosis. . . . Dearest, there's been very little in all this about the important thing, you and me, us, we.

(LATER) How good to hear your voice just now! And how nice and sweet you were about my not writing, and how I do love you altogether! . . . And don't be so unpresumptuous and talk about writing one final letter and so on. For as you see, I have, as I said I would, taken the big and dreadful step and told N the truth, which came as no surprise to her, of course, but it was hard to begin, somehow. And though it's too soon to speak of when and where, we will before very long be together, you and I darling, dearest—with assorted children, of course! (A marriage is an island of privacy totally surrounded by children.) I don't know whether I could go to Haiti or Italy with you in December—that seems like rushing and wd. be too abrupt, I fear, but certainly I can come to you, in whichever place, this winter. You said on phone you wd. probably go to Europe, not Haiti; I like Europe, too, much better—stimulating, lots of places and things to see and people to look up—Haiti sounds too much like the Cape; so DO decide on Italy, dear, and I'll see that you meet all the right people; but maybe we should discuss it all soon.

To Joan Colebrook

December 3 [1950]

It won't work. There's too much of a discrepancy between our emotions. To you, I'm a luxury, to me, you're a necessity. Therefore, I put seeing you before anything else, including my work. You don't: when I just now on the phone suggested that I might come earlier Monday than 12, you said don't, so you could get your daily stint of writing done. I really admire such devotion to creative routine, so that one puts off a meeting by several hours with a lover one hasn't seen for weeks. (You'll say, with that practicality that is one of your greatest virtues and faults, but after all, we'll be together for many hours, in which there will be plenty of time to do and say anything we want to. Oh God!) I admire it but don't envy it. And in this case, it has ominous implications—it's a pretty feeble, commonsensical kind of love that makes such an attitude possible. . . .

I think this is the trouble. Our pasts are too different. Mine is a history of continual emotional and sexual rejections in adolescence and early manhood, then a long period of marriage where there was no rejection but also not (I have come to see of late years) a very intense emotional-sexual experience on either side, and in which I sublimated my sexuality (which I now realize is much deeper and stronger than I'd thought) in writing and thinking and editing; followed by, at the absurd age of 40, the kind of sexual-emotional "awakening" which normally takes place around 20; the knowledge that I am attractive to (some) women, and for the first time a real interest in women; also, last summer, two important fresh discoveries—that I like kids, am good with them, and have a deep feeling for them; and, darling, you, that is, the growth of a relationship unique in my life, a spontaneous, equal, reciprocal, completely open and honest and utterly fascinating relation with a woman, which began on a sexual plane and developed into the strongest emotional tie I have ever felt. . . . You see, I'm not being strategic with you. Even though it all sounds really horrible, the above, to me anyway, and embarrassingly nude, there it is. I dislike especially the abstract words. . . . There is one other thing: my intellectual development was as precocious and "healthy" as my emotional-sexual was the opposite: I began to learn and grow, that way, quite early, and there is a kind of progress, of evolution in that side of my life. In the last 32 years, I now see, the emotional learning I so belatedly am acquiring, or rather the simple idea that there is an important nonintellectual side to one's life and personality, this has paralyzed my intellectual life. I still am in this crisis, don't know if I'll ever emerge; but if I do, I know my thinking will be much different and richer than ever before. . . . Now for you: your growth has been just the opposite of mine. You were early attractive to men, you therefore early developed this side of your nature; and by now you have gone through so much experience of this kind that you are wise, prudent, knowing about it all. You really don't want the kind of love I want to give you (thus my complaint has been that you aren't sufficiently interested in me—as in the business about my Notes on Love, at dinnertime—while you, on the contrary, when I asked you what you meant by the reference to Olive Schreiner's story about the bees, were not delighted at such a close attention to your every word, but on the contrary said to me, affectionately, you shouldn't read my letters so closely. *My* feeling, on the contrary, is that you don't read *mine* closely enough, that you don't answer them in enough detail). Our marriages are also very different: you've made two which haven't worked, I've made only one which has worked (using "worked" in the simplest, most superficial sense, of lasting). This fact has driven you to have lovers, while it has prevented me from the same thing. So now, both of us being middle-aged, though God knows I don't feel so and you don't appear to me to be so, so now you want to "settle down," to make a planned, controlled, harmonious life for yourself, while I want to carry out to the end intensely and recklessly our love. (There's also something of the difference between men and women here.) To continue, on you: Your intellectual-creative development has been as retarded as my emotional development has been: your adolescence and your first-marriage years were spent in conventional noncreative circles; Bernal was your awakening; then over here you changed still more and realized your husband was not your dish (darling, I respect and admire, and sorry the words sound so cold, your hunger, your instinct for this kind of growth, and I hope you feel likewise towards my instinct for the other kind of growth; the marriage with Van Kirk was a regression, though he probably appeared to you different from your first husband, when in fact he wasn't, indeed his personality was deeply hostile to the free life of thought and creativity, even though (or perhaps just because) he superficially had some feeling for it. Your agonies with V show that you really have this deep need for a free and creative life, that you simply cannot "settle down," in this respect anyway, and that is one reason I love you.

So the synthesis of these two strikingly different life histories is that we love each other. (For I know you love me, that's not what's bothering; it's rather how we love each other, what love means to each of us at this present stage of our two lives.) I love you because you seem to me free and lovely and warm, because I can talk with you more freely and with more sense of being understood (or at least of not being misunderstood) than with anyone I've ever known, because I feel that you are like me in many ways, and because you give yourself so generously and can be "yourself" so wonderfully with me. (Also because I like you in bed, but this is not the main reason.) Why you love me I won't venture to say, beyond a speculation that you like my mind. (I know this, not speculation, that you admire some of my ideas and practices about how people should behave to each other, and that you also have a sense of our similarity.)

This is degenerating into a love poem, when I started out to show why it won't work. The trouble is that I simply cannot stay mad at you. But I want to. And yet don't. . . . My mind tells me you aren't for me because of this terrible discrepancy in our pasts. And yet my instinct tells me the opposite. . . . I want to marry you, to live with you for good. Yet my relation with N[ancy] is such that I feel, for a while anyway, that this would mean her shipwreck, and I simply cannot abandon her; she is dear to me, and I love her, in another way; and the kids, oh GOD.

To Nicola Chiaromonte

December 21, 1950

I know, you're absolutely right—inexcusable my not having written in so long—it's not at all, of course, because of any lessening of affection—I've been in a bad mood, everything great effort—also some things, important to me, I don't want to write about. . . .

After nine months, literally, of fooling around, I'm finally getting done with the profile (for *NYorker*) of Roger Baldwin. It's very long—supposed to be 3 parts, about 25,000 words; but as written, is closer to 5 or 6: they will have to cut a lot—but that's only partly why it's taken such a time to do. Main reason is my own indolence-plus-writer's-block; got very little done all summer, due to state of mind. Also, I've made the brilliant discovery, which any idiot would have known already, that in commercial writing one should avoid subjects about which one knows much or has strong personal feelings and convictions. When I wrote about Dick Weil, head of Macy's New York, I did the whole job (2 parts) in 6 or 7 weeks, including getting the research: I didn't know anything about the department store business, and cared less; so I picked up a plausible character for Weil, fitted the data into it, and got a lively piece out of it with little trouble. But with Baldwin, I have to leave out almost everything, have to cover in a few hundred words things I've thought for years about (as, why US liberals went Stalinoid in the early thirties), have to do a job of popularization and condensation that is dull, really, since I'm never finding out anything I didn't know before; also, the material (really a sort of history of civil liberties and of liberalism in the US since 1920) seems important to me; my own conviction, values are involved; I can't toss off something plausible, but have to try to get close to the truth. So one really has to make the kind of effort one makes in writing for one's self. Yet of course one isn't—one is writing to a formula—in the *NYorker*'s case, about the most intelligent and loosest of the commercial formulae, but still a formula; mustn't be too serious, too abstract or difficult; mustn't show feelings or value-convictions directly; have to explain all sorts of things which, if I were writing for myself, I'd assume readers know—or that they'd find out if they didn't. So one gets the worst of both kinds of writing: the responsibility of serious writing (vs. that wonderful carefree who-cares freedom of hack writing), and yet none of the freedom to speak in one's own voice that serious writing gives. Well, I only hope they take the damn thing when I get it done next week. If they don't, we'll really be in the soup.

. . . Ralph Manheim, as usual, is being a trifle malicious when he reports me as a 100% Trumanite. I did approve, 100%, Truman's decision to resist with force the Commies' invasion of South Korea—whole situation seemed to me a replay of all the other crises, from Manchuria to Munich, and nonresistance never worked, never appeased. But the whole political line of Truman—the failure to compete with Commies in freeing, or pretending to in their case, masses from landlords and top dogs—in Korea seemed wrong to me. And in general our foreign policy seems nondynamic, reactionary, defensive. Now that the roof has fallen on us in Korea, I'm damned if I can see WHAT can be done. For the first time it's beginning to seem possible that Russia may win out in the end. The American disease, for such I think it is, goes very deep. Other night I talked to some graduate students in English at Columbia on mass culture— took Gilbert Seldes' new book *The Great Audience*, as my chopping block. One point I made was (quoting German friend) that if the US doesn't or cannot change its mass culture (movies, radio, sports cult, comics, television, slick magazines) it will lose the war against USSR. Americans have been made into permanent adolescents by advertising, mass culture—uncritical, herdminded, pleasure-loving, concerned about trivia of materialistic living, scared of death, sex, old age—friendship is sending xmas cards, sex is the wet dream of those chromium-plated Hollywood glamour girls, death—is not . . . made one neat point: the happy ending is de rigueur in Hollywood, but there is no such thing in real life—everybody's life has an unhappy ending, namely, death. . . . Anyway, we have become relaxed, immersed in a warm bath, perverted to attach high values to trivial things like baseball or football (kids' games really), and we don't function when we get out into the big cold world where poverty, the mere struggle for existence is important, and where some of the people are grownups. . . . Did you see that incredible letter that Truman wrote to the music critic who gave his daughter a bad review? In case you didn't, here's *Time* on it. I rather admire Truman for sending the letter, but what kind of human being does it show him to be, and how lovely to have such a person as President!!!!!!!!!! Truman's a real lumpenproletarian character like Hitler—no sense of fair play (justice), unable to be objective when his own personal interests are involved (justice also)—and then the gutter language (kind of thing for police courts or the flophouse, but in USA, in our warm bath of mass culture, all these distinctions have been melted away. And a President talks like a Bowery bum)—and the nastiness, the brutality (you'll need a new nose)! Really, I think this is one of the big political revelations of the year. . . . But this man, this Bowery flophouse character, is President of the USA, and as such, in no important relation to your and my personal lives. . . .

The kids are developing wonderfully. I love them both, and find both fascinating, to a ridiculous degree. Mike has changed enormously since last summer—has become self-reliant, outgoing, humorous, even a little gregarious.

He's "grown up" or at least taken a large stride away from childhood, overnight. His new school—New Lincoln—is largely responsible; he loves it, talks about it, is interested in what happens there, identifies himself with it; it's really a good progressive school, I'd say . . . Nicky is charming as ever; he was always more stable and outgoing than Mike; he's a great clown, a raconteur who imposes his view of reality simply by virtue of his unself-conscious, intense absorption in what he is trying to communicate—also on occasion a dancer: there was an evening last summer when Nicky, at a Cape party, did a terrific solo to the music of *South Pacific*, all kinds of very professional-looking shuffles and hops and turns, God knows where he picked it up. . . . For that matter, God knows where Mike picks up HIS information: he recently was tops in his class in a current events test, yet I've never seen him read (or heard him talk about) anything except the sports section—or listen to anything on the radio except sports; he must sneak it in behind my back. He's probably going to Exeter next year.

A puzzle: why do adults turn out so badly when children are so good?

To Joan Colebrook [who was traveling in the Southwest and Mexico]

January 23, 1951

. . . Our lives could not have been more dissimilar in the last month. While you've been traveling steadily, I've been sitting here in this apartment, sometimes not going out all day, chipping away at the Baldwin which like some magic substance seems to increase the more I take away from it—I mean the more I write the more remains to be written—like Penelope's web (more in that figure than meets the eye, maybe.) It's not good creation or even work, just will—neurotic blocks all the time so that I stammer over every sentence—but I MUST get it done, since that money is essential—the family is flat broke right now. . . . I've been in such jams before—over a book on the U.S. steel industry, years ago, for instance—but then I just gave up the project after a while. This time I can't because $6000 depends on it. Oh WHY did Baldwin devote his life to civil liberties, and WHY is everything so complicated in the modern world that one gets tired even before one begins to try to unravel and explain it all? Especially to the editors of the *New Yorker* who have all the decent human virtues, but with their readers, present themselves to my eye as a vast blank expanse of political innocence and ignorance to which Everything must be explained.

To Joan Colebrook

March 23, [1951]

. . . Thank you for telling me not to feel depressed, really, it's sweet of you. I'm in a better mood now, perhaps because Dr. Gruenthal [Max Gruenthal, Macdonald's psychiatrist] is forcing me to face up to things, to confront myself and my relationships; I think there's hope for me, and us (not that I didn't always, but at times things become too much). . . . As for those seven women I called before calling Gloria, they were all quite noncompetitive as far as you're concerned, indeed nonexistent except socially for me—Bertha [Gruner] was one, for instance—and I'm quite sure you *do* have seven men around, including blue-angel Pemberton (who's he anyway?), in same category. Only exception might be, but is not, Mary Grand, whom I'll probably see tonight (we're dining with Hatches, and then going on to a party at the Halpers, where Mary will probably be—this Cape society clings all right—trying vainly to think of pun on es-Capism); she's willing and ardent enough, God knows, but always between us, as T.S. says, Falls the Shadow (you), thank God, as T.S. says. . . . I told Gruenthal other day that one of my troubles is I have no personal friends, though I used to have 3 or 4 close ones when I was 20–30; but of late years Nick Chiaromonte and Mary McCarthy are only ones I can think of; and even those I didn't, don't generally talk intimately with; yet I have many, so many more than in past warm intimate *acquaintances*; I establish sociable, friendly relations much more easily than before, but my capacity for friendship seems to have atrophied; keep people too much at a distance; is this at all your own experience? . . . I told Mary that I told Gruenthal, and she said she also regarded me, now that Elizabeth Hardwick is abroad, as her only personal friend on the scene so to speak. Yet we never got around to very personal stuff—odd? . . . Norman Mailer called yesterday, he's rented a room in town and say's he'll be here two or three months; Bea and baby are in Vermont; he invited us to his place tomorrow, and asked me, as a favor, not to get into a political row with Lillian Hellman who may be there too and whom he likes; I promised to be a good boy; his new novel comes out in May. . . . Enclosed are carbons of some of my recent dreams, which I typed out at G's suggestion. I've already given him a verbal account, he says they are very symbolic and also simple, that my unconscious problems lie close to the surface; also, that there's a lot of contradictions in them and in my own statements to him. . . . Joan, my love, I love you and will prove it in not too long a time. . . .

To Niccolo Tucci [former *Politics* contributor and writer]

May 13, 1951

It was kind of you to send me your "non-Marxist" essay, after I was so hectoring and Kefauvering[4] with you on the street about your political views, or lack of them. I apologize for my rudeness. Of late years, I've become more relaxed and even semi-polite about politics, but sometimes the old urge to cross-examine and denounce overcomes me!

I read your essay with intermittent interest. That is, certain formulations (esp. under "The Dandy" section at the end) seemed true and also original, while other parts were to me opaque or else, so far as I could follow, overfamiliar. Your general argument seems absolutely right to me. I've become specially conscious of dreams lately because I'm going to a psychiatrist and so write down the dreams I can remember long enough to get to my desk. My Dr. says I am a very good dreamer, that is, I'm fertile in devices for expressing my unconscious, and also for concealing it. He chuckles, smiles, frowns, looks amazed as he reads the dreams, which are really little stories, aren't they? I've never had such an appreciative audience. If only HE would pay ME for my dreams, instead of the other way round!

To Joan Colebrook

June 19, [1951]

. . . And in your recent letters you . . . still lecture me on my immaturity and ask me where's my manly sense of responsibility etc. When the whole goddam POINT IS THAT I've got to go through a real expression, now, of immaturity and irresponsibility if I'm ever to become really mature and responsible. For years I led a disciplined, maritally faithful, hardworking life—but it was on a false basis, and it began to come apart, and so did I, beginning with 1947. Of course I want to become again productive, self-disciplined, responsible—but there's got to be some inner change and development first—otherwise I'll just go back to what I tried to do between 1947 and the present, that is, to pull myself together by willpower and moral resolves without facing up to my own nature and my own personal history, and without changing anything inside myself—and it won't work, as it didn't work for me then.

. . . Suppose we married. I'd still see in you a lover (the best, most loved, most sexually and emotionally wonderful in my life) and you'd still see in

4. The reference is to Senator Estes Kefauver's recent aggressive questioning of organized crime figures, which appeared on national television. David Halberstam has written that Senator Kefauver became the first politician to benefit from the glare of television.

me . . . a husband (perhaps, probably, ditto ditto). You would want discipline, responsibility, regularity; I, the reverse. I would let my libido float a bit (since I would want to experiment, to explore, to see, belatedly, what women were like and what I was like with them, and since your insistence, which I understand perfectly, on regarding me as the stable, settled, not-in-daytime-and-not-more-than-every-other-night *husband*, would prevent you from really giving me this information (and this reassurance about my own maleness) about women and about myself with women. . . . Right now I'd like wife, but only a wife who is willing and able to let my libido float (or who is, unlike Joan, willing and able to be both a wife *and* a mistress). . . . "Listen, why don't you go ahead and do whatever you want to do without talking about it." Well, YOU listen: my form of action, of being IS "talk," that is, thinking about something and expressing the results in words. Or at least it is that to a large extent. I'm a writer, a person who thinks and analyzes, and when you tell me just to shut up it makes me sore.

To Joan Colebrook

September 11, 1951

. . . And thanks also for your two letters. Delay in replying is due to my not having been near a typewriter for weeks, which in turn is due to esCapeism, living in the present enjoyable moment. Even a letter to you comes under the head of work, since it means sitting down to a typewriter and raising myself to the abstract level of writing words. (SPEAKING words for me is not abstract, or effortful, as you well know. Why is this? Maybe I should be a speaker, not a writer. Had great triumph in P'town [Provincetown] a few weeks ago, at a forum on censorship at the Art Association, with Gilbert Seldes and Mailer as other speakers. I wowed 'em, enraged the fellow-travelers, and made a sensation that became the talk of the town, partly by content of my talk [a defense of absolute free speech, including free speech of Commies, with a blunt denunciation, politically, of communism, thus combining two antithetical stereotypes, siding politically with McCarthy and yet denouncing his tactics as strongly as *The Nation* does], but even more by the form, which was conversational—I've found that if you talk to a hall full of people as if you were talking to three or four friends, that is, if you leave off the full-dress uniform or rhetoric and appear in your shirt-sleeves, you get a kind of anti-rhetorical rhetorical effect that, simply because it is more human and more communicative and livelier, excites and interests and amuses people; I do it because I cannot seem to manage the formal public-speaking effects at all, not out of craft; but it serves quite well; Mailer told me afterward I should cash in on a lecture tour and that some friends of his suggested I should fill the late Robert Benchley's shoes—you remember The Treasurers Report?—which I took as a compliment; my twist, if I ever get around to commercial exploitation, will be to treat serious matters this way, thus engaging sectarians of the Right and the Left, confusing everybody, and I think, bringing out the real seriousness of the subject.) END OF PARENTHESIS.

. . . [I] have never been more conscious of my own [body] than this summer, never spent more time on the sunglared, saltglazed ocean beach or walked more in the enchanted woods around us (we—that is Mike, Nick, and I—have even taken up bird walks, under the stimulus of a youngish Philadelphia, psychiatrist-neighbor, Wharton Sinkler, who is loved by all this summer for his gaiety, gentleness, and intelligent humanity. . . .

No Darling, the difficulties between Nancy and me (which are diminished at the moment, but by no means vanished, nor am I at all certain they ever will be, and don't tell me there are always difficulties between people living together for I realize this, but what I mean is that if there are too many or if they are basic, then there isn't a foundation for living together, though of course it can be done, and most people do it, but not wisely, I think) DON'T prove your point about fidelity. They go back before either of us was unfaithful, and the infidelities were a symptom rather than a cause; in some ways, in fact, things are better between us. But I don't know, really I don't, somehow I've come to feel this summer that there are too great temperamental and even physical differences between us (by physical I mean such things as speed of reflexes, warmth of blood, skin temperatures, style of muscular reactions, and even actual muscular and nervous strength). I don't know. But I do know I must live things out, "run it out" to the (logical) end, and not compromise beyond a reasonable point. Nancy is going back to Gruenthal when we return, in ten days, to NYC. I hope and think it will make a difference to her, will help her, but am less sanguine about us, but, as I believe I have already remarked, I d-o-n-t k-n-o-w.

. . . You write, "Of course you should talk of these things. To whom anyway, if not to me?" Taking you literally, in my fashion, I must tell you that since last spring I have had two "affairs"—God, the English language—one of them, the earlier, of brief duration and no emotional significance, and the other, the later, and indeed current, both longer and much more complete. It's with Gloria [Lanier], as you may have guessed, and I'm not yet prepared to talk much about it and very likely I shouldn't have mentioned it at all, except I felt obligated to, writing to you, because I should have felt playing a double game not to, and I shouldn't have at all were it not that it is important to me, and you told me so wonderfully and honestly about M, and I must do the same, or feel I must. Or else not write you at all. But I want to write you, and feel in some way close to you, and it's all so *different* from what you and I had. Anyway, I'm bemused, and I do enjoy it all tremendously, and I fear that, at present and maybe forever, the root of the matter (faithfulness) is just not in me. It's all very mysterious, and I don't really know what I feel about G except that I enjoy her and vice versa, and maybe, this has occurred to me, it's because she and I are both, as man and woman, still childlike (or, if you like, childish), that is, immature (to say the least), because we both, unlike you, in our 20s and early 30s missed out on Sex pretty much and are now Making Up for Lost Time. Or maybe it's all "just chemical," as they say. I don't know (I'm getting tired of that phrase, as I suspect you are too). . . .

P.S. I just had a $1000 advance from the *NYorker*, do you need some?

To Gilbert Seldes [well-known journalist and critic of popular culture]

October 3, 1951

Let me say, first, on the facts: (1) You misunderstand me on my relations with the Communist Party; I was never a member (though I was, 1940–2, of the Trot-skyists); for about a year, circa 1936, I was a mild fellow-traveler, in a sense I considered myself a radical and ditto the comrades, and I worked with them and gave money to them on some committee to help the sharecroppers; up to then, I was either conservative or nonpolitical (only read Marx, imagine, in 1935!); the 1937 Moscow Trial, of which I read the transcript, caused me to join the Trotsky Defense Committee and to break forever with Commies. (2) [Norman] Mailer didn't "identify" the speaker as a fellow-traveler; he didn't know her; he just agreed with me that, on the basis of her speech, she was one.

    "Slander" seems too strong a term, even granting your whole viewpoint, for my remark that the girl was a f.t. (though not, perhaps, for your own conse-quent characterization of me as a "bastard," "son of a bitch," and a "Mc-Carthyite"). For one thing, I didn't mention her name (since I didn't know it, nor did anyone present), hence your pathetic picture of the ruinous effects on her livelihood and career of my allegation didn't make any sense. For another, I was merely characterizing her political attitude, as it struck Mailer and me, and if the cry of "slander" is to be raised every time, in a private informal conversa-tion, someone disagrees with someone else's political evaluation of a third party, then you'll agree that there won't be much free political discussion possible. Of course, I realize that you don't think I had any real basis for calling her a f.t., and you have a right to that opinion. But it still seems to me far-fetched to argue that she might have been a Catholic or even a Republican. I really don't see how we can settle the question of what is a reasonable basis: I seem to you un-fair and McCarthylike; you seem to me politically ignorant. We'd first have to settle the question of who's right here before we could settle the other one. By the way, I got some slight comfort later on when I chanced to mention our row (or rather, my dear Gilbert, YOUR row) to a Provincetown friend of mine who was in the audience at the forum; he not only agreed that the lady's talk was f.t.-ish but added that she was his tenant this summer and that she subscribed to *The Compass*. (He didn't mind, of course—he just mentioned it as the chief clue he himself had to her possible political orientation.) So your might-have-been-a-Catholic hypothesis will have to be stretched to cover this fact, if you still hold to it.

The issue between us, of course, is much bigger than whether I slandered or didn't slander the speaker. I have long had the impression that you are so distressed by the Budenz-McCarthy tactics (which I condemn, do believe me, as strongly as you do) that you have come to resent and to suspect any vigorous attack on Commies or f.t.'s, feeling that, at best, they can only add fuel to the "anti-red" hysteria, and, at worst, can hurt innocent people. I recall how sharply you reacted, at the Chermayeffs [Serge and Barbara, neighbors of Macdonald in Wellfleet] at dinner summer before last, when I said I didn't think [Owen] Latimore was a Soviet spy but that I did think, from what I knew of his writing, that he was a f.t. Now I have evidence for thinking this, quite a lot, and mostly his own letters and articles. You disagree. Good. But you go much farther (and did that night) and insist that it's not a matter for discussion, where there may be a reasonable case on either side, but rather that the whole notion is so preposterous that anyone who entertains it must be a slandermonger, red-baiter, and general no-good-nik. I resent this attitude; it seems to me unreasonable and, oddly enough, intolerant, and, even more oddly, one that does just what you accuse me of doing: substitutes for facts nothing but invective, and puts an end to discussion.

Also at the forum, you felt obliged to question the good faith of my defense of the Commies' right to free speech, on the grounds that anyone who attacks them as strongly as I had done in my speech and reviles them as enemies of freedom and decency, that such a person could not possibly "really" believe in free speech for them. Your point seems to me unsound logically: the logic of free speech is precisely that you grant it to your worst enemies—after all, naturally you don't suppress your friends. And also unimaginative psychologically: surely I'm only one of a great number of sincere believers in free speech who have upheld it for their most detested opponents, from Voltaire to Holmes with his "real free speech is freedom for the thought we hate." You see, when my [Roger] Baldwin profile appears, that I argue strongly for the Union's position against the Smith Act and other interferences with the Commies' civil rights. This has always been my feeling. For practical as well as ethical reasons. I hated the fascists in the thirties as enemies of all I hold dearest, just as I now do the Commies, but it has never occurred to me to try to take away their civil rights in either case, and indeed I have often gone on record the other way. On the other hand, I must insist on the right to speak out against them as strongly as I feel justified (and they too have the same right vis-à-vis me) without being smeared as one who would suppress them.

Look. I'll be even more careful in future (get that "even") about this f.t. issue (I really DON'T want to slander or be unjust to anyone), if you'll try to be (even) less abusive when someone raises the touchy business. Agreed?

To Nicola Chiaromonte

November 7, 1951

Thanks for your good letter of Oct. 19 and for not being mad at me for not ever answering your one of July 19.

The reason for my silence was mostly that I was in my usual summer state of analphabetic and solipsistic enjoyment, so that, especially in August and September, to sit at a table typing even a letter took more discipline than I had. Also I was, and am, rather ashamed of myself because I've produced so little, and thought so little, and didn't want to have to 'fess up to you. But truth must out sometime, and so here I'm writing at last. My unproductivity, of course, is due to the unsettling effects of love—not Joan, that's all over or at least quiescent, we still correspond—but someone else whom you've not met; it's the most equal relationship I've ever experienced, only pleasure, delight, spontaneity, harmony on both sides, God knows how it will end or IF it will end.

There are great disadvantages, practical ones anyway, to postponing sex to the age of 45. On the other hand, certainly better late than never.

. . . I've run into Lionel Abel twice on the street, we've chatted and I urged him to "ring me up" and he said he would but hasn't. I just don't much like him, never did, he makes me uneasy and restless, not the creative kind but the kind of unease you feel in bed when you can't go to sleep, also he depresses me and makes me feel I don't want to get "involved" at all with him; I imagine he feels much same way about me; we're dogs of a different breed.

Lionel told me something I keep hearing on all sides, from people back from abroad (Dolf Starnberger, editor of *Die Wandlung*, whom I met at Hannah Arendt's other night, was latest): that the USA is becoming more and more unpopular abroad. It is frightening, really. (Get same tale from Joan in Mexico—all the intellectuals hate USA.) People are not FOR Soviet Russia, but they just fear and dislike USA—and think Senator McCarthy runs the country and there is a reign of terror here. (Paole [Milano] said that a friend of his who just arrived was actually afraid to leave his hotel room lest he be picked up by the FBI on suspicion.) In short, Europeans are coming to think of this country as a homogeneous mass of atom-bomb-makers and "red-baiters" and dollar-imperialists. This is one more pressing reason why I think *Politics* must be revived. To communicate directly, in a human voice, with European intellectuals; to express the considerable amount of disaffection, among American intellectuals, with official policies; and to show that the McCarthys and the McCarrans don't by any means have it all their own way. That recent issue of *Colliers* about a hypothetical war against Russia is the sort of thing a revived *Politics* could analyze. So, anyway, I am thinking more seriously than before of trying to get out a mag again. If only my own personal preoccupations didn't so often block my view of History! Of late anyway. But still, as Hannah [Arendt] pointed out to me, after I had put her in possession of the essential facts, as they say in the House of Commons: "Really, Dwight, why in the world can't you have both? Lovemaking can't possibly take up ALL your time or even most of it. So for Christ's sake get down to work in the rest of your time! Plenty of other people have done it." She didn't say just this, but something like it. So I shall try. And, if the effort seems to be failing, shall again consult Dr. Gruenthal, who fixes you up for work as well as for love.

To William Shawn

November 9, 1951

Here's one more suggestion: either a Reporter at Large on the mission which the Catholic Worker group run on Chrystie Street (and their newspaper, also published from there—latest issue enclosed); OR a profile of the remarkable woman who founded the Catholic Worker movement and still actively runs it: Dorothy Day. My preference wd. be latter, as she is a big and vivid personality—she began as a Marxist Socialist around World War I, became converted to Catholicism, and for years has been running this C.W. group; she must be well over 60 by now. Read her column "On Pilgrimage" in enclosed paper, and you'll get an idea of her savor.

The C.W. group is essentially Dorothy Day plus a dozen or so full-time associates, mostly young (around 25) men and women. I spoke there, at one of their regular Friday night forums, last week, and was greatly impressed by both the intellectual level of the some fifty or so youngish people who took part, and by the really Christian, early Christian that is, atmosphere—one of gentle, community-feeling and warm brotherhood.

They are absolute pacifists, ardent pro-unionists, politically extreme radicals distinguishable from Trotskyists only by their anarchistic bent, and they live lives of voluntary poverty. Helping the poor and the underdog is their main activity. They have about 40 beds at their mission, and they feed all comers in two daily breadlines (they make their own whole wheat bread at a farm on Staten Island, and it is as good as Pepperidge Farm bread—they gave me a loaf so I know).

Their newspaper, a monthly, has a circulation now of 65,000, which is about 25,000 more than either the *Nation* or the *New Republic*, and about 40,000 more than the *Daily Worker*, and about 60,000 more than the Trotskyist papers. It had in the mid-thirties over 250,000 circulation, but lost most of it because of their anti-Franco stand in the Spanish Civil War and their anti-war stand in World War II.

They think as little of Cardinal Spellman, almost, as I do. Their relations with the Catholic hierarchy must be interesting. Fact they can exist inside the church is a tribute not only to their own idealism but also to the tolerance that church permits—its house really seems to have many mansions.

Essential story is that here are a few people who are trying to really live up the doctrines of Christ. Since they really put their moral principles into daily practice, instead of just talking or writing about them, their activities are sometimes moving, sometimes comic, but always interesting.

To Dachine Rainer [anarchist friend]

January 24, 1952

Nancy tells me you're lunching (through the courtesy of the very dubious Mr. Kolberg) with Senators McCarran, McCarthy, and Wherry. Well, well well! They are probably the three biggest reactionary bastards in the Senate today—the extreme or lunatic fringe of the Republican Party. Taft is a progressive and an internationalist compared to them. McCarthy this summer made crazy charges against Owen Lattimore and other people in the State Department, that they were Communist agents, Reds, etc. I've read the testimony and—except for Lattimore, who is a "fellow-traveler" but is not, as McCarthy claimed, a Soviet agent—he had no real evidence against any of them. McCarran is even worse—he seems to hate all foreigners except Franco. He is the author of the McCarran Bill that is keeping out of the country almost every politically conscious anti-Communist refugee.

But they are very powerful in the Republican Party and in the Senate, and you MIGHT be able to educate them a little. So, on another sheet, I've put down a few ideas that might be useful. Also, I've collected a few clips along the same lines, which I'd like back. Do try to convince the senators that even foreigners can be useful in fighting the Communists abroad.

To C. Wright Mills

n.d., January 1952

Are you very sore at me?

PR asked me to review your book. I hadn't seen it; I said OK; I read it and thought it was terrible, as, if you've read my review which I assume you have or at least have heard about it, you now know: so—a Problem, should I not do the review, or should do and say what I think and criticize sharply an old pal (and someone I respect, have a strong fellow feeling with as another rebel and bad boy)? I decided to say what I think, since, if the roles had been reversed and you had been asked to review a book of mine that you found was terrible, I should have wanted you to do that (do unto others . . .). Also I thought, and I don't think I'm wrong, that you, too, would prefer that.

Tried to make it clear, in the review, what is the case: that the book doesn't seem to me to represent you at anything approaching your best. Did I? If not, let me hereby say so. In fact, it was only because your past performances and what I knew of your abilities had led me to expect so much more that I wrote so long a damning review. One doesn't bother to so criticize a book by someone from whom one expects little.

Anyway, I'd much like to see you again and to hash over, as much as you will, the book and my review. Maybe we'll both gain. And you're entitled to a comeback! Where are you? Tried your phone—while I was writing the review—but someone else had moved in there. Where can I reach you? That is, if you want to be reached. . . .

To C. Wright Mills

January 30, 1952

Thanks much for your note, and I'm glad, though not at all surprised, that you don't take the review at all personally.[5]

On your two complaints, briefly: (1) I didn't tell reader what book is about, what new facts and or ideas it contained, because, honest-to-god, I didn't know myself—I got so lost in details that didn't seem to add up and in germs of ideas that never got born because you interrupted yourself all the time; the book was one big blur to me, so all I could do was try to analyze why. (2) Your notion of "constructive" and "practical" criticism strikes me as fallacious: it's a critic's job to evaluate a work, to praise the good in it and damn the bad, not to tell the author How to Do It—in fact, such "practical" criticism wd. seem to me, if I were an author, impertinent and presumptuous. Also you can easily extract a positive, heartwarming message from my review if you will just restate my negative points positively, as I say it's bad to shop up those case-history interviews and degrade them merely to "for instance" supports of your own ideas; so that means

---

5. In fact Mills was angered by the review, and if he did not take it personally he considered Macdonald's critique frivolous and without substance. Richard Hofstadter said that Mills was enormously wounded by the review.

(as in fact I wrote) it would have been better if you had given them *in extensor,* let them make their own impression. Simple, see?

Wish we could get out to see you, but fear not for a while—no car, weather poor, and above all right now terribly rushed for time completing profile (of Dorothy Day of the *Catholic Worker,* fascinating woman AND movement), also bringing up to date, with footnotes, the facts and ideas in "The Responsibility of Peoples" and "The Root Is Man," which a little pacifist press in California is reissuing. But if we do see a Saturday or Sunday clear, will phone you and, of course, if you're in town with a couple of hours free, do come see me. I'm very curious to see the something you've created, and you yourself, too.

To Nicola Chiaromonte

February 14, 1952

Pretty impressive this letterhead, eh? This is my first letter on it. No, I'm not an editor, but I now do have an office here [at the *New Yorker*] which they very kindly give me to work in. Marvelous—so quiet and businesslike, fluorescent lights, free paper & pencils, phone, everything but windows (but of course it's air-conditioned, this being USA). . . . Oddly, and sadly, it's Tucci's desk, or rather was. I told him of course I shouldn't usurp his place, but he said not to be silly, and anyway he feels hurt and angry because they tossed him out and wouldn't come back now even if they let him. I gather he was a "squatter," from their viewpoint—they say no fiction writers have desks here, only nonfiction. Poor Tucci, his state seems worse and worse. . . . Florence Samuels just called up for him, recognized my voice, hadn't talked with her in years, odd. She sounded very nice.

Nick, thanks for your letter, and for kind words re my Mills review, which I think WAS about my best, to be immodest. Was trying to work out an informal style, as "close to" the reader as possible without becoming vulgar or superficial. I feel I'm learning about writing, now all I have to do is write. . . . Though I HAVE been slightly productive of late. Just finishing a fascinating (to me) profile on Dorothy Day, founder and still leader of the Catholic Workers. Ever hear of her? The CW's put out a monthly paper, run Houses of Hospitality, live in voluntary poverty, are politically anarchists and pacifists and morally sort of early or primitive Christians.

I'm sorry about your mood of depression and sterility, it's hell I know from my own experience far too well, and God knows what can be done about it but winter it out, so to speak.

. . . On the magazine—I'll certainly not revive it now, if I do at all, until next fall. I do feel more and more in a working and workmanlike mood, and also feel (and an amazing number of people are all the time volunteering the same opinion) that *Politics* is more and more needed now, someday maybe, like Charlemagne, the corpse will come to live again in the hour of its country's need—the country, that is, of the mind and heart, not the one presided over by Harry.

. . . They finally published my Weil profile two weeks ago—sending you the two issues, plus some other stuff might interest you. . . . Mary's new novel, *The Groves of Academe,* is out and she sent me a copy. Alas, me no like. The trouble is she is so damned SUPERIOR to her characters, sneers at most of them and patronizes the rest. Also, usual static quality, even worse than in *Oasis*—acres of intellectual arguments, back and forth, like a tennis match (and about as humanly interesting). WHY does she have to be so goddamned snooty, is she God or something? You begin to feel sorry for her poor characters, who are always so absurd or rascally or just inferior and damned—she's always telling them their slip's showing. She doesn't *love* them, that's the trouble, in the sense of not feeling a human solidarity and sympathy with them—can't create real characters without love, or hate, which is also a human feeling; she has just contempt. And her poor puppets just wither on the page. Is she really like that? She doesn't seem so when I see her. Or is she just kidding *me* along too, and making all kinds of snooty little footnotes in her head as we talk? Funny, she wrote a very good story recently in the *NYorker* about her childhood, best thing I've seen of hers in years, and just because it was *felt* for once, and direct and simple and moving. . . .

To Max Lerner

March 4, 1952

Swell column in today's *Post*—don't ALWAYS think this of your stuff, as you know, so this a real testimonial. . . . Had just same reaction to the one day I sat in on first Commie trial, esp. the absurdity (and the political danger) of making excerpts from theoretical works of Marx, Lenin, Stalin the chief basis for prosecuting the Commies. (Day I was there, some work by Karl Kautsky was introduced. "How do you spell that name?" asked Medina.)

Re your last 2 paragraphs: when I saw Arthur Garfield Hays last year (while researching a profile of Roger Baldwin), he told me—as I recall anyway—that the Commies had asked him to defend them in the first trial and that he had agreed on condition he could run the defense without interference. They had refused, so he said no. So your statement not wholly accurate. Might be worth asking Hays about this, grist for another column maybe.

P.S. Must admit that of late months even so hardened a red-baiter as I am has become alarmed by the treatment of Commies.

To Mary McCarthy

March 18, 1952

Here's some stuff, sorry late but daresay you haven't begun thinking about your talk yet.

There was a discussion meeting of the Committee [on Cultural Freedom] 2 weeks ago you should know about. Dan Bell presided, and began by posing questions: What activities *in the USA* should the committee give top priority at this time to? I had gone prepared to propose that a campaign against McCarthyism should be undertaken, but Jim Farrell got up and said just that, as first speaker. I was second. We both said (1) abroad communism was still great cultural danger and Committee was doing a good job there, but (2) in USA communism as a cultural influence was no longer dangerous, and real danger to cultural freedom now comes from "anti-Communists" like McCarthy and McCarran. Hence right now Committee's chief (not only) target should be McCarthyism. . . . After that, whole meeting was devoted to talking about this question. [James T.] Farrell and I got support from [Richard] Rovere, Bell, Prof. [Koppel] Pinson of Queens College. Opposition (who thought Stalinism should remain chief and indeed, in most cases, only target) was led by Will P. Phillips, [Karl] Wittfogel; former I think mad in a quite logical way, latter, I and many others at meeting think mad in a wild, hysterical way (his wife perhaps responsible—she pushes him, goads him, and he's a weak timid character . . . next day he phoned Bertha Gruner [friend and former *Politics* staffer], said I was "objectively" pro-Stalinist and that I had no right to be in Committee). Arthur Pincus, [Arnold] Beichman (though he later told me he wanted both McCarthyism and Stalinism to be attacked), and Pepik Gordon all backed Will and Karl. Other speakers took a middle position though more against us than for us: Hook (who spoke at length, in very gentle, mild, fatherly way—he clearly fears a split and wants to avoid it at all costs), [Fred] Dupee (sounded very bold and positive, but not clear just where he stood), [Clement] Greenberg (who said let's appoint a committee to study the question), Bert Wolfe, Boris Shub. . . . My general impression was that the "old guard" in Committee had no stomach for anti-McCarthy fight but that they will yield if enough pressure applied (except Phillips and Wittfogel).

Some points that have already no doubt occurred to you too:

1. The Committee's Manifesto (enclosed) says nothing about Stalinism being the ONLY form of cultural repression we oppose, indeed says the contrary.

2. The McCarthyite tendency to harass and penalize teachers, artists, and writers *in their own professional fields* because of real or alleged political activities is the same obliteration of the boundaries between politics and culture, the same trend toward reducing all culture to politics, that the Committee deplores in Soviet communism.

3. A Committee for Cultural Freedom which does not vigorously fight attacks on C.F. from the political right in this country today is a bad joke. It should be called a Committee for Cultural Freedom with Certain Exceptions.

4. That McCarthyism is the chief enemy of CF today in USA even the Committee's "old guard" doesn't deny. They argue only that communism is the chief danger in the long run. I don't think even this true, but granting it is, we cannot just ignore the short run, that is, the actual present situation, as against the speculative future situation.

5. To attack McCarthyism doesn't mean to be silent on Communist cultural infiltration, such as it now is in USA—it is a question not of either anti-Stalinism or anti-McCarthyism, but rather of which is top target for us today.

6. Perhaps our strongest tactical argument is that the best and only way to gain the confidence of European intellectuals, including those affiliated with the Committee, is to vigorously attack McCarthyism over here. This so obvious hardly needs documentation. This morning had a letter from Francois Bondy, who seems to be secretary of the Committee's Paris affiliate (Congress pour la Liberté de la Culture), praising my little squib in New Leader against List's political attack on the Brecht-Weill Beggar's Opera and asking me to write a New York letter for Prevues, the organ of the Congress!

Well, enough—you could make a two-hour speech with all this! By the way, please bring back the material when you come to NYC, as I want to use it to prepare a formal proposal that the Committee commission me to write a pamphlet for them.

Hear you were in NYC lately for that New Yorker party (to which didn't go because not invited), sorry to have missed you. . . . Let's discuss my reactions to your book face to face, okay? We're expecting you for dinner Friday, don't forget (Bowdie [Broadwater, Mary's current husband] too, of course). I think our crucial disagreement is over amount of charity author shows her characters (I was surprised when you said you meant to show Mulcahy as a poor suffering Dosto-evskian—if you used that word—mortal and not just a heel); shall reread book with this in mind.[6]

. . . Have just finished Dorothy Day, two parts (hope to God they don't cut it to one). . . .

6. Mulcahy was the main character in McCarthy's latest novel, The Groves of Academe (1952)—a phony radical who exploits an alleged Communist past to maintain tenure when the grounds for dismissal are academically sound.

To Devin A. Garrity [president of Devin-Adair Co.]

April 7, 1952

. . . You understand, of course, that I consider McCarthy a cheat and a liar and a thoroughly vicious and dangerous political-cultural influence, and that my interest here is simply that of fair play and the free market in ideas. I think booksellers should sell books, and that they have no right to pass on their merits. It's up to the customer to boycott a book if he likes, not the bookseller. I was equally antipathetic to Macy's similar treatment of the Blanshard book [an anti-Catholic polemic].

To Nancy Macdonald

June 11, 1952

Saw Shawn yesterday. He thinks maybe they should not run the Baldwin piece because that quote from *Soviet Russia Today* in 1935 in which B. admits he is interested in civil liberties only as a tactic to help the workers establish their dictatorship—that this will be used by McCarthyites to smear all liberal, civil-libertarian effort. (SHAWN ASKED ME NOT TO TALK ABOUT ALL THIS, AND I AGREED, SO DON'T MENTION IT TO ANYONE.) Shawn does not think piece can be run and omit this (as I don't, also, of course). I pointed out that (1) it's immoral to not tell the truth merely because it may hurt one's own side, (2) not to run article for this reason would amount to "Khvostism" (tail-ism), as the Trotskyists used to call it, to McCarthy would mean the *NYorker* is so scared of McCarthy it daren't tell unfavorable facts about liberalism, and (3) on balance, the article will rouse interest *for* the ACLU, not against it, and hence not to run it will help not hinder McCarthy. Shawn seemed impressed by these arguments. Should think he would be, as they seem far stronger than his reasoning. Hope he changes his mind—and shall bring further pressure to bear later. Only thing worries me is that he doesn't want to run piece for other reasons (it's not on lib-lab line, it's too "serious," etc.) and THINKS it's for these reasons. He's quite neurotic, I fear, and I shouldn't be surprised if he is kidding himself here and suppressing his real reasons. In which case would do no good to convince him about these reasons. . . . Well, we'll see. . . .

I'm leading a sober life, dear, you'll be glad to know. Have bought one pt. whiskey since you left, of which half still remains. And no parties (except small dinner at Laniers last night, where had some martinis). . . . Do you find Parisians anti-USA?

To Gertrude Norman

June 12, 1952

. . . I do get something done by fits and starts, but what used to be called my personal life has been and still is as dippy-bumpy as a plane trip over the Rockies, and has absorbed most of my energies. How did they do it, those old style "geniuses" who loved and "lived" to the hilt without it interfering with Production—in fact, who drew stimulus from it? . . . I'm going through a rather bad time right now. Nancy and the kids sailed a week ago, and I miss them and feel disoriented (I'm more of a family man, I guess, than I'd thought; it's not only the missing, it's also that my self was to some extent defined by my relations with the family, and now I have to make a new self, a painful, puzzling process). Also I feel guilty, remorseful about shipping them off without me, though, rationally, I know it was the right thing to do. Poor Gloria has had to take some of the brunt, she's been lovely about it, too; but things strained there at the moment, wholly because of my own doing—*another* reason for guilt! In fact I have been feeling guilt, worthlessness in last week in the way the books say neurotics do, and in a way up to now I really haven't. Well, guess I'll survive—but how little one knows in advance about one's feelings, and how powerless one is over them! Money problems too. And Gloria's off to Southwest in a few weeks—I think she should, must go, yet dread it. . . . I'll be here all summer, and I'm going to work hard, both on money writing and my own stuff, going to try to get some big project really started and keep at it—a great opportunity, just because I shall be alone, without demands or enticements from outside. So don't feel too sorry for me, this is a passing mood and I'm lucky to have this chance for undistracted work. . . . Sunday I'm driving to Chicago with my mother (who will see her other son there) to take part, at $100 plus expenses, in a round table at the University on Human Rights and Communism.

To Nancy Macdonald

June 14, 1952

. . . Tomorrow mother and I leave for Chicago (Mary [McCarthy] can't go after all, her doc says no, she has gynecological troubles, alas). Mother is so delighted and excited about the trip, it's wonderful. Glad I'm doing it for her sake, though don't at all like idea of using up a week on it, which is about what it will come to. Well, this makes up a little for my past neglect of mother.

Gloria and her kids left, with Robin [Gloria's husband] . . . this A.M. for Baltimore. She'll take a house there, near her parents, in the country probably for a month, before starting West. Robin will drive them out West, on his vacation.

I've begun to nibble at the mountains of paper I've accumulated over the years here in the office. So help me, I'm going to get it all in order this summer, throw away a lot, and file the rest so I don't have to move it all with me every time I move anywhere. Also I'm going to get started on a major project of my own. Also to develop some decent work habits, this summer, alone and on my own, I regard as a crucial test of myself—or rather as a chance to get into the habit of hard, disciplined thinking and writing. I've become very slack of late years, and you're quite right when you say so, darling. But I'm going to make a real try at reforming.

To Gloria Lanier [written from the University of Chicago campus]

June 18, 1952

I'm sitting here taking part (ostensibly at least) in a . . . discussion of (let me look at program) "Communist Tactics and Strategy in Western Europe." Fifty academic characters sitting around a huge table and "formulating" or "suggesting" like hell. Smart fellows, but I keep thinking of you. As I have much on this trip. Darling, I'm so glad you exist.

Christ, what a trip—this country just too big—we drove 12 hours in NY state alone! A lovely rich green kempt landscape, esp. in Central NY. Saw (rather mother did) a sign in window "Dr. MESICK." Many animals killed on the road—woodchucks, cats—something brutal about a car roaring along hour after hour at 60 MPH—one becomes part of the car after awhile—something gross, materialistic about eating up space that way. Yet even so it took us forever to get here. We spent Sunday night at a nice old-style hotel (the Seneca in Geneva, N.Y.). Next day left at 9, got to Buffalo at 11, crossed to Canada and drove all day along N. shore of L. Erie—dull, poor country—not even hills—Canada looks just like USA—only route signs have a crown on top, and gallons are imperial. . . . Crossed back to Detroit at 6, had drink (dry martini) with mother at Statler bar, and saw all prospering businessmen—nice underwater sort of dim place, darling, how I wished you were there—sort of like the Barclay bar, remember. This was only drink of trip—ingested, instead, huge milk shakes and ice cream sodas—a wonderful American roadside service, they give you practically a full quart, with all kinds of sweet goo in it. You'd love it. We then drove all the way to Chicago, foolishly—didn't get there till 3:30 A.M. Tuesday—and not a room in any of the big hotels! Seems all the furniture men in USA are currently in Chicago. A room clerk took pity (poor mother was dead) and sent us to a place way out here by the University. Mother took a room, at $8 per, but I decided to stay up till 7:30 and then take shelter with Dot Wheeler. So I drove around in the dawn. My God, dear, what a city—from the lakefront at least—you see from miles away, through the blue dawn haze, the huge Loop buildings like humped dinosaurs with their long necks up marching planlessly (nothing is planned here, except the Lake Shore Drive which makes our parkways look like alleys) along the shore. The city is integrated with the lake—the buildings often seem to rise up from the beach—and the people bathe, boat, and fish all along the lakefront—thousands of sailboats and motor boats anchored behind breakwaters all along the front of the city. But, dear, cannot go on about Chicago, no time (session is coming to an end)—remind me to tell you more—have many impressions—fascinating city, its raw and shabby and brutal unlike NYC, but also more *alive* more live-able—it's fun to prowl around the streets, architecture flamboyant and varied, something *doing* all the time. I slept at Dot's from 8 to 3 next day (Tuesday). She works, as a secretary in Phillips Petroleum Co., from 8 to 5. Her 2 girls, very nice and pretty and well-mannered, got me breakfast at 4 P.M. . . . Dinner at Dot's last night—I'm staying there, she has a huge apt.—and tonight mother and I (these people here [at session] know so much! They're still talking) with Hedges, Mary, and Hedges Jr.— I speak tomorrow night, and we'll probably start back Friday. I shall be glad to be back, and at work. All the way out here, thoughts were gloomy—I felt *taken away* from my work (which I am anxious to get started) and from you. This week seems a *waste* somehow, but mother is so glad to have the trip that I'm content.

Gloria, I miss you even more than I had expected. You make other women seem pale and dim. . . .

To Michael Macdonald [traveling in Europe with his mother, Nancy]

n.d., Summer 1952

. . . So you like French food! You sure got it better than me, chum—the Automat is my usual dining place (not bad, though, really, but nothing compared to Paris cooking). Now that you can "eat practically everything," Nancy and I will have to whip up some really complicated dishes to regale you on your vacations! Baked Squid with Anchovy Dressing, that sort of thing.

Shall stop sending you *Times* sports sections, as per your instructions, and shall send new *Sport* soon as it is out. (I sent you current issue weeks ago, did you get it?) Shall also look for *Weird Science* (is that the actual name of the mag?).

You ask me who I think will win the Rep. and Dem. Nominations. Well, after much thought plus a glance at the newspapers of the last 3 weeks, I guess Eisenhower and Stevenson. Pretty smart, eh? Seriously, though, Stevenson is TERRIFIC. I followed most of the Dem. Convention on TV (they installed a special set here in my office—so have had to move temporarily into another—so we could all watch the conventions). Spent about 6 hours straight on Friday night last evening, and was much impressed. He uses language beautifully, like Churchill, and gives an impression of being a real individual, not just another political windbag. May even do some work for his campaign. He has 3 sons, as you probably know, and the two youngest (looked about 14 and 16) were with him Friday night and they were very nice-looking boys; the 14-year-old reminded me of you (he was the handsomer of the two!). I gather you're for Stevenson too.

By the way, watching the convention on TV converted me—at least when TV is used to report on current events. It was fascinating. As if you had a cloak of invisibility plus a magic carpet and could float, unseen, up within three feet of anybody you wanted to see and hear him. You catch every little change and flicker of expression, and it's as if the big-shot speakers are talking right to you face to face.

I'm just finishing a long piece on Mass Culture—(a revision, in part of an earlier thing I did in *Politics*) which Seldon asked me to do for *American Perspectives*, a magazine of which he is editing one issue. I'll get $300 or so for it, you'll be glad to hear. . . .

To Gloria Lanier

August 4, 1952

You darling to write me two more letters from Chicago! . . . Am feeling better, sort of purged—sweet, don't worry about me, really, I have Bad Moments, but they go away, and in general I feel much better and work better now than I did at beginning of summer. I write you all this because I don't want to kid you, to pretend, to keep things from you, and I don't want you to do it to or for me either, even if it makes me sad and anxious. . . . Tomorrow if fair shall go to Stamford for late afternoon sail with Wm. Buckley, Jr., and dinner at his house. "We live in a plush house here as befits our station," he writes, inviting me out—now now Gloria, that's just a joke, don't get on your Marxian high horse! He's not a bad fellow, really, just has bad ideas. . . .

To Karl Wittfogel

August 5, 1952

I've read your correspondence with Schlesinger on the [John K.] Fairbank business (including his initial letter of Aug. 24 last that I asked you for and that came safely) and here's my reaction.

I wrote you that F was being denied an entry permit into Japan apparently because the govt. believed he was or had been a member of the Communist

Party, as [Louis] Budenz had just publicly charged before the McCarren Committee. He said he knew F had never been a CP member (and was "sure" you would agree with him on that), and he asked you to submit to the Committee "a statement on your acquaintance with John"—presumably rebutting Budenz's charge that F *had* been a C.P. member.

So far, so simple. Was F, or wasn't he, to the best of your knowledge, a CP member at any time? And were you willing to make a statement on the point to the Committee? But your lengthy reply to this request gets everything all balled up with the broader, and different, question of F's political views and behavior in general, and indeed, largely not even with *that* but with Lattimore's behavior and with our own experiences in trying to combat pro-Communist prejudices among your academic colleagues. Nowhere in this or in your second letter do you even mention the concrete point at issue in S's letter: was F ever a Communist? So I infer that S was right in assuming you agreed with him that the charge was baseless. And I further infer that you do not favor defending a man against a false charge of having been a CP member if you think he is either a conscious fellow-traveler or else is "soft" on the issue. I agree with you, on the basis of the data you bring out and of what I myself knew of F, that F was, perhaps still is, pro-Commie, or at least strongly anti-anti-Commie, and I agree that this is wrong, dangerous, and should be fought vigorously. And so does S agree, of course, as his letters (and his record) make clear.

But how from this follows a refusal to defend him against a false charge of Party membership I don't see, and I agree wholly with S when he calls your attitude here similar to that of the Communists and repugnant to the whole Anglo-Saxon legal tradition with its, to me, admirable discriminations between a general political attitude and a specific act or fact (such as joining the C.P.).

I might add that I thought the personal attack on you in his second letter unjustified, and also the putting you and F in same boat because you had both played around with the Commies (since you some years ago broke sharply and openly with them, while F apparently never has). But on the main issue, I have to agree entirely with him, even to the point that you and he (and I, alas!) "are operating in different realms of discourse," since it was possible for you to write two passionate and lengthy letters on the subject without even touching on what to S and to me appears to be the only point at issue: was or was not F a CP member?

God knows I sympathize with your anger and contempt, Karl, at the whole Lattimore crowd, and also with your almost desperate feeling that they have been getting away with murder while you, with all the right and truth on your side, or at least the great bulk of it, have been made to feel a pariah and a moral leper. I sympathize because such has been my own experience, too. But to refuse to help a man under dishonest attack by telling the truth so far as you know it (which doesn't mean swearing F was never a Commie, which of course only himself, and God, could do, but merely stating that, in your long and fairly close acquaintance with him, you had no reason to believe he was, had no evidence he was), to do this, and to someone with whom you were once on friendly terms too, because you feel (and no doubt rightly) his general political tendency to be dangerous—this is just Stalinism in reverse, and if the war against communism cannot be effectively fought (which I do NOT believe—on the contrary, I think such methods harm our cause) except with such methods, then I say let's fight it ineffectively, because to win that way is to make ourselves into the image of what we are fighting. When you gaze into the abyss, beware lest the abyss gaze into you, says Nietzsche.

Thanks for showing me the letters, sorry I must strongly disagree with your stand, and best personal regards to you as always.

To Henry Regnery [conservative Chicago publisher]

November 16, 1952

I was just about to mail you the enclosed when I got your letter, for which, thanks. Yes, January would be time enough for the grant. Couldn't leave for England before then anyway.

I've just heard that you put up some of the money for that dinner at which McCarthy made that speech slandering (in my opinion, at least, and I do claim some *expertise* in this realm, far more than Sen. McCarthy) [Bernard] Devoto, [James] Wechsler, and Schlesinger. Is this true? If so, I wonder if you and I can, or should, do business together—whether the book on [Aneurin] Bevan I would write wouldn't be something you'd not want to publish. And whether, on my part, I would want to be connected with a pro-McCarthy (taking him as an extreme symbol of a kind of anti-communism with which I am little more, if at all, in sympathy than I am with communism) publishing house. Of course it's possible that your house is not pro-McCarthy, even if you are. (I don't mean to make this McCarthy issue a *personal* matter between us, you understand, any more than it is between me and Bill Buckley, with whom I enjoy pleasant and interesting personal relations despite his politics.) I haven't followed your publications as closely as I should have, or at least I don't have a very clear impression of the politics of your house, if there are such, I mean the general political tendency. Could you send me your last few lists, so I can see for myself?

Thanks—and please excuse the loyalty-oath flavor of this request; this seems to be an age when such discriminations and explorations are unavoidable. Alas.

To Henry Regnery

December 4, 1952

Say, what goes on anyway? I've just been told that acc. to *Chi. Tribune* of Oct 12 last, your name headed the list of members of the Executive Committee for that McCarthy dinner. How does this square with your two explanations to me (which didn't impress me, as you'll recall): (a) you just wanted him to get a hearing, (b) you had never heard him and were curious to do so? These imply a neutral attitude which membership on the committee belies. Where do you stand on this anyway? Are you kidding yourself, or me, or both?

You seemed evasive and/or uninformed in our session here with [Richard] Rovere [liberal journalist]. You weren't willing to defend McCarthy, and yet you didn't seem interested in the evidence Dick and I piled up—you listened with the same deadpan and half-smile I've noted in arguing about Stalinism with fellow-travelers—they (and you) don't try to defend their positions very hard, they admit the facts mostly, but it's clear they (and I think you) have a will-to-believe which is impregnable by evidence.

For example, your citing McCarthy's defense of the Malmedy SS men as an instance of a distinguished crusade for justice. You've been for years specifically interested in "the German question," and yet you apparently didn't know that this crusade for justice was phony, that McCarthy had not a scrap of evidence, and that the whole thing was a fiasco and a farce, if not worse. Just as irresponsible and baseless as his smears of people like Wechsler and Schlesinger. If Rovere didn't happened to have special knowledge of the episode, I'd have been quite taken in. But how come you, of all people considering your interests, didn't know the score? Were you at all shaken, or impressed, by Rovere's evidence? If so, you gave no indication.

And that attempt to dismiss the Beacon Press book as tripe on the basis of a single sentence, which you'd got from a review (you hadn't even read the book, nor, according to what you said, anything else much by or about McCarthy— yet you join a committee to finance a dinner so he can make a major speech)— the sentence about his mania for gambling which—again, thanks to Rovere's knowledge—apparently was justified anyway. What kind of thinking is that? Doesn't seem to show much eagerness on your part to seek out the truth.

And the gall of that listing of Buckley's apologia pro Joe as "a balance sheet" giving both sides of the record! Now honestly, Henry—are you simple-minded maybe? When I objected to that, you didn't defend it, but you didn't back down either—in fact, you simply smiled evasively. But a smile is not an answer.

If you had stood up for McCarthy, it might have been better than all this pussyfooting, since at least it would show that you were conscious yourself of what you thought. As it is—and I assume you are not just trying to put something over—I'm forced to conclude that you have gotten in very deep with this whole Pegler-McCarthy-Utley-Toledano crowd and that you are uneasy about it but don't dare make a study yourself of the whole business to see what's what (lest your psychological base of operations be removed—same way with the fellow-travelers, who are scared lest they have to break with THEIR crowd and base), and that they are pushing you, hurrying you farther and farther along their path, and you're going, but with your eyes tightly shut. I hope you'll someday at least face up to the issue and do some research and serious reading and make up your mind for yourself.

Meanwhile, I don't trust you as a publisher, I think you're committed (only half-consciously) to a McCarthyite line, and so I have to say no to the Bevan project, regretfully, for the terms are very attractive. But I wouldn't write for a Commie house and I won't write for a McCarthyite one either.

To George Counts [well-known liberal educator]

[Late] January 1953

I am very much disturbed by the Committee's action on the Emergency Civil Liberties Committee for several reason.

1. No attempt was made to get some of our people on the program of the ECLC's [Emergency Civil Liberties Committee] coming conference. We did this in the case of the Waldorf Conference, and that Conference's refusal to allow Sidney Hook, yourself, and the other anti-Communists to speak was effective proof of our charges it was a Communist front. It was also a fair procedure: they had their chance to show their true colors. This was, however, not done in this case.

2. "The Communist Front" charge was apparently made recklessly and without sufficient evidence. At least Irving Kristol's Jan. 21 release attempting to defend the Committee action did not produce such evidence. It states that the ECLC has done "very little" and makes no criticism of what it has done. The case rests wholly on the biographies of a majority of the five subjects to have been fellow-travelers in the past, and I note that, except in the case of [I. F.] Stone, they all stop with the 1949 Waldorf Conference. The Korean War took place in 1950, and I'd like to know whether their fellow-traveling extended past that date. Both Emerson and Foreman, for instance, have told me that they resigned from the Progressive Party and its national committee when the pro-Communist majority insisted on blaming the South Koreans for the invasion.

3. I strongly object to the uncritical use of congressional reports, as in calling Fairchild "a member of more than two dozen Communist front organizations" on the say-so of the Un-American Committee. Some fronts mean more

than others; the date of membership is important, also the prominence and degree of participation. Adding up "front" memberships in this undiscriminating way is just what "Red Channels" does, and is bound to be misleading and unjust. It is also unsophisticated—a curious failing for a committee with the composition of ours! (I'm not saying Fairchild has been necessarily misrepresented—it's the principle of such use of "front" statistics that I'm raising.)

There are certainly a lot of fellow-travelers, past and/or present, prominent in the ECLC and on the speakers' list of its conference, nor can I detect any notable anti-Communist names. This is suspicious, and the event may well bear out one's suspicions. But this doesn't justify a flat charge of "Communist Front." I think we were morally wrong to make it. And I'm sure we were tactically inept, since we couldn't back it up. (The fact the ECLC and not we chose to go to the papers with the episode is perhaps an indication of which side had the strongest position.)

Finally, it seems odd to me that a group calling itself a Committee for Cultural Freedom should go out of its way to jump with both feet, on the basis not of actions but of a speculative prediction of future actions, on another group that is organizing a conference on civil liberties. Such trigger-happy vigilance in the present atmosphere of McCarthyism restricts rather than enlarges the area of cultural freedom.

Let me add again that I am not arguing the point as to whether the ECLC is or is not a Communist front, but only the question of principle: is this a proper or effective way to spread cultural freedom or to combat communism? I might also say that I talked at length on the phone this evening with Mr. Clark Foreman in an attempt to see what he had to say in rebuttal, and that he struck me as either very dumb or very devious or perhaps both. He apparently has no regrets as to either the 1948 Progressive campaign or the 1949 Waldorf Conference and denies that either was dominated by the Communists. He insisted that Stone's book blames the Korean War on both sides equally (haven't read it so cannot say) and stated it as his own opinion that it is still a historical mystery as to whether the North Koreans invaded South Korea or vice versa. I asked him if the ECLC had denounced Communist as well as capitalist invasions of civil liberties and he replied they were against all forms of totalitarianism and authoritarianism; when I pointed out the desirability of their specifically taking a stand against Soviet totalitarianism, he replied there were so many different kinds of totalitarianism running around in this wicked world that it would get much too complicated if they were to go into detail on the question. Etc. etc.

Thus, if Mr. Foreman is typical of the top level of the ECLC, it may indeed BE a Communist front. Which would, however, make it all the more unfortunate that we let fly at it in this half-cocked way and so make it easy for it to wriggle off the hook.

To Paul M. Hahn [president, American Tobacco Company]

November 27, 1953

I am preparing an article for the *New Yorker* on the relation of smoking and lung cancer.

As you are doubtless aware, a number of recent studies, notably those of Dell & Hill in England and Graham and Wynder in this country, indicate a strong statistical correlation. The latter announce in the new *Cancer Research* that they have now "proved beyond any doubt" by laboratory experiments that there is a cancer-producing agent in tobacco smoke.

The next step is obviously to identify this agent, so it may be removed. As the *British Medical Journal* editorialized last year, "Intensive research on the chemical constituents of tobacco and tobacco smoke is now needed, and it is surely incumbent upon the tobacco manufacturers to do this . . . so that smoking will become a less dangerous occupation than it appears to be now."

Has the American Tobacco Co. to date appropriated any funds for research into this problem? If so, how much has been appropriated? When? And with what results?

P.S. To Mr. Hahn: Since writing the above I have noticed in today's *Times* your statement characterizing as "loose talk" the medical and scientific evidence to date that there is a connection between smoking and lung cancer. I hope you will not think it impertinent if, on the basis of fairly intensive reading in the large amount of scientific literature that has now accumulated on smoking & lung cancer, I say that the three arguments you bring forward do not seem to me to meet the issue for the following reasons:

On (1): Of course the fact that lung cancer and cigarette smoking have both increased of late years in no way proves that there is any connection between them. But in the scores of monographs I have read, I have not found one yet that says it does. That would be as crude and absurd as claiming that the rise in vacuum-cleaner sales as well as lung cancer "proved" that the latter is caused by using vacuum cleaners. The connection is always made on the basis of studies of lung-cancer victims which compare their smoking habit with those of an equal number of "controls" who do not have lung cancer. On (2): It is true that no one has yet proved that lung cancer is "directly traceable to tobacco," with the possible exception of the new Wynder-Graham study (which, in my own opinion, does NOT prove a direct relationship since it involves mice, whose lung tumors are appreciably different from those of men). But indirect, statistical proof can be very strong, or at least strong enough to warrant taking it, in the absence of any better explanation of the rise in lung cancer and the much greater incidence of it in heavy smokers than in light and nonsmokers, as the best basis we have for trying to go on to the next step and cutting down lung cancer.

On (3): In my reading in the field to date, I have found that it is simply not true that "for every expert who blames tobacco . . . there are others" who say there is no evidence that tobacco is an important cause of lung cancer. This was true ten or fifteen years ago, but in the last five years there has been a great change in the lung-cancer literature, and I would say that since 1948 it would be hard to find one anti-tobacco-cause authority for every five or six pro-tobacco authorities.

This last point can easily be verified. I'd be most grateful if you would refer me to the authorities you have in mind as denying that there is evidence that to-bacco smoking is causally connected with lung cancer.

P.S. to Robert M. Ganger: I note you advertise that Kent's micronite filter re-moves "far more nicotine and tars than any other filter cigarette." Have your own research staff, or some other researchers financed by you, made any studies as to how much, if any, filters cut down on the incidence of lung cancer in smokers?

cc: Parker McComas, President, Phillip Morris
Robert M. Granger, President, P. Lorillard Co.
B. F. Few, President, Liggett & Meyers
Edward A. Darr, Pres., R. J. Reynolds

To Dinsmore Wheeler

December 5, 1953
How could I have let 6 months go by without replying to your letter? Maybe I was waiting to report on the interview with Ian Hugo. He never showed up, or if he did, maybe I was away (I was on Cape with family off and on about a month last summer, rest of time working here) and he left no message. As for my being on the advisory board of the Film Society, of course, delighted and flattered to be. But must warn you that a couple of weeks ago I was at Hugo-Nin film, *Bells of Atlantis*, at a private showing at the Museum of Modern Art, and thought it was terrible—heavy, corny, sentimental, "poetic" and "literary" and "arty" in a way that's now thank God old-fashioned. Also mawkish and egotistical—or is this enough to give a rough idea (and rough is the word I guess, sorry to be such a bastard)? Lest you think this reaction is some kind of perversity, directed at you (since I gather you liked film or at least didn't feel violently contra), let me say that my reaction to it took place before I read your letter (just now) and that I had forgotten completely that you had mentioned Hugo, Nin, and the film.

(My memory is awful, as you know.) In fact I just now got quite a start when I came across their names in your letter.

So if I am honored by election to the Society's advisory board, I'd have to advise them not screen films like *Atlantis*, alas alas. . . .

Buckley, who isn't personally "nasty" (in fact I rather like him that way and have visited him several times at his palatial home in Stamford, though not in last 8 months and probably not ever again as McCarthy has become to me even more horrible than he used to be and now I feel at last a milder horror at Buckley for supporting him) but is so indeed as a political polemicist—he was quoting a crack I made, cannot recall where, about the fact that the liberals talk about witch-hunting and seeing things under the bed, but that difference between today and say, the Salem of witchcraft days or the USA of the Palmer Red Raids days, is that today there really ARE witches like Coplon, and also people named Hiss under the bed. I was objecting to the liberal defensive exaggeration against McCarthy's offensive lies. As for example, McCarthy lied when he called Lattimore a Communist and the No. 1 Soviet agent in USA, but Lattimore lied when he said in retort that he had never had any more sympathy for communism and the USSR than the average US college professor. So too Brownell's implication that Truman appointed White to a high post despite his knowledge that he was pro-Communist because he (T) didn't greatly object to communism is unfair and untrue, but T's speech defending himself was also disingenuous since he implied he had not fired White in order to help the FBI entrap him and other Commies, an excuse that seemed absurd to me at the time and that a day later Hoover revealed to be an untruth, in fact it was apparently the other way round.

Oh well.

. . . I enclose a copy of a recent review of the RSV Bible I did for the *New Yorker*. . . . I've gotten almost as much fan mail on it as I did on the Great Books piece, much of it from (for me) an odd group, namely rather conservative religious people. . . . No of course I didn't go back to 25 reunion at Yale, or any other. Hell with THAT place. Should have gone to Harvard.

Yes I'm wholly freelance except that for months now I've limited myself to *New Yorker* because it pays so much better, and though everybody thinks Nancy and I are rich, fact is we have no savings and manage barely to meet yearly expenses. Have a two-part profile of Barr of Modern Museum appearing beg. next week.

To the Editor, *Manas*

n.d., January 1953

I appreciate the kindly tone of your review of my review of the Hutchins-Adler edition of the Great Books, but not its thinking, which seems to me on the weak side. My review confines itself strictly to the set of books under view, a defensible practice, I think. I found the selection not too bad though marred by dogmatic caprice; I deplored the absence of introductory or explanatory matter and the poor quality of the verse translations; I found the format repellent and noted that one can buy almost all the Great Books in cheaper and more attractive editions, whence I concluded the purpose of publishing the set was NOT to make it easier for Americans to read the Books; and finally, I examined in some detail Dr. Adler's "Syntopicon" (which I not only "argued" is the *raison d'être* of the set, but demonstrated this to be the case, since a simple reading list would have served as well—considering the books can be bought separately more cheaply—if it had not been necessary to have a uniform edition whose pagination would correspond to Dr. Adler's index) and found it to be a useless, pretentious, and absurd project.

This is I think a fair summary of my lengthy review. I did not say anything at all about the following topics which your reviewer seems to think, or to imply, are also of necessity criticized in the mere fact of criticizing the Great Books set: (a) Dr. Hutchins as an educator, moralist, and thinker; (b) the "Great Books idea" as expressed in the movement to read the Great Books in colleges and in adult study groups; (c) the educational system promoted by Drs. Adler and Hutchins at the University of Chicago and at St. Johns College; (d) "the value of the Great Books themselves" (which your obtuse reviewer actually thinks I confuse with "Dr. Adler's presumptuous gadget," the Syntopicon). Since I criticized only the Great books *set*, and Drs. Adler and Hutchins insofar as they are chiefly responsible for the set, it seems a bit unjust for your reviewer to charge me with using "guilt by association." The fact is that my evaluation of the above topics cannot be deduced from my criticism of the set, viz.: (a) While I've never thought highly of Dr. Hutchins as a thinker, I do respect him as a moralist for his pronouncements during the war (though I wish he hadn't also allowed the atom bomb to have been conceived under the grandstand at Stagg Field in his university!) and have still more respect for his educational ideas; (b) I think it at the worst harmless, and at best a very fine idea, to encourage laymen to read the classics, and so am sympathetic to "the Great Books idea"—indeed, the publication of the set seems to me to conflict with this idea, since it is so needlessly expensive and since it does not make the classics more accessible and understandable to the layman; (c) I've given talks at both St. John's and the

U. of Chicago and have spent a little time on both campuses, and I found more intellectual excitement and seriousness there than on any other campus I have come in contact with—hence I think the Adler-Hutchins educational theories have much to be said for them; (d) not only do I value the Great Books highly, but one of my complaints against Drs. Adler and Hutchins *in their capacity as editors of the present set* is that they care so little about these texts that they didn't even commission decent translations (not to mention the barbarous idea of chopping them up in "topics" via the Syntopicon).

If there is to be any talk of "guilt by association," it seems to me it should be directed at your reviewer himself, who, since he evidently assumes that a criticism of Adler-Hutchins as editors of the Great Books set also implies a like criticism of their activities and ideas in other fields, defends them—or at least the latter; he seems willing to throw Adler to the wolves, and here, too, I agree with him; Hutchins is much better of the pair—against charges that I did not make.

Please excuse any undue sharpness of tone that may have crept into this letter. I didn't intend it, and am not angry at all. Just want to be clear and to make some clear distinctions. But some degree of sharpness is often needed in order to cut clearly, as with a razor.

To John Meyers

February 3, 1954

Thanks for your letter and I appreciate the friendly tone, and am genuinely sorry my review distressed you. All I can say is that the "snide" tone wasn't *New Yorkerish* but rather my own—after all, I've done a lot of "snide" writing in my time, am indeed rather an SOB, on paper at least. I LIKE to stick pins into people, especially pretentious people like most of the N[ew] D[irections] 14 writers. And secondly, that I don't see your reasoning about encouraging experimental writers and not being "defeatist" about their products, even if one thinks they are lousy, since "how do you know who might crash through with a wonderful book or painting." This sounds, allow me, a little philistine, like William Lyon Phelps, of the *Sat. Review of Lit,* who are always "encouraging" and "positive." No, the way to get good art and writing is, on the contrary, to be quite merciless toward the second-rate, and to put up only with the best. If a young, unknown writer has the stuff, he will show it and he won't be harmed by his faults being exposed. The avant-garde, just because it does pretend to quality and does look down on the second-rate, should welcome the most stringent criticism. Anyway, so I see it.

Nothing personal in my remarks on the Ford-Tyler anthology—I just thought Parker's introduction insufferably pompous (and badly written) and the anthology a lot of mystification. So I said so. Why not?

Lets discuss it all sometime. And thanks again for writing.

P.S. I cannot, simply cannot, think of the *New Yorker* readers as "slobby" and "philistine," since they seem to like a lot of stuff I've done which I think is quite good—the Barr piece (which you too were kind enough to like), the RSV Bible review, the Baldwin profile, and the Great Books piece. Aren't you being a little snobbish and also provincial in sneering so at the *New Yorker* just because it makes money, has cartoons, and has a largish circulation?

To W. J. Williamson III [Princeton professor of literature]

February 3, 1954

Thank you for your dissent on Hermann Hesse. But I can't quite agree with your reasoning. Imprimis, I *have* "taken the trouble to read" Hesse, namely his *Steppenwolf*, which I thought very arty and pretentious, with huge efforts to be cosmic that were defeated by a lack of talent, and indeed the sheer, vague dullness, of the author. Secundo, I was not and indeed am not aware that critical opinion was so unanimous on Hesse's majority; I was an editor of *Partisan Review* for 6 years and still read a lot of belles lettres and even know a few literary chaps, and believe me, I cannot recall anyone classing him with Kafka or Mann or even [Hermann] Broch; in fact I cannot recall anyone talking about him. (As for Mann's high opinion of Hesse, I note he also thinks *The Greek Tragedy* is terrific; I've recently read, or at least read in, that novel and I have to vigorously dissent—also I have in past noted, haven't you, that Mann's critical acumen is far short of his creative talent?) Finally, of course I didn't mean his subject matter was pretentious, which would be a meaningless statement, but his style and treatment, and while I agree that the adjective might be applied to Faulkner (though scarcely to the dry, precise, underplayed, matter-of-fact style of Kafka) he makes good his stylistic pretentiousness, at least in his best works, because he has the creative energy of a first-rate writer. I mean he can "carry" the weight of a portentous style, while poor puffing and groaning minor-writer Hesse can't.

Since I don't agree as to Hesse's big reputation, I see no reason for having been obliged to back up my sneer. But even if I did agree, I'm not so sure. After all, you simply cannot stop and justify and explain incidental points in a review (and my main point there was the turgidity of Seidlin, not the minority of his subject). Also, it probably wakes up the reader, gives his liver a healthful jolt, to have some pet prejudice or opinion of his given a brush-off. Look what a long letter it stimulated you to.

To Frank Sparks [president, Wabash College]

June 2, 1954

Thank you for asking me to become a member of your department of religion. I am indeed flattered. But, alas, the fact is I'm not at all religious, don't even believe in God, and my interest in KJV [the King James Version] is entirely aesthetic and secular. But it was good of you to ask me, and I am delighted you liked my RSV review.

To Gloria Lanier

June 21, 1954

Clouds have swept away, I feel fine, and I know all will be more than Well! . . . It was dear of you to call me this morning, made me love you even more if that were possible. . . . Leaving for Alabama [for divorce] at three this afternoon, getting back Wed. A.M. early. Called Sam and told him you wanted to go ahead tout suite and would call him. His no. by the way is HA-2060. . . . Told Mother this A.M. finally, she was *delighted*! I knew she liked you but hadn't realized how much. Also, you'll be glad to hear, she has rather dim view of N—which I also knew, but again not how dim. Anyway, she gave three cheers, said I'd been looking like the devil for last year, expects me to Settle Down and Have Fun. She thinks you are "charming, warm, substantial" (not as to figure, I gathered—or at least hoped!). And altogether a Fit Mate for Her Son. . . .

To William Shawn

December 6, 1954

I'll need about $3,000 to pay arrears on my income tax for 1954 (I've paid exactly $75 on it to date—getting divorced is expensive). It would be nice if the *New Yorker* could advance it against the following "purchases": Ford Foundation (should have it in by end of next month at latest); lung cancer (research done, will write it after Ford); [Daniel] Persky [scholar of the Hebrew language] profile; reviews of Melbourne (nearly done) and the ghost book.

The reason I'm so much behind with my *New Yorker* work—I now owe you about $4500—is that I did far too much outside writing this year. I have no other outside commissions and will accept none till I get the drawing account balanced up.

By the way, what do you think of idea of a one-part profile of Norman Thomas as the elder statesman of the left, corresponding to Baruch on the right—his career and life to be sketched in rapidly and briefly, focus to be on his personality and on just what an Elder Statesman does with his time—it's a profession very few of us achieve. Thomas is 70 this year and seems more full of life and zip than he was at 50—has a finger in literally hundreds of pies, all with a distinct flavor of crusading-for-justice. He's a remarkable example of a man who has actually improved with age. Everybody thinks better of him now than they did in 1935, from the Trotskyists to the N.Y. *Times*, which has called him "America's conscience" and not inaccurately either.[7]

To Nicola Chiaromonte

January 18, 1955

I was distressed to learn of your father's death. Please accept my sympathy. I know perhaps a little of how you feel because I still remember the grief when my father died thirty years ago. I also remember him, still, because he knew how to enjoy and give pleasure, to love and to let himself be loved.

. . . It's disgraceful of me not to have sooner replied to your letter—*sooner*, heavens it's been a whole year. I *am* embarrassed. But I've been going through the upsetting, unsettling experience of getting divorced from Nancy and marrying Gloria, and have rarely felt in a mood to write a personal letter. Things are settling down now—we have a very nice place at 56 East 87th, bet. Park and Madison, elegant neighborhood but inexpensive apartment in a rather elderly building; Gloria found it by methods of her own, without benefit of the *NYTimes* real estate section.

Glad you enjoyed reissue of the *Root*; I think I should have been more severe on part 2 in my new notes; you were right about it—also about *Responsibility*, which I feel stands up remarkably well, better than the *Root*. . . . Yes.

[Isaiah] Berlin's *Fox & Hedgehog* [*The Hedgehog and the Fox* (1953)] is excellent, and so is your review in PR of it. Extraordinary to read something which is fruit of actual thinking.

I've a few things in last year, sending you separately most of them. Nothing very ambitious. Now I'm engaged in a very big job, a profile at the Ford Foundation for this mag, no less. Going to Detroit next week to interview Henry Ford II (and, much more exciting) see the River Rouge works for the first time. Odd thing about the Ford Foundation (which spent $60 million last year) is that when you look at most of its projects concretely and in detail they seem all right, some even very praiseworthy, and yet there is a dull patina over the whole business that makes it unreal, uninteresting, unhuman, hard to keep one's mind on. All so abstract—the $$$ they spend don't really belong to anybody,

---

7. In the forties, during the war, Macdonald dismissed Thomas as indistinguishable from bourgeois liberals. He was particularly irked by Thomas's support of the war.

that is not to say person, and they aren't spent to gratify any evil or virtuous wish of anybody. It's all institutionalized, their own division of Behavioral Sciences would say (they invented the term). Only line I've worked out so far is that it's a profile not of people or a person but of money, $$$$.

I've also got a book on mass culture about to commence—Doubleday will probably do it, and, after trade edition, I hope, in one of their excellent Anchor Books (have been dealing with the editor of that series, also the originator, a very intelligent thirtyish-old named Jason Epstein). This ought to be an interesting book to write and to read.

. . . There's a slight chance of my getting over there by next fall, depends on $$$$ which Come In fairly well but also Go Out even more efficiently in my present status. . . . Thank you for writing so explicitly about your personal situation. I was a little angry to learn that you had been somewhat uncandid with me when I saw you. But don't feel so now and am touched & pleased you now write about it. God knows whether your course or mine was best, is best. I won't pretend that many painful and unexpected troubles have now come up between Gloria and me. On the other hand, I feel—now, that is, as against last spring—little guilt or remorse about Nancy. Maybe in part because she seems to be doing all right (though I cannot really tell as I see so little of her). And on the OTHER hand, some of the difficulties in my new life are probably due to unconscious guilt feelings. I'm still, after months of married life with Gloria, not sure what will come even in the next few months. This sound desperate, and it is. What I don't know about human relations! I say human and not sexual because that part, the sexual, is, oddly, more divine than ever. Always. It's the day-to-day living, which I had thought of as no problem at all, which is constantly breaking into painful fragments. Strange and supremely unexpected. . . .

To Stephen Spender

April 25, 1955

You've asked me to put down, for the information of your colleagues, what I think might be done with *Encounter*—assuming I became your co-editor, you to be in charge of the literary side and I to take over the rest.

My chief idea is that *Encounter* should compete with *The New Statesman & Nation* as well as with *Partisan Review*, i.e., that while continuing to print poems, stories, and general cultural articles—which have been, I'd say on the basis of the back issues I've read, on a very high level—it should also go in strongly for political (and cultural) journalism. This shouldn't mean watering down, cheapening, or "popularizing." It's simply a matter of a more topical, timely, journalistically enterprising approach.

Specifically, I suggest (what follows is just what occurs to me now—I'm sure more thought and, especially, some actual experience with the magazine, will produce other ideas and also very likely show some of these to be no good).

(1) A new department of political and topical comment, which I'll do myself, of items varying from a short paragraph or even a sentence to a 2 or 3 thousand word lead article. This would be signed with my initials to make it clear it's simply my own views and not those of the Congress.

(2) An effort to stimulate discussion (the more violent the better—everyone is excited by row) by printing more letters from readers (exp. critical ones, with brief replies by the editors or authors concerned) and by commissioning controversial articles on topics of lively current interest (a pro and a con article on Churchill as a political leader f.i., would be good right now). This dept. of controversy would have to be skillfully handled if it is to avoid becoming a dreary battleground where all-too-familiar viewpoints clash emptily against each other. The topics would be concrete, limited, and the old battle horses like Sidney Hook or Norman Thomas or G. D. H. Cole would be passed over in favor of fresher, livelier antagonists.

(3) More articles on political, social, and cultural topics in the news; more of an effort to go out and get pieces on subjects people are currently thinking about, as against passively choosing from among the material that happens to be sent in. (Not that, with a limited budget, we wouldn't have to use mostly the latter kind—which can be extremely good, of course, as Bell's Notes on Work—but with more aggressive editing, it should be possible to increase the ratio of timely pieces.)

(4) A kind of piece that is seldom written could be encouraged: part reportage, part evaluation, done in an informal personal way, and about some aspect of professional or everyday life. As, Mary McCarthy on shopping in a US supermarket; David Riesman on sociologists' convention; some former *Time* writer on what life is like in Luceland; I could have done something interesting on the McCarran hearing on Lattimore; or some novelist or poet on some kind of political trial or hearing (NOT Rebecca West).

(5) A dept. on mass, or popular, culture which would offer a place for articles on the phenomenon in general, would follow systematically both its more interesting manifestations and also the growing periodical literature, including the academic magazines on it.

(6) One trouble with writing for magazines is that one has to inflate every idea into a full-dress article, that there is no place where one can publish notes, apercus, brief and unconnected paragraphs which one doesn't want to make into a formal article. We could open *Encounter* to this form. (Auden's "World Machine" is a superb example of what I mean, though longer than such notes would generally be.)

I think it would be possible to double or triple *Encounter*'s present circulation by some such editorial reorientation. (If the format and frequency could be changed—the former to a self-cover job about the size of the *New Statesman*, but with each cover using drawings and/or photographs so as to "compose" into a kind of poster, different in layout each time and eye-catching on the newsstands; the latter to a fortnightly—it might be possible to go much higher.) The American circulation, which I understand is only a couple of thousand, could certainly be greatly increased if the magazine went in the direction of political journalism more. Since the *Nation* and the *New Republic* went to seed in the late thirties, mostly because of the self-stultifying line on Soviet communism, we haven't had a decent political magazine. On the other hand, there are perhaps half a dozen cultural magazines on at least a comparable level with *Encounter* and with, to a large extent, the same type of contents—*Partisan Review, Kenyon, Hudson, Perspectives, Sewanee, Accent*. Since I stopped putting out *Politics* in 1949, I've been struck by two things—from letters and from people I run into—(1) how widely it seems to have been read and known, considering that 6,000 was its top circulation; (2) how many people are now hungry for a political-social magazine on some sort of intellectual level.

I hope it all works out. As I told you, I'd enjoy greatly experimenting with this sort of magazine, and I'm sure you and I could work well together.

To Stephen Spender

June 2, 1955

Thanks for your cable and for your letter of May 27. Yes, [Nicholas] Nabokov has written me that [Michael] Josselson is coming to town the first week in June. He hasn't showed yet.

I'm pleased as Punch, from whose editor by the way I had a very nice note the other day, that things are working out. The idea of editing *Encounter* with you seems more attractive than ever. I do hope the question of enumeration, hem hem, can be solved to the mutual satisfaction of both parties.

Thanks for the briefing on the Congress [of Cultural Freedom] and its attitude toward *Encounter*. Sounds positively idyllic. I mean the hands-off policy. Any other would make it impossible to put out a lively magazine, or even a very good one. As for mine toward the Congress, since I know very little of what the Congress has been up to, cannot say in detail. The one impression I have is that the Congress has criticized the American Committee [for Cultural Freedom] for the same general reasons I have. So that's not too bad a basis for a beginning.

Rumors about my superseding Irving [Kristol] have spawned all over town, that is, all over the tiny segment of town occupied by people I know. I said little about it for a while, but of late, when people ask me, I tell them it's been decided except for the matter of salary (assuming things have gone so far there's no point denying the facts—something I'm no good at anyway). Went to a reception given by the Committee for Jules Romains last night and talked with Dan Bell and Sidney Hook. Bell, an old friend and a sensible fellow who's been sympathetic to our (your and mine) objections to the American Committee's exclusive preoccupation with anti-communism (latest is that they have commissioned Bertram D. Wolfe to do a book for them on the coexistence issue, God knows what that has to do with cultural freedom) than with the other side—anyway, Bell says there is some bad feeling in the Committee about my going to *Encounter*, partly because some members prefer Kristol's politics to mine, and partly because (he claims) it was all done sub rosa. Specifically, he said that Hook was sore because you hadn't talked with him about the change when you were over here. I think you should have, even though Hook is not formally involved. But he *is* a member of the Congress executive, and it might have been well to give him the bad news yourself. On the other hand, maybe I'm wrong (and maybe Bell exaggerates Hook's reaction). For when I talked to Hook at the party, he said he wasn't sore at all, that there was no reason you should have talked with him, and said his only problem was why, when he told you, Nabokov, and others at Paris that *Encounter* was too academic and should become more political and journalistic, you had rejected his suggestions, while now this is just what I am supposed to be bringing to the magazine. I said I thought probably the trouble was that you people didn't agree so much with his and Kristol's politics and felt more in harmony with mine. He affected to not understand this at all, and when I pointed to specific issues on which Kristol and I had clashed in the past on the proper way to fight Commies, he dismissed these as trivial differences of opinion as to techniques. He was friendly enough—as he always has been—and did say at one point that he greatly respected my editorial talents, but—leaving it unfinished. I said: "But you think I'm undependable politically." He laughed and admitted this was true. As of course I am, from the Communist-obsessed standpoint of Hook and the other dominant people on the American Committee. (It is odd that, since Hook gave up the chairmanship, the top posts have been occupied by people who share the minority view on the matter of anti-communism—Robert Gorham David, Diana Trilling, James T. Farrell—and yet the actions of the Committee continue to be the other way.) Farrell, too, by the way, whom I also saw last night, said there was a big crisis approaching in the relations of the Committee and the Congress, of which the *Encounter* editorship is one ingredient.

I don't think all of this is too serious. Almost everyone I talked with thought the magazine would be better if it were more political, lively, controversial, journalistic. And I think if we give them an exciting magazine, they will, perhaps a little grudgingly, forget all their fears as to my, and your, alleged "softness" towards the Communist issue. These veteran frontline fighters against communism are anachronisms by now anyway—time for them to move over and let young bloods of fifty take over! The main thing is that *Encounter* can make its way by itself, on the basis of its own qualities and interest, and through the ordinary channels of distribution, with or without the formal blessings of committees.

I'll write you again as soon as Josselson appears and I've talked with him. Meanwhile, let me say that I, too, am anticipating working with you on the magazine. I really think we can do something with it.

To Stephen Spender

June 6–20, 1955

I've had a long and very agreeable talk with Mike Josselson, whom I liked very much, and everything is just about decided. We discussed the Congress's general "line," or rather he outlined it and I kept saying I agreed, as I do. (The chief difference between the Congress and the American Committee seems to be that the former is concerned with defending cultural freedom against all comers and regardless of whether Communists, fascists, or mugwumps are the parties injured, while the latter is not. And here, of course, I find the Congress taking the position I have in my criticisms over the last two years of the Committee. So *that's* all right.) He didn't think the Congress would throw its weight around so far as my own cultural freedom, as editor of *Encounter*, goes, and said they realize that they cannot have an alive magazine unless the editors are given lots of scope. I told him I figured I'd need $12,000 a year (taking into account the lower cost of living in England) and gave him a little memo I had worked up from my own accounts of the last year showing in detail how I arrived at this. I also asked that the Congress pay the passages to and from England of myself and family. He told me he thought both requests reasonable, on the basis of my figures, and that he was sure the Congress would approve. Even though Kristol had been getting "appreciably less." But I gather they are willing to pay more for me because they really want me, which is delightful. He's now off to the Virgin Islands for a vacation with his wife and will get together with me again when they return on the 21st of this month. He said I might consider the deal "practically" closed, and when I asked what "practically" meant, said "75%." So it looks good.

Thanks for your letter, I quite understand now why you didn't approach Hook, and I think your letter to him a veritable masterpiece in the sensibilities-soothing line.

One thing you might find out for me: (a) what would be the English income tax on $12,000 a year; and (b) if, as I believe, the rate is higher than the American tax (which is about $1,700), will it be possible for me to be paid in dollars over here, so that I pay American and not English taxes? I asked Jossel-son, but he was not informed—in fact, he thought British and American in-come taxes are about the same. (Which I'm almost sure is NOT the case.) The point is that if the English tax is appreciably higher, then I'd have to ask the Congress to make up the difference, because my calculation of what I shall need is really pretty close to bedrock.

Josselson said that Irving is leaving October 1, and he suggested I come over the first week in September and attend that Milan conference the Con-gress is holding and write a reportage piece about it for *Encounter*. This is what I plan to do, probably going first to Milan and then to London.

The prospect is exciting all around.

P.S. I'll be coming with Gloria and her two daughters, so you might keep an eye out for a house or apartment (flat) large enough for the four of us.

To Gloria Macdonald

September 15, 1955

. . . Things are finally jelling, after the most incredible amount of backstairs in-trigue. Kristol, with Hook as his patron, has actually won against Spender, and now is to stay on! Spender, who, alas, is even softer and weaker than I'd thought (this from Arthur [Schlesinger], who was in on this afternoon's crucial meeting; and who says that Josselson and Nabokov were far more firm against Hook than Spender!), seems to have accepted the reversal, though I can't imagine the kind of "cooperation" he and K will have in future! So I'm out as Ye Editor. *However*, Josselson (who it appears has been on my side all along but is also worried about the violent reaction of the Americans, some of them, to me) has just (12:30 P.M.) made me this offer: $10,000 a year, I (and YOU, darling!) To live in London, and to (1) write regular articles for *Encounter, Prevues,* and *Der Monat*, (2) travel around to journalistically interesting events and do reportage on them, (3) serve as consultant to the editors of the 3 above mags, giving them ideas, etc. So I said: OK. So *now* I gather it's in the bag that way, *unless* I cannot get the dough out of "Junkie" [Julius] Fleischmann. In some ways, this is better than a full-time editing job—I'd have much more freedom and more time to do my own work.— —BUT, sweet, don't count on it wholly yet, as this organization is Subject to Change Without Notice. Life has moved very fast here lately. Han-nah did very well at her session; we dined together at Greniros [sp?] the other night (we have meal tickets for the best restaurants) and met a couple who make flour (Harris's Best) in Bulawayo, Rhodesia; Mary and the Chiaromontes arrived yesterday so have been seeing much of them (on Sunday I will go with them to the seaside place they are staying at for a few days, then on to Venice).

Yesterday did a lot of shopping (including something I hope you'll like) and saw a very fine private art gallery (old masters). Has no mail come of urgency for me? Haven't gotten anything forwarded. Better write me c/o the Congress Pour la Liberté, etc. 104 Boulevard Haussman, Paris 8, after this (unless I give you a better address). You ask if Spender has changed. No, not at all. He has been very friendly and was obviously enormously delighted (and relieved!) when I told him I would accept J's proposal. *"Then* we *shall* have you!" he cried, in Jamesian fashion. Thanks for the clipping re that unhappy [Harold] Rosenberg article—oddly enough we had just been discussing it. Seems it almost sunk mag when it came out—with first issue.

To Michael Macdonald

September 30, 1955

Very good to get your letter. Ya, I'm still a member of the Yale Club, have even paid my dues for next 6 months. Bruce Barton is a founder of Batten, Barton, Durstine & Osborne (BBD&O), famous advertising firm, and author of *The Man Nobody Knows*, famous (and infamous) best-seller about Christ. I am living here in a garret (literally) up 5 flights of stairs, no running water, $1.20 a night . . . but Mary Mc., who has a nice apartment with an Italian family, lets me write in her place during the day. Venice is the loveliest, gayest place on earth. The most romantic, too. Like Nantucket, it is almost all very old houses. . . .

I got the job with the Congress for C.F., or at least *a* job. My enemies, the Hook faction that dominates the American delegation, objected so strenuously to me as editor of *Encounter* that those who wanted me (the European secretariat, mostly) had to compromise in my doing a series of articles for *Encounter* (and traveling around Europe to get material) and also serving as "editorial consultant" to it + 2 other mags the Congress backs. At $10,000 a year. This is fine with me, as I am free of all editorial responsibility and can travel (expenses paid) and write and be well paid for it. . . .[8]

8. When the news broke that *Encounter* was funded indirectly by the CIA and Macdonald was outraged that he did not know, many wondered where he thought the lavish funds came from. He had worked for little mags throughout his career, and they were hardly noted for large expense accounts.

To William Shawn

n.d., November 1955

This is a fan note. I like you as an editor. I'm thinking especially of your severe bending of the no-personal-editorializing rule in profiles in re my Ford Foundation piece, and the grounds on which you have done it, namely, that only thus could such a piece be either interesting or informative. I also recall, with gratitude, your willingness to let me go to unreasonable lengths, wordwise, in the Bible and Great Books (also the Ford) pieces. Finally, I appreciate your loyal support of the writer in his (my) occasional conflicts with characters like Baldwin and Saudek. All in all, it's a pleasure to work with you. If only you'd wise up about footnotes. But, as Poe used to quote from Bacon (Lord Verulan to him), there is no perfect beauty without some strangeness in the proportions.

To the Editor, *The New Republic*

January 2, 1956

In the January 2 *New Republic*, a TV critic, David Ebbitt, compares me to a vulture, states that I am "especially abhorrent" to him and also more irritating than a bus driver, and confesses "a violent urge" to tell me go soak my head. Since I haven't the pleasure of knowing Mr. Ebbitt—or, indeed, of ever having heard of him—I don't take these strictures personally. And, in fact, the author makes it clear that his animosity is aroused entirely because I am, or at least he conceives me to be, a highbrow.

Now this, I think, is a very sad thing to read in a magazine which itself used to be in the thirties when I read it, proudly and defiantly highbrow. (Let me confess it—Mr. Ebbitt's instinct is right: I *am* highbrow.) It is a depressing sign of the deterioration of liberal journalism that one of your regular contributors could make this charge the basis of a page-long attack on my adverse judgment of *Omnibus* (which was made by the way in the *New Yorker*, a magazine which didn't use to be considered really highbrow, but which by default and by simply maintaining a decent level of writing and thought, of late years has come to have some claim, if only a relative one, to the adjective; it is interesting, by the way, that my colleague here, Phillip Hamburger, also expressed a very low opinion of *Omnibus* when he was writing the *New Yorker*'s TV column). It is also depressing to consider the "highbrow" as a term of abuse as first cousin to "egghead," both being expressions of that philistinism and anti-intellectualism that corrodes our mass democracy. When McCarthy denounces the eggheads, the editors of *The New Republic* have no difficulty knowing where they stand. Why is the tactic any more respectable on the cultural plane? McCarthy dislikes the eggheads because they insist on maintaining certain standards of political behavior, notably in the area of civil liberties; he thinks this is perverse, snobbish, phony, and un-American. Except for the last adjective—and it may come, it may come—this is also the gravamen (look it up, Mr. Ebbitt) of your reviewer's charge against me as a highbrow. Insistence on high cultural standards appears to him perverse and affected—as though our popular culture is suffering from too rigorous criticism! A sad thing.

There is no point in defending here the validity of my evaluation of *Omnibus*. I've expressed myself fully on pages 99 through 103 of the December 3 issue of the *New Yorker*, of which Mr. Ebbitt has given a reasonably fair summary. But I do want to reply, briefly, to his insinuation that I don't know much about (a) popular culture in general, (b) TV in particular, and (c) *Omnibus* in very particular. (a) I have been writing about the movies and other forms of popular culture, off and on, since 1930; the Summer 1953 issue of *Diogenes* (a deplorably highbrow magazine published in, let's face it, Paris, and until lately subsidized by the Ford Foundation that finances *Omnibus*) contains a lead article by me titled "A Theory of Mass Culture"; I am shortly departing for the Salzburg Seminar to give a course in mass culture and am currently working on a book on the subject. (b) In the last year and a half, I have seen a good deal of television owing to children and the acquisition of a TV set. (c) I have seen about 40 *Omnibus* features—20 on my own and another 20 because Robert Saudek, the show's producer, who has all the personal vanity of the artist though unhappily few of the other qualities, was so shocked at my low estimate of his creation when I showed him the article in advance proof, that he could explain my aberration only on the grounds of ignorance. He challenged me to see more, I took him up, and his staff ran off for me, through two sessions of five hours each, kinescopes of features which he considered especially good. I came, I saw, I was not conquered. Three or four of the shows seemed to me definitely good, perhaps ten so-so, and the rest mediocre or worse.

In short, while it is true, as Mr. Ebbitt gloomily suspects, that I have a low opinion of our mass culture in general, this seems not from ignorance or affectation, but from a certain amount of knowledge and, you'll excuse the expression, thinking about the subject over a considerable length of time.

To Hannah Arendt

January 5, 1956

A Puzzle.

At [Elliot] Cohen's party [he was the editor of *Commentary*], you gave as an instance of the corrupting influence of American foundations the fact that you had been asked to serve on some committee at Princeton which has to do with foundation grants and that you will probably accept. When I said why be corrupted, you said because I may be able to steer funds toward some good people who need them.

In short, you recognized that our foundations have their good as well as their bad sides.

Then why was it wrong of me to recognize this in my piece on the Ford Foundation? You said I should have given foundations the drastic treatment I did the Great Books set. But the difference, surely, is that there was no need for the Great Books set and also that whatever novelty it had (such as picking out THE great books and harnessing them to Adler's Syntopicon) was bad; while such things as the Ford's Indian community program or Guggenheim's fellowships are good. (You also recognize this in the Princeton committee, else you wouldn't be willing to be "corrupted" by joining it.)

I may have been less critical of certain Ford projects than I should have (or than you think I should have), but I do insist it was a much more complicated problem than the Great Books (or the Revised Standard Version of the Bible).

All this grows out of my shock (and, I must confess, angry feeling of injustice) at your remark at your New Year's party that since I'd had my chance to criticize seriously the foundations in the Ford pieces and had not taken it, I should now be quiet when the issue is raised again by the *Encounter* affair. As I recall, I had many and sharp things to say about the timidity and the conformity propagated by our foundations, which is the point about the *Encounter* business.

Or perhaps you're *not* joining the Princeton committee? (My impression was that you felt you had to despite everything, but maybe it's wrong.) In that case, I'd say you're being too "pure"—I put the word in quotes because I mean it in a sectarian, formalistic way—that is, the gain in purity is not enough to outweigh the gain in helping good people get some financial support—like some anarchy-pacifists I know who are bothered by having to use U.S. currency. I have a sneaking feeling of sympathy with them, true, but I firmly suppress it and continue to hand out dollar bills (and take them in). As, for that matter, they do, too.

If you do take this position, however, you are logical and the puzzle disappears. But if not, then . . . ?????

P.S. Perhaps you missed the enclosed from today's *Times*? It's the best statement I've seen of the Southern viewpoint (haven't seen yours, of course). Naturally, it's by a New Englander. Let me have back some time unless you want it yourself.

To John Lukacs [well-known conservative historian who became a good friend of Macdonald's]

January 11, 1956

That I haven't until now answered your letters doesn't mean they were not greatly enjoyed. I got into a writer's block, or jam, on revising and adding to the Ford profiles for book publication, and took weeks on it, and couldn't do anything else, or felt I couldn't, till I'd gotten them done, which I just have. . . . And now my departure on the 28 inst. for Salzburg [Seminar] looms close, and I've got to work up some lectures on mass culture, etc. So I'm afraid this cannot be as adequate a reply to your letters as it should.

Thanks, first of all, for [Harold] Nicholson's *Good Behavior*, which came from England and has been, is being read with much appreciation by Gloria and myself. He writes well, though I don't think as well as Beerbohm, Shaw, Strachey, or . . . Herzen; but he's really a cultivated, witty, perceptive writer, and his point of view is "civilized" in the best sense of that word.

No, haven't read *Crowd Culture* [by Elias Canetti] yet, but have ordered it. . . . Re your thanks to me for your $300 raise: I'd hate to think my articles prodded the Foundation into that half-billion program, because (as I show in detail in the last chapter of the book) that program was about as timid, unimaginative, and uncreative a use of money as one could imagine. For instance, to make only one point, why give the $ to ALL the 650 liberal arts colleges?; why not choose the fifty or hundred best ones, big . . . and little, and give them each enough to make a difference?; this way everybody in every college, good or bad or indifferent, gets a 4% pay raise, which is a tip, not a raise; also the $$ doesn't encourage excellence but simply affirms the status quo—and don't think much of the status quo. . . . "Erinaceous" means belonging to the hedgehog family, hence prickly, hence combative (from Greek eris, which I think means war); I picked it up somewhere recently. . . . Yes, I agree McKelway on [John] O'Hara was terrible, even shocking (O'Hara is about the most brutal, insensitive, tricked-up, sensational novelist we have, at least above the Mickey Spillane level; he is really a bad person—snobbish, aggressive, ignorant, facile, with the sentimentalism that usually accompanies brutality—and it shows in his writing. I used to know him in the early thirties; he could never get over his envy of me for having gone to Yale! Interesting to compare him with Fitzgerald, his literary father and mentor—F was a snob too, but a loving one, he makes you feel nostalgic about the Plaza and Princeton of the twenties; there is no love, no charm, no reverence in O'Hara; he is essentially, a bum). . . . Must also agree that friend Rovere's prose style, esp. in the *NYorker*, is indeed often pompous, and always long-winded and inflated; he just doesn't seem to get down to anything, to come to grips. . . . I have just read your massive and eloquent *Epistle Contra*

Herzenum, and the first thing that struck me, with force, was that ten minutes ago and on the preceding page, I had taken exactly the same basic line as you do, in describing O'Hara as a "bad man" and connecting that with his work. Unless this is an unconscious carryover from my first reading of your Anti-Herzen, two weeks ago, it is an indication of something I think we have both come to feel, namely, an extraordinary agreement, despite the most extreme differences as to religion and politics and even as to temperament, between us about basic principles. I'm very glad about this, as to find a benighted, obscurantist, superstitious Catholic like yourself agreeing with me is to make me feel my ideas must have some validity (or, of course, my enemies would say it just goes to show what they have been saying about me all the time!). I'm also glad for other, less egotistical, reasons. . . . On Herzen v Tocq[ueville], I can't pronounce until I have read T's Souvenirs, . . . and also take another look at H's Memoirs. Though I just cannot believe I will ever agree that H was a louse and a liar—to be smug about it. Re the attraction Russian writers have for Americans—namely, that they provide Faith (rather than Love)—this doesn't explain my own liking for the Russians, since I have never sought Faith, not even at 17; reason, skepticism, irony, satire—these were my qualities until the last 10 years, and to a large extent still are, except that somewhere around the middle of editing *Politics*, I began to more and more feel the importance of Love; but Faith never! Voltaire is my man, not Rousseau; the 18th is my century, not the 19th (or, alas the 20th—no, the "alas" is melodramatics, actually I enjoy being against the currents, and also find plenty to like in my times). An ex. of exaggeration surely is your comparing Orwell's *Burmese Days,* a workmanlike and honest novel but no more, with Tolstoy novels, to the disadvantage of the latter! I have read Tolstoy often in the last few years, and, although I am no great fan of naturalism, he always impresses me as about as great a fiction writer as there has ever been; I think it is mostly his intelligence, his sheer power to think, to seize the essentials in a scene and tell them directly and almost without any art at all—it's as if God were writing—without sentiment, impersonally, from no special point of view, clear and fully rounded, with everything in (and yet not the clutter of detail lesser writers put in). He's about as different a writer from Dostoevsky as it is possible to be. In fact, his *fiction* seems to me classic rather than romantic, and to have none of those qualities you describe as typically Russian (while D's fiction has all of them). His own life and his nonfiction writings, on the other hand, do have quite a lot of the Russian about them (though even there, in his moral tracts, it is remarkable how clearly, simply, unenthusiastically he writes without adornment or rhetoric or appeals to emotion. . . .

To Gloria Macdonald

January 31, 1956

They *have* the reservation! Tourist, on the *Flandres* (the one French Line that I have heard is all right in tourist). On June 23!! The only hitch is there are no cabins for 2 in tourist, only for 4, and so all 4 of us will be in one cabin. I don't mind, but I'm going to ask Mike J. if they couldn't loosen up enough to send us Cabin Class. (Of course I'm in an unstrategic position!)

. . . All day yesterday I attended the annual meeting of all the editors of the Congress's publications. We sat around a big hollow square of tables, covered with green felt, Like the UN, and we talked, my God how we talked! [Melvin] Lasky presided. There were also [François] Bondy, [Stephen] Spender, [Irving] Kristol, [Malcolm] Muggeridge, [Minoo] Masani (from the Indian Congress) . . . and several others (an Austrian, some Frenchmen, and a Pole). Oh yes, also [Ignazio] Silone and Chiaromonte. I was made to feel very important. At least, whenever any specific article or series was mentioned, it was usually suggested I do it (or was the type to do it). What they all want seems to be literary journalism or journalistic *belles lettres*—something that is more "actual," livelier, readable than the usual "little magazine" stuff. More reportage, less philosophy. It was a stimulating session, but my God how tiring! Afterwards most of us went to a small party at Bondy's—mild fun—and then to a terrible movie, a French-type gangster film. This morning I've been working on the lectures (they're going to be good dear!). And now, at 11 A.M., I'm waiting for a small (me, Lasky, Bondy) conference to begin. Then lunch with Miloscz (I have a scheme to try to raise some $ in "the States" for him, I want to find out how he and his family are making out). Then another meeting (with a German). Then back to hotel to work on the *Nat. Review* piece. Then dinner with Nicky C.

Only one other date at present: lunch at the Boris Souvarine's. On Thursday [February 2, 1956] I leave for a sleeper and the cars are loaded onto a boat and you wake up in England, where I'll be till I leave for Salzburg on the tenth. . . .

Spender and I dined alone on my first night here. A marvelous meal—lobster bisque, gnocchi, a steak that melted in one's mouth—at a café we chanced on in the Latin Quarter. I like him very much. We talked a lot—about Wordsworth, Kristol (its seems the Milan showdown has made a new man of him, and now he and Spender get on very well), the penalties of being a celebrity (which he knows firsthand), etc. Darling, I'm beginning to ache for you already. Haven't done any sightseeing, because want to "do" them with you this summer.

To Gloria Macdonald

February 6, 1956

Life in London continues to be very interesting Both K[ristol] and S[pender] are putting themselves out . . . for me. Sat. I took K and wife, Bea Himmelfarb, grim of face but very intelligent (she's written a lot about Victorians, did a thing on [Lord] Acton and is now working on a book about Darwin—anyway I took them to dinner at the Café Royale (the literary hangout of the 90's—Wilde, Frank Harris, Shaw, Beerbohm, etc.) We had a really excellent meal, with the kind of service and attention from waiters and so on that seems taken for granted here but is amazing to one used to the rigors of NYC, for about $650 for all 3—living is much cheaper here than in NYC, or even Paris, and then they took me to *Waiting for Godot*, which plays much better than it reads but is still very mannered and slight—"existentialist vaudeville" says K.—superb performances, every character wonderfully taken. Last night Spender took me to dine at the Saville Club. (I'm dining w. Muggeridge at the Garrick on Wed.) It was shabbier, smaller, and less impressive than I'd expected. Also, everybody ate at a common table. I was introduced to most of the few members there (only about a dozen, it being Sunday) and they were all most friendly. Even talkative. Most disappointing. (This famous British reserve and hauteur is a myth—Americans are much ruder and snootier.) Seriously, though, there was a lot of talk, some of it good. I sat next to the head of the BBC's Third Program! S says he is a dull fellow, though very nice. I agree—he reminded me of one of my Exeter teachers—grey and fatherly and somehow unworldly. Somebody asked him if he ever looked at TV and he said, "Heavens, no. I'm just an old-fashioned liberal. I only read books." In the main room there was a small false coal fire run by electricity plugged in front of the fireplace. S was indignant—he wrote at once an item in the "Complaint Book" . . . to the effect that this was very non U and asking for a real coal fire, then went around collecting signatures. Whole atmosphere very gemütlich. I gave a member (he turned out to be a German refugee who is a psychiatrist at Proudmoor, the great asylum for the criminally insane!) a cigar and he bought me a drink. Today, S, K, and I had an editorial meeting at *Encounter* office (which seems even more slipshod and messy than PR used to be) and then we had lunch on the magazine at a "good" restaurant. Not bad, though not so good either. (British food about like USA, far below Paris.) Most of the time I spend in my wonderful room working on Salzburg and the Buckley mag (which is pretty awful—your comments very stimulating, by the way, darling). Now I'm off to Stephen's for dinner, and *who* do you think is to be there? Raymond Chandler. So I can do some mass culture research. I'm curious to meet his wife and kids, to see his place, will continue when I get back, dearest. (Just think how nice it will be when you and I can go out together in London—I'm saving up my sightseeing till then.)

Tues, A.M.—Chandler, poor fellow, disappointing. A pallid, puffy, shaky, elderly Californian—seemed either slightly tight or else a trifle senile—very slow, simpleminded. He's a great admirer and friend of S's wife (who wasn't there, being still in Switzerland—his kids are very cute); his wife died last year, he took to the bottle, Mrs. S. and more friends met him, helped him, saved his life by watching over him; then he saved her life by financing specialist treatment of some disease she had (not specified by Stephen) this fall. Curious story—he and Stephen clearly don't know what to make of each other.

To Gloria Macdonald

February 17, 1956

The students mostly arrived yesterday [at Salzburg Seminar]—there'll be 17 women and 32 men when (and if) they all get here—and I had "interviews" with seven of the 12 signed up for my seminar. The quotes mean I didn't know what to ask or say, and it usually became another kind of interview—I interviewed them about their native land. Disappointed in my students so far—a couple seem to have something, only—but there'll be more. (One of them— one of the bright ones, except she's lunatically aggressive, is niece of Toglatti, head of C.P. in Italy!) But the boys and girls (average age: 30) as a whole look fairly good, and I've met maybe half a dozen of interest. God knows, if the session is at all rewarding it will be because of them—for the permanent staff here, with whom we had to pal around the first two days (friendliness, palship is the keyword here), is pretty ghastly. George Adams, the director, and another fellow named Woodham (I think) are plain and simple Babbitts—big, loud, hearty, anti-cultural—of a type I haven't seen for years. Adams and his wife—a plumb matron with infantile and mildly flirtatious mannerisms, who coos and bats her eyes in the royal good-fellowship like a scout mistress—couldn't have been nicer to me, insisting on driving me to town for my first coffee mit schlag (whipped cream), and very good it was, etc. But why in the world he has anything to do with a place of learning, God knows. (He was dean of Harvard Summer School, another mystery.) If you thought the FF [Ford Foundation] people clods, you couldn't begin to imagine these! There's a third, a younger man, who's about on FF level and a comparative model of social grace. Since these 3 pick the students, it's hard to believe the latter will be very much. But we'll see. . . . Unless you have already decided to fly over, sweet, I think better not because of this disappointing atmosphere. (My 3 colleagues are OK, good fellows and all right to be with, but none will ever set any minds aflame. I now realize I led a very sheltered life in NYC and that the intellectual world is full of people of a very much different quality from those I saw much of in NYC. This is The Provinces, and I must reread *Main Street*.) . . . The Castle—is really more like a huge English country house—is only cold in spots; the bedrooms are warmer than ovens. (Oh my love!) I've been lucky about asthma. No trouble here really, and have to take few pills. Went on a long walk to town, bitter weather, Sat. A.M., and got through all right. A couple of mild, very mild attacks in Paris and London. . . . Very nice library here, and I have a fine big work table and access to a typewriter. So I will get a lot done and, if session proves as thin as it may, will at least be able to cultivate my own garden. . . . It's like going back to boarding school—living together, eating at common tables, always having to meet and greet someone everywhere. I don't terribly like it. So far. Living en masse so to speak. . . . I keep imagining you at table by my side talking to people (the Adamses would *adore* you—and *you'd* probably adore them right back!) And do fly over if you feel an urge. I'm managing between duties . . . to finish the review of Buckley's mag, which I should easily have done in London but of course didn't. . . .

To Gloria Macdonald

February 19, 1956

It's a grey, soft day and the side view from my window—I'm on the 4th floor—is all white with a few vague greenish brown pines and a distant white roof here and there. . . . I've led a very quiet life here, gone out once to a beer place with a crowd (life here tends to be plural), and thrice been into town (which is only 2 miles away—we either walk or take the Seminar station wagon which goes in every P.M.) where I had—in a group of course—coffee mit schlag (whipped cream) at a café. The cafés are crowded even in winter, and very sociable and pleasant; racks of papers from all over the world; people sometimes write whole articles in them; you MUST buy one coffee schlag or bit of pastry, at 5 shillings (20 cents), after that you can sit all day if you like, and waiter won't bother you. . . . I have been working on the *Commentary* review of Buckley's mag, which I am sending off today . . . and which is rather funny I think; also on the lectures, which have been quite successful, the 3 so far: 1 and 2 on Mass Culture in general, mostly defining it (turns out that "kitsch," which I got from Clem Greenberg, a most untrustworthy source, doesn't mean what I thought, but rather just any poor, feeble imitative art—not MC [mass culture] necessarily; the Germans had a field day trying to define it. . . . I'm still disappointed in the Seminar itself (one gets lots of time to oneself, and I hope actually to get Apparitions and most of Persky [a profile] done here, so it's not so bad—also the library is very good, lots of things I want to read, inc. several on MC like [Siegfried] Giedion's book [*Mechanization Takes Command*] and Keuwenhoven's *Made in America*) because (1) as I think I wrote you, the director is the worst Babbitt I've ever seen since I used to interview businessmen for *Fortune*, and his two assistants are equally nonintellectual (God knows how they all got the job, or wanted to for that matter). You'll be pleased to know that our mutual nonfriend Shep[ard] Stone of the FF recently got the Seminar a big $150,000 or so over next five years—grant! (2) the students, though almost all very nice and lively, are much below the level I'd expected, perhaps because the 3 characters who run the place (who are also very NICE, but good God that's not the only thing in life, would rather have a disagreeable but brilliant chap running it—on second thought, Adams, the head, only pretends to be nice, but really is a SOB, I gather—hope to God this letter doesn't get returned here and opened!) are the ones who picked them. The Yugoslavs—3 of them—are perhaps most impressive: two men, both mature and cultivated (one translates Henry James, etc., the other is alleged to be a Marxist theoretician but haven't yet really talked with him) and one woman, a vigorous, stocky, peasant-vital person, not brilliant but lots of good sense and character; she looks as if she . . . was five years ago the country's figure-skating champion. There are also perhaps half a dozen others—a Scotchman, a big Dutchman who runs a newspaper, an earnest, wispy German who's a fan of avant-garde cinema, etc.—who seem to have a lot on the ball. But in general they seem to be either students (and much less argumentative and lively than American students, doubtless because of language trouble) or else professional people (workers in children's publishing houses, advertising agencies, on lesser newspapers, or directors of programs in Swedish and German radio stations). So far, I've not gotten any ideas from them I can use in my book—had hoped to get the "European point of view" on US mass culture. But they don't speak up in class—the other 3 profs find this so too—and its very hard, in fact impossible, so far to get discussion started. Maybe they'll come out more when they get over shyness. . . . They receive my lectures very well, laughing in the right places and listening closely; and I hear there's been a lot of talk about them; but not in class, and not at table or other places outside. I'd expected, as is the case in USA after a talk, that I'd be waylaid with questions, disagreements, etc. But very little. Maybe I scare them. . . . Well, it means anyway that I can work up here a lot. And [Daniel] Aaron & Co. are very gemütlich. We four get on fine and can at least get up a discussion among ourselves. . . . We plan to go into Vienna next weekend. . . . where I'll have dinner with Torberg, editor of the Congress's Austrian magazine.

To Frank S. Meyer [*National Review editor*]

May 4, 1956

. . . Buckley's family's wealth and its Catholicism (which it is fanatic about—I've gone into it at length, in the *Reporter*) has a lot to do with their politics. The fact there are so many Buckley brothers is just a comic touch. . . . (Must omit many of your minor queries, most of which are answered in piece—thus, I obviously DO think Buckley is a poor writer, so why ask me again. As I explained to Murray N. Rothbard [conservative libertarian], I don't think failure or political isolation absurd, my point was that it's comic when an ultra-nationalist pro-private-enterprise-and-property-rights organ shows the same paranoiac defensism as a Marxist splinter group. (NR, of course, is isolated vis-à-vis the intellectuals, whom it is trying to reach, because it's on such a low level, and also, granted, because the intellectuals are mostly liberal; but I'm not a liberal, in fact I'm getting to be more and more of a traditionalist, and it is just the crudity, dullness, and vulgarity of NR that makes me abhor it.) . . . I didn't ignore Clark, had a para on his *New Yorker* pieces which was cut for space; I thought they were garrulous and boring. Didn't mean to overlook your column, but, honestly, don't recall it. I read a lot of things in the mag which I didn't comment on—after all, I was writing an article, not a book—but I didn't omit anything first-rate (there WASN'T anything, alas) to make a polemical point. . . .

The trouble seems to be simply that you like the mag better than I do. . . . In your last paragraph you slide over the crucial point I made, or tried to—that NR is *not* a conservative magazine precisely because it doesn't stick to tradition, to conservative principles, but simply expresses the viewpoint of the Buckley type of anti-liberals, which are much too close to McCarthy for my comfort. Did you read my review in *Partisan Review* of Buckley's book defending McCarthy? What do *you* think of McCarthy, by the way? I consider him the most dangerous figure in many years in US politics—because of his use of lies as the normal, everyday staple of political activity, and because of his willingness to appeal to the lowest and crudest instincts, reflexes rather, in the American psyche. Thank God a couple of *real* conservatives, Watkins of Utah and that other right-wing Republican senator, finally stood up and brought him down! (I also believe, or rather know, that his chief "victim," Lattimore, was in fact consciously working with and for the Commies for years, and that he evaded and half-truthed all through the McCarran hearings. But the trouble is McCarthy called him the No. 1 Soviet agent in the US, and there's no evidence of this, or even that he was a Party member.)

To John Lukacs

May 4, 1956
. . . This seems like a really good college [Northwestern University]. Not a great university like Harvard or even Columbia, of course. The library is poor, there are practically no scholarly "stars" [Melville] Herskovits in anthropology, [Paul] Schilpp [Dewey scholar] in philosophy are all I'd heard of—and latter is a dope I think—no literary magazine. But the students—the ones I have anyway—are

interested, serious, and surprisingly competent; the faculty members seem very unacademic often, and three or four are really interesting, cultivated people, not barbaric specialists; quite a lot one way or another goes on (music, Webster's *White Devil* given by the drama school, avant-garde movies, Hans Kohn and Peter Viereck coming for talks—I'm giving a public address on mass culture in a few weeks); and there's at least one really good top-level person, the one who got me to come here, Moody Prior, dean of the Graduate School. I like teaching a lot—a captive audience five times a week! But seriously it is an exciting, and worth-doing job. I give a small seminar (10) in short-story writing (two of the students are really talented) and larger (40) lecture-and-discussion course in politics & literature since 1930 (reading list enclosed). Nobody else is here that you'd know. Hannah Arendt was at Chicago giving two weeks of special lectures, and I'm talking to David Riesman's seminar there next week (on interviewing, something I've been doing for 30 years without thinking about it!).

To Gloria Macdonald

May 10, 1956

. . . I'm now dead tired—after two-hour talk this A.M. at R[iesman]'s seminar on interviewing. . . . Dinner [at Riesman's] was great fun—must admit you seem right about David . . . at least he couldn't have been "warmer," more friendly and interested; and very nice little dinner party—the [Ruel] Dennys and two other academic couples, lots of lively talk, much of it by me. (I took position that sociology is not and never will be a science, and embarrassed poor David by praising him because he was so imaginatively and brilliantly nonscientific. (I was told later he wants above all things now to be taken seriously as a scientist! But he smiled wanly and was very nice about it.)

To John Lukacs

July 18, 1956

. . . London by the way, is quite all I'd expected, even more. We have a very nice semi-shabby glamorous flat on Percy Street, five minutes from (a) the British Museum and (b) Soho Square, lined with expensive Greek and French restaurants (that is, dinner can cost you all of a pound a head, or $2.80—we go to a neat, clean fresh Indian place in our building, where you get curry, German beer, parata bread, mangoes & cream and coffee for $1.25 or so) and with Sonia Orwell, Clive Bell, and Augustus John for neighbors. I'm doing a piece for *Encounter* on the wonderful, amazing London weekly press (plus the *Times* and *Manchester Guardian*—the *Times* EVERY DAY has a full page of literary, art, and drama criticism which is better than anything in USA)—namely, *Economist, Observer, Spectator, New Statesman* (don't growl—it's not bad for a liblab sheet), *Listener, Times Literary Supplement.*

Maybe *Encounter* wd. be interested in *Miss Lonelyhearts* as the last Quiet American, but can't say because I don't at all understand your point. Nor do I get it being an "innocent" book—I would have said it was quite decadent—it seems French to me, Cocteau kind of stuff, stripped to the gears and full of despair, sadism, je m'en ficheism, etc. AND WHAT does it mean that West and Hiss were the quiet Americans? Either explicate, or send me the article, and I'll see for myself. . . .

Yes, I should much like to meet Peter Mayer. And I shall look up Nicholson. By the way, did you read Isaiah Berlin on Herzen in a recent *Encounter*. I thought it a just and penetrating estimate. Wish you would get over your prejudice and sit down for a few hours with Herzen's *My Past and Thoughts*. If you read Vols. 1 and 2 without being moved, delighted, and impressed, you are a man of profound conviction and limited sensibility.

To John Lukacs

December 19, 1956

As you know by now . . . I've been hors de combat (or rather too much in the combat) in Egypt for weeks . . . when I finally got back, several weeks ago, I had to set to at once and write a long piece about it all, with the printer waiting. Also, I had the most godawful asthma there, because it never rains and hence is very dusty, and this has knocked me out a lot of late—though now back in this salubrious climate it is clearing up. . . . Odd, by the way, that in your note of Dec. 3 you write "Angus Maude is right . . . and all strident British critics of America are right," because the day before I got your letter I met Maude at dinner and had a long and very spirited argument with him on Suez. I don't think he's right at all on THAT, at least, and am delighted Eisenhower and the UN (plus, alas, USSR) stopped the Port Said adventure, for which I see no practical excuse, even if they had taken the whole canal, and occupied Egypt again, it wd. just be Ireland, Cyprus, Algeria, etc. all over—those native peoples just won't take it any more and why should they, it's their country and I say they have a right to go to ruin in their own way if they want without being saved by us whites. But maybe you didn't mean Suez when you praised British critics of USA. . . . So they didn't list Ford F. as one of 25 best books of the year in the *Times*! How comic—maybe they thought it was No. 251. But my old Yale mate Charlie Poore did put it prominently in his rhymed Xmas review of the year in the daily *Times*. (He's not terribly bright, but I'm grateful—also curious; maybe

I've underestimated him!) So far as I can tell from the publisher, the book is a respectable failure, about 4500 sold, will probably just about break even. . . . You say the British and French events show the decline of the West is a myth. You MUST mean Suez. But how can you? I agree the attack was an attempt to assert themselves as powers, but harebrained because (1) world opinion too much against (and this cd. have been foreseen); (2) Nasser regime too popular and solid to be toppled that way (could also have been foreseen); in fact the putsch has guaranteed to make him an even bigger hero to the nationalistic Arab nations; (3) gave Russia a lovely "out" for the rape of Hungary; (4) bitched up Israel's brilliant military campaign (which in 4 days actually won all Sinai and chewed up half the Egyptian army, and which if stumble-footed Eden/Mollet had kept out would have really shaken Nasser, and maybe forced him to make a decent peace with Israel) by giving Nasser an excuse for his military failure (after all cannot fight on two fronts, etc.) and by making the whole thing a UN issue, which means Israel will have to pull out of its military gains. Far from being a sign of potency, it was a sign of weakness; the hysterical attempt of weaklings to "assert themselves," to show how big and strong they are. What would Lord Cromer have said about a British government which couldn't even unseat an Egyptian ruler? But enough.

I've just called Nicholson and left a message for him—look forward to meeting him. His reviews in the *Sunday Times*, or is it the *Observer*, are very good—though he was mean to my dear friend Mary McCarthy this week.

I've finished Tocqueville's *Reminiscences* at last, and the book is much harder to read than Herzen, and somehow narrower, less imaginative, the sensibility far less subtle. I think T had great insights into history, and is best when he is summarizing, in lapidary form, his original and profound generalizations. But as a man, as a personality, bleak, pallid, restricted; hence as a historian or as a memorist defective, though excellent as an analytical thinker. Herzen was an artist, like Marx; Tocqueville more of a professor. . . . Yet there ARE a dozen great pages in the Reminiscences. . . .

You object, in my piece on Asiatic History, contention that "history is, at least partly, a science." As you know, I don't think history is a science and am opposed to the modern attempt to make it one. But I do think that unlike a novel, a work of history must be judged in part by its factual accuracy. While we can never know what REALLY happened, even yesterday, because too many things happen all the time and their relations are too much to be kept in any one mind, that means to me that we cannot have a completely scientifically accurate picture of the past. But this doesn't mean that the reign of a certain Mogul in the 16th century in India cannot be evaluated, on the basis of such data as we have, to be generally this or that; nor does it mean that the Mogul's court historian, who simply praised everything and covered up the bad things, must be accepted as the equal, as a historian, of a more objective modern scholar. If history is not at least partly a science, that is, if it doesn't in some way relate itself to actual events (as against imagined events), then we must accept the rewriting of history by the Stalinists. The reason their history is bad is simply that Trotsky WASN'T a British agent in 1918.

London is more and more pleasurable a place to live in. Gloria has found us a fine new place, two floors of a house, on Carlyle square (THERE was a ghastly historian for you!) in Chelsea, very solid and shabby house furniture, big rooms, tiny electric heaters in each which somehow, after a few hours, do keep the temperature above freezing. We have discovered the Sir John Sloane Museum just off Lincoln's Inn Fields—his own house, built by himself in 1820 and filled with treasures and fantasies he collected and enjoyed; a rich, nonscientific, unmuseumlike pleasure-dome; best thing so far in London (and WHY didn't they use his design for Buckingham Palace, and for other things here?). . . . Mencken? Heavyfooted crude stuff, fatally mannered and predictable, like Carlyle (better, but like); I don't see why so much fuss now made about him; he thought with his blood too much, and swaggered too much; isn't he your type of athletic-virile German?

. . . Just lunched with T. S. Eliot at his club, the Garrick—I gave him a copy of the R[esponsibility] of P[eoples] (which is mostly *The Root Is Man*, you recall, which is NOT being reprinted in the Farrar Straus book), and he wrote me a careful critique, very perceptive, much the most serious and intellectual reaction I've had (except your own). Which goes to show something about conservatism. I find him almost always much closer to my own views, even on politics, than liberals are, and much easier to establish intellectual rapport with.

. . . Speaking of lunches, my other celebrity lunch was with John Strachey. Quite a contrast! VERY hard to establish communication—he thinks Marxism the way to understand history and that socialism is both interesting and valuable, and has never heard of Hannah Arendt nor read Miloscz's *The Captive Mind*; he couldn't understand why his new book isn't going in the USA (as it is in England), thought we Americans must all be corrupted by capitalism; I tried to explain why I, at least, was no longer interested in the kind of political questions he deals with, or rather in the neo-Marxist way of dealing with them; hard going. He is a big, beak-nosed impressive fellow, the very model of a ruddy important MP; yet with a curious naiveté; terribly nice if a little pompous, just a touch. . . . By the way, did you see my demolition of Colin Wilson's *The Outsider* in the *New Yorker* about 2 months ago.

To T. S. Eliot[9]

November 19, 1956

. . . Apropos "They (your and my approach) are both equally removed from actual politics." I lately gave John Strachey a copy and *his* reaction on this was quite different from your own calm acceptance. "Extreme utopianism" is what he calls it, and he finds that, being disillusioned with utopianism, I have now gone to the opposite but similar extreme and become "a defeatist nihilist," which means being still "removed from actual politics." It's curious that what you take for granted, and what is indeed I think necessary if one is to think about such problems seriously, namely detachment from the immediate political context, Strachey sees as a moral sin.

One other thing, besides what you mention, our approaches have in common is that both reject what—at least till recently—has been the fashionable creed, that of progressivism, Marxist or liberal. And I think our reasons for rejecting it are similar—that it doesn't respect the unique quality of each individual and each work of art but crams the particular case into a general theoretical framework that does damage to it.

Your approach is more realistic than mine in that the great cultures of the past have been class, and not classless societies. Your remedy for mass culture, as I see it, is essentially to restore the lines of class (using this in a culture as well as social sense) to wall off again an aristocratic culture from the threat of the masses. And this was actually done, with great success, by the 1890–1930 avant-garde, including yourself, which produced whatever serious painting, music, and writing there was during that period. I must admit my own more democratic remedy seems more and more academic, theoretically untenable but in practice by now almost irrelevant. But I also doubt that it is possible to restore the class-cultural dividing walls, even in the limited way the old avant-garde (sic) did it. I am pessimistic about the future of culture, high or mass.

You object to my "The touchstone would be the extent to which each individual could develop his own talents and personality" that (1) nobody can develop ALL his talents, and (2) the major point, that there must be some "undisclosed set of values here to give any meaning to development" and that "if the persons all have different ethical values how can any political action satisfy them, and if they hold wrong ethic values, will the action be desirable"? On (1): true, no one can develop all of his potentialities; by "his own" I mean those which he chooses to develop (sic) of his free will because they seem to suit what

---

9. Accompanying this letter were extended notes responding to Eliot's assertion that Macdonald's form of radicalism, as expressed in his essays on popular culture and *The Root Is Man,* was consistent with his own form of conservatism.

he thinks as "His" personality; there are dangers both in imposing a form on somebody else's personality and also on letting everybody express freely what he thinks is his personality, but the second seems the safer course. This is related to your (2), on which I'd say: the difference between us is that you have an objective and strong anchor for your ethical values, namely religious belief, while I don't, having, as explained in the essay, to base therefore my ethics (I agree with you, and not with the Marxist-liberalist-progressives, as to (1) importance of ethics and (2) the autonomy, so to speak, of ethics, which means they cannot be deduced from economic or social arrangements but are matters of individual conscience) on a shaky and subjective foundation, namely, my own feeling about what is right and what is wrong (this feeling not whimsical, of course, but coming out of my whole life and thought. Since this is how I arrived at moral choices, I must allow others the same freedom, must respect—in this ultimate theoretical sense—the basis of their own moral systems. As to any political action being able to satisfy persons with many different values—the anarchist theory, which I still hold, is that if people are left free of all coercion to arrange their own collective actions, by a process of trading, reasoning, compromising, they will be able to decide on the course of action which will most benefit them as a group; the variety of ethical (and of other) values, far from being a difficulty, seems to me an advantage, since it insures that the maximum number of possibilities will at least be considered before one is chosen, and since it makes life more interesting because there are many ways things can turn out. True, if a political group holds wrong ethical views (wrong by my standards) then their actions will be wrong (also by my standards), as the Nazis or Stalinists. But I believe that if the Russian and German people had been able to choose the kind of political activity that would "satisfy the particular persons taking part in it," they would not have chosen Nazism or communism because they are extreme, fanatical, rigorously logical creeds and most people are not thus; they are also creeds which demand enormous sacrifices, and again, most people aren't much on sacrifice. In short, I suppose I do still have an optimistic view of human nature, compared to yours, that is, I think if people are left alone they are more likely to do good, or at least not to do harm, than if they are disciplined from outside. Yet even as I write this, I wonder—in the last few years I have become quite opposed, for example to "progressive education" partly because my two boys have been going to such schools—they don't any more—and I have seen the shoddiness of their approach to culture and in other ways I have lost my earlier faith in simple freedom so perhaps you should modify all of the above; it's hard in this kind of argumentation not to be carried too far by the mere structure of one's line of argument, and by one's rhetoric.

Your comments, as the above may show, strike at the heart of my position.

Reading the above over, I see its inadequacy. Perhaps we could spend an hour or two in talk about all this? I think there is fruitful opposition between our viewpoints—that is, they are close enough to engage each other seriously.

To T. S. Eliot

January 3, 1957

. . . Thank you for your note, and delighted you enjoyed my dissection of the Alderman [March—a protest against the Bomb]. . . . The dilemma about longing for classlessness in a class society and vice versa is one I too feel—but may we not both be temperamentally skeptical and agin-the-government (I know that's not your reputation! The agin part, I mean)? . . . I'm not clear what you mean by the unconscious will; I'd have said, from my Freudian indoctrination days, that will was always conscious; I'd like to talk with you on this when you get back from the South. . . . We missed you at New Year's, but John made up a little and we all, I think, had a good time—I did anyway. . . . Good health in The South (trust it's not as far south as Egypt) and I'd like very much to have lunch (on me) when you get back.

To Gloria Macdonald

n.d., Spring 1957

. . . Then we went to the Saville Club to dine with R. Frost. Present: S[pender], K[ristol], C. Day Lewis (whom I talked most with, he's a great charmer, very much in the Allan Pryce-Jones style—but why is his face and brow so wrinkled, lined?—a handsome, clear-cut face, but so lined—like Auden, only not so bad, not puffy and lumpy), Arthur Waley (true to rep., didn't say a word—small, dark, closed man), E. M. Forster (who sat between me and Frost—liked him very much—we discussed D. H. Lawrence, tourism, and Cambridge, where he's a Fellow now), Graham Greene (no contact with), and a couple of others. Frost after dinner in great form; he's a real showman, plays the laconic New England farmer, a little ham but really good at it, and makes many acute observations; a Grand Old Man, his 84-year-old face is big, rugged, lumpy-wrinkled-sagging. Big comic moment as we were all taking leave of him (he was game, stayed an hour after dinner despite efforts of his shepherd, a young American, to get him to go, for his health's sake). He asked me what I wrote, and I said I did book reviews and profiles for the *NYer*; he remembered the Great Books and Bible review, very nice of him. Then Forster, who'd talked w. him all through dinner, came up to say goodbye, and Frost said to him: I'm just getting to know you fellows a little. Mr. Macdonald here writes for the *New Yorker*.

What do YOU WRITE?" Awful, awful pause, while Forster began to mumble and stammer that he had written some novels. I told Frost that Mr. F. had written *A Passage to India*. F. jumped back, "Great heavens, but I've read that many times. So you're Forster!" etc. (He is rather deaf, probably didn't "catch" the name—but odd they shouldn't have discovered who's who during dinner. I suppose Frost's slightly self-centered personality plus Forster's British reticence—he's as British as Frost's American—was responsible. . . . Darling, don't get sore but Frost IS a weeny bit vain—he began his chat after dinner with a lot about what big audiences he had "drawn" over here. But really a G.O.M for all that—lot of humor and wisdom, too—and character. . . . Also, you'll be glad to hear that I went to see the other night at the Film Center Leni Riefenstahl's *Triumph of the Will*, a masterly film about the 1934 Nuremberg Nazi meeting, made at the time for Hitler, and that the faces (there are innumerable close-ups of the spectators, the storm troopers, the youth sections, the soldiers, etc.) after a while began to repel and alarm me. A clumsy gross brutality came up much too often; a lack of sensitivity, grace, even humanity (or if human, in a loutish peasant way); and a humorless, almost insane emotional intensity on many of them, quite scary. Now don't think I am joining you in your Germanphobia—but I must admit some doubts crept in as to whether Germans may not be somewhat quite different from other peoples. And not in a good way. Of course, these were presumably the more fanatic pro-Nazis, but there were so many of them. The leaders were especially repulsive and frightening in a coarse bourgeois way—no style, no restraint—the old Prussian officers, hard-faced and predatory like eagles as they were, were less alarming; they looked as if they had some kind of code, that they recognized some moral principle, however, limited and martial, which would restrain them from acting out whatever neurotic selfish fantasy they wanted to indulge in. . . .

To Roger Strauss

May 17, 1957

I've become unhappy about *Memoirs of a Revolutionist* [anthology of Macdonald's articles] as a title for the book. Everybody around here, including my wife (who has excellent taste in such matters), thinks it is cheap. So do, now, I. Is it too late to change? It almost makes a burlesque out of the book, I fear. I'd rather go back to *The Resp. of Peoples*. Or how about DISSONANCES, with the subtitle: Essays in Political Criticism. (What I'd like is a single word conveying the idea of dissent and of independent criticism that is against the majority ideas, something unorthodox.) I rather fancy *Dissonances*; it sounds well, looks well—T. E. Hulme, you remember, wrote a little book called *Speculations*, and of course

Mencken wrote several volumes of *Prejudices*. If it is not too late, I would like this to be the title.

I'm also unhappy, and rather bewildered, about a note I've just received from Robert Wohlforth, your treasurer (is he the Bob Wohlforth that once worked with the La Follette Committee?) to the effect I owe you $376.75. I wasn't aware of making $145.70 worth of author's alterations over the 10% allowance, but let it pass. I undoubtedly did (though cannot recall being charged for these by other publishers—that is, Vanguard and Reynal). But do most strongly object to being charged $231.05 for killed matter (or, indeed, anything), since what I killed I killed because your people said the book was too long, and since how long the book was to be was not decided until after the stuff had been set up (I have a letter from your people giving me a choice between two different lengths, the letter being written after the galleys were set up), and since I just gave you a big wad of copy, already in type, and it was up to you, not me, to figure out how long a book it would make and to tell me in advance, before setting up the stuff, how much I should eliminate. Nobody told me at any time that there was too much copy, and I don't see why I should bear this loss, since the stuff was already in print and besides it was just a matter of leaving out discrete, separate articles, not of cutting a continuous MS. In which latter case an author might be willing to pay for oversetting so that he could see it all went together). No more space. . . . DO CHANGE THE TITLE.

To Anastasia "Baba" Anrep [daughter of well-known mosaicist Boris Anrep]

November 3, 1957

. . . Don't be sorry you hadn't written; of course I understand; I've been depressed myself ever since walking back into this rattrap. Only thing to be said for NYC is that there are a few of one's friends here and that the delicatessen stores stay open until one A.M. and that you can buy whiskey for $3.50 a bottle. Not very GOOD whiskey but still—whiskey.

No, it is not nice to be home. I miss London, Siena, Bocca di Magre, and you. We do have a better apartment, in same building, bigger and you can see whether it's a sunny day or a black thunderstorm by just looking out the window. Even so, I was dubious about gigantic effort of moving and resettling, but iron-willed Gloria prevailed; and maybe she's right. Though for me it's like moving into a sunnier cell.

Yes, I'm back to writing again, though hardly "without too much strain." After 3 months of almost complete idleness, one's writing muscles become atrophied, mine anyway, and one has to learn all over again How to Do It, like walking again after 3 months in bed. So far I've only done a long review of Jim Agee's last book—it's in next week's issue, look for it—quite good, really, as they are said to say in London. Also most of another long review of Jim Cozzens' new novel, which I think as bad as I think Agee's book is good. (The second Jim is unserious—don't know the fella.) . . .

WHAT is the "lodger's Potomac"? Pontiac maybe. Or is there a new car over here I've missed? Granted these big US cars are heaven to drive, but how ugly and vulgar they are. Now the new models all have 4 headlights, in tandem on each side. And these upswept rear ends, bristling with red lights like some horrible insect. And they are so wide and so long, like a land yacht; the motor and the passengers are just incidental to all those yards of steel boxing, like a Christmas package too elaborately wrapped.

Yes, I'm certainly coming back to London and not later than next fall—not earlier either, probably. I've got to make some $$$ here, also to finish the book on US mass culture. Then its hey for Tottenham Court Road! . . . Day [Gloria's daughter] has been flitting around the art schools trying to find one that is of Sladian standards, vainly. First she spent two weeks at Yale, no go, lots of nice people but dominated by Albers, a doggedly dogmatic abstract-constructivist who doesn't allow the lower classes, that is the first two or three years, to have even a model, all design; then a day at Columbia, rejected as vulgar and provincial; finally, she's now settled for the Art Students League here in the city, which is old-fashioned and full of nice elderly ladies and not so nice but equally amorphous young men and women, but which at least does allow the students to peep at a wholly naked model; she is determined to return to Slade and London after Xmas and I think she will, more or less over Gloria's dead body; it will be that old chestnut, the Irresistible Force meeting the Immovable Body.

The big social event of the season so far for us was the week Bill Coldstream (Sir William to you) spent in NYC. We threw two dinner parties for him and managed to see him here and there practically every day of his stay. It was very nice, ditto Sir William. We even got him to go with us, Gloria and me, to see O'Neill's *Long Day's Journey into Night*, an echt-American play which seemed to baffle him, but he was game, I'll say that. (I was impressed by it—it's a sort of American *Look Back in Anger*—full of wild irrational verbose bitterness and feeling—I didn't respond to *Look Back*, as you know, but *Long Day* got home to me—maybe because, in spite of all temptations, I remain an American.) . . . Keep a lot of my love for yourself. I do wish I could walk down Broadway with you, or just lay eyes on you a moment, even on Tenth Avenue!

To Geoffrey Gorer [British literary critic]

n.d., January 1958

Glad you liked my [James Gould] Cozzens review and thanks for writing. The piece has made a Splash.[10] Dozens, by now scores of letters from rank-and-file readers who were browbeaten by the critics into attempting the book, found they couldn't read it, thought they must be echt-philistine, were relieved to learn there is something to be said on the other side. This is predominant reaction. Not a peep out of either Cozzens or the critics. . . . Yes, the Lady Bountiful business I agree is partly responsible—over here it's the "good guy" syndrome—give him a break, he's worked SO hard. But writers should never be given the tiniest break if we want decent writing. . . . (By the way, I hear C. P. Snow praised the Cozzens novel in the *New Statesman*—maybe it's beginning over your way.) I'm about to do a profile of a fellow (Eugene Gilbert) who makes much money by being the No. 1 authority—at least in business circles— on teenagers, their mores and the way they have become a separate pressure group, like labor or the dairy farmers, in the last 20 years. I recall you had something to say about them in your book on Us, shall reread. Their numbers are multiplying frighteningly—between 1950 and 1965, they are expected to increase 70%, a solemn thought. . . .

To William F. Buckley, Jr.

January 9, 1958

You must be nuts.

I wrote you a friendly note telling you I admired a review by you and was mentioning it in my *Commentary* piece on Cozzens. Also noting that you would enjoy this piece more than my last piece there. And adding some words of praise for a recent issue of N[ational] R[eview].

So now you write me a pompous and priggish note asking if I mean to apologize for my unkind remarks in *Commentary* about NR, and stating that if so (1) you're "not yet prepared to forgive" and will "advise" me when you are, and (2) I should be "man enough" to apologize for my past sins and errors publicly and explicitly.

APOLOGIZE????!!!!

Why you damned whippersnapper, you impertinent pipsqueak, what the hell should I apologize for. I gave your magazine hell, and it deserved it. You

10. Macdonald's *Commentary* review is said to have knocked Cozzens out of contention for the Pulitzer Prize. Norman Mailer was critical, saying, in effect, Macdonald had used a sledgehammer on a flea.

then wrote a silly, top lofty, would-be venomous attack on me (which I did read at the time—you sent it to me, don't you remember), which I felt I didn't deserve, but for which I bore you no grudge. I certainly haven't been waiting for an "apology." You apparently have. Sorry to disappoint you.

You seem to have lost your sense of humor and of reality. It's a cruel world, Bill, and you'll find that writers will express the most UNKIND view of you and your magazine without ever dreaming of apologizing. That's just the way life is. You must be a little dime-store Pope now, with your own magazine and everything—else how could you have such a fantastic reaction to a friendly note written in a (I can now see misguided) spirit of generosity.

Apologize indeed! Who do you think you are, you wretched solemn little sectarian, a sovereign state? And you used to be fun to argue with.

To Roger Strauss

January 16, 1958

1200 copies does seem very small, even allowing for the fact that such a book couldn't be expected to do brilliantly. I'm extremely grateful to you for having done it at all, but don't you think a little more effort could be made? Especially in view of the very good and long reviews it's been getting. (By the way, why didn't your people pass on to me that *Commentary* review? I heard of it by chance. Also David Braybooks, a Yale prof, writes he asked you, that is FS&G, for my address "late in November," got no reply; he finally tracked me down. Am I the forgotten man around your shop? Isn't there any kind of radio program, or other forum, beside Night Beat where I could appear ad majoram gloriam the *Memoirs*? Have you advertised in *PR*, *Hudson*, *New Republic*, and other places? Couldn't something be done about promoting the book among college students? It should appeal to them especially, I'd think. I know authors always feel the publisher isn't "doing" enough for their babies, but maybe, sometimes, he isn't. Or are you?

To Charles Biederman

January 22, 1958

No, I'm not writing on art for this mag. Nor have I ever written anything on art. [Harold] Rosenberg's crack in *Dissent* must refer to some arguments we've had. I actively dislike abstract expressionism, which he's been promoting for years, and I am cool toward abstract constructivism. In fact, I think the abstract tendency has turned out to be a blind alley. Rosenberg seems to think that anyone who attacks the New York School is automatically a philistine. (I like very much, and see as much of it as I can, the work of Picasso, Braque, Gris, Klee, and the other nonabstract Old Masters of modern art, and I spent two months in Tuscany this summer, with great excitement and pleasure, looking at the art and architecture there. But all that, of course, is old hat and philistine to the drum-beaters for action painting and such nonsense.)

Why should I have taken an interest in your art? Have you ever taken an interest in my writing? I must say that if you had sent *me* a friendly work after 17 years, my reaction wouldn't have been a snarl as to why you'd bothered. But then I don't think the only thing of interest about me is my writing. I feel I'm also a person, and that you are one too, and I think it barbarous to reduce one's self to ONLY a writer or an artist. Barbarous because it causes one to behave toward old friends as you have—to actually be irritated to hear from them because one feels they aren't enough interested in one's art or writing!

And come to think of it, you aren't being reasonable even in your own narrow terms. How do you expect me to have seen any of your work? Should I have made a pilgrimage to the Master's study in Red Wing? [Minnesota]? After all, YOU could easily enough follow MY work—not that I feel put out that you haven't—why should you if you don't feel like it—I don't have a monopoly on literary-political culture—you can get it from others—but I feel you feel you DO have such a monopoly, and that you feel it's really outrageous if some one doesn't rally around. I probably wouldn't much like your stuff, if it's as it was years ago when I last saw it, that is abstract constructivist, but I think it intolerable, in human terms, that this should be the only thing of importance between us.

P.S. Come to think of it, I did write a long profile of [Alfred H.] Barr of the Museum of Modern Art 5 years ago. I'll try to dig up a copy if you want to see it.

To Daniel Bell

n.d., January 1958

No, no, how can you be so dense? It wasn't your finding my ultra-leftist past funny that I felt to be condescending in your review. After all, I brought out the humor there myself in *Politics Past* [included in the book]. It was something entirely different: an assumption that you, the reviewer, being a worldly-wise and sensible person, could chuckle indulgently at my will-o'-the-wisp absolutist-utopian romantic political ideas, or moral ideas if you like; can even rather admire the purity of heart that leads to such sweeping judgments on my part, while shaking your wise old head at such youthful folly. This note was often struck in even the most friendly reviews, and I find it irritating and depressing because I don't see why a drastic rejection of what is necessarily means pure-heart-but-wooly-wit; in fact, I think I am the one that has tried to think and to analyze quite objectively, and that you, my sensible old uncle, may, like sensible old uncles in real life, simply be unwilling to go beyond a certain point in "facing up to things," that point being the farthest reach of conventionality—beyond which one must leave the world and confront life. Well, let's discuss it next time we meet.

To Irving Kristol

March 4, 1958

Here it is [requested article, "America, America" for *Encounter*, not accepted]. Hope OK.

I'm shattered to learn you publish [Leslie] Fiedler and me for the same reasons—that we're both provocative. What an abandonment of standards! And why is it funny of me to call him "irresponsible"? Why is this a sign of age? (You seem to have me down as an octogenarian—cf. your comment on my plaint about USA and the aged.) I don't consider myself an irresponsible writer, and like F. I hear little praise of his *Encounter* stuff over here, nor did I run into F. fans over there. And this last piece was exceptionally thin, I thought.

Why did you change the typography of the heads? I preferred the old one. This one just as stingy and less graceful. And the new ENCOUNTER on the cover—not distinguished, thought that reverse plate much better, or the type that fellow designed for it. Last few issues haven't seemed very good to me, no time to go into it.

William Zuckerman [editor, *Jewish Newsletter*]

March 15, 1958

The *Jewish Newsletter* is one of the few periodicals whose arrival I really look forward to. A journalist gets rather blasé about magazines, he reads so many of them. But the *Newsletter* is always interesting—well written, businesslike, full of information, and infused with the fine spirit of its editor, a courageous man with a passion for truth and decency. The specific area in which for ten years he has been seeking out (and publishing) the truth is an especially "sensitive" one. One's natural revulsion at Hitler's extermination of European Jews creates a temptation to regard the state of Israel as sacrosanct and to slur over, or indeed refuse even to think about, the unjust policies of that state toward Arabs and other non-Jews. One must resist this temptation, if only for the honor of the Jews, and Mr. Zuckerman has, as in his excellent lead article in the February 24th issue. There is even a tendency to regard any criticism of Jewish life or Jewish groups as "anti-Semitic," wherefore am grateful to the *Newsletter* for printing Alfred Kazin's excellent series on The Jewish Writer.

To the Editor, *The New Republic*

March 17, 1958

In his clever and generous review of my *Memoirs of a Revolutionist*, Ian Watt quotes me as saying religion "moves me even more than Marxism." This is, of course, just a misprint—"moves" should be "bores"—but what a misprint!

Otherwise I have no complaints though plenty of disagreements, for which Mr. Watts has laid a solid basis by his lucid exposition for the practical, nonabsolutist approach to politics. The trouble is that ideologues, especially those left of center, rarely admit to such flawed and modest aims as Mr. Watt takes for granted. When I criticized the New Deal for not making any "important" changes in people's everyday living, it was not only because I'm a purist, but also because the New Dealers used to talk as if it had; and my endless "baiting" of Henry Wallace and the liberal weeklies will perhaps appear to have some justification if Mr. Watts will look up the enormous moral claims made by Wallace and the liberals in the forties. This is not to deny my political impracticality, merely to suggest it perhaps was more relevant to actuality than Mr. Watts's extremely intelligent review sometimes seems to imply.

To Ian P. Watt [British critic]

March 28, 1958

How extraordinary, these typos, especially the shifting around Watt to Watts in printing my letter! And to make "moves" out of "bores"—was your review in longhand (I recall from my year on *Encounter* that British writers often send in their stuff in longhand and, what is more amazing, British printers work from longhand); if not, then one suspects a cabal in the print shop.

Your letter cheered and delighted me—very nice of you to write it. Esp. the paragraph which the NR editors, with the usual infallible instinct of editors for the vital, jugular vein, omitted. I loved it all, from Mencken to Donald Duck—except I DON'T think the Mark Twain analogy is right, flattering though it is. "Foundered idealism" is too dramatic, too melodramatic, for me—I think, or like to think, I've always been more tough-minded, less open to illusions, than Mark was—and my laughter is not so bitter as his was, in his last phase. The Mencken analogy is better, though I cannot stand his style; I mean that, like Mencken, I really enjoy being disappointed & outraged.

If ever I am in the Bay Area, as you so jauntily call it (I've never been west of Minneapolis), shall certainly call. And if you pass through NYC, do ring me here—I'd like very much to meet you and talk—have a feeling we'd find much to discuss, pleasurably. (I have a weakness for Englishmen, after my year in London, in fact I am absurdly Anglophile, intellectually speaking, and your review confirms this prejudice.) . . .

P.S. The one thing in your letter I don't understand is your characterizing Wallace, et al., as "men of good will"—they were, of course, but that's just the trouble—the worst infamies, the most revolting inhumanities are those perpetrated by Men of Good Will, just because they have a good conscience and are, usually, men of such ruthless, logical principles. Cf. Harry Hopkins and FDR's unconditional surrender policy, the Morgenthau Plan, and the all-Germans-are-Nazis line of the liberal weeklies. . . . But I forgot, sorry, you've read the book.

To Stephenirvingnicholasmike or whoever's around & decides things [editors of *Encounter* and staff of the Congress for Cultural Freedom]

April 16, 1958

I've just received a long letter from Stephen, who's apparently en route to Tokyo. He proposes I rewrite completely the article to make it more "balanced." Since its imbalance is one of the things I like about it, I must decline. It says what *I* want to say, and I didn't write it to express the official, diplomatically sound viewpoint of the Congress pour la etc. It's signed with my name, and if people want to write in and object, by all means, and I'll reply, or try to. But I'm certainly not going to analyze the London and Paris press for the last few months to see how many crimes were committed there as against here—this being one of Stephen's little proposals for further research. As for his general point that Europe is Americanized too—of course, and have no objection to a sentence or two being put in on that—but what struck me, after 14 months over there, was just the opposite, and the article is my reactions, after all, not those of the Congress pour la etc.

But the point isn't the merits of the piece. Presumably the two editors of *Encounter* thought it was OK two months ago—at least it was scheduled for publication first in the April and then in the May issues. However, it seems Stephen had a talk lately with Nicholas, whence this amazing backtracking. A good way to edit a magazine is for the editors to decide what they want and then to print it, without benefit of the counsel, two months later, of General Secretary & Grand Master of International Decorum Nicholas Nabokov.

I'm disgusted with Stephen's letter. If he doesn't want the piece, let him say so and not go meandering around with all those tactful remarks about how "interesting" my ideas are. And why should *Stephen*, not Irving with whom I've dealt up to now on the piece, write the brush-off? Division of labor? Or because he's off to Japan? Am I supposed to negotiate c/o American Express?

If you want to run the article as is (I'm willing to throw in a few sentences as to Europe, too, being to some extent Americanized, but no more, and even there I must perversely insist that I think it still a much better place to live than good ole USA) in the June issue, though by then it will have grown whiskers, OK. Otherwise, let's have it back.

In future, I suggest the London office consult the Paris office at once on receipt of a "controversial" MS, so as to find out immediately what it thinks.

P.S. On second thought, if you don't want the piece at all, would you please pass it on to *Spectator*?

To William Shawn

April 17, 1958

I've just read [Anthony] West's Baudelaire review [April 12, 1958] and, while I suppose it's bad taste for one staff writer to complain to the editor about another, I feel this review is such a scandal that I must do so. For a long time I've been uneasy about West's reviews, especially those like this one (and there are a great many) that attack unfairly and coarsely and with a peculiar venom some great writer whose life or personality West disapproves of. (That smear-job on George Eliot was one example.) But this one really does the limit, and I'm ashamed of the *New Yorker* for printing it.

On the attached sheets I've jotted down some textual notes. Here let me say, in general, that the Procrustean bed of morality on which West stretches his eminent victims fits almost none of the great 19th-century writers (or of any other century's writers). In fact he has a life work cut out for him. When will he get around to Poe, B's American counterpart, a liar, sponger, drunk, and sexual fantast? Or Coleridge (drugs, laziness), Byron (incest, irregular hours), Whitman (homosexuality), Wilde (ditto plus dadaism & snobbishness), Flaubert (who hated the bourgeoisie and the masses as much as Baudelaire and is therefore also partly responsible for Buchenwald and Ravensbruck), Swinburne (infantilism, sado-masochism), Carlyle (impotence, also deplorably ill-tempered), Dostoevsky (an epileptic whose pan-Slavic, authoritarian ideas led directly to Stalinism), Nietzsche (madness, and oh my oh my that awful Superman!), and Verlaine (everything)? About the only 19th-century writer who is completely safe from our Savonarola is Robert Browning, a man of sterling character, positive and optimistic temper, and impeccable family life.

If West could ever back up his indictments, or at least make them appear plausible, then of course he should be heard. And printed. But he can't. Or at least doesn't. I do feel it's a disservice to letters to encourage him.

To Editor, *Encounter*

n.d., May 1958

May I thank Richard Wollheim[11] not only for a most perceptive (and flattering) review of my *The Responsibility of Peoples* [British title for his *Memoirs of a Revolutionist*] but also for stating clearly, indeed brilliantly, his objections to my approach to politics? Mr. Wollheim's criticisms are fundamental and strike, magisterially, the note that has predominantly sounded in other reviews of my book. This note is a peculiar blend of sympathy, even respect, and contempt—a sort of benevolent head-patting. "What a remarkably bright child!" I imagine a child rather dislikes having his or her head patted, however admiringly. Certainly an adult does.

It's not that I think Mr. Wollheim errs in his specific judgments; it's his conclusions I quarrel with. He is right, for instance, to detect an aesthetic tone to my political writings, and even a touristic detachment. I'm very fond of sightseeing and I don't deny that Marx was once my Baedeker to the radical world (though there really was a little more to it than that). I accept, with reservations to be noted later, his clever term "innocent." My reactions to politics have been mainly aesthetic (including in this term the use of the higher reasoning faculties) and moral. Art and morality are oddly joined: both involve value judgments as to what is Good and what is Bad, and such judgments come down, ultimately, to one's own taste and one's own feelings, in rather dramatic contrast to the sphere of science, or of politics, as Mr. Wollheim conceives it—if I read right his sole, whimsical definition: "a system of outdoor relief." For some reason, it is nowadays considered frivolous to base any judgment on one's own taste and feelings; or at least to admit one is doing so. This I see as one effect of our scientized way of thinking. Mr. Wollheim is obviously not a "socialist scientist"; he writes too well, for one thing, good prose being suspect in well-scientized circles, as well it should be, as an uncontrollable injection of aesthetic bacilli into the pure, sterile test-tube of Research. But he is perhaps a philosopher of scientism, a fellow-traveler so to speak, who thinks he ought to go along with the ideology regardless of his own inclinations—"Of course, *personally.* . . . At any rate, he thinks that "aesthetic" and "moral" are bad words and that politics is too serious a business to be left to those to whom such adjectives apply, while I think that the only serious aspect of politics is its relation to art and morality.

Mr. Wollheim defies anyone to say what I have against "Lib-Labism"—that is, modern liberalism of the *New Statesman* variety—"save that it is drab."

11. Richard Wollheim, a British philosopher, art historian, and cultural critic, was soon to marry Day Lanier, Gloria's daughter.

What I have mainly against it is not drabness but hypocrisy. It doesn't act, as he thinks it does, according to principles, but according to prejudices; noble, worthy, and generous prejudices but still—prejudices. That is, a Lib-Lab in the thirties saw Stalin's Russia not as a more terrible version of the czar's Russia but as a Stage in Progress, a Step in the Right Direction—though of course, *personally*. . . . Similarly with Science and Progress: Mr. Wollheim takes what he calls The Long View ("the gradual alleviation of suffering, of disease, of want, the advance of technology") as against The Short View (mine, which he sees as overly concerned with trivia like "the manufacture of bombs" and the spread of mass culture). Now really! The bombs—atomic, hydrogenic, God knows what other impeccably scientific varieties we will be presented with—these fruits of Progress now offer us the shortest view of all, in fact The End. Mr. Wollheim may be right, though it does seem unlikely, but I wish he hadn't invoked Condorcet of all people, the wooden Indian of the Theory of Progress, poor old Condorcet, who took such a Long View that he died in hiding from the Short-View Jacobins who wanted to cut his head off.

What makes it all puzzling is that I have always thought of myself as taking the long view, and of the Wollheimians as taking the short view. That is, I have tried to relate current events to human experience in general, to Reason and Ethics, as against the short-term interests of political doctrines. In fact the political writing I look back on with least pride (and which, for the most part, I omitted from my book) was just that in which I subordinated the ethical-aesthetic approach to what Mr. Wollheim calls the long-term and I call the short-term approach, that is, to the demands of a political program. As, for instance, most of my writing for the Trotskyist *New International* and *Labor Action*, when, far from being "deprived of all the cues that theory and ideology alone can give," far from being without any "principle to support or direct" me, I was in possession of so many cues, principles, and directives—or perhaps better, was possessed by them—that I quite overlooked the most obvious facts of life, as that Lenin, Trotsky, and even Marx, even indeed their basic political ideas, were responsible, far more than I thought, for Stalinism.

Finally, I think Mr. Wollheim exaggerates my Innocence, a little. For instance, he seems to have missed the main point of my title essay, "The Responsibility of Peoples." He does take up two minor points—that "we" did terrible things, too, and that it wasn't a matter of the "national character" of the Germans. But the main point, stated perhaps unclearly but certainly often, was that in a mass society like Nazi Germany's (or ours or Soviet Russia's) it is intellectually absurd and morally unjust to make the general population responsible for crimes they are powerless to prevent—crimes, in fact, they didn't know about until after they were committed. (We Americans didn't know that "our" government was going to atomize Hiroshima any more than those Germans knew "their" government was exterminating the jews—contrary to popular belief, the very existence of the Jewish death-camps was a closely guarded secret; the first news leaked out only in the summer of 1944, when the ghastly "program" had almost been completed.) My object in writing the essay, early in 1945, was not to "allot marks," not simply to simply express horror at the "bare facts" (though that too) but primarily to consider these things in the light of precisely what Mr. Wollheim finds lacking: "some vision of society as it should be, some theory of how it works, some general estimate of what outweighs what." This theory is stated in the essay: (a) "If we can conceive of a modern people as collectively responsible in a moral sense at all, then it must be held accountable only for actions which it takes spontaneously and as a whole, actions which are approved by the popular mores. It cannot be indicted for things done by sharply differentiated sub groups." (b) Modern society has become so tightly organized, sex rationalized, and routinized that it has the character of a mechanism which grinds on without human consciousness or control. . . . More and more things happen to people." (c) "In place of the rigid, unexamined customs which determine the individual's behavior in primitive communities, there is substituted today a complex politico-economic organization which is equally "given" and not-to-be-criticized in its ultimate aims and assumptions, and which overrides with equal finality the individual's power of choice."

This seems to me neither "arbitrary opinion," "immediate reaction," nor "unaided feeling." Nor, for that matter, "like a man at a party." But don't let's quarrel, and let me, glass in hand, renew my thanks to Mr. Wollheim for the kind of review of my book I should have liked to have written had he been its author.

To Irving Kristol

May 21, 1958

No, I'm afraid your arguments have made no dent in the armo(u)r of my obstinacy. As to the specific point, about concluding with the NYorker piece, I will be willing to cut it some more if you insist, but I in turn must insist it be the bitter end of a sour piece. It is exactly the note I want to end on—a note of major questioning of the US way of life. . . .[12]

As to the general issue: I'm obstinate because I think the matter important.

12. Macdonald referred to a piece in the *New Yorker*, October 26, 1957, dealing with the isolated and rootless life of the typical American soldier held captive in the Korean War. It was a devastating portrait of young people without values, stamina, or any sense of self trying then to cope with captivity. Macdonald saw the piece as offering "extremely important data on the American way of Life."

I'm most distressed about the kind of life we've developed over here, and I think it both my privilege and duty to say so. If it leaves a bad taste, well really, I have never cared about that—good taste and bad taste, I mean. I've never understood why one must speak differently of one's country, or one's party or one's friends or relatives, merely because one has a relation to them. I'd write about Nixon as Slippery Dick over here (actually I think he's improved lately, as my parenthesis comparing him favorably to Dulles implies—by the way if Slippery Dick goes out, then the parenthesis should too, for rhetorical reasons) if it seemed apposite to recall that old nickname, and I see no reason why I shouldn't do the same in writing for a foreign paper. I don't seem to feel a kind of group loyalty that many others do feel, for which I'm sorry (hypocritical); and my concept of good manners is that manners apply only to relations between individuals and not to what one says or writes about countries, public figures, or books.

Yours with affection but with undented armor of Missouri mulishness.

To Irving Kristol [marginal note, "Not Sent"]

June 24, 1958

. . . I know you tried to get the piece ["America, America"] into the mag, and thank you again for your efforts. But those Paris boys! You'd think USA was Venezuela, such touchy national pride. And I think they are wrong even practically (obviously they're wrong ethically, can't have sacred cows, double standards in an honest mag), I think people abroad would take *Encounter* much more seriously if it printed drastic criticisms of USA. It would, for instance, be one way of disposing of that hoary canard (which I heard several times after I got back) that the State Dept. finances it. Ah well. Especially nice that the censorship is by a congress for cultural freedom!

I'm by the way not under the illusion that the piece was a masterwork. But it was plenty good enough to print. . . .

To Editors, *Dissent*

July 4, 1958

In your Winter (1958) issue, two old friends, Harold Rosenberg and Paul Goodman, writing independently, have some unkind things to say about the quality of my taste and mind. Now I don't say that it would be impossible to find something critical to say on this topic, but I do feel that my old friends write in a rather smug and sectarian spirit, and therefore that they have quite failed to discover my real weaknesses. I shan't help them there—let them do their own work—but may I at least demonstrate their incompetence.

Rosenberg's strictures are an aside in a manifesto written in his most epigrammatic and gnomic style—if he could just once *develop* a point, he'd become a serious writer. "When Macdonald speaks against kitsch," he writes, "he seems to be speaking from the point of view of art, when he speaks about art it is plain his ideas are kitsch." It is so plain that Rosenberg feels no need to try and demonstrate or even illustrate this sweeping charge. I won't try to rebut it—the evidence is in print, after all—but I would like to show the specific grounds for it. They appear in Rosenberg's statement that "modern art revolts him (me)." I admire and enjoy the work of Gris, Braque, Modigliani, Picasso, Klee, Matisse, etc., which is what most people would call "modern art." But Rosenberg isn't most people, he's a member of a very exclusive club, and by the terms he means simply (or merely) the New York School, or abstract expressionism or action painting or drip 'n drabble (the avant-garde equivalent to rock 'n roll)—anyway the kind of painting that Rosenberg and I have had more than one argument about. (He must mean this because (a) the only place I've written about modern art was in my *New Yorker* profile of Alfred Barr, and (b) the only criticism hostile to any phase of modern art was that directed against abstract expressionism.) To equate this one school with "modern art" and on the basis of this to call me "philistine" (when you say that pardner—smile!), this seems to me a mite sectarian.

I can't here, or at least won't here, go into Rosenberg's general thesis, insofar as I understand it except to say that I agree there is perhaps too much written these days about mass culture—it's become almost as much of an intellectual fad as action painting—and don't agree that Lowenthal was wrong when he wrote, "The counterconcept to popular culture is art." When Rosenberg says that kitsch's counterconcept, its antagonist, is not art but "reality," I don't know what he is talking about. Of course, "reality," whatever *that* means, is different from kitsch (does that make it a "counterconcept"?), but so is it different from art (or high culture). The serious battle today, for all who love literature and art and philosophy and the other forms of the culture we have inherited from past ages, is the battle against the cheapening and debasing of high culture by the lords (and consumers) of kitsch. Agreed that the best way to fight it is for each artist, writer, etc. to do his own work and let the masses have their kitsch (or does Rosenberg still have a soft spot in his Marxistical heart for the masses, it's not clear)—agreed this, I think that critics can profitably, from the standpoint of culture, analyze and expose the corrupting effect of mass culture. It's all these sociologists and Marxologues that have come stampeding into the field that I find superfluous—precisely the ones that Rosenberg, in his sophisticated obscurantism, picks out as the only respectable practitioners. To study kitsch as propaganda is legitimate, pontificates Harold XII, and then makes the mistake (which to be fair to him, is the kind of mistake he rarely does make) of being specific: e.g., the Berelson-Salter piece in *Mass Culture*. What nonsense! This particular piece in the *Mass Culture* anthology, as I pointed out in my review of the book in *Encounter*, was an extreme example of what I call the Academic-Cautious approach to kitsch. After a laborious survey of "198 shorts stories published in 8 of the country's most widely read magazines in 1937 and 1943," replete with statistical tables and other instruments of pedantic torture, the authors triumphantly conclude: "On almost every index—frequency, role, delineation, status, goals—the Americans received better treatment both qualitatively and quantitatively than the minority and foreign groups." The special virtue of such articles, quoth Dr. Rosenberg, is that their "aim is not knowledge alone but action to dissolve the 'old crap' [Engels] by means of a new reality." Well, the reality is not new (unless Dr. R expected the American heroes of magazine fiction to receive worse treatment than minority and foreign groups), the increment of knowledge is minimal, and the line of action has been clear for several generations without any help from Drs. Berelson and Salter (who would be horrified at the very idea). Trouble with Rosenberg as a thinker is he's so damnably abstract. He judges on general, pseudo-philosophical grounds—whence his absurd reaction to the Berelson-Salter article—instead of on those specific grounds where exists all truth.

Likewise with Paul's review of my book—I do like using first names, so *friendly*. He was more charitable than Harold, but also more condescending. It seems I'm outgoing, decent, honest, independent, unspiteful, and brave; in short I have all the Boy Scout virtues. Moreover and in addition, I'm "our best journalist." But this turns out to be a rather mild compliment. For what is a journalist? Alas, an ignorant and superficial fellow, a kibitzer (rather than "a man determined to a goal of action or truth"), a mouther of current slogans, a parasite on the day's headlines "who seems to have no experience of the passion of the intellect." In short, a very different sort of chap from Paul, the one-man academy. (His tone is that of a wise old professor chiding a clever but "unsound" young pupil.) My lack of cultural background is very distressing to Paul, but the three concrete instances he gives seem not such at all: the Greeks *did* condemn the state, using "state" in the Hegelian sense I did in "The Responsibility of Peoples" (the Persians were closer to Hegel's idea of the state); whether Marxism has a richer intellectual tradition than pacifism is, of course, a matter of opinion and not, as Paul pretends, of knowledge, and I think I have a better right to an opinion because I was for years actively engaged in both these camps and Paul wasn't (in fact, it might be hard for the outsider to determine by looking at our careers which of us has been The Man Determined to a Goal of Action and Truth and which has been the kibitzer; Liberty, Equality, Fraternity, my dear Paul, were the watchwords of the French Revolution (1789–1794) and so expressive of bourgeois liberalism. What the devil did they used to teach at Townsend Harris and City College?

Paul accuses me of thinking with my typewriter: (which is true but what's wrong? Thought has to start somewhere) and of having no memory: "Dwight once told me, but he will not remember, that he couldn't remember anything more than three months back—the period, I guess, for researching an assignment and thinking it up with one's typewriter." Well, I do remember, and I also remember, as Paul apparently doesn't, that we were talking about Freudian therapy and my point was that I would be a poor subject because I wasn't much interested in my own past and couldn't remember it very well. So it's not a question of memory in general but of one kind of memory; a writer who actually had to operate only on the basis of his current three months' stock of culture would in fact be the sort of breezy ignoramus Paul thinks I am.

. . . I've been trying to think, using my trusty Remington portable, why Paul feels so superior to and irritated with me, and I've decided it's because he is a very abstract-type thinker while I'm more on the concrete side; or, to put it another way, he is a wholesaler of ideas while I'm a retailer. Paul goes in for big, basic philosophies of life, which he expounds in a confident way; he's way up there in the empyrean, and my own earthbound little typewriter-ideas, always limited to some specific aspect of things, must seem intolerably trivial to him. He specializes in answers while I go in more for questions.

Another difficulty between us is that Paul's temperament is that of the prophet—if Harold is pontifical, Paul is messianic—while mine is that of the artist—or, to be more modest, the craftsman. I find it interesting that he describes me, in a casual aside, as "a very fine writer and craftsman." This is clearly of slight importance to him—and his own writings, so hasty and formless, so obviously dashed off in the heat and so little worked-over, demonstrate this—while good writing is for me a most important quality in a book. I often admire Paul's ideas, when they aren't too cosmic, but rarely his way of expressing them. I know that Paul thinks he is one of the major poets and novelists of our time, because I remember, improbably as it may seem, sitting with him years ago in a restaurant off Astor Place (now what was the name? ah—Conti's!) and having him tell me so in dead seriousness. He also claimed he knew as a matter of scientific truth, not taste, which poems were good (his were) and which bad, and that he could demonstrate this knowledge in such a way as to compel agreement (the demonstration was a flop). Nonetheless—or possibly therefore—I think he is not much interested in the art or craft of writing, and that this is why he reacted to my book so negatively. Otherwise, I really can't explain it. After all, there were at least fifty pages of good writing there.

To John Lukacs

August 4, 1958

... Did you know that *Encounter*, after months of shilly-shallying (first accepting it, then, 2 months later, rejecting it, then a week later accepting it, then a month later finally rejecting it), has refused to print my American Letter on grounds it is "one-sidedly" and unrelievedly critical of the USA, and hence might lose them $$$ from foundations? (It is appearing in the Sept. issue of *Twentieth Century*.)

To John Lukacs

September 3, 1958

... Reason I'm hurried s that I'm this evening enplaning for of all places in the world Hollywood. Fantastic business. *Esquire* magazine offered me $1,000 to do a 4,000-word piece on Dore Schary's movie-in-the-making *Miss Lonelyhearts*, from Nathanael West's novel. Since I've never been to Hollywood, since I'm finishing up that mass culture book, since I admire the novel, and since I cannot see Schary making a movie of it without the most comic and pathetic metamorphoses (which should indicate something of the Hollywood mentality—Miss L. being just about the most uncompromisingly nihilistic book produced in USA in this century), for all these reasons I'm flying out to talk to Dr. Schary and his director, actors, etc.

Shall be staying at all places again the Beverly-Wilshire Hotel, Beverly Hills, Calif., in case you want to cheer me in my exile with a note. Back around Sept. 12. My first Princeton lecture [Christian Gauss lectures on mass culture] is on Oct. 2. I've enrolled you formally as a participant. Then or later, you don't have to attend ALL sessions. Yes, let's by all means plan a weekend chez vous after some lecture you attend.

To Sibyl Moholy-Nagy

September 3, 1958

Was horrified to learn from Gloria how badly I behaved. Had no idea. I do recall sneering at GK [Chesterton] but hadn't realized I'd been so insulting about it. I'm terribly sorry. I really had not slightest intention of any personal criticism of Arno's taste or intelligence, both of which I respect highly. One gets into the habit, at least I do, in the kind of circles I have moved in, of speaking violently about such matters, of telling others "You're crazy" or "Don't be naive," etc., and of pronouncing judgments I'm afraid rather bluntly and even aggressively. But it really doesn't mean anything personally—heavens, the people I've attacked, people for whom I have the greatest respect and whom I see all the time! This is not to excuse myself but just to explain. I'm sure I was indeed bumptious and I apologize profoundly and unreservedly.

Please send me Arno's address (also his first name) so I may write him a note.

To the Editor, *The Twentieth Century* [a London publication]

December 1958

In your editorial preceding my "America! America!" you write: "We would not publish Mr. Dwight Macdonald's spirited and witty comment on American life were not Mr. Macdonald himself a 'good American.'" I must object to this on both factual and logical grounds.

Factual: How do you know I *am* a "good American"? I do have a purely personal affection for some aspects of my native land (and a purely personal dislike for others), but patriotism has never been my strong point, and I don't know as I'd call myself a Good American. I'm certainly a Critical American, and I prefer your country, morally and culturally, to my own.

Logical: You confuse the source of criticism with its validity. A Bad American, cynical and traitorous, might still make perfectly sound criticisms of his country. And if they were sound, it would be your editorial duty to print them. It's in that other place to the East that civic virtue is the indispensable passport to print.

To Czeslaw Miloscz

January 27, 1959

How nice to hear from you again! I'm flattered and most grateful for all you've done to spread my works and name in the Polish-reading public. Already written KULTURA saying, of course, I had no objection to the translation of the Mass Culture essay, so I felt no urgency in replying to your letter.

. . . I agree with you that real, good, authentic folk culture tends to "disappear everywhere" (the only important exception I would say is our own jazz, which is a curious mixture of avant-garde and folk and which has shown great power to survive—the latest jazz school, the progressive, sounds like Bartók, Webern, perhaps even Schoenberg—someone said to me at a progressive jazz concert recently, "The point is not in the notes, it is in the silent intervals between them"—very advanced!). And also that in USSR we have mass culture imposed from above. But I don't see why the nationalization of the means of production favors high culture (Soviet Russia seems to show the opposite), even though you add that while it frees it from the market, it also imposes political pressure on it. Because the political pressure seems to me to debase high culture down to mass culture just as the market does. Very interesting what you write of countries like Poland, the masses being so unorganized (as v USSR and USA) that the elite standards of high culture are the only ones. And about the ultra-sophistication of the young Polish intellectuals. Perhaps in order to have mass culture one must have masses, and in order to have masses one must have a large number of people together, which can only be the case in USA and USSR; in smaller countries, even including England and France and Italy, you can have debasing of high culture and even a feeble imitation of mass culture, but you don't have what you have in USA-USSR, namely the dominance, *culturally*, of mass over high culture.

Have you written anything in the last few years in English or French? I should very much like to see it. As you know, I am a great admirer of your stuff—you combine imagination and acuteness in a way that is not at all common. I wish that *Encounter* would publish more of your things. I always enjoy them.

. . . I trust that in your Selected Writings of Simone Weil (what a pity I don't read Polish) you included that magnificent essay, "The Iliad or the Poem of Force," that I first presented in English in *Politics*. By the way, speaking of *Politics*, thank you for your kind words about that magazine (especially interesting that you used the Henry Wallace article for your official reports!). I am still meeting people who read *Politics* and remember it and who identify me with it (and not with the *New Yorker*) and I must say I like it. True, this is an age of mass culture, but also true that magazines, if they were uncompromising (and, of course, on a decent level), make an impression on people, and on far more of them then one might imagine. Your own Captive Mind is certainly in that category.

To the Editor, *Esquire*

March 2, 1959

In his rather odd note in the March issue on The New Hollywood, Mr. [Arnold] Gingrich [*Esquire* publisher] writes that he is "pretty sure" I would agree with his opinion that "the chief thing wrong with the film called *Miss Lonelyhearts* is that it reminds you, most uncomfortably, of a book called *Miss Lonelyhearts*. Well, I don't at all agree. I suppose it's too much to expect a publisher to read the stuff he publishes, but if Mr. Gingrich had bothered to read my piece he would have found two long paragraphs criticizing *Lonelyhearts* as a movie. They begin, "The film is about as cinematic as the proceedings of the American Iron & Steel Institute," and they go on to sneer at its photography, its direction, its acting, its sets, its dialogue, and its "message." (I seem to have overlooked the special sound effects; maybe they were OK.) I cannot imagine what kind of Grade 6 movies Mr. Gingrich habitually goes to; they must be unbelievably bad if he could congratulate Mr. Schary on the "excellence" of his film.

I called Mr. Gingrich's editorial "odd" because I don't quite get its logic. He seems to want it both ways, to pat his magazine on the back for its bold uncompromising exposé of The New Hollywood, but to give a reassuring pat to Hollywood also and to make it clear there are really no hard feelings at all. May I say there *are* hard feelings as far as I'm concerned, that the kind of inartistic corn *Lonelyhearts* represents makes me very angry indeed? And that as long as we Americans go on being good fellows and positive thinkers, maundering about "double standards" and "peaceful coexistence," we will continue to get the kind of mass culture that Mr. Gingrich seems to enjoy.

To Julia Strachey

June 29, 1959

I've just finished rereading *Cheerful Weather* and I must tell you how much I enjoyed it and admired it. I must also confess that when I first read it, 2-1/2 years ago, I found it baffling; it read to me then like a translation of some ancient Chinese text; I keep thinking I must have missed something, some clue, some connective explicatory matter; the effect was like someone being extremely witty and distinguished in a language one didn't understand. But now, partly because I HAD read it once, partly because English life is more familiar to me, I found it spontaneously delightful, I laughed out loud a number of times (actually!), and I saw that the much that is omitted precisely SHOULD have been omitted in the interest of art. I think it is a masterly little work, and it is one of the few books I've read in some time which I kept wishing would last longer. (I had something of the same experience with *Ulysses* and with *The Wasteland*, that of initial opacity and, a few years later, translucency if not transparency—the great advantage of the "if not" locution is that it may mean either that it IS transparent, in this case, or is NOT, giving both writer and reader a free choice.) Julia, you must publish something soon, I'm sure there are lots of others like me who want some more of your prose. . . . Why don't you let me submit a story or two—if you have such in the treasure-house—to the *New Yorker*?

To Editors, *Partisan Review*

August 11, 1959

I think Elizabeth Hardwick's review of Saul Bellow's *Henderson the Rain King*, clever and often perceptive though it is, mistakes both the author's intention and the special quality of the book. "The fantastic journey is perilous," she writes. "A real man can only be evicted from a real place to make room for the universal destiny, playing itself out among eternal scenery." So she dutifully looks for deep symbolism—and doesn't find it. She thinks Bellow was just kidding when he recently "expressed himself against 'deep readers' and symbolic interpretation," and she magisterially states: "*Henderson* cannot be read except deeply, nor understood except symbolically."

Why not? Why not take it on the surface, as a humorous *tour de force* which gets its effects from the manipulation of rhetoric? I read it so and enjoyed it more than any current novel I've read since *Lolita*, also a fantastic journey, also a verbal *tour de force*, also very funny. *Augie March* seemed to me to be reaching for deep meaning and not quite achieving them, but *Henderson* I thought just right. You can read Reichean theory, existentialism, etcetera into it, but you don't have to; the surface fun and games are enough. I think the effect comes from (1) Bellow's extraordinary ear for language, all kinds of language; (2) the comic vigor and inventiveness of the description; (3) the speech of the natives, with its wonderful combination of pidgin English and formality—doubtless no African native ever spoke that way but doubtless they should, because in some cockeyed way it exactly suggests the quality of the primitive mind; (4) the charm and interest of Henderson himself, who might be garrulous but instead is completely articulate, is one of those rare examples of a fictional genius, outsize and fantastic, who really delivers the goods, that is, he does strike the reader, or at least this reader, as being fully as extraordinary a person as his creator intended him to be. This compulsive monologist should be the biggest bore in creation, instead he is fascinating. I think this is because he is always unexpected and yet his unexpectedness, always, once it has occurred, is just what one might have expected, given his personality. Kind of the way life is. "Henderson, then, is not a 'character,'" Miss Hardwick writes, by which she seems to mean he is not a convincingly real person. True but beside the point. Like saying Pantagruel, with whom Henderson has much in common, isn't believable.

Perhaps Bellow, though I am sure he would be indignant at the suggestion, has learned something since *Augie March*. Perhaps he is pulling in his horns in order to penetrate deeper, perhaps he has given up his ambition to be the great American novelist. (*Seize the Day*, his other post-*Augie* book, also seems to me superb, of course in an entirely different way.) If so he should be encouraged and not damned with praise that is faint, however intelligent.

May I conclude with a few rhetorical questions, including this one? Why has literary criticism become so excessively serious-minded? Why does a critic as clever and witty as Miss Hardwick miss the obvious point about *Henderson* and maunder on about the lack of symbolic meanings? How come Lionel

Trilling writes in your magazine articles about *Lolita*—with whose thesis I agree most wholeheartedly, though it might have been said more succinctly—which say almost nothing about *Lolita*'s chief literary qualities, its stylistic brio and its humor? The genres that one would expect our age to excel in, for all sorts of historic-cultural reasons that the readers of *Partisan Review* know as well as I do, are rhetoric and comedy. Why, then, when they appear, do we not recognize them?

To Kenneth Tynan

August 24, 1959

You didn't ask me, but being an editor at heart I cannot refrain from a few suggestions on US conformists, that is, nonconformists—what a slip.

I suppose you've thought of Norman Mailer; if he weren't a talented novelist, his opinions wd. perhaps be of slight interest; but he is a dedicated hipster and agin-the-government man, and his views are extreme and picturesque.

Dorothy Day, who founded and still heads the Catholic Workers (see my profile some years ago in this magazine), is the best spokesman I can think of for the anarchy-pacifist viewpoint. A charming woman, photogenic, saintly. Next best (for pacifist only) wd. be A. J. Muste who, I think still heads the Fellowship for Reconciliation. (The pacifists are now our most dedicated and energetic political nonconformists; also the most *serious* ones—that is, not just eccentrics or lunatics.)

You must also have thought of C. Wright Mills, the Columbia sociologist. I'm no great admirer of his thought processes, but he is probably the weightiest exponent of the old-fashioned kind of quasi-Marxist leftism you yourself also adhere to. Also very photogenic.

If you want a Trotskyist who can talk your ear off most wittily and raucously (or could 4 or 5 years ago), dig up Max Shachtman, whose Trotskyist group, the Workers Party, merged (I think) with the Socialists a couple years back.[13] He could be a counterpart to Norman Thomas. But maybe too much of the past.

Have you thought of Meyer Schapiro, prof. of art at Columbia, as articulate as your own I. Berlin and even more widely learned, who is now an editor of *Dissent*? Superb face of a Jewish monk, wonderful delivery of highest-level talk, and a very decent and noble person all around. Has been around the non-C.P. left since early thirties. And of course a major art critic and historian.

---

13. Virginia Chamberlain, an old leftist friend of Nancy Macdonald's, said about Max Schachtman, "He was born, he talked, and he died."

To William Shawn

September 15, 1959

I'm a patient man, but—

1. Last winter I handed in the [Daniel] Persky profile.[14] It still has not appeared. When I asked you about it last July, you said it definitely would appear in September. This now seems unlikely. Are you so inundated with material that a piece has to wait 8 months? And I'm embarrassed to think of poor Persky, whom you know how he feels about the piece. It would have been kind not to have made him wait another eternity.

2. Last April I handed in a longish book notice on Hans Jolas's book on gnosticism. I still don't even know if it was printed (I asked you last July and you said you'd find out). If it wasn't printed, I'd like to know why not. I took quite a lot of trouble over it.

3. When I got back from abroad I found a note from an acquaintance, David Bazelon, asking me what had happened to some material he had submitted, through me, to you; he wanted it back. I asked you, I asked your secretary. That *New Yorker* silence, deeper than the midnight hush of the desert, still enshrouds all.

4. Just a month ago I sent you the Mark Twain review (which I was delighted to hear you liked). I gather Whittaker has pondered it, but it clearly isn't scheduled since all the research is still in my office.

5. Where am I? Who am I? What am I? Help! There's somebody down here!

To Ted. Jacobs [member of the Morton Sobell Defense Committee]

September 21, 1959

As I told you on the phone, a careful reading of all the material you sent me has led me to conclude, for the moment anyway, that Sobell was guilty of espionage. I think the sentence was vindictive, and I think he should have been tried separately, since there seems only a very frail connection with the Rosenbergs (and there is no evidence at all of *atomic* espionage, the excuse Judge

---

14. Daniel Persky was a famous Hebrew scholar and a world-class eccentric. The profile finally appeared November 28, 1959. It was one of Macdonald's favorite profiles. Everything about Persky fascinated him. He lived in one room so full of books and papers there was hardly room for his bed. He held court every night in a 14th Street automat. When asked by a caller, "Is this Daniel Persky?" he always replied, "Yes this is the real Daniel Persky." Persky was Lauren Bacall's uncle.

Kaufman used to sentence—also I think wrongly—the Rosenbergs to death and Sobell to 30 years).

As I also said on the phone, what I think should now be done is to try to get Sobell to make a long, detailed statement giving his side of the case. Since he didn't take the stand, and since his lawyers weren't able to break down Elitcher's story (at least not in my opinion), one is left with Elitcher's story and nothing to either refute it or explain it away.

The reason his lawyers give for not putting him on the stand is that in the anti-Communist mood of 1951, Sobell's connections with the Communist Party would have been exploited by the prosecution to injure him with the jury. But since the prosecution at once demonstrated, via Elitcher, in great detail Sobell's Communist membership and sympathies, this reason seems absurd to me. It seems more likely that his lawyers feared he would be unable to sustain cross-examination on his refutation of Elitcher's story. As for Sobell's own explanation, in his single statement, which is that his innocence was so clearly established that there was no need for him to testify, this just doesn't make sense.

But I know one is not supposed, legally, to even wonder about a defendant's not taking the stand, so let's forget this.

I think it might be useful if Sobell would write down (1) exactly what were his relations with the Communist Party—was he a member, a sympathizer, why, how long, etc. (NOT of course any tattle-telling on others in it, if he *was* in it); (2) just why he did go to Mexico (he gives three or four different reasons, some of them contradictory with each other, in his statement) at the particular time he went; (3) his side of the Elitcher story—this would include taking up each of the specific meetings Elitcher tells about and giving his account of what happened (or if the meetings didn't take place, saying so). The last is, of course, the most important point. I have marked on the enclosed copy of Sharp's short *Guide to the Sobell Case* the kind of questions I think ought to be answered. There's also the matter of Elitcher's motivation for bearing false witness against his former best friend, for falsely involving him in a very serious charge merely in order to get off the hook with the government about his own perjury on his C.O. membership. I do wish Sobell would say what his relationship with Elitcher was, exactly, why their friendship cooled, and how he explains E's being willing to testify against him—is E some kind of a monster, and if so why does Sobell think he is, what does he know about him?

I hope something can be done. If you want me to sign a petition or something to have the sentence reduced, I'll be glad to do it (providing it doesn't raise the question of innocence).

To George L. K. Morris

October 16, 1959

. . . Meanwhile, do you remember, but of course you do, our famous meeting with James Joyce? I'm reviewing Richard Ellmann's excellent new biography, which has everything in it but the kitchen stove and our meeting. So I thought I would tell about it in the review (esp. since it seems to have been typical Joyce behavior). It went like this as I recall:

Joyce, looking like a haggard race-track tout (impression of striped sporty shirt, tight coat—or was he wearing a dressing gown?), let us in himself. We followed him down a long hall into his study, where he sank wearily into an armchair. We thanked him for letting us come, told him how much we admired his work, hoped we weren't disturbing him. He said nothing, passed his hand frequently over his face as if in pain or sickness. We tried direct questions. He would answer yes or no and volunteer nothing more. He seemed quite content to sit there in silence until we left. We became more and more desperate. The pauses grew longer. The only specific gambit I recall that we tried—can you think of any other concrete item in the talk—that I said I thought *Ulysses* would make a very good movie, to which he said nothing. (I see in Ellmann's book that others had suggested this to him, with happier results.) I then asked him if he knew the films of Eisenstein, which I said I much admired. He said he did know them. Finally you cleared your throat and said nervously but resolutely that your feared we had to go. This got JJ into action for first and last time. He turned to me and said, "Mr. Macdonald, I understand you're on *Fortune* magazine." "Yes." "An old school friend of mine is shortly going to New York. He is a writer, a very good writer. He needs a job. I wonder if you could put in a word for him at *Fortune?*" I said I could. He told me his name and said he would look me up when he got to New York. Again a long pause. Then we shook hands (or did we?) and he ushered us out—with considerably more cordiality than he had let us in.

Is any of the above wrong? And can you add any details? I should have made notes. Maybe you did.

To the Editor, *The New Leader*

November 3, 1959

In his "Strange Tale of Bruno R." in your September 28th issue, Daniel Bell errs when he writes: "Trotsky refused to consider the alternative of bureaucratic collectivism." On the contrary, Trotsky, in an article in *The New International* of November 1939, entitled "The USSR in War," did consider just that alternative. He wrote (in part):

"If however, onerous the second perspective may be, if the world proletariat should actually prove incapable of fulfilling the mission placed upon it by the course of development, nothing else would remain except openly to recognize that the socialist program based on the internal contradictions of capitalism ended as Utopia. It is self-evident that a new minimum program would be required—for the defense of the interests of the slaves of the totalitarian bureaucratic society."

In fact I was so struck by this evidence of Trotsky's historical open-mindedness (not always his most striking trait) that I quoted the whole passage at length at the beginning of an anti-Marxist piece I wrote in *Politics* in 1946 (happily still available from the Cunningham Press, 3036 W. Main Street, Alhambra, Calif., at a mere $2) called "the Root Is Man."

What puzzles me is how Daniel Bell, who must have read Trotsky's article since he quotes the opening phrase (and since he reads everything anyway) could state that Trotsky "refused to consider the bureaucratic-collective alternative." Trotsky obviously wasn't happy about it, and he didn't go into it at length, but he certainly considered it. A formulation like "a new minimum program would be required—for the defense of the interests of the slaves of the totalitarian bureaucratic society" is earth-shaking, in the context of Trotsky's Bolshevik-Leninist-Marxism. It is distinctly gradualist, even reformist. I'll bet even Max Shachtman hasn't got that far yet. So why not give Trotsky credit for one of his few objective moments?

It also seemed to me that Bell rather slighted Bruno R.—how nice to learn he is still alive. For all his foolishness about the Elders of Zion and his worse-than-foolishness about Hitler and Mussolini being "historically progressive" (I wonder where we've heard *that* before?), Bruno Rizzi—he'll always be Bruno R. to me—did have an important historical *aperçu*. (As did Anton Ciliga in a too-much-neglected book published in Paris in 1938, *The Russian Enigma*.) Burnham vulgarized Bruno R. and Ciliga (and Pareto and Mosca and several others) to the point of nonsense in his *The Managerial Revolution* (as Mills and Gerth observed in *Ethics* of Jan. 1942 and I in *Partisan Review* of Jan.–Feb. 1942, but still Bruno did make an advance in thinking over the usual Marxistical nonsense of the period.

All credit to Bell for digging out the fascinating story of Bruno R. from *Le Contrat Social*—and all credit for that matter to Boris Souvarine as an editor in the first place. But his column puts me in the curious position of defending (mildly) both Trotsky and Bruno R. Is it that my friend Dan Bell is a congenital centrist and hence underestimates both extremes, and that I am the opposite? Ask him. He reads everything.

To the Editors of *Commentary* [response to Hilton Kramer's article attacking the *New Yorker* and its contributors; the footnotes in this letter are Macdonald's]

November 1959

A little of the old steam
A little of the bold steam—
That's what will keep the kramer[15] from the door.
You can snarl at second-rate books,
Find the fraud in all those Great Books,
Twist the tail of Adler, Mortimer J.,[16]
You can polemize with Trotsky,[17]
Show the bible's gone to potsky.[18]

Colin Wilson's epidermis you can flay,[19]
You can judge the Ford Foundation,[20]
Discourse on cinematization
With instances from Griffiths to today.[21]

But
A little of the old steam,
A little of the bold steam—
Or Hilton Kramer's baying at the door.
And
It don't count (no, it don't count)
If it's in that strictly no count,
That provincial adolescent schizophrenic
Deliquescent
Languid effete and congenitally noneffervescent[22]
Rag—and I don't mean *Commentary*.

15. According to Florabel Spurgeon's *Myth and Ritual in the Black Forest* (London, 1905), those woodcutters who had not chopped down their quota of Established Reputations were visited at night by a "kramer," a small rodent-like creature that nibbled at their toes until they got back to work.
16. "The Book-of-the-Millennium Club," *New Yorker*, November 29, 1952.
17. "Varieties of Political Experience," *New Yorker*, March 28, 1959.
18. "The Bible in Modern Undress," *New Yorker*, November 14, 1953.
19. See "Readers Indigestion," *New Yorker*, October 13, 1956, in which I performed for *The Outsider* much the same service I later did for another best-seller in *Commentary*.
20. See *New Yorker*, November 26–December 17, 1955.
21. "The Lost Art," *New Yorker*, March 15, 1958.
22. The adjectives are mostly authentic kramerisms. In my intellectual retirement, I like to compare the holiday doodling of mine listed above with the kramer's apodictic sentence on the *New Yorker*'s treatment of art & letters: "Yet behind this air of relaxation, one

To Julia Gowing [a London friend who asked his opinion of Barzun and Trilling]

November 29, 1959

. . . My opinion of [Jacques] Barzun [is] not very high. I agree with the thesis of *House of Intellect* and most of what he says, but he's so damned civilized, urbane, and genteel. He and [Lionel] Trilling are a pair. I mean, I'm all for civilization (as against beatniks and angries,[23] nice coinage that last) and that's why. I like England, but when an American tries to be urbane—cultivated—it's different from an Englishman; something hollow, inauthentic; the clothes don't fit; he tries too hard, denies himself spontaneity, peculiarity—well, you catch my drift. We Americans have to be intellectual first, civilized afterwards—like Poe or Edmund Wilson or, at a lower level, Mencken & Nathan. [D. H.] Lawrence wrote in his *Studies in Classic American Literature*, in a real American style, what a relief compared to the watery urbanities of Barzun and Trilling.

To the Editor, *The Twentieth Century*

n.d., December 1959

There is something ludicrous in being accused of "literary witch-hunting," as I was by Mr. Colin Wilson in your last issue, because I reviewed adversely two recent best-sellers. Especially when the accusation comes from the author of one of them. Like a millionaire complaining of persecution because his income is taxed and asking why the tax-collector doesn't go after the poor instead. It is true that if *The Outsider* and *By Love Possessed* had not been (a) best-sellers and (b) widely praised in reputable journals, I should not have bothered to review them, since in that case they would have been just two more bad books among hundreds, thousands of others. But it is not true, of course, that I—or any moderately sensible critic—"automatically attacks" any serious book that becomes a best-seller. James Agee's *A Death in the Family* was a best-seller and I praised it at length in the *New Yorker*. Vladimir Nabokov's *Lolita* is a best-seller that I

could not help detecting the terrifying relentlessness with which a serious subject—and a subject, moreover, in which the writer's vital personal response counts for a great deal—had been parodied, trimmed, ridiculed, and finally made boring and absurd by the author's attempt to make it seem completely effortless, utterly common-sensical, and open to the most easygoing attention." (Wow.)

23. The reference is to John Osborne's play *Look Back in Anger* and what were known as the "Angry Young Men" of Britain during the postwar years. Macdonald had little patience with their contempt for the British Establishment. He thought the main character psychotic but not sympathetic, "a self-pitying, bad-tempered mediocrity who lacks the strength and talent to live up to his aspirations."

wouldn't dream of attacking since I consider it the most interesting and moving American novel in years; and there's also *Dr. Zhivago*. But why pile up instances? A critic who conceived it his task to automatically deflate the best sellers would be as balmy as Mr. Wilson, who seems to be suffering not only from a congenital swelled head but also from a closely related complaint: *paranoia literaria*.

Mr. Wilson is "astounded" by my calling Max Beerbohm "a far more original and vigorous thinker than either Mr. Wilson or Mr. Cozzens." I chose Beerbohm deliberately, and I admit a little perversely, because of the tendency among reviewers to confuse seriousness of intention, with which Messers. Wilson and Cozzens are well endowed, with seriousness of achievement, with which they are not. Beerbohm was a determinedly unpretentious, even slightly frivolous writer with a superb prose style and an acute disciplined intelligence. Mr. Wilson, as his letter itself is evidence, is in all those respects just the reverse. Opposites illuminate each other; hence the relevance of Max Beerbohm.

The chief reaction of Mr. Wilson to my review of his book in the October 13, 1956, *New Yorker*, aside from its being "long and very funny," is that it "probably sold more copies than all the enthusiastic reviews in smaller papers." I, in turn find this astounding. And shocking in its naive cynicism. For the review was wholly, ardently unfavorable. If I may quote a few sentences from the conclusion: "Had the Reverend Norman Vincent Peale not been there first, *The Outsider* could have been called *The Power of Positive Serious Thinking*. It is for all its highbrow decor, an inspirational how-to treatise—be glad you're an outsider; face up to life; achieve peace of mind; develop your hidden asset, willpower! . . . As one trudges on through Mr. Wilson's cultural wasteland, it slowly becomes clear that this serious young man is a philistine, a Babbitt, a backwoods revivalist of blood-chilling consistency. . . . 'I will serve nothing but my God and my own soul,' he has his final hero, 'the religious man,' say. Perish all conceptions as knowledge and civilization.'" Apparently Mr. Wilson considers this a soft impeachment—if it sells copies.

I won't reply to Mr. Wilson's laborious sneers at my accent, my waistline, my last book's sales (comfortably under 1,000 as he suspects), my incapacity for "creative work" ("creative" is the last refuge of the 20th-century scoundrel), and my defective *weltanschauung* (I do think he might have left *that* out, a bit personal). But I must object to his "penny a line reviewers" (we get a lot more than that) and also to: "He is . . . in fact, let us not shun the word, a journalist." "Shun," indeed! Of course I'm a journalist. Would that Mr. Wilson were a philosopher.

Dwight Macdonald speaking at the Columbia University counter-commencement, 1968. (*New York Times*)

CHAPTER SIX

BACK TO THE BARRICADES, 1960–1969

"How could Kennedy and Schlesinger and all those bright decent young liberals have gotten themselves into THAT mess?"

These years best illustrate the seeming paradox and contradictions of Macdonald's life—"a rebel in defense of tradition." For it was in the sixties that he reached the height of his reputation as a defender of high culture, with the publication of *Against the American Grain*, a collection of his critiques of the Revised Standard Version of the Bible and the newly revised third edition of *Webster's New International Dictionary*, and articles on the "Decline and the Fall of the English Language." He referred to the collection as his "reactionary essays." He was contemptuous of Britain's "Angry Young Men" and rejected the Beat Generation at home. At the same time he returned to the barricades to defend former Communists Morton Sobell and Junius Scales, to lecture college students on the validity and viability of anarchism, and to support the anti-war movement and the younger generation that manned the barricades. By the end of the decade, after his own participation in the Columbia University countercommencement, he was convinced that "the young were the last best hope of this destructive society." Macdonald now rejected the cold war mantra on the ever-present threat of communism. While he never romanticized the North Vietnamese, as some of his new comrades did, he would not accept an American intervention in what he considered a civil war in Vietnam, in order to stop the spread of communism. His return to political activism, even to civil disobedience, brought a new energy to his life but also separated and alienated him from many of his old comrades on the left. The letters capture the tumult and turmoil of these years and the degree to which Macdonald was at the center of the debates.

To the Editors, *Dissent*

January 5, 1960

Irving Howe claims that if Christ gave his Sermon on the Mount next week, among other routine reactions would be that "Dwight Macdonald would write that while 'Mr. Christ makes some telling points' they suffer from syntactical confusion and a 'woolly pretentious style.'"

But there is this much point to it, which some of your contributors might ponder: that *were* the Sermon woolly and pretentious in style, that would indeed be my reaction, and I should be right, since in that case the Sermon would not be the great moral message it is but a botch, and not only in style. Great ideas can only be expressed in a great style. There is no such thing as a clear message delivered in a confused style; the message is the style and the style is the message. Selah!

Speaking of style, I note that Mr. Howe has been converted to Christianity, since he refers to Christ as "He." (To me, he's "he.") This shows what discoveries can be made if one pays attention to style. And on Mr. Howe's part, what an admirably subtle way of breaking the news!

To Ted Jacobs

February 16, 1960

The letter about the [Morton] Sobell (and other) case in today's *Times* is, you may or may not be glad to hear, the result of your missionary work. That is, I drafted a letter about the Sobell case alone some time ago and asked [Nathan] Glazer, [Sidney] Hook, and [Irving] Kristol to sign it with me. (I thought their names, politically, would carry special weight in such a case.) They thought Gold and Greenglass should also have a word spoken for them, and I really could see no reason why not, since they too were given much too stiff sentences. They also removed almost all the indignation from my original draft on the tactical grounds that attacking Judge Kaufman would be more likely to alienate than to persuade the people who might do something about the sentence. I guess so. Anyway, I agreed. My only fear now is that the letter is so antiseptic that it won't arouse any feelings one way or the other. We'll see.

To George Woodcock

March 22, 1960
Just got the new issue, haven't read it (have been away for two weeks at an absurd film festival in the Argentine—like the country and people enormously, however, MUCH better than Canada), but with my practiced journalistic eye I at once found the letters re my little piece. Would you print the following [response], please.

WHO IS PROVINCIAL?
Some fellow-Americans have objected to my complaints about provincialism in Canadian magazines on the grounds that I write for a "provincially titled and provincially directed magazine" called *The New Yorker*. Without going into the quality of *The New Yorker*, may I say (a) that my objection to the Canadian magazines I reviewed was not that their interest was local but that it was provincial, i.e., that Canadian culture, on their own evidence, is not wide enough or rich enough to sustain such concentrated attention; and (b) that I find it hard to think of New York as a provincial city. Like London or Paris, New York seems to me to be a center of world culture, and indeed, I must confess that it is precisely the rest of the country that strikes me as provincial compared to New York. I say this with no exultation, for, although I have always lived here, I have never much liked the place. Furthermore, I think the concentration of cultural activity in one city deplorable; it would be much better to have half a dozen rivals of comparable importance in each country. But the brute fact is there aren't. Paris, London, and New York are the overwhelmingly dominant centers, and so the adjective "provincial" can hardly be attached to them, and the name *New Yorker*, while it may be objected to as a bit snobbish, cannot really be called provincial.

To Robert Tabor [author of an article on Cuba in *The Nation*]

April 8, 1960
. . . Sorry, too, that I cannot put my name to your newspaper as I don't like it because I think the whole question IS complicated and because the ad reduces it all to one-sided propaganda. Thus, on COMMUNISM, surely not enough to note that the Cuban CP has only 16,000 members. The NY *Times* and *Time*, which I read, have both printed material indicating that there is a lot of Communist influence. Small size of CP not to the point—sympathies of Castro's chief aides and of himself are to the point. CONFISCATION—those 20-year bonds don't seem much of a deal to me; no parallel w. Japan because there a stable govt. but in Cuba who knows; and parallel w. condemnation by govt. of land in USA is absurd, now isn't it really?

But these aren't what bothers me about Castro. It's the wildness of his and his official statements, esp. the ones against USA (blaming US for the blowing up of the *Maine* and even for the war against Spain, which is said to have been waged for imperialist purposes, just to get our hooks into Cuba; that we did get our hooks in is true, but certainly Cuban patriots like Castro then welcomed our help against Spain, and also we didn't take over Cuba as we shamefully did the Philippines; also the official line on the Cuban sugar quota seems to be that it is insulting to Cuban dignity if the USA gives them a break and it is imperialism if USA changes the quota so it no longer favors Cuba); etc. I also don't like Castro's free-handed use of the death penalty for what your ad calls "counter-revolution," for things like dope peddling or black market speculation in currency. True, nobody's been shot yet, but ominous that such penalties should be possible.

I was all for Castro in the first months, but now I am skeptical and worried. On the basis of what I read in the *Times* and in *Time*. If you could show me, by taking specific articles in those papers, that they are printing false or distorted reports, then I would join you. But I'm not prepared to give a general endorsement to the Castro regime in order to fight against nonsense by journalists like Sokolsky.

To Sibyl Mohaly-Nagy

n.d., May 1960

BUT, my dear Sibyl

1. I didn't find *Ben Hur* entertaining, I wish you said why you did.

2. I'm not "dispeptic" ("dyspeptic" usual sp.) About movies, have been writing of them since 1929 precisely because I enjoy them and think they are often entertaining and sometimes art.

3. If BH were in fact "a big historical spectacle decently done" (again I wish you had given some reasons for your view) then I should have praised it. *Birth of a Nation*, *Potemkin*, perhaps even *Citizen Kane* all come inside this category and I admire them very much.

4. What a snob you are! I think the little man in Helena deserves something far better than *Ben Hur* and also that he *might* enjoy it (as he did *Birth* and *Kane*).

5. Wherever did you pick up all this rather antiquated Americanese, so jaunty and forcible-feeble, all those "hells" and "by golly's" and "guys"?

6. And whatever gave you the idea you are "a frivolous person"?

P.S. (7) Your homespun straight-from-the shoulder, down-to-earth, grass-roots note raises, in spite of itself, two interesting questions we must discuss some time: (a) the line between entertainment and art, or rather whether such a line can be drawn; (b) can it be assumed, as you do, that the cinema is not an art form, so that it is absurd to apply to it standards and aesthetic analysis.

P.P.S. (8) Assuming I'm addressing in *Esquire* Little Guys in Helena, Mont. (though of course I'm not; I'm writing for the same people I wrote for in the *New Yorker* and in the *Partisan Review*, that is, for the perhaps small number of them that read *Esquire*; handsome as the pay is, I should not otherwise have been interested in doing the column), anyway assuming this, aren't you being silly when you write that "they should be made to appreciate" (by me) the wonders of *Ben Hur* and other such super-spectacles? I mean, I don't think they need any nudging from me—the film won 11 Oscars and MGM now looks forward to a final gross of 100 millions.

To David Kelly [former classmate of Michael Macdonald at Harvard]

June 21, 1960

You complain of the boring quality of life in our overorganized, routined society, and of the fact it is organized for other ends than those you personally want. True, it is boring and anti-human, this American society we live in—taken as a whole, that is, in its official and mass-culture sense. But the actual people in USA, though more dehumanized by this kind of society than say those in Italy or England (where things have gone less far), still aren't too bad if you can get to them as individuals. And as for being boring, isn't this because you have this ambivalent feeling—rebellion on one hand and on the other the cog-in-machine attitude of the fighter pilot and the paymaster—so you can neither accept society and Make Out nor reject it and have fun at its expense? (For the second alternative is quite practical, even literally—you're wrong when you say there's no market for Menckenian satire and fun-poking—I've been well paid for years for it.)

But why do you feel ambivalent? Why do you think the opportunities for the intellectual are fewer than ever before? There are still lots of Little Magazines, and even the big ones now print more serious stuff than they used to a generation or two ago. What's so terrible about colleges giving tenure to nonacademic writers of note, why is this necessarily one more "stall" in the ox farm? Why not reject US society as a whole but also use whatever chances it offers for your own purposes? I *do* think, I'm afraid, that there is something of a whining tone in your letter (as you point out yourself). Read Ellmann's *Joyce*, and see what he had to put up with—silence, exile, cunning were his watchwords for dealing with society. If you really want to build a cabin and live in it à

TICK! ——— PLEASE
SEND AN **THE NEW YORKER** SWERS TO
No. 25 WEST 43RD STREET
FOLLOWING QUESTIONS AT
ONCE.

EDITORIAL OFFICES
OXFORD 5-1414

July 11, 1960

(1) Have you written any poems?

(2) What are you reading and how
does it strike you? (Answer must
be concrete and detailed. The words
"great" or "greatest" will not be
considered an answer.)

(3) Have you read any poems in
that anthology I gave you?

(4) Have you broken the record,
either way, hitting ball to beach?

(5) How is your serve?

If answer to (1) is Yes, may I see
them? If answer is Yes, let me.

Fred Dupee will welcome us at
his mansion on August 18ᵗʰ. He
warns you that Tony (Tough Tony
~~Dupee~~) is taking tennis lessons at
Rokeby from Roland.

The editors of _Esquire_ seem to

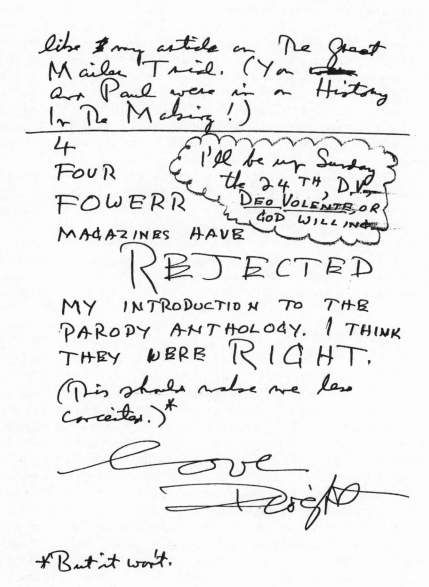

like my article on The Great
Mailer Trial. (You ~~were~~
and Paul were in on History
In The Making!)

4
FOUR
FOWERR

*I'll be my Sunday
the 24TH, D.V.,
DEO VOLENTE, OR
GOD WILLING*

MAGAZINES HAVE

REJECTED

MY INTRODUCTION TO THE
PARODY ANTHOLOGY. I THINK
THEY WERE RIGHT.

(This should make me less
conceited.)*

Love

Dwight

*But it won't.

A typical note that Macdonald often sent to his sons. This one happens to be
devoid of the usual typeovers and insertions. But it does have at least one brief
footnote, a pedagogical form he was addicted to.

la Thoreau, except with wife and babies, quite an exception, go ahead. Though you'd need a few thousand $$$ capital to get started on raising your vegetables. Myself, I'd recommend trying to use society and trying to prevent its using you—no need for a head-on collision. There's perhaps never been a society in which it was easier *economically* for a serious person who disagrees profoundly with it to on the one hand find chances for honest and interesting gain from it and on the other maintain his real independence and do his own work after hours. As for the spiritual and intellectual departments, true USA is a deadening and corrupting place; much harder to be an individualist and rebel than in England or Europe; there I do sympathize with your plaint. But hard is not impossible.

The first thing you ought to do is confront your ambivalence and either become, so to speak, the fighter pilot or the Mencken-Question-of-God type. After that, it's just a matter of making sure you are advancing your interests by what you do and not giving up yours for other people's (except your wife and potential children—but there it is indeed more blessed to give than to receive).

I've probably not answered your letter at all. If so, please excuse it—intentions honorable. Best wishes on your marriage this weekend at which I gather Mike will be present.

To Leo Lowenthal

July 23, 1960

. . . Poe has always fascinated me, in a personal way—I feel he was like me, I sympathize with his absurdities and flamboyances—I admire his intellectual and artistic detachment, his coldness even—to me he is inferior as an artist to Hawthorne and Melville but more gemütlich—his failures are to me more interesting than their successes (except for Benito Cereno and Bartleby)—I dig him (that beat slang does have its place). As for anyone who dismisses him as a hack, let them teach English! I read and reread with delight his most wrongheaded and "fugitive" book reviews because he always wrote so clearly and he got so much intellectual passion into it. Evviva Poe!

On 207–208: you mistake my point; agree Dickens, Balzac, Scott were aware they were writing for the market in general (how could they not have been?). But my point was that they often wrote their own stuff, high level (not Scott—I think he was mediocre all through), and also often wrote kitsch; and the question is whether they were aware of when it was one and when the other. Maybe I am wrong. But to prove it you would have to cite letters or journals that showed this awareness—as, that Dickens when he wrote those appalling pages on the death of Little Nell (which, by the way, I'm using as an unconscious self-parody in an anthology of parodies, edited by me, that Random

House is bringing out this fall) know what he was doing. My impression is he himself was very much moved by Nell's death. . . .

213: [Edward] Shils's piece in *Daedalus*[1] was so bad that I find it hard even to find a point at which to attack. I suppose you have heard of the little scandal at the Congress of Cultural Freedom meeting in Berlin [June 20, 1960], when Will Phillips of PR, an invited guest, arose after Shils had delivered a similar paper and asked, "May I say something?" Shils, who was the chair, is alleged to have replied "No." Will then sat down. I was told audience was on Will's side; Shils is almost crazy, I'd say. I supposed also you noticed that Shils—who has been a pet of the Congress for years—was the organizer of the section in Berlin on mass culture and that he excluded the chief antagonists of his position (you, me, Van Den Haag, Adorno) and included only people like Dan Bell, Irv. Kristol who he knew were on his side; Will P. was there because after all Congress publishes PR, in form at least; and he was not asked to give a paper.

To Gloria Macdonald [in London]

August 5, 1960

. . . Catastrophe disaster irreparable loss utter stupidity—I left my briefcase in the cab that brought me from the station to 87th the night I got back from the Cape; that was almost a week ago and it wasn't turned in; have put ads in papers offering $50 reward, called the police daily, must assume it's gone (didn't write earlier because didn't want to worry you). The devil of it is that it contained (a) the whole week's work on Masscult II and the Mailer piece and (b) several folders of research on avant-gardism and other topics, the most interesting of the course. I wake up at 5 A.M. with a start—where IS it? How COULD I have? Well, it's gone, and I've rewritten the missing pages, partly from memory, partly from the *Post* draft, but all sorts of lovely ideas are probably gone forever (not to mention all that research). Lucky I'd done in final form 3/4 of Masscult II before I left. Shows I'm not to be trusted out alone after dark. A moment's lapse, irretrievable loss, most traumatic experience in years. DON'T sympathize. Wound is covering over. Nothing worse than to do all over what you've done with much labor the week before. I'm an idiot, but why nobody turned it in, of no value to them, my name and address all through it—this is a jungle. I need to live in a

---

1. Edward Shils was a well-known sociologist at the University of Chicago and an important figure in the affairs of the Congress for Cultural Freedom. He totally rejected Macdonald's theories on mass culture. This reference is to his article "Daydreams and Nightmares: Reflections on the Criticism of Mass Culture," *Sewanee Review*, Fall 1957 (Macdonald's reference to *Daedalus* is incorrect).

game preserve. Luckily carbon of Mailer piece here, and I've asked poor Norman to add again his new material.

To Gloria Macdonald

August 31, 1960

. . . Sweet, DON'T be sad. I'll be there on the 10th, and I simply cannot leave earlier because so much to finish before I go. . . . As for the Russells, you may be right. I have only met them couple of times, he did seem a bit dim; she a bit perhaps overpowering. But don't worry about them; I'm sure we'll get on ok with them. . . .

Gather you don't feel strongly about meeting in Paris. In fact, maybe you're right and we should save Paris for later and go off to Cornwall. Honestly, sweet, I'd love to go anywhere with you, wherever you like. You decide and arrange. The main thing is to have a week or ten days of pure vacation with YOU. You don't know how much I need it. And you (that is: and need you). . . . Oh. Dear. You've gotten into a low mood, I've had them myself; people all seem hostile (but, you know, they really AREN'T, not the Spenders, not the Russells, not the Wollheims; just self-centered, like almost everybody, and careless; people like Helen and Baba [Anrep] are rare, we're very lucky to have met them; the rest are ok so long as you don't need anything important from them; the important thing is what is between you and me.

Nicholas, who is still here (he leaves for Cape tomorrow) with me, has actually and of his own motion invited Muffie to have dinner with us tonight and to go to a movie with us (*Beat the Devil* plus *Forbidden Games*, that French film about children I never saw—both at the New Yorker, run by my friend Dan Talbot; I have a *pass*!). I'm delighted; it's the first sign he's shown interest in the other sex. I think he likes Muff because she is, like him, sensible and smart; also because she is pretty. All this mere assumption since naturally we don't discuss such things. Muff [Gloria's youngest daughter Sabina] is very nice with him, I think she likes him too. I'm giving than a roast beef dinner. Mike says he may deign to come too; he's always very toplofty about coming to dinner with les enfants but when he is there he seems to enjoy himself. Shall ask Muff when she sails, and report.

. . . Rahv in this A.M. to get keys and settle things. He will have Ethel once a week. I made inventory of china, silver, pictures. Think he will be a good tenant. We had a long friendly chat.

I've really enjoyed being with Nick the last weeks here; he has his adolescent moods and vapors, but on the whole he's cheerful, undemanding (no interference with work, for instance), and humorous; he even asks me questions about art and politics and letters. With Mike, on the other hand, my relations have rather deteriorated; in fact I am steadily approaching the doghouse that poor Nancy has been in so long; he's wildly moody and emotional, veering between extreme affection and paranoiac suspicion and hostility; odd that he's so bright and so unconscious of himself or of the outside world (logic, for example, just seems to have been left out of his makeup). I think he is a genetic throwback to Seldon [Rodman]. It would have been a catastrophe if he had come to London—though probably you and he would have become fast friends and allies against The Logical Monster. . . . He's gotten his first job, a three-day replacement of someone who is sick, with Francis Thompson, a documentary filmmaker; begins today. He has several other leads, though, and I think he will get placed soon. If he would only SLOW DOWN.

Will you meet me at the airport? It's terribly early. Don't if it's too much for you. Do if you can. I live for the day and you are NOT a displaced person, you're in my heart.

To Michael Macdonald

November 12, 1960

. . . Life here is quiet but pleasant, esp. since I like rain and mist and even that low-keyed but penetrating London cold. We had a large party here [Dwight and Gloria were living in St. Johns Woods, in the house of John Russell, the art critic], first one, other night—V. S. Pritchett, Tony Crossland (C. A. R. Crossland, ideologue of Gaitskell and b.f. [boy friend] of Day at moment), Ken Tynan, Steve Spender, Bill (Sir William to you) Coldstream of Slade School, et al., et feminae. U.S. contingent was Nika Tucci (natch) (he's leaving for States next week) (or so he says, God knows if he IS) (he says he yearns for his children) (maybe he does at that; if so he is a man of enormous self-control), Lillian Hellman (here for opening of *Toys*, which we saw other night, disappointing, terrible production, lines delivered as if it were an Oscar Wilde duchess comedy), and who do you think, Stanley Kubrick. I read he was here to make *Lolita*, called him at studio, found he is living for winter at No. 7 Acacia Road [just down the road from Macdonald]. Fantastic. And how about a job for MMCD [Michael Macdonald]? He was very sympathetic but nothing at moment, all full up. Since I'd already asked him by mail, I didn't press. If any prospects later, will see. He thought you would learn more with [Francis] Thompson than you would as waterboy for a big production. I gathered that if you could show some actual film experience, you would have a much better chance of getting into bigtime stuff later. Not exactly a revolutionary idea. But sound.

Speaking of Kubrick, saw *Spartacus* other morning. Alas. While much better than *Ben Hur*, since Kubrick unlike Wyler has a Griffith-ian cinematic sense, esp. in handling of crowds, it left a bad taste I thought. Maybe those big Roman spectacles now impossible because of slowing-up tendency of the huge technicolor close-ups. Also the dialogue sounds absurd, since it is always 20th century American, like a dubbed film—"Have a good night's rest, Spartacus" (ironical), or when S (having miraculously led a revolt of the gladiators that succeeds, meets his slavegirl inamorata who has miraculously escaped her master) says as his first words: "Varinia! I thought I'd never see you again." Long time no see, Lucius Pompilius. Doesn't work. Script terrible bit of Popular Front sentimentality between [Howard] Fast and [Dalton] Trumbo. Too bad. Kubrick as director reminds me of Albie Booth up against the Notre Dame line—he squirms and even breaks free for some brilliant end runs but in the end he is simply overpowered by sheer weight of the defense—Kirk Douglas was one of the most redoubtable tacklers. . . .

To Thomas H. Rodgers [reader of Masscult/Midcult articles in *Partisan Review*]

February 8, 1961

Your letter of Dec. 12 has made me think more than any other letter—not very many, alas—I've received on my PR articles, which is why it's taken me so long to reply. It's your general point about the obsession today "with hierarchies and status" in culture and my own—innocent I protest—involvement in it that bothers me; also the emotional tone of your letter. Could you have A Point? Or even Several Points? Maybe. Let me react to some of your Points.

You ask "is that what we want?" apropos of my preference for the BBC's cultural stratification over our own radio TV chaos. I say NO, but it's the best we can get. More things interesting to me come over the BBC airwaves than over the USA ones. And I assume, as I always have in my writing, that my readers roughly share my interests—and my cultural level. . . . You say this BBC stratification "may not be so deadly from the viewpoint of passive consumption" but IS deadly from viewpoint of the artist creator. I see your point, but my articles were written for consumers rather than producers.

As to the creator-artist, I'm bothered by your example because I agreed with Jeremy Larner in PR that Roth has been overrated, and I was glad to see him having the nerve to tangle with Kazin, Howe, and Bellow. If one thinks a writer has been overrated by the high priests, how can one say so publicly without attracting the priesthood (and then becoming guilty of stratification in your eyes)? What did you think of my piece in *Commentary* 3 years ago on James Gould Cozzen's *By Love Possessed*? I attacked the low priests but still seems a parallel to Larner.

On your idea of "this national cultural elite front": does it exist? Do you think Allen Tate and PR are co-conspirators? I don't see it. Our culture looks to me, as stated in PR, porous and amorphous to a fault. . . . If you mean that one shouldn't make a "cultural front" with "ex-Marxists, ex-Royalists, ex-Catholics, and ex-Confederates"—this is one of your reproaches—I can only say I have always made such fronts, in the sense of saying what I thought even though it agrees with other positions that in general I don't agree with. If one acts otherwise, one finds oneself in a very sectarian hierarchy indeed. And when you ask (rhetorically) if I think "such an unwieldy cultural front could ever be galvanized into a genuine avant-garde," I reply, as I hope was clear in the essay, that I don't and that I don't think an avant-garde is historically possible today. For stated reasons.

What are Karl Shapiro's difficulties that I should be helping him out of? Only thing I've seen of his in years is a piece in the *Sunday Times* in which he—it seemed to me—quite overbalanced himself in attacking "obscurantism" in modern poetry; I began by agreeing with him and ended by feeling he was impoverishing modern poetry rather than correcting its excesses. But do tell me about those difficulties.

What troubles me about your criticisms is that I feel they are to some extent right. There IS too much categorizing, too much of an air of "this is kosher and this is not, according to the very highest standards," about my essay. As it turned out. But the problem, as I see it, is a lack of any standards at all in USA now, a tendency for the Midcult easily-accessible-good to be substituted for the real good, which is never easily accessible (or not often, anyway). So I think I went too far the other way. But you must try to see the problem I was trying to analyze. Some of your remarks sound as if you don't.

The thing that is most alien to my nature is precisely the esoteric-high-priest attitude. The Tate-Blackmur axis depresses me as much as you—though, and here we get into the really interesting terrain, I must confess that *Hudson Review*, for example, which I suppose is an example of principled Highcultism even more than PR is (politically they are splendidly reactionary), has for years stimulated me more than other quarterlies have. Perhaps my general position— I'm just thinking out loud, fellows—is that I detest highcultism but detest even more low quality; and sometimes you have to choose. What do you think of Max Beerbohm, for instance (a) in general, and (b) as a drama critic?

Well, do let's hear from you—and many thanks for writing. Who are you? Age? Curriculum vita?

To Myron R. Williams [Exeter professor]

April 1, 1961

It was very good to receive here in the heart of Thackeray's Belgravia (that's even our phone exchange) your note about *Parodies*. You're one of the people—not so many of them—I write for, and that the collection gave you enjoyment gives ME ditto. It's sold fantastically well, ten thousand to date I think, which is five times the top sale of any previous book of mine. I can't wait to revise it—already several pearls (as, an Unconscious Parody by Shakespeare—a particularly hollow and Elizabethan-rhetorical passage in Richard III).

. . . As for Mike: he's now out of Harvard (thank God, $2500 plus a year) and—having in his senior year decided that history of art, in which he'd majored, no longer interested him as compared to making movies (God knows what Freudian emulations were involved here—he makes 'em, I review 'em, that kind of thing)—is now employed at $60 a week as casting director for a movie to be made in Puerto Rico by Richard Brook, one of the more highly regarded British stage directors, from William Golding's novel, *Lord of the Flies*. It's an "in" into the movie world that combines intellectual prestige with solid financing, and Mike seems to be doing very well. He's got a lot of flair and is very bright. But I still wish he had maybe become curator of early 19th-century paintings at the Cincinnati Museum. On the other hand he may well be BOTH rich and famous by 30. Anyway, it's his life.

Nick is now a junior at Putney School. It's been a great success—he's worked hard, read all kinds of things, done a lot of things with music, skied, played on the baseball and soccer teams, been elected to the student council, etc. Mike has always been the problem child, Nick the Admirable Crichton. I dare say Nick would have done well at PEA.

Be interesting to see how they come out finally. . . . They are both extraordinary boys, in my unbiased opinion, and I love them very much.

To Mary McCarthy

April 6, 1961

So it's actually happening on the 15th [Mary McCarthy's marriage to James Raymond West, her fourth husband]. Splendid. Of course we'll be there. Just let me know what time on the 15th—also the address of that mairie [town hall], or does every cab driver know?

Thanks very much for your letter—and for the terribly nice things you wrote to Whitney about me, but where do you get that "genially eccentric"? I'm not genial ho ho ho, John Huston is alleged to say; I like Silvers very much, he would be an ideal collaborator, how clever of you to think of him. I'm extremely grateful whatever happens, or doesn't.

On the wedding-breakfast problem, do try for a "workers' wedding" a la *L'Assomoir* (though the Crillon is intriguing, too). As long as it doesn't veer toward the wedding breakfast in *Greed*.

. . . Puzzled by reference to I. Berlin's having done me dirt with Spender before Milan [Conference]. Seem to have forgotten the incident completely. Had always thought of B as a bit of a pal. Though he's shown no eagerness for my company over here.

My state of mind is vastly better than when I saw you. Also my productivity. Though lots of room for improvement, as the report cards used to say, in both. I seem to go through manic-depressive cycles—2 or 3 months of depression and 5 or 6 of mild elation or anyway nondepression—must start keeping track. . . . Thinking of going to Cannes film festival for *Esquire*. Speaking of films, have you seen *Breathless*? A Bout de Souffle, that is; do if not. Couldn't be more different from *L'Aventurra* most ways; just as good though. Also . . . last Monday I joined the Aldermaston March at Whitechapel and walked the last 6 miles to Trafalgar Square. I decided I agreed with them at least 6 miles' worth; also interesting company in the Theater Section—Penelope Gilliatt, the Tynans, Peggy Ashcroft (who passed around a bottle of Vat 69); the admirable-appalling decency and humanity and social discipline of the British—never have 100,000 rebels against the government been less bloodthirsty, and the police so relaxed and nice that if they didn't have those helmets on you'd take them for marchers themselves, except they were cleanshaven—the beard, esp. The fringe beard (which Perelman has described as "the kind once consecrated to old-fashioned sailors and to stage Irishmen") is the oriflamme of insurgent youth here. I could have done with a leeetle more passion even if it had resulted in incidents I should have deplored; something wrong about such a VEG-ETARIAN mob. Also, the beards and slacks and kerchiefs and wild duffle coats tended to become a uniform as one watched them go by (I spent 20 minutes on the sidelines up at Whitechapel before the Theater Section hove in sight), also the faces, while at first each was striking and aesthetic, became types speedily (a young worker or a young city man would have stood out in bohemian contrast but of course there weren't any), and one couldn't tell the Catholic Youth from the Communist Youth except by the banner, nor the Cambridge Peace Society from the Leeds or Birmingham ditto; the only group that stood out was a contingent of Jewish youth, their faces vivid with race, who sang and danced with great verve; nothing vegetarian about THEM! There was some heckling of Frank Cousins when he spoke in Trafalgar Square, by a couple of raucous young men, but then two placid elderly bobbies moved in like Nannies and the hecklers piped down. I really do approve of this English social phlegm, so different from what they were like before Victoria, but I can't help thinking also that something has been leached out of the national character since 1840. The Gordon riots today would mean burning scale models of the prisons, in Hyde Park, with the Fire Dept. standing by.

To Nicola Chiaromonte

April 6, 1961

Distressed to hear from Mary [McCarthy] that you are ill. I wish I could fly down to see you, as much for my own pleasure as yours, but I'm as usual months (years?) behind my journalistic commitments for the *New Yorker* and haven't even dared go to Brighton. Not that I am any model of industry. Just plain neurotic. I now owe the *New Yorker* so much on my drawing account, and I see so little chance of paying it off by production, that I feel like Ivar Kreuger just before the match trust crashed. Fact is, I'm sick to death of doing *New Yorker* "fact pieces" but so far no one has thought of any other, fresher kind of collaboration. I'm 54, or is it 55, I think it is (b. 1906), and I've been explaining things to the public, with molto research, for much too long. Exposition bores me; let them Look It Up themselves, say I. But that's where the $$$$ are in the *New Yorker*, and I owe so many of those $$$$.

Egotistic of me to complain of my lot when you have something really to complain of. Sorry. What filthy luck—though at least you won't have to write fact pieces. Information is the curse of the middle classes.

I've been getting out the *Esquire* column, which I like to do since I make it a rule never to tell the plot (information) as most reviewers for some reason feel they must, and since I can speculate and Pronounce freely and in the first person. My latest edict is that *Breathless* couldn't be more different from *L'A.*—it's closest to the American *Shadows* and the French *Tirez sur le Pianiste*. I also hear that *Zazi dans le Metro* is a good surrealist humor and fantasy; hope to see it when I get to Paris the 15th for Mary's wedding.

I think I told you, with my usual tactfulness, that after 30 years of experiment she has found Mr. Right. Have you met him? Not at all the battered playboy type Bowden had described (though even Bowden, who had special reasons for sourness in addition to the congenital ones, was generous enough to say he rather liked him), but on contrary, a gentle, sweet, responsible family-man type, who may be able to give Mary just the combination of lover and father she needs. I saw a lot of Bowden last summer before I came here, and felt sympathetic for him; he still loves Mary and wants to keep on; or did want to—now he's agreed to the divorce, thank God; yet she was feeling more and more suffocated by the marriage, she tells me, and I can see just why. By the way, did you read that story by David Jackson in the new PR? Very good, I thought, and I wondered if it could be by Bowden; it's about Corso, Venice comes in, and the spirit is Bowdenesque; on the other hand, it's writing in a non-Baroque way which is different from what I've seen of Bowden's prose. On balance, NOT Bowden. . . .

To John Lukacs

June 21, 1961

Forgive my long silence. Due partly to foreign excursions and partly to a disinclination to write—not to you, just to write down words. I seem to have been doing so for such a long time. The excursions were (1) to Paris to assist at the wedding of Mary McCarthy—to a very sweet, gentle, worldly, intelligent career diplomat named James West, who is first secretary of the US Embassy in Warsaw; the wedding itself was simple, in the mairie of the 8th arrondissement (though this does happen to be the most elegant in Paris) with the mayor in tricolor reading out all kinds of precautionary paragraphs from the Code Napoleon, mostly to do with the rights of the spouses if they don't get on, no one can say they weren't warned, also lots on property, all very hardheaded and French; Mary wore a dreamlike woodland green figured chiffon dress with strange hat to match and looked as starry-eyed as if it were her first. Good for her, I say (though you probably want to know if her neck was washed—well, it WAS); this was preceded by v. grand supper at v. chic house of her publishers, French that is, on Rue de Bac, and followed by a luncheon for thirty in the garden of some friend, an American architect, in country near Paris. It's possible to have a good time at such doings, but it does take a little effort; however, I made it and it was Fun. No. 2 excursion was to Cannes Film Festival, where I was less fortunate. In a way it was idyllic—the warmth and sunshine after London were like a blow on the head, and all one had to do was see a lot of movies (no chore for me) and go to various parties of greater or less sumptuousness; the trouble was that the whole operation was so BIG, there were so many PEOPLE there, most parties were closer to a thousand than to five hundred, and one did feel rather lost and massivied; it was like a very populous jungle and God knows who or what you'd run into next; but I don't feel happy in jungles, my ideal life is something more modest and personal. You can read all about it in *Esquire* several months hence. (There was one remarkable film, *Viridiana* by Louis Buñuel (*Un Chien Andalou* and *L'Age d'Or* 30 years ago you remember surrealist and, as they say here, nasty) which was Spain's official entry and turned out to be a very fantastic attack on your church and on its standards, as chastity and charity; he even threw in a visual parody of da Vinci's *Last Supper*, in the course of an orgy; someone in Spain is going to suffer for this, heads will roll;

oddly enough they gave it a golden palm; I agreed on technical grounds, also on emotional—his hatred and scorn of religion is fanatical, and he puts it over—but I think he really went a little too far—the True Church isn't all THAT bad!

Thanks for the news of Mike. He is very fond of you and Helen. (He takes after his father.) He seems to be doing quite well in his chosen career; I was not for it, you know; I thought he should have gone into art history (or art selling) after spending 3 years on it at Harvard; also it seemed more substantial than movies; but, so far, he has been right. At least he's had paying jobs and in his present one he's a success; now he's down in Puerto Rico working with Peter Brook and the others on the actual making of the film; I'm delighted. Brook passed through London recently and called me up to chat about Mike, very nice of him; he was shrewd, said that Mike has terrible work habits, arrives hours late, but is able to make up for it by his energy and enthusiasm and by working till early morning. Yes, he DOES name drop, but I think his snobbishness is venial; he doesn't want to do down outsiders, on contrary he is kind and friendly with them (as, small boys and girls, he's always been remarkably "good" with them); his snobbishness is romantic, he really does adore and admire The Great. Venial, eh? . . .

John, I am simply not in a state of mind to discuss seriously your views on what I should be writing. I feel you are right. But all I can do at present is to keep head above water, or try to. This impasse, this long drawn-out depression must end sometime. I am aware that it exists and that what I now write is not what I should be doing. I look forward to a freer happier future. But at the moment, which seems to have lasted about three years, I'm down here not up there.

I'm grateful for your persistent remarks from the sidelines.[2]

I'm concerned and sympathetic about your emotional problems and joys and troubles. If I may give YOU some advice—don't make any changes until you are sure you cannot exist otherwise—and be very skeptical and coolheaded about it when THAT moment comes. Remember the frying pan and the fire.

As for my plans—I'm leaving London tomorrow, to roam about first in English countryside and then in Italy. My address will be in care of *Encounter*. Sailing back with Nick, my younger son (who joins me in Siena next month), end of August, arriving NYC Sept. 5th.

---

2. John Lukacs, a prolific historian, constantly nagged Macdonald to develop serious discipline and direct his attention to substantial criticism. He greatly admired Macdonald's literary talents but felt that he wasted his time on the politics and culture of the moment.

To Mary McCarthy

July 24, 1961

. . . This is paradise—a large country house, late 18th cent., mile or two out of Siena in midst of the Tuscan landscape which I think most beautiful anywhere, run by Elena Vivante, as great a woman in her way as Hannah [Arendt] who she resembles in vitality and gaiety, and her husband, a dim, odd aesthetic philosopher and gentleman farmer; 15 to 20 borders, English or USA, all people like oneself (intellectuals of one kind or another); like a house party; good feeling prevails, we sit around 45 minutes after lunch, 2 hours after dinner and often rise slightly above small talk. (One of E. Wilson's best qualities is his apathy toward small talk and his flat-footed efforts to lug everybody into big talk.) If you and Jim ever have a vacation, you ought to consider coming here for it. Almost forgot to mention that it is ready-mixed novelistic material, as you might imagine. In fact, there's a woman here, Shirley Hazzard (works for UN in NYC, is English), who has sold 2 or 3 stories to *New Yorker* in last year with a Villa Solaia setting—she's also sold 4 or 5 other ones, is in fact making so much $$$ now as a writer she is thinking of giving up being a bureaucrat. Also Arturo Vivante, one of the sons of the family, has become a standard *New Yorker* writer of late. A nest of singing birds. What YOU could do with this kind of unstructured material is nobody's business! And it really is pleasant, cool, and Siena is always a delight. . . . Among the pg's [paying guests] is Christopher Jencks, Gardner's nephew, very bright, the family brains must have lodged in him, about to become an editor of the *New Republic*. How old one feels! . . . Excuse the dithyramb, of small interest to you. But I do feel, here in Italy (I arrived, in Rome, 3 weeks ago) so much more cheerful and full of beans than I did in England. One is integrated into the landscape (sun so hot, buildings so harmoniously blending into nature, so much charm and beauty everywhere) and never feels lonely, esp. with those Italians everywhere, curious and interested; the most unpromising, even sinister-bandit types break into a lovely smile if you say good day to them (and of course smile first). I was in a low, even desperate mood when I left England, but a few days in Rome changed everything. . . . Gloria is here with me, also Nick (I find him as cheering as Italy; how lucky I am to have such a companionable son). Gloria, Day, and I went for four days to an island about four hours from Rome called Giglio; almost no tourists and even damned few natives; the most clear water and the best beaches one can imagine; by chance we landed in Demo's Hotel, which had no rooms without bathrooms and also very interesting and sophisticated meals; wonderful experience, the whole business. One reason I felt uplifted in Rome was, of course, Nicola and Miriam [Chiaromonte]. We are spending our last ten days in Italy before sailing on the 26th Aug. in Bocca di Magra so as to see some of the C's. (IS THERE ANY CHANCE YOU AND JIM COULD ALSO COME FOR A FEW DAYS AT THE HOTEL SANS FACON BETWEEN AUG. 15 AND AUG. 25? I SUPPOSE NOT BUT I CAN'T THINK OF ANYTHING I'D RATHER HAVE HAPPEN.) I found Nick unchanged, that is good; he looked drawn but he was as vigorous as ever in talking; it is a comfort to know such a person exists; he gave me some good advice on my problems, such as not to drink so much because it makes my belly too big; but the real Chiaromonte touch was—after a dinner I threw at Otello's for the C's, Carmen (whom I have become very fond of), and Mme. Camus (whom I thought v. attractive and simpatico)—to admonish me: "Dwight, you shouldn't DRINK so much." "But I only had a few glasses of wine, Nick." "No. I mean DRINK. All that water. It's very fattening." Maybe he's right. Since arriving in Italy I've drunk very little except wine, and since Nick's warning I've cut down greatly on water. A result is my horrible belly—in London it was like being pregnant, it was one of the reasons I was so depressed, no joke to be overweight; but even this is disappearing in this wonderful land, because I drink v. little except wine and because I've been taking long walks daily w. Nick. . . . Mary, I'm terribly sorry to hear of your slipped disc; is it better? Painful, I believe. What rotten luck. . . . Nick kindly got me a v. handsome Olivetti portable as a present for my Nick, at a discount, via *Tempe Presente*, and so I agreed to write down some Thoughts on Hemingway for them. Which I've been attempting. My main thought is a wonder at how much mileage he got out of a style. And the style today reads as artificially as Euphues; constantly amazing its closeness in rhythm, in simple words, in babytalk repetition to Gertrude Stein. It works fine in trick short stories like "The Killers" and "Hills Like White Elephants," but doesn't work in a novel; even *A Farewell to Arms* is now largely unreadable. . . .

To John Updike

September 25, 1961

I've been meaning to thank you for your extremely kind and intelligent review of my Parody book. Certainly the most interesting, to me, that has appeared [*New Yorker*, September 16, 1961]. I have a few queries and comments.

Think you give too much credit to book's format; cover is indeed good (you ought to see how the cover of the British ed. tried to cozen us into premature jollity—and it's Faber and Faber, that awesome house; I protested but in vain) and the layout inside is dignified; but paper on first ed. was shiny and hard like a geology textbook, the color of cover dismal, and treatment of authors of parodies and authors parodied not consistent. And there were LOTS more typos than the one you found in your Kerouac piece. (By the way, didn't we send you proofs? And what WAS it?) . . .

Agree that the conscious self-parodies were feeble, except for Faulkner's (THAT was a little discovery I'm proud of), but don't see your objection to the unconscious category—much as I admire Dr. J's noble style (and Dr. J, have been reading Boswell), I do think it a bit much on glass. And why is any "suspension of sympathy" needed to enjoy a parody?

Wish you'd included the two items by W. B. Scott in your list of things new to you—I think they're as funny as anything in the book but no reviewer has singled them out, or almost none; delighted you saw Houghton's modest but solid worth.

Aren't you asking Beerbohm to be major when he wanted to be minor? I think trouble with most authors is they're much *too* ambitious. I'm grateful to B for doing a few small things I can reread with pleasure. Nor do I think he belittled nonlittleness in others—in fact you yourself note he embraces "with something like love" the total personalities of his victims. Or perhaps I agree with his sneers at the writers he disliked, like Kipling (though how talented R.K. was? And how vulgar!). Maybe you've put your finger on why I never liked *Zuleika Dobson*.

Your remarks on Joyce as parodist are extremely good—"antic succession of loose-fitting costumes." I hesitated about including the "Oxen of the Sun" parodies because they aren't really parodies but as you say "acts of conquest," and so are neither accurate nor funny, like Beerbohm. But they were so good as pastiche (and as Joyce) that I decided to put them in—also Joyce had to be represented, since his whole oeuvre is parodic in a way. And once in, the reader's enjoyment wd. be increased by identifying them, even at cost of distortion. Sort of a little parlor game. I think you were a bit precious here in your caviling.

On p. 170 don't get your point about parody "subsiding into literary criticism" as the "Victorian concensus disintegrated." (1) Parody was literary criticism from the Smith brothers all through the Victorian age; (2) Lear and Carroll weren't parodists, they wrote burlesque, quite a different thing (see my note on Carroll, where I explain also why such parodies as he did write, for he did write some unlike Lear, don't strike me as very good). And why "subsided" into literary criticism? I'd say *rose* etc.

I do wish you'd explain the last 3 sentences. Nobody I've asked has been able to. How was a serious lit exclusively serious in the Victorian age, what with Dickens, James, Huckleberry Finn, Trollope—and there's a lot of comedy, if not humor, in Dostoevsky—and also Gogol's *Dead Souls*. I agree that, from Joyce through Bellow, Mailer and Nabokov and McCarthy there is a strong humorous element in serious writing now, but whyever does this mean that humor is now "merely trivial . . . recreational . . . distracting"? How can one have too much humor (or too much any good thing)? You imply it's not needed now, in some way. O reason not the need, first. And second, I don't understand your whole notion of humor being less needed sometimes than others, or indeed needed at all. What's wrong with the trivial, recreational, and distractional? And with detachment and dandyism also? I see this goes back to your dissatisfaction with Beerbohm. One doesn't enjoy humor, or art, because it's important, useful, and concentrating, to turn your adjective around, but just because it's pleasurable in and for itself. But I'm sure you agree with those truisms. Yet you seem to be saying the opposite. And your last sentence, forgive me, sounds just a little priggish. Would you apply it, for instance, to Robert Benchley—there's someone whom I would gladly trade for a dozen existential playwrights plus three shortstops. Or rather the other way around.

Don't answer this unless you feel like it and have time. Or perhaps next time you're in the city you could drop into my office here, 18th floor, and we could chat. I'd like to meet you. Thanks very much, by the way, for sending me—or was it your publisher?—*Rabbit Run*. It finally reached me in London. An extraordinary performance, I hear the reviews were stupid. Not surprised. Mary McCarthy, by the way, is a great fan of it, and of *Poorhouse Fair*—so I learned from a MS of interview with her that is to appear in the *Paris Review*. She lays about her and scarcely a reputation is left standing except yours.

P.S. Dutch Schultz's dying words, I suppose it was bad taste and also hard-hearted of me to put them in. I've never been strong on taste, I rather like being in bad taste often. And I look at people I don't know abstractly (also some I do), and I never thought of Dutch as a dying man until I read your perfectly justified objection. He only died in the newspapers for me. To be fair to myself, I shouldn't mind if some one used MY dying words as I did his.

To Arthur Schlesinger, Jr.

November 3, 1961

I am glad you share my concern about the Sobell business, though I knew you would. But I'm really puzzled by your remark, "I do not believe that Mrs. Sobell's activities have advanced her husband's case." Aside from one time I said a few words at a meeting, I haven't been in close touch with her and her committee. But I think it natural—and commendable—that a wife would work hard to get her husband released from an unjustly long prison sentence, and I approve of people kicking up a row in such circumstances. Maybe she's been too obstreperous—that's what you imply—but the line between what's enough of a row and what's too much is not always easy to tread. And, from my slight experience of governments and bureaucracies, I'd say it's better to go too far than not far enough. Anyway, what did you mean by your remark?[3]

Also, can you tell me anything about your negotiations with the Attorney General? Probably not. But is there any hope of Sobell's being released in the near future? . . .

Speaking of films, have you seen that remarkable TV hour-long documentary called "Primary," about the Kennedy-Humphrey battle in Wisconsin? By filmmakers here. I think they are onto something big—using mobile sound and camera to get the most intimate, unstaged kind of reality—most exciting film, technically, I've seen since *Breathless* and *Shadows*. And don't miss Lumet's movie of Arthur Miller's *A View from the Bridge*—the one US film I've seen since returning that is not bad. Not bad at all. Pretty good, in fact.

To the Editor, *Esquire*

November 20, 1961

Bully for Gore Vidal's eloquent exposé of the House Un-American Activities Committee, but who's this "Harry Truman" he quotes as calling it "the most un-American thing in America"? If it's the one who used to be president, then I'd say that this Harry had nerve with him when he attacked HUAC—and Mr. Vidal has either his nerve with him or his memory not with him when he quotes him on the subject.

For on March 22, 1947, this Mr. Truman issued an executive order for the investigation of the political beliefs and activities of every one of the then 2,200,000 employees of the federal government and further instructed his attorney general to draw up a list of "totalitarian, fascist, communist, and subversive groups." A Loyalty Board was set up which could (and did) purge any federal employee it decided was disloyal, without giving him the opportunity to confront his accusers. (This last charming gimmick, after years of service, was recently dishonorably retired by our Supreme Court.) Attorney general's "blacklist" at one time included both the main Trotskyist groups; I went to Washington six or seven years ago, along with Norman Thomas and several others, to testify as to the nontotalitarian and non-Communist nature of the Shachtmanite group, of which I was once a member; unsuccessfully.

Granted that HUAC has a longer and more consistent record of disservice to civil liberties than Harry Truman, still it seems to me tactless of Mr. Vidal to

---

3. Schlesinger may have been referring to the practice of Mrs. Sobell and the defense committee to hawk left-wing literature and sectarian tracts at meetings held to raise money for his defense.

quote the latter in such a context. In the house of the hanged, you don't talk about rope.

To Stephen Spender

January 12, 1962

. . . The old rumors about *Encounter*—and the CCF—being partly subsidized by State Department (or even CIA) funds keep cropping up. Recently I had an encounter (put a question to someone who should know and the same one wouldn't say yes or no) which rather shook me. Say it ain't so, Stephen. If there is any such money involved, I think it must be made public, or rather that it ought to be.

To Hoyt Fuller [black writer]

March 7, 1962

So you wonder where I was in "all those dreary years" when Negroes were being humiliated, etc. Well, I was editing and publishing a little magazine called *Politics*, one of whose regular departments was called FREE AND EQUAL and was devoted to exposing racial discrimination, in particular in our armed forces. This was 1944–1949 when Jim Crow was the rule there; we had a little committee, interracial, called the Lynn Committee, which you have probably never heard of, and we did what we could—this was before Truman began to change things—to publicize the shameful Jim Crowing in the army. Conrad Lynn, now a prominent Negro attorney and an all-out fighter for Negro rights, was our counsel; his brother Winifred, who was penalized in the army because of his race, was the one the committee was named for. Also I have been for many years a contributor to CORE—just today sent them $50. If this is racial prejudice, I hope you find many more such prejudiced persons.

Do have a look at *Politics* in the library.

As for my reference to [Harry] Belafonte, I've looked it up and find that I brought it in because I am writing about Bergman, and Belafonte had asked him to direct a film about Pushkin starring him (B.). And I thought his refusal on the ground that Mr. B. is not a genius admirable because I too think Mr. B is far from a genius—as are many white performers. So I can't see how you can see this as dragged in from more "moldering spite."

I'm trying to be reasonable, but you do put a strain on one.

The enclosed was sent me recently by the author—it appears in the current issue of *Show* magazine. Please read it and let me have your reactions. Mr. Holder makes the point I've been making in *Esquire* only even more strongly—he can speak, as a Negro, with a freedom that few whites can use—namely that Negroes are grown-ups now, big boys, and don't need the kind of condescending head-patting that you, for some reason, think is a mark of a non-racially-prejudiced white person.

More in sorrow than anger, I assure you. . . .

To Geoffrey Holder

March 7, 1962

Thanks very much for sending me your brave and witty "The Awful Afro Trend." You really go to town! I do hope it does some good. Glad to see a slight bow toward *Purlie Victorious*, which I liked enormously, one of the funniest plays I've seen in years, and when Negroes can kid themselves *and* the white supremacists, it is a healthy sign of growing up. (I feel the same way about James Baldwin's essays. And about him—one of the most interesting, lively minds around.) You pack so much thought into every paragraph, and wit. Thanks for writing it.

To the Editor, *Show* Magazine

March 7, 1962

Thank you for printing Geoffrey Holder's witty and courageous "The Awful Afro Trend." It should be read by every white "friend of the Negro"—and by many Negroes too.

As Mr. Holder makes brilliantly clear, it is not only the white supremacists who reduce the Negro to a second-class citizen. His liberal "friends" accomplish the same end by opposite means, by applying to Negro writers and performers a standard more lenient than they would apply to the work of whites. This is condescending and, as Mr. Holder points out, has a bad effect on the recipients of such fatherly pattings-on-the-head.

The insistence of people like Mr. Holder on rejecting such special consideration—I might add James Baldwin, also Ossie Davis, whose *Purlie Victorious* contains the immortal line, "You're a disgrace to the Negro profession"—shows, as the sit-ins and the freedom rides have, that a growing number of Negroes are asserting themselves as full citizens, grown-ups who don't want or need any special treatment. Bravo!

To Martin Panzer [*Esquire* reader]

March 9, 1962

Thank you very much for your letter, and for the decent and reasonable tone. I see what you mean. Agreed I would not have felt it my duty, in Rome when Christians were being martyred, to muckrake Jesus. Of course The Truth should not be spoken at all times. One would have to be a monster of virtue, a

Robespierre, devoid of human feeling (and even common sense) to do so at certain times; also it would be far more immoral than lying. The question is, however, ARE the Jews and Negroes in USA today being "fed to the lions"? Agreed the Jews were under Hitler, but here, now, anti-Semitism seems to me not a clear and present danger—the very horror of what the Nazis did has caused anti-Semitism to be frowned on now—my own experience has been that danger is other way, but I said all that. . . . As for the Negroes, they are certainly discriminated against most shamefully here and now, BUT since 1945 they have been winning, the tide is running in their favor (mostly as result of their own efforts, but also because of that wonderful US Supreme Court under Warren), and my historical calculation is that they are now grown-up enough, and secure enough, to take their place among just people, human beings like all the rest of us, and with the privilege of not being babied or head-patted because of their skin-color. . . . In short, I simply cannot see that it is now here "a matter of life and death" for Negroes and Jews to be exempted from the ordinary give and take of criticism, etc., and I can see damage (to THEM) from continuation of this attitude. Fifty years ago there were hundreds of lynchings of Negroes every year, I mean public affairs not private murders, now there hasn't been one for a long time. As for anti-Semitism, its only public expression is in the propaganda of the crackpot right. I think we can move on to the next stage and admit Jews and Negroes to the adult, normal community of human beings—as the Indians are moving out of the reservations and ceasing to be "wards of the government." But, like everything in life, this has its drawbacks—Jews can't both be exempt wards, protected children, AND also free citizens; and if they are the latter, then they must grin and bear it when a movie critic points out that the Bible says something different from *Ben Hur*. It was 2,000 years ago, for God's sake!

Thanks again for writing. Your cites from Zuckerman (who died recently, as you perhaps know) didn't seem to me very damning. He was too optimistic, granted, but his illusion was a generous and noble one.

To Janetta Somerset Ridgely [editorial writer, *Baltimore Sun*]

March 16, 1962

Your letter—and your editorial—miss the point of the objection raised to Webster's 3 [*Webster's Third New International Dictionary*] by my review, and by all the other reviews I've seen. No sensible person objects to a language changing—I say as much several times in the review. Nor is there any objection to slang—I often use it in my own formal writing. But to say that a usage (as "like" for "as") will become standard English is not the same as to say it *is* standard; similarly a word like "jerk" for a worthless person may become standard but has not yet so become. I did not object to 3's including "like" for "as" or "jerk" for "worthless person"; I didn't object to anything 3 included (in fact I praised 3 for putting in so much slang). The trouble is that 3 accepts them as standard usages (that is, doesn't attach a warning note or label). This is just wrong—that is, if you admit, as 3 does, that there IS such a concept as standard English. The language hasn't changed that much and may never change that much. That large numbers of Americans use "like" for "as" is not in itself conclusive; the majority doesn't always win out because the minority (teachers, lexicographers, writers) has some influence on language—on change too—if only because they are experts and authorities (and taken as such by the majority, or at least by the more ambitious members of the majority). If there were not authorities on usage, as you and R. Gove halfheartedly advocate (halfheartedly since your own letter and editorial are written in standard English, and his dictionary does make a great many authoritative discriminations), the language would degenerate into a kind of pidgin English where no one would know just what someone else meant. Granted that the French Academy makes no sense and hasn't for centuries in its purist attempts—Dr. Johnson remarked on its ineffectuality and, a sensible man, disclaimed any ambition in his dictionary to "fix" the language forever—and also that 2 would have admitted the new common meaning of "careen," I see no reason to go to the other extreme as you and R. Gove want to do (although, as I say, halfheartedly). There's a position between the pedantic purist (and by the way Fowler seems to me not to be that but on the contrary a most intelligent and stimulating analyst of the living language) and the abandoning of all standards.

Have a look at an article by me, "The Great American Massacre," which will appear in *Life International*, in a few weeks.

To Mr. Hook [editor of an English unnamed magazine]

April 30, 1962

The question of commitment was settled for me in the thirties when we battled on *Partisan Review* on the subject against the Communists—and when I read Sartre's absurdities on the subject. I think it is a long-settled issue, and it seems a cultural lag that you people in England are still kicking it around. Therefore no 1500 words from me. Twelve, if you want to use them: "Anyone who thinks the artist should be committed is a damned fool."

To Roy Newton [English Department, Ferris Institute, Big Rapids, Michigan]

May 15, 1962

Thank you for your letter of March 13 about my dictionary review. Glad you liked it, afraid I don't at all agree w. you about 3's including all those scatological words; that is, I favor it, don't see how a serious unabridged could not do so;

sorry they had to leave out *cunt* you bowdlerized so effectively the words on your enclosed pages that I couldn't tell what they were most of the time—surely even a bishop in 1962 could confront them without a heart attack! On "twat"— was it not Browning who innocently thought it meant "some part of a nun's garb" and who wrote a line "cowls and twats" which has become famous? If so then 2 is wrong on it, and 3 is right. Thanks for your letter—no had not heard about Merriam stating that OED was out of print—what nerve!

To Gordon C. Zahn [pacifist activist]

May 22, 1962

Thank you very much for sending me your article ["The Private Conscience and Legitimate Authority," *Commonweal*, March 30, 1962], which I think is a much-needed corrective to my own 1945 piece. Needed now, that is—you are aware, as you write your article, that what was necessary then is not so much now—or rather that another truth now needs to be stated. I agree that individuals are responsible for their actions and that it is disgusting when an Eichmann (or a Keitel) says, "My guilt lies in my obedience." In fact I touched on this point in my essay when I quoted, I think from Hannah Arendt's article in some Jewish magazine, the bewildered cry of the paymaster in the death camp: "But what have I done?" That peoples are not responsible does not mean that NO-BODY (except Hitler or Truman) is responsible. Did you see the later correspondence in *Politics* on my article, by the way? It touched on this point. If you didn't, let me know and I'll see if I can find an extra copy or copies of those issues.

And speaking of Hannah Arendt—have you sent her a copy of your article? If not, please do—mention me—she is at 370 Riverside Drive, NYC. She is now working on an article for this magazine on the Eichmann trial, which she attended, and I'm sure she would like to read your article.

Your Austrian peasant is a great man—such evidence (and how did you find it) makes one proud to be human, since such people are also human. Do you have a factual record of his trial, and his confrontations with those chaplains? If so, you should publish it in the *Commonweal* or elsewhere. It make one proud. . . . I think I should write a letter to *Commonweal*—hope it won't be too late.

To the Editor, *Commonweal*

May 23, 1962

I've only just read Gordon Zahn's excellent article in your March 30th issue, "The Private Conscience and Legitimate Authority," and I hope it's not too late to add my congratulations to the others you must have received.

As Mr. Zahn notes, when I published "The Responsibility of Peoples" in 1945, the world had only learned a few months earlier the scope of the Nazi death camps for the extermination of the Jewish people, and normally decent and sensible people were beginning to talk about punishing the Germans en masse for the crimes they had, it was alleged, collectively committed. But things have changed, and now I agree with Mr. Zahn that we must combat almost the opposite thesis: that no Germans except a handful of top Nazis were morally responsible for the Hitlerite atrocities. . . . But the two are united by a disregard for what I think is the only basis for moral judgment, namely, that the individual is responsible only for his own specific actions, as I argued, and that, as Mr. Zahn does, he *is* responsible for these. The same kind of fuzzy thinking that tried to indict the German people as a whole for actions only a small minority took, or—again taking the individual as a mere cell of the body politic— the fiction that an Eichmann was "only obeying orders" and that the responsibility for his atrocious actions must be put on his superiors, who also were only obeying orders, etc., until finally only Hitler (or Stalin or, in the case of dropping the atom bomb, Truman) is left to bear the guilt.

No, all Germans were not guilty, but some were, those who knowingly played a part in the Nazi atrocities, and that includes State Secretary Dr. Goebbels. In my essay I quoted from a remarkable article by Hannah Arendt in the *Jewish Frontier* of January 1945, from an interview an American correspondent had with an official of a death camp who has been captured by the Russians:

Q. Did you kill people in the camp? A. Yes.

Q. Did you poison them with gas? A. Yes.

Q. Did you bury them alive? A. It sometimes happened.

Q. Did you personally help to kill people? A. Absolutely not. I was only paymaster in the camp.

Q. What did you think of what was going on? A. It was bad at first, but we got used to it. People can get used to anything. This is the most depressing thing I know about human nature.

Q. Do you know the Russians will hang you? A. (bursting into tears) Why should they? What have I done?

"These words ring true," I commented. What had he done indeed? Simply obeyed orders and kept his mouth shut. It was what he had not done that shocks our moral sensibilities. . . . It is not the lawbreaker we must fear today so much as he who obeys the law, and the Germans have always been noted for their deep respect for law and order.

Moral responsibility is an individual affair and cannot be shifted either to the collectivity or to the boss, as that admirable peasant Mr. Zahn quotes understood and as his bishop and his chaplain did not. (They had told him to obey the law). It is exhilarating that such people have existed, and let us hope still exist. That Austrian peasant, insisting on the primacy of his own conscience against the threats of the state and the sophistries of his church, almost makes one believe that God's creation of mankind—or was it the Devil's?—may not have been such a bad idea after all.

To James Sledd [lexicographer]

May 29, 1962

. . . I wish you'd reread the first para. of your May 18 letter. What you seem to be saying is that I should be ashamed of myself because my article has been influential in academic-intellectual circles ("friends of mine in 4 major universities," you write reproachfully, have been "told what to think" by me). Now honestly. The alternatives you present are to write an ineffective article or to accept guilt as the leader of a lynch mob—really, as a leader. But I wrote my piece after much thinking and research, because I was (and still am) convinced that Webster 3 is one more example of the debasement of standards in our cultural life (others are the RSV Bible and the Adler-Hutchins Great Books, both of which I've dealt with).[4] I began with no parti pris, in fact I liked Gove when I spent most of a day with him in Springfield early in the course of my research, and I am convinced he is a sincere and even idealistic lexicographer. Which still doesn't prevent him from being, alas, more than a bit of a dope. In your College English review, which somebody sent me lately, you write, "the serious works of serious scholars should be seriously judged." Why? Or rather, have you never encountered serious works etc. which are, on critical examination, absurd and therefore should be kidded—in a serious way, of course? Also, I think my review was serious, and I can't help it if I get a few satiric ideas every now and then. You also cite the fact that they spent $3,500,000 on it as "sobering." Why, again? That's peanuts for say, Henry Luce, and so we should take his magazines and books seriously?

On para. 2 of your May 18 letter: I've looked up your objections and find: EGO—you're right and can't think how I muffed it. MASSES—does say "pl of Mass," as I wrote, and true if one reads through whole entry, quite long, on MASS one finds a reference to PROLETARIAT, but why not put its chief meaning in

---

4. Macdonald referred to these cultural essays—on the Revised Standard Version of the Bible, the Great Books, Webster's 3rd International Dictionary, and several others—as his "reactionary essays." In his "mass-cult" and "mid-cult" essays he showed utter contempt for the popular culture. Although he was returning to the political barricades, denouncing obsessive anti-communism, supporting the Sobell defense, giving lectures on the viability of anarchism, he was also building a strong defense of cultural traditions. He was beginning in these years to describe himself as a "conservative anarchist."

first time; stupid to conceal things; a dict. is supposed to be useful, not an exercise in research—see what I wrote about Adler's Syntopicon?

COLLOQUIAL *is* a "warning label," it warns you not to use it in formal discourse—and your own review objects to their dropping it so, except for scoring a debater's point, don't see why you object to my accurate description. Webster 2 does not call AIN'T standard English at bottom of p. 111; it calls it "colloquial." Don't see relevance of point re AREN'T since I didn't raise point in my review—but there too it is labeled "colloquial" and not "standard"—if you say that "colloquial" is the same as standard, I ask why they had two categories, and also refer you to your own College English review. As for Gove's five points, he DID say they were basic ones of structural linguistics (as did an earlier book, published by some prestigious academic establishment) and I did say they were "reasonable" and I DID make it clear, earlier in the sentence, that I'm not a die-hard "purist," and so I don't see what your objection is.

I'm not, of course, against English dictionaries and English linguistics generally, and therefore see no reason I should confess to your "innocent friends" that I am. (They must be not only innocent but also stupid, in your terms, to have been taken in by my spiel. In fact you sound paranoiac—conspiracies everywhere, people who should Know Better being seduced by glib arguments, which you assume, as paranoiacs do, are not sincerely meant by the author—otherwise why should I feel guilty because my arguments have convinced people?)

Sorry—got sore. But you do put a strain on one's reasonableness. Did you read my *Life International* piece? As I wrote you, that expressed more fully my ideas about language in general and English in particular. You'll disagree, I'm sure, since I say there that the chief danger to English today is not from the vulgarians but from the academic establishment. But at least it might make clear to you that I'm not "against English dictionaries and English linguistics" and that I'm fighting for the survival of English as a language that can communicate efficiently and pleasingly. "Both the dictionary and the language it records are likely to survive the keening critics," you write in College English, but it's precisely you academic misusers of structural linguistics who seem to me to be the enemies of language. The question is not whether S.L. is valid or not, since on p. 157 I say that "for the scientific study of language" it is "superior" to the approach of the "old grammarians," but whether a literal application of its precepts to such things as teaching and dictionary-making is a good idea. So let's have no more nonsense about my being "against" dictionaries and linguistic studies. . . .

Sorry to sound irritable—but you do irritate me.

To President Kennedy

June 15, 1962

I think you ought to pardon Junius Scales [a Southern Communist from a well-to-do family, imprisoned under the Smith Act]. His six-year prison sentence seems to me excessive in any case, and in this particular one (considering he had resigned from the Communist Party in 1957) monstrous. You can do something about this injustice, and it is your duty to do so.

When two federal judges in Scales's home state plus 9 or 12 jurors who convicted him plus such impeccable anti-Communists as Grenville Clark and Sidney Hook all support the petition for clemency, there would seem to be prima facie evidence that something is wrong. My own hostility to communism dates back to the thirties (such a stance was not then fashionable in liberal circles) as your assistant, Arthur Schlesinger, Jr., can tell you. But this sort of persecution seems to me vindictive and destructive of the very democratic principles which turned me against communism 25 years ago.

To Ernest Callenbach, Editor, *Film Quarterly*

n.d., June 1962

Thanks for showing me your defense of Cinema 16. Yes, there *are* a few things I'd like to say.

I agree there should be a "showcase," as Cinema 16 horribly puts it, for the younger, noncommercial filmmakers. But the display in this particular showcase is cluttered and ineffective because Amos Vogel, though a very nice fellow, can't tell junk from gems. Such a showcase is worse than none because it alienates the more intelligent moviegoers from the art film. (Look how bitter I've become!) Time was, years ago, when I made my pilgrimage regularly to the Fashion Arts Auditorium, but I finally came to agree with Pauline Kael that after an evening of art films, one often wants to go to a movie. So, as you guessed, I have seen few Cinema 16 programs of late. However, Amos was kind enough to send me the program for the last ten years, so I did have a general idea of what they have been offering. And, specifically, I did review the four new (as against revivals) feature films they offered this season. I'm bewildered by your plea: "What Macdonald is in a position to give, if he feels like it, is sensible criticism of Cinema 16's films when they are interestingly good or maddeningly bad." That's just what I did apropos its four new features this season— *The Sin of Jesus, Burial of the Sun, Time of the Heathen*, and *Guns of the Trees*—all of which struck me, for reasons given at length, as "maddeningly bad." Perhaps you thought my criticism not "sensible," but then you should have stated why and defended those films. Instead, you defend merely the general idea of Cinema 16. But the general is always easy to be charitable about; it's when the specific is in question that the problem arises.

The closest you come to the specific seems to concede my point: "As for the 'experimenters,' or the young filmmakers of whose unimaginative *weltschmerz* Macdonald makes rightful fun, they are the only ones we have who are working outside the sponsored film or Hollywood; they are not yet very good, but they are part of our cultural scene, like our painters and composers and playwrights—who do not present a terribly inspiring picture, either. . . ." So the makers of these four films are "unimaginative" and "not yet very good" but since they are "part of our cultural scene" and also "the only ones we have" trying to do something serious, we should be respectful. I don't see why the "yet" implies they will be better later on, but when you eat a steak you are interested in its present, not its future. Nor are Frank, Mekas, Emshwiller, et al. "The only ones we have"—I've praised other, better American art films such as *Shadows*, *Pull My Daisy, The Connection, The Savage Eye*—and have given Cinema 16 credit for showing the first two. But even if they were the only ones we have, I'd still not agree. Critical attitudes in this country have been much too tolerant, as for instance the relaxation of standards in the face of the absurdly inflated vogue for the New York School of drip 'n dribble painting. The *New York Times'* John Canady has been a welcome exception—and look at the going-over he's been given by the faithful—on much the same grounds as you advance for tolerating the noninspiring stuff that Cinema 16 "showcases," as their publicity would say. It's like "progressive" education—I put it in quotes because it should be "regressive"—which has been so permissive that the brighter pupils are discouraged because they are lost in the ruck of mediocrity. Similarly the Cinema 16 approach is encouraging only to the untalented, who should be firmly discouraged, and is depressing and disorienting to the gifted, of whom there are always damned few in any age or art. A generation or two ago the situation was different; then the acceptance, by the critics and the public, of original, pioneering work in all fields was grudging and overcautious. But now it seems to me the opposite is true, and almost anything that has the slightest pretensions to being "serious" is given A for effort, and one is considered immoral and not a good fellow if one points out that a movie can be both serious and a mess. What we need is more birth-control in every branch of art; the young should be discouraged on principle, since most of them are as ungifted as their elders have proved to be; in fact, I really think critics should judge the art film by the same standards they judge the Hollywood film; at least that's what I try to do. . . .

To Mary McCarthy

June 27, 1962

. . . By the oddest coincidence, I was just finishing a (highly unfavorable) review of *Pale Fire* for PR when I got the NR with your lengthy fanfare. Couldn't have been more surprised. I felt it necessary, because you had gone so *very* far and because you do carry a lot of weight, to tack on a final paragraph taking issue with you. What bothered me most was the fact it was for about 14/15ths much the same kind of exegesis and interpretation that poor Dr. Kinbote went in for, and that only in that tiny last paragraph did you make any value judgments, that is, get down to literary criticism. I'm also bothered by such a head-on collision between your taste and mine. I hope you are too. More democratic if so.

Saw Nabokov other night at a very plush party on top of the Time-Life Bldg., champagne at every table, after premiere of *Lolita*. He was very cordial and genial since all he knows so far is that I admired greatly *Lolita*. The movie by the way is good but quite fails to get the spirit of the book.

To John Keliher [Twain scholar and critic of Macdonald's piece on Twain in the *New Yorker*, April 4, 1960, and reprinted in *Against the American Grain*, 1962]

July 6, 1962

. . . God knows where you got the idea I was criticizing Twain for making $$$ with his writings. As you point out, I'm a professional writer myself and get as much $$$ as I can for what I write. Nothing wrong in that. My objection—and Van Wyck Brooks in the *Ordeal*—is that Twain became "respectablized" when he married Olivia, that he came to accept the values of the rich and genteel of his day. Entirely different. Dickens made lots of $$$ from his novels but he was never castrated creatively as Twain was because he didn't accept the bourgeois values. *Hard Times*, a late book, is his most explicit attack on them.

. . . Yes, I'm sure my disappointment in Twain's *Autobiography* was not because I expected him to Tell All and give a Freudian psychoanalysis of himself. (What an idiot you must think me!) I brought in his failure to reveal himself because he himself advanced it, and I give quotes, as the reason d'être of his autobiography. But I gave many other reasons for thinking the book trivial, and except for parts I noted, boring. . . . You accuse me of the most stupid and superficial viewpoint (as that I really think ALL can be told about any person, that I don't realize the deep unconscious motives that of course account for most of any creative efforts, etc); but that ALL cannot be said, that the deeps cannot be plumbed, this doesn't mean that a lot more than Twain got down on paper cannot be expected. Likewise with your thinking it a problem for me, in the essay, to explain how Twain could have written so many bad things and also some very good things, the jester and philosopher, etc.—now really, the whole essay is about that problem—maybe you don't accept my attempts to elucidate it, but to think I'm not aware of it! In fact this is THE great Mark Twain problem, as the literature shows.

In general my approach to art and letters has always been aesthetic rather than philosophical. Ultimately aesthetic discrimination involves values, and values depend on a general way of looking at things which is ultimately philosophical, or anyway based on philosophical assumptions. But a work of art has its own logic and structure, its own use of terms, on which I think it must be judged. That's how I did judge Twain's work—and found it mostly verbose, coarse-grained, and commonplace when it was not vulgar. You approach it in too general, philosophical terms, it seems to me, and therefore read into it merits which are not actually, concretely there.

To T. S. Eliot

July 7, 1962

I don't know whether you have seen the enclosed review of mine (of the new Webster's unabridged dictionary). It's made some stir, almost all favorable to my viewpoint, and I think the subject at least will interest you.

The other day I received, from someone in Cambodia of all places who had read my review, the following verses from your Little Gidding, and I wonder if I might have your permission to quote them in an addition I am making to the version of the review that will appear in a collection of my essays Random House is putting out this fall under the title *Against the American Grain*? I should be most grateful, Your lines beautifully express the approach to language which the editors of that dictionary do *not* have. The verses are:

> Since our concern was speech, and speech impelled us
> To purify the dialect of the tribe
> And urge the mind to aftersight and foresight
>   . . . And every phrase
> And sentence that is right (where every word is at home,
> Taking its place to support the others,
> The word neither diffident nor ostentatious,
> An easy Commerce of the old and new,
> The common word exact without vulgarity,
> The formal word precise but not pedantic,
> The complete consort dancing together)
> Every phrase and every sentence is an end and a beginning.

I do hope you will consent—the lines express just what I mean.

STEINBERG

To Saul Steinberg

September 4, 1962

Just back from vacation to find the attached in an issue I missed. I do think it very bad taste on your part to make copy from a friend's arguments with his wife—at least I cannot believe that the figure at the left end of the sofa, so angularly logical is not me, any more than the quiveringly passionate figure he is embroiled with is not Gloria. The somnolently intuned figure in the easy chair is of course Geoffrey [Hellman].

To W. H. [Ping] Ferry [Ford Foundation executive]

August 9, 1962

. . . If you're so interested in religion, you might like a look at a new book by a brilliant friend of mine named Joel Carmichael, . . . *The Death of Jesus*, which Macmillan is putting out this fall. He argues it really was the Romans whodunit, just as M.M. claimed in *Ben Hur*. Still, a remarkable bit of close reasoning, or maybe special pleading.

Warm congratters on your attack on J. Edgar H.—you're entirely right, as you know—he knows almost as little about communism as McCarthy did. And how shameful (and sad) the Atty. Gen. felt obliged to cover up for him. I bet he agrees with you, but they had either to accept J. Edgar or fight him, and once they'd put the albatross around their neck, they have to say it's a beautiful necklace, really. Sad—and shameful—like much else in way of dirty corners this vigorous broom has avoided. How timid JFK seems compared to FDR.

Have just finished a long review article, 6,000 words or so, on your former employee Mike Harrington's excellent little book on poverty in USA. There's another thing JFK has done almost nothing about.

Only other thing you "ought to know about" my recent activities is that Random House in Oct. is publishing my major essays, mostly cultural, of last 10 years under title: *Against the American Grain*. Ford Foundation piece not included, since it was already in book form. But the Great Books review IS, and how, lotsa laughs. Esp. the appendix re the recent selling campaign. Who says you can take a horse to water but you can't make him drink? That new sales genius has shown this to be untrue. What I specially like is the idea of selling the set on time like a washing machine. How can the public fail to respect culture when it is put in the class of TV sets and automobiles? . . .

To Arthur Schlesinger, Jr.

October 17, 1962

You've probably seen the enclosed column by Jimmy Wechsler on the Junius Scales case, but I send it on the chance. It reminds me that on June 15th last I wrote a letter to President Kennedy about the Scales case.

"You can do something about this injustice, and it is your duty to do so," I wrote, somewhat tactlessly—though power implies moral responsibility. "This sort of persecution seems to me vindictive and destructive of the very democratic principles which turned me against communism 25 years ago."

I have received no answer, not even a form letter. Does this mean the President considers me a crackpot, or my letter that of a crackpot? Or that he thinks the issue so clear that Scales's six-year prison sentence is so obviously just that it's not worth taking notice of a contrary opinion? If neither, then I really would like an answer.

And what do you yourself think about the Scales business?

P.S. There's a parole board hearing to consider a parole for Morton Sobell on October 30th and I've agreed to testify for him at it—C. P. Snow will be there too, the Sobell Committee tells me. I also think, as you know, that the President should have consulted Sobell's thirty-year sentence which seems all out of proportion to his crime. Your main reaction to my letter on that case was that Mrs. Sobell was making a nuisance of herself. Is that also your feeling about Mrs. Scales? I hope Gloria makes a nuisance of herself if I get sent up for a stretch.

To the Editor, *The New Republic*

October 24, 1962

In his reply to Salvador de Madariaga's "Appeal to America," Louis Halle summarily sets down some general principles as justification for our government cosseting the Franco regime in Spain.

"The rule in international affairs has been to accept the existence of a foreign government, whether one approves of it or not, where it appears to be accepted by the people under it (who have the primary responsibility). . . . The best (Washington) can do is to judge the general acceptance, and this only by the absence of popular rebellion on any significant scale. The overwhelming majority of the Spanish people may abhor their present government . . . but they accept it in submitting to its authority. Washington can hardly refuse to accept what they themselves accept. . . . Being courteous to one's ideological opponents is often a necessity of international politics. Otherwise this inflammable world might quickly burn up."

Is Mr. Halle as obtuse as he sounds, or is he just kidding? In either case, I would be interested in his application of the above formulae to our government's policy toward Castro's Cuba, where there has been no popular rebellion as we learned to our cost at the Bay of Pigs and where "the overwhelming majority" submit to Castro's authority with much more enthusiasm than has ever been the case in Franco's Spain. "Washington can hardly refuse to accept what they themselves accept," *dixit* Halle. But in Castro's case, this is precisely what Washington has done, and it has gone much further in the way of active hostility than anything that Mr. de Madariaga proposed. Does Mr. Halle distinguish between the two cases? If so, he might have mentioned it since he does have a lot to say about Cuba (without, apparently, being aware of any such parallel). If not, why not?

This is written at the height of the present crisis, or what I hope is the height, and on the assumption that we will all be alive to discuss the matter in a week or two from now and that this "inflammable world" has not been quickly burned up. President Kennedy's blockade has, of course, nothing to do with the present argument. I hope it will turn out to be justified when we have more evidence than that provided by our modern augurs, the aerial photo experts, but in any case it seems to me precipitate and reckless. The issue should have first been taken before the United Nations; a commission of neutrals should have been proposed to examine the facts; negotiations would have been undertaken;

if, after a reasonable delay, the Kennedy administration felt it must act for the safety of the republic, then such action might have had a moral and rational justification that the present one lacks. (Or might not, depending on the weight of evidence each side brought forth.) As states, this is all beside the point since objecting to Soviet rocket sites being installed in Cuba is quite different from objecting to that country's internal regime or even to its allies. But I would like to know Mr. Halle's discriminations between our policy toward Franco and toward Castro. He might start off from his really marvelous sentence: "Being courteous to one's ideological opponents is often a necessity of international politics."

To Louis Kronenberger [literary critic]

October 23, 1962

I definitely want to do a book in your Litmasters series. Not Mark Twain, I've decided. Alexander Pope would be my choice IF someone has already pre-empted Poe. I don't know why I didn't think of Poe when I was talking to you. For some reason, I have always felt a strong personal affinity to, and sympathy with, Poe. He interests me as a fine example of a professional money-writer, a hack even, who had genius and so was able to turn the most banal kind of market-stuff into something with his personal stamp on it; also who could make hack reviewing into something that is still exciting to read even though we've forgotten most of the writers he analyzed so carefully and sternly; also the inventor of the detective story and science fiction (and also of symbolism—that such a vulgar poet and tawdry journalist-fictioneer should have been the one US writer of the time who influenced as a master the most advanced French writers is interesting). The thing wd. be to show how vulgar and superficial and amateurish and show-offey he was and how all these defects are somehow transcended by the fact of his talent and his inability to ever be out of character (how he was able to write from the head alone and with the most naive, conscious calculation figure out what would make the most sensational display of shock-effect or erudition on his provincial public and yet always be in character, so that his works have a harmony and an interest—since it's always Poe speaking—despite their heterogeneity and opportunism).

Anyway, you get the idea.

If Poe is already spoken for, then I'd very much like to do Pope. (Or, if you get to the stage of having the same person do two, then I'd like to do both.)

To Nicholas Macdonald

October 27, 1962

. . . Warburg's piece is the most sensible I've seen since Walter Lippmann's two columns last week on the Cuba crisis. Isn't it odd and rather terrifying that Kennedy is acting in this crisis the way Hitler and Stalin did—bold, reckless action first, no negotiations, and then maybe we'll talk about it later—while Khrushchev is acting like a sober, responsible 19th-century statesman (Bismarck, Metternich, Gladstone). If we aren't right now at war, it's Khrushchev's doing and not Kennedy's. And we may be by the time this reaches you (or, in that case, doesn't). I hear (but haven't seen the evening papers myself) that Kennedy has turned down Khrushchev's offer to dismantle the Cuban rocket sites if we will ditto our Turkish ones. If true, I think our President is too close to madness for comfort. A colleague here [at New Yorker offices] this P.M. put it: "Kennedy had painted himself into a corner; Khrushchev offers him a plank to step out on; Kennedy kicks the plank away." The only way such issues can be peacefully resolved—or sensibly—is through negotiations, which means compromises and letting each side save face and retire in good order. Kennedy seems determined to carry it all off with a high hand and insist on EVERYTHING. This isn't politics, it's emotional SOLIPSISM (look up the last word) I mean.

So much for world events.

The [Robert Frost] session must have been really something. Your appraisal corresponds with mine at every point: a great performer in both bad and good senses. Odd how many teachers Frost seems to know, and to have known. Thus when I was a year or two younger than you are now, in my final year at Exeter (1924) Frost came to PEA because he knew an English teacher there and went along with a group of us on an excursion to the Isles of Shoals (off Portsmouth, N.H.) and charmed us as he did you. I wrote my best poem under the stimulus of his presence—it was published the next year (must have been my last year at PEA therefore) in the Yale Lit and ran (about) as follows:

> The breaking waves are old men
> With wind-whipped white hair.
> They crawl, roaring, into the beach
> And toss their hair high over the rocks.

Actually, it sounds more like a Japanese hoku (or whatever they call it) than Frost, but it WAS inspired by that trip and Frost's presence. . . .

To Victor Gollancz [British editor of *New Left Press*]

November 23, 1962

I am delighted you like *Against the American Grain* and want to publish it. It's gotten three very favorable reviews over here already (inc. the *Wall Street Journal*)—I enclose an extra copy I have of one, in *Newsweek*. Now on libel points. . . .

I really don't see how the fact that C. P. Snow lost the sight of one eye is relevant to the question of the merit of his novels and his ideas. Milton and Homer were completely blind, after all—I read recently that Snow will retain the sight of his other eye, for which I am very glad. I fear that if I had lived in the 17th century, I should have criticized *Paradise Lost* without making allowances for the author's blindness. To omit this footnote seems to me sentimentality and fuzzy thinking—if I lost a leg tomorrow, I really wouldn't expect critics to lay off my published writing. An author is a public figure and must expect to be treated as such, that is, as an author, regardless of his personal misfortunes. So I don't want that footnote omitted—there's also the confusion that wd. be introduced into standards if critics had to temper their criticism because of the author's private troubles—should one look more genially on a novel because its author's wife had just left him? Etc. As to the lawyer's objections that the formulation "the air seems to be hissing out of the reputation of C. P. Snow" is on the border line of libel (which side does he think it is on, by the way?): if one cannot make such evaluations, how can one write literary criticism? Every "bad" review undermines the reviewee's reputation and so damages him in his profession, but I shouldn't think that even the English courts, so much more severe on libel than ours, would award damages to an author so damaged. If you and lawyer insist, I'd be willing to reformulate the air-hissing phrase, but that's as far as I will go.

. . . To the best of my belief, Cozzens has no idea of libel suits in his head, as I should think the letter I cite from him to me wd. show. (By the way, I omitted in the book a passage about his relations with his wife which showed not anti-Semitism—she is Bernice Baumgarten, the literary agent, as you probably know—exactly but a certain obtuseness on the matter. I did this because it, on reflection, seemed irrelevant to him as a novelist, and also a touch going too far in attack. So you see even I have feelings.) Point is, if he didn't sue on that, he won't sue on mere literary criticisms. By the way, your lawyer didn't read this article very carefully, or he would have known that I *did* reply to Cozzens's letter—telling him about what I'd discovered about "virgin knot untied." He didn't reply to that, as I noted. Tsk, tsk to Rubinstein, Nash & Co.

To Henry Allen Moe [Guggenheim Foundation]

December 3, 1962

. . . I see it's too late to apply for 1963. But I shall apply for 1964 IF the committee will waive my getting statements from sponsors. I've written so much by now that I should think they could decide from my published books. As for my responsibility etc., a call to either Bill Shawn here or Arnold Gingrich at *Esquire* should (at least I so hope) reassure them on THAT. Or I'll stretch a point and ask one of them for a reference if you prefer.

. . . My project is a little book on Edgar Allan Poe, part biography but mostly criticism and cultural history—a writer who has always held for me a very personal fascination, as an amphibian, one of the first between high and mass culture. I have a contract with Crowell-Collier for the book, which would be in a series Louis Kronenberger is editing, but the difficulty is that $2,000 is the top advance they give. It's to be done simultaneously in hard and paper. I have concluded I cannot possibly do it for that—they have huge plans for putting the series in dept. stores and God knows what all over the country, and maybe I'd make a lot more, but maybe I wouldn't. Anyway, I won't go ahead unless I can be sure of $6,000, since it would take me about six months I figure, and I make a lot more than that per annum, and must have a lot more because of children, wife, etc. etc.—at my advanced age.

I think it will be an interesting book. To me, at least. So if one reference is enough, and if the grant is at least $4,000, I should like very much to apply for 1964. Do let me know if you think it's worth my applying—and if it could be *more* than $4,000 that would be delightful. I'm always up against the financial wall, and it would be pleasant to have a breathing space.

To Henry Allen Moe

December 13, 1962

. . . It's kind of you to let me off getting those references. Also to be encouraging about the whole business. And $6,000 wd. do splendidly if you can manage it.

P.S. Thanks for being so unfoundational.

P.P.S. Re your middle name—odd, perhaps fateful coincidence that it is almost Poe's. The "almost" is painful because I remember printing an essay on Poe in PR (by Tate maybe?) in which he came out in title and running heads as "Edgar *Allen* Poe," and the contemptuous and angry note we got from, of course, Edmund Wilson to effect we had no right editing a literary magazine if we didn't know Poe's right name. A terrible moment, though we nonetheless staggered on (with support & articles from Wilson).

To Robert Evett [a *New Republic* editor]

December 21, 1962

Thank you for the proof of [Richard] Gilman's review [*New Republic*, January 5, 1963]. "Not as friendly as I expected it to be" is the understatement of the year. Who in the world IS this Gilman and WHY does he detest my stuff so much? I mean there must be some personal reason (or some extraneous reason, at least), since I refuse to believe the book is as bad as all that. He would have done a better job—as Norman Podhoretz did in *Show*, for instance—had he been less malicious and more fair. But he despises me and my writing so much that he can only scold and rant, as if driven off his head by sheer irritation.

As for "getting my big guns ready"—that really was a MOST unfortunate letter of yours—one doesn't use a gun on a mosquito. And there's no point in replying to a critic who thinks one a pretentious phony. What am I supposed to say—I am not *either*, yaaahh!

Now that the NR has knocked off Kazin (Heller's review I thought as bumptiously obtuse as his book) and myself, why don't you go after really big game? When may we expect an exposé of Edmund Wilson? I suppose you know what you're doing, but I should have thought that the NR would think of Kazin and myself as more or less on their side culturally, to use a word that Mr. Gilman finds especially repellent (as I do, too, see pp. 55–56, and also see my explanation there of why it has become so).

I don't object to serious criticisms, like Podhoretz's, because I can learn from them. But this sort of rant is as educational as a punch in the jaw.

P.S. I've just thought of a possible reason for Mr. Gilman's unremitting animus—revealed in his sentence beginning "But of the art of this moment . . ." on galley 33. Namely, that I criticize contemporary works (which seems to some people to mean I hate the Living Present; see letters to me in my *Esquire* movie column). And the reason, of course, for your printing this kind of review you make clear when you say, hopefully, "it will probably stir up a hornet's nest." Mere abuse isn't enough. Logic, wit, coherence, a rational structure are also needed. And it is fatal to let your animus show through in the way Mr. Gilman does. The readers then become sympathetic with the book or author under attack, if only because of some sense of fair play. So I doubt your editorial opportunism will pay off.

To Vandysot [a reader of Macdonald's film columns]

December 21 [1962]

You're right about *Kane* but, I think, only on the surface. The structural line is indeed the quest by the Luce reporter for the real personality of Kane, what made him tick. But, at least as I read it, the clue to his behavior is social-economic: he was born rich and thus powerful and his tragedy is that he therefore thought that power would solve his personal problems and was furthermore in itself a good thing. His first marriage is wrecked by his preferring power-position to his wife (whom he married for prestige reasons), and his second marriage is a ruin because (a) he pushes his bride into being a big singer (and thinks he can buy her success) and (b) he thinks even after this had failed (and has failed because his wife won't play the game when she realizes she is not a good singer) that she can get the same sort of neurotic satisfaction out of baronial living that he does (she doesn't and prefers to go back to a shoddy but human world of cheap night-club exploitation to the boredom of power-prestige living). His break with Jedediah is similarly because J. is appalled by Kane's assumption that money and power can buy anything—and Kane's attempt to buy J. by giving him the $5,000 check is the last note in their relationship.

On the other hand, I must admit that the Rosebud shot at the end on the burning sled implies that his trouble was Freudian—the sled he used to push down the lawyer who had come to take him from his parents symbolized for the dying Kane the childhood hurt that he had tried by power-money as a man to heal. His whole life was an effort to make up for that initial rejection.

So I conclude that *Citizen Kane* has BOTH social and personal meanings, and so we're both right—and wrong.

But thanks for raising the question, and I think you have a very good point.

Yes, there was a slap at Mailer, I think, and a rather crude one. I'm not at all in sympathy. It was much more complicated than that. A month ago I was at a party given by Mailer and there was Adele, his wife, whom he stabbed. So she at any rate didn't share *Esquire's* opinion. Good.

Partisan Review has reprinted my "Masscult & Midcult" in a pamphlet which they are selling for 95 cents.

To John Lukacs

January 10, 1963

Very nice to see YOU also in that Muggeridgean dinner party—though you shouldn't have shoehorned in that vapid woman (and her ghastly male companions). I know that you were not expecting them, but neither was I expecting HER. You pushed her in on me (and on the Breits, if it had come to that) in the same way she pushed them in on you. Bad form—you really MUST NOT do such things. Social occasions are not free-for-alls. I detest people who bring uninvited guests to my parties. And the way you pushed that damn woman onto me as a fellow guest at the Breits—well really, John! Thank God she didn't come. To be invited to a place is one thing; to ask your hosts if you may take others is another thing (which is what I did with you and Muggeridge); but then to have to include, without notice to the Breits, an unknown woman because YOU, who had no status at all in the whole transaction, had asked her—this seems to me very pushy and vulgar on your part. (That she did the same to you, or tried to, was delicious, I thought.)

I was also upset by some passages at the party—you seemed to have affronted even the kind, tolerant Daphne Shih-Hellman, and wasn't your voice rather loud when you begged me to leave "this dull gathering"? And what did you say to Mrs. Rollo? I remember something about being "cold" sexually or some such nonsense. Anyway, she seemed to be quite angry.

Maybe this is the rough manners of the Hungarian nobility, who, provincially, consider themselves the superior of everybody else. (At those Gauss lectures at Princeton, where you certainly didn't help me, someone asked me, "*Who* is that Hungarian cavalry officer?") Or maybe you think yourself a genius and so exempt from social courtesy? I consider myself a bit of a genius too, and whether this is true or not, have never claimed for myself some special status. Nor will I grant it to you. We geniuses, Hungarian or not, have no right to make others uncomfortable.

So much said, and probably much too strong, let me also say that I can't see any chance of your "Across the Zemen Bridge" being printed in the *New Yorker*. They don't allow footnotes, for one thing, and for another, it isn't good as reportage because you are so self-indulgent as to your own (rather snobbish) reminiscences, and you haven't bothered (or perhaps been able) to transmute your own memories, which might have been moving and interesting, into even journalism. It has some very good things in it, but the whole is vitiated by a kind of emotional SPRAWL, as in a warm bath, which lets in all kinds of details that are merely of interest to you and that fog up the general effect. I suspect you just "knocked it off" in a day or so. Anyway, it would have to be drastically edited to come close to the great goal you set yourself—to render the difference (and similarity) your sensibility found between the Hungary you left in 1946 and the one you found in 1962. The raw materials are there and often very well there, but, in your arrogance, you haven't taken the trouble to make a work of art out of it. Also, why did you omit the most interesting episode you told me: about that uncle or whatever whom you found living in the old style, with a serving maid, etc? Maybe for practical reasons—wd. have gotten him into trouble? Still a pity.

I think you should rewrite the piece—think of the way Proust recaptured his past, f.i. You haven't taken enough TROUBLE with it—it reads like a moderately interesting letter—but you haven't selected and heightened and pruned the loose prose into an actual article, even a journalistic one. You should have more respect for WRITING, even on a reportage level, and less respect for your "genius," a 19th-century term I don't like because of its emphasis on "self-expression." I prefer the earlier idea of craftsmanship, making a work of art that is an impersonal OBJECT. I know that you are convinced that you are writing "the most important book of the 20th century," but this seems to me romanticism.

So there it is between us. Probably hopeless. And yet there is a bond of affection and even general ideas.

One more dismal note, however: I have just consulted my calendar and I find I cannot make that Chestnut Hill conference on February 15 because I had already committed myself to go, on the 16th, to Exeter to talk about James Agee, and the idea of traveling down to your region the day before I have to go all the way to Exeter, in the opposite direction, is just too much at my age. Especially since I had hoped to spend a quiet weekend with your family. I'm extremely sorry—should have looked up things before accepting, but this is the ONE future date I had made—but, unless you can shift the date, and my only other engagement is March 25th at Adelphi College here, I must say No.

To Ned Chase

January 30, 1963

Thank you for your letter about my poverty piece—and for the extremely interesting (and, to me, new) proposals and criticisms you make in the *Commonweal* article. Praise from such an expert as you seem to be is praise indeed. Fascinating facts in your thing—the 50%-plus unemployed among urban Negro youths, the absurd antiquated emphasis in training for farm jobs, the 10 times more spent on school lunch program than on training programs. I hadn't thought beyond a subsidy as a remedy and, from letters and comments, I now think a subsidy by itself wouldn't integrate the poor into society; "they'd only use the bathtubs to store coal"—crack of the reactionaries re public housing; not literally, but as a metaphor—elevators ARE used as latrines, f.i., acc. to those Salisbury pieces. Your training proposals seem to me sound, and a major way of leading the bottom dogs back into the social structure, for they do need to be led or guided.

But I'd like to talk about it with you soon—maybe lunch if you are ever down this way? The response to "Our Invisible Poor" has amazed me—lots of people seem to be concerned at last—and I have the feeling that we are building up to something like 1929–1934, not a depression, but similar in the sense that it suddenly becomes obvious that a large % of the citizenry have become superfluous—then because capitalism collapsed, now because it has developed technologically so as to make superfluous the unskilled—and that government action & spending is the only way to deal with the problem. It's strange how our national mind-set still, even after the New Deal, rejects any rational, planned, overall approach and still is fixed in the Adam Smith mold—judging by Congress, which is after all the most truly representative democratic institution we have.

Maybe now that Kennedy has achieved Inner Security and Self-Confidence (perhaps a bit too much) as result of his Cuban bases triumph, he will be open to some sensible (and drastic) proposals for domestic reform. Let's hope so—it's the only chance. But those damned congressmen—and that damned American public!

To Robert Silvers [future editor of the *New York Review of Books*]

February 28, 1963
. . . Just had a call from Wen Shih, who is Daphne Hellman's husband now, as you probably know. He was enthusiastic about the [*New York*] *Review* [*of Books*] and "To the White House," which he felt sufficiently irreverent; and, more important, he said that he and Daphne might be interested in putting some $$$$ into it. As you probably know, Daphne is very rich but has never up to now done much angel-ing; however, Wen sensibly thinks she (they) might as well spend it on something they believe in as give it to the govt. in taxes for armaments. He is a very clever and also very determined fellow, and I think there might be something sizable forthcoming there. He would like to discuss the business with you, and I told him I would ask you to ring him next week. . . .

Wen's one criticism was, "Why does the list of contributors look like that of *Partisan Review*?" Oddly I had just talked with Barbara [Epstein] and made not that criticism—for you needed Names for first issue and also no reason PR people, myself included, should be discriminated against just because we've been around a long time—but the point that, in future issues, the *Review* will have to develop new, unknown people if it is to survive. I'm sure you agree, if only because old-stagers like myself have so many other commitments and duties we cannot do more than occasional things. Wen mentioned a Negro poet and critic named Leroi Jones, who, he claimed, with proper editing could be "an honest James Baldwin"; my own impression is that Jones is a far-out beat type but maybe Wen is right. Anyway, IF you get the backing—and Barbara tells me you actually may—first order of business should be to comb the little mags and find half a dozen bright boys and girls who can produce competent stuff. . . .

Wen is conscious of being of a younger generation, one that has not "arrived," and one that we must represent and encourage, allowing them to make mistakes (though not at length) provided they have something on the ball. The *Review* should not be the Voice of the Establishment (as PR lamentably is). I know you recognize the danger.

I hear nothing but good about the first issue.

To Robert A. Hume

March 7, 1963

. . . I am glad you enjoyed my writings, and in particular "Our Invisible Poor." As for the contradiction between what the *New Yorker* prints and what it advertises, this has often been commented upon, most recently in the *New Republic* apropos of James Baldwin's recent piece. And for that matter, by myself many years ago, about 1937, in an article on the *New Yorker* in *Partisan Review* called "Laugh and Lie Down." The contradiction is real of course, but (a) nothing can be done about it, and (b) does it make any great difference? Perhaps I have become hardened by ten years of writing for this magazine, or perhaps I have come to a more mature, or at least more practical point of view—namely, that one can read the articles without looking at the ads; or perhaps one could take the cynical view that it is piquant to think of the rich subsidizing such articles.

To Harold Taylor [former president of Sarah Lawrence College, critic, and lecturer on education]

May 2, 1963

Thank you for your review of my book in the H-T [*Herald-Tribune*, April 7, 1963]—most perceptive and intelligent I've seen except maybe for a job in *Village Voice.* . . . I'm getting tired myself of masscult and midcult and wish I hadn't invented those terms which are indeed a little *Time*-like. Also you are right to object to the game of fitting writers into those slots; I was trying to set some fixed boundaries (and I still think we need such), but they became somehow too rigid and exclusive; nothing more boring (and more damaging to art and letters) than "grading" or "rating" artists on such a scale; like the U and non-U business in London. Peccavi! . . . In your penultimate paragraph you don't get my point (doubtless my fault): of course ideas and art and books should be put into circulation for whomever wants to enjoy and use them; my notion of elite not exclusive except in sense that I do think 70%–80% of the population at any time or place, including Elizabethan England, etc., really aren't INTERESTED. Anyone who is odd enough to be interested should have every chance of seeing pictures, reading books, going through college, etc. My elite welcomes all aspirants—their only membership card is their own interest. But such a card is not as common as you perhaps think it is.

Let's discuss it sometime—you have certain liberal presumptions which I don't, since I've never been a liberal (but either a revolutionary or a conservative or my present blend of both), and I dare say I have other prejudices and presumptions you don't.

To the Editor, *New York Times Book Review*

May 23, 1963

It was unnerving to read, on the front page of our most influential book section, a review like Michael A. Musmanno's of Hannah Arendt's *Eichmann in Jerusalem*. The coarse demagogy, the unfairness, the mindlessness. I thought of Vyshinsky at the Moscow Trials.

Mr. Musmanno—I refuse to call him "Judge," a word connected with "justice" and "juridical"—attempts to reduce one of our most distinguished political thinkers to an apologist for the Nazis. He accuses repeatedly a woman whose life has been given to various Jewish causes (as your own biographical sketch shows—I cannot understand how you could have printed that sketch *and* that review; if the one is valid the other is not) of having suddenly and mysteriously become a defender of Eichmann, Himmler, and other murderers of six million of her own people. Style is not all that Mr. Musmanno has in common with Comrade Vyshinsky; to convert Hannah Arendt into an excuser of Nazi genocide is as heroic an undertaking as Vyshinsky's attempt to present Trotsky as a secret agent of the British in 1917.

Mr. Musmanno lifts an eyebrow, as well he might, over Miss Arendt's "suggestion that Eichmann loved the Jews." She suggested nothing of the sort, as his own text makes clear; she merely quoted Eichmann's statement that he "had no hatred for the Jews." It was the reviewer who converted "no hatred" into "love." Miss Arendt's point, of course, reiterated through her book, is that Eichmann was a monster precisely *because* he had no special animus against the Jews, *because* he had no sense he was doing wrong, since he was a loyal and conscientious servant of the state. That the final result of the forms he correctly filled out and the orders he dutifully executed was genocide—this simply was not present to his conscience. It was a nonevent, officially speaking.

This is admittedly a very different view from that of Mr. Musmanno—or of Mr. Hausner, the Israeli prosecutor. It stems from a theory, the evidence for which Miss Arendt gave years ago in her *Origins of Totalitarianism*, about the actual as against the generally accepted, nature of totalitarian bureaucracies. One may disagree about the theory and about the interpretation of Eichmann that follows from it—I myself think the theory is true and, further, that it results in a more profound moral condemnation of the Nazi officialdom than do the familiar stereotypes advanced by Hausner and Musmanno. But it is one thing to disagree with the theory, and to show reasons for doing so, and another to take it as a *defense* of those totalitarian horrors.

I have criticized your journal for printing too many favorable reviews, but if this is your way of redressing the balance, may I implore you to scramble back, with what dignity you can muster, to the *terra firma* of the Positive. May I also protest as dirty pool allowing someone to review a book that ridicules and attacks him and his ideas? Mr. Musmanno was a witness at the Eichmann trial, and Miss Arendt makes fully clear her disrespect for his line of testimony. Or didn't you know.

To John B. Oakes [an editor of the *New York Times*]

June 10, 1963

Your registered letter finally reached me — wasn't home first time it came. Sorry for delay in replying.

I was told by a source I considered reliable that your father changed his name from Ochs to Oakes during the First World War because he wanted to avoid the anti-German hysteria of the times (sauerkraut became liberty cabbage then, briefly, as I recall). But of course you are in a position to know better, and since you tell me the change was NOT made for that reason, I accept your statement. I regret the error—though why you consider "for tactical reasons" is "snide" and "sneering" I don't entirely understand. During that war the Hattenburgs became the Mountbattens, in England, and openly for "tactical reasons," but nobody now thinks any the worse of them for that.

Nor can I see why it shows I am "out of touch" with the *Times* that I called Adolph Ochs "a stuffed shirt." That's a matter of evaluation, not of fact or of inside dope, and I found ample evidence in Berger's history of the paper for my unkind judgment. As for the editorial page, which I understand you've been running of late, I haven't detected enough difference from the previous one to invalidate Mr. Kennan's indignation. Sorry.

Thank you for writing, and I do accept your assurance that Ochs became Oakes during the First World War for nontactical reasons. I suppose you wouldn't like to tell me what they were?

To Nicola Chiaromonte

July 5, 1963

So good to have your letter. I understand your not wanting to write letters; one has a feeling sometimes that just to put down on paper one more sentence is an impossibly heavy weight to lift. . . . No, Fred somewhat misled you: I wasn't ill at all. It was just that I had a complete physical checkup because I felt so weak and rotten most of the time; and after every conceivable test (and some inconceivable ones like pushing a tube up my rectum and then actually blowing air into the colon or whatever it is, like an 18th-century farce—it tickled damnably, very odd sensation, couldn't help laughing), the doc found only one thing wrong: a blockage in the tube leading down from my left kidney, so that I was working on only one kidney. He proposed an operation to remove it, would have meant 3 weeks in hospital; at last moment, Gloria insisted I get a second opinion, so I went to see your pal, Janowitz, who sent me to very big kidney-shot (he actually invented the dye and technique they all now use for x-rays of kidney functioning) and HE said maybe it's congenital, i.e., have had it from birth, in which case no reason to operate. (I don't have to be *perfect*, after all.) So I am waiting six months, then a second x-ray of the kidney, and if it hasn't deteriorated, it will mean it's always been with me and so no operation. Janowitz, by the way, was superb—just the sort of direct, informal, no-side doctor one needs.

After the tests, the doc (a courtly white-haired Hungarian named Lax who, except for his overenthusiasm about having me carved up, I think well of) put me on a dismal diet (no butter, oil, eggs, cheese, potatoes, etc., mostly green vegs, roast or boiled meat, cottage cheese, skimmed milk, saccharine) and also gave me some pills that make you pee a lot and so prevent water making fat; also NO DRINKING, you'll be glad to hear. I have pretty much stuck to this for 3 weeks now, chief exception being I HAVE taken 2–3 drinks per day, which is about a fourth of my former intake; and last week Lax weighed me and I'd actually lost 17 pounds in 14 days, down to 184 lbs. From 201! And I feel (and people tell me look) 10 years younger—you're right, Nick, at a certain age (ours) asceticism pays. . . . As you know, reason and moderation are my guiding stars, and, as those 2–3 drinks per day show, I don't overdo asceticism. But the difference between 3 p.d. and 12 p.d. is much more than fourfold. For the past few years I've really not known what it was to feel simply in good health; I knew it was drink, as did you and Gloria et al., but I know I wouldn't have had the "willpower," or whatever the stuff is called post-Freud, to make any change unless a doctor made me.

Yes, I know the *Observer* reviewer of my book—John Gross, wasn't it? He's youngish (about 30) and used to be an editor at Gollancz. His review WAS indeed an odd combination of respect and condescension, but this has been the tone of most of the more intellectual-highbrow reviewers, esp. the young, so I'm used to it; I'm hoping to get time to review the reviews and draw some conclusions about myself (they DO have a point, several in fact) and about The Age. Their illegitimate objections are that I am for an elite and hostile to the masses, that I write well ("smooth, slick, superficial") and with jokes ("frivolous"), and that I have always had at least one foot, sometimes 1-1/2, in the world of commercial journalism. There valid points are that I have an unacknowledged (thought not unconscious, I assure you) . . . prurient interest [in masscult and midcult] which comes from a moral condemnation of something in me too; and that this shows in my preoccupation with debunking the vulgar and my small interest in praising the superior. But this all premature—won't really know what I think until I begin to actually work, and write, on subject. (Lot of truth in Paul Goodman's quip: "Dwight thinks with his typewriter." And in my rejoinder: "You've got to start somewhere.")

Yes, I hear too that Mary is now rich because of her new sex-novel—$100,000 on just paperback rights alone acc. to *N.Y. Times.*[5] I'm glad for her sake but I agree it's to be hoped she doesn't become too full of her own importance as a writer therefore. You apparently thought she had, from your seeing her en route back to Italy, I gather? Hope your impression was mistaken; would mean a real change in Mary. . . . Lionel A[bel] was very good, I agree, in PR on *Naked Lunch*, and on the shock-obscenity-anti-ideal-ideal now dominant. Things are going farther and farther—the respected firm of Putnam's has just published, unexpurgated, *Fanny Hill*, and now I see some other reputable publisher is bringing out Frank Harris's *My Life and Loves*—both up to now always considered pornographic. As usual I find myself in a divided position: as a civil libertarian (and board member of the NY Civil Liberties Union) I oppose censorship and therefore support the right to publish such works; on the other hand, Harris's book is of slight literary value, *Fanny Hill* of more though still not exactly major, and so argument that can be made for *Chatterley* and *Naked Lunch*, that they're Literature, really doesn't hold. It's like most political civil liberties issues here since 1940: one finds oneself defending the rights of people to be heard whose messages are either eccentric (Trotskyist, DeLeonist) or positively harmful (Communists, racists, fascists). A few weeks ago . . . I was asked by one Ralph Ginzburg, a young publisher-on-the-make, to testify for the defense in a federal case in which the govt. had indicted him for sending obscene matter through the mails. After reading the material complained of (the last issue of *Eros*, a $20-a-year lavishly illustrated hardbound quarterly which in its first year has achieved 175,000 circulation, plus two auxiliary publications), I decided they were of little or no literary or even sex-logical importance and their suppression wd. not do any harm to anybody but Mr. G., but also that they were in no ways obscene or pornographic (far less so than Burroughs or Lawrence). It was also obvious that Ginzburg is exploiting sex the way *Horizon* or *American*

5. Mary McCarthy's novel *The Group*, about a group of Vassar women based on many she knew as a Vassar alumnus.

Heritage (also handsomely laid out, well illustrated, and quite expensive) ex-ploit culture. So I did testify, charging him my usual out-of-town lecture fee ($350, plus another $100 because I had to go to Philadelphia twice). But I was uneasy about it, even though the Philly branch of the Am. Civil Liberties Union had filed an amicus curiae brief supporting Ginzburg. Because while I'm for complete freedom of publication (or ALMOST), maybe one should per-sonally, actively intervene only in cases where more than the mere abstract no-tion of free speech is involved. I don't think I would go to Philadelphia, twice, to testify for some crackpot racist, for instance, though I might sign a petition for his right to speak freely. Maybe I was wrong about the *Eros* business. We lost, by the way, and unless the Supreme Court reverses the decision, Ginzburg may go to jail (maximum is 50 years or so) and be fined (maximum is seven hundred thousand dollars). . . . One reason I did decide yes was that acc. to G's lawyers (a couple of bright young chaps who have done much civil liberties work before, like trying to break the Hollywood blacklist of pro-Communist screen writers) told me the real reason for the *Eros* prosecution was that its lat-est issue, the one complained of, had a portfolio of colored photographs of a Negro man and a white girl embracing, etc. (But nothing pornographic, in fact I thought the photos were very good technically and in much better "taste" than lots of the photos in those "girlie" mags that have been sold for many years openly on the newsstands.) Trouble was (a) they were both nude, and (b) the chairman of the congressional committee in charge of post office appropria-tions is a Southerner. So "miscegenation" (though why such an awful sounding word for it?)—which I have no objection to, but which I daresay any South-erner does—rather than obscenity seems to have been The Point. A few days after the trial, I had a call at the *New Yorker* from someone who said he was "Detective Mamet of the police narcotics bureau." I began to giggle, suspecting a hoax (after all, my narcotics record is clean except for two marijuana ciga-rettes Norman Mailer gave me years ago—the effect is euphoric, one feels calm, lighthearted, benevolent, and there is no hangover and no desire for more later on; much better than that addictive alcohol, which makes one ag-gressive & anti-social; in fact Gloria said she had rarely known me more agree-able), at which Det. M. said, rather offendedly, "Why are you laughing? This IS the narcotics bureau." It turned out he'd read in the *Post* about my testimony that I'd found nothing offensive in the black-white nude photos and he "thought you might be interested to know" that the Negro, a professional model, had been picked up on a narcotics charge; they'd found marijuana cigs in his pad. After some fencing around about marijuana, which I think it's ab-surd to put legally on the same level as heroin, Det. Mamet got down to busi-ness, which was, this being the USA, that he thought a fine *New Yorker* article cd. be done on the work of the narcotics bureau and he wd. be glad to supply any information, etc. Other day I received several tracts from him, put out by the police dept. They want a good press just like every other American, in fact maybe that's now a right of citizenship, too: the right to publicity shall not be abridged and any such curtailment without due cause—like nobody's interested—is cruel and unusual punishment. . . .

I write this from Fred Dupee's mansion up on the Hudson, where Gloria and I are spending a few days in isolation (Fred won't be back till after we leave next week, and Andy [Dupee] set out with Joanna for Europe last week) and most pleasantly. Back to the city for a week shortly and then out to the U of California at Berkeley, where I shall spend two weeks, give two lectures, and have no other duties except to collect the fee. Have never been there, or to San Francisco, most curious. Then a week or two exploring the West, then back to NYC by end of August. . . .

To Isidore Stern

July 26, 1963

Thanks for your letter of June 20 and the kind words about my writing. Yes, as you say, I do indeed think we don't draw the line enough and that we debase standards, etc. But for me the line has never been to exclude sex between Negroes and whites. Indeed I should regard such a line as an expression of racial prejudice. No, of course, I don't condone "anything," and certainly not public sexual exhibitions, with or without children present! Wherever did you get that idea? But (1) I'm a board member of the N.Y. Civil Liberties Union because I believe in civil liberties, including freedom of press (the Philadelphia branch of the ACLU filed an amicus brief in support of the *Eros* defense); (2) I read all 3 of the items the govt. claimed were obscene and did not find any of them to be so (the Negro-white nude series was done, in my opinion, with taste and restraint, and was very good photography—have you seen it, by the way? or are you assuming it must have been lascivious and obscene?); and (3) if I believed (or if someone could demonstrate) that the *Eros* nudes, or any of the many full-color female nudes that now appear in dozens of "girly" magazines, and have for years, without any legal trouble, that these in fact have "incited to rape," I might change my mind on the censorship issue in their case. But I've seen no evidence of any such connection between rape and nudes. I don't think, as I stated in my testimony, that *Eros* is of much literary value, but the question is whether it is obscene, and I simply cannot see it as such, after examining its 4 issues to date. Sorry.

To the Editor, *The New Statesman*

August 12, 1963

Since I have been in California for the past month, I have only lately become aware of Conor Cruise O'Brien's "A New York Critic" in your June 20th issue. I hope it is not too late for a few corrective remarks.

In your July 12th issue Mary McCarthy has explained my political evolution with such generous wit, reason, and imagination that I don't repeat it but will confine myself to three specific points, plus an explanation—he does seem to need them—of the *New Yorker* in particular and journalism in general.

(1) Mr. O'Brien argues that because "about half" the essays in my book are reprinted from the *New Yorker*, "it follows that *Against the American Grain* is not so much against the American grain as all that." But he doesn't mention the provenance of the other half: *Partisan Review, Commentary, Encounter.* Does it also "follow" from them? If so, how inescapable the wickedness of this world!

(2) "Mr. Macdonald constantly reminds us that things are worse in Russia; this not merely keeps him right with the Congress of Cultural Freedom but also reassures his *New Yorker* readers." Now (a) things *are* worse in Russia; and when (1944–49) I published and edited *Politics* (when I was "one of the boldest of American political commentators" and was also renowned for my "prickly and indignant independence") in that golden age of my being—*eheu fugaces!*—I was reminding the five thousand or so buyers of my little Marxo-anarchy-pacifist sheet of this fact of life far more "constantly" (and far more indignantly—after all, Khrushchev is an improvement over Stalin) than I do now—and would the *New Statesman* had at that time displayed the same prickly & indignant independence. And (b) the insinuation that my anti-communism is to keep me "right" with the Congress of Cultural Freedom is snide and, worse, silly; true that I served a year as advisory editor on *Encounter* and that I still contribute to it; but this is because I think it the liveliest intellectual magazine in England, and perhaps in English. And hasn't your reviewer heard of the "America! America!" business, one of those complex affairs that his Simple Simon socialism makes no sense of, since it involved *Encounter* rejecting the article because the editors thought it one-sidedly anti-American, my printing it in *Twentieth Century* and the American *Dissent* (with a foreword that spilled the beans and was much resented by my colleagues on *Encounter*, and, to reduce Simon to hopeless bemusement, my continuing to write for such a journal and their continuing to publish such a writer? Complicated and maybe corrupt on both sides, according to this Simonian view, but let's hear no more of "keeps him right with the Congress of Cultural Freedom."

(3) Let me give Mr. O'Brien a point—he really hasn't done his homework. There is another "organ of Midcult" that has "got hold of" me, namely *Esquire,*

for which I have been writing for the last four years a monthly cinema column. And most contentedly. The reason for my content, as for my pleasure in writing for the *New Yorker*, is that they let me write exactly what I please, without cuts or editorial "suggestions."

This brings us to two questions, and also to the nature of journalism. Am I contented with writing (mostly) for *Esquire* and the *New Yorker* because I am no longer bold, prickly, independent, and generally anti-establishment? Or has writing for such magazines—for not inconsiderable fees, I must confess—made me less bold, etc. It is not clear which question Mr. O'Brien is answering, perhaps both at once and without any conscious discriminating—and always, of course, in the most depressing way. If the first, then I have nothing to add to Miss McCarthy's letter, except to say that Mr. O'Brien's last shot missed fire: I am flattered to be compared to the sagacious Burke and don't at all mind being sneered at by that enthusiast for a dubious Progress, Tom Paine. [Years later O'Brien became a champion of Burke.] But if the second, then I have more to say. Lenin once observed, to cite an authority Mr. O'Brien may respect—that the only serious question in politics is: Who uses whom? So also in journalism. I believe I am using *Esquire* and the *New Yorker* to say what I think needs to be said. I am not the publisher of either magazine and so disclaim responsibility for the advertisements that accompany the texts I supply them, at a fee. Nor am I an editor, and so feel no responsibility for any text they print which is not signed by me. To quote perhaps another acceptable authority, I agree with Trotsky who once remarked that for him a magazine was like an omnibus one takes to reach a destination; if the editor (driver) has a further destination in mind, that is not one's concern, any more than the quality of one's fellow passengers is.

In short, I am not "a New Yorker critic" any more than is Edmund Wilson, who has been writing articles and reviews (and very good ones) for that magazine longer than I have. I cannot see how the central theme of Mr. O'Brien's "review" of my book differs from that "guilt by association" which, when the shoe was on the other, or left, foot, your magazine denounced when it was used by Senator McCarthy.

However, I am quite willing to try on the shoe for size. "The theory that the people who run the *New Yorker* are working in some kind of privileged sanctuary, where they can afford to be indifferent to the reaction of readers and advertisers, hardly belongs on the same intellectual level with most of the rest of Mr. Macdonald's writings," observes Mr. O'Brien. Grateful as I am for the compliment, I must reject it. The fact is the *New Yorker*'s editors *are* indifferent to such reactions; I have been writing for them, in an office on the premises, for some twelve years now, and my copy has been edited and I have had disagreements with the editing (most of which I have won), but not once has an editor said: "You and I understand this, but our readers won't take it." Whatever differing notions they have had—and sometimes they have been right—are always their own, and it's much easier to argue with a person than with a circulation. As for the influence of advertisers, this is a standard bogeyman of Simonian critics. I was six years a staff writer on Henry Luce's *Fortune* and never experienced this pressure, though I recall several instances of advertising being withdrawn because the pressure had been unsuccessful. So with the *New Yorker*: segregation, not integration, is the rule; I have never met a member of the advertising department and I have never heard of any pressure, or even communication, from advertising to editorial. But Mr. O'Brien is skeptical: "The *New Yorker* is, in fact, an immensely commercial enterprise, and such successes are not obtained in the amateurish and absent-minded manner which Mr. Macdonald suggests." His datum is correct—the *New Yorker* is one of the most prosperous American magazines—but the conclusion he draws from it, although impeccable from a Simonian Marxist standpoint, is not.

To Mary McCarthy

September 24, 1963

Thank you for your letter in the *New Statesman*; just the right tone for that malicious exercise in Simple Simon moralizing; also I liked the content. Am I really as appealing and decent as all that? Modesty says no no, absurd, but my love of truth-at-all-costs (here $0.00) says I am. It was loyal, trustworthy, brave, honorable, etc. of you to write the letter, and again thanks. What I liked even more than being so well defended—you really did strike JUST the right note— was the fact you thought of doing it, and did do it. We've been friends a long time, through all sorts of changes, and I felt when I read your letter that friendship, this one at least, is something to be counted on in the flux. I don't mean this is the first time this occurred to me, but your letter put a seal on it. . . .

The reason I haven't thanked you sooner for your N.S. letter was, minor, that I got it (and the Irishman's review) late through the kindness of some friend or acquaintance, and, major, that I had begun a reply to the review which I wanted to enclose to you, and then—as by now you perhaps know—before I got it done, I was suddenly—out in Berkeley, Calif., where I was spending this summer a few weeks giving a couple of lectures (on movies, and on Modern English Abusage) and making myself available to students at office hours—out there at the U. of Calif., a loose kidney stone suddenly moved into a new position and blocked up completely the exit (ureter?) from my left kidney, so that in four hours one morning last August, just as we were about to return to NYC, I was in extreme pain and nausea and, in six hours, was in a hospital for an operation. Which proved to be a major one—a big operation, you might say—taking over four hours and keeping me in the hospital there for over two weeks, after which another two convalescing there, after which back here a few days ago. I'm all right now, but still weak and shocked; that sort of deep-cutting into your body and rearrangement of your insides (there was a congenital blockage as well which had to be revised) is a miracle of modern surgery all right, how do they ever get you up and ticking away again? But it leaves one with a feeling of having been violated in the very center of one's being, in a way one (or at least I) has never experienced and therefore never anticipated (I looked forward to the operation with rational confidence—and even if I hadn't it would have had to be done anyway—and calm, which was justified in the sense that the operation—by mere luck I got a very good and skillful and dedicated surgeon who became a friend—was indeed done efficiently and the later x-rays show all is working very well in that region, but which was not justified in the sense that the post-operative pain for 3 days and nights was something I've never experienced. They can't give you enough Demerol, a less addictive synthesized version of morphine, to deaden the pain for more than, I shd. estimate, half those first days, because of danger of not breathing enough and so getting lungs filled with mucus and so getting pneumonia, v. dangerous in that state) and also in the sense that the psychic wound is much deeper than one might imagine; I still feel this; a protest, a sense of violation, of having been submitted, with of course the most friendly and scientific motives, to an intolerable experience. Badly wounded soldiers must feel this way, or survivors of torture in a concentration camp. It makes it worse, I imagine, if, as was my case, one has never had any hospital or surgical experience, and has always treated one's body as something that can be depended on to meet any demands without any concern for it. The body has now struck back. I feel a little more strong and superior (to my body) every day, but it will take some time before we make a pact, establish a new balance of powers.

Hannah tells me you are coming here in October, so I'll see you then. She's still being hounded about the Eichmann book but is bearing up very well. I approve of her strategy, which she told me this evening on the phone; not to reply publicly to anything yet, but to write a retrospective piece on it all later after the uproar has died down; as she points out, if she tried to answer all the attacks now, she'd spend the next three or four months on it, and it wd. be a sterile and depressing business, also hopeless, since the Jewish establishment has so much more money, personnel, and time than she can command—now including *Partisan Review* (Abel—Will P., months ago, when he called me to ask me to "reply" to Lionel's piece, which I hadn't then seen, said he had forgotten [or maybe didn't know] about A's earlier onslaught on Hannah in *New Politics*—could this be?—if so, he shouldn't be an editor—well, no energy to go into it all, let's talk about it when you come) and also Podhoretz in *Commentary* (last not unexpected). It's a concerted campaign; just this morning I got a document from Israel (letterhead "The Office of the Prime Minister," and a covering letter thereon), and the Anti-Defamation League, etc., are mobilizing the forces; mass hysteria, manipulated like McCarthy days. I do think Hannah maybe reacts a little too strongly and one-sidedly, seeing plots and maneuvers everywhere (though maybe they are there, of course), but I'm with her wholly on the book, which I think her best since *Origins of Totalitarianism.* The striking thing about the hostile reviews is that they don't give any credit to the, to me, obvious strong points of the book.

To Nicholas Macdonald

September 25, 1963

. . . Your courses [Nicholas was at Harvard] sound very good, esp. the two English ones. . . . Why in the devil does a history course come under Soc. Sci.? Don't they have a history dept. any more up there? History isn't a science but a craft and sometimes an art. . . . I think I see what you mean about being depressed and bored at idea of being part of a whole called Harvard, and I think you are right to feel so. No matter how good an institution is, nobody with any intelligence and character, both of which you have abundantly, wants to merge into it, nor does he want to be subsumed by others under the category Harvard Student, regardless of how full of prestige (and let's say on the whole deserved prestige) the category is. But why must this be a bother to you, as it seems to be? Why must you worry about whether 95% (surely too high—though probably 80%) buy school rings and hang Harvard pennants on their walls and delight to think of themselves as Harvard Men? Why not go your way, make use of Harvard for YOUR purposes (and not let yourself be used by Harvard for ITS purposes), and let Harvard and that 80%–90% go their ways? I loved Exeter, or maybe that's too much; I enjoyed it, got a lot out of it, thought it a good school, but never had any "school spirit" and never thought of myself as an "Exonian"; nor did it depress me that most of my classmates were joiners, boosters, true-believers in the myth of P.E.A. I had a half-dozen congenial friends and there were maybe a dozen teachers who, either in or out of the classroom, I respected and felt sympathetic with and who guided me and stimulated me and chivvied me along to new kinds of knowledge; and there was especially the Davis Library on weekends and evenings where I could read anything that took my fancy. The spirit or mana of PEA was all about me and affected most of my fellow students, but it wasn't any business of mine, and they didn't interfere with my pursuing my own interests, so I just ignored PEA as an entity, except maybe to make fun of it sometimes. So with my six years on *Fortune;* I did my work, learned a lot about writing and journalism, was well paid (after the first two years) and had a few good friends there, male and female; it never occurred to me to take any responsibility about *Fortune* as a whole (since I had no control over it, being a writer and not an editor) or to worry much about its more repellent features, which were many; *Fortune* was an entity outside myself and our relation was a cash-contractual one, so many words of splendid (or as splendid as I could make them) prose per month in return for so many dollars; it was it and I was I; never did I think of myself as a member of the team, a loyal, dedicated Fortunian (this irritated Henry Luce).[6] You write: "It is the Whole, the massing together of 4,500 students into a Common Name, the feeling that I am a Harvard Student . . . We are Harvard Students, that I find irreconcilable to (shd. be "with") being free and . . . a human being . . . a person with a particular life, with particular feelings." Of course it is reconcilable, but why do you feel, as you seem to, that you have to reconcile the two modes of being (Harvard Man and yourself)? You don't. This is so obvious, logically, that maybe you should ask yourself whether your mood doesn't come from something more in you than in Harvard-as-a-whole. In you now, that is, of course. If you really ARE an individualist and a noncollectivist (as I know you are in general by temperament and character), then the fact you at the moment let Harvard-as-a-whole get you down, instead of going your own way and cultivating your own interests, of using Harvard for your ends not its ends, as I've said, then maybe this is a false feeling, one that is caused by some quite different malaise of which you are not aware, or which, being aware, you prefer to disguise in a more acceptable garment. . . .

To *Films of the Quarter*

Fall 1963

I've been wondering, for various reasons, whether to keep on contributing to *Films of the Quarter*, but now that Andrew Sarris has been added to the stable, I feel the decision has been made for me. I am not willing to appear under the same ruberic as a "critic" who thinks *The Birds* "finds Hitchcock at the summit of his artistic powers," not to mention similar recent ukases by the Mad Tsarris of Greenwich Village. Nor am I willing to pretend that it's just a matter of taste, a difference of opinion, etc. For I don't consider Sarris a critic; a propagandist, a high priest, even an archivist, but not a critic. His simplistic coarsening of Truffaut's *auteur* theory has produced a dogma so alien to the forms of reasoning and sensibility I respect as to eliminate any basis of discussion. Even if I chance

6. Luce was very irritated with Macdonald because he was spending his time editing a little magazine, *Miscellani*, while he worked for *Fortune*.

to agree with him on some specific movie, as has happened, it is irrelevant. Sometimes a Chinese fortune cookie will hit the mark, too.

Jonas Mekas was not my ideal of a critic, but, since he is a poet and anarchist by temperament, his vagaries are unsystematic and so gleams of perception sometimes shine fitfully through the mist. But Sarris, like certain Marxist sectarians I used to know, is a systematic fool. His judgments have nothing to do with criticism, since he merely applies the party line to each movie, as they did to each event; the actual, concrete film he sees (or rather does not see) is just one more brick to be fitted into his System.

That *Film Quarterly* sees Sarris as a *bona fide* critic like Pauline Kael, Stanley Kauffmann, Gavin Lambert, and myself, to name the four other contributors to the current *Films of the Quarter*—this is one more symptom of that mush-headed confusion and lack of standards I have long observed in most "serious" writing about the movies. (Why, for instance, is the level of "little" movie magazines invariably lower than that of their literary and political counterparts?) Knowing this fact of life, I have made allowances for *Film Quarterly*. I put up with Mekas, I forgave that entire issue recently devoted to Ian Cameron's stolidly uncritical blurb for Antonioni (those *auteur* pundits are most depressing when they praise a director one admires), and I might even have been willing to try coexistence with the increasingly *auteur* orientation of recent issues. But I draw the line at Sarris as a fellow critic. Include me out.

Yours more in anger than in sorrow.

To Nick Chiaromonte

October 14, 1963
Interrupted. Had to spend two days on talk ("Modern English Abusage") at a Catholic college, small, near Philadelphia; but what happened to the other three? At least one spent in bed, just fatigue—can't depend on this body even to get me around any more.

On the Arendt affair—I've been close to the middle of it—don't feel the energy to go into it all. My sympathies are all with her because I think (after rereading the book in hospital) the book is her best since her first, which is very good indeed; and because it is, as you know, the object of a systematic smear campaign by Zionist and Jewish organizations (last week I actually had a personal letter, on the embossed and very grand letterhead of The Prime Minister's Office, from some Israeli cultural official enclosing a long printed report by the Anti-Defamation League of B'Nai Brith denouncing "The Arendt Book," as the headline calls it; I haven't read more than page one, but there I found this gem: "To the extent that the book's research and its author's understanding are glib and trite, *Eichmann in Jerusalem* is a banal book. To the extent that it gains acceptance as a work of unquestioned authority—and undermines the realities of history—it is an evil book."); also because our Jewish intellectual friends all seem to be jumping on it—even former close friends of Hannah's like Kazin and Harold Rosenberg, she tells me. I find this unanimity suspicious, and also the fact that the critics concentrate, as Lionel did, on a few dozen pages about the Jewish Councils and damn the book for them; but even if she is wrong there, and I don't think she is (at least I agree with her when she speculates that more Jews wd. have been saved if there had been no Councils, no organizations at all), what about the other 19/20ths of the book?

But now I am going on too much. I haven't written anything yet for PR on Abel's piece; said I would, but that was months ago; now must see what strength I have and also what pressure of work undone. Shall try to.

I agree with you that Hannah must reply to the factual points raised by the critics (and also that her book is NOT just "a factual report" but is also a polemic, a sermon, and an essay in moral evaluation), but she tells me that she plans to do just this, and has made notes for such a piece, but that if she tried to answer all the attacks, many of them quite long, each specifically and at the moment, she would get little else done. She plans to do a general answer-to-critics later when the dust has settled a little. She IS arrogant, no doubt about it, and also I don't think that Lionel (or the PR boys) were "put up to it" by any Jewish organizations. They are quite capable of being that chauvinistic themselves! (Or, to discriminate, Lionel's piece is merely another expression of his real *hatred* of Hannah, for whatever neurotic reasons, such as was shown in his *New Politics* piece years ago; while Rahv and Phillips's willingness to print his attack is merely an index of their editorial sloth (Phillips told me actually he "hadn't re-membered" the *New Politics* piece!), cowardice (Abel might make himself un-pleasant if they said No—after all, they DID commission a book review), and opportunism (it wd. "open a debate," stir things up, make a splash, and the fact they were doing dirt on an old and frequent contributor by allowing a rabid enemy of hers—one can't say a personal enemy because they hardly knew each other—to smear her book at length—this doesn't seem to have bothered them at all).

But your questions are TOO stimulating, my dear Nick, in my post-operative state. I like your quote from Proudhon, by the way. I liked a good deal of *The Group* but did not think it the best of her novels. I still much prefer *Company; Groves* wd. be second, for me. While I agree this is an improvement, I am put off by the style and the structure. The former seems to be mostly the ver-nacular of the characters themselves (snazzy, spiffy, etc.—note struck on p. 1: "here they were in New York, imagine that," or words to that effect), and this I don't like as well as Mary's own well-groomed, witty style; also, this latter style, Mary's own, often crops up, without any transitional device, so that we have the girls suddenly for a moment becoming Mary and delivering some well-tailored *bon mot*, then relapsing into their coarse patois; this bothered me. As to structure: she tried for something very big, a collective novel, but didn't have the creative force to weld it all together, so that it falls apart into a series of disparate episodes, some weak, some strong, but not adding up to a whole. I too "particularly liked" the defloration episode, which seemed to me not only lucid but also full of human feeling and sensitivity, in a way Mary has not often been before, in her writings. The odd thing is that most of the intellectuals I've talked to, or read, about *The Group* think it is the old Mary, cold and bitchy and superior, and don't at all see—as you do—that, while she does "put down" les girls, on occasion and perhaps habitually, she also strikes, often, a quite new note of sympathy and concern. The character of Norine Schmidlapp, f.i. (she's Eunice Jessup, of course, and what an accurate portrait!), is done with so much empathy (if not sympathy) and appreciation of her comic sublimity that one thinks of Dickens. Or of that art dealer in *The Company She Keeps* (who, you know, later became and still is one of her best friends).

Oh dear, Nick, do you really think the *NY Review of Books* is THAT bad? I'm distressed. Many faults, yes, and sloppinesses, but I still think it far superior to the *NY Times Sunday Book Review*. . . .

But no room or time to discuss. Love, love, love to Miriam and to you—and write soon again—your letters are v. nutritious for me.

To Michael Macdonald

October 26, 1963

. . . Elaine [Tynan] said (as your letters have) that practically everybody in Hollywood either admires me or hates me, depending on whether I've got around to them yet. It's really too bad about types like Lawrence Harvey and Paul Newman because I'm sure that if we met just personally, I'd find, as you both claim, they are intelligent and *simpatico* and they might make same discovery about me. It's just a *professional* clash. Although can't imagine taking [George] Axelrod [a script writer whom Dwight criticized] (Elaine said he was the most recent Dwight-resenter—and for good reason, cf. my piece on *Breakfast at Tiffany's*—you'd met). I hope you at least told Geraldine Page that I think her the best American actress and have said so in print several times! . . .

To Jay W. Jensen [head of the Journalism Department, University of Illinois]

November 29, 1963

I'm most flattered to be asked by you to be nominated for a Miller professorship, and I'm sure I'd enjoy teaching at the University of Illinois for a term (a whole year would be impossible with my other commitments). So I filled out, as you may see, the questionnaire. And then, at the very bottom of the last page, came that affidavit [a loyalty oath].

This ends it for me—see my comments on the form—unless The Authorities will make an exception, which they probably cannot since this is doubtless a pleasant little joke by the state legislature. (And even if they can and will, I should have to think, and take advice, before accepting a post at a university that makes such a requirement.) So it's, I suppose, all off. In future I suggest The Authorities print the affidavit at the *beginning* of the questionnaire, so as to save applicants (some at least) time and trouble.

To the *Herald-Tribune*

January 15, 1964

Your news report on the *Eros* case has just come to my attention. In it your reporter, Albin Krebs, summarizes my testimony for the defense: "He said he considered *Eros* 'nice.'" I did use that adjective but in a much broader context, and I'd be grateful if you'd correct the misquotation. The actual testimony ran:

"Q: In your opinion, does *Eros* No. 4 go substantially beyond the customary limits of candor that we in our country now tolerate and accept in discussion of sexual matters?

"A: No, I should say it goes considerably this side of it.

"Q: By 'this side' you mean considerably within these limits?

"A: I mean the safe side, the legal side, the nice side."

This kind of frivolous distortion runs through Mr. Krebs's story. He ends the first paragraph, after stating that Federal Judge Body sentenced *Eros*'s publisher Ralph Ginzburg to five years in prison and a $42,000 fine, "Mr. Ginzburg said it was a dirty shame." Well, I think it was a dirty shame too, and I'm surprised to find a paper like the *Tribune*, which is usually sensitive to violations of civil liberties, printing this kind of reporting.

Without denying the *Eros* case had its comic aspects and without making any great literary claims for *Eros* and its sister publications—as I made clear on the stand—may I suggest that an injustice has been done and that, if it is not corrected by higher courts, it may have, as Mr. Ginzburg said to the amusement of your reporter, serious effects on freedom of expression? Before I agreed to testify for the defense, I read the complete file of *Eros* and its newsletter, *Liaison*, plus "The Housewife's Handbook on Selective Promiscuity" (which Mr. Krebs gags up as an "erotobiography," but which I thought a serious case history despite its lack of literary interest). None of them seemed to me to push "the customary limits of candor that we now tolerate in discussion of sexual matters" as far as have such works, recently accepted by the federal courts, as *Naked Lunch*, *Lady Chatterley's Lover*, and *Tropic of Cancer*. And if it's a matter of commercial exploitation of sex—which, by the way, is not *ipso facto* illegal, else where would Hollywood be?—then I see no significant difference between Mr. Ginzburg's publications and the dozens of "girlie" magazines that for years have been sold without any legal protest on newsstands throughout the country.

I'm bewildered by your reporter's animus—or rather by your tolerating it—as I was by Judge Body's decision. After my testimony, in which I tried to give some of the recent history of the increasing acceptance by the courts of freedom of expression in novels, plays, movies, and magazines, I was expecting some cross-examination by the prosecution and some questions from the judge. Not a word, not a question. I didn't think I was as persuasive as all that, and it turned out I was right. But I think some dialogue might have been useful. The *Eros* case is more complex and significant than Judge Body thought. Or your reporter.

To Nicholas Macdonald

April 23, 1964

. . . Distressed you are feeling low. Perhaps it is partly the hangover virus. Though probably not mostly that. But don't be depressed about being depressed. It's a natural condition of life, of mine anyway—my psychic graph would look like a roller coaster. And one cannot do anything about the low points, which may last for weeks, even months; just have to endure them, like waiting out a rainstorm in a doorway if you don't have an umbrella.

. . . I went to a party at the Bollingen Foundation for Nabokov the other day, and he rushed up to me and wrung my hand, saying, "Ah, what a pleasure to see you, Macdonald, my grrreat admirer, how beautifully you responded to *Pale Fire*! And our common bond, our mutual discovery—Pushkin's grandfather! Etc. etc." Point being I'd slated *Pale Fire* in PR and had protested in a letter to *Encounter* at their publishing his 12-page essay on P's grandpa, claiming it was a mass of trivial facts without any relevance to P's interest as a writer, in fact an unconscious parody of the American academic research thesis. Point also being he is a real old-style pre-1917 Russian intellectual, full of fun and games— I'm sure his reading made everything come alive, as you write. No, agree *Charmed Life* not one of my favorite McCarthy books either; prefer *The Com-*

pany She Keeps, Cath. Girlhood, and *Groves of Academe*; but where did you get idea it's me AND Wilson; just Wilson, I'd say. Mary once said to me—entre nous please—when I said something to her about Ruel maybe not liking his mother to put his father, satirically, into a book (esp. with that ghastly seduction scene, so cold and humiliating, to Wilson and to her also), Mary said, widening her eyes and looking straight into mine, "But it WASN'T Edmund—so and so (whatever the character's name was) is tall and Edmund is short, also he's a successful playwright and Edmund's plays have always flopped." Well!

To William Bohn

July 6, 1964

Here's my $30 to keep the *New Leader* going. To think I should sink to this—in the Old Days the most flattering adjective I applied to your paper was "Centrist."

But facts are facts, and the *New Leader* now prints some of the best criticism I see, notably Goldman on music, Simon on movies, Bermel on theater, and Kramer on art. (A year ago I should have included Hyman on fiction, but he's come to accentuate the positive and, while I usually agree with his debunkings, I rarely do with his enthusiasms, which may tell something about me, him, and/or contemporary novel.) Sometimes I even read your front-of-the-book pieces, especially when Kristol writes them. I have a weakness for style which I justify—apart from pleasure—by imagining one learns more from a well-written defense of a weak position, as with Kristol's argumentation on poverty, than from a muddled exposition of a line one agrees with.

Evidently my heart has softened since the thirties. Or my brain. Whichever it is, good luck to the *New Leader* of 1964. My week would be poorer without it.

To Ralph Ginzburg

October 12, 1964

Sorry not to have replied earlier to your note of September 13th inviting me to become editor, on my own terms, of FACT. The FACT is I have been abroad and only got back ten days ago, and there was so much accumulated mail that I've only now got down to your letter. Do forgive me.

I'm also sorry that I must say no. You have already given FACT a line and a personality which—even if I left aside your abuse of my name in your promotion, which would be hard, since I think it's not accidental but symptomatic—I don't much like. As I told one of your editors, I think FACT is vulgar and sensational, anything for a journalistic splash. That questionnaire you sent to those

12,000 psychiatrists, for instance, asking them whether Goldwater is psychologically fit to be President, seems to me (speaking as one who hasn't bothered to vote in a presidential election since 1952 but who has registered to vote this year, for Johnson) a foul blow as far as Goldwater goes and, more important perhaps, a cynical exploitation of the psychiatric profession. That, acc. to *Time*, 2,417 answered seems to me to prove merely that, as one might have expected, a sizable minority of psychiatrists—one-sixth—are as zany and irresponsible, when their political prejudices are involved, as those colleagues of theirs who psychoanalyzed Chambers, from their seats in the courtroom, in the Hiss case. If that was what you were after, which you were not (since then you would have asked them about Johnson as well), then I should have no objection. A good practical joke, but not on Goldwater, rather on the psychiatrists.

Although, even then, maybe I WOULD have objected—you see, don't you, that we could never hit it off—since raising such harebrained questions, and infectious ones, seems to me dirty politics. In fact, not politics at all.

So, No. Sorry. Should love to edit a muckraking magazine again, but the muck has to be *outside* the editorial office.

To Mary McCarthy

October 28, 1964

You remember right after the Kennedy-Oswald murders you (and I) thought maybe we should form a committee to get at the truth? (And A. Schlesinger Jr. reacted on the phone to you to effect: why don't you amateurs keep your big feet out of history and leave it to us pros?) Then the Warren Commission was formed and we sat back to wait for its report.

Now the report is out and I wonder what you think of it. Does it set your doubts at rest? If not, which doubts still remain? Was the procedure OK (Leo Sauvage, NYC correspondent of *L'Express*, thinks they should have appointed a devil's advocate who would have cross-examined witnesses on assumption that Oswald was innocent or anyway didn't do it all by himself—Sauvage, as you probably know, thinks Oswald's guilt by no means proved, and that the Warren Report is not at all convincing, and is writing a book to that effect)? How does the literary TONE of the report strike you?

I ask these questions because I've agreed to write a longish review article for *Esquire* on the Warren Report, and it wd. help me v. much if you would jot down any reactions or points, favorable or not. By November 15th or so.

I assume you have a copy of the report—if not please write or wire me here at once and I'll airmail one to you. Most anxious to have your judgment. *Esquire* gives me carte blanche and, if properly done, the piece should be useful—at least I've seen no thorough critical examination of the report in the

American press to date. The general reaction is favorable, perhaps a little too much so. Haven't read enough yet of report to judge it—it does seem v. complete and, in tone, judicious and reasonable.

Don't trouble too much—but do send me rough notes on anything that strikes you as important to be considered.

To Richard Greeman [translator and critic of the works of Victor Serge]

January 4, 1965

Forgive me for not answering your letter about Victor Serge's novels sooner. It wasn't for lack of interest in your project, quite the contrary, but because I got caught in a squeeze-play between unavoidable holiday "festivities" and an even more inexorable deadline for a very long (20,000 words) critique of the Warren Report I've just finished for *Esquire*.

Though I never met Serge (since he couldn't get to this country and I was never in Mexico) I corresponded with him a lot and also printed some things by him in *Politics*, mostly from his very interesting autobiography. So I feel I knew him, in a way—certainly enough to admire him greatly as a man and as a writer. I should think an omnibus of the three novels you mention would be a marvelous idea—I can't think of anyone else who has written about the revolutionary movement in this century with Serge's combination of moral insight and intellectual richness—he's more like such Russian 19th-century intellectuals as Herzen than anybody else (as you write, "his type of human being and of novel are relatively alien" over here—and American readers should have a chance to experience him). Of the novels you mention, I've read only *Ville Conquise*, which impressed me very much. I think Serge was basically a moralist and an artist—which is why he was never effective in Lenin's Russia, not even during the first years of heroic idealism (relative, that is, to what came not very long after). He had a feeling for people and a poet's eye for the meaningful detail, and when these were combined, as in *Ville Conquise*, with an overall political-historical understanding, you get a very rare kind of novel.

So I hope you and Mr. Boyang succeed in your project.

To Mrs. T. S. Eliot

January 19, 1965

May I express belatedly my sympathy? I'm very sorry that Tom Eliot is dead. He was one of the best people I ever knew, and in so many different ways. You know what they were, so I won't say more about them except that he combined three qualities—among others—not so often found together: intelligence, humor, and what I can only call a kind of reckless, generous nobility. From the few times I met him, three stick in my mind: his climbing three steep flights of stairs to visit me in my New York flat around 1948 or 1949, appearing in the doorway looking very smart, even raffish, something of the racetrack about him (Joyce made same visual impression on me only time I met him), in tight-collared, narrow-striped shirt and black homberg, because he was curious to meet me because he liked my then magazine *Politics*, a small-circulation Marxo-anarcho-pacifist monthly whose politics, small "p," couldn't have much appealed to him; second, his reply, at a publisher's party [identified in margin as Roger Straus] here, later, to rather bumptious critic-editor [identified in margin as Norman Podhoretz] who, cigar and glass in hand, began, "Well, Mr. Eliot, my name is XYZ and I only dare to introduce myself because I've already had three martinis!" to which Mr. E. with that sad, gay smile of his, "Well, Mr. XYZ, all I can say is you are more courageous than I am. I should never have dared such a large cigar." And last, that lunch at the Atheneum (sic) Club (ladies annex) which you may remember, when Gloria and I, through traffic miscalculation, kept you waiting, and you were both so nice about it, and the lunch was so lively and pleasant, for us at least. There was some business about Tom's instructing Gloria in how to peel a plover's egg (or was it a gull's egg—no, plover's) for the first time in her life. She still has the shell. And did you once see Eliot plain? Yes, and here's the eggshell to prove it!

Forgive this rambling—thought you might like a snapshot or two of a great man, and dammit I will say it (after all, I'm fifty-eight myself, a mere generation younger than he was), however unfashionable, a good one.

To A. J. Muste

January 20, 1965

No, alas, I cannot sign your Declaration of Conscience because it "escalates" a call for disinvolvement in S. Vietnam into a general statement that could be signed only by a pacifist, I should think. As: "the military resources of the USA in Vietnam *and elsewhere*" being used to suppress freedom, etc. (my emphasis). If by "elsewhere" you mean, say, Berlin, I disagree—and why such sloppy formulations? Nor am I willing to maybe go to jail by advising the young not "to serve in the armed forces even if conscripted"—again a general pacifist stand (and, as you know, I am not a pacifist), with no mention of Vietnam—and later, not "to take part in manufacture or transportation of military equipment." You seem to me to be using Vietnam (where, I agree, we should withdraw, though not "immediately"—if we actually did pull out "immediately" not sure I'd approve at all—we should bargain, compromise, maybe use the de Gaulle formula, but not just suddenly evaporate—after all, Ho Chi Minh & Co. aren't exactly angels either) as a way of broadening your strategy (without saying so frankly) into a general pacifist stance that goes far beyond the Vietnam situation. The Declaration seems to me either devious (in above sense) or ill-conceived and imprecisely (to say the least) formulated. Too bad. I can think of several dozen names from my own address book that might mean a little and who might sign a Declaration that limited itself to the Vietnamese situation and what can be done about it, without requiring illegal acts for general pacifist aims. (Not that I'm unwilling to take part in civil disobedience if it is directed only at "stopping the flow of American soldiers and munitions to Vietnam," by the way—but, not being a pacifist, as none of the names I can think of are, I am not willing to go in for civil disobedience—or even lawful acts—which commit me to a complete pacifist position.)

AJ—I do think you should explain such elementary matters of political logic to your overenthusiastic Young Turks! Am I being nostalgic, or didn't we think more clearly in the thirties? Anyway, look forward to seeing you on February 5th—and I'm most flattered to have been asked to take part in the celebration of your 80th birthday—especially since I'm a mere fifty-eight.

P.S. I am willing to sign the leaflet alone, sans that unfortunate Declaration of Conscience, but that phrase (so blunt, so vague) "immediate withdrawal" bothers me. If I signed something like it in the Dec. 19th document (can't dig it up, no time, files in usual mess), then OK—leave it to you. But if not, then either omit "immediate" (or substitute "immediate negotiations with the N. Vietnamese Government for the withdrawal"), or else omit my name.

To Mrs. Bisdorf

January 31, 1965

It's probably too late now to answer your questions. Yes, I did and do think Dorothy Day is as close to a saint as anyone I have ever met and that she will be canonized. I met her too late in my life to be much influenced by her, and even had I been 20 instead of over 40, I wouldn't have been interested in or converted by her religious beliefs—have never had any interest in religion, or God; much in Jesus, none in Christ. But her anarchistic temperament and politics might have made an anarchist instead of a Trotskyist—certainly I've always had more of the anarchist in me than the Marxist. I suppose the chief thing that Dorothy has given me is an example of a life given to others, without any pride (or false humility either), of a woman who never judges, and reacts with love to the most trying and boring and awful (often) people and provocations. Ever since I wrote my profile of her, I've sent her $25 or so every year for the *Worker* (as, I believe, W. H. Auden also does—and once, at least, I hear, he sent her

$500, when the *Worker* was in one of its chronic crises). She must have been lovely to look at in her wild bohemian days in the Village, and she is still beautiful, I think. That such a person exists is a great comfort, even though I see her rarely (in last two years once at a benefit meeting for the Spanish Refugee Aid that I chaired—her speech was rambling and had little to do with Spain, the topic, but was as usual revealing of a noble, sweet, and generous personality—and once when four or five hundred of us met in City Hall Square during one of those now-abandoned foolish and harmful bomb-defense practice alerts—we refused to go to a shelter and a few of us, including Dorothy, were arrested, at random far as I could see, and spent a few hours in jail—however, I was spared, too far in the middle of the crowd, and so was able to keep a date at Yale College to talk about . . . anarchism!).

Here's slightly cut (by about 1/4) reprint of my review article that takes off from Mike Harrington's book. (Mike himself is one of Dorothy's better creations.)

To Sylvia Solow

March 21, 1965

I remember Herbert for his wit, his subtle intelligence, and, above all, for his feeling for people as people and not as political or moral abstractions. He had an instinct for the human aspects of a situation.

I first met him in 1937 (I think) when I joined the Trotsky Defense Committee shortly after I left *Fortune*. He impressed me by his political experience—he was a veteran of the leftist wars, I a raw recruit—and by his decency and skill in dealing with people, qualities then in short supply on the left, which he showed as impresario of the hearings when John Dewey and the other commissioners went down to Mexico City to take Trotsky's testimony about the Moscow Trials. I always thought Herbert would have made a great diplomat—or politician.

As I don't have to tell you, Herbert had the light touch. He was gay and amusing—hell, he was *funny*. He had humor as well as wit. I remember the time he was trapped, because of some failure of transport, in a country bar, *tête-à-tête* with an extremely good-hearted and extremely boring lady; he returned shaken but not so much he couldn't make a story of it—he could make a story of almost anything—the climax being her anxious question, after he had sat for some time in morose silence, "Do you feel all right, Herbert? Is there something the matter." "Dammit," he concluded, "I just wish I could have said, 'You are the matter.'"

I've always remembered also one of his fantasies—his wit was sub-acid English but his humor was in the extravagant American style—a skit we printed in 1938 in *Partisan Review* shortly after we'd captured it from the Stalinists, doubtless with some aid & comfort from Herbert. (Its companion piece was a satirical review by me of Vol. 1, No. 1 of *Time*, which Henry Luce had rashly reprinted to celebrate his magazine's fifteenth anniversary—curious, that Lucean thread in both our lives.) Under the title "Substitution, at Left Tackle: Hemingway for Dos Passos," he summarized in parallel columns the literary and political careers of the two from 1926 to 1938, with the comrades' precisely corresponding changes of mind about the merit of their novels. One wouldn't think such a document about sad, unhappy far-off things and battles long ago (not such major engagements, either) would make lively reading today, but it is as funny and sharp as ever: scholarly in its documentation, genial and witty in the comments, which are in the underkeyed, throw-it-away English style.

One quality of Herbert's I valued especially was his sense of fair play, his moderation in political and moral judgments (and executions); it was related to his realism—he never refused to see what he didn't want to see. I was interested by Dal Paine's account of Herbert's advice about how to deal with the comrades of Time Inc. Not only because it seemed just and realistic to me, but also because the situation they confronted was partly my fault. At least I was active, in my last year on *Fortune*, in founding the Time-Fortune unit of the Newspaper Guild—the organizational meeting was held in my apartment. I acted from the purest, simplest trade-union motives, but, a year or two after I had left, I gathered that the Communist faction was strong, for a period dominant, and was introducing the usual confusion, finagling, and political nastiness. But in 1936 we were all such innocents that, far from objecting to the organizer the Guild sent to help us, who made no secret of his Communist affiliation, we thought it rather dashing to have a revolutionary Marxist as our adviser. It was a pity Herbert didn't arrive at *Fortune* in time to enlighten us with his weary-eyed experience. I'm sure he would have been courteous and fair to the comrade organizer, giving him as much rope as he needed.

Two other instances of Herbert's fair-mindedness come to mind.

After Carlo Tresca was murdered, Margaret De Silver, dissatisfied with the police efforts (as we all were), hired her own investigator and asked Herbert to look over the evidence he turned up, which was suggestive but far from conclusive. He told her there was no real evidence the Communists had had a hand in it but considerable that a combination of local Italian fascists and gangsters had. I agreed with him—Margaret had also consulted me, but she relied mostly on Herbert, whose talents for this kind of review were greater than mine, or anyone else I can think of. Many of our more "political" friends simply couldn't imagine the murder wasn't a Communist plot.

To David McReynolds

May 14, 1965

. . . I'm appalled by first the bombing of North Vietnam and now the invasion of the Dominican Republic and will do what I can to protest (after Monday the 17th). Have already, in many talks and discussions with students at the U. of Texas last week as a "visiting fellow" for four days, sounded off against both actions—my theory is that since FDR our presidents have been not too bad on domestic policy but terrible on foreign policy. FDR handing over Berlin and Eastern Europe to that nice New Dealer, Stalin, at Yalta; Truman (who did more for civil rights than FDR did) dropping the two atomic bombs; Kennedy and the Bay of Pigs; now Johnson with poverty war and civil rights on one hand, and these two recent reckless and immoral military actions on other. (Eisenhower was best on foreign policy because he never did anything, and for the same reason worst on domestic policy.) I was heartened by students' response (gave four or five talks-plus-questions a day) at U. of Texas—almost no disagreement on bombing N. Vietnam (or on my proposing we get out as soon as possible, on [Walter] Lippmann and [Hans] Morgenthau line) and real enthusiasm for thesis that we have no business at all in Dominican Rep. Can give you some student "contacts" there—but not before the 18th.

I agree that the present crisis is too serious to be left either to the generals or the pacifists. A month or two ago I wrote a long letter to A.J. [Muste] explaining why I couldn't sign that Declaration of Conscience (since I'm not a pacifist) and suggesting another statement be drawn up (not by me—or at least not by me at first, glad to edit and suggest, simply no time now or for next two weeks for job) that would appeal to the nonpacifist majority (even have a list of names, known ones not like the ones that signed the Declaration—talking practically, honor to pacifist idealists, but you really DO need to broaden it—and to drop formulations that only a pacifist could sign) but nothing came of it. Have a look at the letter.

Meanwhile, do send me anything that came out of the May 13th meeting.

SOMETHING must be done—haven't been as alarmed by government actions since Bay of Pigs.

To the Editor, *Washington Post*

May 14, 1965

A friend has just sent me a copy of your May 3rd issue with Jean White's report on the symposium, at the University of Maryland, on "The Nazi Extermination of the Jews: An Assessment of Explanations." I hope it's not too late to ask how in the world Miss White got the impression that "Mr. Macdonald took a middle ground between the positions of Miss Arendt and Mr. Podhoretz." This is, for me, a serious matter because ever since Miss Arendt's *Eichmann in Jerusalem* came out, I have agreed with her thesis that the Jewish leadership's policy of compromise and cooperation with the Nazis, lest worse befall, was a tragic mistake, morally, and practically (as Miss White, in fact, reported I said, which makes it the more puzzling), and have defended it against such critics as Mr. Podhoretz, in an eight-page letter in the Spring 1964 *Partisan Review*. Either I am a spectacularly unclear speaker, or Miss White is a spectacularly incompetent reporter. Perhaps the truth lies midway, as she would say. But whatever the reason for her misconception, the fact is that to describe my position in this issue as "a middle ground" between Arendt and Podhoretz is like saying the symposium was held midway between Washington and New York City.

To the Editor, *Newsweek*

May 31, 1965

Congratulations on your feature article on American Foreign Policy (NATIONAL AFFAIRS, May 17), which was sober, informed, realistic, and fair-minded.

There was one little item that particularly intrigued me. On one page, Dean Rusk—perhaps I should explain he is our Secretary of State—was asked what he considered "the most important achievement of your four years in office." "The steady reduction of the causes of war," he stoutly replied. "We have promoted general recognition that . . . sending divisions across borders involves risks which make such action irrational."

On another page, we read that by now 32,000 American soldiers have been sent across the border of the Dominican Republic.

Even for a Secretary of State, Mr. Rusk's statement is an extraordinary one. How to make sense of it? I see four possible explanations. (1) Mr. Rusk thinks the Dominican Republic has no borders. (2) He thinks 32,000 troops are a regiment, or perhaps a guard of honor, anyway not "divisions" plural, though a phone call to Army Information would have revealed that an American infantry division today, at full strength, numbers 14,496. (3) His promotion of the recognition of the irrational risks involved in "sending divisions across borders" was strictly an export item, for consumption only outside the U.S.A. Or, most likely of all, (4) that Mr. Bundy hasn't got around yet to telling the Secretary of State about the Dominican occupation. I'm sure he will when things quiet down, if they ever do, but right now it's a crisis, so first things first.

To the Editor, *The New Republic* [never published]

July 1, 1965

I must protest the malice with which your art critic, in his account of the recent White House Festival of the Arts, denigrates those of us who supported Robert Lowell's decision not to read his poetry there because of his feeling of "dismay and distrust" about President Johnson's current foreign policy. Although your own columns have consistently and admirably given plenty of reasons for such dismay and distrust, and although it is notorious that of late a large, probably the major, part of the academic-intellectual community has become seriously alarmed by this policy, Mr. Getlein attributes only low motives to our efforts to make ourselves heard. *Sour grapes*: "Its (the Lowell position's) complementary was immediately taken by a hastily organized group which announced that its members, too, disagreed with US actions in Vietnam and the Dominican Republic, and it was a good thing the President hadn't invited them because they wouldn't have accepted." *Boorishness and greed*: "At the Festival itself, it remained for Dwight Macdonald to carve out the best position of all, which was to go to the bash, eat the food, drink the drink, and announce to one and all that he didn't agree with LBJ either." *Paranoia*: "Beneath that level that, as he elegantly puts it, 'the arts had finally made the big scene' there was agitation by the artists, critics and professionals. To many of them, the intent was to take them into camp and cajole them into supporting US policy abroad. The reasoning seemed to go: . . . he's trying to seduce us by showing himself as a big art lover—watch yourself, Jack, and don't be taken in."

The last, though put rather crudely, I think is true, not paranoically but actually: there as an element of seduction at the historical moment, cajolement in the Festival, and I'm glad that many of our "artists, critics and professionals" sensed this, and depressed that Mr. Getlein didn't. The first two attributions of motive I think are due to spite and ignorance.

It is true that the group that signed a statement, published the day after Lowell's letter appeared in the papers, was "hastily organized," but I draw opposite conclusions from Mr. Getlein's inference of unthinking desire to get into the limelight: I admire the enterprise of those who rounded up in a short time twenty well-known intellectuals, and I think it an encouraging sign of the times that they were able to "hastily organize" twenty poets, artists, and writers like, to name a few, Hannah Arendt, John Berryman, Lillian Hellman, Alfred Kazin, Bernard Malamud, Mary McCarthy, Larry Rivers, Mark Rothko, and Robert Penn Warren. Nor do I think the sour grapes implication justified—"it was a good thing the President hadn't invited them because they wouldn't have accepted." No, more was involved than this reduction of hoity-toity vanity— absurd anyway in thinking of the actual personalities of the twenty who signed—something serious, something that would probably not have moved them to such action before the escalation of the war in Vietnam and the invasion of the Dominican Republic: a realization that the administration's "forward" policy abroad, substituting Marines for diplomacy, is rapidly making the US, or us, into what Lowell called "an explosive and suddenly chauvinistic nation" which may end in the role of the Russia of Metternich's time, the gendarme of not Europe but the world. We are seriously concerned, and Mr. Getlein's sneers at "the agitation of the artists, critics and professionals" is illtimed. Why shouldn't we be agitated? And why shouldn't he?

As for myself, Mr. Getlein doesn't seem to realize the full duplicity and tastelessness of my performance at the Festival: for I was one of the twenty who signed the statement supporting Lowell and yet when I was invited to it, the very morning on which the statement appeared in the papers, I accepted. A complicated, inconsistent, perhaps absurd tactic. But I decided, after some thought and consultation, that it might be well to have at least one bad fairy at the christening who could report on just what went on, and so I wired my acceptance to Dr. Eric Goldman, stating I agreed with Lowell and that I should feel free to write about the Festival. I have done so in the July 15th issue of *The New York Review of Books*, a 7,000-word piece that is not only the fullest account but also the only one, including Mr. Getlein's, that analyzes the cultural and political significance of the Festival in depth and with documentary detail I should not have been able to gather had I not been inconsistently and rudely present.

Mr. Getlein makes much of a side-activity I engaged in while I was not taking notes: "The white-bearded savant seemed to be circulating a petition of some sort announcing to one and all that he didn't agree with LBJ either. The feeling of members of what an eminent movie critic dismissed airily as 'the daily sneer press' was that they wouldn't care to invite Macdonald to their houses if that's the way he carries on." Now what's my beard got to do with it? And why "seemed to be circulating"? I did circulate it, with the help of Thomas Hess. And why "petition" (to whom? LBJ? God?) when the document was headed "A Statement to the Press"? And who is that "eminent movie critic"—how archly snide can you get?

To Nick Macdonald

July 6, 1965

. . . About my going to the Johnson Festival: (1) I wired them in accepting that I agreed with Lowell and wd. only come if I recorded some minor culture-political history that wd. have otherwise gone unrecorded; (2) day before I left, after my wire had been sent, Tom Hess of *Art News* (*Digest?*) called me and suggested we might circulate a statement (see my piece for text, which I think mild and dignified) quietly, privately, to people we knew there who might want to back up Lowell and make it clear their presence implied no support for the administration's foreign policy; (3) this we did to perhaps 40 guests, of whom 7 signed; (4) I think it was a public affair—I agree with Lowell that even in such a "private celebration" of arts and letters at the White House certain "subtle public commitments" were involved—hence proper to distinguish, as our statement did, between private-cultural attendance and support of the administration foreign policy, in the present historical moment at least; and (5) LBJ, our host (if you can call him a "host" when he's invited 400 people to the White House, which is not just a white house but a symbol of the present administration, a political, not a private, personal place), took the same line—see my piece—when he didn't receive or greet any of his guests, as Lady Bird did, but limited himself to a brief, and somewhat churlish, speech, and then ducked out without any handshaking and hostly palaver. And (6) re your "not believing in coming as a guest to some place only to turn around and knife him in the back, no matter how worthy the cause," what do you think then of John Hersey's prefacing his readings from *Hiroshima* with the statement I reprint criticizing his "host" for his foreign policy? What is the difference, in taste and politesse, between that and my circulating my statement? The point, as I saw it, and I consulted the people involved in the Lowell protest (and Lowell himself saw nothing wrong), was that it was a public celebration and that, at this particular time, those who attended it had a right to express—to the press, without any fuss, the next day—their disenchantment with the things being done now in Vietnam and Santo Domingo. And also, in my view, a duty. They shouldn't have come then? Maybe. But *I* was there to write about what I saw and heard (the suppressed press releases, etc., I'd not have known of had I not gone), and why not give the others a chance to make the distinction that Lowell and Hersey did?

Well, maybe I was wrong (about the Statement), but I did consider it and I decided it was at least as much a public celebration as a private affair. . . .

To Jerzy N. Kosinski

August 5, 1965

I have read a good deal of your book, [*The Painted Bird*, a fictional memoir of the Holocaust] about an hour skipping and dipping. You have suffered a great deal and you have seen, as a child, repeated scenes of brutality and violence and murder, of the most varied kind, which have left terrible scars, psychological ones. You appear to be trying to tell the precise truth about these things [the veracity of the book was later seriously challenged], and I respect your intention. But I don't like your book, I'm sorry to say, I don't think it is good either as art or as a comment on real life because you haven't been able to transcend your experience, think and feel about it beyond the level of the factual, and so writing is flat, journalistic, without any individual tone; and, from a moral or even realistic viewpoint—taking "realistic" to mean something that encompasses all of life and not just the literal, sensationalistic parts of it—it seems to me not on a very different level from the brutalities and horrors you describe. *The Painted Bird* reminds me of certain documentary films on the Nazi atrocities I've seen. The literal direct description of atrocities, without artistic "distancing" or individual thought or reaction, comes to have a disturbing similarity in its effect on the viewer or reader with the horrors that are shown in this way, although I realize, of course, that the makers of such films intended the very opposite effect, just as you do.

You write you've been "influenced" by my writings, but this is puzzling since I've always commented morally and stylistically on the dark realities I describe—in fact commented a little too much. Perhaps you have not read the first essay in my *Memoirs of a Revolutionist* (Farrar, Straus & Giroux—now in a Meridian paperback), which is called "The Responsibility of Peoples" and is an attempt to come to grips with the Nazi death camps politically and morally.

I'm sorry to have to say all this, but I'm sure you want my real opinion of your book.

To the Editors, *Partisan Review*

n.d., Summer 1965

I didn't sign your statement because, despite a formal impartiality—much to be said against both sides—it asks American intellectuals to reopen a question many of us have come to consider closed: whether there is any justification, moral or in terms of national self-interest, for President Johnson's recent military adventures in Santo Domingo and Vietnam. "Obviously, the time has come for new thinking," you conclude, but to me this is not obvious. I've done my thinking months ago, and it is dismally confirmed in each day's headlines. As for new thinking, let McGeorge [Bundy] do it. Nor do you indicate any new directions of thought beyond such pious banalities as that we must "understand the political and economic problems of rapidly changing countries" and should "support democratic revolutionary groups." Amen, but my own understanding is that revolutionary groups in such countries are rarely democratic and that the Vietnamese scene, North or South, is notably barren of them. So we find ourselves in what your statement calls "a false dilemma" but I call a real one.

I agree that "power politics, the Cold War and Communists" are not "merely American inventions" and that it is "apolitical," and stupid, to assume that "everything would be fine if only the Yanks would go home." But I can't agree that these formulations—surely a little broad for a sophisticated magazine?—fairly summarize what is "simply taken for granted [by] most of the criticism of Administration policy at the teach-ins and in the various petitions we have been asked to sign." Of course Communist sympathizers have added their voices to the chorus—there is one at Rutgers,[7] I note, and I trust PR is defending his unrevolutionary, democratic right to express such wrongheaded opinions so long as he keeps them out of the classroom—but, speaking as one who of late for the first time in fifteen years has been signing petitions, making speeches, and even picketing, I think the protests have deeper, more reasonable grounds than that double standard of morality I find as repugnant as you do. Your own statement gives them: "disastrous violation of any democratic principles" (which, as you note, makes more, not less, Communist sympathizers) and "self-defeating military involvements [which] can be a substitute for political foresight only if we propose to police the whole world, and to imagine that we can do that is to lack even hindsight." The difference is that you don't draw conclusions ("new thinking" is needed) and you object to us doing so. But I think the evidence has been in for some time.

In less than a year—from the first bombings of North Vietnam last February through the Dominican invasion to the commitment of American combat troops in Vietnam and the buildup of our forces there to a projected 200,000 by the end of this year—we have become the most feared and hated nation in the world (feared more for Goldwaterish recklessness than for the success of our use of military power). As Russia in Metternich's time was called "the gendarme of Europe," we are becoming the policeman of the world. "Around the globe—from Berlin to Thailand—are people whose well-being rests in part on the belief that they can count on us if attacked. . . . We will always oppose the effort of one nation to conquer another." So our President on April 7th last. At this writing, we are opposing the effort of North Vietnam to conquer South Vietnam by stepping up our air bombardment of . . . South Vietnam. "U.S. SAID TO PLAN DAILY B-52 RAIDS IN SOUTH VIETNAM" (*NY Times*, Aug. 31). Each B-52 carries fifty-one seven-hundred-and-fifty-pound bombs; "A qualified source said he had verified reports that civilians moved out of the area of a raid in Zone D last Thursday because they could not stand the smell of decomposing flesh." "RECORD AIR DRIVE POUNDS VIET CONG" (*NY Times*, Sept. 4)": five hundred and thirty-two missions in one day "against a wide variety of targets," all in South

7. The historian Eugene D. Genovese, at the time a professor at Rutgers, had come out publicly in favor of the North Vietnamese. Nixon made the professor a celebrity by demanding his dismissal while campaigning for the Republican gubernatorial candidate in New Jersey.

Vietnam. In the next column, a dispatch from the UN: "To Peking's propagandists, working upon unsophisticated Asian masses, the widening use of American bombers, aircraft carriers and mechanized forces is taken to be a godsend. Crude propaganda daily portrays the US as wealthy and racist and as using its superior military technique to crush the aspirations of the awakening colored peoples of Asia."

Unsophisticated the masses, crude the propaganda, but why are we behaving the way Castro and Mao want us to, why are we going in for Kiplingesque idealism, shouldering The White Man's Burden ("The blame of those ye better / The hate of those ye guard") long after more sophisticated imperialisms have let it drop as too weighty an anachronism? Why do we think that, even if we miraculously win a military victory over the Viet Cong—which now, after ten years of massive American economic-military support to its enemies, controls most of the country—our army of occupation can set up and sustain a viable non-Communist government, assuming there is much left to govern after our bombing? And finally, why are *we* asked whether we "really care what happens to the people of Southeast Asia so long as America gets out"? The question is not what will or may happen to these people, but what is happening to them so long as America stays in.

To J. R. Humphreys [Columbia University administrator]

September 9, 1965

I have just looked over the forms, for the first time, the University sent me to fill out for my teaching job, and I find, to my horror and amazement, that I am legally required to sign a loyalty oath! And this in New York State, not in Arkansas or Mississippi. I think this is disgraceful, and I don't see how I can sign such a thing. Not that I have any objection to the content of the oath so far as it concerns the US Constitution (which, in fact, I have come to consider an admirable document, on the whole) though I know nothing of the NY State Constitution and would feel uneasy about swearing to "support" it—but that it's none of their business what a teacher in a private school or university thinks about those constitutions. I suppose if I were a professional teacher, and so dependent for my livelihood on the job, I would pocket my principles and sign. But this is not the case here and so, unless there is a CO exemption, so to speak, allowing those with conscientious scruples to be excused, I feel I must refuse.

I suppose I'm the only person in the state who didn't know about that nasty little 1947 practical joke of our legislature, and I'm terribly sorry to be discovering it so late. Is such an oath required in most states, by the way? In Mass., Conn., Ill., Pa., Calif., for instance? There was a row about a loyalty oath in

Calif. years ago, but I thought it was rescinded—also that it applied only to *state*, not private, colleges; I don't see how they had the gall to impose such a humiliation on teachers in privately financed institutions.

If you want to discuss the point—maybe I've overlooked something—I'll be here Monday from about 11 on.

To Senator Fulbright

September 23, 1965

May I express my admiration of the clarity, courage, and good sense of your September 15th statement on our policy in Santo Domingo? It was the freshest, most inspiring breeze to come from Washington in months, and I am grateful to you—personally, as a citizen, and as an anti-Communist of some thirty years standing. For what bothers me—as I gather it does you—about the administration's Dominican intervention is not only that it is immoral and unjustified, indeed illegal, but also that it has made things much easier for Castro and the Communists throughout Latin America.

I'm preparing a little critical study—not for this magazine—of our recent policies in Vietnam and Santo Domingo. Might I have a copy of the complete text of your Sept. 15th statement? (I've seen only the excerpts the *Times* printed.) The current *Time* states: "In the Senate, Fulbright's colleagues, who had access to the same files (of government classified information) as he, rose one after another to dispute his conclusions." Is this true? If so, would your staff perhaps be able to send me the report on the debate from the *Congressional Record*? (*Time* only mentions Senator Dodd's jejune charge that "Fulbright suffers from an indiscriminate infatuation with revolutions of all kinds." But maybe other senators made more interesting comments on your statement?) Thank you very much for any of this material you can send me—also for the texts of previous statements you have made on our recent foreign policy.

P.S. The enclosed may interest you if you haven't seen it already. A group of us—writers, artists, and intellectuals—sent it to the late Mr. Stevenson last spring a few weeks before his death. He agreed to discuss it with a small delegation—seven of us, including Kay Boyle, Paul Goodman, Nat Henthoff, and myself—and we had an hour-and-a-quarter session with him that left us impressed by his courtesy and decency—he listened patiently and replied to our arguments seriously and in detail—and depressed by the obvious unease he seemed to feel about certain recent foreign adventures, an uneasiness that kept showing through the rationalizations his position forced him to make, such as that the Dominican intervention was solely "to prevent bloodshed" and that we are in Vietnam "at the invitation of the government, to protect it." When one of us asked him if he really thought there was a government there in the normal sense of the term, he said yes, but he didn't look happy about it.

To Dorothy Day

November 4, 1965

Here are copies of the two items in *Politics*. They seem to me v. interesting, historically, and also still relevant (esp. the "Why Burn Draft Cards?" article which, even if it is by yours truly, and all modesty, false or true, aside, strikes me as a rather good statement of the basic civil disobedience position).

Distressed that some have withdrawn their support. My own reaction was opposite. One thing did bother me, though, and I wish you would ask David Miller about it when he gets out of jail and you see him again, and that is a report in the *Times* that he says he is in favor of a Viet Cong victory. For three reasons, two having to do with the *Catholic Worker* creed: (1) it's not pacifism to oppose a war because you want the other side to win, but merely the inverse of our own administration's policy; (2) nor can I see how an anarchist opponent of state power could line up with the Communists, since they are even more statist oriented than our own society. The third reason is, I suppose you'd say, a "prudential" one: it's hard enough to get Americans to see our point of view, namely that this disgusting war in Vietnam should be ended at once and we should stop bombing the people of VN without having to take on the burden of being tagged as adherents of the other side. If Miller really believes that the Viet Cong, and the Communists who run it, offer a morally and politically superior solution, then I'd say he is naive but of course must take his stand. But if he is merely reacting emotionally against our own atrocities, forgetting theirs, then I think he should think it over again.

Anyway, so good to hear from you, and all my best love to you, dear Dorothy.

To Nick Chiaromonte

December 8, 1965

OF COURSE I wasn't in the slightest bit angry at you for your perfectly reasonable criticisms of the propriety of my appearing at that White House Festival, nor would I have been if they had been quite unreasonable, because a friend, or anyway a friend like you, just cannot make me angry. Irritated, maybe, for a few hours, no longer. And I wasn't even that on this issue—indeed, I was much pleased with your crack about how good it was that my circulating that pro-Lowell statement at the party made the whole thing appear like the circus it was! Yes, *Time* actually left out the concluding sentences of my letter, which made it clear I was going in a critical spirit—"I like to review spectaculars and this one promises to be even more spectacular than *Ben Hur* and *King of Kings* put together. So I shall attend the Festival—and report on it in print." Or words to that effect. Those bastards!

What a pity it didn't work out, your Berkeley trip—just so we could have had some time together here. Glad your mother is better.

Nicky isn't causing me worry now (maybe he did once but can't recall)—he's married to that lovely, bright Elspeth Woodcock and a month or so ago they had a boy, named Ethan for some reason by them, who looks like an angry English judge and whom both are crazy about, natural after all. . . .

To Mr. Mayfield

April 5, 1966

Thanks for your letter inviting me to become a member of the Texas Society to Abolish Capital Punishment. I accept with pleasure and enclose $50 as a contribution to your work.

The death penalty seems to me not justified on either practical-social or moral grounds: it doesn't deter (as the statistics show, whether from 18th-century England or from 20th-century American states that have abolished it) and, while an eye for an eye, a life for a life may be Old Testament morality, it isn't Christian ethics. There's also the existential objection that the most atrocious murderers may change into different people during imprisonment, as is shown by the Illinois parole board's recent freeing of Leopold, of the Loeb-Leopold "thrill murder" of Bobby Franks in the twenties, surely as disgusting a murder as there is on record. Death is a penalty that only a god, or God, could presume to inflict, because it is absolute. Not being gods, or God, we must make do with the human compromise of imprisonment plus parole boards to determine when, if ever, the criminal is enough changed to be released again into society.

And in Texas, judging from the statistics in your letter—one-third of all 1964 executions here, and all but one of the victims Negroes—the situation is especially indefensible, since in addition to the above objections, there is also a Darwinian selection, on racial and economic grounds which have nothing to do with social justice or morality, which, even if one favored capital punishment on general principles, should give one pause. . . .

To Mary McCarthy [Macdonald at the time was visiting professor at the University of Texas]

April 11, 1966

. . . "What are you doing about Vietnam?" you ask, properly. Enclosed some clips answering—also some clips showing that editors of the *Texan* share our views. Week or so ago I was chief (and, alas, far as faculty concerned, only) speaker at a campus rally on questions sponsored by the local branch of Students for a Democratic Society; about 300 people, they at least listened, and even applauded at end—even if some campus wit, when I began, "Fellow Americans," remarked not at all *sotto voce*, "another one of his lousy jokes." I couldn't think of any comeback, Shaw would have, alas, but the fact is I said "Fellow Americans" at last minute and with a certain ironical inflection, although I do think of myself as an American and what horrifies me about Johnson's Vietnam escalation is that it's making this country into something I don't like and don't recognize as the country I feel is my own. This is becoming our Peloponnesian War, I'm afraid, and it shows, as with Athens, that despite all the good things about our internal political-social-cultural life, we have become an imperialist power, and one that, partly because of these domestic virtues, is a most inept one. Vietnam (also Santo Domingo) may be our End not only as a world power but also (unlike England and the France that let go of Algeria under de Gaulle's superb double-crossing) as a civilized nation internally. The lack of consciousness on the part of our government frightens me; the only hope is Fulbright and a few senators, plus Kennan and Lippmann, and the intellectual-academic community. Is it enough? The backtracking of the *N.Y. Times* in the last six months on Vietnam is an ominous sign.

To D. Stanley Watson

July 18, 1966

Were back, God what an unlivable city, and so seedy! Every morn, f.i., at 7:30 or so, a mad whining, clanging, banging, screaming-geared operation takes place outside our bedroom windows, on East 87th Street, all for the purpose of collecting the day's garbage; so we get up, or at least are awakened, then; there must be some better way to order these things, maybe in France. Also at all hours of night, from midnight to five A.M., one is likely to be wakened by shrieking, earsplitting fire engines racing through the streets—and when it is on 87th Street itself, by God you know it!—to put out fires which, acc. to recent stories in *N.Y. Times*, are mostly false alarms. (Query: why do fire engines in England merely tinkle a little apologetic bell, while in Italy they make no noise at all, or perhaps they just let it all burn down?) It's a really awful place to live, in any case, and, as I said in my letter, perhaps we may indeed take you up on your offer of the guest house.

P.S. This morning I said a few words at the funeral of Delmore Schwartz, v. sad business, you would have liked him.

P.P.S. What is the name and address of that bookseller in England that you buy current books from? I keep seeing things reviewed or advertised in *Encounter* or *TLS* that I'd like to order—I suppose I could establish a line of credit with him?

P.P.P.S. In the bundle to the Embassy I've also included a copy of a little book of Poe's poems I've edited recently—thought Grace might enjoy it.

To Robert Hivnor

August 17, 1966

Sorry to reply so late to your note about Delmore's funeral, have been occupied w. commitments since I got back from Texas last month (including a memoir on him for *N.Y. Review of Books*, next issue).

By somewhat chance (because I phoned the Hotel Columbia when the *Times* story came out, w. his body unclaimed, and got put onto his aunt, who asked me to clear out the room), I was the one who went around, with two others from here, and packed up things; 4 boxes of books, mostly paperbacks, a few with copious annotations (Rilke and *Finnegans Wake*, which may be of interest), but no MSS except for ten or so notebooks with notes which I couldn't decipher (but which may be legible on closer examination). I'm turning them all over to his brother, from California, who is his heir (no will). It was very sad, a huge clutter of crumpled magazines and dirty shirts, he must have been horribly miserable, a dingy hotel room off Sixth Avenue, a solitary lair. Probably other places where MSS may be found, but not this last one. He died, like Poe, alone and unknown—took two days, evidently, for someone of the *Times* to realize who this "Delmore Schwartz" was, and without the *Times* . . . ?

Sorry I didn't think of telling you about the funeral, didn't know you were concerned, as a friend, shows how out of touch he was, we were, doesn't bear thinking about—best to Mary.

To Stephen Spender [marginal note "Not Sent"]

September 7, 1966

. . . Enclosed on Delmore Schwartz may interest you, case you haven't seen it. Awful, his death, in a cheap hotel off Sixth Avenue; heart failure; room full of crumpled "girlie" magazines, plus lots of paperback books plus half-dozen small note pads with indecipherable notes; no MSS; impression of despair and loneliness (Meyer's poem good, I think); nobody knew for two days until a *Times* reporter recognized his name, and a belated obit (quite good) appeared; I called the hotel, was put in touch with his aunt, who asked me to pack up his "literary remains" from the room, which I did; he must have been very unhappy; probably caches of his books and MSS will be turned up from earlier places he lived in; hope so.

To Dr. Sills

September 9, 1966

Thanks for your note of July 18th saying it's too late to submit my entry on mass culture. On my part also, "needless to say," I regret the Encyclopedia won't include it. I did mean to write it, and my failure to do so appalls me—it's one of a number of such failures to finish articles I've wanted to do and contracted to do in recent years. This particular failure is especially painful to me because mass culture is a subject I've thought a lot about and care about, yet, despite some thought and even some stabs at notes, I kept putting off the actual writing of the entry from month to month, year to year—it must be almost three by now—always there was something urgent, a deadline (what a descriptive term!), to be met; but always this was an excuse, really, there was plenty of time to do it; but I didn't. Yet I wanted to, if only to sum up my ideas on the subject and confront them with those of others, objectively. Maybe I've been writing too long. I feel a reluctance to go into things again and again and again—housemaid's knee, writer's cramp—and yet in this particular subject, so dear to my mind, what an entry might have been done if only I had another month. But I don't, and you've been monumentally patient, patience on a monument, and the only reason I got into all this is to make my apologies and to try to persuade you that my intentions about the entry were serious.

P.S. Now if you could give me till November 1 (1966, of course), well . . .

To R. W. Flint [a reader of Macdonald's obituary on Delmore Schwartz and a frequent reviewer of Schwartz's poetry]

September 12, 1966

Thanks for writing me about my obit on Delmore,[8] and for liking it—I tried to give some sense of what an extraordinary person he was and not only intellectu-

---

8. Macdonald's obituary of Schwartz appeared in the *New York Review of Books*, September 8, 1966.

ally but also emotionally, personally—the most enlivening of companions. . . . I do agree with you, since I read English, that Delmore, whether like Pavese or not, was never able to recapture the "power, humor, wit, conviction, and lyric art" of his first book. I didn't say so in my memoir because I loved him and wanted to commemorate him at his best, which was, after that first explosion of genius, expressed more in his talk than in his writing. But you're right—he didn't live up to his first promise. Something happened, maybe that he kept on with the same rhetoric in his poetry, the same formal style—so different from his free-wheeling, demotic talk—while in his prose stories (which I recently reread in his "Successful Love," surprised you praised them in *Commentary*) he retreated to a basic-English deadpan style that imitated formally the simplicity of "In Dreams Begin Responsibilities" but was garrulous where it was concise, and flat where it was tense. But these are matters of taste, and you may be right about Delmore's later stories, though you don't agree that the one about the track meet, published in this magazine as a matter of fact, in which his brothers kill each other, is a hectic, forced pastiche of "In Dreams (etc.)"? Still, maybe you were right to praise some of those later stories—the one about the genius who didn't make a fortune betting on the races, and why he didn't, was very good. As for blaming "the tragedy on American life," you're of course right, in a way—there must have been something deeply psychotic in Delmore, as in Poe, but don't you think it also significant that so many of our 20th-century poets, the best ones, have been what the English call "mental": Pound, Lowell, Jarrell, Roethke, Berryman, Sylvia Plath? (John Ciardi is an exception, granted.) I agree about the "primitive stamina and shrewdness" being important—as with Auden, the one great success as to long vital genius we have, but he's English, or also, in a smaller way, Frost—though Rexroth, after reading his "Autobiographical Novel," seems to me an instance on my side of the argument, such bland, genial, unperturbed vanity and insensibility is surely a little mad? And if he finally does totter around in his venerable white-haired nineties as the president of the National Academy, I'd say it would be one more instance of the inclement atmosphere of this country to poets.

But I've answered your letter at much too great, and polemical, length; a habit of mine, which will probably confirm you in your belief that you "never met him (Delmore) because, like yourself, Robert Lowell, and others, he seemed to have too much temperament for communication with my dim self." Believe me, your self is not "dim," as expressed in your letter, and I cannot understand your feeling about Lowell, Schwartz, and myself (flattered to be put in their company), and next time I'm in Cambridge—my younger son is an undergraduate there and it may be soon—I hope to have the pleasure of meeting you at last.

To Mr. Dohle

September 19, 1966

Your query to me of last Feb. about "Midcult" got lost in my papers and in my travels (Texas, Mexico, Maine) and only now has surfaced. Hope not too late. Yes, suppose it should be capitalized, and yes, I did invent it—a portmanteau word: middlebrow-plus-culture. See page 37 of my *Against the American Grain* (Vintage Books, 1965), where I first coined the term and also defined it. There I called it "a peculiar hybrid bred from the unnatural intercourse of High Culture with Mass Culture . . . that threatens to absorb both its parents . . . an intermediate form that pretends to respect the standards of High Culture when in fact it waters them down and vulgarizes them." If this definition is too polemical for your dictionary, as it probably is now that we are two centuries more advanced than Dr. Johnson, how about: "an intermediate form between High & Mass Culture that shares some of the qualities of both."

You might also want to include another term I made up, which seems to me useful: "parajournalism" which I defined in the N.Y. *Review of Books* a year or so ago (the *first* article on Tom Wolfe) as "a bastard form that combines the factual authority of journalism with the imaginative license of fiction." Or words to that effect—can't lay hands on the piece.

To Stephen Spender

September 20, 1966

Time printed The Letter, as perhaps you know by now. They only today sent me a copy—I don't read the sheet—and in case you don't know, here's the clip, from last week's issue.

Thanks for your letter of the 12th. I share your doubts and fears about Mel [Lasky] as a wheeler-dealer—he's much like LBJ, I'm afraid—it's not that they are evil or even unethical, just that the moral sense seems to be lacking in their makeup, like people I've been told about who have no tactile sense, so that only the smell of burning flesh tells them they are resting their hand on a hot stove. A lie is a lie only when it's found out. I wouldn't put anything past either of them, since power, success is their only criterion of what is right and what is wrong. As you know, I've long been disturbed by those persistent rumors that the Farfield Foundation was, among other more legitimate things, a bagman, a transmission agency for funds secretly given by the CIA or the State Dept. to the Congress (and via the Congress to *Encounter*). So I'm sympathetic with your own worries about it—odd that Jack Thompson[9] should have struck you,

---

9. Thompson, a CIA agent, was the longest-serving director of the Farfield Foundation, which funded many of the publications sponsored by the CIA for the Congress for Cultural Freedom.

as he did me years ago when I queried him on matter at Jason Epstein's (think I wrote you a letter at time), as somehow, when one came to reflect, not what the lawyers call "responsive."

Anyway, it was unsettling when the *Times* CIA series threw in that sentence about the Congress being a recipient of CIA funds, secretly. A "front," as you write — and do tell me what Josselson replies to your query. When I was in Texas, I got a note from Dan Bell asking me to add my name to a letter that Galbraith, Kennan, Oppenheim, and Schlesinger had printed in the *Times* of May 9th. I finally decided, after reflection, not to, because on reading over the letter carefully I saw that while they asserted about the Congress that "we have no question regarding the independence of its policy, the integrity of its officials or the value of its contribution" and that "the Congress has had no loyalty except an unswerving commitment to cultural freedom," these four distinguished persons did not state directly that they knew, or even that they believed, that the Congress had NOT ever received CIA or US govt. funds. Secretly, of course, if such was the case, the secrecy is my chief objection; had it been openly stated (assuming it is true, of course, which I don't know one way or other), I'd argue that *Encounter*, at least, was one of the few real successes of the CIA's history. So I didn't sign. (The *Times'* "retraction" or apology, by the way, also took the same line: not that their factual statement had been wrong but that no effect on the policy of the Congress or *Encounter* was evident — i.e., they were both splendid, valuable enterprises, etc. But this really was not the issue raised by that remarkable little factual aside in the original articles. So I didn't sign the letter.

Well, too much of this, but it IS disturbing to me, since I was on the payroll for a short time, as it is to you, I am glad, but not at all surprised, to see. I quite agree with you, by the way, that the American editor of *Encounter* shd. not have been connected w. the Congress, so it is a pity that Mel was Kristol's successor (also for other reasons — burn this letter!).

Hoping, dear Stephen, to see you over here some time in the next year — and if we don't make connection then, or even if we do, Gloria and I may well come to visit you and Natasha in Provence — sounds idyllic and thanks for the invite.

To Nicholas Macdonald

September 22, 1966
... P.S. On that N.Y. *Review* article by Stokely Carmichael[10] — and see he's plunged in, again on wrong, or racist side, to the middle of the troubles at that

---

10. Macdonald kept up a running argument with both his sons during the sixties. Nick was on the left and a defender of black militancy. Michael often took a position to the right

new ultramodern Harlem school, where the parents want the white principal replaced by a black, and ALL the Negro teachers, 40 or so of them, half the staff—have joined w. their white colleagues to insist that the white principal be retained because he is qualified and they admire him and like him (actually!). And because they are smart enough, as Stokely is not, to see that professional standards in teaching will be degraded by giving parent or community groups control over the hiring of the teaching staff; today it's "liberal" (heh heh), namely a black community has the right to insist on a principal who has a black skin, but tomorrow it may be "reactionary," i.e., some Birchite racist, whose skin is differently colored from Mr. C's, insisting that in an all-white community only light-colored principals and teachers be employed. . . . But anyway, getting back to what the sentence began to say, re Carmichael's article we discussed on phone, please read the tenth line at the top of page 5 and especially the climactic conclusion: "Responsibility for the use of violence by black men, whether in self-defense or initiated by them, lies with the white community." The words "or initiated by them" are the point; they seem to me to mean that if a Negro mob beats up or kills white people who happen to be in the vicinity, the responsibility is not theirs but that of "the white community"—you and me—because historically we, or at least our ancestors, have mistreated the Negroes, as we (they) have. Suppose the NYC police had not protected Mr. Lisser, the white principal of that school that was opened today with him as principal and w. the Negro leaders, including Carmichael, opposed to his taking office, and suppose that some extremist Negroes, those Black Panther chaps, had jumped him and beaten him and broken his leg, as the white racists did in Granada last week to a Negro schoolboy, then the logic is that these goons are justified because other Negroes had been maltreated by other whites. So all whites, including Mr. Lisser, you, and the many others who have been trying to redress the injustices done to the Negroes by some of our fellow whites, so we must take our beatings, or lynchings, as what's coming to us because of the color of our accursed skin. Or is there something wrong with this interpretation of the logic of Mr. C's statement? If so, do tell me. But first have a look, please, at the best political article I ever wrote, "The Responsibility of Peoples" in the *Memoirs of a Rev.* where I try to explain and illustrate the fallacy, logically, and the repulsiveness, morally, of such attempts to make a whole nation, or a whole race, "collectively responsible" for atrocities that have been committed by only part of them.

---

of his father. Dwight was never really able to justify any "nationalism," black, Jewish, or American. He wrote some stiff attacks on the black militants in columns for *Fortune*. When the SDS was taken over by blacks, he asked that his contribution to their cause be returned. It was.

Moral responsibility must be individual, for what the specific person has done—else we get the gas chambers and the Southern lynch mobs, and, now, Negro ideologues like C. making no distinction between white lynchers and white liberals who have defended their rights, like the mayor of Atlanta and that principal here, Mr. Lisser.

To Harold Hayes, managing editor of *Esquire*

October 5, 1966

. . . As I told you, *my* choice wd. be John Simon. And if *Esquire* hasn't decided, may I suggest you try them out somehow? Pauline [Kael] is a better journalist, but John is a better critic, in my opinion; that is, she will do lively, neatly formulated, clever, and provocative pieces, intelligent as to all that surrounds a movie (culture-socio-politically), not as to its value as a work of art. She seems not interested in that aspect. Simon, on the other hand, writes rather heavily and not very neatly, but he has a much wider and deeper cultural background—sorry to use such awful terms but shorthand, I mean he knows and has thought more about other "fields"—ugh—like books, theater, and art—and also his work seems to me to show an interest in what I think is the point: whether the film is any good aesthetically. With Pauline, you'd have a fairly sure thing, for what you want, I'd say—about like Muggeridge on books—and not ignoble or cheap either (ditto w. Malcolm), quite good and interesting on one level. But with Simon, you'd have a gamble, between a scholastic and not-neat aestheticism and—if it worked out—a much richer and more intellectually daring kind of criticism than Pauline's (BURN THIS LETTER).

My only practical suggestion is that—if you have not already decided—you ask Simon to write a guest column, paying him for it whether used or not but not committing yourself. He seems to me to be the last potentially rich vein of critical ore not already mined by the kultur-explosion, and I think he might be (though God knows no guarantees) just what you're looking for.

To Lawrence Grauman

March 2, 1967

. . . Read your NR review of the book on [Randolph] Bourne w. liveliest interest (and not a disappointed interest, either) and shd. like very much to come to your class on US social criticism, esp. if about Bourne, who I think of indeed as one of my ancestors, in fact, I planned months ago using recent books on him as an excuse to present him, in my *Esquire* column, as a still relevant Ancestor. One sentence bothers me in your review: "Had he lived beyond 32, he would have surely worked through the agony of his misplaced confidence in intellectual solidarity, would have evolved new possibilities for turning culture into power." The two concluding sentences after that don't reassure me, either. "Turning culture into power" strikes a sour note in my ear, sounds like the Dewey instrumentalism that Bourne rejected after his disillusionment with the liberals' pro-war stand; and while Wilson WAS "Messianic"—cf. last two issues of *Encounter*—I don't see Bourne as such; he was moral, true, as any serious social thinker must be, but it seems to me he precisely didn't have the naive, Protestant illusion of Wilson that he was in touch with God and The Right; that's one reason I admire him, indeed. . . . But we can talk about it. . . .

P.S. Thanks VERY much for that superb clip about R. [Roger] Baldwin's introduction to the book by Capt. Bosworth on the Japanese detention camps—shall take notice in column after I've had a look at the book—what gall, brass, hutzbah [sic] on B's part—not unexpected to me after my experiences with RB in re a profile I wrote of him in the *New Yorker* which he didn't like at all and which he tried to suppress, or at least emasculate, by threats of libel suits—not successfully.

To Mary McCarthy

March 27, 1967

Have you paid your income tax yet? If not, would you consider joining me and 10 to 15 other people with some kind of "names" like Cal Lowell (who may come in, he says), Meyer Schapiro, Feiffer, Brustein, Sylvia Marlowe, Hans Morgenthau (haven't asked any, just got idea today) in withholding half your tax because you don't want to pay for the war in Vietnam and other wars, and signing a public statement to that effect? (I hope if you do come in that you would write it, or at least do the first draft—and even if you don't or can't, that you would!)

I got the idea from Chomsky's sentence in his reply in the NY *Review* to Steiner saying he had been withholding half his tax for the past two years—just had long talk on phone w. him, he sounds v. nice and entirely first-rate and serious.

I have thought of tax-withholding before but seemed too much expense and possible legal danger and certain bother—but now I feel I must DO something, must stick my neck out some way—Chomsky says it is technically a crime and one might go to jail (though he hasn't been bothered yet, and my own tax man says it takes them years to get around to actual confiscation or legal proceedings), and I don't at all mind if there is danger, in fact I was rather pleased to hear there may be—I cannot get used to the Vietnam business, every morning I get angry and appalled and ashamed all over, it seems to me to be getting worse and worse, and I want to take some kind of risk to show my complete horror and disgust at what my govt. is doing there.

Or do you have some other idea of an action? Please write me at once one way or other—and if you are sympathetic to the project, suggest some good names, maybe Sandy Calder, do you see him? Or James Jones, is he still in Paris? I've also talked w. Bob Silvers and he says he'll put it on the front page, or maybe he said on the inside of the front page, anyway I think 10 to 15 really good, interesting, well-known names signed to a well-written, strong, and passionate denunciation of the war plus the tax-refusal business would be a very effective gesture at this moment. Do write and advise, etc. (Both Hannah and Auden also have already paid their tax.)

P.S. Silvers tells me your first Vietnam piece is masterly and so did Bowden, actually, last night. He (Bowdie) says you are a good person—I have to agree. Best to Jim D. (He may have even said "noble"—but surely that's going too far?)

To Mike Josselson

March 30, 1967

Thanks for your note of the 15th and the text of the Congress's statement of Feb. 23rd on the CIA subsidy scandal. You write you "expect to have to come out with my own statement sometime" and say you're not sure "just when is the right point." If I might advise, judging from the Congress's statement and your letter, what you say in your own statement rather than its timing is what you should worry about. You and the Congress don't seem to realize that, as a result of the disclosure of the secret CIA funds, the Congress and all its works, including *Encounter*, are in a very awkward, possibly fatal, position, that I'm not the only person who feels betrayed and disgusted, and that the policy the Congress and its leaders have up to now pursued of evading and glossing over the scandal by talk about independence and good works won't work now that there is no doubt that the CIA *was* subsidizing it for years just as all my more radical friends insisted and I, like a damned fool, denied on the grounds they didn't have any hard evidence (as of course they didn't—and couldn't).

Unless the Congress and *Encounter* and its other journals break the continuity with the CIA-dirtied past—i.e., state they DID take CIA money (the Feb. 23rd statement has the gall to say "allegedly!"), either apologize for doing so or if, like you, they are not "ashamed," at least explain why they did so and what good they think has come from it (an argument could certainly be made), state they have not done so since (whatever date—in the Congress's case when the Ford Foundation took over last fall, in *Encounter*'s several years ago when Cecil King took on the whole financing), and also state that the resignations of those executives, editors, trustees, or whatever who were in on the secret have been regretfully accepted. Unless some such break with the past is made, I don't see how the "credibility gap" that has been opened can be closed.

Instead, up to now, everyone has hushed things up, beginning with the letter signed by Galbraith-Schlesinger-Oppenheimer last spring after that one-sentence statement in the *Times* that the CIA had financed *Encounter*. Dan Bell sent me the letter asking me to add my signature, but I didn't because I noticed that while it was strong on *Encounter*'s being independent, serious, honest, and a splendid magazine in general—which I agree it was, in general, the case—it nowhere denied the real charge, which was that the CIA funds had been taken. So it was an evasion, not a lie, but not meeting the issue either. So too the Feb. 23rd statement, which uses "independence" thrice and "integrity" twice but still, even after the fact has been publicly proclaimed throughout the press, tries to dodge and equivocate. And how CAN you, dear Mike, brush off the *Ramparts* disclosures as a "witch hunt"? Doesn't that remind you of anything? There were C.P. witches then and there are CIA witches—one of the Congress's having the witchy name of Holblitzelle!

Do you think I would have gone on the *Encounter* payroll in 1956–7 had I known there was secret US govt. money behind it?[11] If you do, we are really out of contact. One would hesitate to work even for an openly government-financed magazine—it wd. depend on how much real independence one had, and could be sure of—but not many serious writers would edit, or even contribute to, a journal they had discovered was taking secret govt. funds. I think I've been played for a sucker, and I wish I could do something more about it than devoting most of my next *Esquire* "Politics" column to it—like, say, suing the Congress, if only there was the law Spender suggested might be a good idea now in his letter to the *Times* last week, for putting me in a position in which

---

11. Macdonald had heard many charges that the CIA and the State Department were covertly funding publications, particularly *Encounter*. He continued to dismiss such charges even when Nancy wrote him that this was the case. Gloria took one look at the magazine and said it read like a State Department publication. Macdonald wanted the editorship so he could live in England for a year. It appears to have been one of those cases in which his interests shaped his perceptions. People like William Buckley and Daniel Bell found it hard to believe that Macdonald was really unaware of secret funding. See Francis Stoner Saunders, *The Cultural Cold War: The CIA and the World of Arts and Letters* (New York, 1999), pp. 394–395, 411.

my personal & professional reputation is, now that the secret is out, not exactly strengthened, since I can't *prove* I wasn't in on it.

I realize, of course, that it would have been very difficult, most likely impossible, for the Congress and *Encounter* to get the kind of intellectuals to work with them that commanded respect had it been announced how much of the money came from the CIA. It also appears that the CIA was not only a most tolerant and noninterfering angel in many cases, including NSA, but also, back in the McCarthyite days, one of the few sources of big subsidies that dared to fund liberal ventures (like that Latin American teaching program Norman Thomas headed). These excuses could be put forth, and they are worth something. Myself I think there is something inherently wrong about secrecy in such matters—not only the lies that those in charge must tell all the time, but perhaps more important, the impossibility of those not in the know ever being sure there hasn't been any pressure or persuasion or influence—how can mere human beings ask for such trust? The tremendous reaction to *Rampart*'s exposé (which I think was salutary) shows most people feel, as I do, that secret financing is wrong & dangerous. Just today, I see that the President has accepted the advice of his committee and announced that henceforth all secret financing of cultural, educational, and philanthropic private groups will be discontinued. (He and his committee of course defend the past subsidies—saying, in effect, we didn't do anything wrong and we promise never to do it again.) My choice, confronted by the dilemma, either secret CIA funding or no Congress, wd. have been the latter. But you could make a case for the former—only do please realize that you have to come out and make it and recognize that, at least tactically, the Congress is now in a very delicate condition and can't hope to breeze along as before with talk about its "independence" and "integrity" and persiflage about "witch hunts."

Forgive my verbosity, frankness, and, no doubt, priggishness, but I do feel concerned about "the whole business," and not only personally, and it does seem to me that up to now the leading spirits of the Congress haven't indicated in their public statements as much awareness of the dare-I-say moral aspects of the crisis as they might have.

P.S. I am sending carbons of this to J. K. Galbraith, Malcolm Muggeridge, and Stephen Spender. Hope you don't mind.

P.P.S. To give you an idea of how the recent revelations touched off by the *Ramparts* piece on the CIA and the NSA have put the Congress and its activities into a more dubious light than I'd formerly seen them in, there's that rejection by *Encounter* of my "America! America!," a highly unfavorable impression of the American way of life compared to the British and the Italian, I wrote and submitted after my return in 1957 from my year abroad with *Encounter*. "In the whole business," you write, "there's nothing I'm ashamed of—except for that letter I wrote you about your *Encounter* piece on America. My very next trip to the US showed me how much more in touch you were than I was." Okay, but considering that opposition to the article from the Paris "front office" of the Congress played some part in the rejection, how do I know, how can I know (or you either) that your awareness of the secret CIA subsidy played some part in your own conviction that the article was unfair, one-sided, biased, etc.?

To Malcolm Muggeridge

March 31, 1967

I think the enclosed carbon of a letter I've just sent to Mike Josselson will interest you, and I have a feeling you are one of the few big bonzes of the Congress, if not the only one, who may be sympathetic to my criticisms of its public statements on the CIA mess (also *Encounter*'s) and my suggestion for a new policy. Spender—with whom I had a long talk the other day about the business and who thinks, as I do, that a sharp and public break must be made in the continuity of both the Congress and *Encounter* with their CIA-financed pasts if they are to survive with any respect, or perhaps to survive at all, though the letter enclosed is all my own idea and he hasn't seen it—Stephen says you are on some kind of board of trustees set up to oversee *Encounter* when Cecil King began to finance it some years ago. If so, and if you agree with my suggestions, maybe you could raise the question with the board of coming clean publicly about the CIA funds, just stating they existed to begin with, and then either justifying them as means necessary to a good end or raison d'état or whatnot or else expressing regret it happened, and then—the really awkward question—coming to grips with the problem of Melvin J. Lasky. I'm practically certain Spender didn't know the Farfield and Hoblitzelle Foundations were CIA "conduits," partly because I've known him fairly well a long time and it seems out of character, completely so, and partly because long before the *Ramparts* exposé blew the gaff, we were corresponding about our uneasiness about the persistent rumors of CIA money despite the reassurances we had had—but somehow uneasy reassurances—from executives in Farfield and in the Congress when we—quite independently—had pressed them for an answer. I cannot see Stephen going in for such an elaborate and protracted dissimulation—or indeed capable of carrying it off—as wd. explain his part in our mutual worrying and uncertainty, including letters as to his intentions of "having it out once for all" with Josselson. On the other hand, I can easily believe that Lasky WAS in on the CIA deal from what I know of *his* personality, over quite a long stretch of years—he's not a liar or immoral, he just doesn't seem quite openly and almost naively (cynical operators are often very naive, I've found) to have any moral sense. The question appears to him to be not part of real, or serious life. Also other is the fact of his long and close connection with Josselson and the top inside leadership of the Congress from the very beginning, his habituation, like Josselson, to working on a govt. payroll for cultural purposes since 1945 or so (openly of course as publisher of *Der Monat*—if only *Encounter*'s funds had been equally frankly acknowledged!), and his continuing, after he became editor of *Encounter*, to spend a lot of his time working with the top-level executives like Josselson and more recently, I'm told, somebody named Hunt, on Congress business. It seems to me almost incredible—nothing is wholly incredible, I admit—that Josselson knew about the CIA subsidies and Lasky didn't. (I chanced to be in the *Encounter* offices a month or so ago, the day after the CIA-Congress link had first been reported in the press, and Lasky's reaction was really something—good God, what next! Who'd have thought it? Really, Dwight, it's just too much, isn't it—all those years, etc. Mutual head-wagging at the duplicity of the World in which we two innocents had to exist. Later that day he showed me a draft of a statement by the Congress which seemed OK except it said nothing in the way of defense, apology, or contrition about The Point, had it been on the take from CIA or not, indeed didn't mention it—I suggested there WAS a problem there and maybe the statement should meet it. He agreed that was a good point—but the statement that appeared on Feb. 23rd followed his draft and ignored my suggestion.) I have absolutely no evidence that Lasky knew or didn't know about the CIA funds (and how could I? or anybody?), and if you and the other trustees are satisfied he didn't, that's that. But I'm not at all satisfied, and I think some effort shd. be made to find out, perhaps by asking him formally as a starter (but not as a finisher). As of now, I think *Encounter* is compromised by his being the editor, and that he should be persuaded to resign in favor of some Englishman (maybe John Gross? I hear he resigned from the editorial board as soon as he learned of the CIA funds, which shows some moral guts, and he is certainly one of the best of the younger literary men in London, as to writing style, facility, critical acumen, and an extraordinarily broad range of knowledge.) But an Englishman—no reason now that the mag is all English financed, for the Anglo-American co-production front; and an Englishman wd. arouse more confidence than an American at this point.

Well, see what you think, Malcolm, and God bless you and affectionately,

P.S. Should have written you long ago about that "I Like Dwight" tribute in your last book—I came on it as I was reading, with my usual pleasure, in your prose and your irreverence and wit and indignation (and my usual reservations about some of the objects of your irreverence, etc., such as the late Mr. Eliot and what you sneer at but I revere as "INTELLECTUALS") through the volume and suddenly, like a snake in one's path but with the opposite reactions, there was your Tribute, so generous and persuasive and amusing and well-intentioned, even if part of the intention was to expose me as what I've spent most of my life in the higher-brower NYC circles trying to prove I'm not, an instinctive philistine and midbrow. But maybe you're right, how can I resist both you and Norman Podhoretz? Look what happened to the Kaiser and then Hitler when they tried to fight on two fronts! Anyway, thanks. . . .

To Desmond Smith

April 10, 1967

. . . I'm sending you under separate cover, as soon as I can get another copy, the first of Mary McCarthy's series that has just come out in the N.Y. *Review of Books*—masterly, I think—they sent her to Saigon to see for herself—there'll be three more—let me know if you'd like to see them, too, when they appear. . . . I can't seem to get used to what we (or rather "we") are doing in Vietnam, every morning's *Times* is a shock all over again—the death and cruelty and massive destruction, all for no purpose either practical, human, political, or even US self-interest—and every morning I have all over again the question—why are we there, what right have we to be pulverizing with our bombs and blowing to bits with our shells and killing and pushing around with our troops those people, North or South? I think this is the worst thing we have ever done and getting worse daily—today's *Times* says (1) the war dept. has admitted having used fragmentation bombs (each with 800 "baseball-sized" metal balls that shoot out w. compressed air on impact) in N. VN for months; (2) the Navy is thinking of "reactivating" a battleship or two w. 16-inch guns to really tear up the coastal towns, from 15 to 20 miles. I'm ashamed to be an American—since 1936 I've been actively anti-Communist, but now? What price democracy?

To Mary McCarthy

May 17, 1967

This isn't a proper reply to your letter of April 4th which gives me such good advice and which confirms my best suspicions of you—I still am beset with deadlines and other harassments, seem to have no time, my own fault, a dry, hard period for me. I just want to thank you for your letter, to say I agree that tax refusal isn't the way—am now working up a letter of civil disobedience, people over draft age like me trying to share perils of draft-resisters by breaking law against conspiracy to urge draft refusal—more on that shortly. Also to thank you for your absolutely *superb* three pieces on Vietnam in the N.Y. *Review*. One of the best things you've ever done—everybody I meet talks about them, admires them, even some of your hitherto unfans—you realize you DO have some, don't you, Mary dear, as I do. God knows we've both tried hard enough to create them! Even such admit the success of your reportage, its insight & imagination combined with—not so often such a combo—hard, fair, conscientious setting down of just what you saw and heard, in convincing detail.

As you'll see from the last two or three pages enclosed column—the July one, w. is devoted wholly to Vietnam—which was written before I saw the end of your last article, I arrived at a notion of American-style genocide over there that is similar to yours. Not to mention, as you won't be surprised to find, a general agreement on the whole terrible, awful, more and more alarming business: what IS that President doing to us, he seems to be out of control rationally and morally, and it's getting worse now every week, it seems.

I also enclose the column before that (in the issue that has just come out) because you may be interested in what I say about the CIA-*Encounter* affair. It was written six or seven weeks ago, long before Spender-Kermode resigned and Lasky did not. Shall have something to say about that in my next column—really scandalous, I think, the whole affair—maybe Muggeridge (Jim just called, said you had stayed with him in country) showed you a long letter I wrote him early in March on topic? (He hasn't replied, but I shd. imagine he is sympathetic—unless his overdeveloped cynicism makes him say, with Lasky, it's "a storm in the teapot." But I hope not.)

Must run, just wanted to get these in mail now, at last—also to tell you, as if you didn't know, how good your Vietnam things are. And to thank you for your letter—and to promise a real letter soon.

All love, dear Mary.

To Martin Luther King

June 12, 1967

Please accept the enclosed as a token of my admiration for your continuing to insist on nonviolence in your race-relations work, and also for your recent new radical dissent from President Johnson's genocidal war in Vietnam. I agree that our country has become the main center of violence in the world today, also that, since the President seems to pay scant attention to lawful, "orderly" protests, it is now necessary to go on to the next step: civil disobedience. Nonviolent, of course. (I recently debated William Buckley, Jr., on his TV show, *The Firing Line*, on "How to Protest," and before I knew it, he was asking me: "Now you say that you have come to feel so strongly against Johnson's Vietnam policy that civil disobedience, breaking the law is, for you, justified." Well, then with that serene Buckley smile, "Well, then, wouldn't you say that Lee Oswald may have had such strong objections to President Kennedy's policies that he practiced civil disobedience by killing him, and that he was morally justified, according to your own logic?" It took a few minutes to get out of *that* box.)

All good luck to you, Mr. King, in your struggle on both fronts.

P.S. You may recall that we met, briefly, at Wesleyan University in the spring of 1964 when we were both given honorary degrees.

To the Editor, *New York Post*

June 14, 1967

Describing me as "that eminent pacifist," your Mr. Buckley finds it inconsistent of me to oppose our armed intervention in Vietnam while advocating the same thing (allegedly) in the Middle East crisis. As usual, Mr. Buckley is both inaccurate and illogical.

I may be eminent but I am not a pacifist and haven't been since 1949. The statement I signed said nothing about armed intervention but merely called on the President "to maintain free passage in those waters [the Gulf of Aqaba, an international waterway] and so to safeguard the integrity, security and survival of Israel." But even had I advocated armed support (through the UN) defending Israel, which I should have had Nasser's armies seemed likely to "push the Jews into the sea," I see no logical parallel between dispatching American troops and planes to fight a civil war for a regime so unstable and unpopular its own armies won't fight for it (not to mention our bombing of a neighboring country) — between this and sending them to help a country with a stable and popular government to repel an invasion that would probably have resulted in a general massacre had it succeeded. I was for the Berlin air lift, for Truman's sending our troops, with UN sanction, to defend South Korea against Communist invasion, and for British military aid to Malaysia to repel Suharto's terrorist commando raids.

If this be Long John Silverism, let Baron Munchausen make the most of it — as, indeed, he has.

Yours more in anger than sorrow,

P.S. The Baron has a point, a mini-point, when he finds it odd I should want to "uphold our [national] honor." Sorry about that. Not my style, agreed, but didn't seem important enough to refuse to sign.

To Nicola Chiaromonte

July 5, 1967

Of course I know you have no objection to publishing me in T.P. [*Tempo Pesente*, Italian journal edited by Chiaromonte and Ignazio Silone]—you've demonstrated that by doing so, plentifully, leaving aside our personal relations, by which I mean not at all our friendship but rather our deep congruence, over so many years, on the essentials of political events—and arrived at quite independently of each other, of late years too, such as the ending of your letter: "I hate Johnson. I really do. I think he is a catastrophic presence on the world scene." Bravo, bravissima, dearest Nicola! For months now I have been reluctant, shamefacedly, but irresistibly coming to the same conclusion (which I hope was evident in the Vietnam piece [in *Esquire*] I sent you and I think is even more explicit in the one I've done for next month's issue [Macdonald was writing a regular column, "Politics," in *Esquire*]. Our whole training has been against such "subjective" feelings—I mean our Marxist and (classical) anarchist education in looking at history—but I too can't help hating, detesting Johnson, quite personally, as I did Stalin and Hitler. I think as you do he is, himself, in person, a "catastrophic presence on the world scene"—also a ditto in US history, the worst president we've had, the one who's done dirt more than any other on the best of our political tradition, and all the more effectively because of his very abilities. He's no fool and he has a vigorous and terrifying will, like Hitler and Stalin, if only he were the normal kind of "bad"—read "weak"—president like Polk, Buchanan, and the post–Civil War ones, except for Cleveland, a good if limited statesman, and such 20th-century boobs, but benevolent and ineffectual ones, as McKinley, Harding, Coolidge, and Eisenhower! O to regress to those Eisenhowerean years of never meeting any situation head-on, of passive do-nothing-ism—Dulles talked a good brinkmanship crusade but it was all talk when the chips were down as in Hungary. Rusk goes over the brink into action—and clings there forever by his fingernails, let the Marines fall where they may. And how much longer can we absorb those heavy casualties whenever the VC and the NV regulars make a point of exacting them, as they do almost daily now? (Plus the senseless horror of our heavy bombing of Vietnam, N and S, of course, but I'm talking in strictly US practical-political terms.) I don't think either Eisenhower or Kennedy wd. have tried to "bull it through" in Vietnam as Johnson has. I think they were normal politicians, bourgeois leaders w. some calculations of profit and loss to restrain them (McNamara is the only one of the big three in the cabinet who seems to have that kind of prosaic caution), and I agree w. you that Johnson is a catastrophe for us and the Vietnamese.

To Hannah Arendt

August 30, 1967

Greenwood Press—a new house that is specializing in reprinting complete sets of old magazines, notably radical ones—is reprinting, or rather rephotographing, *Politics*. (I've lunched with the head, seen his promotional stuff, talked with people who know him, and it is a serious venture—aimed mostly at libraries, of course.) Now don't do it as a favor to me, for God's sake, do it only if you'd like to, if it would interest you—but would you like to write a short prefacery note to the reissued set? Nothing elaborate, a few pages or so, whatever you think adequate, just giving your ideas on what the quality, meaning, whatever of the mag was in its day, what it did (and didn't do—you know I don't want a blurb, and I know you wouldn't do one if I did want it), just a brief critical-historical evaluation, to be pompous.

I've thought of many people for weeks, but you are the one who I would prefer to do it, the one more on the same wavelength than anybody else living I can think of, I mean the same as the mag's (also you, luckily, didn't contribute to the mag, since we barely knew each other then). Now please, Hannah, only do it if it would amuse you to, not for my sake. Just let me know, soon if possible, either OK or No, thanks, sorry—and if OK, I'll get a set to you. (Doesn't have to be long—just so it places the mag, defines it journalistically and historically.) If you don't want to, I'll either ask Galbraith (keep this quiet though) or else maybe do it myself. And if you don't want, can you suggest somebody better than Galbraith? (His advantage is the opposite of yours—he's NOT on the same beam, w. wd. give his note a certain crossfire interest.) Shd. be somebody of some "name," of course, also some solidity. I'd also thought of Daniel P. Moynihan, but maybe he's too much off the *Politics* radar screen?

To Klodie Osborn

September 6, 1967

. . . Just got back from the NCNP conference in Chicago—Nat. Conference for a New Politics, that is—which was a disaster, alas; the "black caucus" blackmailed, no pun intended, the New Left whiteys, who outnumbered them 7 or some say 10 to 1, into giving them, the b.c. that is, everything they asked for, like a bratty kid being pacified by a permissive parent; 13 propositions, take it or leave it, and indeed if you don't take them, adopt them as the conference's view or we leave (inc. #5, "We condemn the imperialist Zionist war; this condemnation does not imply anti-Semitism)—and #4, "Give total and unquestionable (MUST MEAN "UNQUESTIONING?") support to all national people's liberation wars in Africa, Asia and Latin America . . . ," plus #10, "Make immediate reparation for the historic, physical, sexual, mental and economic exploitation of the black people." And #11, "We strongly suggest that white civilizing committees be established immediately in all white communities to civilize and humanize the savage and beastlike character that runs rampant throughout America." These 13 points were adopted by the whites—who were in a 10 to 1 majority—by a 3 to 1 vote. Next day the whites voted by 2 to 1 to give the black caucus 50% votes in all committees and also in the plenary sessions of the conference itself, the main event when some 2,000 delegates and representatives met to decide things—so the conference became a committee of itself.

Well—see my *Esquire* column two months from now—meanwhile tell Bob that I saw a bit of William Sloan Coffin, the Yale chaplain (he gave a speech at the opening session), v. agreeable guy but hung up on the New Left bit, I think, and he remarked that Yale was well represented there, true, what with Ben Spock, me, him, and others, inc. a David Graham from Maine (Staughton Lynd wasn't there, though). Nor was R. Osborn, damned clever these Osborns.

To Dave McReynolds

October 16, 1967

Sorry to be so late in reply to your Memo of Sept. 19th on the possibility of a campaign for impeaching Johnson. Have been both busy and dilatory. And now (tomorrow) I'm going to the country to get a few writing jobs done, including my first political column for *Esquire*. (Did you know I've given up the movie column and am doing instead, at their request and to my delight, a monthly column on politics?)

I'll be back by Monday, the 24th at latest, but if you want to reach me sooner they have phone here. Meanwhile:

Your memo is one of the most thoughtful and original and interesting political analyses I've seen in a very long time—it should be printed, in toto, in *Liberation*. It wd. make a splash, believe me—and they should do it just as is, no cuts or style changes—the way Byron Dobell, at *Esquire*, launched Tom Wolfe (ugh . . .) By taking his notes on the kandy-kolored [*Tangerine-Flake Streamline Baby*] etc. cars in Calif. (or was it some other thing?) and printing them as was, merely deleting the "Dear Byron" with which Wolfe had begun his 25-page exposition of why he couldn't do the article.

You really, actually, seem to be thinking, not to my surprise—I've long thought you were the best brain around in the pacifist movement, and, as you may recall, I was horrified when you burned up your draft card because such a mind shouldn't be sacrificed by getting jailed—"Save the cadres!" as Jim Cannon perhaps apocryphally cried when the Trotskyist headquarters were on fire years ago and he and other invaluable bureaucrats elbowed the stenogs and mailers to the exit.

But to the point:

(1) I agree that Johnson is the target to aim at—that it is he, personally, who has gotten us into Vietnam (and Dominican) messes, because of his own character, and that to shoot at Rusk, McNamara, and so on is waste of ammunition. Also that he is different from previous presidents from FDR through Kennedy, more ominous, less trusted (for good reason) by people, more psychologically twisted toward personal face-saving, etc. (See Evans-Novak book, if you haven't, New American Library—really unsettling.) Russian peasants used to say, "If only the Czar knew," assuming he would countermand his ministers' injustice, but they were wrong. It's LBJ that is doing it now—and to hell with all that business about his being complex, etc. that Rovere and other decent guys believe in. He is not only, as your memo says, committed to a military-victory-or-nothing "solution" in Vietnam in a political sense, but also in a personal sense. That good old boy jest don't want to lose.

(2) But I think you should consider the impeachment ploy from two angles your Memo hasn't thought of sufficiently: (a) would such an action not arouse such massive emotional backlash, and from the liberals as well as the masses (whoever or whatever THEY are), as to make us anti-war, anti-Johnson people even more isolated than before—as the "Black Power" nonsense has already done in race relations? And (b) on what legal grounds, exactly, are you proposing to impeach the President? Your Memo said nothing about them. Myself, I would not support such a move unless there were constitutional grounds for it (because I am a fan of the US Constitution, on the whole—also because it would be absurd to invoke a legal sanction if it turned out there isn't, in our laws, any grounds for it—okay to stick your tongue out at LBJ, but "impeachment" sounds to me like something that has to be anchored in law—also, of course, as it has just occurred to me, by talking of "impeachment" you, or we, are granting there is a justice to the Constitution and the law, as I don't think would be granted by, let's say, S. Carmichael and some of the hotheads in the WRL and/or pacifist movement who would be delighted to throw up their caps for IMPEACHMENT).

So, in general, I am all in favor of "concentrating our fire" on LBJ—and MAYBE such an extreme move as impeachment might push the *Post* and other liblabs farther toward our position, but maybe it would have opposite effect, as seems to me by now adequately demonstrated by the "black power" fiasco. But we should consider those maybes carefully. Also we should get lawyers to tell us what grounds, exactly, we have for demanding the impeachment of that sob LBJ.

But do print your memo in *Liberation* anyway—it would be one of the most sophisticated political analyses there in years—have you suggested it to AJ?

To Frank Lindenfeld [academic, peace activist, and author of a manifesto on the dialectics of liberation—a make-love-not-war document]

November 11, 1967

I understand your problem about length and have no objection to the cuts you want to make in "The Root Is Man." The only one I suggest you reconsider is the para. on p. 36 beginning "The fact that everybody agrees. . . ." It's not long, and it makes a rather subtle point, I think. But this is just a suggestion; if you are really strapped for space, then omit it too.

P.S. I write "regards" instead of "yours" bec. I read your manifesto and feel a kinship w. you. I can imagine how my old pals, I. Howe and P. Rahv wd. snort in contempt (did you see their long polemics in current *NY Review*; just like the old days, I agreed w. some of each, but more with Rahv than with Howe) "infantile leftism! petty bourgeois romanticism! . . . but can't you *see*, Dwight, it's not POLITICAL! What does he mean, *practically*?????? And they'd be right—as f.i., how "we" are going to practice "self-defense" while continuing to love everybody and fuck everybody in the sun, everybody that's willing of course, and not be part of the system of violence and death—but still I like the spirit and I go along with every word—"philosophically," you understand—I'm all for your utopia, an experiment noble in purpose, as Herbert Hoover said of prohibition. But what's a nice libertarian like you doing in a sociology department?

To Gloria Macdonald

November 19, 1967

. . . Shawn appeared in my office yesterday afternoon, or rather materialized in his silent-butler, unnerving way, like a ghost whose haunting periods are far apart. . . . There Shawn is—came merely to ask if I was still doing the Mailer review—I said yes, half written already but so many other Calls on My Time because of political stuff—and we talked of the war, told him I liked Rovere's piece (and gathered he too was relieved that Dick had finally decided he'd given LBJ too much benefits of too many doubts and was getting out from under on Vietnam). . . . Dr. Shawn Is Worried—I do like him, also respect him, he thinks well, and soberly, seriously, also he does have an old-fashioned conscience—I like that.

So one thing kind of led to another and Bill 'lowed as how mebbe I'd like to do some writin' for his paper after all these years [Macdonald still had his *New Yorker* office but was writing almost exclusively for *Esquire*] and says he'd take most kindly to the idee and I said sure would, Bill—and so maybe, I mean mebbe, what with this Noo Skool proposition I kin kind mosey away from them highbinders over to the Lazy E Writin' Ranch and join the good guys again, or agin. But have to take it slow, they been right good to me over to the Lazy E and a man don't run out on his pals sudden, he does it slow and easy like.

Getting that McNamara piece done at all was a triumph of will and experience—also, if say so myself, character, w. is really habit plus energy over intolerable repulsion, or rather seemed intolerable at time (I spent hour after hour, up to 10, 12 on the last two crucial nights and days, in NOT writing it, in sleepless nervous tension, reading Agatha Christie stories I knew already, dozens of Kipling stories I've known since 14, etc., anything to avoid getting down to the torture-rack of the typewriter—but, w. help of bourbon (had run out of pep pills) did manage to get the thing done, huggermugger, and once bulk was there, was able to improve by rewriting and, more important, to add, in spurts of effort limited to one point only, perhaps the best things in it. Final result reads not badly, not my best goodly either, but my second-best good—I'd have done anything to get out of it (where was Satan? What a missed chance for a soul!)—anything except of course NOT doing it. That void in the issue's lead piece slot HAD to be filled and I had to do it, so I did. Oh God, thought. And then next day to have to drive myself to the 650 words on civil disobedience for the *Times*—they came out better, I think, than McNamara. But there must be pleasanter ways of existing for me at 61, so let's see what the New School offers.

. . . Sorry to inflict all of this on you but as I began to write you, I felt I had to communicate to SOMEBODY a little of what I've been through in the last week, low point was ten days ago when I came back, utterly exhausted from interview in DC with McNamara (just flew down and back, saw nobody, had been up a night or two finishing the piece, turned out to be a third of the whole if not more, and not the worst part) and went to bed for 20 hours—you see, I do it even when you're not around, it's not directed against YOU, my sweet dumkopf! "Principled dumkopf" wd. be more accurate—you do it on *purpose*, yes you do! That splendid brain of yours which can cope w. anything, realistically as well as imaginatively (or intuitively, if you insist) if you give it a chance, and then you switch it off for long periods, you starve it of oxygen, stifle it with reflex prejudices and "feelings," and of course it doesn't do so well, and then MY brain, w. may not be so big but gets plenty of oxygen, i.e., I make the most of what God and my parents' genes have given me—then my brain pushes yours (deliberately) enfeebled one around and there are cries, tears, bellows, recriminations, etc. and it's the End, The Iron Door Is (at last) Closed again, and you're leaving in the A.M. and you never do think God but do let's try when you get back to be better with each other. I'll restrain my too-lively brain and you give more rein to your too-inhibited one, and if we both try hard—and realize we love each other, as is the case and don't forget it—maybe we can rock along on a more even keel and come to love and respect each other not only in general but in particular.

To Robert Lowell [they had participated in an anti-war march on the Pentagon in October 1967]

November 29, 1967

Forgive the italics—you've become dear to me not just formally. A friend. The only person I feel as free, talking, as I used to with poor Delmore [Schwartz]. A rich Delmore too—what an abundantly speculative mixture of imagination & commonsense, wit & passion, sense & sensibility! Well, you get the idea; rather like yours, dear Cal. Also rather like Wilde's, it's recently occurred to me. Oscar was almost always RIGHT (except in his erotic tastes and habits) about all the big issues of his time—social, moral, aesthetic. I'm thinking of lunches w. Delmore and other talk-meetings, but lunches are what I remember most, and he did have an Oscar brio, didn't he? Also the same SCOPE, ready for anything, up to everything, something to say about whatever was on the agenda. I'm also thinking, apropos of Oscar, of the Rupert Hart-Davis collection of his letters; "The Soul of Man Under Socialism," "The Importance of Being Earnest's," and "De Profundis" (the full text, in R.H-D's collection—how remarkable that out of a personal quarrel came a document so full of insight into his own condition—and so, since it is true, or so I think, into all our conditions—all the more remarkable since Oscar was so obviously, overwhelmingly right in all his complaints against [Lord Alfred] Douglas).

But I have gotten off the subject, sorry.

All I had in mind before all these divagations into Delmore and Oscar, was to tell you that your Pentagon poem reads even better in NYRB [*New York Review of Books*] print than it sounded on the phone. You have a great gift, as you must know, in your verse and also in your public ceremonial utterances (as, to name recent example, what you said at the Hilton press-TV conference and what you said outside the Dep. of Justice on Nov. 20, Friday, of stating exactly what *you* want to state, no more and no less. It's not just a "personal you," although I suppose it's that essentially (and that's why it makes a dent, an impression, since the direct, personal voice is absent in most public discourse, poetic or political). But there's another dimension to it, I think—you seem to be able to express yourself both personally, idiosyncratically, and also in words that are related to an objective, current reality, to the historical period—pompous but can't think of anything else at the moment. Your Pentagon poem was extremely personal and yet also quite impersonal because it expressed what others besides you—as, f.i., me—felt about the experience. What I admire is your brevity and your lack of the conventional rhetoric, in both your poems and your public talks. They're connected, I'm sure, no? I mean the brevity and the anti-rhetoric. One of my many writing problems is rhetoric—I can't get away from it enough, it forces my ideas into formulation which, I feel, are not only inefficient (because the form distorts the content—too much, that is; of course any form affects the "content," if indeed one can think of "content" apart from "form") but also long-winded. As in the preceding sentence. How do you do it? I think I know, but I'd like to talk about it with you. When shall we two lunch again?

To the Editor, *Village Voice*

December 21, 1967

Considering the seriousness of the issue, I think your readers may be interested in the full text of a letter I wrote to William F. Buckley, in reply to a "challenge" he gave, in his December 5 column in the *New York Post*, to Dr. Spock and especially me. Mr. Buckley printed most of my reply in his December 16 column and I'm not complaining that he made extensive cuts—even in its truncated version it filled half the column. But I regret Mr. Buckley didn't consult me about cutting for space; I might have suggested alternative cuts that would have better preserved my meaning. Your readers may judge for themselves.

Mr. Buckley challenges me to put up or shut up about civil disobedience and lawbreaking. He proposes a "High Noon" shoot-out in the offices of his magazine on January 4 at exactly 3 P.M. (tick, tock, tick, tock), and he offers to provide young men for me to attempt to subvert into refusing conscription for the Vietnam War, in the presence of TV cameras, a representative of the Department of Justice, and, of course, himself. I must regretfully decline the gambit, for several reasons. How does he get into the act? Who appointed HIM sheriff? Assuming the government needs more evidence of my lawbreaking than I've given in writing and verbally (twice with TV cameras in action), why should I provide it in the offices of the *National Review*, a magazine for which, as Mr. Buckley knows, my admiration is not excessive? Martyrdom, if it comes to that, can be staged under more dignified conditions.

But I deny his assumption that the Department of Justice needs any more evidence than Dr. Spock and myself have copiously, tediously provided, including what Mr. Buckley quotes from our remarks at the press conference that set him off. He chides us, indeed, for issuing a brazen "defi" to The Law. He quotes my statement, "What we're doing is not just dissent, it's a deliberate violation of the law," and remarks: "Mr. Macdonald is being as plain as any man can be." But not plain enough for him, it seems, since a few inches further on, in one of those dizzying trapeze leaps of illogic that make his writings so charming, he finds we are "a foxy lot" with a "subtle ace up their sleeve," namely: "The draft card turns out not really to be a draft card, but a facsimile. Take them to the grand jury and all of a sudden, in the privacy of the chamber, they will plead the Fifth Amendment, and the government will not have a prosecutor's case."

My draft card, and Dr. Spock's and those of our 2000 coevals who have by now signed a "Call to Resist Illegitimate Authority"—which notifies the authorities that we are illegally conspiring to support and encourage young men to resist the draft—our cards are not even facsimiles. They are nonexistent. I burned mine, for instance, in 1948 during a demonstration against peacetime conscription.

As for "taking the Fifth," we would be as illogical as Mr. Buckley if we did so since it would negate the two purposes we have in mind by taking a stand of civil disobedience: to make it awkward for the authorities to continue to prosecute young draft refusers without also prosecuting their elders who are breaking the same law, and to bring about a demonstration trial, which the press would not ignore, in which the immorality, and the illegality, of the Vietnam War could be thoroughly explored by the defense. I agree with Dr. Spock that the authorities have no ardent wish for such a trial. If they decide to risk it, there will be no need of "High Noon" melodramatics presided over by Sheriff Bill to give them evidence for indictment. Nor will there have to be a rendezvous at the *National Review* if they want to arrest us. I'm in the Manhattan phone book, and Dr. Spock can be found on the nearest picket line.

To Collector of Internal Revenue

January 15, 1968

As a patriotic American concerned for my country's good name, I can no longer find it in my conscience, or in my common sense, to continue to pay taxes in support of my government's military operations in Vietnam. The enclosed check for $731 is 25% less than the $975 due for the fourth-quarter installment of my 1967 income tax. This is my rough estimate of the proportion which would go toward the prosecution of President Johnson's increasingly senseless and genocidal war.

If 25% is too high, please let me know, with supporting figures, and I will remit the balance due. If it is too low, I shall expect a refund. I want to have no part, financially or otherwise, in this dirty business. I'm sure you will understand my feeling, unofficially.

P.S. It's too late for the 1968 tax forms, but for the 1969 ones may I suggest you consider including a line stating the exact percentage of the income tax that will go for the Vietnam War? And perhaps also another line or two giving a statistical projection for other wars imminent or in progress—Laos, Thailand, Cambodia, Burma, Malaysia? China I don't expect—too many variables, and too massive ones. Maybe most practical thing would be a box—with deductions to be estimated later—in which the taxpayer could check off the wars of his choice.

To Joan Colebrook

January 15, 1968

. . . More and more involved on Vietnam. Indictment of Spock, Coffin, et al. in Boston last week ominous new escalation of LBJ's campaign against domestic dissenters. If Coffin (Yale chaplain, and w. much religious backing) comes, can Dwight be far behind? We had a v. good press conference last Thursday (see *Times* Jan. 12 for a fairly full, and for once fairly fair, account) in which we supported the five Boston indictees and challenged the Dept. of Justice to include us. Two serious, sober, nonhippy young men gave us their draft cards, w. TV cameras buzzing & blazing, to hand on to D of J., an open conspiracy.

We'll see. My impression is that we've a lot more support than I'd expected, this war is too disgusting. I made a mini-speech (picked up by *Times*): "I have reluctantly decided that civil disobedience is the only adequate answer to the immorality and the illegality of what our government is doing in Vietnam. This is the first time in my life I have felt obliged to violate the law."

You are worried lest the USA be "forced into isolation (Yankee Go Home)." I'm worried that we won't be—Yankee Stay Home is my slogan in the consulship of LBJ. Maybe we could do some good abroad, as in the time of the Marshall Plan, backing up countries that don't want to be Communized; but the LBJ military all-out methods produce the opposite result—the means are so atrocious they infect the ends.

Well, goodnight, dear Joan, see you soon I hope.

To Mark Raskin

January 25, 1968

I'm a little disturbed by your gnomic note of the 22nd.

Agree it would not be *pro bono publico* if "the best people" (us—let's not quibble) "should be in the can over the next decade"—though, to be literal, it wd. be at worst, w. time off for good behavior, half a decade. But I don't understand your second sentence: "I am very anxious that those who have done what they are doing realize the possible penalties." Leaving aside the confusion of tenses, I would say that we—that is, you and I and the other ringleaders of the Resist group—started the whole action in order to challenge the government to arrest us so there would be a "show trial," with maximum publicity because of the eminence of the defendants, which would challenge the legality, and would impugn the morality as a side effect, of the Vietnam War. There was also a secondary objective: to try to share the legal guilt of the young draft-resisters our statement encouraged. So if we didn't realize the possible "penalties," we damned well should have—else what was the point of the whole business?

God knows I share your disinclination to be imprisoned, for all sorts of personal reasons, interestingly different for me at 62 than for you at 33 (or so I'm told your age is, I'd have guessed, from your talk, a decade later, this is meant as a compliment) but strong for both of us in that our productive work would be, to say the least, interrupted. And I won't pretend I'm not relieved that I wasn't included along with Spock and Coffin, the stars so to speak, in the first five chosen, by some legalistic abracadabra I don't understand, for indictment. Paul Goodman and myself and others did try to get into your act, as you know, at that press conference two weeks ago. No success so far, which was OK by me. I've no desire for martyrdom (the only way one can get into the history books without talent, as General Burgoyne says in *The Devil's Disciple*).

My point is, dear Mark, that while I'm in favor of the most vigorous and far-ranging defense of you five—and for us later fives if it comes to that, God forbid—I think we must, if it comes to a choice, put the general question, the legality of the war, before the personal, the First Amendment defense. And we, that is, our lawyers, must all hang together or else. . . .

But perhaps I misread your note. Could we talk about it next time you're in New York, for my sake as much as for yours? I *won't* be seeing you in Boston next Monday, by the way, because I have to rally round a draft-resister at Whitehall Street that morning, but if you pass through the city that afternoon, could we have an hour together? I can be reached here, always. Or suggest some later date.

To Leroy Harvey

January 30, 1968

The course I took with Canby at Yale was in writing—"advanced writing," or maybe "composition"—think too early for that awful locution "creative writing." Can't recall why I took it, since I was already writing a lot for all the publications—it was in my junior or senior year—maybe because I was curious to discover the rules for doing what I was doing (was the only "writing" course I remember taking in school or college—they weren't so common then, of course).

Or maybe in reaction against the "romantic" lecturers who dominated the Yale English Dept. and whose method I disdained as what I later called "mid-cult"—Tinker, French, Berdan. Canby was not romantic, certainly—his appearance, manner, and mentality were those of a rather dim, cautious, snuffy clerk in a legal or insurance office, one notably unimaginative even for that profession. Can't recall any stories, anything specific—the idea of anecdotes in conn. with Canby is absurd—just a deadening academic mediocrity in responding to our writing, or our ideas. I seem to recall that several of my literary friends also took the course and that we made fun of him among ourselves—we were very clever and we thought we were very advanced (as we were, God knows, compared to Canby)—and used to bait him, in the polite, underkeyed style of the '20s, in class. It was hard to make an impact, however, since he seemed to have no personality—couldn't get a rise out of him—he was a function of the sober, respectable academic mentality, and there was no way, short of mayhem and obscenity (neither of which even occurred to us then, circa 1926), to push his reactions out of well-worn professional grooves.

Professor Pierson (name sounds familiar but can't recall knowing him, only Norman Holmes Pearson—who might also have made the remark) is right about Canby's two-dimensionality. Very good. Assume you're "doing" Canby—scraping the bottom of the barrel even for a Ph.D. dissertation, I'd think—in same spirit I once "did" James Gould Gozzens.

Hope this of use to you—quote as you like for your thesis.

P.S. Canby was one of the last pure examples of what I call (page 50–1 of *Against the American Grain*) "academicism." Norman Cousins, who succeeded him (though with a hiatus, probably) as ed. of the *Sat. Review*, is an equally fine example of "midcult." A corruption, to gain a larger audience—Canby's *Sat. Rev.* had maybe 60,000 at top, Cousins' now has 600,000, I'm told—of a sterile, stuffy genre which did have integrity, vis-à-vis the crowd-pleasing style of mid-cult, although a dead kind of integrity. Hell with both.

To James Malcolm Williams

April 24, 1968

I've already signed your statement calling for the impeachment of President Johnson, months ago, and I agree with your recent letter pointing out that it's still a useful & necessary task. As always with Mr. Johnson, his credibility gap is gapping. His idea of stopping the bombing of North Vietnam is to continue it on a scale as massive, in tonnage, as before (though not in geography—but that he now "spares" 85% of the North Vietnamese people from our bombs also suggests we were destroying them before we, or he, decided to spare them) while our military operations roll up every week casualty lists much as before. As for his Lincolnesque renunciation of the presidency—not that Lincoln, a practical and nonhypocritical politico, wd. have made such a gesture—we'll see. The quip here was (after it turned out that LBJ was sending the bombers, still, hundreds of miles inside the boundaries of North Vietnam): If that's his idea of stopping the bombing, what does he mean when he says he won't run again?

I don't trust him around the corner, not even up to the corner, and it's not inconceivable he may be "drafted," not too willingly, as The Great Peacemaker. (Though after all these weeks of stalling on the site for the negotiations—"I will go anywhere to make peace"—and even rejecting Warsaw—which Rusk agreed to, as Drew Pearson has revealed—one wonders. . . .)

The awful thing is that while I'm grateful for his taking for the moment a de-escalating line (more or less, as above) and even more for removing his catastrophic presence from the White House (also more or less), I don't trust him either way. He'll double-cross us by making peace (as a ploy for getting himself "drafted"—to get us into some more Vietnams in 1968–1972) or by not making peace, as seems his present line. I realize this is illogical and unfair (though how can any unfairness measure up to LBJ's policies?), but I think I can back up either suspicion. So up the impeachment!

To Joan Colebrook

May 16, 1968
Here's that first Mailer column—parody not bad, I think—hope you enjoy, anyway.

And do look at my next *Esquire* column, out June 15th, where I really go into things.

Sorry I was so overbearing at lunch—which I did enjoy, and even, such perversity, enjoyed our talk! My only defense (for my overbearingness, alleged by you, constantly, and doubtless truly) is that to every point you made a dozen counterpoints occurred to me, instantly, from experience and knowledge, also from my native wit, of which I still retain some, and so I had this uprush of argumentation—data, rationality, simple common sense—that did possess me and forced entrance through my mouth, despite my fondness for you and my sincere will to SHUT UP. But I couldn't, nor will I ever, I'm afraid, so there's no hope in future if we get on serious topics like Vietnam and McCarthy and LBJ—dearest Joan, you know you actually asked me whether I voted for Henry Wallace in 1948—if you're that vague, how can we talk except (in my case) in shouts?

So let's NEVER bring up any political topics again—to me you seem to be as ignorant and irrational—and, indeed, pixilated—on the topic of communism as I do to you. I can't understand your recent (last 10 years or so) evolution towards what seems to me a narrow, uninformed, hard-line, and even at times paranoiac (sorry . . .) anti-communism (I'd put it in quotes, for I think your and LBJ's kind of anti-communism, like the first McCarthy's, is giving the world over to communism) any more than you do my gradual change of mind, in the last 15 years, about "communism" and its threat—the change being that I see more and more that there are all kinds of communism, some quite agreeable to me (and to the national interests of my country.) And most recent change of all, in the last 3 ghastly years of LBJ's Vietnam insanity, for the first time has made me less worried about Soviet (or Nazi) violence as a threat to the peaceful status quo than I am about our own ditto.

I think this is an extension of my old political viewpoint, in the thirties and forties and fifties, that I've not changed my values. You doubtlessly think the same—so we can't talk about it anymore, it seems—at least whenever we do, the result is as the other day—you seem uninformed and unreasonable to me, and I seem overbearing to you. (Can't resist pointing out that your objections to my argumentation are always on form—don't shout, don't interrupt, let ME say something, etc.—while mine are always on the subject matter—can it be simply that my voice is louder?)

Well, love, dear Joan, but God knows what we can talk about next time we meet.

To Noam Chomsky

June 3, 1968

Good to see you again yesterday in Boudin's office—sorry shan't be seeing you in Boston as a witness (bec. wd. like to have an hour or so talk w. you) since B., after his aide had asked me to the Sunday meeting for briefing as a witness, changed his mind, remarking that I have been "in too many places too often," i.e., too deeply involved, for his purposes. Can see that, but why didn't he think of it earlier? Was he put off by my interventions at the Sunday meeting, which were all along line of that I had thought I was breaking a law, was being civilly disobedient, and that such had been my understanding of whole point of Resist; that we were going from lawful pressures to defiance of the (draft) laws?

This brings me to one of the reasons I'm writing you. It seemed to me, from yesterday's meeting & from the *Times* reports of the trial, that the defendants have been too much influenced by their lawyers to make a legalistic, rather than a political, defense; to rest their case too much on the First Amendment and too little on the illegality and immorality of the war and the illegality of the draft act. True that latter defense probably isn't going to win, while former (1st amend.) has good chance, or *some* chance; hence the lawyers emphasized it. But also true that it was other line that motivated us all, was reason we all stuck our necks out in the first place; to get a "show trial," a political-moral confrontation w. the govt. on Vietnam. (Also we wanted to share the perils of the young who refused to be drafted—and a 1st amend. defense certainly doesn't do that, since they can't possibly claim they are merely exercising their right of free speech, since they have taken a specific action, violating the law.)

This line of the lawyers leads to things like Coffin's May 31st exchange w. the prosecutors:

Q: It was not your intent to persuade anyone to turn in his draft card?

A: That's correct.

Q: It never entered your mind?

A: There might be an outside chance. But it was not my intention. Their decision had already been made.

True that Coffin, like the rest of us, didn't try to persuade any youth to violate the draft laws—not bec. we didn't want them to but bec. we didn't feel had the moral right to urge them to a course that was much more likely to get them imprisoned than us. But also true that we—or at least I—(a) knew that our attacks on the Vietnam War and our repeated statements that we wd. aid and comfort all youths who refused to be drafted for it (and were willing to take whatever legal penalties might be imposed on us for this encouragement) might move some of them to break the law who mightn't have otherwise; and (b) we welcomed such a decision—as I myself did when my younger son, Nick, turned in his draft card last December, without any specific persuasion from me but of his own accord—and hoped that many more wd. be encouraged to take such a stand by the support we tried to give them in Resist.

The lawyers naturally want to get their clients off but, I thought from yesterday's meeting at least, they have imposed this ambition on the clients (and the witnesses) to the exclusion of the main reason for the whole trial. OK to "take the first" but not at expense of the rationale we all began with.

My second worry, as I told you briefly yesterday, is that the defendants haven't made any general, lengthy statements on the legal and moral issues of the Vietnam War. Probably because it's been the prosecution's case up to now. But now the defense is beginning, and I think it essential that some of them try to get into the record such a statement. The court will almost surely reject it, true. But the press may not—the *Times* MIGHT run it, and certainly the liberal weeklies would—coming from one of the defendants, such a statement wd. be "news," they have a special advantage in getting public attention for their views (w. you and I, f.i. don't have) and it wd. be a pity not to exploit it. Such statements cd. be either short and personal, or long and documented. But they should be made, now, during the trial. Again that's one of the reasons we all took our course of Resist action, the hope of getting a public platform.

To the Editor, *New York Review of Books*

June 20, 1968

HELP SDS. This is a personal, and urgent, appeal for money. The SDS—Students for a Democratic Society—which played a major part in the recent and, in my opinion, beneficial disturbances on the campus of Columbia University, is about to be evicted from its New York headquarters. It needs $3,400 for the down payment on larger, cheaper offices in a friendly cooperative building. This will be a permanent solution for at least one of its problems. I hope you will contribute.

"In the last ten months," writes Anita Simpson of the SDS regional staff, "the New York office has been evicted from three locations. The charges against us have always been vague—'bearded, unkempt people in the corridors,' 'other tenants request your relocation'—but the message is always emphatic: 30 days to get out, lease not withstanding. As long as our organization is kept in packing cases, it is dead. Our printing equipment is sitting idle, its installation frustrated. To end this nonsense, we would like to locate in a co-op building. We have an option on a loft in such a building on Prince Street. Its cost is $3,400 down and a monthly charge of under $100. This is less than half of our present rent. Please don't let the voice of SDS be stifled . . . Hail Columbia!"

It's always hard to write a "begging letter," and this one is especially hard for me because, as a member of the Old Left, I've long had, and still do, mixed feelings about the New Left, especially about the SDS or, as they disarmingly style themselves, the Students for a Democratic Society. Their political line—if one can use so definite a term, an attractive aspect of the SDS being that its organization is open, democratic, indeed anarchistically porous—has often seemed to me alienated to the point of nihilism, while their methods have sometimes been both deplorable, from a libertarian viewpoint, and, from that of making friends and influencing people, counterproductive. The only justification for such ideology and such tactics would be that there is a revolutionary situation in this country, which there obviously is not, in general. But on two particular, and major issues today, Vietnam and race cum poverty, there is such a situation, I think. The follies and the injustices of the Establishment, in these two cases, are so extreme and so indurated as to make necessary the use of the extra-legal pressures. Like, for example, the occupation—or, more accurately, the "liberation," as the phrase was—of certain buildings on the Columbia campus to which the students had a moral right, from concrete use and interest, that they successfully asserted against the abstract ownership of the trustees; for a while, anyway. The other condition, also met by the Columbia sit-ins, for revolutionary, extra-legal tactics is that there will be a broad response to the minority action from the majority directly involved—in this case the Columbia undergraduates—a general recognition that such actions, while unlawful and even, at first, statistically undemocratic, are the only ones adequate to the historical situation: the kind of outrageous defiance of the Establishment which can shove it off its dead-center stasis towards basic reform. Like what the Sorbonne students are doing; they may not topple de Gaulle, or they may, but the old place won't be the same again. Nor will Columbia.

So, on balance, I'm for SDS and I think the Establishment needs its shoving, and I hope you'll help SDS to survive—and to keep shoving.

P.S. Please make checks payable to "Students for a Democratic Society" and send them to: Students for a Democratic Society, 50 East 11 Street, New York 3, N.Y.

To Shirley Hazzard [novelist and essayist]

July 1, 1968

Sorry to be so late in replying to your letter of May 23rd telling me why you wouldn't give to SDS. Fact is I got so many similar letters—25 or 30, none of them as thoughtful as yours, and some of them much less so—I figured I'd make a general *apologia pro propaganda sua*, re SDS and Columbia strike, and Ivan Morris gave me a chance to do so in the *NYRB*—and I enclose the issue, see p. 41–2, if you haven't already.

On your points—I have to agree: the kids are a group, an Establishment of their own (BUT I like it better than others I know), and of course "profound ideas on complicated questions will probably continue to emanate, as usual, from individuals and not from groups." (Why probably—surely, I'd say.) Your two main propositions seem to me truisms. And of course I don't think it's enough justification (for ME) for SDS to keep "shoving" the Establishment—depends on which direction it's being shoved, and I liked the direction at Columbia. Well, we really must have a chat, Shirley, such simple confusions between us.

Also, what's all that about the letter being mimeographed and yet beginning "Dear Friend" and calling itself a "personal appeal"—as if something phony ("by the way")—you don't expect me to write them by hand, do you? And "Dear Friend" is like "Dear Sir" or "Dear Comrade," doesn't really MEAN it, and the "personal appeal" was mine (and I did write it, so why not? Personal *from* me, not personal to recipient—really, you ARE being difficult, Shirley!).

To the Editor, *New York Review of Books*

July 11, 1968

I'm grateful to Ivan Morris [Columbia University professor] for an opportunity to explain why I concluded, after visiting the campus to see for myself, that the Columbia student strike was a beneficial disturbance. My fund-raising letter for the New York Chapter of SDS, which stimulated his Open Letter to me, was undertaken mostly because I admired the Columbia SDS for the spirit and courage with which they gave the initial stimulus to the strike. . . .

But first let me deal with Professor Morris's specific accusations—or, more accurately, assumptions. He accuses "the leaders of the demonstrations" of a "resort to violence," including arson, and me of justifying "violence of this kind." But so far as I know in my five visits over six weeks to the campus, or read in the not overly sympathetic (to the strikes) *New York Times*, there was remarkably little violence: scuffles between "jocks" and strike sympathizers around Low Memorial (black eyes, bloody noses total damages, and the jocks weren't exactly pacifists), vulgar taunting of the police and some throwing of pop bottles at them when they invaded the campus those two frightening nights—I deplore the taunts and the missiles but much more so the invasion—and minimum resistance when the police cleared the occupied buildings, unless Professor Morris considers, as the cops do, that going limp and refusing to move when ordered by a policeman are categories of "violence." No, that commodity was monopolized by New York's Finest, as they used to be called, and they used it freely, sending a dean and a university chaplain to the hospital along with many students and some faculty members. Or perhaps by "violence" he means the immobilization of Dean Coleman in his office? I don't justify that—I'm against restricting the freedom of movement of Dow recruiters, or, indeed, anybody, but it seems not a crucial charge: the dean could have freed himself by a phone call to the campus cops; that he didn't was a tactical decision: he and his three immobilizees were not threatened, were well fed and treated by their own account, and they emerged from their ordeal unruffled, unstuck, and unindignant; anticlimax.

Or by "violence" does Professor Morris mean the occupation of the buildings (which I do justify)? If so he confuses illegality with violence. I oppose the latter, on tactical as well as principled grounds, and I've criticized . . . the romantic exhortations of certain New Left and Black Power leaders for a scorched-earth policy aimed at bringing on a "revolutionary" catastrophe. . . . I've lost some of my inhibitions about illegality. In certain circumstances—as when an administration, of a nation or a university, chronically ignores lawful protests against its destructive policies—it seems to me more moral to break a law with Dr. Spock than to obey it with President Johnson or President Kirk [president of Columbia University]. (This is also, by the way, a bourgeois reaction.)

I've written so much that I haven't space for much detail on my own reasons for backing the strike. When I first read about it in the press, I was against it on general principles: I don't approve of "direct action" that interferes with the freedom of others, nor would I see justification for a minority occupying college buildings and closing down a great university—or even a small, mediocre university. That was in general. But, as had often happened in my life, the general yielded to the pressure of the particular. On Friday I went up to Columbia to see for myself. I was egged on by my wife, who was sympathetic to the strike, on *her* general principles, and stimulated by Fred Dupee who, when I phoned him to ask what in the world was going on, said: "You must come up right away, Dwight. It's a revolution! You may never get another chance to see one." I came up and he was right. I've never been in or even near a revolution before. I guess I like them. There was an atmosphere of exhilaration, excitement—pleasant, friendly, almost joyous excitement. Neither then nor on any of my four later trips to the campus did I have any sense of that violence that Ivan Morris sees as a leading characteristic of the six weeks. Everybody was talking to everybody else those days, one sign of a revolution; Hyde Park suddenly materialized and as abruptly dispersed, all over the place; even the jocks were arguing. It was as if a Victorian heavy father had been removed from his family's bosom (or neck)—later I got a load of President Kirk on TV and I realized my simile was accurate—and the children were exulting in their freedom to figure out things for themselves. A fervid rationality was the note, a spirit of daring and experiment, the kind of expansive mood of liberation from an oppressive and worse, boring tyranny that Stendhal describes in the Milanese populace after Napoleon's revolutionary army had driven out the Austrians. The SDS putsch became a revolution overnight: like the Milanese, the Columbians had realized with a start how dull and mediocre their existence had been under the Kirk administration.

But what really changed my mind about the sit-ins was my own observation of two of the "communes," as the occupied buildings were ringingly called; Mathematics Hall, which I was let into—after a vote, everything was put to a vote in the communes—on Friday, and Fayerweather Hall, into which I was allowed to climb—all access by window—on Monday afternoon before the Tuesday morning police raid. Mathematics was the Smolny Institute of the revolution, the ultra-left SDS stronghold (said to have been liberated by a task force led by Tom Hayden in person) while Fayerweather was the Menshevik center—the "Fayerweather Formula" was an attempt on Monday to reach a compromise with the administration, but Dr. Kirk was as firmly opposed to it, doubtless on principle, as was Mark Rudd of the SDS. The two communes nevertheless seemed to me very much alike in their temper and their domestic arrangements. Rather to my surprise (as a reader of the *New York Times*), the atmosphere in both was calm, resolute, serious, and orderly; I saw no signs of vandalism, many efforts to keep the place clean and the communal life disciplined. . . . The communes were forever having meetings, must have become as deadly as a nonstop political caucus, but at least it was, or seemed to be, participatory democracy—which discussed the tactics to be used if the jocks tried to put them out as against those suitable for resisting the police. Everybody had his say as far as I could tell—had same impression at the Hamilton Hall sit-in before the second police raid—and the conclusion arrived at was sensible: resist the jocks because their armament was muscular only, hence the fighting would be on equal terms; don't resist the police because they had superior force—clubs, guns, tear gas—and also were trained in violence (this proved a true prophecy). . . . In general what struck me about the two communes I visited was the resourcefulness and energy with which the students were meeting problems they had never had to think about before, such as getting in and distributing food supplies, arranging for medical first aid, drawing up rules for living together in an isolated society . . . with some decorum and harmony, electing leaders, working out a line in democratic discussion that had to keep changing to meet the latest development in the complicated interaction between the white communards, the blacks in Hamilton Hall, the sympathizers and the opponents of the strike on the campus, the administration, the trustees, and the various faculty groups, plus the community in Harlem and in the immediate neighborhood. My impression is that the communards met these problems rather well, showing that intellectuals can be practical when they have to be. Also that they got a lot of education, not paid for by their parents, out of those six weeks, and that so did the thousands of students who milled around on the campus arguing tirelessly the questions raised in the first place by the SDS zealots. I'm told that one of the jocks admitted under pressure of debate, that while he still didn't think a tiny Minority had any Right, etc., he had learned more in those six weeks than in four years of classes.

To Fritz Stern [professor of history, Columbia University]

July 12, 1968

Thanks for your note of June 6th and apologies for taking so long to reply. I enclose the current issue of the *NY Review of Books*, in case you don't see it, with an explanation by me to a colleague of yours as to why, in detail and from some firsthand observation, I was favorably impressed by the recent Columbia sit-in strike, and by the SDS leaders who got it going. (See next issue but one of *NYRB* for Ivan Morris's reply to me, and mine to him.)

Don't hope this will change your mind about the strike—you must have had more chances than I to see for yourself, after all—but do hope you may be persuaded that something more than "moral obtuseness" was involved in my judgment. Also that I am NOT "saying, in effect (or in any way) that any action . . . can be justified provided it is directed against the Establishment." That wd. be against my whole past way of political thinking, and my present one too (must I add?). Ends don't justify means—that's why I broke w. the Stalinists in 1937 when it wasn't fashionable. Also why I founded, w. my former wife, Nancy (who really IS the organization, and a marvelous job she's done, too) Spanish Refugee Aid. It grew out of our "Packages Abroad" program, in *Politics* mag. (1944–9), whose aim was to help those European radicals who were both anti-fascist and anti-Stalinist.

Well, I really don't think I need to prove my *bona fides* to you, or to anyone.

My fund-raising letter for SDS tried to make clear my general reservations about that organization, also my specific enthusiasm for its part in what I regard as a beneficial subversion of the status quo at Columbia. You may disagree but you have no right, Seth Low Professor of History though you are, to be "appalled" by "the moral obtuseness" of my argument. (That DOES rather stick in my craw.)

Especially since the moral obtusity seems to me to be yours. In your last paragraph, you note your generous support of SRA in the past (for which my, and Nancy's thanks, $1,000 IS a lot to have given) and then add: "I confess that seeing your name on that (SDS) appeal makes me hesitate to continue my support. I would have thought that the Spanish refugees . . . deserve a better spokesman." Maybe they do, but I'm all they've got right now—at least if you reduce, as you seem to, SRA to me as chairman—and I don't see the justice, or the logic, of your threatening to punish them because they're stuck with me. Not *their* fault, really—and do suggest a successor. Believe me, it was a bottom-of-the-barrel choice two years ago when I accepted the job: Jim Farrell, Mary McCarthy, and Hannah Arendt had all done their bit, and there seemed to be nobody but me. Might add that after Hannah wrote *Eichmann in Jerusalem*, we got a few protests along your line: if that anti-Semitic Semite is your chairman, then. . . . She offered to resign but we—the SRA board, that is—thought that our friends, like you, would not in general penalize the refugees for the chairman's lapse, if any, and in fact this proved to be the case: receipts have risen every year, as you doubtless know, and are now at $175,000 per annum. Quite something, and I hope you'll continue to help us along despite your disagreement with the chairman as to the Columbia strike.

Thanks again for your letter, and forgive my running on so.

P.S. Those Students for a Restructured University (SRU) who put on that para-Commencement with Prof. Erlich, Erich Fromm, Harold Taylor, and myself as speakers—they're really more my type than SDS. But they didn't ask me to raise $$$ for them, and now the Ford Foundation has given them $10,000, glad to read, w. is three times the sum my letter raised for SDS.

To *New York Review of Books* [concerning the Columbia sit-in]

August 22, 1968

Ivan Morris now proposes a "homemade definition" of "violence" that fits his argument like a glove. But if controversialists bully words in this Humpty-Dumpty style, discussion won't get far. "The question is who is to be master," Mr. Dumpty explained to Alice, adding that he paid extra when he made his words work hard, as when "glory" had to mean "a nice knockdown argument." I'd rather not think how much overtime Professor Morris had to pay "violence." So let's try a real, manufactured definition, one in a dictionary. The two on my desk give: "Proceeding from or marked by great physical force or roughness; overwhelmingly forceful" (Funk & Wagnalls) and "Acting with or characterized by uncontrolled, strong, rough force" (Random House). I think my eminent friend would have to agree that these don't describe the tactics of the student strikers and do describe those of the police when they were called onto the campus, twice, by Dr. Kirk and Dean Truman to help them run their university.

The analogy between the taking over of President Kirk's office and a hypothetical occupation by Professor Morris of my apartment fudges over the difference between the personal and the professional, spheres—making distinctions isn't his forte. It takes a heap of living to make an office a home, and although from Dr. Kirk's laments about the brutalization of his office—he was so shook up that he forgot to express similar regrets about the brutalization of students by the cops he called in—one realizes that for an inured bureaucrat his office *is* his home—still, in the real not bureaucratic, world, the students took over an office, a more legitimate object of occupation because of its public, professional function. If my friend and his cronies hijacked my office, I'd temporize, partly because I'd be curious to see what their "rifling" of my disordered correspondence files turned up and partly because I would recognize an obligation to negotiate, really negotiate, not just in form.

On the burning of Dr. Ranum's research papers, I gave three possibilities: perhaps some nut fanatics from among the students, perhaps ditto from outside the campus, perhaps police provocateurs. I did judge it unlikely—giving reasons—that strike leaders had anything to do with this disgusting, and counterproductive, act of petty revenge. Now Professor Morris omits the first two categories and implies the cops were my chief suspects, adding he's never met anyone "even among those most sympathetic to the demonstrators, who doubted it was their doing." But *whose* doing, the responsible leaders or some irresponsible followers? It makes quite a difference—as noted, distinctions aren't his strongest point—and until our police, who seem better at cracking skulls than at sleuthing, on the Columbia campus at least, solve the crime, he knows just what to do about it, which is nothing.

And why does my friend assume he's won the argument when he triumphantly concludes: "I take it that the right to make omelettes in this particular fashion is restricted to people whose objectives Mr. Macdonald happens to support"? Oh dear, more distinctions. As a supporter, and former board member, of the New York Civil Liberties Union, let me state the obvious: (1) There is no general moral "right" to break the law as the student strikers did when they occupied the buildings (or as the 1936 sit-down strikers did when they occupied the Detroit automobile plants). (2) Whether one supports such actions or not depends on (a) whether one agrees with the aims of the lawbreakers, (b) whether one thinks the actions, the means are congruent with the ends and so won't corrupt or subvert them, and (c) whether one believes that lawful means have been tried and have failed. I've recently conspired with Dr. Spock, Chaplain Coffin, and many others I know as well as I do them to give support and encouragement to young men who violate the Selective Service Act; I'm also refusing to pay 25 percent of my federal income tax; both illegal actions that seem to me—as those of the Columbia strikers did—to satisfy requirements (a), (b), and (c) given above. (3) Therefore, if the jocks or the Birchers take over Hamilton Hall and refuse to leave until the trustees agree to begin building again that unfortunate gym in Morningside Park (this time on a lily-white basis, no place for the black community at all, top or bottom, segregated or not), when they appeal to me for support, enclosing a marked copy of my friend's letter, I'll have to say sorry, all a misunderstanding, you're on your own, baby, as far as I'm concerned.

Finally, Professor Morris's letters do raise, in however fuzzy a form, a serious problem. I tried to meet it in some of my remarks at a para-Commencement mounted by the strikers on the campus last spring while the official one was going on at the Cathedral of St. John the Divine:

"While I find your strike and your sit-ins productive, I don't think these tactics can be used indefinitely without doing more damage than good to the university. It would be a pity if Columbia became another Latin American–type university in which education is impossible because student strikes and political disruptions have become chronic. Nor do I think that our universities should be degraded to service as entering wedges to pry open our society for the benefit of social revolution. I'm for such a revolution but, I don't think it is a historical possibility in the foreseeable future in this country, and premature efforts to force it will merely damage or destroy such positive progressive institutions as we have. Their only effect—if any—will be to stimulate a counter-revolution which will have far more chances of success.

"An example of this kind of tactics—one can hardly call it thinking—is a recent manifesto by Tom Hayden in the June 15th issue of *Ramparts.* 'The goal written on University walls,' he begins, was 'Create two three, many Columbias' (a reference to the late Che Guevara's 'Create two, three, many Vietnams in Latin America'—one is enough for me, and also his effort didn't turn out a very solid enterprise, speaking in terms of history, not rhetoric). It meant expand the strike so that the US must change or send its troops to occupy campuses. . . . Not only are these Columbia tactics being duplicated on other campuses, but they are sure to be surpassed by even more militant tactics. In the future it is conceivable that students will threaten the destruction of buildings as a last deterrent to police attack. Many of the tactics learned can also be applied in smaller hit-and-run operations between strikes; raids on the offices of professors doing weapons research could win substantial support among students while making the university more blatantly repressive. . . . The Columbia students . . . did not even want to be included in the decision-making circles of the military-industrial complex that runs Columbia. . . . They want a new independent university standing against the mainstream of American society, or they want no university at all. They are, in Fidel Castro's words, 'guerrillas in the field of culture.'"

This program might be called "Building Socialism in One University" and it would have the same effects on the campus as Stalin's "Building Socialism in One Country" did on the Soviet Union; as in that case, the means would vitiate the ends and the result of Hayden's "hit-and-run operations," raids on professors' offices and chronic guerrilla warfare, would not be socialism, and certainly not culture, but a Hobbesian chaos of mindlessly reflexive "confrontations"— how he gloats over provoking the academic authorities into becoming "more blatantly repressive"!—about which a safe prediction is that it would undoubtedly be nasty, brutish—and short. An even safer prediction is that the campuses won't be Haydenized. A lot of capital has gone into our universities, and the bourgeois trustees and state legislators who control them are not about to turn over these plants to Mr. Hayden's, and my, revolution. He talks grandly of "the students" throughout his article, but this is as undiscriminating as Professor Morris's references to "the demonstrators." A majority of Columbia students responded to the SDS initiative because the demands were limited and reasonable—a brighter administration would have granted them before things got ugly, and "the military-industrial complex" wouldn't have been even dented—but, in a recent (June 6th) poll by Columbia's Bureau of Applied Social Research (C. Wright Mills was its co-founder), only 19 percent of the student respondents favored (as Mr. Hayden and I did) the tactics of the demonstrators, while 68 percent were against them. The actual occupation of the buildings was carried out by a large group—about 700, many of them Barnard girls—but it was still very much a minority, and even among these activists there was dissent from some of the more "militant" and uncompromising tactics of the SDS leadership, as in the big Fayerweather Hall "commune." The para-Commencement at which I spoke, for example, was organized not by the SDS but by the Students for a Restructured University, who had split from the SDS-dominated strike committee because they had the same objections to Building Socialism in One University that I expressed above. (The SDS was dubious up to the last day, when they did join, worried lest even a mock imitation of the real thing was not too great a concession to bourgeoisdom, since parody implies some parallelism.) The other speakers were two university chaplains, Jewish and Protestant, Dr. Ehrlich of the Economics Department, Harold Taylor, and Erich Fromm, and it was a beautiful occasion, spirited and friendly and digni-fied, with an audience of some 4,000, including 300 members of the graduating class in their caps and gowns.

When Columbia reopens this fall, I hope there will be no more High Noon showdowns between the Kirk administration and the SDS revolutionar-ies, and that both will compromise their principles for the sake of Columbia—and of sanity. The SRU has received a grant of $10,000 from the Ford Foundation to study and formulate proposals for reform, and something may come of this. Before Ivan Morris writes a third letter asking why I raised funds for the SDS instead of the SRU, let me explain that the former asked me and the latter didn't, perhaps because it wasn't in existence at the time; also that SDS is broader, and looser, than its Haydenesque and Ruddite infantile ultra-leftists (and I even like *their* spirit); and finally that the strike was needed and that SDS lit the fuse. "If we succeed in reforming Columbia," John Thoms of the SRU is quoted in the June 10 *Times*, "it will be because of the radicals." I agree with him.

The threat to Columbia this fall will come not from the SDS but from the petty, vindictive, and inept policies of the Kirk-Truman administration. By re-fusing to drop criminal trespass charges against hundreds of demonstrators and by supplementing them with suspensions, President Kirk and the trustees are sailing their ship into the minefield that blew it up last spring, setting the stage for a second round of student protest, police violence, and general uproar (this time, it won't be so creative, I think, and much more unpleasant). If Columbia is ever Guevaraized, the credit will go to Dr. Kirk more than to Tom Hayden.

The new undergraduate dean, Carl Hovde, wants the criminal charges dropped but is against academic amnesty for the strikers. Most of the faculty (78 percent) and even the students (70 percent) agree with him. The usual argument is that if you violate the rules, or the law, as a demonstration of principle, it is not logical to ask to be let off paying the penalty. Maybe not logical, but standard procedure in the other kind of strike: the first union demand is always that strikers shall be rehired without discrimination and that illegal acts of pickets shall not be prosecuted by the company. The 1936 Detroit sit-in strikers occupied far more valuable properties than five college buildings and for a much longer time, causing losses of hundreds of millions to the automobile companies, but the settlement of the strike provided no punishment for them. Of course, they won. And the demonstrators so far have not won. But let's be clear: the denial of amnesty is for that reason, not because of any moralistic nonsense about paying the price, etc. The Columbia bureaucrats think they can operate without settling the strike, i.e., granting amnesty. I don't. We'll soon see which view is right.

To Donald Harrington

October 8, 1968

I should like to join the Emergency City Committee to Save School Decentralization and Community Control.[12] I have long thought that our city's public schools were not educating most of their pupils, that the chief trouble was the centralization and routinization of methods and authority in the Board of Education, and that giving the communities involved more say is the most promising way of breaking up the present stasis and letting in some fresh air—and imagination. I'm also impressed by the efforts the Ocean Hill–Brownsville local board has been making of late to get something going, and I think it would be a tragedy if the present suspension is carried on long enough to destroy this first flowering of decentralization.

Several weeks ago I was asked to sign a statement, "The Freedom to Teach," circulated by an Ad Hoc Committee headed by Michael Harrington and Tom Kahn. After considerable hesitation—not long enough, it now appears—I did so because I thought the ten teachers fired by the Ocean Hill board had gotten a raw deal: the examiner who reviewed the evidence found in every case the specific charges unsubstantiated; I also thought it was necessary

12. This letter and some that follow deal with the Ocean Hill–Brownsville controversy concerning school decentralization and the demands of minority communities for community control. It became a struggle between black community activists and the Jewish-dominated American Federation of Teachers, and helped mark the decline of the alliance between Jews and blacks in the city.

to protect trade union rights against arbitrary actions. I accepted the assurance in the statement that "Decentralization is not the issue" and that "The United Federation of Teachers has pledged its full cooperation to make the reorganization succeed."

Recent events, however, seem to me to indicate that decentralization *is* the issue and also that the [Al] Shanker leadership in the UFT is not in favor of it, as the Ad Hoc Committee's statement implies, nor neutral, but definitely against it. I mean the threat of a third city-wide strike by Mr. Shanker in order to enforce the return of the teachers to Ocean Hill, and today's report in the *Post* that two UFT vice presidents, John O'Neill and George Altomare, have been removed by the Shanker leadership because of their opposition to a third strike, and also, in Mr. O'Neill's case, according to him, because of his publicly expressed views favoring decentralization and not favoring another strike.

Even were the position of the UFT as strong on the issue of the ten discharged teachers as I thought it was three weeks ago—I now have reason to believe that, in some of their cases too, decentralization *was* the issue—I should still prefer the alternative of allowing the Ocean Hill experiment to continue without the unwanted teachers (and also without setting any precedent, making it, as Mr. McCoy lately proposed, an independent school district, an ad hoc exception to all rules, for the moment), I should still prefer this to the alternatives of either destruction of the Ocean Hill embryo or another city-wide UFT strike. Finally, even as conventional trade union tactics it seems to me overkill to threaten indefinite paralysis of the city's public schools in order to bring pressure to bear on one recalcitrant segment thereof.

So I am as of today resigning from the Ad Hoc Committee to Defend the Right to Teach, with regret, and joining your group to Save School Decentralization and Community Control, also with regret. But it seems necessary.

To Mayor John Lindsay [of New York City]

October 16, 1968

The enclosed carbon of a letter I wrote a week ago might interest you.

I send it now because I've just read about the mob rudeness you endured at a Brooklyn Jewish center when you tried to reason with the crowd about the school situation. That outburst of mass feeling was, to me, unexpected. Perhaps to you also? And of course it can't be blamed on Mr. Shanker or the union. Not directly at least. But it's one more of a series of events, or symptoms, that caused me to shift my sympathies—as the enclosed makes clear—rather drastically from Mr. Shanker's UFT a month ago to Mr. McCoy's Ocean Hill–Brownsville a week ago. And now that the Shankerized UFT has actually struck the whole school system a third time, it seems clear where the blame lies for the disaster.

Although Mr. Shanker's UFT got the most visible support first, I hope you are coming to realize that there is a trend the other way now and especially among the kind of independent liberals who voted for you, as I did. The report of the N.Y. Civil Liberties Union last week is one example.

We don't want you to break the union—perhaps that job can be entrusted to Mr. Shanker, who seems bent on a Götterdämmerung showdown, alas—but we do ask you not to let his pettifogging, vindictive "union contract" tactics destroy the very promising beginnings of real, as against professional, teaching that has begun in Ocean Hill.

To Wells Kerr [former professor at Exeter]

November 4, 1968

. . . How good to hear from you—and that tone, and also the handwriting (so much better, more controlled than mine ever was, you must have gotten coaching in England) just as ever.

Afraid I can't recall your suppression of my attack on Stearns of Andover— no, wait a minute, something does stir dimly, did he write a foolish inspirational book and did I write a sensible uninspiring review of it for the *Exonian*? Ah yes, it comes back . . . vaguely, like a feeble, gnatlike, irritating ghost . . . and I thought you were stuffy and you thought I was cheeky and we were both right.

By God, Wells, if only we'd flourished in our respective roles 40 years later—it wouldn't have been any walkover for you, over you rather, truth would have triumphed and you'd have been lucky to get off with an apology, a public one, and promise to write a foreword, in the next issue, to my demolition of Mr. Stearns—after we had withdrawn our occupying forces from your sybaritic quarters in Dunbar Hall, of course!

Strange how different it all is now—and how sympathetic in general I am to the Young, they're the best generation I've known in this country, the cleverest and the most serious and decent (though I wish they'd READ a little—also I hate that obscenity bit, Up Against the Wall Motherfucker turns ME off, nor do I like—though must accept, wryly—that "shit" has become an ordinary word of parliamentary discourse, nothing obscene or vulgar intended, they just use it the way we would say "nonsense." . . .

To the Editor, *New York Times*

November 18, 1968

I've recently spent a day exploring four of the Ocean Hill–Brownsville schools, and I had the same impression Alfred Kazin did: something remarkable is happening out there, a deeply imaginative experiment that may have lessons for all ghetto schools—assuming Mr. Shanker ever allows them to open again.

The atmosphere was friendly and relaxed; I was allowed to wander where I liked, sometimes without a guide. There was no fighting or violent horseplay in the corridors between classes; I gather this is most unusual in such schools. (One exception in six hours: two obstreperous boys were making a row outside a classroom they had been asked to leave; they were quickly controlled by a white teacher, later backed up skillfully by a black one, without anger or threats but with patient firmness.)

The relation of the teachers—most of them were young, male, white, sophisticated, and bearded—with their black pupils was not at all what I'd expected from teacher friends' accounts of ghetto schools in "normal," or unstuck, times. The teachers talked quietly, directly, and without pulling rank on their students, who responded in the same manner: easy, informal, and serious. "Discipline" seemed to be no problem, or, more accurately, it was irrelevant since some kind of dialogue and sympathy had been miraculously established between the teachers and the students.

It will be tragic if Mr. Shanker and his United Federation of Teachers are able to destroy this promising experiment in community control. I wish, by the way, the U.F.T. pickets would stop passing out that Sept. 20 ad from the *Times* supporting them against Ocean Hill. I did sign it, but by Oct. 8 I had learned, as I should have known, that Mr. Shanker's union has been actively sabotaging decentralization since last spring; also that its complaints about denial of "due process" at Ocean Hill were half-truths when they weren't baseless. So I resigned, as have at least two other of the 25 signers. If the U.F.T. must distribute that misleading document, they might at least revise the list of signers.

To Philip Toynbee

May 9, 1969

Thanks for your note of long ago about the Harrington-Macdonald row in *NYRB* and for your appreciation, as a fellow journalist and craftsman, that I had him "hands down" (whatever that means). Nice of you to write me, esp. on this technological-style level (most letters were on the issues, and most were anti my view of them), and it cheered me up. Things more and more depressing here, re the black-white "confrontations," if only they wd. be elliptical, devious, circuitous, sly, Machiavellian, anything but direct and Hemingway-tough— *machismo*—I wish they'd have less balls, or at least show less, be more cowardly and sensible and willing to compromise. Fires set at CCNY every day . . . fellow from Harvard told me yesterday the Widener librarians are worried about SDS "militants" mixing up their file catalog cards (w. cd. be done by merely taking out a few here and there) and so now countermove (counterrevolutionary we used to say) is to raise funds for making duplicate Xerox copy of the Widener cards.

To Robert Lowell

July 21, 1969

. . . I liked being with you out there [conference at Aspen Colorado], you're a good companion and I'm glad we're friends. . . . Fixed here for summer, occupied in gardening (two sea-gardens plus more prosaic kinds, Gloria turns out, once she has her own 1/2 acre to work on, to be earth-plant oriented) idling, hovering, overseeing building (by a sweet, able, undependable—4 hours his working day if in energetic mood—youngish refugee from Madison Ave. & Princeton) of a hexagonal writing-studio-cum-summer-house on front lawn, and even a little unavoidable writing. But will be loose in fall and see you then in town—unless you all plan a trip down here in w. case guest room yours long as you like. I'm also pursuing, *entre nous*, a delightful (and mutual) love affair w. a local girl, quite young. Nine months, in fact, name of Queenie, pug-terrier mongrel. My Dog Queenie, can see what Joe Ackerley meant. . . .

To Mary McCarthy

September 12, 1969

Thanks for Nicola's letter, hope I haven't kept it too long.

One reason for my delay—aside from fact that I, like you, apparently, these days find it hard to think in the old political terms and am dissatisfied w. the new varieties, and even harder therefore to *act*—is that it was for me a puzzling exposition. So much I agree with, as always in the time I've known Nick—the rejection of progress, democracy, Marxism, socialism, and communism (as these terms are perverted by the left pietists), the refusal to be bullied in the name of "the masses," the insistence on social justice as a precondition of a decent new order, etc. But there's that vagueness about What Is to Be Done now, concretely, that you rightly complain of, and also flashes of a disturbing, to me, kind of anti-popular elitism. I'm for elitism in culture but not in politics (that sphere I'm with Nick's M. Proudhon: people know better what their interests are than any specialized corps of political leaders or New Deal reformist bureaucrats, people have more common sense and decency—if they can find a way of acting cooperatively together without being crushed into mass-action forms by demagogues, bourgeois manipulators, or Communist authorities— than their "leaders" have. I do believe in people—Rousseau was more right than Hobbes—and I think Nick maybe doesn't any more. "Modern man, as they call him, just does not give a damn for democracy, liberty, or anything that is not crudely material and stupidly mythical at the same time (like space travel)." Well, yes and no—don't like the ring of it somehow. On the moon junket, f.i., do we really know what the people (as apart from the editorialists and the Cronkites and the *Life* editors) thought about it? Only evidence I've seen is that the part of our society that showed the least interest in moonacy was the blacks (who often are found agreeing w. the top classes in these polls but here, bec. they had a sense of their own interests, were admirably "alienated").

On socialism and aristocracy, I agree w. you that Nick has an interesting, and new, point. He should develop it.

On that, I thought of your talk w. Pham Van Dong when I read the obituaries of Ho in the *Times*—there was a man—and a poet! What a contrast in style and background to our own LBJ and RMN!

It was good to have a glimpse of you again, dearest Mary, and hope to see you in NYC before you return to Paris. Give me a ring at *NYorker* (or home: GR-3-0835) if you have some free time—shall be more in NYC than here after next week, when my stint at Hofstra begins.

To Paul Lauter

October 1, 1969

I'm sending in card saying I'll sign the "New Call," with some misgivings—not sure tactically shrewd to broaden the front at this moment, when seems chance of pushing Nixon on Vietnam withdrawal—introducing economic inequalities (3), educational and ecological horrors (4), and the chronic American racial injustices (5) seems to me to dissipate our Resist thrust (and maybe will turn off, or bore, new recruits). But I agree in general and in principle, so I'll sign.

But the statement on the (alleged) "persecution" of the Black Panthers I can't sign for several reasons. In general, it assumes, as I'm afraid I do not, that the indictments of various Panther members in various states and for various crimes are frame-ups. I'm not so sure—not sure even about Huey Newton—on basis of press reports I've read—maybe and again maybe not. Is it conceivable, f.i., that Bobby Seale WAS involved in that torture-murder of a Panther informer in New Haven? He was talking at Yale at the time, and while the Panthers seem to have changed their spots, thank God, in a nonviolent direction in the last year, there's a lot of violence on the black scene and how can one be SURE it's a frame-up before the trial? Did you see a piece in the *Village Voice* about a month ago on this case? It rather shook me, esp. bec. it was more sympathetic than not to the Panthers.

I think it is likely that the police establishment is out to get the Panthers, but that doesn't mean, as the statement implies, that all the charges are necessarily false.

Also, I think it rhetorical exaggeration—the kind I've always objected to on the left from the days of Browder to those of Rudd—to write: "We recall the Rev. Niemoller's description of how he was silent while the Nazis struck at the

Jews, Communists, and other political opponents, only to discover that no one remained to protest when they got to him." We aren't as yet in a parallel situation, historically speaking, to the Germany the Nazis took over—can't see Nixon, or even his atty. gen. (a most hateful man) or even J. Edgar, as totalitarian demagogues like the Nazis. Might be some similarity (though would have to be qualified, as yet) if you were talking about the Spock trial, the Milwaukee 14 case, and, certainly, the current Chicago "conspiracy" trial. But the Black Panther cases differ in being—formally at least—prosecutions for specific crimes of violence. Think it is wrong for Resist to take a position on them in general, and on any particular case until the evidence is as clear as it was, or seemed to be, in the Sacco-Vanzetti, Tom Mooney, and Scottsboro cases. As it wd. have been—in my opinion—to stick our necks out for Alger Hiss. (I think he was proved guilty as charged by Chambers of perjury beyond a reasonable doubt.)

Finally, I'm puzzled a little by: "But even if the Panthers' program were as violent as charged, the First Amendment theoretically protects them against police repression." A little bec. of violent intentions and violent acts are not the same thing acc. to 1st Amend. But IF the P's program were as violent as the cops charge (which I don't think it was, and, as noted above, don't think it has been for the last year or so), then one might reasonably infer they might go in for criminal violence, it wd. be one factor to be taken into consideration before Resist made this blanket assumption all the cases are political frame-ups. Sticking that sentence in shows a certain bias, prejudgment, overconfidence, I think.

A 1966 reunion: Standing (from left), Heinrich Blucher, Hannah Arendt, Dwight Macdonald, Gloria Macdonald. Seated, Nicola Chiaromonte, Mary McCarthy, Robert Lowell. (McCarthy Papers, Vassar College Library)

CHAPTER SEVEN

CIRCUIT-RIDER PROFESSOR, 1970–1982

"The Young are the last best hope of this self destructive Society."

During these last years of his life, Macdonald suffered from periodic writing blocks. Although William Shawn permitted him to keep his office at the *New Yorker*, he did very little writing for the magazine. His work for *Esquire* greatly declined. As he found it difficult to write, he was drawn more and more to the frequent offers of visiting professorships in colleges and universities. Despite growing difficulties, physical and mental, Macdonald proved to be a successful teacher. He took his job seriously, put a great deal of effort into his preparation and particularly in the detailed grading of papers. His students for the most part admired him and looked forward to their meetings with him. But Macdonald did not look after himself. He was a heavy drinker and a chain smoker. Gloria and his two sons were shocked by his death. He died on December 19, 1982, of congestive heart failure brought on by bronchial asthma and a gastrointestinal hemorrhage. He had been active to the very end, teaching a course at Yale and granting a long interview to two enthusiastic students of his writings.

To Mr. Masin [editor at Greenwood Press]

March 17, 1970

I return this to you and not to Miss Harrington because I want to be sure that my wording, and not that of her copy editors, is retained in the many places I have indicated. Really, such bossy and pedantic editorial interference I've never experienced. See, for ex., on p. 4 change of my "Dorothy's bright young men" to "Dorothy Day's bright young men"; also I've marked on that page one ex. of dozens throughout, changing contractions like "don't" to "do not"—dammit, I've been writing for 40 years and I know what I'm doing and I prefer contracting such verbs and who the hell are your copy editors to "correct" me like a schoolboy? Also what an absurd waste of time—my kind of writing "don't" (which is perfectly good English) often seems better bec. looser, informal . . . why bother with such nonsense?

Also see p. 10, please, where Miss H's copy-wreckers have destroyed syntax of sentence at top by putting in parenthesis (they have no *ear* . . .); AND deleting lower down on page "or Wobblies" after "the I.W.W." (do they think "Wobblies" not up to Greenwood's high standards of formal usage, or what for God's sake?) AND, 2 lines down, changing "cops" to "police"—do your copy editors wear wing collars?—and even if they do, what bloody business is it of theirs if I want to call 'em "cops" and not "police"????

So please see that things are put back as were in places where I ask it to be done. (Some, maybe most of copy-editing changes either neutral or improvements—I'm not unreasonable.) And please send me a final proof—as you'll see I've rewritten 3 pages and added another of new footnotes—so I can see for myself it's been done. I promise not to make any major (more than a few words) changes and not to add anything.

"Mr. Masin tells me," Miss BH writes, "that he wants to have your essay set as soon as it's returned; therefore he asks that you forgo seeing the manuscript again." I do—but I want to see galleys. And as for the time element: you had my MS two or so weeks when I finally called you and asked about it; then you said it wd. be sent me on Monday (the 9th) to my L.I. address. Actually, it wasn't sent until that Wed., acc. to postmark, and I got it Friday. (Miss H's copyniks are as dilatory as they are officious, it seems.) . . . So I think you can take another couple of days and let me see proofs, eh?

To Richard Peltz [administrator, University of Wisconsin at Milwaukee]

April 7, 1970

Enjoyed very much my stay at UWM and wouldn't mind at all returning for a term next year, if you want me and if there is a special, amateur slot open, as you thought might be the case. I'd be interested in one or two of the three following possibilities:

(1) Writer in Residence—*you* define it.

(2) A seminar in Edgar Allan Poe, his life, works & reputation.

(3) A lecture course in American Political Fiction, from Hawthorne to Mailer:

Hawthorne: *The Blithdale Romance*; "Endicott and the Red Cross"; "The Maypole of Merry Mount"; "My Kinsman, Major Molineux"; "The Great Stone Face."

Melville: *The Piazza Tales* (inc. *Benito Cereno* and *Bartleby, The Scrivener*) plus *Billy Budd.*

Edmund Wilson: *Patriotic Gore* (selections)

Harriet Beecher Stowe: *Uncle Tom's Cabin*

Henry Adams: *Democracy*

Henry James: *The Bostonians*

Harold Frederick: *The Damnation of Theron Ware*

John Dos Passos: *The Big Money*

Nathanael West: *Miss Lonelyhearts*

Mary McCarthy: *The Portrait of the Intellectual as a Yale Man*

Lionel Trilling: *The Middle of the Journey*

J. F. Powers: *Morte d'Urban*

Ralph Ellison: *Invisible Man*

Robert Penn Warren: *All the King's Men*

Norman Mailer: *Armies of the Night*

So do let me know if any of the above strike your (collective) fancy; and most grateful if you will pass them on to proper authorities.

P.S. Also prepared to do a course on History of Cinema w. did at Texas 1966 and Santa Cruz (U of C) 1969—but this not your province, have written Adolph Rosenblatt about it—maybe cd. do it plus 1 of above, interdisciplinary. . . .

To the Editor, *New York Times*[1]

May 3, 1970

"At Yale, police fired tear gas at a crowd of youths who gathered in New Haven, 12,000 to 15,000 strong, to express support for nine Black Panthers facing a trial there." Not true. No tear gas was fired by police at the 15,000 demonstrators who gathered on the New Haven green on Friday and Saturday afternoons. I was there and the only cops I saw—just three—were relaxed, passive, glazed with boredom.

Mr. [Fred] Hechinger must be referring—unless he is even more out of touch with actualities than I'd expect a *Times* editor to be—to the teargassing of a few hundred demonstrators long after the two big rallies were over. I was there, too and, I saw the splendid work of the student marshals—backed up by Black Panther leaders who kept bullhorning, "Please leave the green and go back to the old campus . . . the Panthers ask you to avoid any violence"—in shepherding all but a few hundred by the eleven P.M. curfew back to the liberated, peaceful Yale turf. The tear gas was directed against this tiny group—heavy barrages but no cracked heads, no charges by either the police of kamikaze-balaclava ultra-leftists—and it did move them, nonviolently as it were, up to the old campus where Allen Ginsberg was on stage to soothe uninflated masses with his opiate chanting. The slogan of the weekend wasn't "Up against the wall, mother-bleeper" or "To the barricades!" but rather "oooOOOM . . ." repeated *da capo*.

I'm sure Mr. Hechinger shares my relief at the nonconfrontationary nature of the Yale weekend, a tactical agreement whatever our longer-ranged hopes are, and so I wonder how he wrote a falsehood like the above? (One that reflects, by the way, on not only the rebellious students—and more power to them—but also on the police, who were admirably controlled by their chief.) Also, why does the *Times* habitually exaggerate, editorially and in its news columns, the violence of student demonstrations? And, in the present instance, the potential violence, like worrying about eggs, indeed full-fledged fighting cocks, when you hear a rooster crow. That lengthy report on some Black Panther girl who bought a shotgun in Dayton, plus other superheated forebodings in your news columns—and of course in other media, the *Times'* sins are not

---

1. Macdonald attended a weekend of astonishing protests and demonstrations at Yale University in support of the Black Panthers on trial in New Haven. The president of Yale, Kingman Brewster, publicly stated that the defendants could not get a fair trial because of a "nationwide effort to smash the Black Panther movement. . . ." Macdonald was sympathetic toward Brewster's stand. Although he rejected the separatism of current black nationalism, he agreed that the racial climate did not allow for a fair trial.

original—such tendentious reportage may well have scared away thousands from a gathering that was less destructive to life, limb & property than the routine American Legion convention.

These are rhetorical questions to which I don't know the answers—speculations aren't answers. But you of the *Times* might stop and think about them.

To Pauline Kael

August 9, 1970

I hope I didn't insult you more than normal other night at Dan Talbot's—didn't mean to—if I did say things out of line even for your—my style, please forgive—blame it on drink plus that stupid movie (oh, sorry—there I go again!) which irritated me because everybody else, especially my wife, affected to find it interesting. . . . Anyway, reason I'm writing is that I just came across, in ordering my shelves, the *New Republic* for Nov. 5, 1966—that's pretty old even for my compost heap—and came on your review of *Red Desert* and *Georgy Girl* (latter mostly about *Morgan!*). And read it all, quite long, and liked it a lot—AND (here's the point at last) I saw how your approach to film differs from mine—or rather, since we both knew that, I saw what you emphasize in a movie that I don't, AND, here's real point, I wished that I'd thought of the socio-cultural-audience points you make about both *Morgan!* and *Red Desert* and had put them into my reviews of same (see D . . . M . . . on Movies, pp. 339 and 406) at least in capsule form. On the other hand, you might have put in some of my aesthetic points too. Though actually both our lines coincide in an interesting way, not only did we both have same basic objections to the two films, but also there's a lot more art in yours and sociology in mine than I admitted the other night in my drunk-irritated mood. Do have a look at my reviews. You got the book? I asked them to send you a copy. If not, let me know and I'll send you one—in exchange for your last collection, which I *don't* have. . . .

To Kate Manheim [daughter of the translator Ralph Manheim]

November 3, 1970

. . . I'm frantically busy here [at the University of Wisconsin, Milwaukee] and desperately "visible," as the press agents say—an Agnew of the left, a cultured Billy Graham, a Walter Cronkite of the campus—forever talking, talking, talking on everything—literature, movies, politics, my past (lots of room in THAT subject)—to TV interviewers (only local stations), dinner meetings of women journalists, English graduate students, film enthusiasts—endlessly explaining, discussing, expanding, and/or refining (that is, contracting) this theory, those facts with my students, who are most of them even younger than you but who listen to me w. considerably more interest, or perhaps just tolerance, perhaps bec. I prepare my remarks more thoroughly than I do for you. . . .

To Bob Greenblatt [anti–Vietnam War leader]

November 24, 1970

. . . I went along [with the group's declaration] bec. I believe in your (our) cause, more desperately in last three days—never thought I'd come to think of LBJ as not our MOST disastrous president but Nixon is pushing me that way. Lyndon was at least a predictable lunatic but Dick seems to have no form to his paranoia, just random impulses—I suppose that commando raid on the POW camp seemed a good idea at the time.

To Jane Elkoff [Harper College student]

December 28, 1970

Your letter has just surfaced on my disorderly desk, sorry to be late in replying. . . . Your many questions interested and moved me v. much and shall try to answer some of the easier ones—a hard job bec. they are the right questions, hence not easy ones ("what is the answer?" mused Gertrude Stein on her deathbed, then, w. her last gasp, revised it to "what is the question?").

Yes, lots of masscult pervading campus and classroom life (I know bec. have been teaching this fall at U of Wisconsin, Milwaukee—program of course enclosed) but also not lots, but some, of its antithesis, the real stuff, and enough for me. I've never expected utopia. A few dozen kids & profs there were my kind and the library was excellent and it was enough to live on, and enjoy . . . also, if students generally were able "to fully appreciate and discriminate in books they read" between the "noble & ignoble, true & false," then, in general, there'd be no need for them to be students—or me to be a prof.

I do not know how to extend that judgment (bet. noble-ignoble—I LIKE that formulation—and true-false) to my life. You write, "Has it been for you enough of a solution to express the truth in an atmosphere that proclaims what you disagree with? Can even a deeply personal art-for-art's sake (commitment) keep alive today? Is there a way to preserve quality without escaping?" Yes, it has been enough, for me, to write and speak my truth, and taste, in a generally hostile cultural atmosphere: (a) while it's worse here in USA today than has been elsewhere in past, as in renaissance Italy or pre-1800 France or England or Periclean Athens, still it was always hard going for the truth-art-ethic minority—cf. what happened to Jesus, Socrates, Bruno, also failure of contemporaries to see greatness of Donne, Blake, Shakespeare, Piero della Francesca, the later Rembrandt; (b) a relatively small, say 1% to 5% of mass population in post-1800 period, brotherhood of readers, lookers, listeners, thinkers, has been enough in this period to creatively encourage them, to serious artists from Baudelaire to Eliot, from Manet to Picasso. . . . As for "preserving quality without escaping" — if above two statistic points are valid, it's possible to "escape" from masscult, and from the vast majority today, in taste and politics, into a community big enough to be an alternative world (on a much higher plane, mentally, morally, aesthetically, humanly) that feeds one enough for creative survival. Thus my little radical-cultural mag, *Politics*, 1944–1949, had six thousand subscribers top (as v. as many millions for *Life* or *Reader's Digest* or *Saturday Evening Post*), but they were plenty for me as an editor and writer, they wrote more in letters I wanted to answer than I could answer, there was a dialogue on a level, and of an intensity, that the mass mags, or even the much bigger (hundreds of thousands, not thousand) middlebrow mags couldn't and didn't provide.

"Escapism" is a cant word of the mass philistines, cultural & political — just as "relevant" is ditto of the campus leftists, who have their mass-philistine-conformist aspects, too. . . . Question is what you are escaping from, and toward what? . . . Two current noncultural examples are the young draft-resisters and the hippie-yippie "dropouts" from our society — their "escapism" from the Vietnam War and the legal-governmental-respectable structure of which it is an expression, this seems to me an escape into life — whatever the constrictions of prison, exile, or ad hoc jerry-built communes, they are less cramping, in moral and human terms, than the conventional tracks the present American establishment has laid down for young to follow. . . . (Maybe not the hippie-yippie "thing," esp. in its drug-dropping aspect, some ways seems to me MORE restricting than even middle-class USA life-styles — still can see whey they want to get out from under . . . and if some alternative is ever found that is satisfying to human needs, it will be along the lines of the disreputable hippie yippie revolt . . . running away from a clear & present danger, even if you don't know where to go, is more sensible than freezing into your responsible post, like the Roman sentries in Pompeii (you can see their lava-embalmed corpses to this day, heroic but not intelligent) who manfully refused to "escape" from a dangerous spot. . . . But still, those "communes" don't sound so great, now, and so an open question for me.)

I left the Trotskyist movement in 1941 after 2 years as a member, for much more concrete reasons than a desire for "difference, quality, and variety" — though this was also involved: namely that its internal organization didn't seem to me democratic, i.e., that the party structure gave too much repressive power to the leadership and too little expressive power of dissent, or even questioning to the rank and file. . . . Too much like cause ("Stalinists") we'd been fighting for so long. . . . I've always been temperamentally an anarchist — the top-down authoritarianism of Marxism bothered me even when I was a Trotsky-ist; my idea of good politics—though not of good culture—is a system that works from the bottom up. . . . Might add, re your worry about "escapism," that my comrades in the movement, even those who agreed w. my criticisms of lack of democracy, and indeed, especially them, used that very term in trying to dis-suade me from leaving the party: you should not run away (or escape), their ar-gument ran, but rather stay with us and fight for reforms, for a better party from within. . . . But I saw no hope of success in such a nonescapist struggle (as I don't within our mass culture, the beaches of Hollywood and Madison Ave. are white with the bones of nonescapist fighters-from-within) and figured (I still think correctly) that if I didn't get out, I would not only not prevail as a reformer but wd. also become myself part of what I was fighting. . . . Silence, exile, cun-ning were James Joyce's (my party name was James Joyce) watchwords in his struggle with masscult.

As to your own choices of what to do after graduation—aren't they too many? I mean, can you really be that open—and multi-talented—so that "a life of service, healing—e.g., child psychology," or one of "self-protection and es-cape—a farm," or "defiance, art, and fear" (dilettantist tasting of the youth "counterculture"), or "a compromise between service-utility and aesthetics, namely architecture"—so that these are all possibilities for you now? You're only 19, true, but still you ARE 19 and that's not a kid—Elizabethan males that old were ship captains or poets, USA males now fight in Vietnam (or refuse to)—you must be more formed, thus limited than that spectrum. . . . I think your first job is to narrow alternatives down, to sit and think for a while about yourself and your talents and your interests—few w. a gift for child psychology, for instance, wd. make good architects, I imagine, and vice versa. . . . Ulti-mately you'll do what you want to do most strongly, but the more you are con-scious of yourself (by reflection, introspection, nonacting), the better you can get down to the real strength of your needs and desires, w. is not always and maybe not usually the strongest on the surface. . . . I'd advise you to escape for a while from action, involvement, decision into yourself and see what comes up from your unconscious depths. . . . Always better to put off a decision than to rush into one prematurely, that is, superficially bec. you make it without know-ing who you are. . . .

To [Yale] Classmates of '28

January 29, 1971

The $25 enclosed for the Alumni Fund is 2,100% (by my figuring) of my total contributions to the fund to date (1929–1971) which were, or was, $1 extracted under pressure—let's make it 100% donors, fellow, don't worry about amount, just give SOMETHING; I did—years ago.

Until recently, I'd never thought of Yale as one of my Worthy Causes, quite the contrary. It was an educational bust for me in the twenties, boring, irritating, philistine, uncongenial. But in the last decade, from my occasional visits, it seems to have enormously improved both educationally (far better for undergraduate education than Harvard, I'd say, just reverse of the situation in the twenties—I'm told there are 75 faculty members teaching undergraduate English as v. 35 at Harvard, f.i.) and, under Brewster, politically from my old-new-left standpoint.

Also I'm actually being paid by dear old Yale for teaching a seminar this term in American Political Fiction, from Hawthorne to Mailer. Billy Phelps must be revolving like a squirrel in whatever purgatorial cage the gods have appointed for the eternal punishment of professorial popularizers—maybe he has to lecture on "The Outlook for the Novel Today" to three ladies' clubs per diem, all composed of Women's Lib members. But peace to Billy's vanilla-ice-cream-suited ashes! After forty years, Yale seems to have become the kind of campus I relate to, as we now say. Maybe it will prove a mirage by the time I get to the end of this term—but meanwhile I'll risk $25 on it.

To Mr. Litt [*Esquire* reader]

February 1, 1971

. . . Shall try to answer, briefly and inadequately your difficult questions about voting.

I too feel impaled on the horns of the dilemma you outline: on one hand, voting in national elections in a mass country like USA means either nothing or worse, something in reverse of what one voted for (as in 1964 when I voted for that bastard LBJ against my anarchist principles); yet on the other hand, or horn, seems puristic and sterilely virtuous not to take trouble to pull down that lever lest one be deceived or corrupted, since in many elections there IS if not a good at least a lesser evil. As you know from the Politics column [in *Esquire*], I refrained from pulling down the lever for Humphrey—just couldn't somehow—yet now I wonder if I was right—could he have been as disastrous as Nixon has turned out, in Indochina and at home? Must admit hard to believe. I thought Nixon was an opportunist and so wd. do an Eisenhower and really get out of Indochina—he's proved to be as nutty an idealist as LBJ when it comes to admitting his great country is in the wrong, and acting on it, as de Gaulle did when he got out of Algeria (a much harder job than getting out Vietnam since there were a million French *colons* there as against o American settlers in Vietnam, not to mention the direct double-cross of the very people who had put him in power). . . . But would HHH have done it either? Recently saw again Di Antonio's superb documentary, *The Year of the Pig*, and believe me, HHH's appearances there don't make one very hopeful—he seems to be even more bogus and true-believing about the war than LBJ was.

About only practical rule of thumb on voting I've developed is that the smaller the electoral region, the more likely it is one can find a real alternative to vote for—local elections here for school boards or city councilmen are more likely to produce real issues than state elections and latter than national ones; also elections for congressmen or senators more likely than those for President. This bec. people aren't idiots about their interests, and smaller the electoral body more chance of some candidate campaigning on concrete, specific, limited issues on w. the voters can have some informed opinion.

To Linda Tomoshok [Yale student]

December 27, 1971

Thanks for your query of Sept. 5 about your grade in the Stiles seminar, w. I haven't answered till now bec. it's hard to answer. Without offense to you—and making me look amateur as teacher, too, wonder is I'm now answering. My Presbyterian upbringing. . . . Well—fact is your paper on *The Possessed* WAS v. good, and deserved its A. BUT it was first term paper I got and then I got other papers that I thought—forgive me—were even better, and so I gave them A+. And A++ and even A+++. So I thought—since term papers were the most important factor, no tests after all (next time I'll give class quizzes—as you'll recall, the class hooted down this proposal as kindergarten stuff and I weakly went along—wrongly, I think)—so I thought I had to discriminate between your paper and those 3 or 4 others, and so I gave you a "high pass." And then the highest whatever it was, can't recall—TERRIFIC? SUPER? something like that. I also thought "high pass" was quite a good mark—seems it isn't—one of our co-seminarians called me up, distressed with it to my surprise, and said he needed the highest grade (PLUPERFECTO?) to get a scholarship and I wrote the registrar (dean?) and changed his grade to that, naturally. He, too, was "an active participant in class," and I did value both of you for that, should have made THAT maybe, the chief criterion. But I didn't. Maybe wrong—next time. . . . And next time I'll grade all term papers at same time. . . . Terribly sorry—and if I can still retroactively up your grade, and it makes any difference to you as to your academic future, tell me how to do it and I will. Gladly.

Hope you understand—and shd. like to see you again—recall our lunch w. pleasure—doubt if will be at Yale for a while, maybe some time as an E. Stiles fellow, not as prof—perhaps you'll give me a ring next time you're in

NYC and drop in for a visit, or drink? I'm at *New Yorker,* 25 East 43, 18th floor. . . .

To Miriam Chiaromonte

January 19, 1972

Bob Silvers [editor, *New York Review of Books*] gave me the terrible news yesterday, and I'm still dazed by it. I knew Nick had a bad heart and for years, of course, but I somehow was unprepared emotionally—I really never thought he'd die, leave us, and I can't get used to the idea of my world permanently without him. It's the most *depriving* death in my life since my dear father died—also suddenly, of a heart attack—in 1926. Well, I suppose that we—you and I—shd. be grateful such wonderful, generous, and always lovingly dependable people existed for us. But it's hard to think of them not being around, ever. When my father died I broke out in rashes and cried, next morning, when I saw my mother making breakfast for my brother and me but not for him. And for the past 24 hours, I've had recurring spasms of grief when I thought Nicola will never, never be there, or anywhere, again. . . . And especially when I thought of his last note to me two weeks ago, reassuring me we were still friends, explaining about the mixups in getting his latest (last!) book to us—w. by the way still hasn't arrived wd. like it v. much sometime but don't worry now, please—and enfolding me in his affection and intelligence. . . . Ever since we met in 1944, he's been my best friend, the one person—despite recent political-cultural disagreements, w. were so painful to us both—I felt closest to, morally and intellectually, also personally. The one person, except my poor dear father, that gave me the feeling of being valued for myself, individually, not for my brains (though also for them too) or achievements, just for myself—a personal love and respect—as I felt for him too, but it was not quite an equal relationship, emotionally—I now think—more like a father to a son, despite our almost equal ages, a good father, like mine, and one who, unlike mine (not that that made me love my father any less, or Nick any more), shared my intellectual interests and was also a brother in that we could talk about things on the same level. . . . As passage from *The Great Gatsby* has kept coming to mind in last day and I've looked it up, as a stab at what Nick was like to his friends:

"He smiled understandingly—much more than understandingly. It was one of those rare smiles with a quality of eternal reassurance about it, that you may come across four or five times in a life. It faced—or seemed to face—the whole eternal world for an instant, and then concentrated on *you* with an irresistible prejudice in your favor. It understood you just so far as you wanted to be understood, believed in you as you would like to believe in yourself. . . ."

Well, dearest Miriam, you know all this. He was a good man and a good friend and even at his most "difficult," w. was plenty of late years (as mine too, of course w. him), I loved and respected him and I'm sure our recent political disagreements wd. have yielded to lengthy and unquiet discussions w. will never take place now. ("Differences of opinion," he wrote in his last letter. "I certainly do not attach enough importance to political strife today to let it so much as come near my personal feelings.") . . .

To U.S. Board of Parole, Washington, D.C.

February 25, 1972

May I suggest, with reasons, that you grant a parole to Ralph Ginzburg at an early date?

My name is Dwight Macdonald. I am a journalist, editor, and literary critic. From 1929 to 1936 I was an associate editor of *Fortune*; from 1937 to 1943 an editor of *Partisan Review*; from 1944 to 1949 the editor and publisher of *Politics*; from 1960 to 1966 the movie critic of *Esquire*; and from 1951 to the present, a staff writer on the *New Yorker*. My books include: *The Ford Foundation* (1956); *Parodies: An Anthology from Chaucer to Beerbohm* (1960); *Against the American Grain: Essays on Mass Culture* (1962); *Dwight Macdonald on Movies* (1969); and *Politics Past* (1971).

I first met Mr. Ginzburg at his trial in Philadelphia, where I testified in his defense. I agreed to do so because the charges against him (as the publisher of *Eros* magazine, *The Housewife's Handbook of Selective Promiscuity*, and a vulgar but, I thought, nonpornographic newsletter seemed to me, as a longtime critic of mass culture, absurd in the historical context of what was then being publicly sold, without legal challenge, on public newsstands, in bookstores, and in movie theaters. By "then" I mean those far-off, innocent, dewy-eyed days of long ago—must be all of five years now. As for the loosening of legally tolerated sexual mores in the years Ginzburg has been fighting his case in the courts—here I find myself at a loss for a comparison. Maybe the Marquis de Sade and Elinor Glyn (whose *Three Weeks* was the 1906 of *Eros*) being caught in the same police dragnet? Except his disciples aren't imprisoned now. I'd say myself neither his nor hers should be, but certainly if his aren't, hers shouldn't be.

In my testimony at the Philadelphia trial, I didn't claim that *Eros* was of any great cultural value—in fact I insisted it wasn't. My point was a social and historical one: that its sexual explicitness, "obscenity," "prurient stimulation," etc. were much less offensive to our then prevailing standards of public morality than were many other books, magazines, and movies that were circulating freely without legal interference. Test cases had been staged, but they had been almost all resolved in favor of the defendants—until Mr. Ginzburg came along. Then the roof fell in. Five years, later reduced to three, but still much too long—as, indeed, any prison sentence would have been even then—and certainly now. It's out of all proportion to the offense—do have a look yourself at *Eros* and *The Housewife's Handbook* and even that tasteless newsletter—and compare their sex-charge with that delivered by your local movie and magazine distributors as routinely as the daily milkman.

The reduction of Mr. Ginzburg's sentence from five to three years is a covert judicial recognition of this overt fact of life: a (partial) recognition that justice had somehow miscarried in his case. My plea is that you carry on this admirable realism by releasing him on parole at the earliest legal opportunity.

I understand that your function is not to review the justice or injustice of the conviction and sentence—my excuse in bringing these matters up is that I think they are relevant to your basis of decision on parole—but only to decide whether the prisoner's release on parole would (a) improve the chances of his rehabilitation, and (b) benefit society. My feeling is that an early parole for Ralph Ginzburg would do both.

(a) The problem of "rehabilitation" doesn't arise in Ginzburg's case since he has always been, from my reading of his career, quite "habilitated" to our present society. He is not a criminal (or radical) type but just the opposite: a bourgeois entrepreneur who accepts, indeed welcomes, the present American legal-economic system as the necessary foothold for his commercial enterprises—his latest being the ultra-capitalist *Moneysworth* magazine. His vociferous (and justified) complaints about what's been done to him—as his tearing up the Bill of Rights, on camera, as he entered prison—are protests of betrayal by the system he believes in, not acts of defiance against an alien system.

(b) His early release would "benefit society" in the sense it would show, as the reduction of sentence (partially) did, that the American legal system is not blindly routinized, that its institutions, including your board, are realistically flexible enough to redress an obvious miscarriage of justice (partially again, not your fault, you come late) in the case of Ralph Ginzburg. If you're worried about his good behavior after release, I'd be delighted to have him paroled in my care or custody or whatever the term is. I don't think I'd be running any great risk.

"The law is a ass," concluded Mr. Bumble, speaking as a respectable being in Dickensian England. I hope we—you and I—can do better.

To John Leonard, Editor, *New York Review of Books*

October 9, 1972

The day after I sent you my bill of complaints about copy-editing butchery of my Swanberg review, I received $350 for it from your business dept. Injury added to insult.

What did you pay Ken Galbraith for his lead review in this week's issue? If it was on a per-word basis, then it wd. have been around $150, w. is what you paid me for my second lead review of Roth's *Our Gang* last year, about same length. And niggardly and penny-pinching—about 10 cents a word. *NYRB* or *PR* pay around that and they don't have 1,500,000 circ. plus all those ads plus all those profits, for the Sulzbergers but not for Ken and me—if you did pay him $150. But if you pay the same (measly, tightwad) $350 for any lead review re-gardless of length, then let me suggest you pay more when the lead review runs double or triple length—and send me another $350. Yes, I know you want to pay more and are embarrassed by the bus. dept.'s stinginess, dear John—you're a decent pro like me & Ken and your other contributors, you're on our side bec. you're one of us, right—also as a pro you want to get good reviews and you know the bus. dept. is underpaying you out of the market—only reviewers w. other sources of income than writing, or w. academic or other ambitions to "make" the *Times* and edge onto the map—only such can afford to write for your mag. I'm not in either category and I think $350 an insult-injury for what I gave you, inc. that crucial 3–4 page add I spent 2 days and 1 night on, quite needlessly bec. review plenty long & good enough already—too much both in-deed for $350, but I have an unprofessional, amateur joy-cum-duty feeling of obligation to make it as good as possible. . . . So I suggest, if you DO think $350 rather skimpy, you send in an expense account for me (w. will be glad to con-coct—3 days hotel & meals @$35 plus 3 days extra thought, research & writing at $75, say, we can cook it up. . . . Also that you go to mat w. them re *Times Book Review* rates in general . . . wd. still not be Maecenes-Medici lavish, not even *Esquire* lavish. . . . And what DID you pay Ken?

To Henry Luce III

October 23, 1972

I'm very pleased you liked my review of the Swanberg book on your father—and thanks for telling me so.

I did indeed make quite an "effort" on the piece—way beyond the call of duty—because I analyzed Swanberg's biography and compared it with my own recollections of Henry when I worked for him—and in those days often with him as an editor—on *Fortune* from 1929 to 1936, the more it seemed to me that Swanberg was one of those simplistic "liblabs" (I called them later when I was fighting the Stalinists, from the left) who see everything in black and white. So he colored Henry black when in fact he was often smudgy grey—politically—and sometimes at least off-white (his papers, even in the Goldsboroughian thir-ties were, domestically, always anti-racist and sympathetic to labor; also, later they early spoke out against McCarthyism, though you'd never know it from Swanberg). As you know, I was politically opposed to him in the thirties when I worked for him—and continued to be so after that, too. But politics isn't everything. What disgusted me about Swanberg's book, as I thought of my own experience with Henry as a person, was his failure to see, bec. of ideological prejudice, how complex, riven, and agonized a man he was—a good man gone wrong (from my political standpoint) but a good man—and an interesting, sympathetic one that I always like to deal with, as writer to editor—he had no "side," he listened, he was curious and alive. I came to dislike Ralph Ingersoll, but I liked Henry—invited him and Lila to my (first) wedding and they came and it was nice and natural. Even at his most maddeningly obtuse, and he could be maddeningly obtuse as you must know, I respected him because he was a man, a *mensch*, not a stuffed shirt or a hypocrite but another struggler like me. Later he may have changed, don't know, Swanberg gives data to suggest so, but I can't believe he ever changed into the pompous dullard of Swanberg's caricature.

Well, enough—I really liked your father—and thanks for your note.

To George Abbot White [Matthiessen archivist]

November 13, 1972

. . . I don't recall . . . addressing the SDS at the Hotel Barbizon (Plaza?) in June 1960. Do you have a clip or something about it? . . .

On [F. O.] Matthiessen—knew him v. slightly at Yale, also saw a bit of him in late thirties when we were on opp. sides of Stalinist barricades—at Yale he was a quiet, v. intelligent—subtle figure, also a gent, as he was always (quite a contrast to his Stalinoid bullyboy associates). . . . He was about the only one who from beginning wrote for our de-Stalinized and pro-Trotskyist *Partisan Review*—despite his political disagreement w. us, he agreed w. us—as few of that crowd did—that literature was one thing, politics another. So he admirably contributed a few reviews to our whiteguard socialfascist rag. . . . One specific glimpse of him I retain: sitting next me (and could Mary McCarthy or maybe Phil Rahv been on his other side—quite possibly—sure he felt more at home w. us then w. them) at the critical session (or perhaps "workshop") of the spring 1937 (38?) Am. Writers Congress, w. Granny Hicks in chair . . . and we kept throwing monkey wrenches into the machinery (remember I praised Trotsky's prose style and Hicks became ruffled and shrill like an enraged sparrow . . . and Matty, despite some nudges and whispers from me at especially outrageous moments, kept silent, uneasily but quite firmly. . . . Often wondered why he clove to the comrades so long, way after the pact, in fact at the 1949 Waldorf Conferences of the NCASP, as you doubtless know, he was a platform speaker at the writers panel—this time we were hopelessly apart, physically and historically . . . see p. 32-b of *Politics* for Winter 1949, though of course you have.

To Fred Dupee

December 1, 1972

. . . All last spring and summer, up to middle of August, I was in a writing block and working stasis remarkable even for me of late years—sat at desk in study most of day but mood so numbly drear almost nothing emerged, not even letters. "Each morning I get up with the sun (or anyway by 10:30)/And find at night no work has been done."—remember "Fascinatin' Rhythm" circa late '20s? . . . Then just before Labor Day two reviews I'd rashly promised in spring (the *Times* on Swanberg's Luce biog. and the *Columbia Forum* one I had sent you, Erik [Wensberg, editor of *Columbia Forum*] says you liked it, glad) became due and overdue and both editors pressed, swore huge gaps wd. result and general disaster if I didn't come through . . . so I got down to them at last. (As usual had many pages of notes and drafts) and FORCED them through one after another, plus, in the next month, a long piece on "My Favorite Movies" for an anthology plus some brief book notes for this mag (more writing than I've done in several years). . . . And now I'm feeling more interested in writing, also more competent to do it (response to both reviews has been amazing to modest me) . . . BUT just bec. I have been till lately grinding out the stuff, I haven't got around to answering your welcome letters. . . .

My own news is (apart from Lazarus Lives tale just told—& my fingers are crossed about that) mostly that from Jan through May I'm going to be teaching in English dept. at U Buffalo—same courses did at Umass (Am Pol. Fict, Hawthorne to Mailer; and seminar in Poe)—coldest, windiest place in USA everybody says but the salary is persuasive. . . . Suppose you know Nick Chiaromonte died suddenly, heart attack, in Rome last spring? Great loss to me—despite political-social differences late years, felt a deep bond w. him, and respect. . . . And a few months ago my poor brother [Hedges Macdonald] also died unexpectedly—in Orlando, Fla., whither he and Mary and my nephew had just moved, finding San Diego not to their taste (except, I imagine, politically). Hedges was increasingly bowed down, crippled, distorted by arthritis in last 4–5 years as you know—last time I saw him, winter before last, he was doubled over and looked sadly old and feeble (but w. humor and gentle smile and ditto wit intact). . . . But one doesn't usually die of arthritis—he seems to have just gotten weaker and weaker, and some minor infection was too much. (They'll never know exactly, my nephew writes, bec. Hedges, so typical, articulated in will that no autopsy be performed!) Have been going through old letters—really old, from '20s on—w. view to doing some kind of memoir, intellectual autobiography, w. will be my next large project (notes, glimpses rather than a consecutive narrative) . . . many heartbreaking views of Hedges when we were all young and hopeful—many of you, too, of course, NOT heartbreaking, of course, but moving and interesting. . . . In fact, one problem is it's so fascinating to *read* the past that it's hard to leave off and try to work out a style and a form (a formless, anarchistic form, hardest kind to find) in which to convey the experience of (a) the past and (b) recapturing the past 20 to fifty years later. To combine (a) and (b) is the problem, wouldn't you say? Solution is made more difficult (though if I reach one, it will be the more enriched) by fact that I've kept everything—letters to me from my parents when I was at PEA and all my own over last 50 years, either bec. they were kept and returned later to me (my parents, Dins—heavens, what a quantity there, for a decade—1928–1938—and Dot) or else, later, bec. I made carbons of my own letters always (even my love letters to Gloria, she didn't like that at all when she years later chanced to find out, I can see her feelings but what can I do, I seem to have a passion, a lust for documentation, for preserving my past). I'm now glad I did and have all the pleasure of a dirty old man voyeuristically tompeeping at his own past, Dwight's Last Tapes. . . . And there's quite a lot of more solid, or at least less personal, stuff in those "archives" too, I'm discovering. . . . Love to Andy and tell her that I reciprocate her antiquarian feeling about me and consider her a large and inalterable feature of the landscape of MY past and will oppose to the death her being in any way updated, revised, or urban-renewed.

To Ruth Gay

July 2, 1973

No, I haven't disposed of my papers—should have years ago when you could get a tax benefit if you donated them to a library—missed the boat. But I've been planning to get around to disposing of them, and your letter is therefore "interesting." Yale is one of the two libraries I'd prefer as depositories of my, by now, fairly copious letters & MSS etc. (Other of course is Harvard.) I've kept everything (within reason—no laundry bills)—from my schoolboy letters to my parents from Exeter (1920–1924) up to now. Because (a) I am an antiquarian at heart, fascinated by the past, and (b) I've always thought—conn. with (a)—that when I got old (as now—67 ain't no chicken) I'd like to review my past as preserved in letters from and to me (I've always made carbons of letters I write, even love letters, I'm afraid—you see, a real 100% historian, or chronicler). But I've never had "time" to do it, up to now. . . . This summer I may get around to the review (and ordering) of all those cartons—just one or two can't wait, jobs first. . . . We'll see. . . . Until then, I wouldn't want to deposit the stuff anywhere (though I suppose I could have access, no?). . . . But real problem is that it's all in great disorder—geological layers that only I can decipher—or is this really true and not an excuse for putting it off? . . . Maybe if I did "deposit" the stuff in your library, some bright sympathetic grad student or librarian could set it into order (along my lines, the ones I roughed out after a test-boring) to suit my purposes—w. include an intellectual autobiography (my past & thoughts, my life & hard times) w. I really must get at soon.

So maybe we can do business by the end of the summer (when I go back to SUNY-Buffalo for a year teaching English—grad seminar in Poe and undergrad course in Am. Political Fiction from Hawthorne to Mailer). . . . Depends on if I can get a few weeks free (w. likely, almost nothing on fire at moment but one never knows). To get some idea of what IS there in those cartons and what I can do with it. . . . Will let you know in a month.

One question can be settled now: do you pay anything, and if so, what wd. you think my papers (assuming they're as important as your letter assumes they are)—might be worth to the Yale Corporation, which I gather is strapped of late but is still much richer than me? Just an estimate (assuming you pay *anything*)—wd. depend of course on your inspection of the goods for sale.

To Wendy [Freedman, Ph.D. student, SUNY Buffalo]

October 10, 1973

To my surprise, I don't like your thesis at all, nor do I find it of any interest (to me), nor, in fact, have I been able to read very much of it, I'm afraid.

The attached notes will show that I've tried to read it, also (I hope) why I dislike (or more accurately, can't read) it. They're at least detailed and specific.

I hope you won't take my criticisms personally, though shouldn't blame you if you did—your book did keep rousing the critical beat in me, again and again I resolved to skip a bit and make a fresh start and not get angry and supercilious, always with no success. There was always some new cause of offense, something else to sneer and jeer at. . . . Sorry.

Actually I'm not sorry. The differences between your and my approach to Don Juan, or even our understanding of what it IS, are so great that I'm beginning to see them as a chasm so deep that it can't be bridged by discourse (though the 10 pp enclosed try to, since that's my only way of thinking or writing—and fact I kept scratching the itch, the sore, for so long, is significant) and indeed to be more geological than personal. That is, I know you're not *personally* stupid—but your thesis is stupid (plus other unflattering adjectives). Why I went on and on has bemused me—and will you too no doubt. Surface, bec. I found so many openings for criticism, on each new page I flipped to (always hard to resist for my kind of mind). More deeply, bec. it slowly grew on me that trouble wasn't your talents (though must confess you cd. do w. a little more lit-erary skill—but I don't get sore at Dreiser or Dewey) but rather the method you use in analyzing Don Juan. And this method it more and more dawned on me, w. why went on so long, kind of fascinating, is death to poetry and the artist and any feeling for art . . . is reductive . . . takes the mickey out of the whole busi-ness by using a terminology (and the perceptions that go with it as either cause or effect or both) that misses the whole point of art—its pleasure, superficiality, fun, nonsense, beauty, form, spontaneity, etc. etc. etc. . . . Well, do read my notes—they read pretty well to me on second look, lots of laughs & food for thought—and if you want to talk about the whole unhappy business, I'm at your service, room 64, annex a, 831-4439.

To William Shawn

February 6, 1974

I've talked with the people at the Yale Library MS division and they definitely want my letters and papers, w. they looked over several weeks ago in my Augean office. They've also put me onto a chap at Strand Bookstore who will look over my books and make an offer for the ones (about 2/3 I'd guess) I don't want to keep.

Once I've gone through the papers and books, roughly, to decide what goes to Yale, what to Strand, and what to me, both outfits will send in movers and strip the office bare. I began the job Xmas vacation and am coming down tomorrow for three days to carry it on, but there's just too much to be got through in that time. So the actual move will take place during the Spring va-cation here—March 15–25—when I can be in office to make sure who takes what out. Sorry couldn't clean it out sooner, but you've seen the place and can believe me when I tell you there's not only 20 years' accumulation of MSS, let-ters, and books from time I first came to NYorker but also masses of papers from much earlier I've stored there, going all the way back to schoolboy letters from PEA and early '20s. (I keep EVERYTHING. The Yale archivists are delighted, of course.)

I'm most grateful for your forebearance through a whole decade when I've not contributed much to the mag—various causes, chiefly of late years my re-luctance to write, that's why I'm teaching, after all—about my continuing to squat in the office. And when and if the writing spirit moves me again, the NYorker will be the first outlet—or better, home—I'll think of.

To Joe Fredan [chairman, English Department, SUNY Buffalo]

April 8, 1974

As I've told you, I have enormously enjoyed my year and a half teaching here, and I'd like to keep open for both of us the option of coming back for one or maybe both semesters in 1975–6. . . . *My* decision will depend on how things work out at John Jay—i.e., whether (a) I want to keep on there, and (b) if so, whether I cd. arrange to take a semester off. (As I've told you, the only reason I'm shifting to Jay is that unlike SUNYAB, it is only 2-1/2 hours from our cottage in East Hampton, where I long to spend the fall and spring commuting to NYC for 2 days a week. Why didn't you think of locating the new campus in Scarsdale?

I hope we (the Eng. Dept. and I) can work out a return visit because my tour of duty at SUNYAB has been incomparably more pleasurable—and stimulating—than any of the six or seven I've had in last 15 years at other universities, from Santa Cruz to Amherst (U. of Mass.) to Milwaukee (U. of Wis.) to Austin (U. of Texas). The students, both graduate and undergraduate, are livelier, more variegated, and more serious about their work (that goes for a recent semester at Yale, too) and so is the faculty (in this dept. at least). And so much is going on in the campus, esp. in movies. It's Shangri-la—high thinking and low living (also frostbite), comradeship, liberty-equality-fraternity! Anyway, I like it very much—also I think I've improved as a teacher here, so now I feel I'm not WHOLLY amateur. Also, specifically I WOULD like to give my Poe class again—for undergraduates—it's much more developed and refined the third time round, believe me—and Poe seems to become more "relevant," intellectually and culturally, every month. Also I like to talk about him to a sympathetic if slightly captive audience—in fact, if I were a millionaire, which I'm not (maybe another $1,000 cd. be squeezed onto my "line" when and if I return?), I'd gladly pay SUNYAB for the privilege of exploring once more that magic terrain with another eager little boy-scout troop!

So for the record, if things can be worked out, I WILL RETURN or SHALL? or both: intention plus simple futurity).

Not the least of SUNYAB amenities, need I say, has been your own play-it-by-ear unbureaucratized chairmanship—I'll miss those wisecracks: not very good perhaps always maybe, but a lot of them—dependable, that's what one wants in friends, or chairpersons.

To Herman Kahn [Yale University archivist]

June 19, 1974

Yes, as I told you on phone, I'm delighted to accept $15,000 for the "correspon-
dence, papers, and other materials" you and Ruth and that pleasant young assistant removed, with my help—we did buckle to!—from my *New Yorker* office
"some months ago." It seems a most generous offer, works out to be $200 and
$300 per carton, depending on whether you got 50 or 75—but anyway more
than I expected. Anal-retentive virtue is rewarded, also pack-ratism. Some of
cartons were duds, I'm sure, but some were not—and only that grad student
who's ordering the mélange will ever know—look forward to his neatening up
when I come up to Yale next month—expect all sorts of mislaid treasures to
emerge!

We'll formalize/finalize details re accessibility & use then. . . . Nice of you
to express "pride & satisfaction" in the acquisition of my archives. My relations
w. Yale seem to be getting warmer the longer I'm distant from my 1924–1926 undergraduate experience—I even sent $1 to my alumni class agent last month—
"tokenism," true, but a token is something, and up to now I've not, on principle,
tokened anything. Can the bulldog change his spots? Apparently yes, as of post-
1945. . . . Anyway, it all makes me feel good—if only my archives weren't
housed in that ghastly Gothic library: approaching the desk to prosaically file a
withdrawal slip is like staggering up to take communion in a particularly Holly-
woodesque stage set, one expects Lady Diana Manners (she of the *Miracle, you*
remember?—Max Reinhardt at his most Reinhardtesque) to receive your call
slip. John Russell Pope the perpetrator, I think? Or was it James Gamble
Rodgers? No, he committed Harkness, I've just learned—previously I'd attrib-
uted Harkness to Ralph Adams Cram. Or is Rodgers a double murderer? . . .
Well, hope the medieval archery-slits (could J.G.R. or J.R.P. have foreseen the
Panther weekend?) Will admit enough light for me to pore over my *incunable*
next month—hope you have anachronistic electric lights. . . .

P.S. Yes, I'd like the $15,000 to be paid in three annual instalments, beginning
1975.

P.P.S. A few more cartons will be forthcoming—recent stuff plus things I'd
stashed down here or in my NYC apt. Seems no end to my retentiveness—
nothing of great $$$ value probably—yet will round out the chronology
("What! Will the line stretch out to the crack of doom?" as Macbeth com-
plained—and I'm afraid it will, to my doomcrack at least. But that's one virtue
of my "archives," I'd say, completeness over (my God) fifty odd years. . . . If you

and/or your funding patrons, want to ante up more for such future "accessions," OK by me—but the Yale U. Library, MS. Division will get them regardless.

To Anthony Battaglia (SUNY at Buffalo undergraduate]

June 26, 1974

Thanks for your Gogol-Poe paper, which came a few days ago and which I've begun to read and which, not to prolong your possible suspense, strikes me as, so far—about 1/4 to 1/3 into, you didn't number the pages—the most interesting paper I've read in some 15 years of visiting professorships—and that goes for a few Ph.D. theses too.

In your covering letter, you write: "This paper was generated by inertia rather than by the force of inspiration. It was forced out. I should have dropped the course when I had the chance. I became exhausted in April [the cruelest month] and disappointed for what seemed another case of 'lapsed potential' on my part. The way in which I burlesqued the concept of independent study, like the way in which I just couldn't record my more acute insight, is symptomatic with [of] my being. . . . I plan to quit school . . . and find out how life is related to art. . . . At this point I have no ideal. The only thing that compels me anymore is the fear of being (or becoming or having been all along) a mediocrity."

Well, do let me assure you, on the basis of the portion of your paper I've so far read (you really SHOULD number pages—also a bit more attention to syntax and spelling wd. be welcomed), you need not fear the charge of mediocrity. Your thoughts are often original, sometimes peculiar, and usually serious—i.e., not "mediocre." Even your spelling & syntax is/are odd [see P.P.S. at end].

I've made many notes on the MS and will make many more when I get around to finishing it in a week or so, but for the moment, let's get down to brass tacks. I gave you an Incomplete grade several weeks ago, before receiving your supracompleta—like "superfecta" in betting—paper, and now I'll change the grade to "A" if you'll send me your Social Security (and/or other numbers needed) for Sharon's purposes.

As for your final quote—"But release me from my bands / with the help of your good hands," I do so "my tricksy spirit," and then "to the elements / Be free, and fare thou well!"

P.S. Under separate cover, I'm sending you a copy of my ed. of EAP's poems.

P.P.S. Do you really live in a place called Fredonia? I mean, isn't that the name of a mythical kingdom in a Marx Bros. film, or maybe Fields? I mean why boggle at Gogol?

P.P.S. As your magisterial first para . . . Also, p. 5 by my reckoning, your summary on Gogol: "His writings compose a universe in which all that is good and noble has been lost amid a mire of triviality." (You see more than that in Gogol, as later expressed, but this is a good first-approximate reading.) . . . Or, many pages on: "Searching for the 'word,' Poe heard in far-off rooms sounds that were barely audible and less recognizable." (Though as you'll see, I suggest deleting last 3 words—but maybe not, on 2nd thought.) . . . Or next page, coinage of "psychologistics." . . . But you get my point—you have knack for phrase.

To Harrison Salisbury [National Institute of Arts and Letters]

July 7, 1975

As a veteran movie critic/historian, I've wondered why playwrights are eligible for the Institute while movie directors aren't—at least I assume this, since Miller, Williams, and Hellman are members and Welles, Hawks, and Kubrick—who are certainly as creative and significant in Am. Culture—are not.

The explanation seems to be that (1) movies weren't until the last few decades considered serious art, like plays, by the stuffily conservative types who created and dominated the Institute; and (2) a false analogy, really a semantic confusion, between a theatrical director (or an orchestral one) and a movie director. I assume by now most members of the Institute wd. agree that cinema is as much high art as theater (and indeed in last 30/40 perhaps the more interesting one). As for (2), the symphony or play director is in fact an interpretive artist, like an actor or a pianist (who are also excluded from our club whose doors are open only to "creative" types, including, how perceptive, critics like me), that is, he interprets a work somebody else has created. But the movie director is the creator himself, he shapes and controls the work the way the composer and the playwright do, using script-writers (what movie script is more famous than the movie, as any play is than the director's mise-en-scène?), actors, cinematographers, et al. to express *his* views.

So I propose we change our criteria for membership (and thus also forwarding prizes) to include film directors just as we now do playwrights. Could you take this up with the committee you chair? Glad to appear for questions, discussion, etc. or whatever—don't know what the "channels" are.

Specific problem that crystallized above—have been vaguely wondering about it since I was elected—is that at the first meeting of that committee on next year's literature award w. you kindly suggested I chair (and a very enjoyable experience it's been, so much to read!) we were confronted with the problem of choosing the recipient of the five-year drama medal and none of us could think of any playwright remotely on a level of most recipients (as I recall they included O'Neill, Odets, Miller, Williams). In fact none of us four present (Barth, Levin, Boyle, and me—Ciardi, Bishop, and, alas, Miller didn't show) had gone to the theater much of late, movies were our speed and scene. . . . Maybe Miller will come up with somebody, or maybe not. . . . But if "drama" could also mean "cinema" (and why not? That amorphous, bastardized new art of our time is related to music, literature, and painting but most closely to the theater), and if movie directors could be considered original creators of art, then we could give the 1976 drama medal to Orson Welles (Kubrick wd. be my choice for 1981) and a grand master (*Kane* and *Ambersons*) with an *oeuvre* of lesser works that is extensive and interesting. . . . Also putting our imprimatur (at last!) on the open secret that cinema is art would get us more in step—with a belated hop/leap—with the cultural zeitgeist. Institutions (and Institutes) need such periodical self-shakings like a dog emerging from water.

I do hope a rethinking of categories can be done.

To Cynthia Merman [editor at Harper and Row]

September 8, 1975

Re. your queries of Aug. 5: I think a collection of Rosa Luxemburg letters—a selection, rather—is an excellent idea, also I think it would be widely (and well) reviewed and might even sell (I'm no expert on that). . . . She was a great woman as well as a major left-Marxist leader and theoretician; also a most talented writer—Trotsky alone occurs to me as comparable that way among 20th-cent. revolutionaries. Also a most vivid, passionate, and intellectually interesting personality. Emma Goldman—whose anarchism had more in common with Rosa's brand of Marxism than either seemed to realize—had her woman's heart and her decency, culture, and common sense—but not her brains. (Had Doctorow been a German and written a *Ragtime* about turn-of-the-century Germany, I bet Rosa wd. have played the major role that Emma does.)

The only specific references about her as a person rather than a political leader I can suggest—and you probably know both—are (1) Hannah Arendt's splendidly critical appreciation in the NY *Review* 3 or 4 years ago, (2) a "Rosa Luxemburg: Letters from Prison," we ran in the June 1938 *Partisan Review* (w. introduction and a postscript, "The Death of Luxemburg; A Newsreel," by myself). They are tender, delicately written, very personal ("quiet, reflective greys" as v. the "virile reds" of her political persona, was my formulation) and extremely moving. Hell of it is that, in our unscholarly way, we forget to mention the German source from which Eleanor Clark (now Mrs. Robert Penn Warren) made "the first rendering in English." Maybe Eleanor remembers—you shd. ask her your questions in any case. Hannah certainly wd. know—they're all to Sonia Liebknecht—and would also know where other more personal and less political letters may be found. (I agree w. your slant but don't be too pedantic about it—Rosa was too large and varied a person to be Procrusteanized into "personal rather than political" writings—there was plenty personal feeling (and style) in her politics . . . and plenty of sane verve in some of her letters to Kautsky, Lenin (?), Liebknecht, et al. So too her political and personal emotions blend together in the prison letters we printed.

To James Atlas [biographer of Delmore Schwartz]

October 8, 1975

Farrar Straus sent me the first 75 pages of your MS weeks ago—too many weeks, sorry, summer sloth—and I read them with even more interest than I'd expected.

You've done a remarkable research job on his early years, the factual narrative is extraordinarily dense and your comments imaginative and acute.

My one major criticism is that the style is often clotted and verbose. You say perfectly sensible things in such a long-winded, heavy-breathing way that one might suspect you were trying to hide a thinness of content behind a screen of verbiage in the usual academic way. But in fact the content is rich both as to information and your own interpretive comments on the data. So it's puzzling why you use such a backing-away, overwritten style, esp. in the first 20 or 30 pages. Hope this is a first draft. And that you'll drastically cut, condense, simplify (stylistically) the second draft.

There are no reference notes. Are you planning to give sources for the intimate details—sometimes as to what he was feeling at a certain point—which must have come from interviews w. friends and family? In back w. line and page reference, as Ellmann did in Joyce? I think this essential.

I've made queries and comments on 20 or so pages, w. will send you if you like. Or, better, if you can come see me in NYC sometime between Oct. 20 and 25, we could talk about it—in w. case, if you've done more chapters you might send them to me here in advance.

You've got the makings of a superb and definitive biography of Delmore, but a lot of water cd. be squeezed out of the prose.

To Mark Shechner

November 3, 1975

Sure I will be delighted to blurb you for the Guggenheim, *ça va sans dire*, if my French still holds up. . . . And do send me those chaps. on Trilling and PR, will read w. pleasure.

Now I have a favor to ask *you* (and Alan and Howard and other pals in

SUNYAB Eng. Dept.). I want to come back for 1976–77 year—see enclosed letter to Slotin—and wd. appreciate you-all keeping an unobtrusive eye on things there and maybe putting in a word if occasion arises. Low-profile stuff. My guess is that Leslie [Fiedler] has mixed feelings about my return from John Jay Elba—but at least they're mixed. Rat reasons for leaving sinking JJ—but more elevated ones for going back to SUNYAB where I had best students & most stimulating/simpatico colleagues in my 15-year trek through 10 campuses.

Yes, saw the *Newsweek* take-out on Bellow, quite good survey for a newsmag, I thought, interesting facts and, esp., pics. . . . He did cosmeticize his role at LBJ's unfestive Festival, as you note, but what else cd. he do? To confront the truth, beg. w. his refusing to join Lowell in not reading there and flimsy/odd reasons he made public for so doing: citizen has duty to honor the presidential office no matter what his views on the President's actions (flimsy) and Vietnam escalating OK bec. Ike and JFK had started the escalator and LBJ couldn't back down, his only objection being to the Dominican caper, odd, indeed, Jesuitical/perverse—I suspect [Edward] Shils in woodpile. Also his un-wave-making behavior at the Festival (episode of half-signing then, under [Ralph] Ellison's pressure, unsigning my "petition" I told you about; also his reading from his work w. no ed. comment like a good little boy as contrasted w. [John] Hersey's (not exactly an Abbie Hoffman type) insisting on reading from his *Hiroshima* AND drawing an awkward moral—to pick up the syntax 3 inches above: To confront the truth/actuality of his role at the Festival wd. have forced Saul to the kind of new self-understanding and rejection of his old values that Ivan Ilyich had to make. Well, one can hardly expect that—he wasn't dying of cancer, after all.

Thanks for your . . . Bellow piece, a most impressive survey, the main hypothesis about him, psychologically & aesthetically sustained and also varied w. asides and/or related . . . notes confirming them. Can't go into your general ideas here without writing another piece—hope we'll meet before too long, talk is better—will say only that you are developing a great style (one lapse, though, on p. 43 "vintage Bellow" is a gourmet cliché by now—eating-drinking metaphors about art don't somehow ever work). Three exs. of what I like (all exs. of your knack for condensing a large perception into a neat, hard, witty formulation: p. 69, "Steiner is Reich with liftoff; anthroposophy is orgonomy in orbit"; 75, "Moses Herzog's symptomatology (shouldn't it be "symptomology"?) Has become Charlie Citrine's wisdom." (The para this ends is one of your best, I thought—Bellow's philosophizing has always seemed to me, too, more static than music.) P. 75, "Humboldt's real gift to Citrine, it appears, was the gift of gab. (new para) Thus it is that a novel that is manic at the start turns increasingly depressive as it goes on."

I've one general criticism: you are too serious in sense you are more aware of Bellow's defects as a thinker (w. are plenty) than you are sensitive to his virtues as an artist (taking art as play, fooling around, "putting on," mystification). Two examples: (1) You treat *Henderson* at length (and perceptively) but you don't mention the quality that I enjoy most in it (*Henderson* is second only to *Seize the Day* in my canon—interesting STD is almost always put first by everybody in print and talk, by the way, bec. no philosophical bullshit and no "vitalistic" overkill, as in *Augie*, is my guess—and that's why, or because it's so short)—To resume: that quality is humor. Maybe bec. B was writing about a WASP for once (hence distanced, humor requiring distancing) or bec. the scene is an imaginary Africa (freeing his rhetorical brio to soar above an actual milieu to w. he feels responsible in other novels as a realist (of sorts). Whyever, he cuts loose in *Henderson* and keeps building a picaresque hero and locales into increasingly grotesque comic dimensions. It's a very *funny* book. But you complain it's not intellectually consequent, not serious. "A voice within him cries incessantly, 'I want, I want, I want,' though it never specifies what exactly it is after," you write. But poor id-ridden Henderson doesn't have a clue as to what his inner voice is "after" (that's the point) and to demand he, or his creator, must "specify"—and "exactly" yet!—what it is like asking Bellow to put his crazy-sane hero through a psychoanalysis. It might clear his mind but wd. certainly delete his raison d'être in the novel: his gigantic, irrational, nonsensical Rabelaisian instinct for low comedy that somehow is also a criticism of life. . . . Later you complain that Bellow "is . . . coy in refusing to tell us what Henderson's trouble really was and what his cure represents. It is no wonder that the conclusion has satisfied almost no one." Glad you said "almost" bec. the ending satisfied one reader, me. It is an appropriately inconclusive end to a splendidly inconclusive book: Henderson's trouble, by my reading, is that his id is natural and the USA milieu he lives in is not—he's sane his way, w. is id-primitive, and his wife and other friends and neighbors are sane in their superego, 20th-cent., sophisticated (had connotations to this adj, too) way. And he finds what he is looking for in an (imaginary) Africa, where id and superego lie down together in peace. This is his "cure" (it's as absurd to apply such a term to the rain king as it wd. be to the lion-cub he brings back, w. will be as uncured and undomesticated in USA as will Henderson. So his long safari quest, and the novel recording it, is a failure, curewise. But a success artwise. You reproach Bellow precisely for his most courageous triumph as an artist—his insistence on sustaining the comedy of natural instinct in an unnatural world to its logical end when "Henderson leaps out into the snows of Newfoundland . . . and dances and capers around the plane like a Hasidic rabbi." This bothers you ("not dramatically credible"), but it seems to me to flow from the preceding novel (w. you praise, on the whole). Also what's wrong w. a Hasidic rabbi—the Hasidim have always struck me as a particularly enlivening and attractive part of your race, so friendly and gay and humorous—those jokey stories!—compared to your heavyweights in the Old Testament. . . .

To James Atlas

February 17, 1976

Your discouraged note of the 12th to hand. (Do call me "Dwight," by the way—think we've got beyond, or should have, the Mr. stage.) I understand your mood, what w. my continued carps and those of Gertrude's [Buckman] letter w. I kick myself for having shown you—I'd forgotten HER carps, maybe bec. not directed at me but also bec. I didn't take them (or her) seriously. But don't you either—she's a limited, schoolmarmish, prickly/pedant type—and the diff. bet. her and my carps is simply that mine proceed from a basic sympathy with and confidence in you as a biographer and in your ability as a thinker and writer.

The trouble with the MS now is, I think—and you say your editor was of same opinion—that you've gotten bogged down in the rich data your energetic researching has turned up and you've allowed it to overwhelm your own personal pleasure in writing—and good writing never comes but from such pleasure. The two areas you sometimes feel free to kick up your heels in—to generalize, to push around the data—are both essential ones: you're very good, fertile in ideas, and also your style loosens up, on (a) Delmore's psychological complexities (putting it mildly!), their origin in his family/childhood years and their bursting up from his unconscious constantly to wreck his intellectual triumphs; (2) your literary evaluations of his work. The two big ones: Delmore's twisted psyche was the terrible x in his life and career, and the wonder is he did so much, even in the last black years, that transcended it and rose into poetic and critical health. And it's always a great plus when a writer's biographer can illuminate his subject's work—after all, the reason one is interested in his biography—as well as his life and personality. As you do when you now and then shed the burden of factual chronicle and indulge your deeper lusts (or higher capabilities). You even can relate—when you're running free—D's psyche, his life & Hard Times, to his literary productions, show how the former shaped the latter—and without reducing the value of the work.

The MS so far (except for those last 40 or so pages that you say you wrote after my first strictures, w. are MUCH superior to what went before, in style and in freedom of generalization) is, as I said last week, too much a chronicle and not enough a history: the details take over and the general outline is lost. Oddly enough, in MS to date you meet the big intellectual challenges (in psychological and literary interpretations) much better than the humdrum, unchallenging, "kitchen work" job of factual narrative. You're often free and eloquent in such big moments but almost always stiff, clumsy, and boring in retelling the minutiae of D's month-to-month life.

I say "oddly" but it's not odd to me—I've had same problem myself and have observed it in other writers, as Poe's *P.M.* in which the big imaginative challenges are met superbly while he can't manage the kitchen work of making his fantastic tale plausible except by throwing in huge sections of undigested factual stuff from voyages and natural histories that don't work—Defoe could do it bec. he *wasn't* at all imaginative. . . . Or the contrast between the stiff, off-putting transitional material in *Billy Budd*—the kitchen work—and the great writing of the high scenes they botchily connect.

So what to do? My suggestions:

1. As you said when we talked last, no point in reworking what's been done up to now until you get it all down on paper. Then you can decide which chronicler's details should be omitted as repetitious or as blurring the general form of book you see emerging when you look back at end. As for now as you approach the half or more still to be written, I'd suggest that (a) you put in any data you think might POSSIBLY be necessary when you review it all at end, BUT also, a bit contradictorily, you do more preliminary editing than you've done up to now (assume you're getting the feel of the general structure and form more and more as you go along) so as to save yourself any later chores (like condensing, omitting, etc., The Facts) you can. . . . But, to reverse my field again, if you think there's any reasonable chance of factual items being NECESSARY (for a full rounded view of D), I'd stick them in, provisionally.

2. Your general approach should be that you're the boss, not the Facts, and that you have no obligation to trudge through D's life month by month and record all the details you've admirably dug up, that in general if a factual item doesn't interest you (i.e., if you can't think of much to say about it from YOUR point of view, you should omit it as probably repetitious or trivial, but in any case not stimulating to a flight of Atlasian commentary. In that case out with it. You're a writer, with your own peculiar viewpoint on D, not a congressional investigating committee. The latter is supposed to be a recording Angel and so to set down all the data (since it couldn't have an end structure in mind), but you are a poet and a critic, like D, and you should only record what gives YOU pleasure, your focus should be narrowed to your own whims, crotchets (within reason). Thus you will enjoy writing about D—and the reader will enjoy reading what you write about D.

3. In short, be a (literary) man, not a (research) mouse. Enjoy yourself as a stylist, simplify and generalize acc. to YOUR taste & pleasure & fun, kick those Facts around, ignore them if they don't strike you as important to YOUR view of D. You have by now done such an extraordinary amount of factual digging that

you have earned the right to make such deletions of the raw material (and you must do it anyway since book is already too long). Also, I think your own understanding of D and his works is broad and deep enough for me to trust your simplifications. Finally, for a paradigm of the approach I recommend, see Lytton Strachey's *Eminent Victorians*, w. I've just read for 4th or 5th time with usual delight. He goes too far, agreed—his profiles are skeletonesque if you know much about the subjects, as by now I do, also skewed—but he gets the essence of Chinese Gordon, F. Nightingale, and the rest better than more scholarly works do—and what a pleasure to read—and, I imagine, for him to write. . . . Omission, generalization, intensification—in the interests (in general) of both writer and reader—that's your cue.

To Theodore Gill [department chairman at John Jay College]

March 4, 1977

I'm out here [University of California, San Diego] for a one-month gig as a Visiting Prof.—talking with classes on my various specialties de la maison (goddam this elect. typewriter, they're so advanced in Calif. natch that no backward unelectrified machine available) and making some public appearances, see enc. schedule—and am enjoying it enormously: climate, professors, and busdrivers incredibly humane cf. to NYC counterparts; and pedestrians are a protected species—cars stop half a block away to wait for your decision in case you deign to cross the street, rather embarrassing if you're not a king; and a splendid library, a million vols, and just what one wants at least in the humanities—not bad for a mere 10,000 campus, also one as recent a vintage as JJ, namely about 14 years. . . . The two talks so far have been succès d'estime in that the audiences were attentive and appreciative, judging from absence of coughing & rustling, presence of (laughter) or at least (giggles) and level of questions period; but not success quantitywise, mean average pop. about 60, almost no students, due partly to the usual faulty staff work (publicity too little and late, other celebs—Baraka, Dubos, Marcuse—competing for same time, etc.) but mostly to my charisma, w. is v. elitish (most of those present seemed to have been *Politics* subscribers, judging from talks then and later—We Happy Few!)

What are chances for a semester at JJ next fall, or the winter-spring of 1978? I'm probably going to be living in NYC most of the time anyway, and I'd love to return to JJ if it suits your plans too. Would you look into and let me know in the next month or so. I'd be most grateful.

To Cathy Hellman

October 5, 1977

Gloria tried to reach you on phone in city last week to express our love and sympathy about Geoffrey's death, w. I heard of almost by chance (the *New Yorker* checker called me re. the obit—often miss the *Times* here). So I'm using a last stray bit of *NYorker* stationery to write you about the oldest friend I'd still "kept up with" from Yale, or indeed earlier. . . . Geoffrey was someone one *did* keep up with (in feeling at least, of late years), and I think it was because of his own steadiness and tolerant, genial humanity, w. I flatter myself I shared in my own rambunctious way—anyway, I always felt easy in his company, despite temperamental/intellectual/political that steadily widened after the thirties. I also *enjoyed* his company, not so common between anarchist and troglodyte types, maybe because we liked to laugh at, and with, each other. At Yale we were both ironic, harem-scarem mockers of The Establishment—our '28 philistine/stockbroking-to-be classmates. (1929 put an end to THEM!) He was much funnier then than I, even though I was chairman of the *Record*. . . . Later we became part of different Establishments—he of the *NYorker*/genteel/social one, me of the Trotskyist/intellectual one, later anarchy-pacifist-alienated one. But we always enjoyed, liked, respected each other. Odd we were both on *NYorker* writing staff 1951–65, or maybe not so odd. . . . One big row I recall from the late '30s, w. also shows our mutual bond: the big elevator strike, he came to a party at my (and Nancy's) place, 3 flights up, and HE TOOK THE SCAB ELEVATOR! The only guest who did—I heard the thing creaking, darted out, found Geoffrey calmly taking off his rubbers, in *flagrante delicto*, outside the door, pounced on him shouting "Out, you darn scab-lover!" or some such (not "fascist," never sank that low), and he said, "Oh come *on*, Dwight" or such, don't be a fool, THREE flights! And then—either (a) he left huffily, or (b) I let him in after a stern lecture w. he endured as an adult to a child in tantrum. Don't remember—but sure we both giggled at some point, also that next time I saw him we were still friends. . . . Later—this postitively my last senile anecdote, but thought you might enjoy such glimpse of *temps perdu*—I sent him carbon of my first piece in the now radical but anti-Stalinist *PR* (1937) w. was about the *New Yorker*, called "Laugh & Lie Down," for his expert vetting and criticism. And he responded w. 4 or 5 pages of single-spaced numbered factual or ideological objections (still have MS), some of which I adopted, all of which I answered. Very cool, clever, reasonable, detailed objections, as ditto my replies. Reflects credit on both of us, I think.

Forgive garrulity—shall miss him, dammit—best love,

To Tom Toper [a marginal note reads: "NOT SENT—Drunk? Senile? Bit of both? Such expansive garrulity to a stranger. It was late at night—woke up realizing it wouldn't do."]

October 20, 1977

Thanks so much for your fan note about *Discriminations*. You're one of a very select group ("we happy few") who bought it. Viking-Grossman kept it a dark secret, went out of print after 3/4 years last year w. under 2,000 copies sold; and the bastards refused to do it in paperback (as, to be fair, have many others, despite the best efforts of friends and agents) bec. the hardcover, w. they overpriced @ $15, did so badly. Never had such a hard-cover flop before—always did at least 3/4 thousand; and always paperback later.

Ford Foundation has been o.p. for decades (even that did over 3,000, tho no paperback). But I do have in my larder still a few copies of *Against the American Grain* (hard cover), and you may have one from me @ $5, postpaid, if you act NOW (going back to NYC Oct. 29th). Also, same price *DM on Movies* (hardcover, 493 pp., Prentice-Hall, 1969); and at $1.00 my *Politics Past* (paper, Viking, 1970—reissue of *Memoirs of a Revolutionist*, 1957). All these now o.p.— I lay in a few copies for friends—and fans—at o.p. time.

Thanks again for telling me you enjoyed *Discr.* I write to please . . . my peers and I don't agree with Benchley who in "Take the Witness" (2-1/2 pp.) wrote he was perfectly willing to be judged by a jury of his peers "if such exist." (Shd add that "peers" does not mean "equals.")

P.S. Curious to know why you thought I was "a bit disingenuous in explaining the title" of *Discriminations*. When you say that, pardner, *smile!*—my rep is built on honesty—indeed, some critics say "ingenuousness," or more generously, "innocence."

P.P.S. How'd you ever get on the *Post* (even) w. a name like "Toper" w. its suggestion of "toper" and "torpor"? Are you the only Toper in NYC phone book?

To Nicholas Macdonald

November 28, 1977

. . . I am feeling better now than I have in years—as you can see from garrulity of this note—gayer, more energy, even began writing in the Memoirs after 5 years of nonwriting! All began last Monday with awful asthma attack I've had in last 10 years (was there one in NYC 2 years ago?)—Gloria rushes me to South Hampton Hospital (what a 30 minutes) where lovely, loving, expert emergency unit [operates] day and night—was hitched to . . . intravenous tube, oxygen mask, finally got morphine shot went to sleep. Stayed in hospital 4 days, massive treatment, came out Friday and since then no wheezes, feel a lad of 45 again. Doc & I think, I hope over hump am back to health at last. Details when see you—shall be in NYC again bet. Dec. 10 and 15.—Show this to Nancy, please. . . .

To Russell A. Fraser [biographer of R. P. Blackmur]

December 7, 1977

Sorry to reply so late to yours of almost a year ago, but I've had a long siege of illnesses and have only lately emerged into the world. . . . To answer minor query first: (a) of course you may quote, far as I'm concerned, from Blackmur's letters to Schwartz, in fact as you later seemed to realize, letters belong to the recipient only physically, the writer retaining the copyright; odd but just, I think. . . . Speaking of Delmore, what did you think of Atlas's biography? I thought well of it as back cover attested but I'd be curious to have your opinion as a pal of Blackmur whose relations w. Delmore were let's say variable.

Mine, too, must confess. Only time I saw much of him was that on the whole unfortunate Gauss Seminar I gave on Kitsch a long time ago. My memories not golden, probably mostly my fault. (I didn't prepare it for a high academic audience, in fact I took it much too lightly—another exoteric performance but the ambience was esoteric/academic and my craft ran into a lot of unrespected depth mines. Not a few, I must say, detonated by your friend, R.P.B., as chairman. I recall complaining to him after one particularly ungemütlich session: "But, Richard, I thought the chairman was supposed to be friendly to the speaker, or at least neutral, not to trip him up all the time.")

I remember the final dinner, I think at the Nassau Inn, with B and a couple of other profs or grad students, you know the kind of genial/suspicious, edgy gathering, and he kept matching me drink for drink and indeed pressing "one more" on me (which I took, wrongly it turned out, as a sign of unacademic fellow-feeling), and then, when some stern visaged scholar asked one of those whendidustopbeatingyour wife? questions, which gave me the choice between venial error and invincible ignorance, then my chairman intervened with a rueful smile (but duty is duty) before I could answer (ha! ha!) and rephrased the question, lest the speaker hadn't quite caught the drift, in a sharper and, I must admit, more unanswerable form, not omitting a sincere side-glance at the speaker (me) that positively radiated a hope, against all the evidence of the last two hours, for enlightenment.

Well, that's a cadenza run up from malicious memory 20 years later and 100% nonfactual. But maybe 50% truthful. *Se non è vero, è ben trovato . . .* what was odd, about both of us, was that after the lectures (and RPB's chairmanship was certainly undercutting of the speaker, me anyway, though not as extreme as in the above fantasia), when I went over to his place for the usual wake, in my case it was a lot of fun, as wakes are said to be, and very "wet," and we both, doubtless for that reason, enjoyed talking (I can't recall a single exchange, or even a single subject), though at arm's length. He wasn't my kind of critic, too esoteric, nor I his, too exoteric.

Luck to your biography/memoir and do send me a copy if any lying around free—maybe I'll get a handle on RPB, as they say in Marin County.

P.S. Nothing in above is copyright and everything may be reproduced free, gratis, and without cost. Or, of course not—also free.

To Fred Dupee

February 19, 1978

. . . Why didn't I respond to [your] friendly query, w. I especially appreciated after those Two Days That Shook our Friendship? Since, do believe me, that edifice, such as it is, was shaken, often and violently, during the drive back from your camp (and that absurd argument about Wm. Buckley, Jr., both of us hopefully at cross purposes and the Question, as W.B. Jr. wd. smirkingly suggest in his TV show, wasn't ever defined w. any clarity, typical leftist muddleheadedness—I mean you & Gloria kept saying how bad, evil, vicious he was politically while I kept insisting he did so have personal charm & was a hard guy to hate. How he would have reveled if he could have overheard us!). And my rudeness at dinner, my smug, know-it-all sneers, fortissimo, at you & (especially, alas) Andy, the innocent bystander if ever there was one. (Enc. among other material is a clip file I made last spring when I got back and began to read the press and discover that she was right about Mobutu, and I very wrong.) Climaxed by my loftily dismissing the both of you after you'd, probably, told me to slow down, with something like "Trouble is just . . . I think faster than you do." Oh God! I'd drunk a lot (and drank a lot more in next month) to numb the pain of that split vertebra—w. healed itself, finally (w. help of $260 Jack-Kennedy-fitted brace of steel, leather, elastic webbing), by early Sept., but it was hell esp. first 2 months. A partial, v. partial excuse. I was moved the next A.M. when you came in and put your arm around my shoulder and asked me how the back was and otherwise showed friendship.

And by the time we left, my feelings toward you (I never had, or have had, any animosity, though irritation yes, toward Andy who was my actual antagonist that evening. Do give her my love) had cooled off and even begun to warm up again. Soooo . . . to quote a fall of 1927 letter from you to me which came to hand recently—I've been browsing among old letters, in hopes, not yet granted, of getting on those "memoirs": "It's not spite that's kept me from writing sooner . . ." rest of sentence being, "though your letter made me pretty mad at first." (I seem to have written you a letter after that ill-omened Bowdoin visit; we do seem to get on each other's nerves a lot, but if our friendship has weathered so many storms & hurricanes so long, w. it has far as I'm concerned, I guess we'll just have to put up with them and enjoy the placid interludes, which in my memory are the norm. "I couldn't see how after the way you acted up here," you continue, "you could still sit down and pass lofty cold-blooded judgments on me."

Well, this time anyway I'm apologizing (3/4 anyway), so *that's* a gain, eh?

Hard to say WHY I haven't at least written you a note about my health, etc. It's been on my mind for many weeks now, a guilty burden, I keep beginning letters to you both in my head in bed and then putting it off the next day. Short answer to your query: by end of Aug. last my back had mended and I was over the postoperative depression (3 weeks in hospitals having my prostate, what else, out). Then in September a 3-4 week bout of bronchial asthma v. bad (can't lie down, fitful sleep sitting up, wheezing & gasping always) w. finally cured by experimental young doc in E. Hampton clinic who finally found that cortisone (strong medicine, tricky) worked. And so far this winter no real asthma attacks, just a whiff of inhaler when needed. So health OK physically. But mentally not, for months all I've really wanted was to lie down and sleep—actually FEEL drowsy a lot of the day, must spend well over 12 hours in bed. This either cause or effect, probably both, of a general deep sadness and feeling of boredom and futility, in short a depression that's chronic. . . . So I didn't write and haven't done much of anything for months. Maybe I shd. try lithium, w. helped Cal Lowell, but my doc is v. conservative and says it's dangerous, constant blood tests, etc., and at moment I'm on a milder nostrum, Elavil. . . . We'll see. . . . Fact I can now write you may be significant. . . . One stroke of good luck budgetwise (and also psychewise—Fred, you must know of course that the suffix "wise" is OK usage, long & honorable linguistic lineage? Even if now used mostly by Madison Ave. types). . . . That stroke is Bob Brustein's asking me to be a CBS "fellow" at the Yale Drama School for this semester: two sessions back to back, Monday/Tuesday, one a vague affair I call "Conversazione with Dwight Macdonald," 30-40 students, no credit, I talk on some topic like mass culture or myself for 45 minutes, then we kick it around; not bad fun so far, they often heckle and even ask questions; other 5 aspiring playwrights I meet for 2 hours Tuesdays and comment on, or rather get them to argue and comment on, scripts of plays they have written. What the hell do I know about play writing? One of them seems talented. And one of them, while not without talent (relative to class) is a Hitler fan, personally not ideologically, you understand; he thinks Hitler was a genius politically (w. is possible) AND militarily (w. is not).

Also I discovered, over a couple of beers after first class, that he believes it possible that Hitler not only didn't order the death camps to gas to death the Jews and Gypsies but didn't even know that Himmler and other wicked aides were operating that vast death machine. Seems nobody has found any official orders from Hitler about setting up or running the camps. . . . This depressed me so much I could only wave a dispirited hand when we parted, impossible to smile. An academic friend says there's a sort of parody "revisionist" school of young historians who are out to rehabilitate Hitler simply bec.—as my student said—everybody has always assumed he was a monster. . . . Must stop now, later may try to write you about this drowsy depression that has settled over me, constant feeling of physical weakness, chronic low spirits. . . . Or maybe this letter marks the beginning of the upward swing of manic depression. . . .

To Grillo [Felix della Paolera, Argentine literary and film critic]

July 8, 1981

Do you keep au courant w. the *NY Times* and the *New Yorker* on the Timmerman case? I've been clipping items on it, including the *New Yorker* excerpts of *Prisoner Without a Name*, and if you haven't seen them should be glad to send them to you. . . . Well, that was SOME party, your farewell bow (hope not for too long), eh? Quite a bash, won't forget it in a hurry. . . . Please thank Borges for the inscribed book & photo. I've sent Mailer's to him and he replied: ". . . I'm delighted he autographed them for me, but suspect it may speak less of his admiration for me than my admiration for him (whatever that means). I've been asked several times by South American reporters who I thought were the best writers down there, and always answer 'Borges and Marquez (I disagree on Marquez—D.M.). . . . I think they are probably the two best writers alive in the world today.' So it may be just a papal blessing, but I'm still delighted. God, what a mind. When I told these S. American reporters of my regard for him, they said, 'But he's a right-winger.' And I said, 'Who gives a fuck? When you're that good it doesn't matter any more. Your influence goes all the way past politics.'" . . . I'm puzzled by the reporters dismissing Borges (or anyone) as "a right-winger"—such archaic language in 1981—and also by Mailer's acceptance of the charge in defending Borges. . . . Norman still has a lot of unexamined ultra-leftist prejudices buzzing in his busy bonnet.

Hope you're well, Grillo, and not too bothered by your present rulers. . . .

To Gerardus H. Wynkoop [Yale Class of '28 scribe]

June 25, 1982

I didn't read your Class Letter until yesterday—and a very amusing letter it was—so I missed the bargain picnic of all time, that "do" in Worcester.

Sorry the enclosed ten bucks is all I can give now to the Class Fund. Will be wealthier next year, so more then.

The quote from Whitman and the comic poems were fun—you should burst into song more often!

I'm puzzled by Bob Osborne's message: "Tell Dwight that his paragraphs about Roger Baldwin were superb: so perceptive of that decent man." My two-part profile of Baldwin appeared in the *New Yorker* and I remember it chiefly because Roger threatened to sue me and the magazine if Shawn didn't print a retraction or fire me. (He did neither, of course.) Several things graveled him about my piece, especially my unfavorable estimate of him compared to Norman Thomas and my (justified) criticism of his voting, in the Union board meeting, to keep quiet about the forced evacuation of the California Japanese-Americans because FDR claimed it was a military necessity. Thomas argued the other way, and of course he was right. That action was one of the biggest blots on FDR's escutcheon (on which, in my opinion, there were plenty of dirty spots).

To John Rossi

May 13, 1982

No, of course my view of the Waldorf Conference as "Stalinoid" hasn't changed. How could it? No new data far as I know.

On your second query: my reaction to the Hellman/Wills view of the period in *Scoundrel Time*. I read that lamentable book most carefully for certain reasons and I think that, while she is herself still anti-Stalinist (her break came late, in fact, when I got her to sign a manifesto in 1969 protesting Moscow's persecution of Sinyavski-Daniel), she regards Mary and myself as "premature anti-Communists." Her disgraceful lawsuit against Mary shows this. . . . Whaddya . . . mean, or rather what does Wills mean, by our getting "carried away by anti-communism"? We've been anti-Soviet since the '30s and far from being "carried away," we were never cooler than at the Waldorf Conference.

Yes, I've noticed that the elders are angered by Hellman's book while the juniors admire her "courage." Some courage—did you see couple years back that standing ovation those cretins at the Oscar ceremonies gave to Lilian? Down here there are lots of liberals, not all of them young either, who are horrified by my refusing to have Alger Hiss as a cocktail guest because he was a traitorous Soviet agent. . . . Not surprised you list Navasky as one of those neo-Sovieters, suspected it for some time. . . . How absurd: pro-Sovietism rears its head again among the young and/or ignorant, after so many decades of disillusionment. And when the Soviet bureaucrats no longer believe in their own mystique.

To Nicholas Macdonald

June 8, 1982

. . . My health has never been better, ever since they pumped 45 pounds of water out of me at the hospital. Asthma almost cured, can (and have) walked miles w. no bad effects—and that's something for a sedentary 76-year-old! . . . Writing Dan Walker, thanks for address, hope Zack [Nicholas and Elspeth's oldest son] gets the part. . . . Good God, both my grandsons seem to be geniuses! Unbelievable—or would be did I not know the dear boys. Hey, how come Harvard on list of colleges for Ethan [Nicholas and Elspeth's youngest son]? You didn't like it when you were there. *And why not Yale?* It's by far top choice for undergraduate teaching today—Stanford comes in a poor second. . . . Yes, agree a good sign Ethan wants to go to college away from his NYC home. . . . Don't share your admiration of V. Woolf on movies. Seemed to me vague and pretentious—what can she mean by all that guff about movies being inherently abstract? . . .

INDEX

A NOTE ON THE EDITOR

Michael Wreszin's biography of Dwight Macdonald, *A Rebel in Defense of Tradition*, was published in 1994. Mr. Wreszin has also written biographies of Oswald Garrison Villard and Albert Jay Nock. Born in Glen Ridge, New Jersey, he studied at Syracuse, Colgate, and Brown universities, receiving a Ph.D. from Brown. After teaching at Wayne State and Brown, he is now professor emeritus at Queens College and the Graduate Center of the City University of New York, and lives in New York City.